THE GOSPEL OF JOHN

THE GOSPEL OF JOHN

Introduction, Exposition and Notes

BY

F. F. BRUCE
D.D., F.B.A.

WILLIAM B. EERDMANS PUBLISHING COMPANY
GRAND RAPIDS, MICHIGAN

ISBN-10: 0-8028-4915-6
ISBN-13: 978-0-8028-4915-1

TO

BARRY AND BETTY HALE

PREFACE

THIS exposition of the Fourth Gospel, like my expositions of Ephesians (1961) and the Epistles of John (1970), is intended chiefly for the general Christian reader who is interested in serious Bible study, not for the professional or specialist student. Textual, linguistic and other critical questions have been touched on lightly; the chief aim has been to communicate what I myself have learned of the Evangelist's meaning and message.

This work has taken shape over a period of nearly thirty years. In 1953 I began to contribute, in quarterly instalments, 'An Expository Study of St John's Gospel' to *The Bible Student* of Bangalore, India, at the invitation of the editor, Alfred McDonald Redwood. By the time *The Bible Student* ceased publication in 1960 (two years before the editor's death), the first seven chapters of John had been covered. The work was then set aside for several years. Then, in 1971 and 1972, mainly out of a desire to clarify for myself certain problems in the passion narrative of the Fourth Gospel (especially with regard to the trial of Jesus), I contributed to *The Witness* eighteen articles on 'St John's Passion Narrative' and six on 'St John's Resurrection Narrative'. Later, in 1977, the editor of *The Witness*, the late Cecil Howley, suggested that I might reproduce in its columns the expository study which had appeared previously in *The Bible Student* (revised where appropriate) and carry on until I had covered the whole Gospel. This I proceeded to do (with the good will of his successor as editor, John Polkinghorne), and when *The Witness* was merged with *The Harvester* from the beginning of 1981 the exposition continued to appear in *The Harvester* month by month until it was completed in December 1982. I am grateful to my publishers for giving me the opportunity to prepare the work for publication in book form.

The haphazard and topsy-turvy way in which much of the work originally appeared means that a good deal of overlapping and inconcinnity has had to be removed. It would be over-optimistic to suppose that this removal has been as thorough-going as it should have been. The introduction and notes have been added for the present form of publication.

I am conscious of my deep indebtedness to many previous expositors: some of this indebtedness is expressly acknowledged, but much of it must remain unacknowledged, because most of what I have read or heard about the Gospel of John over many years has been integrated with my own thinking about the Gospel and cannot now be analysed into its sources. My chief conscious indebtedness is to the work of C. H. Dodd. Also, for much of my career as a teacher of Biblical Studies I was fortunate in having two colleagues who specialized in the study of this Gospel—Dr Aileen Guilding in the University of Sheffield and Dr Stephen Smalley in the University of Manchester – and my understanding of the Gospel was greatly strengthened through my association with them.

The biblical text which is printed at the head of each section of the exposition is my translation from the Greek of the Nestle-Aland edition of 1979.

F. F. BRUCE

CONTENTS

ABBREVIATIONS

AB	Anchor Bible
ad loc.	At the place (cited)
AV	Authorized (King James) Version
BJRL	*Bulletin of the John Rylands (University) Library*
BNTC	Black's New Testament Commentaries
CBC	Cambridge Bible Commentaries (on the New English Bible)
CBQ	*Catholic Biblical Quarterly*
CBRF	Christian Brethren Research Fellowship
EQ	*Evangelical Quarterly*
ExpT	*Expository Times*
GNB	Good News Bible
Hist. Eccl.	*Ecclesiastical History*
HTCNT	Herder's Theological Commentary on the New Testament
HTR	*Harvard Theological Review*
IB	*Interpreter's Bible*
ICC	International Critical Commentary
IEJ	*Israel Exploration Journal*
JQR	*Jewish Quarterly Review*
JTS	*Journal of Theological Studies*
LXX	Septuagint (Greek Old Testament)
MNTC	Moffatt New Testament Commentary
NCB	New Century Bible
NClarB	New Clarendon Bible
NEB	New English Bible
NICNT	New International Commentary on the New Testament
NIGTC	New International Greek Testament Commentary
NIV	New International Version
n.s.	new series
NT	New Testament
NTC	New Testament Commentary
NTS	*New Testament Studies*
op. cit.	The work (by the same author) cited (above)
OT	Old Testament
PEQ	*Palestine Exploration Quarterly*

PGC	Pelican Gospel Commentaries
Q	Qumran
1QS	*Rule of the Community* from Qumran Cave 1
3Q15	'Copper Scroll' from Qumran Cave 3
11QMelch	'Melchizedek document' from Qumran Cave 11
11QTemple	*Temple Scroll* from Qumran Cave 11
QD	Quaestiones Disputatae
RB	*Revue Biblique*
RSV	Revised Standard Version
RV	Revised Version
SBLDS	Society of Biblical Literature Dissertation Series
SBLMS	Society of Biblical Literature Monograph Series
SBT	Studies in Biblical Theology
SNT	Supplement to *Novum Testamentum*
SNTSMS	Society for New Testament Studies Monograph Series
TDNT	*Theological Dictionary of the New Testament*
TNTC	Tyndale New Testament Commentaries
WBC	Word Biblical Commentaries
ZDPV	*Zeitschrift des Deutschen Palästina-Vereins*
ZNW	*Zeitschrift für die neutestamentliche Wissenschaft*

INTRODUCTION

1 THE EVANGELIST AND HIS GOSPEL

The Fourth Gospel, like the three Synoptic Gospels, is anonymous: it does not bear its author's name. The title 'According to John' is a label attached to it when the four Gospels were gathered together and began to circulate as one collection, in order to distinguish it from its three companions. It is noteworthy that, while the four canonical Gospels could afford to be published anonymously, the apocryphal Gospels which began to appear from the mid-second century onwards claimed (falsely) to be written by apostles or other persons closely associated with the Lord.

As early as the ascription of this Gospel to 'John' can be traced back, it is regularly assumed that the John in question was John the son of Zebedee, one of the twelve. There is indeed positive evidence for another 'disciple of the Lord' called John,[1] living (probably) in the Roman province of Asia to which John the son of Zebedee, according to tradition, migrated from Palestine in the later part of the first century; but no one in antiquity, as far as we can tell, ascribed the Fourth Gospel to this other John rather than to the son of Zebedee. This other John is referred to by Papias, bishop of Hierapolis (c. AD 130), as 'John the elder' (or 'presbyter') – 'elder' being a designation given especially at that time to Christian leaders of the generation next to the apostles.

A concentric series of arguments for identifying the Fourth Evangelist with John the son of Zebedee was propounded in classical form by B. F. Westcott. According to him the internal evidence of the Gospel indicates that it was written (a) by a Palestinian Jew, (b) by an eyewitness, (c) by the disciple whom Jesus loved, (d) by John the son of Zebedee.[2]

That the Evangelist was a Jew seems to be clear. The debates between Jesus and the religious leaders in Jerusalem on the finer points of Jewish legal interpretation, reproduced in the central chapters of the Gospel, could not well have been grasped or recorded in those days by an author who was not himself one of 'the Jews'. True, the Evangelist frequently speaks of 'the Jews' in a way that suggests that he is distancing himself from them, but when he does so, he regularly means 'the other Jews' (as distinct from himself and his associates) or else, occasionally, the Judaeans (as distinct from the Galilaeans). As our exposition below emphasizes repeatedly, it is always important to ascertain who precisely 'the Jews' are in each place where the expression occurs.

That the Evangelist was (by origin at least) a Palestinian Jew seems equally clear. If, as seems probable, the Gospel was published in the province of Asia some sixty years after the events which it narrates, we should not be surprised that it reflects not only the situation in which those events took place but also the situation in which they were finally recorded and published. But the Evangelist gives the impression of personal acquaintance with the scenes of Jesus' ministry which he describes, especially those in and around Jerusalem – even if it is something of an exaggeration to say that he knows his Jerusalem 'as a Euston taxi-driver knows his London'.[3]

A few scholars have gone farther in maintaining the Palestinian character of the Evangelist and his Gospel, arguing that while the Gospel (like all the other NT books) has come down to us in Greek, it was nevertheless written originally in Aramaic, the vernacular of Palestinian Jews.[4] This is quite improbable. Naturally, if Jesus and his disciples habitually spoke in Aramaic, we might expect to find Aramaisms in the Greek form of their sayings (just as the English spoken by Scottish Highlanders or by Welsh people reflects the idioms of their native Celtic speech); and this indeed we find in all four Gospels. But unless a piece of objective evidence is forthcoming (such as part of an Aramaic text of the Gospel which bears no sign of being a translation from the Greek), there is no reason to doubt that the Gospel of John as such was a Greek composition from the beginning.

An argument for the Palestinian provenance of this Gospel which was not available to scholars of earlier generations has been provided by the discovery and study of documents emanating from the religious community which had its headquarters at Qumran, north-west of the Dead Sea, for about two centuries before AD 70.[5] Their significance need not be exaggerated (it is salutary to recall that nearly every fresh discovery in Near Eastern religious history of the relevant period has been hailed in its day as the key to the solution of the problem of the Fourth Gospel).[6] Yet some affinities there are between the two bodies of literature. Characteristic Johannine expressions such as 'the light of life', 'the sons of light', 'doing the truth', 'the works of God' are paralleled in the Qumran writings. Both John and the men of Qumran see the universe in terms of sharply contrasted light and darkness, good and evil, truth and falsehood. But even if John appears to 'draw from a common reservoir of terminology and ideas which were well known to the Essenes',[7] the new element in his use of these terms should not be overlooked. When he speaks of 'the light of life', he is not thinking in abstractions, nor is he primarily concerned with a body of teaching or a holy community; for him the true light is identical with Jesus Christ, the incarnate Word. W. F. Albright, one of the first scholars to draw attention to the Qumran affinities of the Fourth Gospel, wisely emphasized the 'wide gulf between the doctrines of the Essenes and the essentials of Johannine teaching': he listed four of these essentials, relating to the function of the Messiah, the salvation of sinners, the ministry of healing and the gospel of love.[8]

Was the Evangelist an eyewitness? In one place there is an emphatic and explicit claim to eyewitness authority. That is where the piercing of Jesus' side after his death on the cross is related (John 19:35): 'he who has seen it has borne his testimony' (i.e. this is the testimony of an eyewitness). It is not said who the eyewitness is – whether he is the Evangelist himself or someone on whose evidence the Evangelist relies. Again, in the epilogue to the Gospel the 'disciple whom Jesus loved' is said to be the one who 'bears witness to these things and wrote these things' (21:24). The statement that he 'wrote these things' could be understood to mean that he caused them to be written, that his was the testimony underlying the record; but the statement that he 'bears witness' to them implies firsthand testimony. 'These things' probably include not only the incident narrated in chapter 21 but others recorded in the main body of the Gospel. In particular, the beloved disciple is said to have been present at the Last Supper (13:23), at the cross (19:26 f.) and at the empty tomb (20:2–10); it may readily be inferred that he is the authority for those phases of the passion and resurrection narratives, if for no more.

The identification of the beloved disciple with John the son of Zebedee has been argued on negative and positive grounds. On the negative side is the absence from this Gospel of the name of John (or of his brother James, for that matter), apart from the statement at the beginning of the epilogue that 'the sons of Zebedee' were among the seven disciples who met the risen Lord by the lake of Galilee (John 21:2). The absence of any mention of John or James is the more remarkable when one considers the part played by name in this Gospel by other members of the twelve – not only more prominent members like Simon Peter and Andrew but less prominent members like Philip, Thomas and Judas 'not Iscariot'.

On the positive side is the presence of the beloved disciple at the Last Supper. If it is proper to infer from Mark 14:17 (and Synoptic parallels) that only the twelve were present with Jesus at the Last Supper, then the beloved disciple was one of the twelve – certainly not Peter (from whom he is distinguished in John 13:24) and probably not any of the other disciples mentioned by name in John 13–17. His recurring designation as 'the disciple whom Jesus loved' implies a deliberate avoidance of his personal name. So also in the epilogue, where he is evidently one of the seven disciples who figure in the incident of the appearance at the lakeside, he is expressly distinguished from Peter (John 21:7, 20) and by implication also from Thomas and Nathanael; we should think of him then as one of the sons of Zebedee (whose names are not given) or as one of the two other disciples listed but not named in John 21:2. So far as the sons of Zebedee are concerned, he cannot be identified with James: James was put to death by Herod Agrippa I, according to Acts 12:1 f., during his brief reign as king of Judaea (AD 41–44); it was not with regard to James that the rumour spread at a later date 'that that disciple was not going to die' (John 21:23).

At the supper table (John 13:24), at the empty tomb (John 20:2–10) and at the lakeside (John 21:7, 20) the beloved disciple is specially associated with Peter; in the early days of the church John appears repeatedly as a companion of Peter (Acts 3:1–4:23; 8:15–25; cf. also Gal. 2:9, where Peter and John, with James the Lord's brother, are associated as 'pillars' of the Jerusalem community). In the early chapters of Acts Peter is so much the dominant partner that John is relatively a lay-figure beside him; indeed, we have very little information in the NT about John the son of Zebedee as a named individual. He and his brother James were described by Jesus as *Boanē-rges*, explained as meaning 'sons of thunder' (Mark 3:17). We may guess that they were so described because of their impetuous nature. It was James and John who proposed the calling of fire from heaven to consume the inhospitable Samaritans (Luke 9:54); it was John who reported how he and his associates tried to stop a man who was casting out demons in Jesus' name because he did not belong to their company (Luke 9:49). James and John incurred the resentment of their fellow-disciples on one occasion by appearing to steal a march on them in a bid to secure preferential status for themselves in the coming kingdom of Christ (Mark 10:35–45). Along with Peter, they belonged to an inner group of three disciples admitted to exceptionally close association with their Master (Mark 5:37; 9:2; 14:33).

Our scanty knowledge about John the son of Zebedee is such that it is difficult to go along with a highly respected scholar who judges it to be a 'moral certainty' that the Fourth Gospel was not written by him[9] – unless indeed it is held to be a moral certainty that it was not written by any eyewitness. The scholar referred to (C. K. Barrett) suggests that the Evangelist (not himself an eyewitness) was a disciple of the apostle John, one of those whom he gathered round himself after his migration from Palestine to Ephesus.[10] He is not so rash as to try to identify this disciple with Papias's 'John the elder', although this identification has been proposed by some students of the Fourth Gospel. We do not know enough about John the elder to bring him into close association either with his namesake the apostle or with the Fourth Gospel.[11]

The eyewitness testimony discerned in the Gospel is mainly that of the beloved disciple, and therefore of the apostle John (if his identity with the beloved disciple can be established). But if it was a disciple of his who wrote down (or wrote up) the Gospel on his behalf, he also may have been an eyewitness of some of the incidents recorded. It has been conjectured that he was a Jerusalemite. Was he, for example, the disciple who was 'known to the high priest' (John 18:15 f.)? Was he, further, the witness of the piercing of Jesus' side (John 19:35)? It is safer to ask these questions than to supply the answers.

Professor Barrett suggests that the Evangelist was the author of the first twenty chapters of the Gospel and that the epilogue (chapter 21) was added when the work was edited for publication – presumably by the group responsible for the 'we know' of John 21:24. This group – the Johannine school or community – certainly played some part in relation to the Gospel.

If the 'Johannine tradition', as it is called, was primarily preserved in the memory of one man, the disciple whom Jesus loved, he might indeed have said, as P. H. Menoud put it, 'la tradition, c'est moi' ('*I* am the tradition').[12] Yet it would be a mistake to picture him as cherishing his reminiscences in solitude for many decades. J. A. T. Robinson, who has been for long a vigorous defender of the apostolic authorship of the Gospel, attaches much more than marginal importance to John's associates. The Johannine tradition, in his view, did not 'come out of the blue round about the year AD 100'; rather, there is 'a real continuity, not merely in the memory of one old man, but in the life of an on-going community, with the earliest days of Christianity'.[13]

It is the tradition thus preserved and handed down that forms the only recognizable 'source' of the Fourth Gospel. It would be foolish to deny that the Evangelist knew the other Gospels; with some of them at least he was probably acquainted. But he did not rely on them as *sources*.[14] Still less ground is there for postulating other written sources on which he may have drawn. Rudolf Bultmann distinguished a signs-source and a sayings-source.[15] But the signs and the discourses are too interdependent to be sorted out into separate sources.

The historical tradition preserved by the beloved disciple and transmitted among his associates is independent of those traditions represented in the Synoptic Gospels, but no less authentic.[16] It is not part of our present purpose to trace the history of the 'community of the beloved disciple';[17] suffice it to say that it does not appear to have had close links with the great church of Ephesus.

In the early part of the second century that church still ranked as a Pauline foundation; only later did it lay claim to John as its apostle *par excellence*.

The historical tradition was not simply *preserved* by John and his disciples. The sayings of Jesus and incidents from his ministry which it enshrined formed the basis for further meditation, instruction and preaching; it flourished as a living and growing tradition, but remained faithful to its historical basis.

In arranging and recording this tradition, the Evangelist shows remarkable skill in various ways and not least in character-portrayal. The Samaritan woman (chapter 4) and the once-blind man of Jerusalem (chapter 9) are well-drawn and unforgettable personalities; and it is almost entirely to this Evangelist that we owe the vivid traditional picture of the personality of Mary of Magdala. Scholars have discussed the dialogue form in this Gospel and distinguished it from that found in the other Gospels,[18] but perhaps the most remarkable testimony to its dramatic realism is borne by Dorothy Sayers when she says, with regard to her sequence of radio plays, *The Man Born to be King*, that when John is the authority for any scene, 'the playwright's task is easy. Either the dialogue is all there – vivid and personal on both sides – or the part of the interlocutor can be readily reconstructed from the replies given'.[19]

2. THE FOURTH GOSPEL IN THE EARLY CHUCH

Not long after the publication of the Fourth Gospel, it was brought together with the three Synoptic Gospels to form the fourfold Gospel, and for the most part it was in this form rather than as separate documents that the four Gospels henceforth circulated. The use of the codex (a book more or less as we know it, with leaves and pages), which early Christians preferred to the scroll (a long strip of writing material, containing perhaps as many as a hundred columns of text, which had to be wound and unwound round a central rod), made it practicable for all four Gospels to be contained together in one book.

Some of the earliest pieces of NT manuscript which have survived to this day exhibit part of the text of the Fourth Gospel. The earliest known fragment of any part of the NT is a tiny piece of one leaf of what was once a codex of this Gospel. This is the papyrus fragment of John's Gospel in the John Rylands University Library of Manchester, containing a few words from John 18, and dated about AD 130. Henry Guppy, who was Rylands Librarian from 1900 to 1948, said with pardonable exaggeration that it must have been written 'when the ink of the original autograph was scarcely dry'.[20] In the authorized catalogue of NT papyri it is listed as Papyrus 52.

Two other papyrus codices of the Gospel of John come from the end of the second century; they belong to the Bodmer Library at Cologny, near Geneva. One of them, Papyrus 66, contains most of John 1–14 and substantial portions of the remaining chapters; the other, Papyrus 75, contains most of the Gospel of Luke followed by John 1–11 almost in its entirety and portions of chapters 12–15.

Yet another papyrus codex is Papyrus 45, in the Chester Beatty collection in Dublin; it belongs to the first half of the third century and, with other biblical papyri in the same collection, was probably the property of a Greek-speaking country church in Egypt. When complete, Papyrus 45 contained the Greek text of all four Gospels and Acts; parts of these five documents are preserved even in its present mutilated form.

In the earlier part of the second century the Fourth Gospel was recognized and quoted by gnostic writers at least as much as by those whose teaching came to be acknowledged as more in line with the apostolic tradition. There are affinities to its thought and language in the letters of Ignatius, bishop of Antioch (*c.* AD 110), and in the collection of hymns called the *Odes of Solomon* (from about the same period), which have a gnostic flavour.[21] Polycarp, bishop of Smyrna (writing *c.* AD 120), quotes from 1 John, knowledge of which might be thought to presuppose knowledge of the Gospel of John too.[22] Hippolytus states that the gnostic Basilides (*c.* AD 130) quoted John 1:9 (about the true light coming into the world) as a gloss on the creative word 'Let there be light' (Gen. 1:3);[23] if he is right, then that is the earliest known explicit quotation from the Gospel of John.

The *Gospel of Truth* (*c.* AD 140), a gnostic work coming either from Valentinus or from one of his disciples, has several echoes of our Gospel if not direct quotations. To Valentinus the incarnation doctrine of the prologue (John 1:14) was not so objectionable as it would have been to many gnostic teachers: 'when the Word came into the midst', says the *Gospel of Truth* (26:4–8), '. . . it became a body (*sōma*)' – perhaps John's term 'flesh' (*sarx*) was too 'carnal' to be palatable to the writer, but 'body' (*sōma*) was acceptable. However, later he says, 'those who were material were strangers and did not see his form or recognize him. For he came forth in flesh (*sarx*) of such a kind that nothing could block his progress' (31:1–7). Here 'flesh' is conceded, but not in the sense of ordinary flesh: this flesh is not material or subject to physical limitations, but is rather as free from them as was Jesus' resurrection body, to which closed doors presented no barrier (John 20:19).[24]

A disciple of Valentinus named Heracleon, who died *c*. AD 180, is the first known commentator on the Fourth Gospel. His commentary has not survived independently, but it is repeatedly quoted by Origen (AD 185–254) in his own commentary on this Gospel: it is evident from these quotations that Heracleon's commentary was of a highly allegorizing character.[25]

Acknowledgement of the ready use which second-century gnostic writers made of the Fourth Gospel cannot blind us to the fact that 'at every crucial point the Gospel is in tension with the Gnostic point of view, indeed repudiates it'.[26] Only by a forced exegesis which went against the grain of this Gospel could Gnostics make it serve their purpose.

Apart from the Gnostics, the first writer who makes anything like a quotation from this Gospel is Justin Martyr who, in a discussion of baptism, says, 'Christ indeed said, "Unless you are born again you shall not enter into the kingdom of heaven." It is evident to all that those who have once been born cannot re-enter their mothers' wombs.'[27] This is most probably a memory-quotation of John 3:3–5. But Justin does not cite this Gospel explicitly where he might have been expected to do so – for example, in his teaching about the pre-existent Word (*logos*) of God that became incarnate in Jesus Christ.[28] He has nothing to say of the authorship of any one of the canonical Gospels, but refers in general to the 'memoirs of the apostles'.[29]

Justin's disciple Tatian, however, has more positive testimony to give. He seems to have been the first person to conceive the idea of unstitching the units of which each of the four Gospels is made up and rearranging them so as to form one continuous narrative. Tatian's arrangement, published *c*. AD 170, was called the *Diatessaron* – a Greek musical term meaning 'harmony of four'. It was probably first compiled in Greek, but it became very popular in a Syriac version in the upper Euphrates and Tigris area – the region to which Tatian belonged. In the fourth century Ephrem, most eminent among the fathers of the Syriac church, wrote a commentary on the *Diatessaron*. So attached were the Syriac Christians to this form of the Gospels that it was only with difficulty that Bishop Rabbula of Edessa (AD 411–435) got them to accept the separate Gospels in the Peshitta edition – the edition which has remained the 'authorized version' of the Syriac Bible.

In Tatian's *Diatessaron* the Gospel of John provided the framework into which material from the other Gospels was fitted at appropriate points. Here, then, is adequate evidence for the recognition of John's Gospel as one of the authoritative records of the story of Jesus – indeed, as a specially authoritative record.

To around the same period as Tatian it has been customary to assign the anti-Marcionite prologue to the Gospel of John, which precedes the text of this Gospel in some Latin manuscripts.[30] More recently serious arguments for dating it considerably later have been put forward.[31] Even so, this is a convenient point to mention it.

Marcion, a native of Pontus in the north of Asia Minor, was so extreme a devotee of Paul that he held him to be the only apostle who preserved the pure message of Jesus. All the other apostles relapsed into Judaism, he maintained, and corrupted the message. Finding that the bishops of Asia Minor were unwilling to take him seriously, he went to Rome *c.* AD 140, hoping perhaps that the leaders of the Roman church might show themselves more enlightened and unprejudiced. But he was equally unsuccessful with them, so he withdrew his followers from their communion and formed a 'Marcionite' church. He published a canon or closed list of Christian scripture, comprising one gospel writing (an edition of the Gospel of Luke who, as Paul's companion, might be expected to be true to the pure message of Jesus) and ten letters of Paul. His action stimulated a reaction on the part of the catholic church, and what are called the anti-Marcionite prologues to the Gospels have been viewed as part of that reaction. That prologue to John's Gospel, extant only in a corrupt Latin translation, runs as follows (when obvious corruptions have been emended):

> The Gospel of John was published and delivered to the churches by John while he was still in the body, as a man of Hierapolis, Papias, John's dear disciple, has related in his five exegetical[32] books. He wrote down the Gospel at John's dictation. But the heretic Marcion was thrust out by John, after being censured by him for his contrary opinions. He had carried writings or letters to him from brethren in Pontus.

Whatever be the date of this enigmatic piece of information, it appears to be dependent on statements of Papias, bishop of Hierapolis in Phrygia (*c.* AD 130), whose five-volume *Exegesis of the Dominical Logia* (no longer extant) was accessible in some monastic libraries of Europe in the Middle Ages. But if so, the information has suffered in transmission, partly because of defects in the rendering of the Greek text into Latin and partly because of subsequent copying errors.

That Papias was a disciple of John is affirmed by Irenaeus[33] but denied by Eusebius.[34] Since he was contemporary with Polycarp (*c.* AD 70–156), who was certainly a disciple of John, he could, so far as chronology is concerned, have served as amanuensis when the Fourth Gospel was being written down. But the statement to this effect in the prologue may have arisen from a misunderstanding

of what Papias wrote. Papias may have said that 'they [the churches
to which this Gospel was delivered by John] wrote it down at his
dictation' (in Greek 'they wrote down' could easily be misread as
'I wrote down').[35] As for Marcion's being 'thrust out' by John, this
is so improbable as to be practically impossible. The truth more
probably is tht he was repudiated by Papias, when he visited him
at Hierapolis as a messenger from fellow-Christians in Pontus. The
author of the prologue wished to emphasize how thoroughly Marcion and his teachings were rejected by reputable church leaders.

An even more enigmatic account of the origin of the Fourth
Gospel is given in the Muratorian Canon, the earliest known 'catholic' list of NT books, compiled in Latin and probably at Rome
towards the end of the second century.[36] According to this
document:

> John, one of the disciples, wrote the Fourth Gospel. When his fellow-
> disciples and the bishops urged him to do so, he said, 'Join me in fasting
> for three days, and then let us relate to one another what shall be
> revealed to each.' The same night it was revealed to Andrew, one of the
> apostles, that John should write down everything in his own name, and
> that they should all revise it.

The compiler was no doubt dependent on some tradition or
other for the account, but the only item of historical worth that it
contains is the implication that others in addition to the Evangelist
himself shared responsibility for the publication of the work – and
that may have been an intelligent inference from John 21:24.
Then the compiler goes on:

> And therefore, although varying principles are taught in the several
> books of the gospels, yet it makes no difference to the faith of believers,
> since everything is set forth in them all by one directing Spirit, con-
> cerning our Lord's nativity, his passion, his resurrection, his converse
> with his disciples and his twofold advent – first in lowliness, without
> honour, which is past; secondly in royal power and glory, which is yet
> future. No wonder, then, that John so explicitly lays claim in his letters
> also to these experiences one by one, saying of himself, 'What we have
> seen with our eyes and heard with our ears and our hands have touched
> – this is what we have written.' Thus he claims not to be a spectator
> and hearer only but also a writer of all the Lord's wonders in due order.

He insisted on the consentient witness of all four Gospels to one
and the same faith and on the eyewitness character of John's record.
His free quotation of 1 John 1:1, 3a, is applied to the contents of
the Gospel. His emphases probably bear some relation to theological controversies of his day.

By the end of the second century, then, the Gospel of John was generally acknowledged throughout the Christian churches as one of the four canonical gospel-writings. Our principal witness from this period is Irenaeus, who went from his home in the province of Asia shortly after AD 177 to become bishop of Lyon in the Rhone valley. Irenaeus was familiar with Christianity in the eastern and western parts of the Roman Empire; he also maintained close association with the church in Rome. His statements about the books of the NT, like his statements about Christian doctrine as a whole, reflect the consensus of Christian belief over a wide area.

To Irenaeus, the fourfold character of the gospel record is as axiomatic as the four quarters of the world or the four principal winds (or, as we should say today in an idiom which was not available to him, the four cardinal points of the compass).[37] Not only was he sure that the Fourth Gospel was authoritative; he had no doubt of the Evangelist's identity: 'John the disciple of the Lord, who leaned back on his breast, published the Gospel while he was resident at Ephesus in Asia.'[38] The Evangelist, that is to say, was the beloved disciple of John 13:23, and his name was John.

In this as in other matters Irenaeus attached importance to the testimony of reliable Christian tradition, and with regard to the Fourth Evangelist he relied on one specially important bearer of tradition – Polycarp, bishop of Smyrna. On one occasion he had occasion to remonstrate with Florinus, a former acquaintance of his, whom he had known in Smyrna many years before, and wrote to him as follows:

> I remember the events of those days more clearly than those which have taken place recently, for what we learn as boys grows up with our lives and becomes united to them. So I can describe for you the very place where the blessed Polycarp sat and discoursed, how he came in and went out, his manner of life and his bodily appearance, the discourses which he used to deliver to the people, and how he would tell of his converse with John and with the others who had seen the Lord, how he remembered their words, and what things he had heard from them about the Lord, including his mighty works and his teaching. . . .[39]

It is inevitable that we should identify the John of whom Polycarp spoke with that John who, according to Irenaeus, published the Gospel at Ephesus. Polycarp, who was at least eighty-six years old at the time of his martyrdom in AD 156, could well have known in his earlier years men and women who had met Jesus and who lived on into the eighties and nineties of the first century.

Another letter in which Irenaeus associates Polycarp with John was sent to Victor, bishop of Rome (c. AD 190), when Victor proposed to excommunicate people who celebrated Easter on a

fixed day of the month, after the Asian manner, and not on a fixed
day of the week. Irenaeus pointed out that the Asian manner had
venerable precedent: Polycarp had followed it 'along with John the
disciple of the Lord and the other apostles with whom he
associated'.[40]

By the time of Irenaeus the only exceptions to the general
acknowledgment of the Johannine authorship of the Fourth Gospel
were the *Alogoi*, a group of people so called because they refused
to accept this Gospel with the *logos* doctrine of its prologue (and
also because *alogoi* as a common Greek adjective means 'witless
ones').[41] The one person of consequence among them was a presbyter of the Roman church named Gaius, whose only deviation
from current orthodoxy was his rejection of the Fourth Gospel and
the Apocalypse. His main reason for rejecting them seems to have
been his opposition to Montanism, a charismatic movement which
arose in Phrygia about AD 156. The Montanists claimed that
Christ's promise to send the Paraclete was fulfilled in the emergence
of their movement, and that their founder, Montanus, was the
Paraclete's mouthpiece. Since the Fourth Gospel was the source of
all teaching about the coming Paraclete (John 14:16, 26; 15:26;
16:7), Gaius's rejection of this Gospel undergirded his rejection of
Montanist claims.[42]

From Irenaeus onwards there is virtual unanimity in the church
on the canonicity and authorship of the Fourth Gospel. His contemporary, Clement of Alexandria says that, after the first three
Gospels had been written, 'John, last of all, conscious that the
bodily (i.e. external) facts had been set forth in those Gospels, was
urged on by his disciples and, divinely moved by the Spirit, composed a spiritual (i.e. allegorical) Gospel'.[43]

3. THE MESSAGE OF THE FOURTH GOSPEL

The purpose of the Gospel is stated in John 20:30 f.: it is to bring
the readers to faith, or to confirm them in faith. Faith involves
both believing *in* and believing *that*: believing in Jesus is emphasized as the way of life throughout the Gospel, but believing in him
implies believing certain things about him – that he is 'the Christ,
the Son of God'. These are not two separate designations: for John,
to believe in Jesus as the Messiah is to believe in him as the Son of
God (and this is true of the other Evangelists also).

The Fourth Evangelist wrote for a world very different from that
in which the saving events took place. For the people of this new
world Jerusalem and Palestine were geographically remote, but
more than that: the way of life which had been followed there sixty
years earlier, and which formed the setting of the gospel narrative,

belonged to a world which, they felt, had passed away for ever. The climate of opinion in which they lived was not greatly concerned about historical fact and geographical location. An insistence on historical fact and geographical location, it was thought, tended to obscure the universal relevance of eternal truth. Eternal truth belonged to the spiritual realm, the realm that really mattered; historical fact and geographical location were too closely tied to the passing material order. Such a question as who was or who was not king of the Jews in AD 30 could have only local and temporary relevance, even if the answer to it determined whether Jesus was rightly or wrongly sentenced to death by Pontius Pilate.

John himself attached the utmost importance to eternal truth, which he identified with the divine self-expression, the Word that existed in the beginning with God. But he insisted that eternal truth was uniquely manifested in time and place – in Palestine, during the governorship of Pontius Pilate – when the Word appeared on earth in the human life of Jesus of Nazareth. Far from depreciating the material order, John affirms that the Word became *flesh*. It is the man who was crucified as king of the Jews in AD 30 that is king of the realm of truth; those who are truly devoted to eternal truth will gladly listen to him as his obedient subjects.[44]

But within John's general Hellenistic environment can we think of one particular category of reader that he might have in mind? Whom are the arguments deployed in the great debate of his central chapters designed to convince? These central chapters are largely devoted to one sustained debate between Jesus and the religious leaders in Jerusalem – a debate which was carried on in the following decades between the followers of Jesus and the synagogue authorities.

The destruction of the Jerusalem temple and the cessation of the sacrificial worship in AD 70 made little difference to Jewish life in the dispersion. The debate between the disciples and the synagogue authorities reached a critical stage around AD 90, when one of the prayers in the synagogue service was reworded so as effectively to exclude the followers of Jesus.[45] It was probably against this background that the Fourth Gospel was published, in order to bring members of synagogue congregations in that area of the dispersion where the Evangelist and his associates lived (and in other areas too) to faith in Jesus as the Messiah of Israel, the Son of God, the Revealer of the Father.[46] Among members of synagogue congregations those most likely to be impressed were perhaps Gentile God-fearers who regularly attended synagogue services. (The record of Acts illustrates how this was so in Paul's mission-field a generation earlier.)

But, whoever may have formed the original target for the Evangelist's persuasion, his persuasive power has proved effective with readers of many diverse types. Not unnaturally, readers of a philosophical or mystical turn of mind have found this Gospel specially congenial. But its message has spoken directly to the condition of much more unlikely hearers. For example, the members of the Christian Industrial League, an organization dedicated to Christian aid among the residents of Chicago's Skidrow, have said 'that in their work they have found that St John's Gospel is the best for dealing with these tough, hard men. Its straight, unequivocal words about sin and salvation somehow go home and carry conviction to the most abandoned, while its direct invitation wins a response that nothing else does'.[47] Together with many others throughout nineteen centuries, such hearers and readers find in their own experience an echo of the confession which first authenticated the Evangelist's record: 'We know that his testimony is true.'[48]

And this is his testimony: 'God so loved the world that he gave his only Son' (John 3:16). It was out of love for the world that God revealed eternal truth to the world. Eternal truth is inseparable from eternal love. Both inhere in the life of God, and Jesus is the embodiment of both, as he is the embodiment of the divine life itself: 'God gave us eternal life, and this life is in his Son' (1 John 5:11).

As the prologue to the Gospel puts it, Jesus is the eternal Word or self-revelation of God, expressed in many ways at various times, but finally incarnated in a human life. As the whole Gospel emphasizes, Jesus is the eternal Son of the Father, sent into the world for the world's salvation. The revelation of the Father which he imparts means the salvation of the world: the revelation and the salvation are consummated together in Jesus' laying down his life on the cross.

The relationship which the Father and the Son eternally bear to each other is declared to be a coinherence or mutual indwelling of love. Jesus is in the Father; the Father is in him. And the purpose of Jesus' coming to reveal the Father is that men and women may, through faith in him, have eternal life – may, in other words, be drawn into this divine fellowship of love, dwelling in God as God dwells in them.[49]

It is of the essence of the gospel that the life in which the eternal Word became incarnate was the life of a real human being of flesh and blood. There is nothing docetic about Jesus' humanity. It is equally of the essence of the gospel that the events in which Jesus revealed the Father were historical events – in particular, that the crucial outpouring of divine love actually took place 'on an April day about AD 30, at a supper-table in Jerusalem, in a garden across the Kidron valley, in the headquarters of Pontius Pilate, and on a

Roman cross at Golgotha'.[50] Moreover, Jesus' words are as truly revelatory events as his actions are. The Evangelist records words which were really spoken, actions which were really performed. His record of these words and actions includes their interpretation, in which their inward significance is disclosed and faith is quickened in Jesus as the Revealer of the Father and the Saviour of the world.

The source of the Evangelist's interpretation of Jesus' words and actions is clearly indicated in his record. He reports Jesus' promise that the Holy Spirit, the Paraclete, would come to guide his disciples into all the truth, especially by bringing to their remembrance all that Jesus had taught them and making it plain to them.[51] In reporting this promise, the Evangelist implies that he himself experienced a rich fulfilment of it, as he pondered the significance of what Jesus had done and said during his ministry, as he shared with others what he and his companions had seen and heard, and as he finally caused the contents of this Gospel to be set down in writing. If in this Gospel the words and deeds of Jesus appear to have undergone 'transposition into a higher key'[52] than that with which we are familiar in the Synoptic Gospels, this is the effect of the Spirit's enabling the Evangelist to adapt the story of Jesus to a different public from that for which the earlier Gospels were designed. The Spirit was, among other things, to serve as a trustworthy interpreter; his interpretative ministry is clearly to be discerned in the Gospel according to John.

Interpretation (which in the Gospels involved, at an early stage, translation from the Aramaic which Jesus normally spoke into Greek) may take a variety of forms. A word-for-word transcription or translation is scarcely an interpretation in the usual sense of the word. Today one would 'interpret' the words of Jesus by transposing them from the Hellenistic Greek in which they have been preserved into a late twentieth-century idiom (whether English or any other language). Interpretation may result in an abridgement or a summary (it is widely believed, for example, that the speeches in Acts are literary summaries of what was originally spoken at much greater length). It may, on the other hand, result in an expanded version of what was said; if so, it will probably include a good deal of paraphrase. If the effect of such an expanded paraphrase is to bring out the sense more fully, then the use of this form is amply justified.

Plutarch, in his *Life of Brutus*, describes what happened in Rome on the morrow of Julius Caesar's assassination:

Antony and his supporters demanded that Caesar's will should be read in public, and that Caesar's body should not be buried in private but with the customary honours. . . . Brutus agreed to these demands. . . .

The first consequence of this was that, when it became known that according to the terms of his will the dictator had presented seventy-five drachmas to each Roman citizen, and had bequeathed to the citizens the use of his gardens beyond the Tiber, . . . a great wave of affection for Caesar and a powerful sense of his loss swept over the people. The second consequence was that, after the dead man had been brought to the forum, Antony delivered the customary funeral oration over his body. As soon as he saw that the people were deeply stirred by his speech, he changed his tone and struck a note of compassion, and picking up Caesar's toga, stiff with blood as it was, he unfolded it for all to see, pointing out each gash where the daggers had stabbed through and the number of Caesar's wounds. At this his hearers lost all control of their emotions. Some called out for the assassins to be killed; others . . . dragged out benches and tables from the neighbouring shops and piled them on top of one another to make an enormous pyre. On this they laid Caesar's corpse and cremated it. . . . As the flames began to mount, people rushed up from all sides, seized burning brands, and ran through the city to the assassins' houses to set fire to them.[53]

A vivid enough account, to be sure. But how was Caesar's will read, and what exactly did Mark Antony say in his eulogy? A satisfying answer to these two questions is provided in a well-known English interpretation of Plutarch's narrative – not a word-for-word translation but an expanded paraphrase in which it is Antony who reads Caesar's will aloud *after* he has excited the indignation of the crowd by exhibiting Caesar's torn and blood-stained robe and exposing his wounded corpse. Antony's whole speech, from its low-key exordium:

> Friends, Romans, countrymen, lend me your ears;
> I come to bury Caesar, not to praise him –

to its ringing peroration:

> Here was a Caesar! when comes such another?[54]

is a translation of the freest kind, a transposition into another key; but Shakespeare's genius enables him to put the right words into Antony's mouth, 'endeavouring as nearly as possible' (in Thucydidean fashion), 'to give the general purport of what was actually said'.[55]

What Shakespeare does by dramatic insight (and, it may be added, what many a preacher does by homiletical skill), all this and much more the Spirit of God accomplished in our Evangelist. It does not take divine inspiration to provide a verbatim transcript; but to reproduce the words which were spirit and life to their first believing hearers in such a way that they continue to communicate their saving message and prove themselves to be spirit and life to men and women today, nineteen centuries after John wrote–that is the work of the Spirit of God. It is through the Spirit's operation that, in William Temple's words, 'the mind of Jesus himself was what the Fourth Gospel disclosed';[56] and it is through the illumination granted by the same Spirit that one may still recognize in this Gospel the authentic voice of Jesus.

Bibliography[1]

1. *Commentaries*

BAILEY, R. F. *The Gospel of S John: An Introductory Commentary* (SCM Press, London 1940).

*BARRETT, C. K. *The Gospel according to St John: An Introduction with Commentary and Notes on the Greek Text* (SPCK, London ²1978).

*BEASLEY-MURRAY, G. R. *John*, WBC (Word Books, Waco, Texas, forthcoming).

*BERNARD, J. H. *The Gospel according to St John*, ICC. Two volumes (T. & T. Clark, Edinburgh, 1928).

BROWN, R. E. *The Gospel according to John: Introduction, Translation and Notes*, AB. Two volumes (Doubleday, Garden City, N.Y. 1966, 1970).

*BULTMANN, R. *The Gospel of John: A Commentary*. Translated by G. R. Beasley-Murray, R. W. N. Hoare, J. K. Riches (Blackwell, Oxford, 1971).

FENTON, J. C. *The Gospel according to John* NClarB (Clarendon Press, Oxford, 1970).

FINDLAY, J. A. *The Fourth Gospel: An Expository Commentary* (Epworth Press, London, 1956).

HENDRIKSEN, W. *Exposition of the Gospel according to John* NTC. Two volumes (Baker, Grand Rapids, Michigan, 1953, 1954).

HOSKYNS, E. C. *The Fourth Gospel*. Edited by F. N. Davey (Faber & Faber, London, 1954).

HOWARD, W. F. 'The Gospel according to John' *IB* 8 (Abingdon, Nashville/New York, 1952).

HUNTER, A. M. *The Gospel according to John* CBC (University Press, Cambridge, 1965).

KELLY, W. *An Exposition of the Gospel of John* (T. Weston, London, 1898).

---

[1]. The bibliography is confined to works accessible in English. Commentaries marked with an asterisk (*) are designed for the more advanced student.

LIGHTFOOT, R. H. *St John's Gospel: A Commentary* (University Press, Oxford 1956).

LINDARS, B. *The Gospel of John* NCB (Oliphants, London, 1972).

MACGREGOR, G. H. C. *The Gospel of John* MNTC (Hodder & Stoughton, London, 1928).

MARSH, J., *The Gospel of St John*, PGC (Penguin Books, Harmondsworth, 1968).

MORRIS, L. *The Gospel according to John* NICNT (Eerdmans, Grand Rapids, Michigan, 1971).

NEWBIGIN, L. *The Light has come: An Exposition of the Fourth Gospel* (Eerdmans, Grand Rapids, Michigan, 1982).

SANDERS, J. N. *A Commentary on the Gospel according to St John*. Edited and Completed by B. A. Mastin. BNTC (A. & C. Black, London, 1968).

*SCHNACKENBURG, R. *The Gospel according to St John*. Translated by K. Smyth, C. Hastings and others. HTCNT. Three volumes (Burns & Oates, London 1968, 1980, 1982).

*SMALLEY, S. S. *The Gospel according to John* NIGTC (Paternoster, Exeter; Eerdmans, Grand Rapids, Michigan, forthcoming).

TASKER, R. V. G. *The Gospel according to St John* TNTC (Tyndale Press, London 1960).

TEMPLE, W. *Readings in St John's Gospel*. Two volumes (Macmillans, London 1939, 1940).

VINE, W. E. *John: His Record of Christ* (Oliphants, London 1948).

WESTCOTT, B. F. *The Gospel according to St John* (1880). With a new introduction by A. Fox (James Clarke, London, 1958).

*WESTCOTT, B. F. *The Gospel according to St John: The Greek Text with Introduction and Notes*. Two volumes (John Murray, London, 1908).

2. *Other works*

ASKWITH, E. H. *The Historical Value of the Fourth Gospel* (Hodder & Stoughton, London, 1910).

BACON, B. W. *The Fourth Gospel in Research and Debate* (Unwin, London, 1910).

BARRETT, C. K. *Essays on John* (SPCK, London, 1982).

BARRETT, C. K. *The Gospel of John and Judaism* (SPCK, London, 1975).

BOICE, J. M. *Witness and Revelation in the Gospel of John* (Zondervan, Grand Rapids, Michigan, 1970).

BROOMFIELD, G. W. *John, Peter and the Fourth Gospel* (SPCK, London, 1934).

BROWN, R. E. *The Community of the Beloved Disciple* (Geoffrey Chapman, London, 1979).

BURNEY, C. F. *The Aramaic Origin of the Fourth Gospel* (Clarendon Press, Oxford, 1922).

BURY, R. G. *The Fourth Gospel and the Logos-Doctrine* (Heffer, Cambridge, 1940).

CHAPMAN, J. *John the Presbyter and the Fourth Gospel* (Clarendon Press, Oxford, 1911).

CHARLESWORTH, J. H. (ed.), *John and Qumran* (Geoffrey Chapman, London, 1972).

COLWELL, E. C. *The Greek of the Fourth Gospel* (University Press, Chicago, 1931).

CROSS, F. L. (ed.) *Studies in the Fourth Gospel* (Mowbray, London, 1957).

CULLMANN, O. *The Johannine Circle*. Translated by J. Bowden (SCM Press, London 1976).

CULPEPPER, R. A. *The Johannine School* SBLDS 26 (Scholars Press, Missoula, Montana, 1975).

DAVEY, J. E. *The Jesus of St John* (Lutterworth Press, London 1958).

DE JONGE, M. *Jesus: Stranger from Heaven and Son of God* (Scholars Press, Missoula, Montana, 1977).

DODD, C. H. *The Interpretation of the Fourth Gospel* (University Press, Cambridge, 1953).

DODD, C. H. *Historical Tradition in the Fourth Gospel* (University Press, Cambridge, 1963).

DRUMMOND, J. *An Inquiry into the Character and Authorship of the Fourth Gospel* (Williams & Norgate, London, 1903).

EDWARDS, H. E. *The Disciple who Wrote These Things* (James Clarke, London, 1953).

FORTNA, R. *The Gospel of Signs*, SNTSMS 11 (University Press, Cambridge, 1970).

FREED, E. D. *Old Testament Quotations in the Gospel of John* SNT 11 (Brill, Leiden, 1965).

GARDNER-SMITH, P. *St John and the Synoptic Gospels* (University Press, Cambridge, 1938).

GREEN-ARMYTAGE, A. H. N. *John Who Saw* (Faber & Faber, London, 1952).

GUILDING, A. *The Fourth Gospel and Jewish Worship* (Clarendon Press, Oxford, 1960).

HARRIS, J. R. *The Origin of the Prologue to St John's Gospel* (University Press, Cambridge, 1917).

HARVEY, A. E. *Jesus on Trial: A Study in the Fourth Gospel* (SPCK, London, 1976).

HEADLAM, A. C. *The Fourth Gospel as History* (Blackwell, Oxford, 1948).

HENDERSON, R. A. *The Gospel of Fulfilment* (SPCK, London, 1936).

HIGGINS, A. J. B. *The Historicity of the Fourth Gospel* (Lutterworth Press, London, 1960).

HOLLAND, H. S. *The Fourth Gospel.* Edited by W. J. Richmond (John Murray, London, 1923).

HOLWERDA, D. E. *The Holy Spirit and Eschatology in the Gospel of John* (J. H. Kok, Kampen, 1959).

HOWARD, W. F., *Christianity according to St John* (Duckworth, London, 1943).

HOWARD, W. F. *The Fourth Gospel in Recent Criticism and Interpretation.* Revised by C. K. Barrett (Epworth Press, London, [4]1955).

HUNTER, A. M. *According to John* (SCM Press, London, 1968).

JOHNSTON, G. *The Spirit-Paraclete in the Gospel of John* SNTSMS 12 (University Press, Cambridge, 1970).

KÄSEMANN, E. *The Testament of Jesus: A Study of the Gospel of John in the Light of Chapter 17.* Translated by G. Krodel (SCM Press, London 1968).

KYSAR, R. *The Fourth Evangelist and his Gospel: An Examination of Contemporary Scholarship* (Augsburg, Minneapolis, 1975).

LIGHTFOOT, J. B. *Biblical Essays* (Macmillan, London, 1893), pp. 1–44 ('Internal Evidence for the Authenticity and Genuineness of St John's Gospel'), 45–122 ('External Evidence for the Authenticity and Genuineness of St John's Gospel'), 123–193 ('Internal Evidence for the Authenticity and Genuineness of St John's Gospel'), 194–198 ('Additional Notes').

LINDARS, B. *Behind the Fourth Gospel* (SPCK, London, 1971).

LOFTHOUSE, W. F. *The Father and the Son: A Study of Johannine Thought* (SCM Press, London 1934).

MANSON, T. W. *On Paul and John*, SBT 38 (SCM Press, London, 1963).

MARTYN, J. L., *The Gospel of John in Christian History* (Paulist, New York, 1978).

MARTYN, J. L. *History and Theology in the Fourth Gospel* (Abingdon, Nashville, [2]1979).

MORRIS, L. *The Dead Sea Scrolls and St John's Gospel* (Westminster Chapel Bookroom, London, 1960).

MORRIS, L. *Studies in the Fourth Gospel* (Paternoster Press, Exeter; Eerdmans, Grand Rapids, Michigan, 1969).

MUSSNER, F. *The Historical Jesus in the Gospel of St John*, QD 19. Translated by W. J. O'Hara (Burns & Oates, London, 1967).

NOLLOTH, C. F. *The Fourth Evangelist* (John Murray, London, 1925).

OLSSON, B. *Structure and Meaning of the Fourth Gospel*, CB:NTS 6 (Gleerup, Lund, 1974).

PAGELS, E. H. *The Johannine Gospel in Gnostic Exegesis*, SBLMS 17 (Abingdon, Nashville/New York, 1973).

PAINTER, J. *John: Witness and Theologian* (SPCK, London, 1975).

POLLARD, T. E. *Johannine Christology and the Early Church* SNTSMS 13 (University Press, Cambridge, 1970).

REDLICH, E. B. *An Introduction to the Fourth Gospel* (Longmans, London, 1939).

ROBERTSON, A. T. *The Divinity of Christ in the Gospel of John* (Revell, New York, 1916).

ROBINSON, J. A. *The Historical Character of St John's Gospel* (Longmans, Green & Co., London, ²1929).

ROBINSON, J. A. T. *Redating the New Testament* (SCM Press, London, 1976), pp. 254–311 ('The Gospel and Epistles of John').

ROBINSON, J. A. T. *Twelve New Testament Studies* SBT 34 (SCM Press, London, 1962), pp. 94–106 ('The New Look on the Fourth Gospel'), 107–125 ('The Destination and Purpose of St John's Gospel').

SANDAY, W. *The Authorship and Historical Character of the Fourth Gospel* (Macmillan, London, 1872).

SANDAY, W. *The Criticism of the Fourth Gospel* (Clarendon Press, Oxford 1905).

SANDERS, J. N.*The Fourth Gospel in the Early Church* (University Press, Cambridge, 1943).

SAUNDERS, E. W. *John Celebrates the Gospel* (Abingdon, Nashville/New York, 1968).

SIDEBOTTOM, E. M. *The Christ of the Fourth Gospel* (SPCK, London, 1961).

SMALLEY, S. S. *John: Evangelist and Interpreter* (Paternoster Press, Exeter, 1978).

STRACHAN, R. H. *The Fourth Gospel: Its Significance and Environment* (SCM Press, London, ³1941).

WILES, M. F. *The Spiritual Gospel: The Interpretation of the Fourth Gospel in the Early Church* (University Press, Cambridge, 1960).

WRIGHT, C. J. *Jesus the Revelation of God: His Mission and Message according to St John* (Hodder & Stoughton, London, 1950).

NOTES

1. Papias *Exegesis of the Dominical Oracles*, quoted by Eusebius, *Hist. Eccl.* 3.39.4. See F. F. Bruce, *Men and Movements in the Primitive Church* (Exeter 1979), pp. 132–136.

2. B. F. Westcott, *The Gospel according to St. John* (London 1880), pp. xxiv f. See F. F. Bruce, 'Johannine studies since Westcott's Day', contributed to the 1966 reprint of Westcott's *The Epistles of St. John* (London ³1892) issued by the Marcham Manor Press, Appleford, pp. lvii–lxxvi.

3. A. R. Short, *The Bible and Modern Research* (London 1931), p. 178.

4. E.g. C. F. Burney, *The Aramaic Origin of the Fourth Gospel* (Oxford, 1922); J. A. Montgomery *The Origin of the Gospel of St John* (Philadelphia, 1923).

5. See the essays collected in *John and Qumran*, ed. J. H. Charlesworth (London 1972).

6. Quite recently even the records of Ebla in Syria (3rd millennium BC) have been pressed into service; cf. M. Dahood, 'Ebla, Genesis and John' *The Christian Century*, April 15, 1981, pp. 418–421.

7. W. F. Albright, 'Recent Discoveries in Palestine and the Gospel of St John' in *The Background of the New Testament and its Eschatology* ed. W. D. Davies and D. Daube (Cambridge 1954), p. 169.

8. *Ibid.*, p. 170.

9. C. K. Barrett *The Gospel according to St John* (London ²1978), p. 132.

10. *Ibid.*, pp. 133 f.

11. When the author of 2 and 3 John calls himself 'the elder' in the superscription of these two letters, he probably uses the designation in a different sense from Papias and other second-century Christian writers. Writing to Christians who were so much younger than himself that he could address them as his 'little children' he refers to himself by the term of affection which they were accustomed to use in speaking of him.

12. P. H. Menoud *L'évangile de Jean d'après recherches récentes* (Neuchatel/Paris ²1947), p. 77.

13. J. A. T. Robinson, 'The New Look on the Fourth Gospel' in *Twelve New Testament Studies* (London 1962), p. 106.

14. Cf. P. Gardner-Smith *St John and the Synoptic Gospels* (Cambridge 1938).

15. R. Bultmann *The Gospel of John* (Oxford 1971), pp. 6–9 *et passim*; cf. R. T. Fortna *The Gospel of Signs* (Cambridge 1970).

16. Cf. C. H. Dodd *Historical Tradition in the Fourth Gospel* (Cambridge 1963).

17. Cf. R. E. Brown *The Community of the Beloved Disciple* (London 1979); also O. Cullmann *The Johannine Circle* (London 1976); R. A. Culpepper *The Johannine School* (Missoula 1975).

18. Cf. C. H. Dodd, 'The Dialogue Form in the Gospels' *BJRL* 37 (1954–55), pp. 54–67.

19. D. L. Sayers *The Man Born to be King* (London 1943), pp. 33 f. See also her comments, quoted on p. 409 (on John 21:24), with regard to the eyewitness claim of this Gospel.

20. *Catalogue of an Exhibition Illustrating the History of the Transmission of the Bible* (Manchester 1935), p. 4; cf. C. H. Roberts *An Unpublished Fragment of the Fourth Gospel in the John Rylands Library* (Manchester 1935).

21. When J. Rendel Harris discovered the *Odes of Solomon* in 1909 and suggested that they might even be of first-century date, the German scholar Adolf Jülicher is reported to have said, 'Then all our criticism of the Fourth Gospel is *kaput*' (T. R. Glover *Cambridge Retrospect* [Cambridge 1943], p. 73).

22. Polycarp *To the Philippians* 7:1: 'For every one who does not confess that Jesus Christ has come in the flesh is an antichrist' (loose quotation from 1 John 4:2 f.).

23. Hippolytus *Refutation of Heresies* 7.22.4.
24. Cf. C. K. Barrett, 'The Theological Vocabulary of the Fourth Gospel and the Gospel of Truth' *Essays on John* (London 1982), pp. 50–64.
25. Cf. E. H. Pagels *The Johannine Gospel in Gnostic Exegesis* (Nashville/New York 1973).
26. S. C. Neill *The Interpretation of the New Testament 1861–1961* (Oxford 1964), p. 210.
27. Justin *First Apology* 61.4 f.
28. See p. 63, n. 4 (on John 1:1).
28. Justin *First Apology* 67.3; *Dialogue with Trypho* 106.1 Elsewhere in the *Dialogue* (81.4) he mentions John the apostle as author of the Apocalypse.
30. The anti-Marcionite character of this and companion prologues and a date between AD 160 and 180 were defended by D. de Bruyne, 'Les plus anciens prologues latins des Evangiles' *Revue bénédictine* 40 (1928), pp. 193–214; A. von Harnack *Die ältesten Evangelien-Prologe und die Bildung des Neuen Testaments* (Berlin 1928).
31. J. Regul *Die antimarcionitischen Evangelienprologe* (Freiburg 1969), argues for a date not earlier than the fourth century.
32. The Latin text reads *extremis* ('last'). This appears to be a corruption of *externis*, a translation of Greek *exōterikois*, which was in turn a corruption of an original *exēgētikois*.
33. Irenaeus *Against Heresies* 5.33.4.
34. Eusebius *Hist. Eccl.* 3.39.2.
35. In the imperfect tense *apegraphon* means either 'I wrote down' or 'they wrote down' (according to the context); in the aorist 'I wrote down' is *apegrapsa* and 'they wrote down' *apegrapsan* (often written *apegrapsā*). Cf. J. B. Lightfoot *Essays on the Work entitled 'Supernatural Religion'* (London 1889), p. 214.
36. Cf. A. Ehrhardt, 'The Gospels in the Muratorian Fragment' in *The Framework of the New Testament Stories* (Manchester 1964), pp. 11–36. He presents a powerful case for regarding the Latin as the original text, not a translation from Greek; he even suggests that the compiler may have been one of the Latin-speaking popes at the end of the second century. A careful, but not conclusive, argument for a fourth-century date is set out by A. C. Sundberg, 'Canon Muratori: A Fourth-Century List' *HTR* 66 (1973), pp. 1–41.
37. Irenaeus *Against Heresies* 3.11.11.
38. Irenaeus *Against Heresies* 3.1.2
39. Eusebius *Hist. Eccl.* 5.20.5, 6.
40. Eusebius *Hist. Eccl.* 5.24.16.
41. Epiphanius *Heresies* 51.3.
42. Cf. Bar-Salibi *Commentary on Apocalypse* Introduction; Eusebius *Hist. Eccl.* 2.26.6, 7; 3.28.1, 2; 3.31.4; 6.19.3. Gaius'a arguments were rebutted by Hippolytus in a lost treatise *Concerning the Johannine Gospel and Revelation*, perhaps identical with his *Chapters against Gaius*, of which fragments survive in a Syriac translation.
43. Clement *Hypotyposes*, quoted by Eusebius, *Hist. Eccl.* 6.14.7.
44. John 18:33–38 (see pp. 352–354).
45. See p. 215 (on John 9:22).
46. See W. C. van Unnik, 'The Purpose of St John's Gospel' *Studia Evangelica* 1 = *Texte und Untersuchungen* 73 (Berlin 1959), pp. 382–411.
47. A. M. Chirgwin *The Bible in World Evangelism* (London 1954), p. 113.
48. John 21:24.
49. This is expressed in an eloquent and memorable passage by C. H. Dodd, *The Interpretation of the Fourth Gospel* (Cambridge 1953), pp. 199 f.
50. C. H. Dodd, *ibid.*
51. See exposition of John 14:26 and 16:13 f. (pp. 305, 320f.).

52. P. Gardner *The Ephesian Gospel* (London 1915), p. 284.
53. Plutarch, *Life of Brutus* 20.1–4, cf. his *Life of Caesar* 68.1; *Life of Antony* 14.3 f.
54. Shakespeare *Julius Caesar*, Act 3, Scene 2.
55. Thucydides, *History* 1.22.1.
56. W. Temple *Readings in St John's Gospel* (London 1939), p. xxxii.

Analysis of the Gospel of John

EXPOSITION

CHAPTER 1

PROLOGUE (John 1:1–18)

The prologue to the Fourth Gospel sets forth the theme of the whole work.[1] The narrative as a whole spells out the message of the prologue: that in the life and ministry of Jesus of Nazareth the glory of God was uniquely and perfectly disclosed. This message, of course, is not peculiar to the Fourth Evangelist among the NT writers; it is summed up concisely in Paul's affirmation that 'the God who said, "Let light shine out of darkness", has shone in our hearts to give the light of the knowledge of the glory of God in the face of Christ' (2 Cor. 4:6). The same parallel between the work of God in the old creation and his work in the new creation is drawn in the Johannine prologue.

The prologue is composed in rhythmical prose – hardly, as some have suggested, in poetry. It may have been originally a separate composition which has been integrated with the Gospel by having two preliminary sections of narrative dovetailed into it – verses 6–8 and verse 15, recording the beginning of the witness of John the Baptist. This and similar suggestions (such as that it was composed after the Gospel and then prefaced to it) are speculative at best. It is certainly the work of the Evangelist himself, if we may judge from the way in which it anticipates the various forms in which the main theme of the Gospel is presented in the chapters which follow. Several of the key-words of the Gospel – life, light, witness, glory (for example) – appear in the prologue. But the most characteristic term in the prologue, the term 'Word', does not reappear in the body of the Gospel in the sense which it bears in the prologue. Nevertheless, in what it says about the 'Word', the prologue shows us the perspective from which the Gospel as a whole is to be understood: all that is recorded, from the banks of Jordan to the resurrection appearances, shows how the eternal Word of God became flesh, that men and women might believe in him and live.

1:1 In the beginning was the Word, and the Word was with God, and the Word was God.

It is not by accident that the Gospel begins with the same phrase as the book of Genesis. In Gen. 1:1 'In the beginning' introduces the story of the old creation; here it introduces the story of the

28

new creation. In both works of creation the agent is the Word of God.

No doubt the English term 'Word' is an inadequate rendering of the Greek *logos*, but it would be difficult to find one less inadequate. In a version or commentary intended for scholars it might suffice to retain *logos* untranslated, but it will not really do to retain it in a work intended for the general reader, like James Moffatt's translation. Moffatt's translation of the Gospel begins with the statement, 'The Logos existed in the very beginning,' and this is justified by the observation that ' "Logos" is at any rate less misleading than "Word" would be to a modern reader.' But if *logos* is not completely meaningless to an ordinary reader, it probably suggests something like 'reason', and that is more misleading than 'Word'. A 'word' is a means of communication, the expression of what is in one's mind. J. B. Phillips renders the clause 'At the beginning God expressed himself', and he safeguards the personal quality which the Evangelist assigns to the divine self-expression by continuing: 'That personal expression, that word, was with God . . .' . Phillips agrees that his rendering is not one hundred per cent accurate, but says that a number of his readers have told him that it does convey some positive meaning to them, whereas they find the rendering 'word' (whether capitalized or not) too ambiguous.[2]

There is a famous passage in Goethe's *Faust* where Faust grapples with the translation of this clause, attempting to hit on the *mot juste* for *logos*, until at last he thinks he has found it: 'Im Anfang war die *Tat*' – 'In the beginning was the deed, the action'.[3] And while this is not the whole meaning, it is part of it. If we understand *logos* in this prologue as 'word in action' we may begin to do it justice.

The term *logos* was familiar in some Greek philosophical schools, where it denoted the principle of reason or order immanent in the universe, the principle which imposes form on the material world and constitutes the rational soul in man. It is not in Greek philosophical usage, however, that the background of John's thought and language should be sought. Yet, because of that usage, *logos* constituted a bridge-word by which people brought up in Greek philosophy, like Justin Martyr in the second century, found their way into Johannine Christianity.[4]

The true background to John's thought and language is found not in Greek philosophy but in Hebrew revelation. The 'word of God' in the Old Testament denotes God in action, especially in creation, revelation and deliverance.

In the creation narrative at the beginning of Genesis we read repeatedly that 'God said . . . and it was so'. This can be expressed in other terms, as in Ps. 33:6, 'By the word of the LORD the heavens were made'. But when this latter form of language is used, the way is open to personify 'the word of the LORD' and treat it as his agent or messenger. Similarly, alongside the statement that 'the LORD said to Isaiah . . .' (Isa. 7:3) we may be told that 'the word of the LORD came to Isaiah' (Isa. 38:4). Again, the two statements are synonymous, but in the latter of the two 'the word of the LORD' can be pictured as a messenger sent by God to the prophet.

An even more telling instance of this usage appears in Ps. 107:20. There men are portrayed suffering near-mortal sickness and crying to God for help, whereupon

> he sent forth his word, and healed them,
> and delivered them from destruction.

In a famous passage in the Book of Wisdom (18:14, 15) the angel of death which wrought such havoc in Egypt on the first passover night is identified with God's 'all-powerful word' which 'leaped from heaven, from the royal throne' into the doomed land, wielding the divine command as a 'sharp sword':

> and stood and filled all things with death,
> and touched heaven while standing on the earth.

Here the personification is more detailed and circumstantial than anything we find in the Hebrew Bible. But it is recognizably a development of the prophetic conception of God's word as his messenger, unerringly fulfilling his commission, as in Isa. 55:11:

> my word . . . that goes forth from my mouth
>   . . . shall not return to me empty;
> but it shall accomplish that which I purpose,
>   and prosper in the thing for which I sent it.

'In the beginning', then, when the universe was brought into existence, the divine Word by which it was brought into existence was already there. And the language which follows shows that our Evangelist has no mere literary personification in mind. The personal status which he ascribes to the Word is a matter of real existence; the relation which the Word bears to God is a personal relation: 'the Word was with God'.

This statement has profound theological implications, but these implications are not involved in the choice of the Greek preposition *pros* to denote 'with'. True, in literary Greek this is not a common sense of *pros*, but *pros* in this sense can be paralleled within the fourfold Gospel in the most ordinary and everyday context. When the Nazarenes say of Jesus in Mark 6:3, 'are not his sisters here with us?', the Greek word translated 'with' is *pros*. The Word of God is distinguished from God himself, and yet exists in a close personal relation with him; moreover, the Word shares the very nature of God, for 'the Word was *God*'.

The structure of the third clause in verse 1, *theos ēn ho logos*, demands the translation 'The Word was God'. Since *logos* has the article preceding it, it is marked out as the subject. The fact that *theos* is the first word after the conjunction *kai* ('and') shows that the main emphasis of the clause lies on it. Had *theos* as well as *logos* been preceded by the article the meaning would have been that the Word was completely identical with God, which is impossible if the Word was also 'with God'. What is meant is that the Word shared the nature and being of God, or (to use a piece of modern jargon) was an extension of the personality of God. The NEB paraphrase 'what God was, the Word was', brings out the meaning of the clause as successfully as a paraphrase can. 'John intends that the whole of his gospel shall be read in the light of this verse. The deeds and words of Jesus are the deeds and words of God; if this be not true, the book is blasphemous'.[5]

So, when heaven and earth were created, there was the Word of God, already existing in the closest association with God and partaking of the essence of God. No matter how far back we may try to push our imagination, we can never reach a point at which we could say of the Divine Word, as Arius did, 'There was once when he was not.'[6]

1:2 This (is the one who) was in the beginning with God.

This might appear to be little more than a repetition of the second clause of verse 1, but it is more than that. This divine Word of whom I speak, the Evangelist implies, is the one who, according to the earlier scriptures, was with God in the beginning; he is probably referring to passages where divine wisdom is personified and described as being present and active at the creation of the world. Thus, in Prov. 8:22–31 Wisdom claims to have been the Creator's master workman:

> The LORD possessed[7] me at the beginning of his way,
>   before his works of old.
> Ages ago I was set up,
>   at the first, before the beginning of the earth. . . .
> Then I was beside him . . .

The Evangelist makes it plain that the Word of which he speaks is also the Wisdom described by psalmist and sage in OT times, and he goes on to declare that Word and Wisdom alike became incarnate in Jesus Christ.[8]

1:3 **All things came into being through him, and apart from him not even one thing that has come into being came into being.**

This rendering is somewhat clumsy because it is excessively literal, but the excessively literal rendering is designed to make the Evangelist's point clear. God is the Creator; his Word is the agent. The two parts of the verse say the same thing, first positively ('through him everything came into being'), and then negatively ('apart from him nothing that exists came into being'). This twofold affirmation sums up the teaching of Gen. 1, where the record of each creative day is introduced by the clause 'And God said'. In Ps. 33:6 this is interpreted as meaning that 'by the word of the LORD' the heavens (and everything else) came into being; in the Wisdom literature it is similarly interpreted to mean that all things exist by his wisdom (cf. Prov. 3:19; 8:30; also Ps. 104:24). The Johannine prologue is not the only place in the NT where this creative agency is ascribed to the pre-existent Christ. In Col. 1.16 f. Paul states that 'in him (and "through him") all things were created . . . and in him all things cohere', while Heb. 1:2 speaks of the Son of God as the one 'through whom he made the worlds', and in Rev. 3:14 he introduces himself as 'the Amen . . . the beginning of God's creation' (where 'Amen' may be a variant on Heb. *'āmôn*, 'master workman', of Prov. 8:30). No literary dependence is probable between one and another of these passages: the teaching which they convey is antecedent to them all and therefore impressively primitive.

The adjective clause 'that has come into being' (the perfect tense denoting the present state of existence resulting from the past 'becoming') is attached in a number of versions to verse 4. Thus the RSV margin suggests, as an alternative to the punctuation preferred in the RSV text, 'without him was not anything made. That which has been made was life in him.' Similarly the NEB text renders, 'no single thing was created without him. All that came to be was alive with his life'. This punctuation is supported by the majority of ante-Nicene Christian writers (both orthodox and heterodox) who quote the passage; indeed, as Westcott says, 'it would be difficult to find a more complete consent of ancient authorities in favour of any reading than that which supported the second punctuation' (i.e. that of RSV margin and NEB text). It has also been claimed that this punctuation gives a better balance to the construction. But it may be urged on the other hand that a sentence beginning 'In him was life' is more in accord with Johannine usage, and (most conclusive argument of all) that it is extremely difficult to make sense of 'That which has been made was life in him' or 'All that came to be was alive with his life'. 'Despite valiant attempts of commentators to bring sense out of' this construction, says B. M. Metzger, 'the passage remains intolerably clumsy and opaque',[9] whereas, whatever may be said of the stylistic balance of the rendering more traditionally familiar to readers of the English Bible, its meaning is crystal clear. Accordingly, we keep the adjective clause in verse 3, and find in verse 4 a statement not about created things but about the creative Word.

1:4 In him was life, and the life was the light of men.

The statement that life was in the Word is amplified later in the Gospel – especially in John 5:26, from which we gather that the Word (or 'the Son', to use the language of the later passage) shares by the Father's good pleasure that self-existent life which belongs to the Creator as distinct from the creature. In John 5:19–29 it is because the Son shares this self-existent life with the Father that he is able to impart life to others; so here the statement that 'in him was life' probably implies a life-giving agency on the part of the Word. (The relation God/Word in the prologue corresponds to the relation Father/Son in the discourses of the Gospel.) But the life which inheres in the Word is here expressly said to have a special importance for one part of the creation – the human race. 'The life was the light of men' (human beings, *tōn anthrōpōn*). This is true both of the natural illumination of reason which is given to the human mind and of the spiritual illumination which accompanies the new birth: neither can be received apart from the light that resides in the Word. But what the Evangelist has in mind here is the spiritual illumination that dispels the darkness of sin and unbelief.

1:5 And the light shines in the darkness, and the darkness did not overcome it.

In the first creation, 'darkness was upon the face of the deep' (Gen. 1:2) until God called light into being, so the new creation (in which the Word is God's agent as effectively as in the earlier one) involves the banishing of spiritual darkness by the light which shines in the Word. Apart from the light (as is emphasized repeatedly in the body of the Gospel) the world of mankind is shrouded in darkness.

The exact force of the aorist *katelaben* must be determined by the context; this suggests that 'overcame' (cf. RSV) or 'mastered' (NEB) is prefereable to 'comprehended' (AV) or 'apprehended' (RV). This is true of ordinary light: a little candle can dispel a roomful of darkness and not be dimmed by it. Light and darkness are opposites, but they are not opposites of equal power. Light is stronger than darkness; darkness cannot prevail against it. The lie is thus given to those dualist systems which envisaged light and darkness as equally and eternally opposed to each other. Now that the Word has come into the world, 'the darkness is passing away and the true light is already shining' (1 John 2:8). The light of the world could not be overcome by the power of darkness, for all its hostility; similarly darkness cannot overcome (*katalabein*) those who walk in the light (John 12:35).[10]

Light and darkness are to be understood ethically rather than metaphysically: 'light' is a synonym of goodness and truth, while 'darkness' is a synonym of evil and falsehood.

1:6–8 There came a man, sent from God, whose name was John. He came for the purpose of witness, to bear witness concerning the light, that all might believe through him. *He* was not the light, but (came) to bear witness concerning the light.

Here we have the first of two brief narrative sections dovetailed into the prologue (the second comes at verse 15). Their insertion may remind the reader that the author is not concerned simply to state timeless truths, but rather to show how these truths are anchored in human history.

In all three Synoptic Gospels the record of Jesus' public ministry is introduced by an outline of the ministry of John the Baptist. In the Acts of the Apostles the ministry of John plays a similar part in Peter's address in the house of Cornelius (10:37) and in Paul's synagogue address in Pisidian Antioch (13:24 f.); and when the question arises of filling the vacancy created in the ranks of the twelve by the defection of Judas, Peter's condition for the replacement is that he must be 'one of the men who have accompanied us during all the time that the Lord Jesus went in and out among us, beginning from the baptism of John' (1.21 f.). This Evangelist is faithful to the pattern of the primitive preaching: all its essential elements are reproduced in his record. The life which was the light of men was first publicly manifested on earth when witness was borne by the man sent from God, whose name was John.

In this Gospel John is never identified as 'the Baptist'. Our Evangelist is careful to distinguish other figures in his narrative who bear the same name – as when he distinguishes 'Judas not

Iscariot' (14:22) from Judas Iscariot – but no other John than the Baptist is named by him. The traditional explanation of the non-mention of any other John in this Gospel is that the only other John in Jesus' circle, John the son of Zebedee, had a major responsibility for the production of the work. It is difficult to think of a better one.[11]

John, then, was sent to bear witness. A fuller account of his witness appears below in verses 19–34 and later in 3:27–30 (cf. 5:33). The theme of witness, here introduced, pervades the whole Gospel. The witness to the truth of God's self-revelation in the Word is manifold: it comprises the witness of the Father (5:32, 37; 8:18), of the Son (8:14, 18), of the Spirit (15:26); the witness of the works of Christ (5:36; 10:25), the witness of the scriptures (5:39), the witness of the disciples (15:27), including that of the disciple whom Jesus loved (19:35; 21:24). The purpose of this manifold witness, as of John's witness, is 'that all might believe'; it is the purpose for which the Gospel itself was written (20:31).

In pointing out that John himself was not the light, but a witness to the light, the Evangelist may have had in mind a group of people, surviving at the time when this Gospel was written, who looked back to John as their founder and venerated him as the one through whom God had made his final revelation to mankind, the last and greatest of the prophets. We know very little about this group, if indeed it existed; but some emphases in the Gospel would be specially appropriate if the Evangelist knew of such people. (It is doubtful if we should think in this connection of the twelve disciples at Ephesus, mentioned in Acts 19:1–7, who knew no baptism but John's.)[12]

If the Evangelist denies that John was the light, we should not forget that Jesus later speaks of him as 'the lamp that burns and shines' (5:35). The function of a lamp is to let the light be seen; that was Jesus' estimate of the quality of John's witness.

1:9 The true light, which enlightens every human being, was in the course of coming into the world.

The participial phrase 'coming into the world' might be attached grammatically either to 'light' (in which case the participle *erchomenon* is nominative neuter) or to 'human being' (in which case the participle would be accusative masculine). The latter construction is adopted in AV. But 'coming into the world' is repeatedly predicated in this Gospel of him who is the eternal Word and the true light. It is from this true light that all genuine illumination proceeds. Whatever measure of truth men and women in all ages have apprehended has been derived from this source. Justin Martyr was not wrong when he affirmed that Socrates and the Stoics and others who had lived in conformity with right reason (*logos*) were really, if unconsciously, directed by the pre-existent Christ[13] – although his use of *logos* was different from our Evangelist's. But the illumination that the Evangelist has primarily in mind is that spiritual illumination which dispels the darkness of sin and unbelief; and it was by coming into the world that the true light provided this supreme illumination – and provided it for all mankind. He is the light 'which enlightens every human being' in the sense that the illumination which he has brought is for all without distinction. True, there are those who refuse to come to the light (cf. John 3:19 f.). If they remain in darkness, it is not because there is no illumination for them, but because they deliberately prefer the darkness. Here, then, we have an anticipation of the theme which is elaborated more than once throughout the Gospel – that Jesus is 'the light of the world' (8:12; 9:5).

1:10 **He was in the world and the world came into being through him, and the world did not know him.**

The construction is paratactic; here, as so often, our Evangelist prefers to set a series of co-ordinate principal clauses side by side, without indicating the logical connection between one and another. If we were to replace John's parataxis by a freer use of subordinate clauses, this sentence might be reconstructed thus: 'He was in the world but the world, although it owed its existence to him, failed nevertheless to recognize him.' The world (*kosmos*) is the universe, referred to in verse 3 as 'all things'. The divine revelation ranged freely through the universe which God created, but all too often it was not acknowledged by those to whom it came. By 'the world' the Evangelist understands in particular the world of mankind, alienated from God, which, in Paul's words, 'did not see fit to acknowledge God (Rom. 1:28), even although 'since the creation of the world (*kosmos*) his invisible nature, namely, his everlasting power and divinity, has been clearly perceived in the things that have been made' (Rom. 1:20).

The divine Word, then, was in the world already, before that special 'coming into the world' for which the appearance of John was the signal (verses 6–9) and which is the theme of this Gospel as a whole. The world's general response to that special 'coming' was in keeping with the general response to the Word in earlier ages. The ambivalence of the term 'world' (*kosmos*) in the Johannine writings can be discerned in these first occurrences in the prologue. The world is God's world, created by him through the agency of the Logos. There is no basis for dualism in the Evangelist's thought – no independent principle of evil belonging to another universe than that which God created. Apart from the divine Word, nothing that exists came into being. If the world as made by God has nevertheless become the 'godless world' (as the NEB renders *kosmos* in appropriate Johannine contexts), that is because of its refusal to acknowledge the revelation of God or respond positively to his overtures.[14] Yet the world remains the object of its Creator's love: if the presence of the Word in the world causes a division between the minority who acknowledge him and the majority who do not and are thereby self-condemned, God's purpose in sending his Son into the world is 'not to condemn the world, but that the world might be saved through him' (John 3:17).[15]

1:11 He came to his own place, and his own people did not receive him.

'His own place' translated the neuter plural *ta idia*; 'his own people' translates the masculine plural *hoi idioi*. (The phrase *eis ta idia* with which this verse opens reappears in the passion narrative, in John 19:27, where the beloved disciple takes the mother of Jesus 'to his own home'; cf. also 16:32.)

This is not a mere repetition of verse 10; it particularizes what was said more generally there. The Word of God, which came to the world of mankind in general, came in the form of special revelation to the people of Israel, in law, prophecy and wisdom, and in mighty acts of mercy and judgment such as no other nation experienced (cf. Deut. 4:7, 8; Ps. 147:20). But repeatedly the testimony of God's spokesmen to Israel was that his message was ignored: 'From the day that your fathers came out of the land of Egypt to this day [the eve of the Babylonian exile], I have persistently sent all my servants the prophets to them, day after day; yet they did not listen to me, or incline their ear, but stiffened their neck' (Jer. 7:25 f.). The Evangelist is thinking not only of what happened in those earlier days of Israel's history; he has in mind what happened when the Word 'came to his own place' in an unprecedented manner, and his plan is to amplify this in the record which follows. Those who were 'his own people' would have none of him when he came. Stated thus starkly and absolutely, the paradox is grim. But the grimness is not unrelieved. Had none at all received him, darkness would have prevailed indeed. But some did receive him gladly, and showed themselves thus to be truly 'his own people'. Over the first main division of the Gospel, to the end of chapter 12, we might write the words 'his own people did not receive him', but over the next division (chapters 13–17) we might write the words which immediately follow in our present context: 'But as for those who did receive him . . .' – and it is of those that we read at the beginning of chapter 13, 'He had set his love on his own people who were in the world, and he loved them to the uttermost'. As in OT times, so now, it is the believing remnant which embodies the true people of God and provides the visible guarantee of the fulfilment of all his promises to them.

1:12, 13 But as for those who did receive him, to them all he gave authority to become God's children – to those who believe in his name, who were born, not from blood nor from the will of flesh nor from the will of a man, but from God.

Spiritual birth and the new life to which it is the gateway are prominent themes in the Gospel of John. The remnant which gave the Word a welcome when he came into the world received the birthright to all the blessings and privileges which his coming was designed to impart. These blessings and privileges are summed up in this, that they were admitted to membership in the family of God. To enter God's family one must receive his Word – in other terms, one must believe in his name.[16] The 'name' is much more than the designation by which a person is known; it means the real character or sometimes, as here, the person himself. To receive him who is the Word of God, then, means to place one's faith in him, to yield one's allegiance to him and thus, in the most practical manner, to acknowledge his claims.

The verb in verse 13, *gennaō*, originally meant 'beget' rather than 'give birth', but (especially in the passive) came to be used indifferently in the sense 'to be begotten' or 'to be born'. So in John 3:4 Nicodemus, misunderstanding Jesus' language about the new birth, asks if any one can 'enter into his mother's womb a second time and be born', where the verb is *gennaō* (in the passive) but the meaning is clearly 'be born'; and the same verb is used unambiguously in that sense in Jesus' illustration in John 16:21: the mother who has given birth to a child forgets her labour pains 'for joy that a human being has been born (*gennaō*, passive) into the world'. In any case, where a spiritual experience is in view, begetting and birth are alike figurative terms.

Verse 13 anticipates the fuller statement of the new birth which is to be made in chapter 3. There, the difference between the two orders is emphasized: 'What is born from the flesh is flesh, and what is born from the Spirit is spirit' (3:6). So here, the repeated negatives insist that birth into the family of God is quite different from physical birth. This divine birthright has nothing to do with racial or national or family ties. It is spiritually irrelevant to be descended from Abraham in the natural order if one is not a child of Abraham in the only sense that matters before God – by reproducing Abraham's faith. Physical birth, membership of a family in the natural sense, is a matter of blood-relationship. It is the product of bodily desire ('flesh' here has no pejorative implication); it results from the will of a man (*anēr*, a member of the male sex, not simply *anthrōpos*, a human being, or, as one might have expected, two *anthrōpoi*). But spiritual birth, entry into the family whose Father is God, depends on quite different factors – the receiving by faith of him whom God has sent.

Some Old Latin (pre-Vulgate) witnesses to the Gospel text have an interesting variant (for which they have the partial support of a few Syriac manuscripts), in which the plural 'who were born' is replaced by the singular 'who was born'. The construction would then be: '. . . to those who believe in the name of him who was born, not from blood . . . but from God'. This variant reading may have been designed to provide explicit Johannine testimony to our Lord's virgin birth; but the fact that it is completely unattested in the Greek textual tradition is sufficient in itself to rule it out of court.[17]

1:14 And the Word became flesh and pitched his tabernacle among us. We looked on his glory – glory such as an only-begotten son (receives) from a father, full of grace and truth.

In the seventh book of his *Confessions*, Augustine tells how, not long before his conversion, he was introduced to a Latin translation of some Neoplatonic writings and found in them much that (to his mind) resembled the teaching of this prologue. 'I read there that God the Word "was born not of flesh nor of blood, nor of the will of man nor of the will of the flesh, but of God". But that "the Word was made flesh and dwelt among us" – that I did not read there'.[18] The differences between our Evangelist and the Neoplatonists, then, were more important than the resemblances – and even these were more superficial than Augustine realized.

This is the event to which the preceding statements of the prologue have been leading up: 'the Word became flesh'. It is evident from the first two epistles of John that a form of docetism was widespread in the area in which the Johannine literature appeared – a teaching which denied that Jesus Christ had 'come in the flesh' and disunited the earthly Jesus from the heavenly Christ (cf. 1 John 4:1–3).[19] Here and there the Gospel of John betrays awareness of this teaching and uses a form of words which excludes it. The Evangelist might have declared in the present text that the eternal Word took manhood or assumed a bodily form, but no such

declaration would have been so uncompromisingly anti-docetic as
the declaration that 'the Word became flesh'. The humanity, the
'flesh', which was taken by the divine Word at that point in time
was and remains as perfect as his divine nature; yet it is *our* human
nature (apart from sin) that he took, and not some 'heavenly humanity' of a different order. ('Heavenly humanity' is a proper
expression to use of the resurrection life of our Lord and his people,
in the light of 1 Cor. 15:44–53, but not of his earthly life.) To
expand the implications of the incarnation of the Word in terms of
historical or systematic theology would carry us beyond the Evangelist's intention.[20] What he is concerned to emphasize here is that
God, who had revealed or expressed himself – 'sent his word' – in
a variety of ways from the beginning, made himself known at last
in a real historical human person: when 'the Word became flesh',
God became man.

It is this scripture, more than anything else in the NT, that
provided the foundation for the doctrine of the person of Christ
formulated in the Creed of Nicaea (AD 325) and the Definition of
Chalcedon (AD 451).[21] 'The great advantage – I had almost said the
trump card – of Christianity was its belief in the Incarnation, in a
Saviour who was at once God and man. . . . In denying the con-
substantiality of the Son with the Father Arius broke down the
bridge which Christianity had built between a transcendent Deity
and the insignificance of man.'[22] The truth of God incarnate safeguards the Christian doctrine of God the Father and the Christian
doctrine of man as well as the doctrine of the person of Christ.

The further statement that the incarnate Word 'pitched his tabernacle (*eskēnōsen*) among us' harks back to the tabernacle (*skēnē*) of Israel's wilderness wanderings. The tabernacle was erected
by God's command in order that his dwelling-place might be established with his people: 'let them make me a sanctuary', he said,
'that I may dwell in their midst' (Ex. 25:8). So, it is implied, as
God formerly manifested his presence among his people in the tent
which Moses pitched, now in a fuller sense he has taken up residence on earth in the Word made flesh.[23]

Not only so, but among Greek-speaking Jews the noun *skēnē*
and cognate words, like the verb *skēnoō*, which is used in this
clause, were commonly associated with the Hebrew verb *shākan*
('dwell') and its derivatives, such as the biblical *mishkān* ('tabernacle') and the post-biblical *shekînāh* – a word which literally
means 'residence' but was used more particularly of the glorious
presence of God which resided in the Mosaic tabernacle and Solomon's temple. When the tabernacle was completed, 'the cloud
covered the tent of meeting, and the glory of the LORD filled the
tabernacle' (Ex. 40:34). Similarly, at the dedication of Solomon's

temple, 'a cloud filled the house of the LORD . . . for the glory of
the LORD filled the house of the LORD' (1 Kgs. 8:10 f.). So, when
the Word became flesh, the glorious presence of God was embodied
in him, for he is the true *shekînāh*.[24]

The glory which shone in the tabernacle and temple, veiled in
the mysterious cloud, was but the foreglow of that excelling glory
which shone in the incarnate Word, veiled from those who had no
mind to come to the light, but manifested to faith. The Evangelist
looks back and sees how the whole earthly career of the incarnate
Word, and pre-eminently the sacrifice of the cross which crowned
that career, revealed the glory of God. 'We looked on his glory'[25]
– the testimony of the Evangelist and his fellow-disciples – might
serve as a sub-title for this Gospel; 'glory' is one of its principal
keywords. The glory which shone in the incarnate Word was glory
such as a father bestows on his best-loved son. We are reminded
of the paraphrase of 'Thou art my Son' (Ps. 2:7) in the Targum on
the Psalms: 'Beloved as a son to his father art thou to me.' The
adjective *monogenēs* ('only', AV 'only begotten') is one of the LXX
terms used to translate Heb. *yāḥîd*,[26] but another aspect of the
Hebrew word's meaning is conveyed in the LXX by *agapētos* ('beloved'). Thus in Gen. 22:2, where Isaac is called Abraham's 'only
(*yāḥîd*) son', the Septuagint renders the adjective by *agapētos*.
Isaac was not in the literal sense Abraham's 'only' son, but he
was his best-loved son, his 'unique' son, on whom he bestowed all
that he had. Greater still is the glory bestowed by God on his only
Son –

> Of the Father's love begotten,
> Ere the worlds began to be –

and such, says the Evangelist, was the glory which 'we looked on'.

The standard English versions (but not NEB) take the phrase 'full
of grace and truth' to refer to 'the Word'. This is because the
adjective 'full' (*plērēs*) is nominative, and so should be in concord
with the nominative *logos*. But there is sufficient evidence to show
that in Hellenistic Greek *plērēs* could be used indeclinably, agreeing with a noun in any case. We could thus take 'full of grace and
truth' as agreeing with the nearer noun 'glory', although 'glory' is
in the accusative case (*doxan*); and this is rendered the more probable when we consider the background of these words.

Moses in the wilderness asked a boon from God: 'I pray thee,
show me thy glory.' The reply was: 'I will make all my goodness
pass before you, and will proclaim before you my name "the
LORD" ' (Ex. 33:18f.). For God's glory – the attribute which is
distinctively his – is his goodness. Accordingly, in fulfilment of his

promise, 'the LORD descended in the cloud and stood with him there, and proclaimed the name of the LORD.[27] The LORD passed before him, and proclaimed, "The LORD, the LORD, a God merciful and gracious, slow to anger, and abounding in steadfast love and faithfulness. . ." ' (Ex. 34:5 f.). These last words spell out the goodness which is God's surpassing glory. But the Greek words of John 1:14, translated 'full of grace (*charis*) and truth' (*alētheia*), are readily recognizable as a rendering of the last phrase of Ex. 34:6, 'abounding in steadfast love (Heb. *ḥesed*) and faithfulness' (Heb. *'ĕmeth*). The glory seen in the incarnate Word was the glory which was revealed to Moses when the name of Yahweh was sounded in his ears; but now that glory has been manifested on earth in a human life, 'full of grace and truth'.[28]

1:15 **John bears witness concerning him and has cried aloud: 'This is he of whom I said, "He who is coming after me has taken precedence over me, for he existed before me"'.**

In this second narrative section dovetailed into the prologue (for the first see verses 6–8) we have a piece of the following narrative anticipated (cf. verse 30). The narrative which follows the prologue gives an account of John's witness. Here part of that witness is summarized, so as to make it clear that the light to which John is said to have borne witness in verses 7 and 8 is identical with the incarnate Word of verse 14. The present tense, 'John bears witness', may indicate that while John himself was long dead by the time the Gospel was written, his witness remained (and remains). Similarly the perfect tense 'has cried' implies that while John's proclamation was a past event, the substance of what he proclaimed is permanently true.

John had announced the near advent of the Coming One before he was able to point to a particular person and say 'This is he'; when at last he saw the sign described in verse 33, he could thenceforth point to that person and say, 'This is the one I meant'. The Coming One appeared later in history than John did, but he took precedence over John (the one whose way is being prepared is greater than his forerunner). His precedence over John, however is expressed in exceptionally emphatic terms. John does not simply say *pro mou ēn* ('he was before me') but *prōtos mou ēn* (literally 'he was first in respect of me'), that is to say, 'he had absolute primacy over me' or better, as NEB renders it 'before I was born, he already was.' The reader who comes to this after reading the earlier part of the prologue has no difficulty in understanding John's witness: he is speaking of the Word that existed in the beginning with God and in the fulness of time became incarnate among men.

1:16 Because we have all received from his fulness, even grace upon grace.

Logically, these words follow immediately on the closing words of verse 14 (verse 15 being parenthetic). The incarnate Word was full of grace and truth, and from that fulness of his, says the Evangelist, we have all drawn. 'We all' probably denotes not only the Evangelist and his original associates, who saw the glory of the Word made flesh, but the readers of the Gospel also, and indeed all who share the blessing pronounced in 20:29 on 'those who have not seen, and yet have believed'. This plenitude of divine glory and goodness which resides in Christ (cf. Col. 1:19; 2:9) is an ocean from which all his people may draw without ever diminishing its content.

In the phrase 'grace upon grace' the preposition is *anti* but no satisfactory sense can be obtained by pressing it to mean 'instead of' here.[29] What the followers of Christ draw from the ocean of divine fulness is grace upon grace – one wave of grace being constantly replaced by a fresh one. There is no limit to the supply of grace which God has placed at his people's disposal in Christ: our Evangelist, like Paul, has proved the truth of the assurance: 'My grace is sufficient for you' (2 Cor. 12:9).

1:17 Because the law was given through Moses; grace and truth came through Jesus Christ.

Grace and truth were not absent from God's ways which he made known to Moses; on the contrary, as we have seen, he revealed himself to Moses as 'abounding in steadfast love and faithfulness' (Ex. 34:6), and the same language is repeatedly used throughout the OT as a summary of his character (cf. Ps. 86:15). But our Evangelist likes to set the old order and the new in antithetical terms. Even in the law which was given through Moses, intimations of grace and truth were not lacking, but all that was manifested of these qualities in OT times was disclosed in concentrated fulness in the incarnate Word. Here, then, as in Paul's writings, Christ displaces the law of Moses as the focus of divine revelation and the way to life. This Gospel emphasizes in a series of presentations that the new order fulfils, surpasses and replaces the old: the wine of the new creation is better than the water which was used in Jewish religion (John 2:10), the new temple supersedes the old (2:19), the new birth is the gateway into a sphere of life

which cannot be entered by natural birth, even natural birth into
membership of the chosen people (3:3, 5), the living water of the
Spirit which Jesus imparts is far superior both to the water in
Jacob's well and to the water which was ritually poured out in the
temple court at the feast of Tabernacles (4:13f.; 7:37 ff.), the bread
of heaven is the reality of which the manna in the wilderness was
but an adumbration (6:32 f.). Moses was the mediator of the law;
Jesus Christ is not only the mediator but the embodiment of grace
and truth. 'What God was, the Word was.'

Here, in the statement that grace and truth came through Jesus
Christ', the incarnate Word is given a name for the first time.
Usually in this Gospel 'Jesus' is his personal name, while 'Christ'
is a title or designation – 'Messiah' or 'Anointed One'[30] – but in
this place 'Jesus Christ' appears to be used as the twofold name by
which he was commonly known among Greek-speaking Christians.

1:18 **No one has ever seen God; the only-begotten, (himself)
God, who has his being in the Father's bosom, is the one who
has declared him.**

God, being pure spirit, is invisible to physical eyesight. Not even
Abraham, 'the friend of God', not even Moses, 'whom the LORD
knew face to face' (Deut. 34:10) could see the divine glory in its
fulness. When Moses asked that he might see the glory of God, he
was told, 'you cannot see my face; for man shall not see me and
live' (Ex. 33:20). He was instructed instead to stand in a hollow in
the rocky slope of Sinai while the glory of God passed by, and
there, said God, 'I will cover you with my hand until I have passed
by; then I will take away my hand, and you shall see my back; but
my face shall not be seen' (Ex. 33:22 f.). We should perhaps say,
less anthropomorphically but equally metaphorically, that Moses
saw, so to speak, the afterglow of the divine glory. To this extent
was it true that Moses could 'behold the form of the LORD' (Num.
12:8); but the glory on which even Moses could not look has now
been displayed among men and women.

'Who has seen him and can describe (*ekdiēgēsetai*) him?' asked
Ben Sira concerning God (Sir. 43:31). He left his question unan-
swered, but now an answer is forthcoming; one who has not only
seen him but has his being in his bosom has declared (*exēgēsato*)
him.[31]

The weight of the textual evidence here favours the reading
monogenēs theos, 'God only-begotten' or 'the only begotten, (himself) God'. Not only is it attested by early authorities, including
the two earliest known (the Bodmer papyri 66 and 75); the tendency
would inevitably be to replace it by the commoner *monogenēs*

hyios ('only- begotten son'), whereas, if the commoner reading were original, it is difficult to see what could have impelled any scribe or editor to replace it by the unparalleled *monogenēs theos*. This unparalleled reading is supported both by the principle that the more difficult reading is to be preferred and by transcriptional probability. There is a rather late and weakly attested variant reading which exhibits the adjective *monogenēs* alone ('the only-begotten'); it might be argued that this simple reading was the original and was amplified in two ways: by the addition of *theos* in a few early texts and by the addition of *hyios* in the rest. But this is unlikely; why would anyone think of adding *theos* to form the unique phrase *monogenēs theos* if the Evangelist had not first written it so? If *monogenēs theos* is the original reading, then the Evangelist is repeating what he said of the Logos in the third clause of verse 1: since the Logos was God, the Only-begotten is God in that sense, for the Logos and the Only-begotten are identical.

The statement that the only-begotten exists in the Father's bosom may remind us of the description of Lazarus in Abraham's bosom in Luke 16:22 f., or of the beloved disciple occupying a similar position of nearness to Jesus at the Last Supper in John 13:23. In those two passages the expression denotes a place of special favour next to the principal person at a banquet; it may have the same meaning here, but there is also a suggestion of the mutual love and understanding of the Father and the Son and of the Son's dependence on the Father. Only one who fully knows the Father can make him fully known. The same sense is conveyed by the 'aerolite from the Johannine heaven' embedded in the Synoptic record: 'no one knows the Father except the Son and any one to whom the Son chooses to reveal him' (Matt. 11:27; cf. Luke 10:22).

In the other places where the verb *exēgeomai* appears in the NT (all in Luke's writings) it means to tell or narrate (Luke 24:35; Acts 10:8; 15:12, 14; 21:19), and that is its meaning at the end of John 1:18: we might use an English word derived from the Greek verb and say that the Son is the 'exegete' of the Father. In origin the verb is compounded of *hēgeomai* ('lead') with the prefix *ex*; one French scholar (M.-E. Boismard) takes it in its etymological sense and renders the verse: 'No one has ever seen God except the only-begotten; he has led the way into the bosom of the Father'.[32] This is an improbable construction, even if it does give the preposition *eis* its classical sense of 'into'. (By the first century AD *eis* was well launched on its process of encroachment on the sphere of *en*, which it was ultimately to displace altogether.)

How the Son declared the unseen God to men, functioning thus as the living Word in the world, it is the evangelist's purpose to relate in the record to which these eighteen verses form the prologue.

A. JESUS' MINISTRY BEGINS (John 1:19–2:12)

I. The witness of John (1:19–34)

1. JOHN AND THE DEPUTATION FROM JERUSALEM (1:19–28)

1, 19, 20 This is John's witness. When the Jews sent priests and Levites to him from Jerusalem to ask him, 'Who are you?' he confessed and did not deny: he confessed, 'I am not the Christ.'

John's witness has been mentioned and quoted in the brief narrative sections dovetailed into the prologue: now the Evangelist gives a continuous account of it (verse 19–34). The first example of his witness here given is his reply to a deputation sent out by the religious establishment in Jerusalem.

Here for the first time we come upon the use of the term 'the Jews' in this Gospel to denote not the people as a whole but one particular group – here, the religious establishment in Jerusalem, whether the Sanhedrin[33] or the temple authorities. Elsewhere it is occasionally used (as in John 7:1) to mean the Judaeans as distinct from the Galilaeans, while at other times it has quite a general meaning. Attention to the sense which the word bears in each place where it occurs could save the reader from supposing that the Evangelist (who was himself a Jew) had an animus against the Jews as such.

At the time when John commenced his public career as a preacher of repentance in the Jordan valley, there was a widespread sense of expectancy abroad, especially among those pious Israelites who were 'looking for the redemption of Jerusalem' (Luke 2:38). The sudden appearance of this strange preacher and baptizer, displaying the authentic marks of the prophets of old, made a deep impression on his fellow-Israelites. Less than a century before (63 BC) the native Hasmonaean dynasty had fallen and the land of Israel was incorporated in the Roman Empire. This loss of independence and the failure of the hopes that had been pinned to the Hasmonaean priest-kings brought about a revival of the ancient hope of a Messiah from the line of David.

John indeed was born into a priestly family and so belonged to the tribe of Levi, not Judah (to which David and his family belonged); but his parentage may not have been known to the populace at large. In any case, there was a wide variety of messianic hope, and alongside the expectation of a Messiah of David's line there is evidence of the expectation in some quarters of an 'anointed one' of Aaron's line.[34] At any rate, people began to wonder who he was and what he claimed to be; as another Evangelist says 'the people were in expectation, and all men questioned in their hearts concerning John, whether perhaps he was the Christ' (Luke 3:15). This is the background of the question 'Who are you?' addressed to John by the deputation from Jerusalem: 'People are wondering whether you are the Messiah or not; what have you to say yourself?'

Since John's reply was a negative one, it is strange that it should be introduced by the words 'he confessed and did not deny'. We might have expected 'he denied that he made any such claim'. But the Evangelist will have us understand that even John's denials were part of his positive witness or confession. Had John made such a claim, he would have found many willing to accept it. The designation 'Christ' represents Gk. *christos*, the verbal adjective of *chriō* ('anoint'); it is the counterpart of 'Messiah', which represents the verbal adjective of Heb. *māshaḥ* ('anoint'). The Hebrew word is applied in the OT to kings and high priests, and occasionally to prophets.[35] But John refused to entertain any messianic claims for himself, whether royal, priestly or prophetic. It has sometimes been thought that the emphasis with which the Evangelist reports John's denial reflects the survival, around the time when the Gospel was written, of a group of people who maintained that John was the sent one of God *par excellence*; but evidence of this is hard to come by.

1:21 **So they asked him then, 'What are you, then? Are you Elijah?' 'I am not,' he said. 'Are you the prophet?' 'No,' he answered.**

If John was not the Messiah, he might be some other figure of end-time expectation. For example, a post-exilic prophet had communicated this divine message to Israel: 'I will send you Elijah the prophet before the great and terrible day of the LORD comes' (Mal. 4:5). The expectation of the returning Elijah remained alive; and John certainly bore some of the marks of Elijah. His very dress – he 'was clothed with camel's hair, and had a leather girdle round his waist' (Mark 1:6) – must have reminded people of the description of Elijah in 2 Kings 1:8: 'He wore a garment of haircloth, with a girdle of leather about his loins'. But while anyone could imitate Elijah's dress (cf. Zech. 13:4), no mere imitation could reproduce the note of judgment and the call to repentance which sounded both in his message and in John's. Was John, then, Elijah? Or, at least, was this what he claimed to be? No, said John.

In the Synoptic record the association between John and Elijah is repeatedly affirmed, not least in Jesus' words to his disciples: 'Elijah has come, and they did to him whatever they pleased' (Mark 9:13). But nowhere is it suggested that John made such a claim for himself, and in this Gospel he expressly refuses to make it.

If he was not Elijah, however, there was another figure of OT prophecy with whom he might be identified. 'Are you the prophet?' said John's questioners. He had no need to say 'Which prophet?' for he knew which one they meant. Moses, in his farewell speech to his people, told them that when they wished to ascertain God's will, they must not have recourse to divination and necromancy, like their pagan neighbours: when God had any communication to make to them, he would raise up in their midst a prophet like Moses and speak through him. The voice of this prophet should be treated as the voice of God (Deut. 18:15–19).

These words of Moses were early understood to point to one particular prophet, a second Moses, who would exercise the full mediatorial function that Moses had exercised. In the obituary appreciation of Moses at the end of the Pentateuch it is recorded that 'there has not arisen a prophet since in Israel like Moses, whom the LORD knew face to face' (Deut. 34:10). It came to be believed that the prophet like Moses would not be raised up until the end of the age. In some circles, especially among the Samaritans, the Messiah was envisaged in terms of this coming prophet,[36] and our Evangelist leaves his readers in no doubt that the promise was fulfilled in Jesus. John repudiated the idea that he was the prophet like Moses as emphatically as he repudiated the idea that he was Elijah.

1:22, 23 **So they said to him, 'Who are you? We must give some answer to those who sent us. What do you say about yourself?' He said, 'I am the voice of one calling in the wilderness, "Make straight the way of the Lord",' as Isaiah the prophet said.**

The members of the deputation felt frustrated. John was clearly an 'eschatological' figure, with his preaching of imminent judgment to be administered by the Coming One. Yet he refused to be identified with any of the figures of popular eschatological expectation. What, then, was his own account of himself? What kind of answer were they to take back to the people who had sent them?

John says, in effect, 'If you wish to find me foretold among the oracles of the prophets, you may identify me with the "voice" which calls for the preparation of a way for the LORD in the desert'. The other Evangelists quote Isa. 40:3 as a prophecy of John's ministry; here John quotes it in this sense himself. In the original context the prophet hears a voice calling for the levelling of a path through the eastern desert so that the God of Israel may lead his people home from exile.[37] In the NT application of the oracle, the desert becomes the wilderness of Judaea in which John preached his message of repentance. The twofold corpus of prophecy which runs from Isa. 40 to 66 begins by proclaiming good tidings to Zion of the return of her exiled children, but goes on to tell of a greater redemption, wrought not by the edict of a Cyrus but by the passion and triumph of the obedient Servant of the LORD, and concludes with the promise of new heavens and a new earth. The NT writers reinterpret the glad tidings to Zion in terms of the Christian gospel, the message which began to be inaugurated when John prepared the way for the greater one than himself. The redemption which he was to accomplish was now on the eve of its appearance, and it was John's high honour to be the voice announcing its near approach.

1:24, 25 Some Pharisees also had been sent, and they asked him, 'Why do you baptize, then, if you are not the Christ, nor yet Elijah nor the prophet?'

The translation of verse 24 is disputed. One question is whether this is the same deputation or a different one. Quite clearly it is the same one: the question of verse 25 presupposes John's answers given in verses 20–23. A more difficult question relates to the phrase *ek tōn Pharisaiōn*. Does the preposition *ek* mean 'from' or does it mean 'some of' – i.e. has it 'partitive' force? The RSV takes it in the former sense: 'Now they had been sent from the Pharisees.' But it is unlikely that the Pharisees would be in a position to send members of the temple staff as a deputation from themselves. The NEB rendering is nearer the mark: 'Some Pharisees who were in the deputation asked him . . .'. If the deputation was sent by the Sanhedrin, then the Pharisees, who formed an influential minority in that body, could insist on having some of their own number included among those who were sent. This is more probable than that a separate Pharisaic deputation was sent.

The party of the Pharisees was specially conscientious about keeping the law in minute detail, although the obligation to keep it lay on every member of the covenant-community of Israel. The Pharisees, who first appear in history towards the end of the second century BC, were spiritual heirs of the Hasidaeans or pious groups who played a noble part in defence of their ancestral religion when Antiochus Epiphanes (175–163 BC) attempted to abolish it (cf. 1 Macc. 2:42; 7:14; 2 Macc. 14:6). At an earlier date those pious

groups receive honourable mention in Mal. 3:16–4:3; their devotion
to the law is reflected in Ps. 119.

The term 'Pharisees' means 'separated ones' (Heb. *pᵉrûshîm*);
it has been variously explained, but in practice it emphasized their
separation from everything that might convey ethical or ceremonial
purity (even the eating of produce on which the tithe had not been
regularly paid). They built up a body of oral tradition, which was
designed to adapt the ancient principles of the written law to the
changing situations of later days and thus safeguard those principles
against being dismissed as obsolete or impracticable. In this they
were distinguished from their chief rivals, the Sadducees, who
maintained the authority of the written law alone and who also
rejected as innovations the Pharisaic belief in the resurrection of
the body and in the existence of orders of angels and demons (cf.
Mark 12:18; Acts 23:8).[38] They banded themselves together in local
brotherhoods or fellowships. Josephus, who claims to have regulated his own life by Pharisaic principles from the age of nineteen,
reckons that there were some 6,000 Pharisees in his day (*Antiquities*
17.42).[39]

The Pharisees would be specially interested in the religious implication of John's activity, and particularly in his warrant for
baptizing. Their question suggests that baptism in their eyes was
an eschatological rite, to be administered by one of the expected
figures of the end-time. The community of Qumran and other
Essene groups made a special feature of bathing in purifying water,
invoking as their authority such passages as Ezek. 36:25, where the
God of Israel tells his people how, in the time of restoration, 'I
will sprinkle clean water upon you, and you shall be clean . . .'.[40]
The men of Qumran considered themselves to be the righteous
community of the end-time, and John in his turn was commissioned 'to make ready for the Lord a people prepared' (Luke 1:17).
His baptism was apparently distinctive in that he administered it
personally; it was not self-administered, as proselyte baptism was.[41]
John had supreme authority for his baptismal ministry: 'he who
sent me to baptize with water' (verse 33) was God. That being so,
his personal status was unimportant; he was an instrument in God's
hand for the introduction of someone greater than himself.

**1:26, 27 John answered them, 'I baptize in water. Among you
there stands one whom you do not know, the one who is coming
after me. I am not fit to untie his sandal-strap.'**

The emphatic '*I* baptize in water' prepares the reader for the
mention of someone else who will baptize in a different medium.
For the moment John does not speak of this different baptism, but

he does speak of the one who will administer it. He is the one for whom John is preparing the way as forerunner, the one who is coming after him. By all accounts the forerunner is less important than the person for whom he prepares the way; John underlines his own relative unimportance in comparison with the Coming One by saying that he is unfit even to perform such a lowly service as untying his sandal-strap for him. 'Every service which a slave performs for his master', said one rabbi,[42] 'a disciple will perform for his teacher, except to untie his sandal-strap.' Even that menial service John thought himself unworthy to perform for the Coming One. But in fact, in preparing the way for that Coming One, John was discharging a far more honourable ministry than any of his hearers could have realized.

1:28 **This took place in Bethany in Transjordan, where John was baptizing.**

Bethany in Transjordan is so called to distinguish it from the better known Bethany near Jerusalem (cf. John 11:1). Its location cannot be certainly established. The variant reading Bethabara, meaning 'place of the ford' (cf. AV), was known to Origen (*c.* AD 231), who preferred it on geographical grounds.[43] His preference was probably based on local information; the same reading appears in the Sinaitic Syriac version of the Gospels. The place evidently lay in the Peraean part of Herod Antipas's tetrarchy (it was John's activity in Peraea that incurred Herod's enmity, and it was in the Peraean fortress of Machaerus that he was imprisoned and put to death).[44] It has been identified by some with the Beth-barah of Judg. 7:24, by others (more plausibly) with the Beth-nimrah of Josh. 13:27.[45]

2. THE COMING ONE'S IDENTITY (1:29–34)

1:29 **Next day John sees Jesus coming to him, and says, 'See! there is the Lamb of God, the one who takes away the sin of the world!'**

'Next day' presumably means the day after John met the deputation from Jerusalem. Some weeks probably had elapsed since Jesus received baptism at John's hands; he had been away since then, but now he is back, and John draws the crowd's attention to him. When John began to announce the approach of the Coming One, he did not know who that Coming One was; now, as he goes on to explain, he is able to identify him with a particular person, thanks to a sign which he has received.

But the designation with which he greets Jesus' appearance is startling – at least, it must have been so to those who heard it for the first time. To us the designation 'Lamb of God' is so familiar in Christian speech and art that we can scarcely realize how strange it must have been in the ears of John's audience. Many attempts have been made to discover the background of John's phraseology, but probably no one usage accounts for the complete background, and even if the complete background could be discovered it would not entirely account for the New Testament usage, which has a new and creative element in it.

Some of John's hearers may have been familiar with a form of apocalyptic imagery in which the messianic champion was depicted under the guise of a horned ram or lamb.[46] This imagery is taken up in the New Testament Apocalypse, where the victorious and exalted Lamb appears as the leader of the faithful people of God (Rev. 7:17; 17:4, etc.), but here the imagery is reshaped to express the Christian gospel, for the Lamb has won the victory by being slaughtered and has thus procured redemption for many (Rev. 5:6 ff.). Although the Greek word used in the Apocalypse (*arnion*) is not the same as that used in John 1:29, 36 (*amnos*), yet it is noteworthy that these two Johannine documents are the only New Testament writings to use a word meaning 'lamb' as a title of Christ.[47]

Among possible antecedents for John's language we might think of the lamb to be provided by God, mentioned by Abraham in Gen. 22:8 (cf. John 8:56), or of the passover lamb, which was evidently in the Evangelist's mind in the passion narrative (cf. John 19:36). But Abraham spoke of a lamb for a burnt offering, not a sin offering, and the passover lamb was not prescribed as a sin offering. If there are sacrificial overtones in John's choice of the word 'Lamb', then a sin offering is the sacrifice of which one may most readily think since this Lamb 'takes away the sin of the world'. In the levitical law, indeed, a lamb is not the characteristic animal for a sin offering; but behind John's language may be discerned the Servant of the LORD who suffered 'like a lamb that is led to the slaughter' and gave himself as 'an offering for sin' (Isa. 53:7, 10).

Some scholars find a more explicit reference to the Isaianic Servant in John's language: behind the Greek *amnos* they see the Aramaic *ṭalyā*.[48] Aramaic *ṭalyā*, they say, can mean both 'lamb' and 'servant'; indeed, it has been pointed out that in one Palestinian Syriac text *ṭalyā* is used in the sense of 'Servant' in Isa. 52:13.[49] So, it is argued, John may have spoken of the *ṭalyā* of God, and the Aramaic word could have been rendered *amnos* ('lamb') or *pais* ('servant'). Even so, the argument is precarious. That the Isaianic

Servant contributed to John's thought and phraseology, however, is probable enough, especially if we recall the quotation already made in verse 23 from the same body of evangelical prophecy.

The verb *airō* is rightly rendered 'take away' or 'remove' here. Where the *bearing* of sin is in view, the verb commonly used is *anapherō*, as in Heb. 9:28; 1 Pet. 2:24. The two ideas, of course, are not mutually exclusive: the bearing of sin by another involves its removal from the one on whom it formerly rested. Here the sin which is removed by the Lamb of God is that of 'the world' (*kosmos*); the universal note so struck is heard again in the course of this Gospel (e.g. 3:16 f.; 4:42; 6:51) and in the First Epistle (2:2; 4:14). The reader of the Gospel as a whole finds John's proclamation much less cryptic than its first hearers must have done with no such context to guide them to its meaning. The 'world' embraces all without distinction of race, religion or culture (cf. John 12:32).[50]

1:30 'This is the one of whom I said, "After me comes a man who has taken precedence over me, because he existed before me." '

This testimony has already been quoted in the prologue (verse 15). Formerly John has to speak of this person in general terms; now he can point him out.

1:31 'And I did not know him, but it was in order that he should be made manifest to Israel that I came baptizing in water.'

As has been said already, not until he witnessed the promised sign did John know who the Coming One was. But he knew that his own baptismal ministry was divinely intended to serve as the curtain raiser for the public appearance of this Coming One.

1:32 John bore witness as follows: 'I have looked on the Spirit descending like a dove from heaven, and it remained on him.'

The reference is, of course, to something that happened when Jesus came up out of Jordan, after being baptized by John. But this Gospel nowhere states explicitly that Jesus was baptized by John. To inquire into the reason for this silence would lead us unnecessarily into the realm of speculation. The one feature in the total baptismal incident to which John makes reference here – and emphatic reference at that – is one which bore a special significance for him.

The descent of the Spirit on Jesus marked him out as the Davidic ruler of Isa. 11:1 ff., of whom it is written, 'the Spirit of the LORD

shall rest upon him', as the Servant of whom God says in introducing him in Isa. 42:1, 'I have put my Spirit upon him', and as
the prophet who announces in Isa. 61:1, 'The Spirit of the Lord
GOD is upon me, because the LORD has anointed me . . .' This was
the occasion when, in the words of Acts 10:38, 'God anointed
Jesus of Nazareth with the Holy Spirit and with power'. That the
Spirit came upon Jesus 'like a dove' is recorded also in the Synoptic
Gospels (Matt. 3:16; Mark 1:10; Luke 3:22); Luke's wording is 'in
bodily form, like a dove'. Early parallels to the dove as a symbol
of the Spirit are hard to find. There is one from around AD 100:
Rabbi Ben Zoma commented on Gen. 1:2 ('the Spirit of God was
hovering over the surface of the water'), 'like a dove which hovers
over her young without touching them'.[51] We may recall John
Milton's apostrophe of the Spirit at the beginning of *Paradise Lost*:

> Thou from the first
> Wast present, and with mighty wings outspread
> Dovelike satst brooding on the vast Abyss
> And mad'st it pregnant.

**1:33 'And I did not know him, but he who sent me to baptize
in water – it was he who said to me, "The one on whom you see
the Spirit descending and remaining on him, this is the one who
is to baptize in the Holy Spirit".'**

Again John repeats that he did not know the Coming One's
identity up to that moment, but when he saw the descent of the
dove, he recognized the sign of which he had been warned by God
in advance. Now ignorance was displaced by certainty: this was
the Coming One – or, as it is put here, 'the one who was to baptize
in the Holy Spirit.'

Here at last we have the antithesis to John's statement of verse
26: '*I* baptize in water'. The implication was that the one whose
way John was preparing would administer baptism of a different
kind; now the nature of this baptism is disclosed. In Ezekiel's
prophecy of restoration, God promises not only to purify his
people with clean water but also to impart to them a new spirit –
his own Spirit (Ezek. 36:25–27). If the cleansing with water was
associated with John's ministry, the bestowal of the Spirit was
reserved for one greater than John. Now this greater Baptizer stood
revealed before them. He who had himself been so signally anointed
by the Spirit was uniquely qualified to impart the same unction to
his people – although, as is emphasized later in this Gospel, the
full impartation of the Spirit could not take place until Jesus was
glorified (John 7:39).

1:34 'I saw it myself, and so I have testified that this is the Son of God.'

The visible descent of the dove confirmed for John the truth that was simultaneously proclaimed by the heavenly voice which acknowledged Jesus as God's beloved Son.[52] While the designation 'Son of God' belonged *ex officio*, in terms of Psalm 2:7, to the one whom God acknowledged as his Messiah, it is in no merely official or formal sense that the designation is given to Jesus. It is plain, and nowhere more so than in this Gospel, that for Jesus himself it expressed the essential relationship which he bore to God as his Father. This filial consciousness is a most impressive feature of his inner life, in so far as the Gospel records permit us to penetrate the shrine of his personal devotion. In the experience of his disciples, perhaps, his Sonship as Messiah was appreciated before they grasped the deeper dimensions of his relationship to the Father. But actually the Sonship manifested in Jesus' messianic service was grounded in his eternal Sonship. This emerges with special clarity and emphasis in the Fourth Gospel, but it is taught in the Synoptic Gospels as well. There it is because Jesus is antecedently the Son of God that he is sent into the world as the last and greatest of God's messengers (Mark 12:6); it is because of the Son's unique and mutual knowledge of the Father that he is commissioned by the Father to communicate that knowledge to others (Matt. 11:27; Luke 10:22).[53]

II. The First Disciples (1:35–2:12)

1. THE FIRST DISCIPLES CALLED (1:35–51)

1:35–37 Next day John was standing again with two of his disciples, and looking at Jesus walking he said, 'See! there is the Lamb of God!' His two disciples heard him speak, and they went after Jesus.

The 'next day' was the day after John bore the testimony recorded in verses 29–34. The care with which the successive days are enumerated in this part of the narrative (1:29, 35, 43; 2:1) suggests that it is based on the recollection of a participant in the events described, who bore imprinted on his memory ever afterwards the detailed sequence of his first acquaintance with Jesus.[54] There would, in fact, be nothing against the supposition that this participant was one of the two disciples of John mentioned here, the one whose name is not given. John had many disciples; although these two became disciples of Jesus, others remained in John's company so long as he lived and some continued to regard themselves as his disciples after he died. As on the previous day,

Jesus was seen walking past them, and John directed his disciples'
attention to him, repeating the title which he had already given
him: 'the Lamb of God' (see verse 29). Hearing this, the two
immediately set off after Jesus. (The verb 'went after' or 'followed'
is in the aorist tense; it may be taken as an instance of the 'ingressive' aorist: 'they became his followers'.)

It is not certain what response John expected his disciples to
make to his words, but they left their teacher's side at once and
hurried after Jesus to catch up with him. They certainly did not
grasp the depth of meaning which modern readers find in the title
'the Lamb of God'; but they probably understood that John was
pointing this man out to them as the Coming One of whom he
had spoken before. No wonder, then, that they were eager to know
more of him.

**1:38, 39 Jesus turned and looked at them coming after him.
'What do you want?' he said to them. 'Rabbi', said they to him
(that is to say, 'Teacher'), 'where are you staying?' 'Come', said
he, 'and you will see.' So they went and saw where he was
staying, and they stayed with him that day. (It was about the
tenth hour.)**

Jesus knew very well what they wanted: his question was intended simply to give them an opportunity to say what was in their
minds. What they wanted was to get to know *him*, but this might
have sounded presumptuous; they contented themselves with asking where he was staying. A few words exchanged with him on the
spot, as they stood there, would be good; to be invited to accompany him and enjoy a more private and leisurely conversation
would be better. The respectful title 'Rabbi' (literally 'my great
one') is translated by the Evangelist for the benefit of his Greek
readers. In the course of the first century AD it came to be applied
in a rather technical sense to one ordained as a teacher after an
appropriate course of rabbinical training,[55] but it was given to Jesus
as a courtesy title by those who recognized in him a teacher sent
by God, as Nicodemus did (John 3:1).

The invitation for which, perhaps, they had scarcely dared to
hope was forthcoming at once, as it still is to those who wish to
get to know him better: 'Come, and you will see'. So they went
with him to his lodging and spent the rest of the day with him.
The 'tenth hour' (reckoning from sunrise) was about 4 p.m., when
men began to leave their work for the day.[56] What he said to them
is not recorded, but it was enough to convince them that John was
not mistaken; this was indeed the Coming One, the expected Mes-

siah. Such wonderful news could not be kept to themselves: their friends must share it with them

1:40–42 **Andrew, the brother of Simon Peter, was one of the two who heard John's words and went after Jesus. The first thing he did was to find his brother Simon. He said to him, 'We have found the Messiah' (that is to say, 'the anointed one'); and brought him to Jesus. Jesus looked at him and said, 'You are Simon the son of John: you will be called Cephas' (that is to say, 'Peter' or 'Rock').**

In later Christian decades Simon Peter's name was so familiar that Andrew is here identified as his brother,[57] even if Andrew makes his appearance on the stage of this Evangelist's history before Peter does. (The other disciple remains unnamed.) Andrew's first act after making Jesus' acquaintance was to bring his brother Simon to make his acquaintance too. RV translates literally 'his own brother Simon', giving the pronoun *idios* its full classical weight; but by this time *idios*, when followed by a noun, was tending to lose its emphasis and to be used as a simple possessive pronoun.[58] The pronoun is emphatic in its double occurrence in verse 11 above, where it is not followed by a noun.

'We have found the Messiah,' said Andrew. This Semitic verbal adjective does not appear in the New Testament except in his Gospel, where it is found twice – here and in 4:25; In both places it is interpreted by the Greek equivalent *christos*. In the OT the verbal adjective is used to denote the king of Israel ('the LORD's anointed', as in 1 Sam. 16:6, etc.), the high priest ('the anointed priest', as in Lev. 4:3, etc.) and once, in the plural, of the patriarchs in their rôle as prophets ('my anointed ones', Ps. 105:15). While the messianic expectation at the outset of the Christian era took a predominantly royal form, in actual fulfilment Jesus proved himself to be Messiah *par excellence* in all three rôles: prophet, priest and king. What Andrew would have meant at this time by the title Messiah cannot be stated with certainty; his understanding would no doubt have been coloured by contemporary forms in which the hope of Israel was cherished. But as he and his fellow-disciples came to know Jesus better, earlier conceptions of the Messiah and his achievement were displaced in their minds by the actual character and ministry of Jesus.[59]

Andrew, then, brought his brother to Jesus; and in later years, when Simon Peter performed such mighty works in the name of Jesus – in Jerusalem at the first Christian Pentecost, in Caesarea when Gentiles first heard and believed the gospel, and in places much farther afield – Andrew must have recalled with deep satisfaction that day when he brought his brother and their Master together. No one can foresee, when he brings a man or woman to Jesus, what Jesus will make of that person.

But Jesus himself saw what he could make of Andrew's brother, and expressed his purpose in his salutation. Simon Bar-Yoḥanan, the full name by which Simon was known, is abridged Simon Bar-Yona in Matt. 16:17 and translated 'Simon son of John' here. With such a man as this he could begin to found his new community. An affinity has sometimes been traced between Jesus' renaming of Simon and a late rabbinical parable told to explain why, in Isa. 51:1, Abraham is called 'the rock' from which Israel was hewn. 'A certain king', the story goes, 'desired to build a palace and his workmen dug deep to find a firm foundation. After two lengthy spells of digging, soundings were taken, but only morass was found. At length, however, they struck rock (*peṭra*) and he said, 'Now I can make a beginning''.'[60]

Whether something of this sort was in Jesus' mind or not, he hailed Simon as *Kepha*, an Aramaic word meaning 'rock'.[61] This was the form (Cephas) by which Paul commonly named him, adding a final -*s* to adapt it to the Greek tongue (cf. 1 Cor. 9:5; Gal. 1:18, etc.). More often, however, the Aramaic word was translated into Greek in the form *Petros* (used in our present text). Discussions about a possible variation in meaning between Greek *petros* and *petra* are beside the point here; for a man's name the masculine form *Petros* had to be used, whatever its precise nuance might be.

1:43, 44 **Next day he resolved to leave for Galilee, and found Philip. Jesus said to him, 'Follow me.' (Philip was from Bethsaida, the town of Andrew and Peter.)**

Andrew, it appears, had brought his brother to Jesus during the evening of the day whose events are narrated in verses 35–42. Now we move on to the day after that. But who was it that 'resolved to leave Galilee, and found Philip?' It is most natural to think that it was Jesus. But why then is the noun 'Jesus' inserted before the next verb 'said', as though there were a change of subject? May not Andrew or Peter have found Philip, who was their fellow-townsman?[62] If it was Andrew who found him, that might give additional point to the word 'first' in verse 41; it would then mean that the first person whom Andrew found and brought to Jesus was his brother Simon, but the next person was Philip. But in view of the formal ambiguity of the language, we cannot be sure. It may be that Jesus, setting out on the road to Galilee, found Philip making the same homeward journey from the place in Peraea where

John was baptizing, and invited him to join the company of his followers. 'Follow me' or 'Come after me' occurs here for the first time in this Gospel; we should probably recognize a note of authority in the command: the hand on the shoulder and the words to match the action – 'You come along with me'.

Moffatt makes Jesus find Philip after his arrival in Galilee: 'Next day Jesus determined to leave for Galilee; there he met Philip and told him, "Follow me".' But this is not the natural way to understand the narrative.

Bethsaida means 'house of the fisherman' or 'Fishertown'. It lay a short distance east of the point where Jordan enters the Lake of Galilee, perhaps near the place where the natural harbour of el-'Araj is still located. Some time before 2 BC Philip the tetrarch had refounded it (apparently including the neighbouring settlement now called et-Tell) and renamed it Julias, after Augustus's daughter Julia. The reference in John 12:21 to 'Bethsaida of Galilee' as Philip's home does not necessarily point to the west shore of the lake: in popular usage 'Galilee' included some territory east of the lake. ('Judas the Galilaean', mentioned in Acts 5:37, actually came from Gamala, east of the lake.)

1:45 Philip finds Nathanael and says to him, 'We have found the one of whom Moses wrote in the law, and the prophets too – Jesus son of Joseph, from Nazareth.'

This is how the number of Jesus' followers has gone on increasing to this day, as one has found another and shared the good news with him or her. The other early disciples mentioned in these verses figure in the lists of the twelve apostles given by the Synoptic Evangelists; it has therefore been widely supposed that Nathanael also appears in those lists under the patronymic Bartholomew (i.e. the son of Tholomai or Ptolemy). In Matt. 10:3, Mark 3:18 and Luke 6:14 Bartholomew is linked with Philip (not so, however, in Acts 1:13).

What Philip says to Nathanael means much the same as what Andrew said to Simon (verse 41) but instead of calling Jesus the Messiah he describes him as the one of whom Moses and the prophets wrote. The rôle of Jesus as fulfiller of the OT scriptures is emphasized in various ways throughout this Gospel. He is the prophet of whom Moses spoke in Deut. 18:15–19 (cf. verse 21 above); he is the Lord's anointed whose coming, foretold by the prophets, was to establish worldwide righteousness, peace and the knowledge and fear of God. In referring to our Lord as 'Jesus son of Joseph, from Nazareth', Philip gave him the full designation by which he was currently known: to a man's personal name was appended the name of his father (real or reputed) and of his home-town.

1:46 Nathanael said to him, 'Can anything good come out of Nazareth?' 'Come and see', said Philip to him.

Nathanael himself was a Galilaean from Cana (cf. John 21:2). The form of his question implies that among other Galilaeans Nazareth (on which the emphasis lies) enjoyed no high repute. We have no other evidence that Nazareth was regarded unfavourably, but that is not surprising, as Nazareth was an unimportant place. It was the fact that Jesus spent most of his life there that first 'put it on the map'. (The earliest Jewish reference to it comes in a Hebrew inscription excavated at Caesarea in 1962 which lists places in Galilee to which members of the twenty-four priestly courses emigrated after a pagan city was founded on the site of Jerusalem in AD 135.)[63] People who live in country districts know how one small place may have an exceptionally bad reputation among its neighbours, but such a local reputation does not usually find its way into literature. At any rate, Nathanael's bantering question received the only adequate answer: 'Come and see'. Honest inquiry is a sovereign cure for prejudice. Nazareth might be all that Nathanael thought, but there is an exception to prove every rule; and what an exception these young men had found!

1:47 Jesus saw Nathanael coming to him. 'See', he said, 'an Israelite indeed, in whom there is no deceit!'

To Nathanael's surprise, Jesus greeted him on his approach as if he knew him quite well. And what an encomium Jesus gave him! The point of the encomium is best understood from the conversation which follows, with its reference to the narrative of Jacob's ladder. 'Here is a true son of Israel', Jesus' words may be paraphrased, 'one who is all Israel and no Jacob'. Whatever the etymology of the name Jacob may be,[64] it was traditionally associated with deceit. When Isaac said to Esau, 'Your brother came with deceit (LXX *dolos*, the word used here by John), and he has taken away your blessing', Esau replied, 'Is he not rightly named Jacob (Heb. *ya'ăqōb*)? For he has supplanted me (*ya'aqᵉbēnî*) these two times (Gen. 27:35 f.).

In spite of Nazareth's unenviable notoriety, Nathanael's transparent generosity of heart made him willing to come and see this Nazarene whom Philip declared to be the one foretold in the law and the prophets. Jacob, for all the over-reaching deceit associated with his name, received a vision of God which changed his character, and was given the new name Israel to mark that change (Gen. 28:10 ff.; 32:24–28). While Israel is actually derived from the Hebrew verb *śārāh* ('strive'),[65] there was current in the first century (as we may see from Philo of Alexandria) a popular etymology which explained by the name by the Hebrew phrase *'ish-rō'eh-'ēl* ('the man who sees God');[66] and there may be some allusion to this etymology here. For Nathanael, this typical member of the true believing Israel, receives a promise that he and his companions will experience such a vision as was granted to Jacob.

1:48 **'How do you know me?' said Nathanael to him. 'Before Philip called you', said Jesus in reply, 'when you were under the fig tree, I saw you.'**

With an allusion to something known only to Nathanael and himself, Jesus let him understand that he knew more about him than he could have conceived possible. We can only surmise what the significance of the fig tree was. C. F. D. Moule has suggested that the expression 'under the fig tree' denoted 'accurate knowledge of a person's whereabouts and movements'.[67] Or perhaps it was a place where Nathanael had recently sat in meditation and received some spiritual impression. It is impossible to be sure. Certainly the shady foliage of the fig tree made it a suitable tree to sit under in the heat of the day. It was under a fig tree that Augustine sat meditating when he heard the voice singing 'Take up and read!' and found his soul flooded with heavenly light as he took up and read the closing words of Romans 13.[68]

1:49 **Nathanael answered him, 'Rabbi', you are the Son of God; you are King of Israel.'**

Whatever doubts Nathanael may have had vanished instantaneously. The one who manifested such intimate knowledge of his movements and his thoughts was certainly the one to whom the ancient scriptures pointed forward. He addresses Jesus by the courtesy title Rabbi ('Teacher'), but proceeds to give him far loftier designations than that. In effect he acclaims him as Messiah, using two messianic titles conjoined in the second psalm where God says to the anointed King of Israel, enthroned on the holy hill of Zion, 'You are my Son; today I have begotten you' (Ps. 2:6 f.). To the Evangelist as he wrote, 'the Son of God' had a much greater depth of meaning than this, but we need not suppose that, at such an early stage in his career as a disciple, Nathanael meant much more by it than he meant by 'King of Israel'; they were alternative ways of denoting the Messiah. In the context of the Gospel record,

however, both titles convey to the reader a fuller significance than
Nathanael could have given them.

1:50, 51 **Jesus said to him in reply. 'Do you believe because I
told you that I saw you underneath the fig tree? You will see
greater things than these. Indeed and in truth I tell you'**, he
went on to say to him, **'you will all see heaven opened and the
angels of God ascending and descending on the Son of Man.'**

Whatever degree of supernatural knowledge Jesus's words about
Nathanael's fig-tree experience had evinced, Nathanael would be
confronted with much more wonderful and conclusive tokens of
Jesus' true identity than any such words as these. Nor would these
promised tokens be witnessed by Nathanael alone: the transition
in verse 51 from the second person singular to the second person
plural ('you will all see'[69]) indicates that his fellow-disciples would
witness them too.

In announcing one of these 'greater things', Jesus uses, for the
first time in this Gospel, his characteristic word of solemn affirmation, 'Amen' (translated 'Verily' in AV and RV, 'Truly', in RSV).
In the Synoptic Gospels 'Amen, I tell you' occurs with the single
'Amen'; its duplication (as here) is distinctively Johannine.[70]
'Amen' is in origin a Hebrew word meaning 'steadfast' or 'sure';
from the same root come the ordinary Hebrew words for 'belief',
'faithfulness' and 'truth'. It was used in the liturgy (cf. Ps. 41:13,
etc.) to express the assurance that a prayer (e.g. for the glorifying
of God's name) would be fulfilled. On Jesus' lips it confirms the
certainty and trustworthiness of what he says, and was preserved
untranslated in the Greek-speaking church as his *ipsissima vox*,
proclaiming his unique authority.

The words which follow may be a Johannine parallel to the
Synoptic prediction of the day when the Son of Man will be manifested on the clouds of heaven 'with great power and glory' (cf.
Mark 13:26; 14:62).[71] But here the imagery is taken from the
account of Jacob's vision at Bethel, when he saw 'a ladder set up
on the earth, and the top of it reached to heaven; and, behold, the
angels of God were ascending and descending on it' (Gen. 28:12).[72]
In this application of Jacob's vision, however, the union between
earth and heaven is effected by the Son of Man: he is the mediator
between God and the human race.[73] Not only so: the occasion to
which the words of Jesus point is none other than his crucifixion.
On a later occasion, speaking to a Jerusalem audience, he said,
'When you have lifted up the Son of Man, then you shall know
that I am He' (John 8:28). His being 'lifted up' is his exaltation,
though his enemies intended it for degradation; the cross is the

supreme manifestation of his glory. By the cross heaven is thrown wide open, God draws near to man, and man is reconciled to God.

> As to the holy patriarch
> That wondrous dream was given,
> So seems my Saviour's cross to me
> A ladder up to heaven.

The designation 'the Son of Man' does not appear to have been a current title for the Messiah or any other eschatological figure. Jesus could therefore use it of himself without the risk of being misunderstood because of associations which might have controlled his hearer's conception of its meaning. He was free to take up the expression and fill it with what significance he chose.

The expression probably had an OT background in the 'one like a son of man' (i.e. a man-like figure) who, in Daniel's vision of the day of judgment, was divinely invested with universal authority (Dan. 7:13, 14).[74] Jesus enriched it by fusing with this figure the figure of a righteous sufferer portrayed here and there throughout the OT, not least in the 'Servant Songs' of Isa. 42:1–53:12. Thus he could speak of the suffering of the Son of Man as something that was 'written' concerning him. By suffering and vindication Jesus, the Son of Man, has become his people's deliverer and advocate.

Students of the Synoptic Gospels distinguish passages which speak of the suffering Son of Man from those which speak of his coming in glory. But in this Gospel no such distinction is made: the suffering of the Son of Man is caught up into the glory, so that the glory is revealed pre-eminently in the suffering (cf. John 12:23).[75]

NOTES

1. Cf. C. K. Barrett, 'The Prologue of St John's Gospel' in *New Testament Essays* (London 1972), pp. 27–48.
2. E. V. Rieu and J. B. Phillips, 'Translating the Gospels' *The Bible Translator* 6 (1955), pp. 157 f.
3. J. W. von Goethe *Faust*, line 1237.
4. According to Justin, *First Apology* 5.3, 4, the *logos* or right reason which enabled Socrates to discern truth and expose falsehood, the *logos* for the sake of which he was sentenced to death, is the *logos* which later became incarnate in Jesus Christ. See also p. 8, and compare the quotation from Augustine on p. 39.
5. C. K. Barrett, *The Gospel according to St John* (London ²1978), p. 156. On the construction of the clause see E. C. Colwell, 'A Definite Rule for the Use of the Article in the Greek New Testament' *JBL* 52 (1933), pp. 12–21: on the rendering 'the Word was God' he says, 'This statement cannot be regarded as strange in the prologue of the gospel which reaches its climax in the confession of Thomas' (p. 21).

6. Socrates *Hist. Eccl.* 1. 5.2. This proposition was explicitly condemned by the Council of Nicaea (AD 325).

7. RSV and NEB follow LXX in using the verb 'created' in the first clause. Arius and his followers seized eagerly on this LXX rendering as showing that the Son of God was originally created, and their opponents were embarrassed in trying to get round this argument. In fact, they were both mistaken: the personification of wisdom here and elsewhere in the OT is a figure of speech, but it is one which provided several NT writers with a conceptual and verbal framework for portraying Christ as the personal, not merely personified, wisdom of God – begotten, not created.

8. The statement of verse 2 might also be taken as an answer to the Creator's rhetorical question in Isa. 44:24, 'I am the LORD . . . who stretched out the heavens alone, who spread out the earth – who was with me?' or to the question prompted by his words in Gen. 1:26, 'Let us make man . . .': 'Who was with him to whom he said this?' 'This', says the Evangelist, 'is the one who was in the beginning with God.'

9. B. M. Metzger *A Textual Commentary on the Greek New Testament* (London/ New York 1971), p. 196, n. 2.

10. Cf. Wisdom 7:29b, 30: 'Wisdom is superior in comparison with light, for light is succeeded by the night, but against wisdom evil does not prevail.'

11. See Introduction, p. 3.

12. Although they knew no baptism but John's, it is improbable that Luke represents them as John's disciples; when he uses the word 'disciples' without qualification, as he uses it of them in Acts 19:1, he regularly means 'disiciples of Jesus'.

13. Justin *First Apology* 46.2, 3 (see p. 63, n. 4).

14. See F. F. Bruce *The Epistles of John* (Pickering & Inglis 1970), pp. 59–64.

15. Where the prologue speaks of the coming of the Word, the body of the Gospel speaks of the sending of the Son.

16. The expression 'many believed in his name' is used in John 2:23 in a weaker sense, of people who accorded him an outward assent without an accompanying inward allegiance.

17. The Greek reading, moreover, 'is in accord with the characteristic teaching of John' (B. M. Metzger *A Textual Commentary on the Greek New Testament*, p. 197). Among modern English versions, the Jerusalem Bible is exceptional in opting for the minority reading with the singular.

18. Augustine *Confessions* 7.13, 14. Augustine evidently knew the singular Old Latin reading of John 1:13 mentioned above.

19. See F. F. Bruce *The Epistles of John*, pp. 16 f., 104 f., 140–143.

20. See H. D. McDonald and F. F. Bruce, 'The Humanity of Jesus Christ' *CBRF Journal* 24 (1973), pp. 5–23; D. J. A. Clines, 'God in Human Form: A Theme in Biblical Theology' *ibid.*, pp. 24–40.

21. See J. N. D. Kelly *Early Christian Creeds* (London 1950), pp. 205–331 and, for a popular account, F. F. Bruce *The Spreading Flame* (Exeter 1970), pp. 302–315.

22. H. I. Bell *Egypt from Alexander the Great to the Arab Conquest* (Oxford 1948), p. 107.

23. If Ex. 25:8 is indeed in the author's mind, it will have been the Hebrew text and not the LXX, which renders 'I may dwell' (Heb. *shākanti*) as 'I will appear' (Gk. *ophthēsomai*).

24. In Sir. 24:8 it is to Wisdom that God assigns a place for a tent (Gk. *skēnē*), saying, 'Make your dwelling (*kataskēnōson*) in Jacob, and in Israel receive your inheritance.'

25. The verb *theaomai*, used elsewhere in this Gospel in the general sense of seeing or looking (John 1:32, 38; 4:35; 6:5; 11:45), is used here of contemplating the

life of the historical Jesus in such a way as to recognize the divine quality (the 'glory') in it, and so to attain that knowledge of him which is the true vision of God. This is expressed in other places in the Gospel by *horaō* or *theōreō*. See C. H. Dodd *The Interpretation of the Fourth Gospel* (Cambridge 1953), p. 167.

26. It is used in Judg. 11:34 of Jephthah's daughter, and in Tobit 3:15; 6:14; 8:17 of Raguel's daughter Sarah and Tobit's son Tobias. In other Greek versions it is similarly used of Isaac in Gen. 22:2, 12 (so also in Heb. 11:17). In Luke 7:12; 8:42; 9:38 it is used of various only children. In the Johannine writings it is used of Jesus in relation to God (cf. verse 18; 3:16, 18;1 John 4:9). The word etymologically means the only one (*monos*) of his/her/its kind (*genos*). With reference to Jesus as the Son of God the traditional rendering 'only-begotten' (cf. Latin *unigenitus*) is retained here, as the Evangelist perhaps associated *-genēs* with the verb *gennaō* (used in verse 13), thus taking the compound *monogenēs* in the sense of either 'only-begotten' or 'begotten of the only One'.

27. The reference is to the ineffable name spelt with the four consonants YHWH, commonly transcribed Yahweh ('Jehovah' in the older versions). It is not the etymology of the name, but its significance as unfolded in God's dealings with his people, that is 'proclaimed' or 'declared'. In this sense (but more fully) Jesus, in his prayer of consecration, claims to have 'declared' the Father's name to his disciples (John 17:5, 26).

28. In *Grace and Truth* (London 1975) A. T. Hanson expresses dissatisfaction with Chalcedonian Christology which, he observes, is (together with the bulk of traditional Christology) dependent on this Gospel; but it is to John 1:14, viewed as a restatement of the divine name revealed in Ex. 34:6, that he turns to find a firmer christological basis than that laid down by the Chalcedonian divines.

29. Philo uses the preposition *anti* in something like this sense when he says that God varies his gifts (*charites*), withdrawing those of which the recipients have had enough, storing them up for future bestowal, and giving others in place of (*anti*) them, 'and always new ones in place of (*anti*) earlier' (*On Cain's Posterity and Exile*, 145).

30. See comment on verse 20 (pp. 46f).

31. In Job 28:27 the subject and object are reversed: it is God who has 'declared' (LXX *exēgēsato*) wisdom.

32. His bosom, in contrast to his back, the only part of him which Moses was permitted to see (Ex. 33:23). See M.-E. Boismard, ' "Dans le sein du Père" (Jn. 1,18)', *RB* 59 (1952), pp. 23–39.

33. The Sanhedrin, from the beginning of the second century BC to the outbreak of the war against Rome in AD 66, was the supreme court of the Jewish nation. Under the Roman occupation of Judaea it controlled internal Jewish affairs. The reigning high priest was *ex officio* president and it comprised seventy other 'elders'. At this time it was dominated by the 'chief priests' (members of the families from which the high priest was drawn), who belonged to the party of the Sadducees; but the views of the Pharisaic minority could not be ignored (see p. 250.).

34. In the Qumran community three figures were expected to arise at the end-time: 'a prophet and the anointed ones of Aaron and Israel' (1QS 9.11) – the last two being otherwise translated 'the priestly and lay Messiahs'.

35. See comment on verse 41 (p. 57).

36. See comments on John 4:19, 25 (pp. 108, 111). Compare the expectation of an end-time prophet in the Qumran text quoted in n. 34.

37. Isa. 40:3 seems to have been invoked to justify the Qumran community's withdrawal to the wilderness of Judaea (1QS 8.13–15).

38. The Sadducees are not mentioned in this Gospel, perhaps because their party

had disappeared by the time it was written. The leading chief priests (e.g. Annas, Caiaphas) and their families belonged to the Sadducean party.

39. On the Pharisees see Josephus *Jewish War* 2.162–166; *Antiquities* 18.12–15; cf. also J. Bowker *Jesus and the Pharisees* (Cambridge 1973); E. Rivkin *A Hidden Revolution* (Nashville 1978).

40. For further implications of Ezek. 36:25–27 in the following narrative see comment on verse 33 (p. 54).

41. Cf. H. H. Rowley, 'Jewish Proselyte Baptism and the Baptism of John' *From Moses to Qumran* (London 1963), pp. 211–235; also J. A. T. Robinson, 'The Baptism of John and the Qumran Community' *Twelve New Testament Studies* (London 1962), pp. 11–27.

42. Rabbi Joshua ben Levi (c. AD 239), as reported in Babylonian Talmud, tractate K'thûbôth 96a.

43. *Commentary on John, ad loc.*

44. Josephus, *Antiquities* 18.119.

45. One edition of the LXX renders Bethnimrah by *Baithanabra*, a form which looks like a conflation of Bethany and Bethabara.

46. E.g. in 1 Enoch 90:9–12; *Testament of Joseph* 19:8. See C. H. Dodd *The Interpretation of the Fourth Gospel* (Cambridge 1953), pp. 230–238.

47. In 1 Pet. 1:19 where *amnos* is used in relation to Christ, it is used not as a title but as a simile, with reference probably to the paschal lamb.

48. It is the feminine form of *ṭalyā* that Jesus used when telling Jairus's daughter to get up: 'Talitha cumi – Little girl . . . arise' (Mark 5:41).

49. So J. Jeremias *TDNT* 5, p. 702, n. 356 (*s.v. pais theou*).

50. For a more restricted use of the term 'world' see John 7:7; 14:17; 15:18 f., etc.

51. Babylonian Talmud, tractate Ḥāgîgāh 15a.

52. For the voice see Mark 1:11 where its wording – 'Thou art my Son, my Beloved; in thee I am well pleased' – seems to combine the acclamation to the Lord's Anointed in Ps. 2:7 ('Thou art my Son') with the introduction of the Servant in Isa. 42:1 ('my chosen, in whom my soul delights').

53. Cf. G. Vos *The Self-Disclosure of Jesus* (Grand Rapids ²1954), pp. 195–226, on 'The Sonship of Jesus in the Fourth Gospel'.

54. This is more probable than that the successive days in this part of the narrative are designed to reflect the seven days of Gen. 1:3–2: 3; cf. T. Barrosse, 'The Seven Days of the New Creation in St John's Gospel' *CBQ* 21 (1959), pp. 507–516.

55. This formal ordination involved the laying on of hands (Heb. s'mikhāh); cf. J. Newman *Semikhah* (Manchester 1950); A. A. T. Ehrhardt, 'Jewish and Christian Ordination' *The Framework of the New Testament Stories* (Manchester 1964), pp. 132–150.

56. Some writers say that John followed the 'Roman' reckoning and counted the hours from midnight. Pliny the Elder is sometimes cited in support of this view. But what Pliny says is that the Romans (like the Egyptians) defined the civil *day* as lasting from midnight to midnight (*Natural History* 2.79.188). They divided the period of daylight (from sunrise to sunset) into twelve *hours*, and the period of darkness (from sunset to sunrise) into four watches. Cf. John 4:6, 52; 19.14.

57. See P. M. Peterson *Andrew, Brother of Simon Peter* (Leiden 1958).

58. Cf. Acts 24:24 for another instance of the 'exhausted' use of *idios*: 'his (own) wife Drusilla'.

59. See comment on verse 20 above (pp. 46f).

60. The parable is preserved in the mediaeval collection *Yalquṭ Shim'ônî* (1.766). The two earlier soundings were taken in the days of Enosh, when 'men began

to call upon the name of the LORD' (Gen. 4:26), and in the days of Noah, who 'found favour in the eyes of the LORD' (Gen. 6:9).

61. The corresponding Hebrew word is *kēph*, which is found in the sense of 'rock' in Job 30:6 and Jer. 4:29.

62. It is implied in Mark 1:29 that, by the time Jesus began his Galilaean ministry, Peter and Andrew had taken up residence at Capernaum, west of the lake (cf. John 2:12).

63. Cf. M. Avi-Yonah, 'The Caesarea Inscription of the Twenty-Four Priestly Courses' in *The Teacher's Yoke*, ed. E. J. Vardaman and J. L. Garrett (Waco, Texas 1964), pp. 46–57. It is only from the 4th century AD onwards that Nazareth became a place of any importance, but human settlement in the area is attested as early as the Middle Bronze Age (between 2000 and 1550 BC.

64. It is derived from *'āqēb*, 'heel'; *ya'āqōb* means 'he seizes by the heel', and hence, by extension, 'he overreaches'.

65. Cf. Gen. 32:28, 'you have striven' (*śārîthā*).

66. Philo *Allegorical Interpretation* 3.186.

67. C. F. D. Moule, 'A Note on "Under the Fig Tree" ' *JTS* n.s. 5 (1954), pp. 210 f.

68. Augustine *Confessions* 8.29.

69. The addition of 'henceforth' before 'you will (all) see' is of late attestation and is probably borrowed from Matt. 26:64.

70. NEB renders the double 'Amen' of this Gospel: 'in truth, in very truth'. The locution, according to B. Lindars, 'is a recurring sign that John is making use of a saying of Jesus from his stock of traditional material' (*Behind the Fourth Gospel* [London 1971], p. 44).

71. The phrase 'son of man' is a Hebrew and Aramaic idiom meaning simply 'a man', 'a human being'. In Aramaic, the language which Jesus appears normally to have spoken, 'the Son of Man' would have meant 'the Man'. On occasion Jesus may have used this expression as a substitute for the pronoun 'I' or 'me' (see comment on John 3:27), but usually a further significance is implied in his use of it. The Greek form *ho hyios tou anthrōpou* appears in the NT only with reference to Jesus and almost always on his own lips. Only once (John 5:27) is it used of him without the twofold definite article.

72. It is possible to render the Hebrew, '. . . the angels of God ascending and descending on *him*' (i.e. on Jacob). According to a rabbinical traditional preserved in the late commentary *Genesis Rabba* 69.7 (on Gen. 28:17), Jacob's ladder stood on the site of the future temple; this involved understanding Beth-el etymologically ('the house of God') and not geographically.

73. In Ps. 8:4 'the son of man' (Heb. *ben 'ādām*) stands in synonymous parallelism with 'man' (Heb. *'ĕnōsh*), both expressions being used in the generic sense.

74. The phrase 'one like a son of man' in Rev. 1:13; 14:14 (*hōs hyios anthrōpou*) does not belong to this category; it means (like the Aramaic phrase *kᵉbar 'ĕnāsh* in Dan. 7:13) 'a man-like figure'.

75. See S. S. Smalley, 'The Johannine Son of Man Sayings' *New Testament Studies* 15 (1968–69), pp. 278–301; B. Lindars, 'The Son of Man in the Johannine Christology' in *Christ and Spirit in the New Testament*, ed. B. Lindars and S. S. Smalley (Cambridge 1973), pp. 43–60; E. Kinniburgh, 'The Johannine "Son of Man" ' *Studia Evangelica* 6 = *Texte und Untersuchungen* 102 (Berlin 1973), pp. 64–71. Cf. p.277, n. 22.

CHAPTER 2

2. THE SIGN AT CANA (2:1–11)

2:1, 2 On the third day there was a wedding in Cana of Galilee, and Jesus' mother was there. Jesus also was invited to the wedding, and his disciples too.

'The third day' is probably to be counted from the event last mentioned, the call of Nathanael. The reckoning is, as usual, inclusive; we should say 'two days later' (Moffatt). The distance from Bethany beyond Jordan (1:28) to Cana cannot be measured precisely because we do not know where the former place was, but it was presumably a distance which a group of young men could walk without great difficulty in two days. Less probably we might suppose that the wedding took place two days after their arrival in Galilee. Some interpreters see a symbolic significance in 'the third day'; Jesus' manifesting his glory (verse 11) on the third day has been held to adumbrate his resurrection. It is very doubtful if the Evangelist had any such thought in his mind.

Cana, the home of Nathanael (21:2), has been traditionally identified with Kefr Kenna, 4 miles from Nazareth on the road to the lake. There both Greek and Roman churches claim to mark the site of the changing of water into wine; the visitor is even given a minuscule drink of wine to commemorate the occasion. But a more probable location is Khirbet Qana, a ruined village some 9 miles north of Nazareth. This is supported by Josephus's information that Cana, where he had his headquarters when he took up his military command in Galilee in AD 66, lay in the Plain of Asochis,[1] which includes Khirbet Qana but not Kefr Kenna.

The mother of Jesus appears twice in this Gospel – here, and at the cross (19:25 ff.). There is also an allusion to her in 6:42. In none of these places is she referred to by her personal name Mary. This may simply be to prevent confusion with other women of that name mentioned in the Gospel. Attempts have been made to view her allegorically in this Gospel – as personifying Israel or the church, for example – but their validity is very doubtful.

It is traditional to invoke Jesus' presence at the wedding as setting the seal of his approval on the divine ordinance of marriage – and rightly so. There is a world of difference between his taking part in this joyful celebration and the attitude of those Essenes who disdained marriage.[2]

2:3 When wine had run short, Jesus' mother said to him, 'They have no wine.'

Such a festal occasion might be prolonged for a week, and for the wine to run short before it was due to end was a serious blow, particularly damaging to the reputation of the host. Mary may well have had some responsibility for the catering; at any rate she knew that in such a crisis she could not do better than call upon her Son's resourcefulness. Probably she had learned by experience that to draw his attention to a need was a sure way of getting something done.

2:4 Jesus says to her, 'Why trouble me with that, lady? My hour has not yet come.'

Mary probably failed to realize adequately that since her Son had left home (some months before) something had happened which must make a difference to their former relationship. He had been anointed with the Holy Spirit and had received power to undertaken the special work which his Father had given him to do. Now that, after the long 'silent years' at Nazareth, he had entered on his public ministry, everything (including family ties) must be subordinated to this. This at least lies behind his surprising answer to her, translated in the older versions as 'Woman, what have I to do with thee?' The English word 'woman', used thus in the vocative, carries with it a flavour of disrespect which is not present in the original. (Perhaps the Ulster expression 'Woman dear' would convey the sense fairly well.) Our Lord addressed his mother by this same term (Gk. *gynai*, vocative of *gynē*) when he hung on the cross (19:26); and indeed the term was consonant with the utmost courtesy, being translatable as 'madam' or 'my lady'. But when the NEB makes him say 'Your concern, mother, is not mine', it misses the point, which is that 'mother' is precisely what he did *not* call her. If she sought his help now, she must not seek it on the basis of their mother-and-son relationship.

The rest of his reply is even more difficult to translate with confidence. The Greek wording *ti emoi kai soi* may mean either 'what have I to do with thee?' (RV) or 'what have you to do with me?' (RSV). Which alternative is to be preferred must be decided by the context, and the present context points to the latter alternative. To translate the Greek more or less word for word, as the Douai-Rheims-Challoner version does – 'what is it to me and to thee?' – is to give excellent sense but, unfortunately, not the sense of the original. The sense of the original is better conveyed by two more recent Catholic versions – R. A. Knox's 'Nay, woman, why

dost thou trouble me with that?' (which has been partly borrowed
in the rendering above) and the Jerusalem Bible's 'Woman, why
turn to me?' (which sounds rather too peremptory). The kind of
action she wanted him to perform, for the limited purpose she had
in mind, was not in keeping with his messianic vocation; perhaps
is smacked too much of the turning of stones into loaves of bread
(one of the Synoptic temptations). Even if the action were to be
the vehicle for a manifestation of his glory, the time for that had
not yet come. The full manifestation of the glory would not take
place until the Son of Man was lifted up. Yet he did grant her
implied request, but granted it in a way which manifested in anticipation the glory later to be revealed in its fulness. 'It is an axiom
of our Gospel that the transformation of the symbolical into the
"real" can only come about with the bestowal of the Spirit, which
in turn cannot take place till after Jesus death'.[3] Even at that early
stage in the ministry, however, the lesson of that future transformation could be taught by an acted parable.

**2:5 His mother says to the servants, 'Do whatever he tells
you.'**

Mary knew (despite her Son's unforthcoming reply) that the
situation was saved when it had been committed to him. She did
not know what he would do, but she knew he would do the right
thing. Hence her instructions to the servants or waiters, given in
a tone which confirms our impression that she was in some position
of responsibility at the feast. The recorded words of Mary are few;
these particular words have an application beyond the immediate
occasion which called them forth.

**2:6–8 Now there were standing there, in accordance with the
Jews' purificatory practice, six stone water-jars, each holding
some twenty gallons. Jesus says to them, 'Fill the jars with
water.' And they filled them right up. Then he says to them,
'Now draw (some water) and carry it to the chief steward.'**

The stone jars which stood at the door where the feast was going
on would have been quite similar to stone jars from that period
which have been found here and there in Palestine in our own day.
Each, says the Evangelist, held two or three 'measures' (AV 'firkins')
– a 'measure' (Gk. *metrētēs*) being equivalent to eight or nine of
our gallons.[4] They stood there to supply water for rinsing the
guests' hands and for washing the various vessels required for the
feast, in accordance with the old-established tradition mentioned
in Mark 7:3 f. The way in which our Evangelist speaks of 'the

Jews' purificatory practice' (cf. 'the Jews' passover, verse 13) suggests that he is writing for a largely Gentile constituency. But the
reference to their 'purificatory practice' here gives the clue to the
spiritual meaning of the present narrative. The water, provided for
purification as laid down by Jewish law and custom, stands for the
whole ancient order of Jewish ceremonial, which Christ was to
replace by something better.

The servants, mindful of Mary's instructions, followed Jesus'
directions and filled the six jars with water. Then he bade them
draw some more water from the well and carry it to the chief
steward. The usual view is that it was the water in the six jars that
was turned into wine. But the verb *antleō* ('draw') naturally implies
drawing water from a well (cf. the noun *antlēma*, 'something to
draw with', in 4:11). The suggestion made here is that what was
turned into wine was the water drawn from the well after the filling
of the jars. The filling of the jars to the brim indicates that the
appointed time for the ceremonial observances of the Jewish law
had run its full course; these observances had so completely fulfilled
their purpose that nothing of the old order remained to be accomplished. The time had come therefore for the new order to be
inaugurated. The wine symbolizes the new order as the water in
the jars symbolized the old order.

The 'chief steward' or head waiter was in charge of the place
where the banquet was held. Since he superintended the supply of
food and drink to the wedding guests, it was the servants' duty to
take what they had drawn to him before it was served to those
reclining at the table. The table here was one running round three
sides of the room (Latin *triclinium*); the chief steward is called 'the
rule of the table' (Gk. *archtriklinos*).

**2:9, 10 When the chief steward had tasted the water made
wine, and did not know where it came from (the servants who
had drawn the water knew), he calls the bridegroom and says to
him, 'Every one serves the good wine first, and then the inferior
stuff when people are drunk; *you* have kept the good wine till
now.'**

The common practice was so well known as to be proverbial.
The guests were supplied with the best wine first; as the feast
progressed they became less particular about the quality of what
was offered them. But for some reason which the chief steward
failed to grasp, the best wine on this occasion had been reserved to
the end of the feast. The point of the Evangelist's narrative is missed
entirely by those popular commentators who suggest that the water
remained water all the time, but that Jesus had it served up under

the name of wine in a spirit of good-humoured playfulness, while
the chief steward accepted it in the same spirit and said, 'Yes, of
course, the best wine! Adam's wine! But why have you kept it to
the last?' Other commentators, at a less popular level, have noted
the literary affinities between the chief steward's surprise and Greek
stories of the introduction of wine to the human race by Dionysos.[5]
But these affinities are verbal, not material. Jesus action was, in
C. S. Lewis's terminology, a 'miracle of the old creation': the
Creator who, year by year, turns water into wine, so to speak, by
a natural process, on this occasion speeds up the process and attains
the same end.[6] But if it is a miracle of the old creation, it is a
parable of the new creation. Christ has come into the world to
fulfil and terminate the old order, and to replace it by a new
worship 'in spirit and truth' which surpasses the old as much as
wine surpasses water.

**2:11 Jesus did this as the first of his signs in Cana of Galilee,
and manifested his glory, and his disciples believed in him.**

'We looked on his glory,' said the Evangelist of the incarnate
Word in his prologue: now he has narrated the first of a sequence
of 'signs' in which, throughout the body of the Gospel, that glory
was shown, leading up to the surpassing glory of Jesus' self-obla-
tion. As the glory was manifested, faith in him was quickened and
strengthened in the hearts of His disciples.

Several words are used in the NT to denote Jesus' mighty works.
The word which actually means 'mighty works' (*dynameis*) is not
found in this Gospel; in fact the word *dynamis* ('power'), of which
dynameis is the plural, is totally absent from it. Another word is
terata ('portents' or 'miracles'), which is never found in the NT
unaccompanied by *sēmeia* ('signs'). The NT miracles are not *mere*
miracles; they are all signs of some underlying reality. Only once
in the Gospel of John does *terata* occur – in the general statement
of 4:48: 'Unless you see signs (*sēmeia*) and wonders (*terata*) you
will not believe.' John prefers to call the miracles of Jesus 'signs'
(*sēmeia*) pure and simple.[7] Jesus himself (in this Gospel) calls them
his 'works' (*erga*).[8]

3. RESIDENCE IN CAPERNAUM (2:12)

**2:12 After this he went down to Capernaum with his mother
and brothers and his disciples, and they stayed there for a short
time.**

Capernaum (*Kefar-naḥum*, 'the village of Nahum') lay on the north-west shore of the lake of Galilee; hence one went down to it from Cana or Nazareth. It lies about 16 miles ENE of Cana, and is commonly identified with the locality known in Arabic as Tell-Ḥum. (This identification is taken for granted nowadays by the Israeli authorities.) It appears that the holy family as a whole moved from Nazareth to Capernaum, where Jesus had his headquarters for the greater part of his Galilaean ministry recorded by the Synoptists (cf. also John 6:24, 59). The statement that they stayed there 'for a short time' (literally 'not many days') may simply mean that a few days after they settled there Jesus and his disciples went up to Jerusalem for the Passover (verse 13).

The most natural understanding of our Lord's brothers is that they were children of Joseph and Mary, he himself being Mary's firstborn.[9] The disciples will be (in the first instance) those whose call is recorded in chapter 1.

B. JESUS REVEALS THE FATHER IN THE WORLD
(John 2:13–12:50)

I. Ministry in Judaea (2:13–3:36)

1. IN JERUSALEM AT THE FIRST PASSOVER (2:13–3:21)

(a) Cleansing of the Temple (2:13–22)

2:13 The Passover of the Jews was at hand, and Jesus went up to Jerusalem.

Our Evangelist repeatedly refers to festivals as festivals 'of the Jews'[10] – not because he himself was not a Jew by birth and upbringing (he was), but because many of his readers would be Gentiles, unacquainted with the details of the Jewish sacred year. It is unnecessary to suppose that he was in this way depreciating the festivals as belonging to a now superseded order; his language is simply descriptive. The Passover, commemorating Israel's deliverance from Egypt, was celebrated annually on the anniversary of that deliverance, 14 Nisan (at the March-April full moon), and was followed immediately by the week-long festival of Unleavened Bread (15–22 Nisan). Three Passovers are mentioned by John, the other two being those of John 6:4 and 11:55 ff.; only the last of these is mentioned in the Synoptic record. The present Passover was probably that of AD 28; Jesus went up to Jerusalem for it as he had been brought up to do (cf. Luke 2:41).

2:14 He found in the temple those who were selling oxen,

sheep and pigeons, and the moneychangers sitting (at their tables).

The oxen, sheep and pigeons were the animals principally used in sacrificial worship at the temple. It was a convenience to worshippers to be able to buy them as close as possible to the place where they were to be sacrificed. The setting up of stalls for this purpose in the outer court of the temple must have taken up much room that could have been used for worthier purposes. It may well be that it was only in a temporary emergency that they were set up within the temple precincts; the evidence is inadequate to speak with certainty about this.[11] Nor is there evidence for the common idea that the sale of the animals was a means of lining the pockets of the chief priests. The money-changers also performed a convenient service for visitors to the temple, who might bring all sorts of coinage with them and require to have it exchanged for something more acceptable. The word for 'money-changer' in this verse is *kermatistēs* (a dealer in small coins), from Gk. *kerma*, plural *kermata* (small coins). That is verse 15 is *kollybistēs*, from *kollybos*, the commission charged for the transaction. But the etymology of the words is of secondary importance for their meaning. Many people took the opportunity of a visit to the temple at this season to pay the annual half-shekel, contributed by Jewish men of twenty and over throughout the world for the maintenance of the temple. The only coinage acceptable for this purpose was Tyrian (because of the exceptional purity of its silver content); two Jews would frequently pay their contributions together with the Tyrian stater or tetradrachm (the coin which was to pay the joint contributions of Peter and his Master in Matt. 17:27).[12] From 25 Adar onwards (nineteen or twenty days before Passover) exchange tables for this purpose were set up in Jerusalem.[13] The commission charged might be 12½ per cent.

2:15, 16 Making a whip of cords he drove them all out of the temple, both the sheep and the oxen; he poured out the money-changers' small change and overturned their tables, and said to the pigeon-sellers, 'Take these away from here. Do not make my Father's house a trading establishment!'

B. F. Westcott, probably rightly, sees in this incident a commentary on Mal. 3.1 ff. ('the LORD whom you seek will suddenly come to his temple; . . . and he will purify . . .'), following on Zech. 14:21: 'there shall no longer be a trader in the house of the LORD of hosts on that day'. The second of these passages may indeed be echoed in Jesus' remonstrance.

The improvised whip was useful for driving the animals out. Some preachers and others who express surprise that Jesus should have used force of this mild kind even on animals have probably had little experience in moving cattle about in the streets and open spaces of a busy town. Modern drovers can rely on the help of dogs, but this was not available. Whatever the degree of force that was used, the action took on nothing of the riotous character that would have attracted swift and sharp intervention from the Roman garrison in the Antonia fortress, which overlooked the temple area on the north-west and communicated with the outer court by two flights of steps (cf. Acts 21:35).

What Jesus did is best classified as an act of prophetic symbolism. If he had Zech. 14:21 in his mind when he protested against his Father's house (cf. Luke 2:49) being turned into a supermarket, we may recall that the preceding verses of Zech. 14 tell how all nations will go up to Jerusalem to worship. The only place within the temple precincts which was open to people of 'all nations' (apart from the Israelites) was the outer court (sometimes called the 'court of the Gentiles'); if this area were taken up for trading it could not be used for worship. Jesus' action reinforced his spoken protest.[14]

2:17 His disciples remembered that scripture says: 'Zeal for your house will consume me.'

It is not clear whether they remembered this text on the spot, or called it to mind later, when they reflected on these things after his resurrection (cf. verse 22). What the scripture says (Psalm 69:9) is 'Zeal for your house has consumed me'; the change to the future tense has regard to the perspective of the cleansing act: the zeal for the house of God which Jesus manifested on that occasion would yet be the death of him. The following clause of Psalm 69:9 ('the reproaches of those who reproached you fell on me') is quoted by Paul in Rom. 15:3. 'In both cases it is assumed without argument that the passage refers to Christ. Are we to believe', asks C. H. Dodd, 'that each of these writers, neither acquainted with the other's work, selected by accident the two halves of a single verse for use as a "testimony" – and that from a psalm which is not, in any obvious sense, "messianic"?'[15] It was, he implies, no 'accident'; the psalm was in general use from primitive Christian days as a *testimonium*.

2:18 The Jews said to him in reply, 'What sign can you show us for doing this?'

'The Jews' here are members of the establishment, especially the temple authorities, as in Mark 11:25 f. Their request for a 'sign' was misguided: what sign could have been more eloquent than that which they had just witnessed?[16]

2:19–21 Jesus said to them in reply, 'Destroy this sanctuary, and I will raise it up in three days.' So the Jews said, 'This sanctuary was built in forty-six years; will _you_ raise it up in three days?' But _he_ was speaking about the sanctuary of his body.

In the Synoptic narrative of Jesus' trial before the Sanhedrin, he is charged with making a statement very similar to that here recorded by John: 'I will destroy this temple, made with hands, and in the course of three days I will build another, made without hands' (Mark 14:58). Those who brought this charge against him are called 'false witnesses', not because their testimony was a complete fabrication, but because it was given in opposition to him who is 'the faithful and true witness'. Their testimony could not be admitted because of internal inconsistencies. That Jesus had said something of the sort, and that in public, is evident from one of the taunts hurled at him by passers-by while he was on the cross (Mark 15:30). But for our knowledge of what he really said we have to thank this Evangelist.

His words provided a motif which was taken up later in the church – the replacement of the doomed material temple (cf. the charge against Stephen in Acts 6:13 f.) by a new and spiritual temple (cf. 1 Cor. 3:16; 2 Cor. 6:16; Eph. 2:21 f.; 1 Pet. 2:4 ff.).[17] In this connexion it is to be noted that, whereas the word for 'temple' in John 2:14, 15 is _hieron_, denoting the whole complex of buildings and courts, the word in verses 19–21 is _naos_, denoting the sanctuary or the holy house proper (comprising the vestibule, the holy place and the holy of holies). It was the _naos_, rather than the _hieron_ as a whole, that was regarded as the dwelling-place of God.

The reconstruction of the temple in the form which it had at this time was begun by Herod the Great early in 19 BC. The main part of the work was completed and consecrated in ten years, but other parts were still being carried out; in fact, the finishing touches were not put to the whole enterprise until AD 63, only seven years before its destruction. The 'forty-six years' of verse 20 are reckoned from the beginning of the reconstruction. (A curiosity of exegesis, going back to the time of Irenaeus in the late second century AD, treats them as indicating Jesus' age at the time, in the light of John 8:57, with the corollary that the addition of the three subsequent years

of his ministry would equate his life on earth with the first seven
of Daniel's seventy 'weeks'!)[18]

The Evangelist explains that the words of Jesus referred to his
body, the living habitation of God on earth, which in fact was
raised from the dead within three days of death and burial. This
explanation could not have come to his mind until the historical
fulfilment had taken place, as indeed he goes on to say explicitly.

**2:22 So, when he had been raised from the dead, his disciples
remembered that he said this, and they believed the scripture
and the word that Jesus had spoken.**

This applies to much that is recorded in this Gospel: only in the
light of later events was the significance of all appreciated (cf. John
12:16), and that by the illuminating aid of the Spirit (cf. John
14:26). The 'scripture' which the disciples believed might be the
total corpus of prophecy which was fulfilled in Jesus' ministry and
resurrection, not least those passages which are referred to, implicitly if not in express quotation, in John's account of this incident. The temple-cleansing in its own way, like the changing of
the water into wine in another way, is a sign of the impending
supersession of the old order by the new.

The question of the chronological relation of John's account of
the temple cleansing to the Synoptic version which dates it during
Holy Week is not easy to answer; an adequate answer, indeed,
would require a separate excursus.[19] It seems probable that John
takes it out of its chronological sequence and places it, with programmatic intent, in the forefront of his record of Jesus' Jerusalem
ministry. If his readers understand the significance of this incident,
they will know what the ministry was all about.

(b) Superficial faith (2:23-25)

**2:23 While he was in Jerusalem at the passover during the
festival, many believed in his name, when they saw the signs
which he did.**

Verses 23-25 of this chapter probably serve as an introduction
to the Nicodemus episode of chapter 3. It is frequently said that,
while Jesus in the Synoptic Gospels deprecates the faith that must
be supported by a sign (cf. Mark 8:11-13), the Jesus of the Fourth
Gospel performs signs expressly to call forth faith. A passage like
the present one shows that the antithesis is not so sharp as is often
represented (cf. also John 4:48). Jesus made a clear distinction
between those who were superficially impressed because they saw
the bare signs and those who penetrated beneath the surface and

grasped the truth that was signified by the signs (cf. John 6:26). Nicodemus came to positive conclusions about Jesus through seeing the signs which he performed, but he was slow to appreciate their spiritual inwardness. There are two levels of believing in Jesus' name – that spoken of in John 1:12, which carries with it the authority to become God's children, and that spoken of here. The former level involves unreserved personal commitment, the practical acknowledgment of Jesus as Lord, but it will not be attained so long as 'we see the signs but see not him'.

2:24, 25 But Jesus for his part did not entrust himself to them, because he knew every one, and had no need to rely on the testimony of others regarding any one, for he himself knew what was in human beings.

Other leaders and teachers may be misled at times into giving their followers more credit for loyalty and understanding than they actually possess; not so Jesus, who could read the inmost thoughts of men and women like an open book. It was only those whose faith and allegiance were beyond question that he admitted into the inner secret of his person and purpose. So too in the Synoptic record, it was not until the apostles, in the face of all appearances to the contrary, confessed him spontaneously as Messiah, through the lips of their spokesman Peter, that Jesus 'began to teach them that the Son of man must suffer many things' (Mark 8:31).

He who is the Word incarnate has immediate apprehension of the mysteries and complexities of human nature. He does not depend on spoken words as the index to inward thoughts and feelings; the hidden depths of every heart lie open to his penetrating insight. This is revealed in one conversation after another in the following chapters – in those which he holds, for example, with Nicodemus, with the woman of Sychar, with the invalid at Bethesda. In each case he goes straight to the root of the trouble. Thus, in the opening sentences of chapter 3, he pays scant attention to Nicodemus's complimentary salutation, but insists on the truth which Nicodemus most needed to learn – the necessity of being born anew.

NOTES

1. Josephus *Life* 86, 207.
2. Cf. Josephus *Jewish War* 2.120.
3. G. H. C. Macgregor, *The Gospel of John* (London 1928), p. 52.
4. The metric equivalent is given in GNB (British edition): 'each one large enough to hold about a hundred litres'.
5. Cf. R. Bultmann *The Gospel of John* (Oxford 1971), pp. 118 f. He points out the coincidence of the date of the Dionysos festival, January 6, with the date

of the later Christian festival of the Epiphany, for which John 2:1–11 was a prescribed lesson. But the reason for choosing this lesson for Epiphany ('Manifestation') lies in its recording how Jesus on this occasion 'manifested (*ephanerōsen*) his glory' (verse 11). Bultmann calls this episode 'The Miracle of the Epiphany'.

6. C. S. Lewis *Miracles* (London 1947), p. 163.

7. It is often said that seven of these 'signs' are recorded in this Gospel, beginning with that at Cana and ending with the raising of Lazarus (cf. John 12:18). But it is difficult to be sure: not all the miracles described by John are explicitly called 'signs'.

8. Cf. John 5:36; 7:21; 10:25, 32, 38.

9. This was the view apparently of Tertullian (*Against Marcion* 4:19; *On the Flesh of Christ* 7) and certainly of Helvidius of Rome (c. AD 380). The apocryphal *Protevangel of James* (9:2) regarded them as sons of Joseph by a previous marriage; this view was later defended by Epiphanius (*Against Heresies* 78). The denial that they were Mary's children was due (in part at least) to the growing belief in her perpetual virginity. Jerome (*Against Helvidius*) propounded a third view – that Jesus' 'brothers' were actually his first cousins, sons of Alphaeus by 'Mary of Clopas', whom he inferred from John 19:25 alongside Mark 15:40 to be the Virgin's sister. Jerome regarded it as a strong argument for the correctness of this view that it safeguarded Joseph's virginity as well as Mary's, he himself being convinced of the superiority of virginity over the married state. See also R. E. Brown, K. P. Donfried, J. A. Fitzmyer, J. Reumann (ed.) *Mary in the New Testament* (London 1978), pp. 65–72, 270–278.

10. Cf. John 5:1; 6:4; 7:2; 11:55.

11. The 'booths of the sons of Ḥanan', where doves and other sacred offerings might be bought, were normally set up on the Mount of Olives (Jerusalem Talmud, tractate *Pēʾāh* 1.6). But it has been argued that, because of a dispute with the sons of Ḥanan, the temple authorities may have allowed rival vendors to sell such wares in the outer court, and that they were newly installed there when Jesus saw them and made his protest. See V. Eppstein, 'The Historicity of the Gospel Account of the Cleansing of the Temple' *ZNW* 55 (1964), pp. 42–58.

12. The stater or tetradrachm was reckoned as equivalent to one shekel.

13. According to the Mishnah, 'on the first day of Adar they give warning of the shekel dues, . . . on the fifteenth thereof the tables were set up in the provinces, and on the twenty-fifth thereof they were set up in the temple' (tractate *Shᵉqālīm* 1.1, 3).

14. See further p. 263 for the comment on John 12:20 (the Greek visitors who asked to see Jesus). For a suggestive study of the incident in the light of the OT background see C. K. Barrett, 'The House of Prayer and the Den of Thieves' in *Jesus und Paulus*, ed. E. E. Ellis and E. Grässer (Göttingen 1975), pp. 13–20.

15. C. H. Dodd *According to the Scriptures* (London 1952), p. 58. There is a further probable quotation from the same psalm in John 15:25. Cf. 19:28.

16. Cf. the parallel in Mark 11:27–33, where Jesus replies to the 'chief priests and the scribes and the elders' (i.e. members of the Sanhedrin) who came to him in the temple precincts and asked him, 'By what authority are you doing these things, or who gave you this authority to do them?'

17. Cf. R. J. McKelvey, *The New Temple* (Oxford 1969).

18. Irenaeus *Against Heresies* 2.33.4. Cf. B. W. Bacon *The Fourth Gospel in Research and Debate* (London 1910), pp. 395–408.

19. That John's chronological setting is the historically correct one has been maintained, among others, by W. Temple *Readings in St John's Gospel* (London

1939), pp. 175–177; D. L. Sayers *The Man Born to be King* (London 1943), p. 35, n. 1.

CHAPTER 3

(c) Nicodemus and the new birth (3:1–21)

3:1 There was one of the Pharisees, a man named Nicodemus, a ruler of the Jews.

Nicodemus has been identified by some with one Naqdimon ben Gorion, a wealthy Jerusalemite who, according to the Talmud, was entrusted with supplying water to pilgrims at the great festivals.[1] But the arguments for this identification are quite inconclusive. The Pharisees (mentioned already in John 1:24) exercised an influence on the general public out of all proportion to their numbers. They formed a minority group in the Sanhedrin.[2] The description of Nicodemus as 'a ruler of the Jews' implies that he was a member of the Pharisaic group in the Sanhedrin (cf. also John 7:50).

Nicodemus may be regarded by the Evangelist as one of the 'many' of John 2:23.[3] It is possible, however, that the Greek conjunction *de* with which he is introduced at the beginning of John 3:1, has adversative force: '*But* there was one of the Pharisees . . .' . Nicodemus, like the others, had been impressed by the signs which he saw without realizing their deeper significance, *but* there was in him a sincere willingness to learn more to which Jesus responded by 'entrusting himself' to him more than he did to many others.

3:2 This man came to Jesus by night and said to him, 'Rabbi, we know that you have come as a teacher from God; no one can do these signs which you do, unless God is with him.'

It is best to take the statement that Nicodemus's visit was paid at night as a simple factual reminiscence, without giving it an allegorical interpretation, as though the darkness without reflected the darkness of Nicodemus's understanding, which required to be illuminated. Nor need we enquire why he chose to come at night – whether he did not wish his colleagues and others to know of his errand, or chose a time when Jesus was likely to be undisturbed, so that there would be leisure for a long conversation.

Nicodemus may have been deficient in comprehension, but at least he was not blinded by prejudice, like those religious leaders whose reaction to the words and works of Jesus was to put them down to demonic activity (cf. John 8:48, 52; Mark 3:22 ff.). Even if he did not grasp the significance of the signs, he recognized by their character that they could not be wrought except by the power of God. Therefore, although Jesus did not belong to one of the acknowledged schools of sacred learning, this leading teacher in Israel saluted him as an equal with the title 'Rabbi' – a mark of respect which meant more coming from Nicodemus than it did on the lips of the two young disciples of John 1:38. Nicodemus's conclusions were valid so far as they went, but they did not go far enough. Jesus saw beyond his words of greeting to the state of his soul, and answered him in language which, baffling and unintelligible as Nicodemus found it, was carefully calculated to speak to his condition.

3:3 Jesus answered him, 'Indeed and in truth I tell you, unless one is born from above, he cannot see the kingdom of God.'

Most of the speeches and conversations recorded in the Gospels and Acts are brief summaries, and this helps to explain at times the apparent abruptness of transition from one thought or topic to another. But the abruptness is probably true to life here. Whatever Nicodemus's expectation about the course of his talk with the Galilaean rabbi may have been, he was quite unprepared for words like these, introduced as they were by the double 'Amen' (cf. John 1:51).

The kingdom of God in the OT is presented on occasion as his eternal and universal rule: 'The LORD shall reign for ever and ever' (Ex. 15:18); 'The LORD has established his throne in the heavens, and his kingdom rules over all' (Ps. 103:19). But more particularly his kingdom or kingship is manifested on earth where it is accepted and obeyed by men – that is to say, among his people Israel, or at least among the righteous in Israel. Members of other nations might submit to his rule by incorporation as proselytes in the commonwealth of Israel; people who did this were sometimes said to 'take on themselves the yoke of the kingdom of heaven'. A proselyte in effect entered on a new life in thus assuming the yoke of the kingdom of heaven. 'The proselyte', it was said, 'is like a new-born child'.[4] Such a person might fittingly be described as 'born from above' or 'born anew'.

In the Synoptic record it is insisted that 'whoever does not receive the kingdom of God like a child shall not enter it, (Mark 10:15; Luke 18:17; cf. Matt. 18:3).[5] No wonder, therefore, that Jesus stresses 'how hard it is to enter the kingdom of God' (Mark 10:24). It is very difficult for a person with adult experiences to revert to the simplicity of childhood. And, while a convert to Judaism from paganism could be understood as starting life all over again, how could such language be applied to a true-born Israelite?

To 'see the kingdom of God' meant to witness (and have a share in) the final consummation of God's kingly rule, when it would be accepted and obeyed universally.[6] This future aspect of the divine kingdom is also set forth in the OT, notably in the book of Daniel (cf. Dan. 2:44; 7:14, 27). To a Jew with Nicodemus's upbringing, seeing the kingdom of God would mean participation in the age to come, the resurrection life. In this Gospel as in the others 'the kingdom of God' in this sense is interchangeable with 'eternal life' (compare 'to enter life' in Mark 9:43, 45, with 'to enter the kingdom of God' in verse 47). The 'regeneration' in Matt. 19:28 (RSV 'the new world') is another synonym. But Jesus speaks of a regeneration to be experienced here and now. To be born 'from above' or 'anew' (Gk. *anōthen*) in the sense which his words have here is to be 'born from God' in the sense of John 1:13, to enter immediately into the life of that coming age. We who have read the prologue to the Gospel know that those who are thus born into the divine family, becoming children of God, are those who have received the incarnate Word, believing in his name. But Nicodemus knew nothing of this; hence his bewildered reply.

3:4 Nicodemus says to him, 'How can a man be born when he is old? Can he enter into his mother's womb a second time and be born?'

Repeatedly in conversations recorded in this Gospel, Jesus makes a statement which is misunderstood; the expressed misunderstanding then gives him the opportunity of unfolding his meaning more plainly. On this occasion, had he been talking of proselytes from paganism, Nicodemus would have understood him well enough; but it would have appeared that his enigmatic words were intended to apply to Nicodemus himself. But in what sense? As Nicodemus remarked, a repetition of natural birth, or a reincarnation, was out of the question. Justin Martyr was probably referring to this passage when he said, 'It is clear to all that those who have once been born cannot re-enter their mother's wombs.'[7] Or was Nicodemus giving a figurative reply to what he understood as a figurative challenge? In that case perhaps he meant that when a man is grown up and set in his ways, he cannot be expected to change his nature and start all over again. At any rate, he did not understand Jesus' insistence on the necessity of a new birth; Jesus therefore repeated his statement in rather different terms.

3:5 Jesus answered, 'Indeed and in truth I tell you, unless one is born of water and Spirit, he cannot enter into the kingdom of God.'

Like the earlier statement in verse 3, this one is prefaced by the solemnity of the double Amen. There is no difference between seeing the kingdom of God and entering into it, any more than there is between seeeing life (John 3:36) and entering into it (Matt. 19:17; Mark 9:43, 45). Neither is there any difference between being born anew (or born from above) and being born 'of water and Spirit'; but the latter way of putting it echoes OT phraseology and might have been calculated to ring a bell in Nicodemus's mind. If he thought it impossible for one to acquire a new nature in later life, let him recall that God had promised to do this very thing for his people Israel: 'I will sprinkle clean *water* upon you, and you shall be clean . . . , and a new *spirit* I will put within you' (Ezek. 36:25 f.). This 'new spirit' was God's own Spirit: 'I will put my spirit within you' (Ezek. 36:27). The promise to Israel through Ezekiel was amplified in the vision of the valley of dry bones, when the prophet obeyed the divine command: 'Prophesy to the breath, prophesy, son of man, and say to the breath, Thus says the Lord GOD: Come from the four kinds, O breath, and breathe upon these slain, that they may live' (Ezek. 37:9, RSV). In that passage of Ezekiel, as in the present passage of the Fourth Gospel, it must be remembered that one and the same noun in Hebrew (*rûaḥ*) and Greek (*pneuma*) may be rendered 'breath', 'wind' or 'spirit' according to the context.

The promise in Ezekiel had primary reference to a national revival, but a secondary application to individuals was not unknown. The cleansing with water in Ezek. 36:25 was invoked as biblical authority for the baptism of proselytes. John the Baptist called on his hearers, true-born Israelites though they were, to enter the repentant and believing remnant of Israel, the 'people prepared for the Lord', by accepting baptism at his hands; but he pointed out that, while he administered a baptism in water, another would come after him and baptize them with the Holy Spirit. Both his own ministry and that of the Coming One were necessary to fulfil the prophetic promise. Now the Coming One in person urges Nicodemus to accept the promise in its fulness – the new birth 'of water and Spirit'. The kingdom of God is a spiritual order which can be entered only by spiritual rebirth.

The Evangelist was writing in a day when, for the followers of Jesus, John's baptism has long since been absorbed in Christian baptism. If even John's baptism taught the necessity of a new beginning, Christian baptism even more emphatically symbolizes the new beginning for every one who by faith-union with Christ shares his death and burial in a spiritual sense and rises with him to newness of life. It is a pity when reaction against the notion of baptismal regeneration by an *opus operatum* leads to the complete overlooking of the baptismal allusion in these words of Jesus.

3:6, 7 'What is born of the flesh is flesh, and what is born of the Spirit is spirit. Don't be surprised at my saying to you, "You must all be born from above".'

By natural birth people become members of an earthly family; to become members of the family of God, to receive the spiritual nature which alone can gain admittance to his kingdom, a birth 'from above' is necessary. An antithesis is drawn between the realm of the flesh and that of the Spirit, but those who have been born into the former may be reborn into the latter through the divine Word who, belonging as he did eternally to the spiritual order, yet became flesh for the regeneration of mankind. When once this antithesis is appreciated, there is nothing strange in the insistence that two distinct 'births' are necessary for entrance to the one order and to the other. Jesus was speaking personally to Nicodemus, but his words held good for others as well as Nicodemus; hence the transition to the second person plural in the statement: 'You must all be born from above.'

3:8 'The wind blows where it pleases, and you hear its sound but do not know where it comes from or where it goes; so it is with every one who is born of the Spirit.'

Here it is specially necessary to remember the wide range in meaning of Gk. *pneuma*; it is used twice in this verse, being translated first as 'wind' and then as 'Spirit'. Indeed, a case has been argued for rendering the first part of the verse 'the Spirit breathes where he pleases . . .', but the following words about hearing the sound but not knowing provenance or destination are more appropriate to the wind. As in the vision of Ezek. 37, however, the operation of the wind is a parable of the work of the Spirit. As the coming or going of the wind cannot be controlled by human power or wisdom, so the new birth of the Spirit is independent of human volition – coming neither 'from the will of flesh nor from the will of a man', as John has already put it in his prologue (John 1:13). The hidden work of the Spirit in the human heart cannot be controlled or seen, but its effects are unmistakably evident.

3:9, 10 'How can this be?' said Nicodemus in reply. 'Are you the teacher of Israel', answered Jesus, 'and do not understand these things?'

Nicodemus is still unable to grasp the sense of Jesus' words. He himself had probably taught others the conditions required for admittance to the kingdom of God, for enjoying the life of the age to come, but he had never heard these conditions expressed in the terms which Jesus now used. Keeping the commandments of God, doing his will day by day, were terms which he would have understood; but what was meant by this strange language about being 'born of the Spirit'?

The description of Nicodemus as 'the teacher of Israel' implies that he had some standing among the rabbis of his day. He might therefore have been expected to comprehend Jesus' teaching, which was not a complete innovation but was implicit in the Hebrew scriptures – and not in the prophets only. The safe passage of Noah and his family through the flood, to start life anew in a new world (Gen. 6:13–9:19), the redeemed Israelites' crossing the sea of reeds to be a people set apart for God (Ex. 14:15–15:21), Naaman the Syrian's 'baptism'[8] in Jordan, whereby 'his flesh was restored like the flesh of a little child, and he was clean' (2 Kings 5:14) – these and other OT incidents were parables of the truth which Jesus was endeavouring to convey to Nicodemus. The Naaman incident in particular was regarded as a precedent for proselyte-baptism. But from none of these scriptures had Nicodemus learned the lesson that for Jews by natural descent, as well as for proselytes, the life of the age to come and participation in the kingdom of God could be attained only through the gateway of regeneration.

3:11 'Indeed and in truth I tell you, we speak what we know and bear witness to what we have seen, but you do not accept our witness.'

From here on the dialogue between Jesus and Nicodemus passes into a monologue on the lips of Jesus, and the monologue then passes almost imperceptibly into a meditation by the Evangelist on the subject of the new birth. Those versions which use quotation-marks have to be more decisive about the point of transition from monologue to meditation than was necessary for the older versions. The RSV makes the monologue end with the last word of verse 15, and this is probably right (the NEB postpones the closing quotation-marks to the end of verse 21, thus merging monologue and meditation in one).

Jesus used words which his disciples must often have echoed as he emphasizes that the gospel is no hearsay message but one based on personal experience and testimony. The language of the disciples may be recognized here in the plural 'we' and 'you'. Similar assurance is given by John to the Christian readers of his first epistle:

'that which we have seen and heard we proclaim also to you' (1 John 1:3). The witness of Jesus is one and the same, whether delivered personally by himself (cf. verse 32), or in the words of Holy Writ (John 5:39), or in the testimony of his disciples (John 15:27). But no matter which form it took, his witness was all too often refused, whether during his early ministry or in the later ministry of his disciples.

3:12, 13 'If I have told you of the earthly things and you do not believe, how will you believe if I tell you of the heavenly things?' And no one has ascended into heaven except the one who descended from heaven, the Son of Man (who is in heaven).

What are the 'earthly things', which are set in contrast with the 'heavenly things'? The language here is reminiscent of several passages in the wisdom books. Agur the son of Jakeh, disclaiming the possession of wisdom, asks, 'Who has ascended to heaven and come down?' (Prov. 30:4). The implication is that only in heaven can divine wisdom be found. Similarly the Greek book of Wisdom says, 'We can hardly guess at what is on earth, . . . but who has traced out what is in the heavens? Who has learned thy counsel, unless thou hast given wisdom and sent thy holy Spirit from on high?' (Wisdom 9:16, 17).[9] So here, divine wisdom belongs to the Son of Man. He has not had to go up to heaven to acquire it, but he has come down from heaven to impart it.

The most natural way to understand the 'earthly things' is to take them as including what Jesus has just been talking about.[10] It may seem strange to classify the new birth as an 'earthly' subject, since it is in its very nature a birth from above; but it is 'earthly' in the sense that it takes place on earth and can be illustrated from earthly analogies. In Jesus' teaching the new birth belongs to the elementary stage. There is much more to be learned after this first lesson is grasped, but how can anyone who fails to appreciate this go on to understand the fulness of God's revelation in Christ? Among the 'heavenly things' which have no earthly analogy may be mentioned the Son's eternal relation with the Father and his incarnation as man on earth. These are completely beyond ordinary human experience; to know them we are dependent on one who has come from God to disclose them, the Son of Man.

The clause at the end of verse 13, 'who is in heaven', is absent from our oldest manuscripts of John (Papyri 66 and 75) and from the leading representatives of the Alexandrian text, but its presence is supported by an impressive array of other witnesses. If it was present in the original text of the Gospel, one can understand how a scribe or editor omitted it on the ground that the Son of Man was not in heaven but on earth as he spoke these words. If, on the other hand, the clause was not part of the original text of the Gospel, it is difficult to see why any one should have added it. The clause is not necessarily part of what Jesus said to Nicodemus; it may be an explanatory comment added by the Evangelist, comparable to the clause 'who has his being in the Father's bosom' in John 1:18. In that verse 'no one has ever seen God'; here 'no one has ascended into heaven'. There the only-begotten is the revealer of the Father; here he is the unfolder of heavenly truth. It is not surprising then to find a relative clause here parallel to that in the earlier passage. By the time the Evangelist wrote, the one who came down from heaven had ascended up where he was before; heaven, in any case, is where he belongs.[11]

3:14, 15 'And as Moses lifted up the serpent in the wilderness, so the Son of Man must be lifted up, in order that every one who believes may have eternal life in him.'

Nicodemus had failed to grasp the teaching about the new birth when it was presented to him in terms drawn from Ezekiel's prophecy; now it is presented to him by means of an object-lesson, from a story with which he had been familiar since childhood. During one of the outbreaks of unrest during the Israelites' wilderness journeys, they were plagued by 'fiery serpents' and many of them died because of the serpents' poisonous bite. The survivors appealed to Moses in contrition and confession, Moses interceded with God for them, and in accordance with the divine instruction he 'made a bronze serpent, and set it on a pole; and if a serpent bit any one, he would look at the bronze serpent and live' (Num. 21:5-9). If one of those bitten Israelites, who looked and lived when he was at death's door, had been asked how he felt, he might well have said that he felt as if he had been born all over again and received a new lease of life. That was a renewal of natural life, but here it serves as a parable of the receiving of spiritual life. The setting of the bronze serpent aloft on a pole in the midst of the camp of Israel is a picture of the Son of Man's being raised aloft on the cross. But the verb used for his being 'lifted up' (Gk. *hypsoō*) is carefully chosen; it denotes not only literal lifting up in space but also exaltation in glory. In this Gospel Jesus is glorified by being crucified (cf. John 8:28; 12:23, 32, 34). He who descended has now once more ascended up on high, but he has ascended by way of the cross; the cross on which he was lifted up became the ladder of his ascent to the Father's presence (cf. John 1:51).

There was no healing virtue in the bronze serpent in the wilderness. In itself it was a mere *nehushtan*, a piece of bronze; when in later days people paid homage to it as though it had some inherent sanctity or power, good King Hezekiah broke it in pieces (2 Kings 18:4). It was the saving grace of God that healed the bitten Israelites when they believed his word and obeyed his command. But in the Son of Man who was lifted up there resides infinite healing virtue, far more potent than anything which was experienced by the Israelites in the wilderness. They were cured of a physical disease and received a prolongation of mortal life, but it is eternal life that the Son of Man ensures to those who look to him. The teaching of the prologue (John 1:12, 13) is thus confirmed by the words of Jesus. Here is the answer to Nicodemus's question: 'How can this be?' The new birth is experienced, the kingdom of God is entered, through the saving work of Christ, accepted by faith.

This is the first place in this Gospel where the frequently repeated phrase 'eternal life' (*zōē aiōnios*) occurs. Primarily this means the life of the age (*aiōn*) to come, resurrection life, which believers in Christ enjoy in advance because of their union with one who is already risen from the dead. In the Gospel of John that meaning is certainly present, but eternal life here is the very life of God which resides in the eternal Word ('in him was life') and is communicated by him to all believers.

The 'must' in the clause 'the Son of Man must be lifted up', as in Mark's repeated insistence that 'the Son of Man must suffer', is the 'must' of the divine purpose, foretold in the writings of the prophets.

The phrase 'in him' in verse 15 is probably to be taken with 'may have eternal life' rather than with 'believes'. The Greek is *en autō*, whereas *eis auton* is regularly used when reference is made to believing 'in him' (as in verse 16).

With verse 15 Jesus' conversation with Nicodemus probably comes to an end (cf. RSV); in verses 16–21 we have the Evangelist's application to the reader of the significance of that conversation.

3:16 For such was God's love for the world that he gave his only-begotten Son, in order that every one who believes in him should not perish but have eternal life.

It is not the Evangelist's intention to gratify our curiosity about Nicodemus's response to Jesus' words; readers may draw their own conclusions from Nicodemus's two further appearances in this Gospel (John 7:50 ff.; 19:39 ff.). His intention is rather to set forth in terms of universal applicability the lesson that Nicodemus was taught.

If there is one sentence more than another which sums up the message of the Fourth Gospel, it is this. The love of God is limitless; it embraces all mankind. No sacrifice was too great to bring its unmeasured intensity home to men and women: the best that God had to give, he gave – his only Son, his well-beloved. Nor was it for one nation or group that he was given: he was given so that all, without distinction or exception, who repose their faith on him (*eis auton* here, as against *en autō* in the preceding verse), might be rescued from destruction and blessed with the life that is life indeed. The gospel of salvation and life has its source in the love of God. The essence of the saving message is made unmistakably plain, in language which people of all races, cultures and times can grasp, and so effectively is it set forth in these words that many more, probably, have found the way of life through them than through any other biblical text.

To 'perish' (*apolesthai*) is the alternative to having 'eternal life' or (as verse 17 puts it) to being 'saved' (cf. 8:24, where those who refuse to believe in Jesus will 'die in their sins').

3:17 For it was not to judge the world that God sent his Son into the world, but in order that the world might be saved through him.

The judgment referred to here is clearly adverse judgment, condemnation. If the incarnate Word came into a world of sinners, how could his judgment be anything other than adverse? But, says the Evangelist, it was not for judgment that he came (cf. John 12:47: 'I did not come to judge the world, but to save the world'). If there appears to be a formal contradiction between this and John 9:39 – 'For judgment I came into this world' – the context both there and here will resolve it.[12] When in the Synoptic record Jesus announces that 'the Son of Man has authority on earth to forgive sin' (Mark 2:10), he takes his hearers by surprise. They might have inferred from Dan. 7:13, 14 that the Son of Man had authority on earth to pronounce judgment – but to pronounce *forgiveness*? His teaching and his work have brought forgiveness near. The separation between those who accept his forgiveness and those who refuse it is inevitable; but the latter are self-judged. The responsibility for their self-judgment cannot be laid at the door of 'the *Saviour* of the world' (John 4:42; 1 John 4:14). If he came so that those who believe in him should not perish, how can those who reject his gift of life do other than perish? It is nowhere suggested in Scripture that all must be saved, whether they will or not; it is implied that only those who persistently turn their backs on God's salvation will be deprived of it.

3:18 He who believes in him is not judged; he who does not believe has been judged already, because he has not believed in the name of God's only-begotten Son.

The judgment, as in verse 17, is that adverse judgment which is inherent in the act of turning away from the truth, which is embodied in Christ. For those who put their trust in him there is no such condemnation. John does not use the terminology of 'justification' by faith, but he teaches it in his own language as plainly as Paul does in his.

In a gallery where artistic masterpieces are on display, it is not the masterpieces but the visitors that are on trial. The works which they view are not there to abide their question, but they reveal their own taste (or lack of it) by their reactions to what they see. The pop-star who was reported some years ago to have dismissed the Mona Lisa as 'a load of rubbish' (except that he used a less polite word than 'rubbish') did not tell us anything about the Mona Lisa; he told us much about himself. What is true in the aesthetic realm is equally true in the spiritual realm. The man who depreciates Christ, or thinks him unworthy of his allegiance, passes judgment on himself, not on Christ. He does not need to wait until the day of judgment; the verdict on him has been pronounced already. There will indeed be a final day of judgment (John 5:26–29), but that day will serve only to confirm the judgment already passed. Those who believe in the name of the Son of God, as we have already learned (John 1:12), become God's children; for those who will not believe there is no alternative but self-incurred judgment.

3:19-21 And this is the judgment: that the light has come into the world and people loved the darkness more than the light, for their works were wicked. For every one who does things that are bad hates the light and does not come to the light, in case his works should be exposed. But he who does the truth comes to the light, so that his works may be shown to have been wrought in God.

The essence of this judgment is now stated in terms of light and darkness. Christ was the true light shining in the darkness, the light which came into the world to illuminate every one. But what if some will not come to the light? What if they actually prefer the darkness? Such an attitude is the sin against the Holy Spirit which by its very nature is irremediable. There are some who, like Paul on the Damascus road, need to be struck blind by the light in order to be brought to their senses – but what if Paul, even so, had turned his back on the glory of that light and refused to obey the heavenly vision? What hope could there have been for him?

As the prologue to the Gospel has implied that only a few received the living Word when he came into the world, while most of those who were by right 'his own' gave him no welcome, so here it is suggested that mankind as a whole prefers darkness to light while only a minority 'does the truth' and comes to the light. This was so during Jesus' ministry; perhaps the Evangelist means that it was still true when his Gospel was being composed.

In a well-ordered polity those who practise evil practise it secretly; they do not wish to be found out and brought to book. Law-abiding citizens have no need to practise such concealment. In the Evangelist's thought the coming of the light necessarily involves the separation of those who welcome it from those who avoid it for fear that it should reveal them and their conduct as they really are.

Our Evangelist delights to use contrasting terms; good and evil, love and hatred, life and death, salvation and judgment, light and darkness, truth and falsehood. The positive terms in these antithetical pairs are largely interchangeable – good, love, life, salvation, light, truth. So here, where we might have expected 'he who does what is good' in verse 21 as the correlative of 'every one who does things that are bad' in verse 20, we have 'he who does the truth'. In the OT 'to do truth' or 'to deal truly' means in effects 'to act honourably' (cf. Gen. 32:10; 47:29; Neh. 9:33). Those whose lives and actions are of this sort have no reason to avoid the light. On the contrary, the true light is their reward. 'Blessed are the pure in heart, for they shall see God' (Matt. 5:8). Their works are 'wrought in God', says John – 'in union with Him, and therefore by His power' (Westcott).[13]

No explicit mention is made here of those who have never had the opportunity of believing in Christ, those on whom the light in its fulness has never shone. But John's words probably unfold the principle of their judgment too. As the eternal Word came to men and women before becoming incarnate in Christ, so it is with the light of God. If men and women are judged by their response to the light, they are judged by their response to such light as is available to them. All true light is in some degree an effulgence from him who is the light of the world. Those who accept the partial light that is available to them will gladly accept the perfect light when it shines on them. Those who refuse the light, in whatever fashion it shines on them, pronounce sentence on themselves.

2. JOHN'S FURTHER WITNESS TO JESUS (3:22–36)

3:22, 23 **After this Jesus came with his disciples into the Judaean land, and he spent some time with them there and baptized. John also was baptizing at Aenon, near Salim, because there was much water there, and people were coming to him and being baptized.**

The opening clause of this new section is strange. Jesus has been talking to Nicodemus in Jerusalem, and Jerusalem was in Judaea; how then could he come from Jerusalem into 'the Judaean land' (or 'the land of Judaea')? One answer to this question assumes some displacement of the original arrangement of the text, but such an assumption is precarious in default of manuscript evidence and indeed usually raises other problems. As we shall see when we come to John 4:38, this short narrative (verse 22–30) prepares us for the events of chapter 4. It is simplest to understand 'the Judaean land' as the country districts of Judaea, outside the city.

This is the only Gospel of the four which ascribes a baptismal activity to Jesus during his earthly ministry – even so, according to John 4:2, he did not baptize personally but by the hands of his disciples. This baptismal activity seems to have been an extension of John's ministry; it is certainly not suggested that it marked the beginning of the promised baptism with the Holy Spirit (John 1:33). John himself was continuing his baptismal ministry. He had moved away from Bethany beyond Jordan, where we first met him, to 'Aenon near Salim'. The exact location of these places is disputed, but a strong case has been made out by W. F. Albright for identifying them with sites in the region of Samaria (which at this time was part of the Roman province of Judaea). 'Salim', he says, 'cannot be separated from the well-known ancient town of that name, south-east of Nablus, nor can it be quite accidental that there is an 'Ainun in the immediate vicinity. The near-by sources of the Wadi Far'ah are extremely well provided with water.' (The earliest reference to 'the well-known ancient town', as Albright calls it, may be in Gen. 33:18, if av is right in rendering 'Jacob came to Shalem, a city of Shechem'.) The name Aenon ('Ainun) means 'springs', which would provide the 'much water' (literally 'many waters') required by John for baptizing.[14]

3:24 **For John had not yet been put in prison.**

The added comment of verse 24, 'John had not yet been put in prison', might seem superfluous; if he was free to go on baptizing, self-evidently he had not yet been imprisoned. The point of the comment (whether we owe it to the Evangelist or to an editor) appears to be that the events here recorded are earlier than anything narrated in the Synoptic Gospels in relation to Jesus' ministry.[15] In the Synoptic account Jesus' Galilaean preaching of the kingdom of God began 'after John was arrested' (Mark 1:14). But as far as the end of John 4 we have the account of an earlier ministry of Jesus carried out mainly in the south, concurrently with a later phase of John's ministry. When we come to John 5:33–35, John is referred to in the past tense, implying that, even if still alive, he was no longer in circulation.

3:25, 26 So a dispute arose on the part of some disciples of John with a Jew about purification, and they came to John and said to him, 'Rabbi, he who was with you beyond Jordan, the one to whom you bore witness, look, he is baptizing and they are all coming to him!'

The dispute probably concerned the relation of the baptismal ministries of John and Jesus to 'the Jews' purificatory practice' alluded to in John 2:6, but it served to foster some disquiet in the minds of John's disciples about what seemed to them to be a competitive ministry carried on by Jesus. The study of the Qumran texts during the past thirty years has thrown new light on the practice of ceremonial purifications in various Jewish communities about that time. What Josephus says about John's baptism has probably more relevance to some of those other purifications: 'he taught that baptism would appear acceptable in God's sight if people underwent it not to procure pardon for certain sins but with a view to bodily cleansing when once the soul had been cleansed by righteousness'.[16] Josephus's explanation fails to do justice to the essential element of repentance in John's baptism.

The singular reading 'with a Jew' is somewhat better attested than the plural 'with Jews' of AV and NEB but is slightly odd in the context.[17] Such a conjectural emendation as 'with Jesus' or 'with the disciples of Jesus' would deserve more serious attention if there were any independent evidence for it.[18] Perhaps John's disciples did not know what Jesus was doing until the disputing Jew (or Jews) mentioned it to them in the course of the argument about purification. 'Our master ought to know about this', they said, and set off to tell John. It was particularly disturbing in their eyes that so many should now be flocking to Jesus whereas formerly they would inevitably have flocked to John.

3:27, 28 John replied, 'No one can receive anything unless it has been given to him from heaven. You yourselves bear me

witness that I said, "I am not the Christ" but "I have been sent ahead of him".'

Each man, says John, has his allotted gift or ministry from God; his responsibility is to fulfil that. John was appointed to be a herald and witness of the Messiah; he might well be content to have fulfilled that commission. All gifts come from God, including the gift of serving him in this or that capacity. The idiom with which John's answer begins (literally, 'A man can receive nothing unless . . .') reflects an Aramaic usage of the term *bar'ēnāsh* (literally, 'a son of man') to express something that is true of human beings in general and is particularly applicable to the speaker.[19]

John is not so disquieted at his disciples' news as they themselves are: he reminds them that he had already made it plain that he was not the Messiah (John 1:20) but had come baptizing to make ready the way for the Coming One. The forerunner's gifts and tasks were different from those of the Coming One, but both alike were bestowed 'from heaven'.

3:29, 30 'It is the bridegroom that has the bride. The bridegroom's friend, who stands and listens to him, rejoices greatly because of the bridegroom's voice. This joy is mine, and it has been fulfilled. He must grow greater; I must grow less.'

At a wedding the best man[20] does not complain because he is not the bridegroom; he is there to assist the bridegroom and to see that all goes well as he secures the bride of his choice. The best man is satisfied if the wedding goes off successfully and the bridal couple rejoice in each other's company. So John is satisfied now that he has introduced Jesus to the faithful in Israel. In OT days (and in some other cultures) the king – especially Israel's divine King – was regarded as married to his people or land; this is the point of the promise to Zion in Isa. 62:4 f.: 'you shall be called "My delight is in her" (Hephzi-bah), and your land "Married" (Beulah); for the LORD delights in you, and your land shall be married . . . as the bridegroom rejoices over the bride, so shall your God rejoice over you.' John's words may therefore have the further implication that Jesus is the true King and Messiah of Israel. (There may be a similar implication in Jesus' own statement in Mark 2:19 that the wedding guests[21] cannot be expected to fast 'as long as they have the bridegroom with them'; and the picture of 'the Bride, the wife of the Lamb' in Rev. 21:9 ff. tells its own story.) John, as the forerunner preparing the way for Messiah's entry on the scene, may now retire satisfied when Messiah has come and begun to be accepted by his own people.

John betrays no sense of envy or rivalry. It is not easy to see another's influence growing at the expense of one's own; it is even less easy to rejoice at the sight.[22] But John found his joy completed by the news which his disciples brought.

> It takes more grace than I can tell
> To play the second fiddle well –

but John manifested a generous share of this rare grace. He came to bear witness, and when he saw so many attracted to Jesus because of his witness, he rested content. 'He must grow greater; I must grow less' are John's last recorded words in this Gospel.

3:31, 32 **He who comes from above is above all. He who is from the earth has his origin from the earth and it is from the earth that he speaks. He who comes from heaven (is above all) – he bears witness to what he has seen and heard, yet no one receives his witness.**

As in verses 16–21 the Evangelist adds his meditation to the words of Jesus which come to an end in verse 15, so now, in verse 31–36, he adds his meditation to the words of John which come to an end in verse 30 (after which RSV rightly places closing quotation marks).

It is because the incarnate Word 'comes from above' and 'is above all' that 'he must grow greater' while John and everyone else 'must grow less'. There is no suggestion of evil in being 'from the earth', but rather one of limitation. Even John's witness, excellent as it was, was subject to limitation because, while he was 'a man sent from God' (John 1:6), he did not come down from heaven as the Son of Man did. Jesus' own witness is of supreme validity because, when he speaks of heavenly things, he bears witness to what he has seen and heard in the heavenly sphere. The bracketed words ('is above all') at the end of verse 31 should probably be omitted, as in RV margin and NEB;[23] this leaves us with the clause: 'he who comes from heaven bears witness to what he has seen and heard' – a reading described by B. F. Westcott as 'much more impressive'. There is an echo here of verse 11; 'you do not receive our witness' there is caught up by 'no one receives his witness' here.

3:33-35 **He who has received his witness has confirmed that God is true; for he whom God sent speaks the words of God; it is not by measure that he gives the Spirit (to him). The Father loves the Son and has given everything into his hand.**

Jesus' witness is God's perfect truth. He is God's perfect messenger and delivers God's message perfectly. Those who accept Jesus' witness therefore attest the truthfulness of God, as though they affixed their seal to the divine message. The statement that 'no one receives his witness' at the end of verse 32 is thus not absolute, any more than the statement in John 1:11 that 'his own people did not receive him' is absolute. On both occasions the Evangelist immediately adds a qualification.

God had sent many messengers to convey his truth to the world; their line ended with John the Baptist. Each of them received that measure of the Spirit which was necessary for him or her to bear true witness.[24] But upon the Son of God the Spirit 'remains' (cf. John 1:32, 33), as was foretold in Isa. 11:2; 42:1; 61:1. It is not in carefully measured portions that the Spirit is given to him. That this is the sense of the last clause of verse 34 is implied by the following statement that the Father has given everything into the Son's hand. In itself, the clause 'it is not by measure that he gives the Spirit' might be construed as though Christ were the subject, and such a construction would accord with reality, even if it is not what the Evangelist is primarily concerned to say at this point. He who has received the Spirit in this unmeasured and abiding fulness is 'he who baptizes with the Holy Spirit' (John 1:33), and he does not pay scrupulous attention to the 'nicely calculated less or more' when he dispenses the heavenly gift. His people may then become faithful witnesses in their turn, telling with confidence what they too have 'seen and heard' (cf. 1 John 1:3).

Twice in this Gospel we read that 'the Father loves the Son' – here (verse 35) and in John 5:20. The verb here is *agapaō*; in the other place it is *phileō*. The alternation of these two verbs in identical statements illustrates the Evangelist's propensity for varying his choice of synonyms. Verse 35 provides a counterpart to Jesus' own saying in the Synoptic record: 'All things have been delivered to me by my Father' (Matt. 11:27; Luke 10:22). The Son is the Father's envoy plenipotentiary, his perfect spokesman and revealer.[25]

3:36 He who believes in the Son has eternal life. He who disobeys the Son will not see life, but the wrath of God remains on him.

The simple affirmation that 'he who believes in the Son has eternal life' sums up what has been said already about the new birth by which believers in Christ become God's children (cf. John 1:12 f.; 3:3 ff.). The Son has received from the Father authority to bestow spiritual life, the life of the age to come, here and now on those who receive him in faith and accept his witness (cf. John 5:20 f., 25 f., 17:2).

Since faith in the Son of God is the only way to eternal life, those who refuse to have faith in him deny themselves the enjoyment of that life which is in his gift. This saving faith comprises believing and obeying; hence, as frequently in the NT, *apeitheō* ('disobey') is used here as the antithesis to *pisteuō* ('believe'). To 'see' life, like 'seeing' the kingdom of God in verse 3, means to participate in it, to experience and enjoy it. To 'see life' has as its antithesis to 'see death' (as in John 8:51). Since those who will not obey the Son cut themselves off from the benefits of his sin-removing work, their persistent impenitence leaves them exposed to the wrath of God – to the retribution which is integral to his moral universe. The eternal life which believers receive involves their being accepted by God as righteous in Christ; apart from this divinely provided way of righteousness men remain liable to the judgment of heaven – in the language of verse 18, they are 'condemned already'.

NOTES

1. Babylonian Talmud, tractate *Ta'anith* 20a.
2. Josephus *Antiquities* 18.15, 17.
3. Cf. M. de Jonge, 'Nicodemus and Jesus: Some Observations on Misunderstanding and Understanding in the Fourth Gospel' *BJRL* 53 (1970–71), pp. 337–359.
4. So said Rabbi Jose (c. AD 150), according to Babylonian Talmud, tractate *Yᵉbāmôth* 48b.
5. It has been argued that the discourse with Nicodemus is an expansion of the Synoptic saying, received by John along an independent line of transmission (B. Lindars, 'John and the Synoptic Gospels: A Test Case' *NTS* 27 [1980–81], pp. 287–294).
6. The question who has a share in the age to come was discussed in rabbinic Judaism. The prevalent answer was that 'all Israel has a portion in the age to come' (Mishnah, tractate *Sanhedrin* 10.1) – all, in fact, except those who by deliberate apostasy or exceptional wickedness put themselves outside the covenant.
7. Justin *First Apology* 61.4.
8. In the Greek OT Naaman's dipping in Jordan is expressed by the verb *baptizō* in the middle voice. According to one line of rabbinical thought, Naaman was an outstandingly worthy proselyte, worthier even than Jethro, because while Jethro confessed 'that the LORD is greater than all gods' (Ex. 18:11), implying that other gods might exist, Naaman confessed 'that there is no God in all the earth but in Israel' (2 Kings 5:15); so *Mekhilta* (rabbinical commentary on Exodus), tractate *Amalek* 3.
9. Rabbi Gamaliel II is reported as having said to the Roman Emperor, in a debate with him, 'You do not know what is on earth; how should you know what is in heaven?' (Babylonian Talmud, tractate *Sanhedrin* 39a).
10. Less satisfactory suggestions are that the 'earthly things' relate to the law and the 'heavenly things' to the gospel, or that the 'earthly things' are what Jesus taught during his Palestinian ministry while the 'heavenly things' belong to the further truth revealed by the Spirit after Jesus' departure (John 16:13).

11. To ascend into heaven so as to have access to the divine mysteries was an aspiration cherished by many more than actually attained it. Of those who attained it in the NT record Paul heard things which might not be uttered (2 Cor. 12:3 f.), while the seer of Patmos was commanded to write down and publish what he saw and heard (Rev. 1:19; 4:1). But the supreme revealer does not pay an exceptional visit from earth to heaven; his habitual home is in heaven, and from there he pays a temporary visit to earth. See C. Rowland *The Open Heaven* (London 1982), pp. 52–57, etc.

12. See p. 220.

13. This ethical use of the light-darkness antithesis is characteristic also of the literature of the Qumran community, where men are divided between the lots of the Prince of Light and the Angel of Darkness, so that the 'sons of light' practise truth and righteousness while the 'sons of darkness' practise falsehood and iniquity (1QS 3.18–25).

14. Perhaps at the confluence of the Wadi Baida and the Wadi Fara'a, where there is an ample supply of spring water. See W. F. Albright *The Archaeology of Palestine* (Pelican Books 1960), p. 247.

15. The importance of this chronological datum for the comparative study of John and the Synoptic Gospels was appreciated by Eusebius (*Hist. Eccl.* 3.24.11, 12).

16. Josephus *Antiquities* 18.117. The Essenes, according to Josephus, took a purifying bath in cold water each day before their midday meal (*Jewish War* 2.129). There were people known to rabbinical tradition as 'morning bathers' because they practised a ritual washing at dawn before they took the name of God on their lips, thus exceeding the righteousness of the scribes and Pharisees, with whom they engaged in controversy (Tosefta, tractate *Yadayim* 2.20). They may have been akin to the 'daily bathers' (*hēmerobaptistai*) mentioned by Epiphanius (*Recapitulation* 17). In addition to such (possibly competing) communities we may recall the hermit Bannus, who 'bathed in cold water day and night, with a view to purity', and to whom the young Josephus attached himself for a time (Josephus *Life* 11).

17. But the plural 'Jews' is attested by Papyrus 66.

18. The emendation *Iēsou* ('Jesus') was conjectured by R. Bentley; somewhat more probable is O. Holtzmann's conjecture *tōn Iēsou* ('those of Jesus', i.e. the disciples of Jesus, whose baptismal activity is mentioned in John 4:2. But neither has any ancient attestation.

19. See p. 67, notes 62, 64 (on John 1:51).

20. The bridegroom's friend was the *shôshbîn*, who arranged and presided over a Judaean wedding (arrangements at a Galilaean wedding, like that at Cana in John 2:1;11, were somewhat different).

21. Literally, 'the sons of the bridechamber' (i.e. all the invited guests).

22. George Müller, writing of his lately deceased colleague Henry Craik, said, 'While at Teignmouth, I became acquainted with Mr Craik, and *his warmth of heart towards the Lord* drew me to him. . . . When in the year 1832, I saw how some preferred my beloved friend's ministry to my own, I determined, in the strength of God, to rejoice in this, instead of envying him' (Introduction to *Passages from the Diary and Letters of Henry Craik of Bristol*, ed. W. E. Tayler [London 1866], pp. xii, xiii).

23. The textual evidence for and against the omission is rather evenly balanced; of our two earlier witnesses, Papyrus 66 retains the words 'is above all' and Papyrus 75 omits them.

24. According to Rabbi Acha (4th century AD, as quoted in the rabbinical commentary *Leviticus Rabba* 15.2 (on Lev. 13:2), the Holy Spirit rests on a prophet only 'according to the measure' (*bᵉmišqal*) of his commission.

25. See p. 45 (on 1:18).

CHAPTER 4

II. Jesus and the Samaritans (4:1–42)

4:1–3 So, when Jesus learned that the Pharisees had heard it said, 'Jesus is making more disciples than John, and baptizing them' (although it was not Jesus himself who was baptizing, but his disciples), he left Judaea and went back again to Galilee.

The dispute about purification which sprang from the concurrent baptismal ministries of John and Jesus (John 3:25) had wider implications than appear on the surface. The Pharisees viewed both preachers with critical reserve (cf. John 1:24). If, then, the increasing number of those who came to receive Jesus' baptism produced feelings of resentment in the minds of John's disciples, and a measure of estrangement between them and Jesus' disciples, the situation might be exploited by the Pharisees to the disadvantage of John and Jesus alike. One could wish that more were known of the details of the situation, thus briefly referred to by the Evangelist. As has been said above, John and Jesus were not the only leaders of 'baptismal' movements in Judaea around this time. But the once-for-all initiatory baptism administered by John, and then by Jesus (if only through his disciples), had a significance quite distinct from the repeated purificatory dippings of those other movements.

As for the parenthetical statement that 'it was not Jesus himself who was baptizing, but his disciples', it breaks into the course of the sentence (rather like the parenthesis in John 4:8) and has been thought to be the work of an editor. It does not, however, contradict the substance of the previous verse or the report of John 3:26. He who acts through a duly appointed agent is the real author of the act performed. When later, in the new believing community constituted on the day of Pentecost, baptism was administered 'in the name of Jesus Christ' (Acts 2:38; cf. 10:48), the apostles were acting as the agents of their exalted Lord and not by their own authority. So it was in this earlier phase of his ministry. It has indeed been suggested that the present reference is to the post-Pentecostal baptism, antedated to the earthly career of Jesus, and that this explains the saving parenthesis of verse 2, inserted (on this hypothesis) by someone with a historical conscience. But we are dealing with an actual situation in that earlier Judaean ministry of Jesus which preceded the main course of his Galilaean ministry.[1]

If there was any likelihood of an attempt to drive a wedge

between his work and John's, Jesus would forestall it. His regard
for John was such that he could not tolerate the very possibility or
appearance of a cleavage, so he withdrew from Judaea and returned
to Galilee, which he had left some months before to attend the
Passover in Jerusalem (John 2:13).

**4:4-6 And he had to pass through Samaria. So he came to a
city of Samaria called Sychar, near the piece of land which Jacob
gave to Joseph his son; and Jacob's well was there. So Jesus,
tired after his journey, sat as he was by the well; it was about
the sixth hour.**

Samaria lay between Judaea in the south and Galilee in the north;
any one, therefore, who wished to go from Judaea to Galilee 'had
to pass through Samaria' unless he was prepared to make a detour
through Transjordan, with its largely Gentile population. Jesus on
this occasion took the direct route from south to north, and arrived
in due course at the place here called Sychar, a name not previously
attested. It is commonly identified with the modern village of
'Askar, on the slope of Mount Ebal, a mile or two north-east of
Nablus and about half-a-mile north of Jacob's well.[2] The identification may well be right, although the two names are probably not
related – *'askar* is an Arabic term for a military camp, and would
not be known in Palestine before the seventh century AD.[3] The
place-name Sychar was known in the first half of the fourth century: the Bordeaux pilgrim (AD 333) says that Sychar lay a Roman
mile distant from Shechem (modern Balata); he distinguishes it also
from the neighbouring Neapolis (modern Nablus). The name may
also be preserved in that of the spring 'En Soker, mentioned in the
Talmud[4] (which may be identical with the plentiful fountain still
existing in 'Askar).

The piece of land which Jacob gave to Joseph is mentioned in
Gen. 48:22, where Jacob on his deathbed says to Joseph, 'I have
given to you rather than to your brothers one mountain slope
(Heb. *shechem*, 'shoulder') which I took from the hand of the
Amorites with my sword and with my bow'. (This military conquest is otherwise unchronicled in the OT, unless it is a variant of
the incident of Gen. 34:25 ff., which is unlikely.)[5] Many years
later, when the Israelites occupied Central Canaan, they buried
Joseph's bones, which they had brought from Egypt, 'at Shechem,
in the portion of ground which Jacob bought from the sons of
Hamor the father of Shechem for a hundred pieces of money (or
a hundred sheep, according to NEB); it became an inheritance of
the descendants of Joseph' (Josh. 24:32; cf. Gen. 33:19). The place
therefore had ancient and sacred associations. Joseph's tomb is still

pointed out in the neighbourhood; it is covered with a dome, like many another *weli* (monument of a holy man) in the Islamic world.

Whatever doubt there may be about the site of Sychar, there is little or none about the identity of Jacob's well (325 yards S.E. of Joseph's tomb), which has been recognized since early Christian times. In the days of Jerome (*c.* AD 400) a church stood there; the Crusaders built another seven centuries later. Both of these were destroyed by Muslims. The site is now marked by an unfinished Orthodox church, begun early in the present century; the well-head lies in the shadow of its crypt, no longer exposed to the sun and open air, as it was in Jesus' time.

The Greek word here translated 'well' in *pēgē*, meaning 'spring' or 'fountain'; in verses 11 and 12 the word used is *phrear*, which denotes a dug-out well or cistern. Both words are appropriate to Jacob's well; it was dug, indeed, but it is fed by an underground stream, which rarely gives out.[6]

The sixth hour, reckoned from sunrise, would be noon – a natural time of day for a weary traveller to seek rest and refreshment. While our Evangelist insists that it was the divine Word that became flesh in Jesus, he insists at the same time that what the divine Word became was *flesh*. He emphasizes those traits which attest our Lord's genuine humanity; this is no impassible visitant from another realm, untouched by our ordinary infirmities. The description of Jesus tired after his journey and sitting down for rest has inspired one of the immortal lines of the *Dies Irae*: 'Seeking me thou sat'st there weary' (*quaerens me sedisti lassus*).

4:7, 8 A woman of Samaria came to draw water. Jesus said to her, 'Give me a drink'. (His disciples had gone off into the city to buy food.)

Women usually came to draw water in company, and at a cooler time of day. This woman evidently came alone; possibly she did not seek the company of her neighbours (or they did not seek hers), so she deliberately chose a time when they were not likely to be around – but it is easy to speculate. Jesus' request would normally have seemed a most natural one from a tired and thirsty traveller to a woman who was drawing water; but it surprised her. The implication of the parenthesis in verse 8 is that his disciples would have drawn water for him, had they been there; but they had gone to buy food. The 'city' was presumably that to which the woman belonged. Strictly observant Jews would have thought they were incurring defilement if they ate food which had been handled by Samaritans; however, certain dry kinds of food were regarded as being less susceptible of defilement than most.

4:9 The Samaritan woman said to him, 'How is it that a Jew like you can ask a drink from a Samaritan woman like me?' (Jews do not use the same vessels as Samaritans.)

The religious differences between Jews and Samaritans were serious and deep-rooted.[7] The cleavage between Samaria and Judah in the days of the Hebrew monarchy might have been healed after the Babylonian captivity, but the returning Jewish exiles rejected an offer of co-operation from the Samaritans, whose racial and religious purity they suspected. The resultant hostility was sharpened by the erection of a rival Samaritan temple on Mount Gerizim about 400 BC, and the destruction of this temple by the Hasmonaean ruler John Hyrcanus about 108 BC did nothing to improve relations. And quite apart from inherited animosity, many a Jew would not dream of asking a favour from a Samaritan, for fear of incurring ritual defilement. This scruple would be intensified when the Samaritan was a woman, for there must have been a considerable number of Jews who held the view which acquired the status of religious law a generation or two later, that all Samaritan women must be assumed to be in a perpetual state of ceremonial uncleanness. This Samaritan woman's surprise was natural.

The Evangelist's explanation of her surprise – another of his typical parentheses – is not simply that (as the older versions have it) 'Jews have no dealings with Samaritans' but more specifically that (as the NEB renders it) 'Jews and Samaritans, it should be noted, do not use vessels in common'.[8] If the woman complied with Jesus' request, he would have had to drink from her vessel, since he had none of his own. This would have involved a risk of ceremonial pollution for a Jew even if the owner of the vessel had been a male Samaritan, but the fact that the owner was a woman made that risk a certainty, from the standpoint of a strictly observant Jew. No wonder that Jesus' request astonished the woman; by asking such a favour from her he had shown most unexpected goodwill.

4:10 Jesus said to her in reply, 'If you knew the gift of God and who it is that is asking you for a drink, you would have asked him and he would have given you living water.'

Jesus does not pursue the subject of the Jewish-Samaritan cleavage which she had introduced, but lifts the topic of conversation to another plane. Had she known who was sitting at the well-head, and what he was able to bestow, she would have got her request in first. Water, in a land subject to drought, is appreciated as a true gift from God. Any traveller in Palestine quickly learns how indispensable it is. But Jesus now speaks of a greater gift of God than the purest earthly spring can supply. In the sign at Cana (John 2:6 ff.) and in the conversation with Nicodemus (John 3:5) water has already figured in a spiritual sense. Here the water in Jacob's well, symbolizing the old order inherited by Samaritans and Jews alike, is contrasted with the new order, the gift of the Spirit, life eternal. The expression 'living water' was in current use to denote spring water or running water as distinct from the water collected in a cistern. We may recall how in Jer. 2:13 the God of Israel speaks of himself as 'the fountain of living waters' which his people have forsaken in favour of cisterns hewn out by themselves. At best the water in those cisterns would be stagnant; as it was, they proved to be 'broken cisterns, that can hold no water'. Running water aptly illustrated the fresh and perennial supply of God's grace, as it does in these words of Jesus.

4:11, 12 'Sir', said she, 'you have no bucket and the well is deep. Where then do you get this "living water" from? Are you greater than our father Jacob, who gave us this well and drank from it himself, as also did his sons and his cattle?'

When Jesus spoke of 'living water', the woman thought he meant fresh spring water like that of the spring which feeds Jacob's well. The strange obviously had no bucket (Gk. *antlēma; cf.* the verb *antleō* in verse 15) or anything with which to draw water from the depths of the well (the word used here is *phrear*). Even today the well is over 100 feet deep, and it must have been deeper then. Canon H. B. Tristram, a Palestinian explorer of the last century (and author of a standard work on *The Natural History of the Bible*), is said once to have sat thus by the well and read the fourth chapter of John. At that time the well was not built over; as he read he grew drowsy in the hot sun, and his Bible fell from his hands into the well. It was not recovered until several years later, during an unusually dry winter.

The woman's failure to comprehend Jesus' words about living water is comparable to Nicodemus's failure to comprehend his words about the new birth (John 3:4).[9] Any one who could make and fulfil such a promise must indeed be greater than Jacob, and this the woman thought unlikely. (Her question, introduced by the negative particle *mē*, implies the answer 'No'.) Jacob had with much trouble dug this well (*phrear*) for his family and descendants. There is no reference to the digging of the well in the OT narrative of Jacob; it probably belongs to the context of Gen. 33:18–20. The question indeed arises why it was necessary to dig a well at all in a neighbourhood so well provided with springs. Probably strained relations with the people who lived in the vicinity made it advisable for him to secure a separate water supply; we may compare his father Isaac's trouble in this matter with the tribes of the Negev (Gen. 26:15–33). The Evangelist no doubt discerns a deeper significance in the woman's words; the descendants of Jacob, whether Samaritans or Jews, were still content with spiritual refreshment inferior to that bestowed by Jesus.

4:13, 14 Jesus replied, 'Every one who drinks from this water will thirst again; but whoever drinks from the water that I shall give him will thirst no more: the water that I shall give him will become a spring of water within him, water bubbling up to eternal life.'

The woman's last question had been incredulous; how could a chance passing Jew be greater than the patriarch Jacob? But Jesus takes up her question seriously. The water in Jacob's well was good water, undoubtedly (it still is), but it could not satisfy one's thirst indefinitely. Those who drew water there and enjoyed its refreshing properties grew thirsty again and had to come back for another draught. The frequent comparison of the law to refreshing water in the rabbinical traditions suggests that Jesus is here offering something superior not only to the water in Jacob's well but to the legal religion of Jews and Samaritans alike. It is conceivable that his words may have rung a distinctive bell in a Samaritan ear. The (admittedly much later) Samaritan liturgy for the Day of Atonement says of the Taheb (the Samaritan counterpart to the Jewish Messiah), 'Water shall flow from his buckets' (language borrowed from Balaam's oracle in Num. 24:7).[10] Was this stranger promising to give what the Taheb was expected to supply?

The Evangelist might well have added to Jesus' words about the water that he would give the same comment as he added to similar words on a later occasion: 'he said this with regard to the Spirit' (John 7:39). For the Spirit of God, imparted by our Lord to his people, dwells within them as a perennial wellspring of refreshment and life. The soul's deepest thirst is for God himself, who has made us so that we can never be satisfied without him. 'Christ satisfies a man not by banishing his thirst, which would be to stunt his soul's growth, but by bestowing upon him by the gift of his Spirit an inward source of satisfaction which perennially and spontaneously supplies each recurrent need of refreshment' (G. H. C. Macgregor). The fountain of living waters may thus be found resident in the personal life of men and women; with joy they may draw water from the wells of salvation (Isa. 12:3) and know that, as they partake of that saving draught, they are tasting the true

heavenly gift, the life of the age to come. It is of a spring (*pegē*),
not a hewn-out cistern, that Jesus speaks here (in the Greek text
the participle 'bubbling up' or 'leaping up' agrees with 'water', not
with 'spring').

**4:15 The woman said to him, 'Give me this water, Sir, so that
I shall not thirst nor come all the way here to draw it.'**

If the stranger can really do what he says, then certainly he is
greater than Jacob. But the woman's thought continues to move
on the mundane plane; she still imagines that Jesus is talking about
material water and bodily thirst. How grand it would be if she had
a supply of this miraculous water and had no more need to make
the daily journey to Jacob's well! (If the place where she lived
occupied the site of modern 'Askar, she would have passed the
fountain 'En Soker and also crossed a stream on her way to Jacob's
well; perhaps she preferred not to join her neighbours in drawing
water from the sources which they frequented.) Her response is
parallel to that of the Galilaeans to whom Jesus later spoke of the
life-giving bread from heaven: 'Sir, give us this bread always' (John
6:34).

**4:16 'Go and call your husband', said he to her, 'and come
here.'**

Her misunderstanding could evidently not be corrected so long
as the conversation was carried on in terms of thirst and water.
Hence what appears to be an abrupt change of subject is introduced
– one which is calculated to lead on to a further unfolding of the
heavenly truth already hinted at, without the use of the water
metaphor.

**4:17, 18 The woman said to him in reply, 'I have no husband',
'You did right', said Jesus, 'in saying that you have no husband.
In fact, you have had five husbands, and now the man whom
you have is not your husband. You have told the truth.'**

The woman was taken aback by the abrupt change of subject,
the more so because the stranger touched on a phase of her life
about which she was naturally sensitive. Still, he was only a stranger
and would not know her history, so she could put him off with a
bare statement of her present position: 'I have no husband'. But
the stranger obviously knew much more about her than she suspected: he knew that her statement was the truth so far as it went,
but that it was not the whole truth, so he proceeded to let her
understand just how much he did know about her.

Jesus' words in verse 18 may be taken as a literal summary of her chequered married life. We do not know why she had had so many husbands: perhaps one after the other had divorced her because of some 'unseemliness' in the sense of Deut. 24:1, or she may have lost some of them by death. And now she was cohabiting with a man to whom she was not regularly married, possibly because of some legal impediment. Hence her answer, 'I have no husband', was formally true but potentially misleading. Have these words of Jesus, however, a deeper meaning than that which lies on the surface? As so often in this Gospel, we get the impression that this may be so, but we have no assurance what this deeper meaning may be.

A time-honoured interpretation sees in these words a reference to the religious syncretism which characterized the Samaritan population in the days following the planting of non-Israelite settlers in Samaria by the Assyrian kings. On this showing he woman represents the Samaritan community, despised by the Jews as being hybrid in race and religion. Her five husbands are the pagan deities whose worship was brought into Samaria by the settlers from five Mesopotamian and Syrian cities mentioned in 2 Kings 17:24; the sixth, to whom she was not regularly married, is the true God of Israel. It is remarkable that the prophetic imagery could be so reversed that idolatry could be represented by legal marriage and the worship of the true God by an illicit union. Interpreters who are not given pause by this will not be unduly disturbed by the fact that the pagan deities originally worshipped by the settlers were seven in number, not five (2 Kings 17:30 f.) and that they were worshipped simultaneously, not one after another. Other expositors, realizing that the details do not correspond, are content with a vaguer allegorization, suggesting that the Evangelist is concerned to condemn religious syncretism in general rather than the Samaritan variety in particular.[11] A verdict of 'Not proven' is the kindest treatment that can be given to such interpretations; and until something more like proof is forthcoming it is best to conclude that the woman is reminded of her many disappointments in personal relationships in order that she may appreciate the more the deep and lasting satisfaction that Jesus brings.

4:19, 20 'Sir', said the woman to him, 'I perceive that you are a prophet. Our fathers worshipped on this mountain, but you (Jews) say that the place where worship should be offered is in Jerusalem.'

A stranger who could read the woman's life-story like an open book was no ordinary man; such insight betokened the gift of prophecy. Now the Samaritans did not recognize the canon of post-Mosaic prophecy which forms the second division of the Jewish Bible. In their belief, the statement of Deut. 34:10, 'there has not arisen a prophet since in Israel like Moses', remained absolute and valid until the rise of the second Moses, the Taheb or great prophet of the new age, to whom they looked forward.[12] Between the first and second Moses no prophet could be expected. If therefore the woman meant the term 'prophet' seriously, she was already on the brink of the great discovery about this stranger's identity at which she was shortly to arrive: a man who could tell her all that she ever did could be no less than the Coming One himself.

But first, since she was talking to a 'prophet', the conversation must take a religious turn. There are some people who cannot engage in a religious conversation with a person of a different persuasion without bringing up the points on which they differ. If a Jew and a Samaritan conversed about religion, one of the chief points at issue between the two communities had to be aired. What was the place which the God of Israel had chosen out of all his people's tribes to cause his name to dwell there? Where must his people have recourse to worship him? The authoritative text was Deut. 12:5, which directs them to seek the place of God's choice and present their offerings to him there. But that text does not specify the place of God's choice; it leaves it to be inferred. The Jews and the Samaritans drew different inferences about its whereabouts. The Jews located it 'in Jerusalem', the Samaritans 'on this mountain' – i.e. Gerizim, overlooking Shechem – to which they could look up as they talked by the well. And whereas the Jews' edition of the Hebrew Bible spoke of 'the place which the LORD your God will choose', the Samaritan edition read: 'the place which the LORD your God has chosen' (the difference hanging on the presence or absence of a *yod*, the smallest letter in the alphabet). The Samaritan reading implies that the divine choice had already been made known. Not only was Shechem the first place where Abraham built an altar on his entry into the promised land (Gen. 12:6 f.); in the Samaritan Bible the Decalogue (both in Exod. 20:17 and in Deut. 5:21) is followed by a further direction (anticipating Deut. 27:2–7 and 11:30), which indeed ranks as the tenth commandment: 'And when the LORD your God brings you into the land of the Canaanites, which you are entering to take possession of it, you shall set up large stones and plaster them with plaster; and you shall write upon them all the words of this law. And when you have passed over the Jordan, you shall set up these stones, concerning which I command you this day, on Mount Gerizim. And there you shall build an altar to the LORD your God, an altar of stones; you shall lift up no iron tool upon them. You shall build an altar to the LORD your God of unhewn stones, and you shall offer burnt-offerings on it to the LORD your God; and you shall sacrifice peace-offerings, and shall eat there; and you shall rejoice before the LORD your God. That mountain is beyond the Jordan, west of the road, towards the going down of the sun, in the land of the Canaanites who live in the Arabah, over against Gilgal, beside the terebinth of Moreh, opposite Shechem'. There, on Mount Gerizim, the blessings were pronounced on Israel after the settlement in Joshua's day (Josh. 8:33; cf. Deut. 27:12), and there, in later days, the Samaritan temple stood. To this day it is the holiest place on earth in the eyes of the small Samaritan remnant – and incidentally, by dogma rather than by measurement, the highest mountain in the world.[13] The place 'in Jerusalem' where the Jews believed worship should be offered was the temple first built by Solomon, rebuilt by Zerubbabel and later embellished by Herod, but that temple was a latecomer among the shrines dedicated to the God of Israel. Was there one single passage in the five books of Moses to which the Jews could point in support of their claim that Jerusalem and not Shechem was the place of God's choice? What (the woman may have thought to herself) would this Jewish prophet say to that?

4:21–24 Jesus said to her, 'Believe me, woman, an hour is coming when you will worship the Father neither on this mountain nor yet in Jerusalem. *You* worship what you do not know; *we* worship what we know because it is from the Jews that salvation proceeds. But an hour is coming – in fact, it is already present – when the true worshippers will worship the Father in spirit and truth; such are the worshippers that the Father seeks. God is Spirit, and so those who worship him must worship in spirit and truth'.

The answer the woman received was quite different from anything that she could have expected. The time when there was any point in the argument about the claims of Gerizim versus those of Zion had come to an end. A new order was now being introduced which rendered such questions out-of-date and meaningless. The important question is not *where* people worship God but *how* they worship him. And part of the 'how' of worshipping him is disclosed in Jesus' language about worshipping him as *the Father*. Jesus habitually spoke of God as his Father – we have seen how spontaneously he referred to the temple as 'my Father's house' (John 2:16) – and addressed him as Father (cf. John 11:41; 12:27 f.; 17:1, etc.); and he taught his followers to do the same. How readily they did so is evident from the wide circulation in the early church of the invocation 'Abba, Father' (Rom. 8:15, Gal. 4:6), following their Master's example (Mark 14:36).

This revelation of the essence of true worship, as Jesus unfolds it, appears simple and indeed obvious, when once it is presented to us – yet not all that obvious, when we think of the considerable number of Christians who make the same mistake as the Samaritan woman (and with less justification), imagining that a man or woman cannot worship God properly unless he or she worships *with them*. The sense of Jesus' teaching was well caught by William Cowper:

> Jesus, where'er thy people meet,
> There they behold thy mercy-seat;
> Where'er they seek thee, thou art found,
> And every place is hallowed ground.

Even with regard to the time now past, Jesus makes no pronouncement on the claims of the rival sanctuaries. But with regard to the general dispute between the Samaritans and the Jews, he declares the Jewish worship to be more intelligent than that of the Samaritans – perhaps because the promised deliverer of all Israel (Jews and Samaritans alike) was to come from the tribe of Judah, as even the Samaritan Bible foretold (Gen. 49:10); it was therefore from the Jews – the descendants of Judah – that salvation was to proceed for Israel and the world in general.

The affirmation, 'It is from the Jews that salvation proceeds', stands as an effective answer to the charge of anti-Jewish bias frequently laid against this Evangelist nowadays.

The prophets had spoken of a coming day when not one central sanctuary alone, but the whole earth, would be the habitation of the name and glory of God. While the manifest consummation of this hope, associated as it is with the universal knowledge of God, lies in the future even from our perspective, yet to faith the conditions of that coming age are present already. Hence 'an hour is coming' in verse 21 is followed in verse 23 by 'an hour is coming – indeed it is already present' (compare the reverse order in John 5:25, 28). Here is an instance of this Evangelist's 'realized eschatology'. Just as, in chapter 3, the life of the age to come may be possessed and enjoyed here and now, so in chapter 4 the worship of the age to come may be rendered here and now, by those true worshippers, so desired by the Father, who worship him 'in spirit and truth'. Spiritual worship, genuine worship, cannot be tied to set places and seasons. And such worship is seen to be the more appropriate when we consider the nature of the God to whom it is offered.

'God is Spirit': it is not merely that he is *a* Spirit among other spirits; rather, God himself is pure Spirit, and the worship in which he takes delight is accordingly spiritual worship – the sacrifice of a humble, contrite, grateful and adoring spirit. This affirmation of our Lord's was not entirely new; it but crowns the witness of psalmists and prophets in earlier ages, who saw that material things could at best be the vehicle of true worship but could never belong to its essence. Sincere heart-devotion, whenever and wherever found, is indispensable if men and woman would present to God worship which he can accept.

4:25, 26 **The woman said to him, 'I know that Messiah is coming' (that is to say, Christ);**[14] **'when he comes, he will declare all things to us'. Jesus said to her, 'I am he – the one who is speaking to you.'**

The woman, probably beyond her depth, says in effect, 'A day is coming when all these religious problems will be cleared up for us'. For 'I know' some early witnesses present the reading 'we know'. The place occupied in much Jewish expectation by the Messiah of David's line was occupied in Samaritan expectation by the great prophet of the future, the one foretold by Moses in Deut. 18:15. This 'prophet like Moses' would naturally be in a position to explain all mysteries; in this respect he would discharge a ministry like that assigned to the returning Elijah in Jewish expectation. It is further noteworthy that in Samaritan tradition this prophet to come is called the Taheb or 'restorer', for this also recalls Jewish beliefs about Elijah (cf. Mal. 4:4–6; Mark 9:11–13). (Another disclosure which the Taheb would make related to the place where the sacred vessels of the Mosaic tabernacle had been laid up in hiding.)[15]

This remarkable stranger, whom the woman suspected to be a 'prophet', had given a ruling on the true worship of God; but the absolutely authoritative ruling would be given by the great prophet of the new age, when once he appeared. Was she testing Jesus, to see what he would say?

If she had begun to have an inkling about his identity, it was now confirmed. He whom the Jews expected as the promised prince of the house of David was at the same time the one whom the Samaritans (and others) expected as the prophet like Moses. She had not known at first who it was that asked her for a drink of water, but now she understood how he could make a claim that marked him out as greater than their father Jacob; it was the Coming One in person who sat thus by the well and spoke so wonderfully to her.[16]

4:27 At this point his disciples came and were surprised that he was talking with a woman. However, none of them said 'What do you want?' or 'Why are you talking with her?'

The disciples who had gone to the city to buy food now returned. Their surprise at finding their Master talking to a woman was no doubt all the greater because the woman was a Samaritan, but for a rabbi to engage in conversation even with a true-born Jewish woman was regarded by many as a waste of time that might have been more profitably spent. The classical comment on this verse is provided by the words of Yose ben Yoḥanan, a rabbi of the second century AD, 'Prolong not conversation with a woman', together with the editorial remark of whoever was responsible for preserving his words: 'That is to say, even with one's own wife; how much more with a neighbour's wife. Hence the wise men say, "He who prolongs conversation with a woman brings evil upon himself, ceases from the words of the law, and at the last inherits Gehanna".'[17]

However, the disciples knew from experience that their Master always had good reason for what he did, even when it was strange and unconventional, so none of them asked the woman what she wanted with him or asked him why he was talking to her.

4:28–30 So the woman left her waterpot and went off to the city and said to the people, 'Come here, see someone who has told me all that I ever did. Can this be the Messiah?' They came out of the city and made their way to him.

The arrival of the disciples brought the conversation to an end; the women went off to the city to tell the people about the remarkable stranger she had met. She forgot the water of Jacob's well in her excitement at receiving the living water of which Jesus had spoken. The wellspring of perennial refreshment was now bubbling up within her. Her abandonment of the waterpot is a parable of the renunciation of the old ceremonial, practised by Jews and Samaritans alike, on the part of those who through faith in Christ have received the divine gift of eternal life. If she had avoided the company of her fellow-citizens before, she was a changed woman now: she must seek them out and share her news with them.

When the stranger by the well revealed so surprisingly intimate an acquaintance with the details of her private life (compare his words to Nathanael in John 1:48), she concluded that he must be a prophet; now it had been borne in upon her that he was not only *a* prophet but *the* prophet, foretold byMoses, for whom she and her fellow-Samaritans were waiting. When the end-time prophet came, they knew that he would explain all mysteries to them; surely, the woman said to her neighbours, this must be he, since he had revealed such comprehensive familiarity with her personal history? Her words, 'all that I ever did', may well have been the hyperbole of excitement; in any case, one who knew the points on which he had laid his finger would certainly know everything else about her.

They were impressed by her story, and decided to see for themselves. We must picture them approaching the well during Jesus' conversation with his disciples after their return.

4:31–34 Meanwhile his disciples were begging him to take food: 'Eat something, Rabbi'. But he said to them, 'I have food to eat that you do not know about'. So the disciples began to say one to another, 'Has any one brought him something to eat?' Jesus said to them, 'My food is to do the will of him who sent me, and to complete his work.'

The disciples had brought food in the neighbouring city; now, while the woman had gone off to tell her story to the people of Sychar, they kept on entreating their Master to eat some of it. There is a parallel between Jesus' earlier conversation with the woman about water and his present conversation with the disciples about food. Tired and thirsty though he was (and probably hungry as well), he appears to have been refreshed and invigorated by the opportunity of imparting spiritual help to a soul in need. 'Man does not live by bread alone'.

Just as the woman had misunderstood his first words about the living water, taking them in a material sense, so the disciples now imagine that he is talking about physical food. Jesus therefore has to enlighten them further. This is a recurring pattern throughout the discourses recorded in this Gospel. (The disciples' question, 'Has any one brought him something to eat?', is cast in a form implying the answer 'No'.)

'Man lives by everything that proceeds out of the mouth of the LORD', Moses had said (Deut. 8:3); and no one demonstrated the truth of this principle so thoroughly as Jesus did. To listen to the Father's voice and to do his will were the joy and strength of his life.[18] And towards the end of his ministry he could say to the Father, 'I glorified thee on earth, by completing the work which thou gavest me to do' (John 17:4). Part of the work which the Father gave him to do was to communicate his blessing to the woman of Sychar, and through her to the other inhabitants of that place; the satisfaction which he now experienced through doing the

Father's will in this respect was greater than any satisfaction which bread could give.

4:35-38 'Do you not say, "Yet four months and harvest comes"? See, I tell you: raise your eyes and look at the fields; they are white, ready for harvest. Already the reaper is receiving his wages, as he gathers fruit for eternal life, so that the sower and the reaper may rejoice together. In this you have the fulfilment of the saying: "One sows and another reaps." I sent you to reap a harvest for which you have not toiled; others have toiled, and you have entered into their toil.'

The point of the saying about the four months in this context is not quite clear. Some suppose that the incident took place in December or January, four months before the normal harvest-time. In that case Jesus' meaning would have been: 'You say that four months have to elapse before harvest is ripe; but look at this harvest waiting to be reaped!' – referring to the people of Sychar who were coming out to the well to see him. In support of this view it has been argued that the synagogue readings for the period which fell four months before Passover included Exod. 2:15 ff., where a well figures in the story of Moses, and the following chapter, where the words occur: 'you shall serve God upon this mountain' (Exod. 3:12; cf. John 4:20).[19] But this is far-fetched: the well of Exodus was in Midian, not in Samaria, and 'this mountain' was Horeb, not Gerizim. In Greek the words 'Yet four months and harvest comes' have a rhythmic form which suggests that we have to do with a popular or proverbial saying, meaning 'Four months from sowing to harvest'. (The interval was normally nearer six months than four, but the word *tetramēnos* may simply denote an interval which calls for patience, but will not be unduly prolonged.) Jesus' words would then mean: 'You always say, "Four months from sowing to harvest" – but look: the seed has newly been sown and here is the harvest already!' (referring to the approach of the people of Sychar). This is a more probable interpretation.

The adverb 'already' may be attached either to the end of verse 35 or to the beginning of verse 36; either punctuation suits the context, but the latter has more point.

Jesus himself was the sower; now his disciples had an opportunity to share his joy by helping to reap the harvest which had sprung from his conversation with the woman and her witness to the other Samaritans. This harvest would not be consumed in due course, as an ordinary harvest would; it would endure for eternal life.

The saying quoted in verse 37 seems to mean that while one may

sow and another reap, the labours of both are necessary if a crop
is to be harvested; that is why sower and reaper alike have a right
to share in the joy of harvest home. But Jesus may have in mind
another sower than himself, if John 3:23 is rightly understood to
point to a ministry of John the Baptist in that very area.[20] John
was the last of the goodly succession of prophets and righteous
men who had faithfully sown the seed of the word of God but had
not lived to see the harvest. Then came Jesus, proclaiming the
arrival of the divine kingdom which they had foretold. He came as
that kingdom in person, the *autobasileia*, as Origen so finely put
it,[21] the very embodiment of the good news which he brought. He
is the Sower *par excellence*; more than that, he is himself the grain
of wheat falling into the ground and dying, so as to produce an
abundance of fruit (John 12:24).

It is the privilege of his disciples in all generations to reap the
harvest that continues to spring from this good seed.

**4:39 Many of the Samaritans from that city believed in him
because of what the woman said when she testified: 'He told me
all that I ever did.'**

The living water which the woman received from Jesus had
certainly become an overflowing fountain in her life, and others
were coming to share the refreshment that she had begun to enjoy.
Let us not grow weary in well-doing; the most unlikely soul may
prove the most effective witness.

**4:40–42 So, when the Samaritans came to him, they asked him
to stay with them; and he stayed there two days. Many more
believed because of what he said, and they said to the woman,
'It is no longer because of your talk that we believe; we ourselves
have heard him, and we know that this is indeed the Saviour of
the world.'**

That Samaritans should invite a Jewish teacher to stay with them,
with no fear of a rebuff, shows how completely he had won their
confidence. The 'harvest' was not limited to those who came out
to see him at the well; others in the city believed in him during his
brief sojourn among them. We may wonder if this was the same
'city of Samaria' as was evangelized by Philip a few years later; if
it was, the events that took place at this time could explain the
ready credence which great crowds gave to Philip when he 'proclaimed to them the Christ' (Acts 8:5). This might be a further
fulfilment of the principle of verse 38; others had toiled and Philip
entered into their toil. (Some indeed, like Oscar Cullmann, have

suggested that the Evangelist had Philip's mission in mind at this point.)[22]

But for the woman's witness, her fellow-townsfolk would never have come to know Jesus; but they could not rely on her witness alone: they must know him for themselves. Second-hand acquaintance with Christ or hearsay belief in him cannot be a substitute for personal knowledge and saving faith. Now they were able to prove for themselves that all she said about him was true. He was not only the prophet like Moses, but also the Saviour of the world. This title appears twice in the Johannine writing (the other instance being 1 John 4:14); it is in line with the statement of John 3:17, that God sent his Son into the world 'in order that the world might be saved through him'. The use of the title in this context suggests that the Samaritan mission represents the first outreaching of Jesus' grace beyond the confines of Judaism.[23] The same pattern is repeated in the apostolic history, in conformity with Jesus' own direction: 'you shall be my witnesses in Jerusalem and in all Judaea and Samaria and to the end of the earth' (Acts 1:8).

III. Healing of the Nobleman's Son (4:43–54)

4:43, 44 After the two days, Jesus set out from there for Galilee. For Jesus himself bore witness that a prophet has no honour in his own home.

Thus Jesus completed his journey from Judaea to Galilee mentioned in verse 3. The two days are those which, according to verse 40, he spent with the Samaritans at Sychar. The proverb of verse 44, 'a prophet has no honour in his own home', provides a further comment on his departure from Judaea (verses 1–3).[24] All three Synoptists also record him as quoting this proverb (Matt. 13:57; Mark 6:4; Luke 4:24), but with reference to his home town of Nazareth, where 'he marvelled because of their unbelief' (Mark 6:6). Here, however, his 'home' (Gk. *patris*, as in the other three Gospels) is not Nazareth or Galilee, but Judaea – not so much because of his birth at Bethlehem (cf. John 7:42), as because Judaea, and more particularly Jerusalem, constituted 'his own place' (Gk. *ta idia*), the headquarters of 'his own people' (*hoi idioi*), who 'did not receive him' (John 1:11). It is to the religious leaders of Jerusalem that Jesus says in John 5:43, 'I have come in my Father's name, and you do not receive me'; it is of people in that city that the Evangelist later says that though Jesus 'had performed so many signs in their presence, they would not believe in him' (John 12:37).

4:45 So, when he came into Galilee, the Galilaeans received

him, having seen all that he did in Jerusalem at the festival – for
they themselves had also gone to the festival.

If Jerusalem reject him, however, Galilee welcomed him. His
fame had reached the northern territory before he himself did,
carried by Galilaeans who had been in Jerusalem for the passover
of John 2:13 ff., and had seen 'the signs which he did' (John 2:23).
It was not until a year later that his Galilaean following began to
dwindle (John 6:66).

**4:46, 47 So he came back to Cana of Galilee, where he had
made the water wine. Now there was a certain nobleman, whose
son was sick at Capernaum. When he heard that Jesus had come
into Galilee from Judaea, he went to him and begged him to
come down and heal his son, for he was at death's door.**

The Evangelist emphasizes that the place where Jesus first manifested his glory on what was in any case a joyful occasion (John
2:1–11) was now to witness a further manifestation of that glory
in a time of desperate need. On the former occasion old life was
transformed into new life; on this occasion life is snatched back
from the brink of death.

The Greek word translated 'nobleman' is *basilikos* ('royal'), an
adjective derived from *basileus* ('king'). Most probably we should
envisage this man as attached to the entourage of Herod Antipas,
tetrarch of Galilee (4 BC – AD 39) who was popularly called 'king'
(cf. Mark 6:14), although the Roman Emperor withheld the full
royal title from him. Some have suggested an identification with
Chuza, Herod's steward (Luke 8:3). It is less likely that the man
was attached to the service of the emperor, who was also called
'king' (*basileus*) by his Greek-speaking subjects (cf. John 19:15);
Galilee was not at this time part of the imperial province. There is
a variant reading *basiliskos* ('petty king'), attested by Codex Bezae
and some Coptic and Latin witnesses (cf. Vulgate *regulus*, whence
'ruler' in the Douai-Rheims version). There is nothing to suggest
that this man was a Gentile, as was the centurion of Matt. 8:5–13
and Luke 7:2–10, whose 'servant' (*pais*, Matthew) or 'slave' (*doulos*,
Luke) was cured on one occasion when Jesus was in Capernaum.[25]

News of Jesus' wonderful 'signs' in Jerusalem had been spread
throughout Galilee by the pilgrims returning from the recent passover. Jesus' arrival in Galilee – just in time, as it seemed – must
have been eagerly grasped by the anxious father as the last hope
for his sick son.

**4:48 So Jesus said to him, 'Unless you people see signs and
wonders, you will never believe'.**

Jesus' recent experience in Jerusalem was fresh in his mind. Many had accorded him a superficial belief there when they saw his signs without appreciating their deeper meaning (John 2:23). Was the same situation to recur in Galilee? But these words to the nobleman may well have been intended as a test of his faith. (This is the only instance in this Gospel of the word *teras*, 'wonder' or 'miracle' – a word never found in the NT except in association with *sēmeion*, 'sign'.)[26]

4:49, 50 The nobleman said to him, 'Sir, come down before my boy dies'. Jesus said to him, 'Be on your way; your son lives'. The man believed the word that Jesus spoke to him and went his way.

The nobleman was in no mood to discuss the nature of his faith; he knew what he wanted, and he was sure that Jesus was the only one who could do it. So he begged Jesus to come down to Capernaum with him at once – perhaps by chariot – before his boy (*paidion*) died. Unlike the centurion of the Synoptic record, he did not ask Jesus to speak but a word and work the cure by remote control, but this was the response he received to his entreaty; 'Your son is better already'. Life, almost extinguished in the battle with death, had suddenly gained new strength from Jesus' reviving word and won the victory.

The father was content: he was not interested in signs and wonders but in his son's life, and his ready acceptance of Jesus' assurance proved the quality of his faith. So he went on his homeward way (*eporeueto*, imperfect tense).

4:51 As he was now on his way down, his slaves came to meet him with the news that his son was alive and well.

One always goes down (*katabainō.* as in verse 47 and 2:12) to Capernaum or any other place at the lakeside; the lake lies 695 feet below (Mediterranean) sea level. The welcome news brought by the slaves (*douloi*), 'Your son lives', corroborated Jesus' words, which the nobleman had already believed.

4:52, 53 So he ascertained from them the hour at which he had taken a turn for the better. They told him, 'Yesterday, at the seventh hour, the fever left him'. The father recognized that it was at that hour that Jesus had said to him, 'Your son lives'; and he himself believed, together with his whole household.

The cure had taken place suddenly, at the seventh hour – that is, about 1 p.m. Probably the father could have got home the same day, but his confidence in Jesus' word was so strong that all anxiety left him and instead of hurrying home he completed some other convenient business. He was sure that the boy's cure took place at the moment when Jesus spoke the life-giving word; that was why he asked the slaves when he had taken the turn for the better (*kompsoteron eschen*, aorist), and their answer confirmed his conviction.

On the previous day the nobleman had believed Jesus' reassurance; now, together with his household (wife, children, slaves and other dependents), he believed in Jesus personally, acknowledging him as the sent one of God.

4:54 This again was a second sign that Jesus did when he had come out of Judaea into Galilee.

Just as Jesus' 'beginning of signs' was performed on an earlier occasion when he had newly returned to Galilee from Judaea (John 2:11), so this 'second sign' was performed immediately after his next return from Judaea. The signs performed in Jerusalem (John 2:23) do not come into the reckoning here. The Evangelist is thinking only of Galilaean signs at this point.

NOTES

1. See comment on John 3:24.
2. Cf. G. A. Smith, *Historical Geography of the Holy Land* (London, [25]1931), pp. 367-376.
3. Cf. W. F. Albright, *The Archaeology of Palestine* (Pelican Books, 1960), p. 247.
4. Babylonian Talmud, tractate *Soṭa* 49b, tractate *Mᵉnāḥôth* 64b; Jerusalem Talmud, tractate *Shᵉqālim* 5.48d.
5. Later embellishments of the conquest appear in Jubilees 34:2-9 and *Testament of Judah* 3:1-7:11. A place-name Sakir occurs in Jubilees 34:4, 7; it might be identical with Sychar, but there is no way of proving this.
6. Cf. C. Kopp, *The Holy Places of the Gospels* (Edinburgh/London, 1962), p. 156.
7. See R. J. Coggins, *Samaritans and Jews: The Origins of Samaritanism Reconsidered* (Oxford, 1975).
8. Cf. GNB: 'Jews will not use the same cups and bowls that Samaritans use.' The widespread modern acceptance of this interpretation is probably due to D. Daube, *The New Testament and Rabbinic Judaism* (London, 1956), p. 382. But it has more recently been pointed out that Augustine understood the sentence thus: 'You see that they [the Samaritans] were aliens: indeed, the Jews would not use their vessels. And as the woman brought with her a vessel with which to draw the water, it made her wonder that a Jew sought drink of her – a thing which the Jews were not accustomed to do' (*Tractate 15 on St. John*, 4.11). See T. E. Pollard 'Jesus and the Samaritan Woman', *ExpT* 92 (1980–81), pp. 147 f.
9. J. Rendel Harris, 'A Lost Verse of St. John's Gospel', *ExpT* 38 (1926–27), pp.

342 f., inferred from the Armenian version of Ephrem's commentary on the *Diatessaron* that the question, 'Where then do you get this "living water" from ?' was originally followed by the words: 'He said, "My water comes down from heaven".'

10. A. E. Cowley, 'The Samaritan Doctrine of the Messiah', *Expositor* series 5, 1 (1895), p. 163. On the Taheb ('restorer') see comment on verse 19 (p. 108).

11. Another kind of allegorization, after the manner of Philo, is ascribed to the Evangelist by W. L. Knox, *Some Hellenistic Elements in Primitive Christianity* (London, 1944), p. 64, n. 2: 'The five husbands are the five senses and the sixth man the natural soul which can never be the true "husband" of the highest element in man, which can only be the Spirit' (typified by the living water). This is quite like the interpretation of Heracleon, but what was natural for him with his gnostic presuppositions seems less natural for a twentieth-century English scholar.

12. The wording of Deut. 34:10 echoes the promise of Deut. 18:15, 18 f., a promise which in Samaritan belief was to be fulfilled by the coming of the Taheb. See John 1:21 with comment (p. 48).

13. The adjoining peak of Ebal (3074 feet, 938 metres, above sea level) is visibly higher than Gerizim (2849 feet, 868 metres, above sea level), but this makes no impact on the dogma.

14. Compare the comment on the similar wording of John 1:41 (p. 57).

15. On the Taheb see J. Macdonald, *The Theology of the Samaritans* (London, 1964), pp. 362–371. While the literary evidence for the Taheb expectation is much later than the NT, the belief that he would reveal the whereabouts of the tabernacle or its furnishings is incidentally attested by Josephus's account of an enthusiast who, in AD 36, led a large body of Samaritans to Gerizim, promising to show them the sacred vessels in the place where Moses had buried them (*Antiquities* 18.85).

16. It is noteworthy that Jesus could unambiguously disclose his identity to a Samaritan woman when he deliberately refrained from doing so to the Jewish authorities in Jerusalem; see John 10:24 and the comment on that verse (p. 230).

17. *Pirqê 'Abôth* 1.5.

18. Repeatedly in this Gospel 'he who sent me' on Jesus' lips (cf. Mark 9:47) is another way of saying 'my Father'. Sometimes both expressions are used together: 'the Father who sent me' (cf. John 6:44; 8:18; 12:49; 14:24).

19. Cf. A. Guilding, *The Fourth Gospel and Jewish Worship* (Oxford, 1960), pp. 206–211.

20. Cf. J. A. T. Robinson, 'The "Others" of John 4.38', in *Twelve New Testament Studies* (London, 1962), pp. 61–66.

21. Origen, *Commentary on Matthew* 14.6 (on Matt. 18:23).

22. O. Cullmann, 'Samaria and the Origins of the Christian Mission', in *The Early Church* (London, 1956), pp. 185–192.

23. If, in the interests of Gospel harmony, it be asked how this narrative can be squared with Jesus' forbidding his disciples to enter any city of the Samaritans (Matt. 10:5), the reason for that prohibition lies not in any feeling of contempt or hostility for the Samaritans, but rather in the fact that the period prescribed for the Mission of the Twelve was so short that they would not have time to visit even all the Jewish towns on their route.

24. Cf. R. H. Lightfoot, *Locality and Doctrine in the Gospels* (London, 1938), pp. 146 f.

25. On Capernaum see John 2:12 with comment (pp. 72 f.).

26. See comment on John 2:11 (p. 72).

CHAPTER 5

IV. Ministry in Jerusalem (5:1–47)

1. HEALING AT THE POOL OF BETHESDA (5.1–9a)

5:1 After this there was a festival of the Jews, and Jesus went up to Jerusalem.

The central chapters of the Gospel of John are chronologically related to various festivals of the Jewish year;[1] cf. John 6:4 (Passover), 7:2 (Tabernacles), 10:22 (Dedication), 11:55 (Passover again). As for the festival mentioned here, its identification is quite uncertain. There is a variant reading which has the definite article before 'festival'; 'the festival of the Jews' would probably be Tabernacles. But the weight of the evidence favours the absence of the article.

Some attractive arguments have been put forward for identifying this festival with New Year's Day (the festival of Trumpets, as it is called in Lev. 23:23–25). This was the identification preferred by B. F. Westcott. In 1908 J. Rendel Harris pointed out that the popular belief mentioned in the interpolation after verse 3 belongs to a class which in the folklore of many nations is associated with New Year.[2] A weightier argument has been developed by Dr. Aileen Guilding. She shows how the discourses of these central chapters are closely related to those passages of the Pentateuch which were prescribed for synagogue reading at the festivals which form the setting of the respective discourses, and in particular that the judgment theme of the discourse in chapter 5 is characteristic of the lessons for the season of Trumpets.[3]

5:2, 3a There is in Jerusalem at the sheep gate a pool called in Hebrew Bethesda. It has five colonnades, and in these there lay a crowd of infirm people – blind, lame, paralysed.

In this rendering the phrase 'sheep gate' corresponds to the Greek adjective *probatikē* ('pertaining to sheep'). The noun qualified by this adjective is not expressed, probably because at the time of which the Evangelist is thinking every one knew it. (Jerusalem may have been in ruins for several years when this Gospel was written, but the Evangelist envisages it as it was when he knew it, and describes its natural features in the present tense.) AV renders 'sheep market'; this is less probable than 'sheep gate', although the sheep gate would probably lead to the sheep market. NEB 'at the Sheep-

Pool represents the usage of later Christian tradition, in which the name *Probatikē* (Latin *Probatica*) tends to replace Bethesda. But it probably does not represent the Evangelist's meaning here: it involves taking *kolymbēthra* ('pool') as a dative, which leaves the verb 'is' without a subject and makes rather odd Greek. The sheep gate is mentioned three times in the book of Nehemiah (3:1, 32; 12:39), from which we gather that it was an opening in the north wall of the city, a little way west of the 'upper chamber of the corner' (the 'corner' being the north-east corner of the city wall).

The name of the pool is given variously in our principal witnesses: Bethesda, Bethzatha, Bethsaida[4] (the last of these forms is probably due to confusion with the fishing town on the Lake of Galilee, mentioned in John 1:44). That Bethesda (Heb. *bêth 'esh-dāh*, 'place of outpouring') is the true form was settled fairly conclusively in 1960, when the text of the Copper Scroll from Qumran was first published. The place is clearly named on that Scroll in the form *Beth'eshdāthain* – *'eshdāthain* being the dual number of *'eshdāh*: 'the place of the twin outpourings'.[5] But why the dual number? The pilgrim from Bordeaux who visited Jerusalem in AD 333 recorded that 'inside the city is a pair of pools with five arcades, which pools are called Betsaida'. This testimony is confirmed by the evidence of recent excavations on the site, which is close beside the Church of St Anne, in the northeast quarter of the Old City. Excavations have indeed been carried out there from time to time since Napoleon III acquired the site for France in 1856. It is now clear that there were two adjacent pools, a northern and a southern, and that the trapezoidal area which they occupied was surrounded by four covered colonnades, one on each side, with a fifth one on the ridge of living rock separating the two pools.[6] It was in the shelter of these colonnades that the crowd of variously afflicted persons waited in hope of healing.

An early expansion of the text, first appearing in the Western and Caesarean recensions, completes verse 3 with the participial phrase, 'waiting for the movement of the water', and then continues: 'For an angel (of the Lord) went down into the pool at a certain time and disturbed the water. So the person who stepped in first after the disturbing of the water was made well, whatever his disability has been' (cf. AV, verse 4).[7] While we cannot credit (or debit) the Evangelist himself with this information about the angel, it probably reproduced the popular belief about the cause of the healing properties ascribed to the water. That the water was indeed disturbed from time to time, and that it was deemed advantageous to get into the pool on these occasions, may be gathered from verse 7.

The twin pools were part of a large reservoir system, being filled from the great reservoirs called Solomon's Pools (south-west of Bethlehem). Fragments of the stone piping through which the water was led have been found in the vicinity of Bethesda. But the reference to the periodic disturbance of the water has suggested that the pools also received water from an intermittent spring (possibly a chalybeate spring, to judge from ancient references to the redness of the water).[8]

5:5 There was a man there whose infirmity had lasted for thirty-eight years.

It is not said that the man had lain continuously in one of the Bethesda colonnades all this time; we should understand rather that he was brought there regularly when the 'disturbing' of the water was expected, in the hope that one day he might be able to get in first. It is not said what precisely his infirmity was; it was evidently some form of lameness or paralysis, since he was unable to go down into the water in time without help (verse 7), and there is a suggestion (verse 14) that it was the result of some sin of his own. Those interpreters who allegorize the Samaritan woman's five husbands try to allegorize the thirty-eight years of this man's disability, linking them with the thirty-eight unecessary years that the Israelites spent in the wilderness (Deut. 2:14), as though the man symbolized the nation frustrated in its endeavour to reach the promised land. This will convince whom it will. But a contrast may be seen between the precarious chance of healing in the pool and the efficacious word of Christ. In that case, the water of Bethesda, like the water in the stone pots at Cana (John 2:6), or the water of Jacob's well (John 4:13), might illustrate the rites of the Jewish religion, or even the divinely-given law, as contrasted with the salvation brought near in the gospel.

5:6, 7 When Jesus saw him lying there, and recognized that he had been like that for a long time now, he said to him, 'Do you want to be made better?' 'Sir', said the cripple, 'when the water is disturbed, I have no one to put me into the pool; while I am coming myself, someone else gets down in front of me.'

Jesus' question went home to the heart of the trouble. Did the man really want to be cured? It may seem a strange question, but it was possible that, after so many years in that condition, the man preferred not to face the challenge of a normal healthy life. If the water, in the Evangelist's mind (and this is not certain), represents the law, the point might be that while the law can show the way of life ('Do this and you will live'), it cannot impart the will to choose life, still less impart life itself.

The cripple evidently shared the current belief in the curative properties of the 'disturbed' water. His reply to Jesus' question indicates that it was lack of opportunity, not lack of will, that kept him from profiting by these properties. To call his reply 'a feeble excuse', as C. H. Dodd does,[9] goes beyond what is warranted by the evidence. At any rate, so far as the range of our influence stretches, if any one says, 'I have no one to help', let it not be because we were found wanting there.

5:8, 9a Jesus said to him, 'Get up, lift your pallet and walk.' The man was made better on the spot; he lifted his pallet and walked.

The healing of this man plays a part in John's narrative comparable to that played in the Synoptic narrative by the healing of the paralytic of Capernaum (Mark 2:1–12 and parallels), The healing words of Jesus to both were the same. But the man at Bethesda did not receive the assurance that his sins were forgiven (see verse 14); the scandal caused by the Bethesda incident had another basis (see verse 9b).

The bed, as it is called in the older English versions, was a mat or pallet of straw, easily rolled up and carried on the shoulder (Gk. *krabattos*, as also in Mark 2:9, 11, 12). In verses 8 and 9 the verb 'walk' is *peripateō*, literally 'walk about' (as also in Mark 2:9; Acts 3:6). The sequence of the verbs is significant; of course the man had to be 'made better' before he could lift his pallet and walk. What made him better, then? Nothing but the enabling command of Christ, to which his will responded obediently. Thus he received power to do what a moment earlier had been quite beyond his capacity.

2. THE FATHER AND THE SON (5:9b–29)

5:9b, 10 Now on that day it was the sabbath. So the Jews said to the man who had been cured, 'It is the sabbath; you are not allowed to lift your pallet.'

In John's record of Jesus' Jerusalem ministry, as in the Synoptic record of his Galilaean ministry, it is his infringement of the traditional interpretation of the sabbath law that first brings him into serious conflict with the religious authorities. (Cf. Mark 2:23–3:6, where it is his sovereign attitude to the sabbath, and not the disputes of Mark 2:1–22, that aroused the deadly hostility of his opponents.)

The 'tradition of the elders' distinguished thirty-nine categories of work which might not be undertaken on the sabbath; the thirty-ninth of these was the carrying of a load from one dwelling to another. By this standard the man's action in carrying his pallet home was a violation of the sabbath law.[10]

Here, as regularly in the Gospel of John, it is important to mark who exactly 'the Jews' in question are: in this context they are members of the religious establishment in Jerusalem.

5:11–13 He replied, 'The man that made me well, it was he that told me to lift my pallet and walk.' They asked him 'Who is the man who told you to lift it and walk?' But the man who had been healed did not know who it was, for Jesus had taken advantage of the crowd that was there to slip away.

The man defended himself against the charge of sabbath-breaking by the plea that he was acting by another's command. The lifting of his pallet, in fact, was one of the conditions for his cure. But in his reply there may be the implication that one who was able to work such a cure must be possessed of peculiar authority, and that to obey such a person's command seemed a clear duty. Similarly, in the Synoptic account of the healing of the paralytic of Capernaum, the power given to the paralytic to get up from his pallet, shoulder it and go home is the outward and visible sign to the bystanders of the Son of Man's authority on earth to forgive sins (Mark 2:10–12). In Jesus' eyes, the sabbath was given to be a blessing and not a burden to human beings, and it was most worthily kept when the purpose for which God gave it was most actively promoted. He therefore regarded acts of healing and relief not as permitted exceptions to the prohibition of work on the sabbath, but as deeds which should be done by preference on that day, because they so signally fulfilled the divine purpose in its institution.

The man's defence did not indeed exonerate him in the eyes of the custodians of the law, but at least it suggested that the primary responsibility for his action lay with the person who had told him to perform it. Evidently he did not know so much as his benefactor's name (unlike the blind man in John 9:11). Jesus, in keeping with his common policy, shunned publicity for acts of this kind, and the presence of the crowd around the pool of Bethesda made it easy for him to disappear as soon as the cure was accomplished.

5:14–16 After this Jesus found him in the temple and said to him, 'See, you have been made well. Do not sin any more, in

case something worse happens to you.' The man went off and told the Jews that it was Jesus who had made him well. And therefore the Jews began to persecute Jesus because he did this on the sabbath.

A little later, Jesus recognized the man in the temple precincts, just south of the place where the healing had taken place. He gave him a word of advice, in terms which may suggest that in this case the man's disability had resulted from his own sin. He should take warning and not repeat the sin (or continue in it), for fear of suffering something worse. The 'something worse' might well be eternal death. Jesus was far from thinking that sickness and suffering were necessarily the result of one's sin; his reaction to the disciples' speculation about the blind man in John 9:2 f. provides evidence enough of that. But in the case of this man, he knew what the cause of his infirmity was, and let him know that he knew.

Now that the man had ascertained his benefactor's identity, he was able to tell the authorities ('the Jews') what he could not tell them when first they asked – it was Jesus who had cured him. Some commentators have denounced his action as ungrateful; others have thought his intention was to give credit where credit was due (as the blind man did in John 9:11). Our Evangelist throws no light on this question; he is not concerned with the man's state of mind but with the controversy to which his information gave rise.

The man might have acted in ignorance of the technicalities of the law, but Jesus, as the authorities very well knew, had acted with full appreciation of the issues involved when he bade him carry his pallet on the sabbath. Inciting others to break the law (as they understood it) was worse than breaking it oneself. Therefore they launched a campaign against Jesus which was not relaxed until his death some eighteen months later.[11]

5:17, 18 But Jesus answered them, 'My Father has been working until now, and I am working too.' Therefore the Jews sought all the more to put him to death, because he not only broke the sabbath but also called God his own Father, making himself equal to God.

When Jesus' attitude to the sabbath was challenged in Galilee, he appealed to the purpose for which the day was given: 'The sabbath was made for man, not man for the sabbath; so the Son of Man is lord even of the sabbath' (Mark 2:27 f.).[12] Here, in Jerusalem, he invokes another principle, one which exercised the minds of many rabbis. Did God keep his own laws? In particular, did he

keep the sabbath law? But how could he, since plainly his provi-
dential care over his creation was unceasing? One story tells how,
around the time when this Gospel was written, four eminent rabbis
visited Rome and were challenged on this very point. By an ingen-
ious argument they maintained that God carried no load outside
the limits of his own dwelling (heaven and earth), and lifted nothing
to a height which exceeded his own stature. Therefore all that he
did fell within their interpretation of what was admissible on the
sabbath.[13] Other authorities dealt with the problem without having
recourse to such dialectical subtleties. But on one point they were
all agreed: God was active all the time, on sabbath days as much
as on ordinary days.

But Jesus' reply presupposes a view of the matter which finds
expression also in Heb. 4:3–10 (and also here and there in the
writings of Philo of Alexandria)[14] namely, that God's seventh-day
rest (or *sabbatismos*), which began when creation's work was finished, has never come to an end; it is still in being. The point made
by the writer to the Hebrews is that this rest of God is still available
for his people to enter and enjoy. The point made by Jesus is
different: 'You charge me with breaking the sabbath by working
on it', he implies; 'but although my Father's sabbath rest began
when he had completed his work of creation, and is still going on,
he continues to work – and therefore so do I.' He justifies his
action on the ground that he is but following his Father's example.

Had he said, 'God works on the sabbath day, and therefore I
am free to do so too', his words would have given offence enough
to his hearers. But the manner of his reference to God as 'my
Father' was more offensive still: it suggested rather pointedly that
he was putting himself on a level with God. In their synagogue
services of prayer and thanksgiving the Jews were accustomed to
address God as 'our Father'; but Jesus appeared to be claiming
God as 'his own Father' in an exceptional, if not exclusive, sense.

To Greeks there would be nothing extraordinary in such a claim:
they habitually thought of certain outstanding men as godlike
(*theioi anthrōpoi* or *theioi andres*) in the sense that they were
endowed with an unusually generous share of the divine nature.[15]
But for Jews the line of demarcation between the divine and the
human was strictly drawn; it was unthinkable that any one should
be comparable to God (Isa. 40:25).[16] It was the fatal desire to be
like God that had driven Adam from paradise and precipitated the
son of the morning from heaven.[17] Yet here was a man whose
words and actions implied a trespass across the inviolable boundary
that separated God from mankind. That such a man should be alive
and at large constituted a danger to the community which tolerated
him. But the law of blasphemy was so strictly framed that it would

be difficult to prove in court that Jesus' words constituted blasphemy within the terms of its definition.[18] Only if, in further debate, he went on to use language which did amount to technical blasphemy could he be convicted on a capital charge.

5:19 So Jesus said to them in reply, 'Indeed and in truth I tell you: the Son can do nothing on his own initiative; he can do only what he sees the Father doing. Whatever things he does, these are the things that the Son does likewise.'

The controversy which arose out of the healing of the cripple on the sabbath now opens out into an extended monologue in which Jesus expands the meaning of his words in verse 17, and shows in what sense he claims to be equal with God. There is no thought of any independent action on his part: his claims do not contravene the Jewish refusal to countenance a 'second principle' alongside God. Philo might speak of the *logos* as a 'second God' (*deuteros theos*);[19] but such language, taken at its face value, infringes the sovereignty of the one true God. No such language is used in this Gospel. Jesus is the Son in a unique sense, to be sure, but as the Son he maintains an attitude of perfect submission to the Father. It is for the Father to initiate; it is for the Son to obey. It is for the Father to show the Son what to do; it is for the Son to follow the Father's example. C. H. Dodd discerned an 'embedded parable' in verses 19 and 20: Jesus draws an analogy from his own boyhood experience in the carpenter's workshop, when he learned to imitate the things he saw Joseph doing, thus serving his apprenticeship against the day when he in his turn would be the carpenter of Nazareth.[20] The activity which originates with the Father, then, is manifested in the Son. In the following verses two forms of this activity are particularly dwelt upon – the impartation of life and the execution of judgment.

5:20 'For the Father loves the Son and shows him everything that he himself does, and he will show him greater works than these, to give you cause for marvel.'

That 'the Father loves the Son' has been affirmed already in this Gospel (John 3:35); it is immaterial that the verb here is *phileō* whereas in the earlier occurrence it is *agapaō*. The unity between the Father and the Son is a unity of perfect love, in which, it might be said, the Father is 'Thou' to the Son's 'I'.[21] If the Father's love for the Son is stressed here, the Son's reciprocal love for the Father is unfolded in John 14:31, where it is this obedient love that leads the Son from the upper room to the garden, and thence to the cross. The Son sees what the Father shows him, and by his consequent word and action reveals the Father's mind, into which he enjoys such uninhibited insight.

Jesus' opponents had been scandalized because of a comparatively minor work that he had performed – the healing of a cripple. He justified this action – sabbath day as it was – by an appeal to the example of God: if the Father worked on the sabbath, so must the Son. And now that his defence has scandalized them more than his original action had done, he goes on to assure them that, because he is the Son, he has the authority to perform much greater works than that one, as he perceives the Father's will and gives effect to it. If what he has done already has taken them by surprise, what they have yet to see will give them real cause for wonder.

5:21 'For as the Father raises the dead and gives them life, so the Son also gives life to whom he will.'

In Jewish belief God, and none but he, was the raiser of the dead; this was one of his chief prerogatives and one of the greatest tokens of his power. In the great synagogue prayer called the *'Amidah* or 'Eighteen Benedictions', which may go back to pre-Christian times, the second benediction addresses God as follows:

> Thou, O Lord, art mighty for ever; thou quickenest the dead; thou art mighty to save. Thou sustainest the living with loving-kindness, thou quickenest the dead in great mercy, thou supportest the fallen, healest the sick, loosest those who are bound, and keepest faith with those who sleep in the dust. Who is like thee, O Lord of mighty acts? Who is comparable to thee, O King, who bringest to death and quickenest again, and causest salvation to spring forth? Yea, thou art faithful to quicken the dead. Blessed art thou, O Lord, who quickenest the dead![22]

It is against this kind of background that Jesus' claim is to be evaluated. He does not claim simply to be an instrument in God's hand for restoring the dead to life, as Elijah and Elisha were; he asserts that authority has been given him to raise the dead not merely to a resumption of this mortal life but to the life of the age to come. It is not only that eternal life is granted to those who believe in him (cf. John 3:15, 16, 36); it is that he exercises the divine prerogative of imparting this life. How he does so will appear anon. But first he claims a parallel authority to that of giving life to whom he will.

5:22, 23 'Neither does the Father judge any one, but he has committed all judgment to the Son, in order that all may honour

the Son as they honour the Father. One who fails to honour the Son fails to honour the Father who sent him.'

From ancient days God had been acknowledged as 'the Judge of all the earth' (Gen. 18:25). His judgment was constantly being exercised in the lives of men and nations; but at the end of time, it was believed, he would consummate his work of judgment in one last assize. Then, in fact, he would combine his twin prerogatives as raiser of the dead and judge of all. But, as the Son has claimed authority to raise the dead, so now he claims authority to execute final judgment; indeed, he states that the Father has placed this authority within the Son's sole jurisdiction and does not exercise it himself. How this claim is to be reconciled with the statement of John 3:17, that 'God did not send his Son into the world to judge the world' (cf. John 12:47), will appear more clearly as the discourse proceeds.[23] But the Father's purpose in committing all judgment to the Son is noteworthy. It is that the Son may receive the same honour as is given to the Father.

When Paul speaks of the exaltation with which Christ's obedience to the point of death was rewarded by God, how he received 'the name which is above every name, that at the name of Jesus every knee should bow, and every tongue confess that Jesus Christ is Lord' (Phil. 2:9–11), he uses language which implies that Christ, by divine decree, receives honours which belong to the God of Israel alone. For it is the God of Israel who says, 'I am God, and there is none else; . . . to me every knee shall bow, every tongue shall swear' (Isa. 45:22 f.). But when Christ receives such honours, the glory of God is not diminished or given to 'another'; it is rather enhanced, for Christ receives these honours 'to the glory of God the Father' (Phil. 2:11). When the Son is exalted, the Father is glorified. So here the honouring of the Son is the Father's good pleasure.

An ambassador receives the honour due to the sovereign whom he represents; dishonour to the ambassador is an insult to his sovereign. The Son is the Father's envoy plenipotentiary. The Father bestows the authority and the Son exercises it; the Father sends and the Son is sent. Yet so completely one are the Father and the Son, so perfectly does the Son manifest the Father, that no one can at the same time refuse the Son's claims and pay honour to the Father. Jesus' opponents thought they could do this very thing, but they were mistaken.

5:24 'Indeed and in truth I tell you: whoever hears my word and believes the one who sent me has eternal life; such a person

does not come into judgment but has passed out of death into life.'

How does the Son impart life? By his 'word', for the word which he speaks is spoken not by his own authority but by the Father's. To pay heed to the word spoken by the Son is to give credence to the Father who commissioned him and in whose name he speaks. This 'word' is the Son's whole message to the world.

The incident of the cripple at the pool of Bethesda is a 'sign' of this truth; as he received bodily healing through the enabling word of Christ, so it is through his word that men and women receive life on the spiritual plane. The Son, we have already been told, 'gives life to whom he will' (verse 21). Now we are told who those people are to whom the Son chooses to give life; they are those who in faith receive his life-giving word. Further, they receive the assurance that they will not 'come into judgment'. As in John 3:18, the judgment here in view is the adverse judgment reserved for those who reject the Son, but 'the one who believes in him is not judged'. The believer does not need to wait for the last day to hear the judge's favourable verdict; it has been pronounced already. Nor do believers need to wait for the last day to experience the essence of resurrection; here and now they have 'passed out of death into life'. This anticipation of a favourable verdict and resurrection life sums up what in more recent times we have come to call 'realized eschatology'.

5:25 **'Indeed and in truth I tell you: an hour is coming – in fact, it is already present – when the dead will hear the voice of the Son of God; and those who hear it will live.'**

For those who put their faith in the word which Christ speaks, a veritable day of resurrection dawns. Apart from him in whom alone resides that life which is the light of men, we are dead; when he comes and speaks his life-giving word, those who hear it are raised from spiritual death. In him the invitation once given through a Hebrew prophet acquires fresh fulness of meaning: 'Incline your ear, and come to me; hear, that your soul may live' (Isa. 55:3). And should it be asked how the dead can be expected to hear, another Hebrew prophet will help us to answer the question. When Ezekiel was commanded to prophesy to the most unpromising congregation that ever a preacher faced, 'O dry bones, hear the word of the LORD' (Ezek. 37:4), it was the breath of God entering into them that enabled them to respond. It is the same Spirit who now enables the spiritually dead to hear the voice of the Son of God and enter into life.

5:26, 27 'For as the Father has life in himself, so he has granted to the Son also to have life in himself, and he has given him authority to execute judgment, because he is Son of Man.'

None but God the Father, unbegotten and uncreated, inherently possesses life-in-himself. He is in his very being 'the living God'. Human beings, in common with all other living things, do not possess life-in-themselves; their life is derived from God, the source and stay of all life. To the Son alone, begotten but not created, has the Father imparted his own prerogative to have life-in-himself. Indeed, the Son's investiture with this prerogative is a necessary condition of his exercising the other prerogatives of raising the dead and executing judgment to which he has already laid claim. Nor is the Father's bestowal of life-in-himself on the Son something which began with his ministry on earth, or with the Incarnation; it is an eternal act, part and parcel of the unique Father-Son relationship which existed already 'in the beginning'. In the eternal order the Father, as Father, imparts to the Son, as Son, that life-in-himself which it is the Father's to possess and impart; on the temporal plane the Son reveals that life to men and women. So, elsewhere in the Johannine writings, the Son is depicted as the very embodiment of that 'eternal life which was with the Father and was made manifest to us' (1 John 1:2). So dearly does the Father love the Son; so truly does the Son reflect the Father.

Hitherto in this discourse the designation 'the Son' means 'the Son of God'; this is made explicit in verse 25. But in verse 27 the authority to pass judgment is given to the Son 'because he is *Son of Man*'. Why? In Daniel's vision of the final judgment it is to 'one like a son of man' that universal and everlasting dominion is given by the Ancient of Days (Dan. 7:13 f.). It is this OT passage more than any other that lies behind Jesus' use of the designation 'the Son of Man' – although here as elsewhere he transcends and transforms the OT foreshadowing by his interpretation and fulfilment of it.[24] His pronouncing of judgment is the reverse side of his life-giving act. His presence in the world inevitably involves judgment, in the twofold sense of the Greek noun *krisis* – discrimination and condemnation. When he comes, there is a discrimination or separation between those who welcome the light and those who shun it. The former receive life; the latter are self-condemned. He does not come to condemn the world; his desire is that the world may be saved. But the *effect*, if not the *purpose*, of his coming is the judgment of those who will not receive him. Moreover, the judgment which is being determined now will be finally promulgated on a coming day, as Jesus proceeds to show.

affirmation of OT

5:28, 29 '**Do not be surprised at this; an hour is coming in which all who are in the tombs will hear his voice and come out – those who have done good, for the resurrection of life, and those who have done evil, for the resurrection of judgment.**'

The emphasis on 'realized eschatology' in the immediately preceding words of Jesus does not rule out all thought of a future eschatology. The raising of men and women from spiritual death to life in Christ during this age anticipates the bodily resurrection at the end of the age. There is a close connexion between the two resurrections. The fact that here and now the dead come to life as they hear the voice of the Son of God is the guarantee that his voice will raise the dead at the last day. This twofold aspect of resurrection is mentioned again in John 6:40, 54, where Jesus, in his Capernaum discourse on the bread of life, insists that it is those who have eternal life through faith in him who will be raised by him at the last day. It finds clearest expression in the narrative of the raising of Lazarus (e.g. in John 11:24–26).

As the present resurrection does not exclude the future one, so the future judgment is not excluded by the present one. Daniel had foreseen the day in which 'many of those who sleep in the dust of the earth shall awake, some to everlasting contempt' (Dan. 12:2). (As S. P. Tregelles and others have pointed out, Daniel may not have in mind a *resurrection* for the latter company: his view may be concentrated on the resurrection of the righteous.)[25] Now it is made plain that the 'one like a son of man' whom Daniel had seen in an earlier vision (Dan. 7:13 f.) is to be the agent of God in resurrection as well as in the exercise of mediatorial sovereignty. But when the day of final separation comes, and life or condemnation is apportioned to men, there will be nothing arbitrary about the judicial decision. That decision will simply be the ratification of a decision made in this life. 'Those who have done good' (literally, 'the good things') are those who have come to the light; 'those who have done evil' (literally, 'the evil things') are those who 'loved the darkness more than the light, for their works were evil' (John 3:19–21). The former group have eternal life already; the others are 'condemned already' (John 3:18).

3. THE SON'S CREDENTIALS (5:30–47)

5:30 '**I can do nothing on my own initiative. I judge as I hear, and my judgment is just, because it is not my own will that I seek, but the will of him who sent me.**'

We recall the affirmation in verse 20, that the Son does nothing on his own initiative; he follows the Father's example. The affirmation is here repeated with special reference to the work of judgment: the judgment pronounced by the Son is the judgment which he has first heard passed by the Father. Such judgment cannot be other than just, for it is that searching and unerring judgment carried out by the light when it shines into the darkness and shows everything up for what it really is.

To give effect to the Father's will was the Son's lifelong food and drink (cf. John 4:34; 6:38). Because this is his unchanging principle of action, he can safely leave his vindication in the Father's hands. The Father does indeed vindicate the Son and provides credentials for him which convey a direct message to unprejudiced minds.

5:31, 32 'If I bear testimony of myself, my testimony is not true. It is another who bears testimony of me, and I know that the testimony which he bears of me is true.'

A testimonial to oneself is no testimonial. No one can witness his own signature. If Jesus' claims were made without the Father's authority, there would be no obligation on his hearers to accept them. This argument was in fact brought against them by his opponents during a later visit to Jerusalem: 'You are bearing testimony of yourself; your testimony is not true' (John 8:13). But to this he could answer. 'Even if I do bear testimony of myself, my testimony is true' – because it was confirmed by the Father's testimony (John 8:14, 18). This note of testimony or witness-bearing, first introduced in John 1:7, is a dominant one in this Gospel. and forms the subject of the remainder of chapter 5.[26]

The 'other' who bears testimony of him in verse 32 is most probably the Father: the other forms of testimony mentioned in the following verses are subordinate to his. Jesus 'knows' that the Father's testimony is true just as he 'knows' that the Father's commandment is eternal life (John 12:50) – by that immediate inward awareness which belongs to the unity of mind that binds the Son and the Father together.

5:33–35 'You have sent to John, and he has borne testimony to the truth. I do not accept testimony from any human being, but I say this in order that you may be saved. John was a lamp, burning and shining, and you were pleased to enjoy his light for a time.'

When John is first introduced in this Gospel, he is said to have come to bear testimony to the true light (John 1:7). An instance of this testimony was provided by his reply to the deputation sent to him by the religious establishment in Jerusalem, recorded in John

1:19–28. To this occasion Jesus now refers, John, in his reply to the deputation, told them of the Coming One whose way he was preparing, and later he pointed to Jesus as this Coming One, and testified that he was the Son of God (John 1:29–34).

Jesus did not rely on human testimony to confirm his claims; but (although John is not the 'other' of verse 32) John's testimony might have been expected to weigh with those who recognized him as a messenger of God, and the acceptance of his testimony would have set them on the way to salvation and life.

When the Evangelist first speaks of John, he makes it plain that John 'was not the light, but came to bear testimony of the light' (John 1:8). But if John was not the light (*phōs*), he was a light-bearer, a lamp (*lychnos*) – one that burned brightly and illuminated all around. The purpose of a lamp is to show the light, and John discharged this duty right well. As he proclaimed the near approach of the Coming One and the new age, many of his hearers were attracted by his preaching and were glad to think that the long-expected day was so near, even if they trembled at the same time because of his announcement of wrath for the unrepentant. But instead of taking urgent action while John's lamp still burned, they procrastinated, and now that lamp had been removed. But here was the Light of the world himself, with greater accreditation than even John could supply.

5:36 'But I have greater testimony than John's. The works which the Father has given me to accomplish, the very works which I do, testify of me that the Father has sent me.'

One of the ways in which the Father testified to the Son was in the works which he gave the Son to do (cf. verses 19, 20). By doing these works, Jesus showed himself to be the Son of God. These works were summed up in the achievement of the world's salvation, the prime purpose of his coming into the world (cf. John 3:17). The individual works which contributed to this one comprehensive 'work' were 'signs' to those who had eyes to see that Jesus was indeed the sent one of God. The Father, by giving him these works to do, and the Son, by doing them, provided an assurance which was doubly sure.

5:37, 38 'And the Father who sent me, he has borne testimony concerning me. You have neither heard his voice at any time nor seen his form; and you have not his word remaining within you, because you do not believe the one whom he has sent.'

By commissioning Jesus to carry out the service proper to the

Messiah, God marks him out as the Messiah. But there is a further way in which God has borne testimony to him – by the heavenly voice which acclaimed Jesus as Son of God at his baptism, together with the impartation of the Spirit to him in a visible form, which convinced John the Baptist. When the Baptist refers to this experience in John 1:32–34, he refers only to the descent of the dove, not to the heavenly voice nor yet indeed to the baptism itself. The readers of the Gospel were presumably sufficiently familiar with the story of Jesus' baptism by John to be able to fill in these details for themselves.

Jesus' present hearers, however, had never received such audible or visible communication of the Father's testimony to the Son.[27] But that testimony had been communicated to them in yet another form. God had sent his word to the people of Israel 'in many and various ways' (Heb. 1:1); but had they accepted it? Those at any rate who were now being addressed showed that they had not, by their refusal to lend credence to the incarnate Word. Jesus was the fulfilment of all the revelation previously given by God through prophets and wise men; those who appreciated the import of that preparatory revelation would have recognized Jesus as the one to whom it pointed forward, as the 'Son' in whom God had spoken his perfect and final word 'in these last days' (Heb. 1:2). It was possible to have a minute knowledge of the letter of those writings which enshrined the former revelation and foreshadowed the final revelation, and yet not have the divine word which those writings recorded dwelling in their hearts.

5:39, 40 'You search the scriptures, because in them you think to have eternal life; yet they are the writings which bear testimony of me, and you refuse to come to me in order to have life.'

'Search the scriptures', the AV rendering of the first clause of verse 39, is excellent advice. But the men whom Jesus was addressing were already diligent Bible searchers. The form of the verb may be either indicative or imperative, but the indicative is more appropriate in the present context.

The verb itself (*eraunaō*) implies keen scrutiny, tracking down the message of the Scriptures. The tragedy was that these people, for all their painstaking exploration of the sacred writings, had never found the clue which would lead them to their goal. The goal at which they aimed was eternal life, but that life could be received only through him to whom the Scriptures bore witness. The Scriptures are able to make their readers wise as regards salvation, but they make it plain that this salvation comes only 'through faith in Christ Jesus' (2 Tim. 3:15). Time and again it is affirmed in rabbinic literature that the study of the holy law is the way to the life of the age to come;[28] the NT affirms that this life is found in him who 'is the end of the law, that every one who has faith may be justified' (Rom. 10:4). By refusing to come to him, the people to whom Jesus was speaking missed the life which they sought.

There is some slender evidence for a variant punctuation of verse 39: 'You search the scriptures; these writings in which you think to have life are those which bear testimony of me.'[29] The sense is not materially affected. Either way, the reference is to the OT. That the NT testifies of Christ is so obvious as not to require affirmation; but it is equally true that the OT testifies of him, and this was the justification for its retention by Christians as an integral part of Holy Writ. If the OT did not testify of Christ, it would have had little religious relevance for Christians; the fact that it does bear witness to the living Word (as he in turn bears witness to it) means that in it God speaks as truly to his people today as he did to their predecessors two and three thousand years ago.

5:41, 42 'I accept no glory from men, but I know you: you have not the love of God within you.'

The theme of witness (*martyria*) now merges into that of glory (*doxa*). The 'signs' which Jesus performed manifested his glory (2:11); in particular, the 'sign' at the pool of Bethesda manifested his glory as lifegiver and judge. Those who refused to admit such testimony deprived themselves of life and exposed themselves to judgment. Had Jesus conformed to their ideas of what the Messiah would be and do, they would readily have honoured him. But why should he seek such honour as they could give, when by doing the Father's will he could have the glory which God bestows – glory such as the only-begotten receives from the Father (John 1:14)?

'I know you' probably means not merely that he knew that the love of God was not present in their hearts; it means that he knew *them* with that penetrating insight by which 'he himself knew what was in man' (John 2:25), and was thus able to discern that they had no love for God within themselves. By 'the love of God' here is most probably meant their love for God; the genitive 'of God' in other words, is objective. Had there been any love for God in their hearts, it would have manifested itself by their acceptance of the one who came to them in the name of God. 'This is the love of God, that we keep his commandments' (1 John 5:3), and chief among his commandments is this: 'that we should believe in the name of his Son Jesus Christ (1 John 3:23).

5:43 'I have come in my Father's name and you do not accept me. If someone else comes in his own name, you will accept *him*.'

The judgment incurred by those who refused the Messiah who came with credentials was this: they would readily follow a false messiah who had no credentials but his own claim. An outstanding fulfilment of this prediction came about in AD 132, when one Simeon ben Kosebah claimed to be the Messiah of David's line, and led a revolt against Rome. His claim was supported by Akiba, the most eminent rabbi of the day, who hailed Simeon as the 'star out of Jacob' foretold by Balaam in Num. 24:17. But Simeon's messianic pretensions involved himself, his supporters and the people of Judaea in the most fearful ruin. It is not necessary to suppose that he is particularly in view here – there were several similar pretenders in the period between AD 30 and 70 (cf. Mark 13:6)[30] – but he provides the best known example.

5:44 'How can you believe, when you accept glory from one another and do not seek the glory which comes from the only God?'

The tense of the verb 'believe' is aorist (*pisteusai*, aorist infinitive); the initial act of faith may therefore be implied: 'How can you put your faith (in me)?' To admit the claims of Jesus would have won them 'the glory which comes from the only God';[31] but at the same time they would lose the esteem of their peers, which meant so much to them, as it means so much to most people. The situation is summed up later by the Evangelist in 12:43; 'they loved the glory of men more than the glory of God.' Thus they could have little sympathy with one who saw so clearly the difference between true glory and false, and desired his Father's approval above everything else.

5:45 'Do not suppose that *I* will accuse you before the Father. Your accuser is Moses, in whom you have placed your hope.'

In the divine lawcourt their unbelief incurred sure judgment, but the Son of Man would not be their prosecutor, or chief witness against them. Had he chosen to act in such a capacity, it would have fared ill with them; but he had come to save, not to judge. No: the chief witness for the prosecution would be one whose name they held in high veneration. Moses, through whom God had given them the law on which they relied (cf. Rom. 2:17), would testify against them. As Paul put it: 'all who have sinned under the law will be judged by the law' (Rom. 2:12).

5:46 'For if you believed Moses, you would believe me, for it was of me that Moses wrote.'

Among all the scriptures which they searched in the belief that they would find life there, they paid chief devotion to the Mosaic books. But these, like the other scriptures, bore witness to Christ. If their devotion to Moses and his writings was more than lip-devotion, they would accept the testimony borne by these writings to the one who was in their midst. But their repudiation of him showed that at heart they repudiated Moses and the prophets. Herein lay their condemnation. For men and women are regularly judged by the light that is available to them.

If it be asked if any particular scripture was in Jesus' mind when he said that Moses wrote of him, we may think specially of Deut. 18:15: 'the LORD your God will raise you up a prophet from among you, from your brethren – a prophet like me', a text to which there are repeated allusions to this Gospel.[32]

5:47 'But if you do not believe his writings, how will you believe my words?'

The testimonies of Moses and Jesus are so closely interrelated that to believe one is to believe the other; to refuse one is to refuse the other. Jesus by his own testimony, did not come to annul the law and the prophets, but to fulfil them (Matt. 5:17). The promise that God had given through them was fulfilled in him. The words of the Lord of the prophets are all of a piece with the words of the prophets. By rejecting Jesus' words, his opponents rejected Moses' witness, and the one whose prevailing intercession they hoped would be exercised on their behalf on the great day, as it had so repeatedly been exercised on their ancestors' behalf in the wilderness, would turn out to be their accuser instead of their advocate. We may compare Abraham's closing reply to the rich man in Luke 16:31: 'If they do not listen to Moses and the prophets, they will not be convinced even if one should rise from the dead.'

The conflict between Jesus and the religious establishment in Jerusalem, begun in this chapter with his claim to be the Son of God, continues to be waged with increasing intensity throughout the Gospel until it reaches its climax in the passion narrative: 'by our law he ought to die, because he has made himself the Son of God' (John 19:7).

NOTES

1. For the expression 'festival of the Jews' see comment on John 2:13 (p. 73).
2. J. R. Harris, *Side-lights on New Testament Research* (London, 1908), pp. 37–78).

3. A Guilding, *The Fourth Gospel and Jewish Worship*, pp. 70–91.

4. The first hand of Papyrus 66 has Bethsaida; Papyrus 75 has Bethzatha (which is also written by a corrector in Papyrus 66).

5. 3Q15, column 11, line 12. Cf. J. M. Allegro, *The Treasure of the Copper Scroll* (Garden City, N.Y., 1960), pp. 53, 165 f.; J. T. Milik, in *Discoveries in the Judaean Desert*, III (Oxford, 1962), pp. 214, 271, f., 297.

6. Cf. J. Jeremias, *The Rediscovery of Bethesda* (Louisville, Kentucky, 1966); M. Avi-Yonah, 'Excavations in Jerusalem – Review and Evaluation', in *Jerusalem Revealed*, ed. Y. Yadin (New Haven/London, 1976), pp. 21, 24; J. Wilkinson, *Jerusalem as Jesus knew it* (London, 1978), pp. 95–104. Origen (*c.* AD 231) says that there were four colonnades round the pool and another one in the middle (*Commentary on John*, Catena fragment 61, on John 5:2). Over a century later Cyril, bishop of Jerusalem (*c.* AD 348), who apparently knew the ruins of the structure, writes to the same effect, adding that it was in the middle colonnade that the sick people lay (*Homily on the Cripple at the Pool* 2).

7. See G. D. Fee, 'On the inauthenticity of John 5:3b–4', *EQ* 54 (1982), pp. 207–218.

8. Eusebius (*Onomastikon, s.v.* Bezatha/Bethsaida), who says that the pools collected rain-water, speaks of the 'remarkably red' colouring of the water; similarly the Bordeaux pilgrim says, 'The water of these pools is turbid and its colour is scarlet' (*in modum coccini*). M. Avi-Yonah ('Excavations in Jerusalem', p. 24) locates the healing in a cave east of the twin pools: 'The waters of a nearby brook were gathered in this cave and, because of their reddish colour, were held to have healing properties.' He holds that the twin pools were of Hasmonaean date (before 63 BC) and had fallen into disuse at the time we are dealing with, having been replaced by the Birket Israïl (of Herodian date). But the Copper Scroll from Qumran implies that the twin pools were in use in the period between the ministry of Jesus and the writing of the Gospel.

9. C. H. Dodd *The Interpretation of the Fourth Gospel*, p. 320.

10. Mishnah, tractate *Shabbāth* 7.2.

11. The Greek verb *ediōkon* ('persecuted') in verse 16 is in the imperfect tense, denoting continued action.

12. Cf. *Mekhilta* (rabbinical commentary) on Exod. 31:14 for the observation of the second-century Rabbi Simeon ben Menasya: 'The sabbath is delivered to you; you are not delivered to the sabbath.'

13. *Exodus Rabba* (rabbinical commentary) 30.9 (on Exod. 21:1).

14. Cf. Philo, *On the Cherubim* 26; *On the Sacrifices of Cain and Abel* 8. Philo does not use the word *sabbatismos*, whose first occurrence in Greek literature is in Heb. 4:9.

15. Philo (*Life of Moses* 2.188) and Josephus (*Against Apion* 1.279) indeed call Moses *theios*, but by *theios* they mean no more than 'divinely inspired'.

16. 'The mind is self-centred and godless when it deems itself to be equal to God' (Philo, *Allegorical Interpretation* 1.49). With the Jew Philo contrast the Greek author of the *Corpus Hermeticum* (11.20): 'Unless you make yourself equal to God, you cannot apprehend God; for like is apprehended by like.'

17. Gen. 3:5; Isa. 14:13 f.

18. Cf. Mishnah, tractate *Sanhedrin* 7.5: 'The blasphemer is not culpable unless he pronounces the Name itself' (i.e. the ineffable name spelt with the four consonants YHWH). By the time of the codification of the Mishnah (*c.* AD 200) the law was perhaps more strictly framed than it had been in the period before AD 70.

19. Philo, *Questions and Answers* (on Gen. 9:6), quoted by Eusebius, *Preparation*, 7.30.

20. C. H. Dodd *Historical Tradition in the Fourth Gospel* (Cambridge 1963), p. 386, n. 2.

21. The Jewish philosopher Martin Buber has been quoted in this connexion: 'How powerful, even to being overpowering, and how legitimate, even to being self-evident, is the saying of *I* by Jesus! For it is the *I* of unconditional relation in which the man calls his *Thou* Father in such a way that he is simply Son, and nothing else but Son. Whenever he says *I* he can only mean the *I* of the holy primary word that has been raised for him into unconditional being' (*I and Thou* [Edinburgh, 1937], pp. 66 f.).

22. S. Singer *The Authorised Daily Prayer Book* (London, 1939), pp. 44 f.

23. See verses 24, 27, with comment (pp. 131 f.); also John 8:15 f. (p. 189).

24. See comment and note on John 1:51; 12:34 (pp. 62, 67, 268 f., 277).

25. Tregelles took the words to mean: 'these (who awake) are for everlasting life, and those (who do not then awake) are for shame and everlasting contempt' (*Remarks on the Prophetic Visions in the Book of Daniel* [London, 1883], pp. 165–170); similarly B. J. Alfrink, 'L'idée de Résurrection d'après Dan. XII, 1.2', in *Studia Biblica et Orientalia*, I = *Analecta Biblica* 10 (Rome 1959), pp. 221–237.

26. Cf. J. M. Boice, *Witness and Revelation in the Gospel of John* (Grand Rapids, 1970); A. A. Trites, *The New Testament Concept of Witness* (Cambridge, 1977), especially pp. 78–127.

27. What of the many OT incidents in which God was seen or heard (e.g. Gen. 32:30)? John implies that what was seen or heard was his *logos* ('word') or his *doxa* ('glory'); cf. John 12:41, with its reference to Isa. 6:1.

28. Cf. the aphorisms of Hillel: 'The more study of the law the more life; . . . if one has gained for himself words of the law he has gained for himself life in the age to come' (*Pirqê 'Abôth* 2.7).

29. This reading is attested by a few Old Latin and Old Syriac witnesses and by Payrus Egerton 2.

30. For the appearance of a succession of such charlatans in AD 44 and the following years see Josephus, *Antiquities* 20.97–99, 177–172; *Jewish War* 2.258–265, with comments by P. W. Barnett, 'The Jewish Sign Prophets – AD 40–70: Their Intentions and Origin', *NTS* 27 (1980–81), pp. 679–697.

31. The AV rendering 'the honour that cometh from God only' is a mistranslation; it is not based on a different Greek text. There is, however, a textual variant in the verse; some ancient witnesses omit 'God'; thus yielding the meaning, 'the glory which comes from the Only One'.

32. Cf. John 1:21; 4:19; 6:14; 7:40, 52 with comments (pp. 48, 108, 145 f., 183, 186).

CHAPTER 6

V. Ministry in Galilee (6:1–71)

1. THE FEEDING OF THE MULTITUDE (6:1–21)

6:1, 2 After this Jesus went away across the sea of Galilee – that is, the sea of Tiberias. A large crowd followed him, because they saw the signs that he was performing on those who were sick.

'After this' – the same formula of transition as is used at the beginning of chapters 5 and 7 – most naturally refers back to the healing at the pool of Bethesda and its sequel. It has been argued, indeed, that chapter 5 originally came between chapters 6 and 7. If this were so, then 'after this' would refer back to the healing of the nobleman's son (4:46–54): Jesus was at that time on the west of the lake and could easily cross to the eastern side, as he is here said to have done.[1] The 'sea of Galilee', called Kinnereth in the OT (Num. 34:11, etc.) because of its shape (the word means 'lyre'), came to be known as Lake Tiberias from the city which Herod Antipas founded on its west shore about AD 20 and named in honour of the Emperor Tiberius. The lake had probably not acquired this new name at the time of Jesus' ministry, but it was generally so known by the time this Gospel was written (cf. John 21:1).

The crowd that followed Jesus, to judge by their attitude as the narrative develops, apparently belonged to the class described in a Jerusalem setting in John 2:23: they were impressed by the signs which they saw, but they yielded Jesus an adherence which was only superficial because they did not appreciate the inward import of the signs.

6:3, 4 So Jesus went up on the high ground, and sat there with his disciples. (Now the Jews' festival of Passover was at hand.)

The 'high ground' is the sharply rising terrain east of the lake, well known today as the Golan heights. From there one overlooks the level plain east of the river and the lake. In such a spot Jesus repeatedly sought solitude and rest with or without his disciples (cf. Mark 3:13; 6:46; 9:2).

A parenthical note indicates that this was just before Passover. Three Passovers are mentioned in this Gospel; for the first (John

2:13) and the third (John 11:55 ff.) Jesus went up to Jerusalem, but for this one he remained in Galilee. John's purpose in mentioning the Passover may be not only to fix the time of year at which the following incident took place; he probably thought the Passover season particularly appropriate both for the incident and for the discourse which arose out of it.

6:5, 6 Jesus looked up and saw that a large crowd was coming to him, so he said to Philip, 'Where shall we buy bread so that these people may eat?' (He said this by way of testing him; he himself knew what he was going to do.)

This is the one 'sign' from the period before the passion which is common to this Gospel and the Synoptic record (not surprisingly, since this is the only chapter in this Gospel which touches on the phase of Jesus' Galilaean ministry covered by the Synoptic record). There are points in this narrative, then, at which the Synoptic evidence can be adduced to explain the Johannine account, and *vice versa*. For example, John does not say, as Mark does (Mark 6:34 f.), that the crowd had been listening to Jesus' teaching all day, but this explains his concern about feeding them.

There are several places in the Gospel of John where individual disciples are named, as against the general reference to 'his disciples' in parallel accounts in the other Gospels. Here John is the only Evangelist who particularizes the rôles of Philip and Andrew in the discussion about ways and means of feeding the crowd. Since Philip came from the neighbouring town of Bethsaida (cf. John 1:44), it was natural that he should be consulted about places where food might be bought. But lest any reader should imagine that Jesus himself did not know where bread might be bought or how it could be supplied, the Evangelist adds a parenthetical comment to the effect that he put the question to Philip to see what he would say, since he already had a plan of his own.

6:7–9 Philip replied, 'Two hundred denarii worth of bread would not be sufficient for them, for each to have a little bit.' One of his disciples, Andrew, brother of Simon Peter, said to him, 'There is a boy here who has five barley cakes and two small fish, but what are these among so many?'

Philip did some quick mental arithmetic. Since a denarius was acceptable as a day's wage for a casual labourer (Matt. 20:2), it would presumably buy a day's supply of bread for an average family. But Philip reckoned that even if 200 *denarii* could be raised, that sum would not go nearly far enough to meet the present need.

(The figure of 200 *denarii* is mentioned also in Mark 6:37, but there it is 'the disciples' who mention it, not Philip in particular.) It is hardly worth while nowadays to try to translate *denarius*. In 1611 'penny' was good enough, but in these inflationary days this year's modern equivalent will be out of date next year. 'Eight months' wages' is the NIV rendering for 200 *denarii* here.

The particularization of the disciples who took part in the discussion, together with other incidental details, may bespeak the recollection of an eyewitness. Andrew draws attention to one individual's provisions which had come under his eye. John is the only Evangelist to mention that the five barley cakes and the two fish belonged to a boy in the company; he had presumably brought them for his day's lunch. The flat barley cakes had been baked on a gridiron or on hot stones. While the other Evangelists use the ordinary word for fish (*ichthys*), John calls them *opsaria*,[2] indicating that they were two small (perhaps salted) fish to be eaten as a relish along with the cakes of barley. In view of the size of the crowd, this tiny meal was scarcely worth mentioning: Andrew drew attention to it simply to underline its ludicrous inadequacy for so many hungry people. But it was enough for the Lord's purpose.

6:10, 11 **Jesus said, 'Make the people sit down.' (There was much grass in the place.) So the men sat down, about five thousand in number. Then Jesus took the cakes, gave thanks and distributed them to the people who were sitting down, and similarly as much of the fish as they desired.**

The 'grass' is another eyewitness reminiscence; Mark 6:39 notes that they sat down on the *green* grass. The plain here (the Butaiha) is very fertile, and in March or April the grass would not yet be burnt brown by the heat of high summer.

Two different words for 'men' are used here: Jesus said, 'Make the people (*anthrōpoi*) sit down', but John adds that 'the men (*andres*) sat down.' The former word includes women and children; the latter denotes men only, and appears in all four Gospels – Matthew indeed emphasizes the point by adding the words, 'apart from women and children' (Matt. 14:21). These 5,000 men would have constituted a ready-made guerrilla force to any one willing to become their leader, and verse 15 suggests that a leader is just what they were looking for.

Mark adds that, in accordance with Jesus' directions to the disciples, the crowd was arranged in groups of fifty and a hundred. He who 'knew what he was going to do' had no need to panic when confronted by this huge catering problem: he proceeded about his work with perfect orderliness.

The verb rendered 'gave thanks' in verse 11 is *eucharisteō*, from which we derive the term Eucharist ('thanksgiving'), commonly used of the Holy Communion. But this in itself would not require a eucharistic significance for the feeding; the verb is perfectly common and untechnical in Greek. If Jesus used the regular form of thanksgiving on such an occasion, he would have said, 'Blessed art thou, O Lord our God, King of the universe, who bringest forth bread from the earth.' According to the Synoptic record, he gave the bread to the disciples, who in turn distributed it among the crowd. Philip had tried to calculate how much would have to be spent for each person to have 'a little bit'; but in the event they were able to eat as much as they desired. When the Lord gives, he gives with no niggardly hand. As in the other Gospels, the multiplication of the bread and fish is implied rather than asserted.

6:12, 13 When they were satisfied, he said to his disciples, 'Gather the bits that have been left over; let nothing be wasted.' So they gathered them, and filled twelve baskets full of bits from the five barley cakes left over by those who had eaten.

When the Lord supplies his people's needs, there is abundance but no waste. His directions to the disciples convey an important practical lesson. To waste food which we do not need, when so many live at starvation level, is an insult to the divine giver. When this practical lesson has been digested, there may be a further spiritual lesson. However plentifully the Lord bestows his grace, he has always enough and to spare for others; he is never impoverished by the generosity of his giving. So too his people, when they imitate his liberality, will prove the truth of the proverb: 'One man gives freely, yet grows all the richer' (Prov. 11:24).

After all the crowd had been satisfied, more was gathered up than had been available before the meal began. Some have seen in the *twelve* baskets a significant coincidence with the number of the apostles; perhaps there is a hint that the Lord not only supplied the need of these 'lost sheep of the house of Israel' but had enough left over to supply the need of all twelve tribes.[3]

6:14 So, when the people saw the sign which he had performed, they said, 'This is indeed the prophet that is coming into the world!'

The people who had been fed with bread and fish thought they had factual evidence that the prophet like Moses (foretold in Deut. 18:15–19) was present among them.[4] As their forefathers had been fed miraculously in the wilderness in the days of the first Moses, so the one who had now fed them miraculously in another wilderness must be the second Moses, the great prophet of the end-time whose advent so many in Israel were expecting. A rabbi of a later date is credited with the observation that 'as the first redeemer caused manna to descend, . . . so will the last redeemer cause manner to descend',[5] and the general idea seems to have been current in the first century. The Evangelist does not suggest that the people were wrong in identifying Jesus as the coming prophet; he does suggest that they were wrong in interpreting his significance on a material and external plane. When the true interpretation of his significance was made plain to them, most of them took offence.

6:15 When Jesus then knew that they were going to come and take him by force, to make him king, he withdrew again on to the high ground, alone by himself.

If this was the second Moses, he would surely do for them what the first Moses had done for their ancestors and deliver them from oppression. This time no long journey was necessary to bring them to the promised land: the promised land now was national independence right where they were. If the Galilaeans did not live directly under Roman control, as their brethren in Judaea did, their ruler Herod Antipas was a creature of Rome, and they experienced no feelings of patriotic pride as they contemplated the Herodian dynasty. The Herods stood or fell with the Romans: to oppose the one was to oppose the other. It may well have been in the hope that Jesus would lead the cause of liberation that the crowd came to him on this occasion (verse 5): his feeding them there in the wilderness confirmed their assurance that he was indeed the man of the hour.

Their attempt to make him king does not necessarily mean that they recognized him as the Messiah of David's line. Elsewhere in this Gospel it appears that the Messiah and the prophet were distinguished in public expectation (John 1:19-25; 7:40-42); they were certainly distinguished in the thinking of the Qumran community.[6] We should not, indeed, assume that the rank and file of the people kept the various aspects of the eschatological hope neatly separated in their minds, any more than their modern successors do. Jesus had already shown his power to banish disease; now he had shown his power to banish hunger. If only he would show his power to secure his people's liberation, nothing could stand in his way. Here, surely, was the leader for whom they had been waiting; with him as their captain and king, victory and freedom were as good as won! If he would not take the initiative and present himself to them as their leader, they would compel him to do so. But Jesus recognized in their action a recurrence of one of his wilderness temptations. He knew that this was not the way in which he was to fulfil the Father's will and win deliverance for his people. So he avoided the crowd's unwelcome attention by withdrawing to the Golan heights – not this time with the disciples (whom he sent back across the lake) but in solitude.

John provides no wider political context for this incident; the situation had changed out of recognition by the time he wrote his Gospel, and he had quite another purpose before him in relating the feeding and its sequel. But it is illuminating to read John's account in the light of the Galilaean context which Mark supplies. According to Mark, the twelve had just returned from a mission in Galilee which had quite spectacular results, but which excited the hostile interest of Herod Antipas. Herod had recently got rid of John the Baptist, but now it seemed that he had on his hands a greater menace than John. Jesus therefore took the twelve to the east side of the lake, out of Herod's territory, so that they might have a time of quiet after the recent excitement. But such excitement had been caused among the Galilaeans by their mission that they followed them, and even overtook them, so that when Jesus and the twelve reached their place of retreat, they found that a great crowd of Galilaeans had got there ahead of them. Jesus fed their minds with words of life and their bodies with loaves and fishes because in his eyes they were 'like sheep without a shepherd' (Mark 6:34) – words which, as T. W. Manson used to emphasize, did not mean a congregation without a pastor, but an army without a captain (as in 1 Kings 22:17).[7] He knew how easily they might find the wrong kind of captain (one after their own heart though he might be), and be led by him to disaster. Against the background which Mark supplies, John's statement that the crowd tried to force Jesus to be their king is readily intelligible.

6:16–18 When it was evening, his disciples went down to the sea, got into their boat and were on their way across the sea to Capernaum. It had now grown dark, and Jesus had not yet come to them. The sea, moreover, was being stirred up because a strong wind was blowing.

According to Mark 6:45, Jesus 'compelled' (*anankazō*) his disciples to embark and go back across the lake; perhaps he saw that they were being infected with the crowd's excitement. Mark adds (6:46) that Jesus himself had gone up to the high ground to pray; what John has just told us shows how urgent an occasion for prayer it was.

The disciples, then, crossing to the west side of the lake by

themselves, had to make headway against a wind that was not only
strong but contrary (cf. Mark 6:48). 'The atmosphere, for the most
part, hangs still and heavy, but the cold currents, as they pass from
the west, are sucked down in vortices of air, or by the narrow
gorges that break upon the Lake. Then arise those sudden storms
for which the region is notorious.'[8]

6:19–21 **So, when they had rowed about twenty-five or thirty
furlongs they saw Jesus walking on the sea and drawing near
the boat, and they were seized with fear. But he said to them,
'It is I; stop being afraid.' So they willingly took him into the
boat, and in no time the boat reached the land for which they
were making.**

A 'furlong' (Gk. *stadion*) was rather less than our modern furlong; they had rowed about three miles. From the neighbourhood
of Bethsaida across the lake to Capernaum would be about five
miles. Some commentators suggest that John means that they had
been hugging the shore all the time, and that they caught sight of
Jesus walking *by* the sea. To be sure, the phrase *epi tēs thalassēs*
does bear this meaning where the context requires it (as in John
21:1), but the same phrase is used in the Synoptic account of the
present incident (Matt. 14:26; Mark 6:48 f.), where it certainly
means '*on* the sea'. Matt 14:25 uses the phrase *epi tēn thalassan*
('on the sea') in the same sense, and both Matthew (14:24) and
Mark (6:47) say that the boat was 'in the midst of the sea'. True,
the wording of the Synoptists cannot determine the exegesis of
John, but it is not John's practice to tone down the miraculous
element in the gospel narrative. Moreover, there would have been
no cause for fear if the disciples had seen Jesus walking *by* the sea;
it was the sight of him walking *on* the sea that made them cry out,
thinking (as we are told in Mark 6:49), that it was an apparition.

Jesus' reassuring words quieted their fears. The present imperative (*mē phobeisthe*) means 'Don't go on being afraid', i.e. 'Stop
being afraid'. Since he was there, there was nothing to worry about.
There are places in this Gospel where the words *egō eimi* have the
nature of a divine designation (as we shall see on 8:24, 28), but here
they simply mean 'It is I'. (How else would one say 'It is I' in
Hellenistic Greek than with the words *egō eimi*? The man cured
of blindness uses the same words of himself in John 9:9).

As soon, then, as they realized that it was really their Master
that they were seeing, and no apparition, the disciples gladly took
him on board with them. There was no more trouble. Mark (6:48,
51) fills in the details by telling us that it was 'about the fourth
watch of the night' – i.e., not long before dawn – that he came to

them, and that the wind fell as soon as he entered the boat. Probably dawn was breaking as they came safely ashore at Capernaum.

2. THE BREAD OF LIFE (6:22–71)

6:22–24 **The crowd that was standing on the other side of the sea had seen that there was no boat there but one, and that Jesus had not gone into the boat with his disciples but his disciples had set off (in it) alone. Other boats had (meanwhile) come from Tiberias to the neighbourhood of the place where they had eaten the bread after the Lord gave thanks. So then, next day, when the crowd saw that Jesus was not there, nor yet his disciples, they themselves embarked in those (other) boats and came to Capernaum looking for Jesus.**

The sense of these three verses is reasonably plain, though the construction is complicated. The complication is due mainly to the interposition of the sentence about the 'other' boats (verse 23), which is a parenthesis. The crowd, we are told, saw that the disciples had set off in their boat without Jesus, and there was no other boat which could have taken him across; yet in the morning he was not there. If verse 24 had followed immediately on verse 22, the reader would naturally have asked, 'How did the crowd get across by boat, since there were no boats there but that in which the disciples had embarked?' The answer is provided by verse 23: other boats had come across from Tiberias to the east side of the lake – perhaps the strong gale from the west (see verse 18) had blown them across during the night. The phrase 'next day' (Gk. *tē epaurion*) at the beginning of verse 22 relates to the action of verse 24. The parenthesis in verse 23 is in very much the same style as that of John 4:2.

The crowd, then, made sure that Jesus was nowhere in the vicinity, and that there was no sign of the disciples returning to fetch him, so they crossed to the west side to look for him.

6:25, 26 **When they found him on the other side of the sea, they said to him, 'Rabbi, when did you get here?' Jesus said to them in reply, 'Indeed and in truth I tell you: you are looking for me not because you saw signs but because you ate of the (barley) cakes and were filled.'**

When the people landed at Capernaum, they found Jesus there, and naturally wondered how and when he had got across since they knew he had not embarked in the disciples' boat.

Jesus gives them no direct answer to gratify their curiosity, but tells them that their motive in seeking him out is an unworthy one. They were attracted to him because he had fed them, and they imagined that they had found in him the leader for whom they were looking. But they had missed the real significance of the feeding. When in verse 14 they are said to have seen 'the sign which he had performed', we are to understand that they saw the external action. But here it is implied that they failed to see what lay beneath the external action: the 'signs' now denote the things signified. According to the Synoptic narrative, even the twelve 'did not understand about the loaves, but their hearts were hardened' (Mark 6:52; cf. Mark 8:14–21), so it was not surprising that the crowd failed to grasp the message. But while the Synoptic narrative simply leaves us with the feeling that beneath the surface of the miraculous feeding there was more than met the eye, John proceeds to bring that hidden meaning to light, by recording Jesus' discourse about the bread of life, delivered in the synagogue at Capernaum (cf. verse 59).

The discourse falls into three parts, with an appendix.

(a) The true manna (6:27–34)

6:27 'Do not work for the perishable food; work for the food that endures to eternal life, the food which the Son of Man will give you. It is he whom God the Father has sealed.'

The discourse begins and ends with an interchange between Jesus and his hearers, and is punctuated by further interchanges. There is nothing out of the ordinary in this: it is part of what has been called 'the freedom of the synagogue'.[9]

The contrast here between perishable and spiritual food is similar to the contrast between material and spiritual water in Jesus' conversation with the woman at the well (John 4:10 ff.). As the water in Jacob's well could not provide the soul-refreshment which 'living water' provided, so food which 'perishes with the using' (cf. Col. 2:22) might sustain physical life but could not impart life eternal. As Jesus in chapter 4 is the giver of that water which bubbles up to eternal life in those who receive it, so here he is the giver of the food whose properties are such that those who eat of it will never hunger again.[10] He avoids using the term 'Messiah' or any other which would have appealed to his hearers' militant aspirations. The designation 'the Son of Man' suited his purpose well enough; it was not current coin in their religious or political vocabulary and could therefore bear whatever meaning he chose to put on it.[11] The Son of Man, he says, is the one whom God has 'sealed' – that is to say, the one whom God has appointed as his certified and authorized agent for the bestowal of this life-giving food. If the aorist tense of the verb 'sealed' (Gk. *esphragisen*) suggests that we identify the sealing with one particular event, we should probably think of our Lord's baptism (cf. John 1:32–34).

6:28, 29 So they said to him, 'What shall we do in order to work the works of God?' Jesus replied, 'This is the work of God: you must believe in the one whom he has sent.'

Jesus had told them to work for the food that is imperishable: what kind of work (they asked) is this? As they had to do their common daily work to earn their daily food, so (they supposed) to receive the food which imparted eternal life they would have to perform tasks especially prescribed by God. What were these tasks? Jesus assures them that God's basic requirement for those who would receive the food which imparts eternal life is faith – faith in the 'messenger of the covenant' whom God had sent in accordance with his ancient promise (cf. Mal. 3:1). The people (rightly) understand him to mean that he himself is the messenger referred to. They ask him, therefore, to supply further confirmation of his implicit claim to be the sent one of God.

6:30, 31 So they said to him, 'What sign do you perform, then, so that we may see it and believe in you? What work do you do? Our fathers ate the manna in the wilderness, as scripture says, "He gave them bread out of heaven to eat".'

It might have been thought that the sign they had seen was sufficient attestation of Jesus' claim, but they want another. For many, the feeding of the multitude marked him out as the second Moses (verse 14). Let him give further evidence of being the second Moses. If Moses had given their forefathers manna in the wilderness, let the second Moses vindicate his authority in a similar way – not by a once-for-all feeding but on a more lasting basis. It may be that the the narrative of the giving of the manna (Ex. 16:11–36) formed part of the scripture lesson in the synagogue that sabbath.[12] Jesus' words about 'the food that endures' might in any case have reminded them of the bread from heaven which their ancestors ate, although even the manna came under the description of 'perishable food' (cf. Ex. 16:20). In later times the rabbis taught that the new age would be marked by the restoration of the gift of manna, and there are some indications that this idea was current in the first Christian century (cf. the reference to 'the hidden manna' in Rev. 2:17). So the people may have meant: 'In the messianic age the gift of manna will be renewed; give us manna, and we shall know that the messianic age has truly dawned'. The scripture which they

quote about the manna is Ps. 78:24, which may indeed be regarded
as the text for the present discourse (cf. also Ps. 105:40; Neh. 9:15).
The loaves and fishes were a timely provision indeed, but they
were earthly food, not bread from heaven. One who could give
them bread from heaven would beyond all doubt be the prophet
like Moses.

**6:32, 33 So Jesus said to them, 'Indeed and in truth I tell you;
it is not Moses who gave you the bread out of heaven, but it is
my Father who gives you the true bread out of heaven. For the
bread of God is that which comes down from heaven and gives
life to the world.'**

Jesus reminds them that it was not Moses, but God, who gave
their forefathers the manna in the wilderness. And God, who fed
his people with material food in those earlier days – and in fact still
did so[13] – was now offering them spiritual food, heavenly manna,
life-giving bread. Like the loaves and fishes with which the multitude had recently been fed, the manna which Israel ate in the days
of Moses was also material food, 'bread out of heaven' though it
was. But there is another kind of bread which comes down from
heaven – true, real bread sustaining the inmost and most lasting life
of men and women – and it is of no perishable or material nature.

The expression 'the bread of God' is used occasionally in OT of
the 'showbread' (cf. Lev. 21:6, 8, 17, 21, 22; 22:25). The manna
is called 'bread of the mighty' or 'bread of the angels' (Heb. *leḥem
'abbirim*) in Ps. 78.25. But here 'the bread of God' is the bread
which God supplies: like the manna, it comes down from heaven,
but unlike the manna, it gives life – eternal life – to all mankind.

6:34 So they said to him, 'Sir, give us this bread always.'

Like the Samaritan woman, who said, 'Sir, give me this water'
(John 4:15) when she heard Jesus speak of the living water which
he could give, the congregation responds to his words about the
true bread with an eager request that they may receive this bread
for evermore. But they still understand his words in a material
sense; he therefore uses a new form of words to make his meaning
plainer.

(b) Jesus the food of eternal life (6:35–51)

**6:35 Jesus said to them, 'I am the bread of life. The one who
comes to me shall not hunger, and the one who believes in me
shall never thirst.'**

Jesus' hearers had not understood what he meant by the 'bread of God which comes down from heaven and gives life to the world.' Now he tells them plainly what he means. In the former section of the discourse he had spoken of himself as the giver of this bread; in this section he identifies himself with it. 'For Jesus is himself the gift of which he is the giver.'[14] He has come to give himself that men and women may live by him. To partake of the bread of life they must come to him, they must believe in him. This total self-commitment to Christ, this appropriating him by faith, is the secret of eternal life and perpetual soul-refreshment.

This is the first of the distinctive 'I am' sayings of this Gospel (where Jesus uses *egō eimi* with a predicate).[15]

6:36-38 'But I told you that you have seen me indeed but do not believe. All that the Father gives me will come to me, and I will by no means reject the one who comes to me, for I have come down from heaven, not to do my own will, but the will of him who sent me.'

The words 'you have seen me indeed but do not believe' echo those of John 5:36-38, but those earlier words were addressed to people in Jerusalem, and these addressed here are Galilaeans. In the present context, the words sum up the sense of what was said in verse 26: they had seen Jesus providing food for the multitude, but did not penetrate by faith into the true significance of what he did. They had not come to him and believed in him in the only sense that matters. Unlike the Evangelist and his associates, they had not 'looked on his glory' (cf. John 1:14); thus they had not yet been able to partake of the bread of life.

Yet Jesus had the assurance that many would indeed come to him in faith and receive the life-giving bread, for it was the will of his Father that they should do so. Men's blindness cannot frustrate the saving work of God. God is at work by his grace in the world, and those who come to Christ come to him by the 'sweet constraint' of that grace. And when they come, they find that Christ undertakes the entire responsibility for their full and final salvation. He does not turn them away when they come, nor does he subsequently disown them. At a later stage in this Gospel he claims to have lost none of those whom the Father had given him, apart from that one who deliberately severed himself from Christ (John 17:6-12).

In the work of salvation the Father and the Son are completely at one, the Father giving the believing community to the Son, the Son receiving and guarding those who come to him, because he is utterly devoted to the Father's will. The doing of the Father's will

is the purpose of his coming into the world and it is the very
sustenance of his life on earth (cf. John 4:34).

In the first part of verse 37 the pronoun 'all' is neuter singular
(Gk. *pan*), denoting the sum-total of believers. In the second part
('the one who comes') each individual member of that sum-total is
in view. This oscillation between the community as a whole and its
individual members reappears in verses 39 and 40.

**6:39, 40 'And this is the will of him who sent me, that I should
lose nothing of all that he has given me, but raise it up at the
last day. For this is my Father's will, that every one who sees
the Son and believes in him should have eternal life, and I will
raise him up at the last day.'**

In verse 39 'all' is neuter singular (*pan*) as in verse 37a, and when
Jesus says that he will 'raise *it* (*auto*) up at the last day' he speaks
of the sum-total of his people. In verse 40 'every one' is masculine
singular (*pas*), and when Jesus says that he will 'raise *him* (*auton*)
up at the last day' he speaks of each individual believer as in verse
37b.

In their perfect unity of will and purpose the Father and the Son
stand engaged for the salvation of all believers. This is equally so
whether we think of believers as making up one entity (verse 39)
or think of each separate member of this entity (verse 40). No
believer need fear being overlooked among the multitude of his or
her companions in the faith. The community as a whole, and each
member of the community, having been given by the Father to the
Son, will be safely kept by the Son until the consummation of the
resurrection life 'at the last day'. To treat John's eschatology as
exclusively 'realized' is to overlook those passages where Jesus is
described as raising his people up 'at the last day' (see also verses
44, 54; 11:24; 12:48). There is no textual evidence for removing
such passages from the Gospel, as though they were later editorial
additions. The 'last day' is the time indicated in John 5:28 f., when
'all who are in the tombs will hear his voice and come out.' Those
who come to Christ receive the resurrection life in measure here
and now, but they will receive it in its fulness when they are
clothed in bodies of glory.

The seeing of the Son spoken of in verse 40 is much more than
the superficial seeing of him, unaccompanied by faith, which has
been mentioned in verse 36; it is that divinely-imparted vision
which discerns the glory of God in the Word become flesh. According to C. H. Dodd, the verb *theōreō* is used here, as in verse 62,
'for the discerning vision which recognizes the eternal reality behind or within the phenomenal facts of the life and death of Jesus

Christ'.[16] It is not that the verb *theōreō* in itself has this sense (in John 2:23 it was used of seeing Jesus' signs with no adequate appreciation of their significance); it is the appropriate context that bestows this fulness of meaning on it.[17] The possession of eternal life now and the hope of resurrection 'at the last day' are two things which God has joined together for those who have come to Christ in faith.

6:41, 42 So the Jews complained about him because he said, 'I am the bread which came down from heaven.' 'Is this not Jesus the son of Joseph', they asked, 'whose father and mother we know? How does he say now, "I have come down from heaven"?'

On this occasion 'the Jews' must be the synagogue congregation in Capernaum, or rather the leaders of the congregation. The phrase is used more generally here than in 5:18, where it was the teaching establishment in Jerusalem that was so incensed by the way in which he spoke of God as his Father. He was a visitor in Jerusalem, but he was a resident in Galilee; this was what offended his hearers. How could a man with whose family they were well acquainted make such a claim as he did? How could he provide, much less be, the food of immortality? How could he be the bond between heaven and earth?

Here, as in John 1:45. Jesus is known as 'the son of Joseph', whereas in Mark 6:3, in Nazareth, he is known as 'the son of Mary'. The words 'and mother' are lacking here in some authorities, including the first hand of Sinaiticus, but they are present in the overwhelming majority of witnesses, including the oldest of all, Papyri 66 and 75. The audience's language need not imply that Joseph was still alive: it means 'We know who this man's parents were; how could he have come down from heaven?' (That Jesus' family was known in Capernaum has been indicated in 2:12.) John and his readers understand that the Capernaum congregation had no inkling of the mystery of the Incarnation – of the fact that Jesus, while he entered human life by a real birth, was at the same time the eternal Word.

6:43, 44 Jesus answered them, 'Do not complain among your-selves. No one can come to me unless the Father, who sent me, draws him, and I will raise him up at the last day.'

Their complaint was not directly addressed to Jesus, but it is from him that the answer comes. He urges them to stop this exchange of scandalized criticism: they would not arrive at the truth that way.

The first clause of verse 44 repeats in different language the thought in the first clause of verse 37. Those who come to Christ are here described as being drawn to him by the Father; in John 12:32 it is Christ who, by being 'lifted up from the earth', draws all without distinction to himself. One way or the other, the divine initiative in the salvation of believers is emphasized. The responsibility of men and women in the matter of coming to Christ is not overlooked (cf. John 5:40); but none at all would come unless divinely persuaded and enabled to do so. And every one who comes to him will gladly acknowledge:

> He loved me ere I knew him;
> He drew me with the cords of love,
> And thus he bound me to him.

Then for the third (but not yet the last) time in this discourse the resurrection of the believer is emphasized as the final and crowning stage of the saving work which Christ undertakes to accomplish in every one who comes to him.

6:45, 46 'It is written in the prophets, "And they will all be taught by God." Everyone who has heard, and learned, from the Father comes to me.' (Not that any one has seen the Father, except the one who is from God – he has seen the Father.)

By 'the prophets' we are to understand the second division of the Hebrew Bible. The quotation comes from Isa. 54:13, where the restored city of Jerusalem receives the assurance: 'All your children shall be taught by the LORD.' The new age – the kingdom of God – to which these words pointed has now dawned with the coming of Jesus, the true Wisdom of God. In the NT the restoration of Zion after the Babylonian exile, celebrated in Isa. 40–66, is treated as a parable of the restoration effected by Christ. With the words quoted here we may compare the promise of the new covenant in Jer. 31:31–34, also interpreted of the Christian age by the NT writers (cf. 2 Cor. 3:4–4:6; Heb. 8:6–10:18): ' . . . I will put my law within them, and I will write it upon their hearts; and . . . they shall all know me, from the least of them to the greatest, says the LORD.'

If, as some believe, Isa. 54 was included in the appointed synagogue lessons for this period of the year,[18] then the words quoted by Jesus may have been fresh in the minds of many of his hearers. He wishes them to understand that the time for the fulfilment of these words has now arrived, and that they will show that they have been taught by God – in other words, that God's word abides in them (John 5:38–40) – if they come to him who is in their midst as the Son of God. The Father 'draws' men and women to Christ (verse 44) by enabling them to appreciate who he is – as he enabled Peter (6.68 f.; cf. Matt. 16:17). Those who receive this divine illumination and respond to it show by their coming to Christ that they are children and citizens of the new Jerusalem, as the prophet foretold.

Verse 46 appears to be a characteristic comment by the Evangelist; if it is so, it might be placed between brackets. Hearing the Father and learning from him do not imply seeing him: 'no one has ever seen God' (John 1:18). Only the Son, the one who comes from God, has seen the Father, but those who see the Son for what he really is see the Father in him (cf. John 12:45; 14:9). But to see the Son for what he really is requires the eye of faith; hence the next words of Jesus emphasize afresh the necessity of faith.

6:47 'Indeed and in truth I tell you: he who believes has eternal life.'

Jesus has already said that it is the Father's will that every one who believes in the Son should have eternal life and be raised up at the last day (verse 40); here he makes it plain that every one who believes in the Son has eternal life here and now, without waiting for the last day: he already anticipates the conditions of the coming resurrection age which will be ushered in by the last day of the present age (cf. John 3:36a). It is to the believer that the Son mediates that vision of God which he himself enjoys immediately and uninterruptedly; and with the vision of God eternal life is bestowed.

6:48–50 'I am the bread of life. Your fathers ate the manna in the wilderness – and they died. This is the bread that comes down from heaven, so that one may eat of it and not die.'

Jesus is not only the living bread in contrast to perishable food (verse 35 over against verse 27); he is the life-giving bread, delivering those who receive him from the power of death, which even the manna could not achieve for those who ate it. The Israelites of the wilderness generation fed on manna, and yet they died. For all its wonderful properties as 'the grain of heaven . . . the bread of the angels' (Ps. 78:24 f.), it could not impart *eternal* life; those who received it sustained bodily life by it, but even so they died at last. The true heavenly bread, by contrast – that is, the Son of God himself – bestows spiritual life on those who 'eat' of him (i.e., appropriate him by faith); and this spiritual life is maintained by him and safeguarded from the menace of death.

6:51 'I am the living bread that came down from heaven. If any one eats of this bread, he will live for ever. Yes, and the bread which I will give is my flesh, (given) for the life of the world.'

In these words the lesson of the preceding verses is summed up and driven home. But if Christ is not only the giver of 'the food that remains to eternal life' (verse 27), but the living bread in person, then it follows that what he gives is himself: how does he do this? He provides his own answer: he is to give his flesh for the life of the world.

The reader of John's record can recognize this language as sacrificial, remembering, for example, the Baptist's designation of Jesus as 'the Lamb of God, that takes away the sin of the world' (John 1:29). To give one's flesh can scarcely mean anything other than death, and the wording here points to a death which is both voluntary ('I will give') and vicarious ('for the life of the world'). When we recall the apt description of this Gospel as 'the gospel of fulfilment',[19] we may think of the voluntary and vicarious self-offering of the Servant of the LORD in Isa. 52:13–53:12. The Servant's death was to bring blessing to 'the many' (Isa. 53:11 f.), from Israel and the Gentiles alike (cf. Isa. 49:6); so Jesus takes the widest view of those who are to benefit by his death: he will give his flesh 'for the life of the world'. The worldwide scope of his saving work has been emphasized already in this Gospel: the Son of God was sent 'that the world should be saved through him' (John 3:17); he is, as the Samaritans confessed, 'the Saviour of the world' (John 4:42). But Jesus' hearers in Capernaum were far from grasping the implications of his statement. The third section of the discourse is devoted to a fuller setting out of these implications.

(c) Partaking of the Son of Man (6:52–59)

6:52–55 So the Jews held a heated disputation among themselves. 'How', they said, 'can this man give us his flesh to eat?' Jesus said to them, 'Indeed and in truth I tell you: unless you eat the flesh of the Son of Man and drink his blood, you have no life in yourselves. He who eats my flesh and drinks my blood has eternal life, and I will raise him up at the last day; for my flesh is real food, and my blood is real drink.'

The dispute which ensued among the members of the congregation was hot and stormy: 'they fought' (*emachonto*), says John. They knew that Jesus was not speaking literally; they did not suppose that he seriously implied cannibalism. Yet that was the natural sense of his words; it was an offensive way of speaking, they thought, even if he was speaking figuratively. And if he was speaking figuratively, they could not fathom what the figurative sense of his words might be. Some had one interpretation, some another; and a wordy strife broke out among them. Is it too far-fetched to see in this wordy strife an anticipation of the perennial controversies in which Christians have engaged over the meaning of their Lord's words of institution: 'This is my body, which is for you' (1 Cor. 11:24)?

Before answering their question, 'How . . . ?' Jesus amplifies his contentious statement. The amplification was more offensive than the original statement. The law of Moses imposed a ban on the drinking of any blood whatsoever (including the eating of flesh with the blood in it); the idea of drinking the blood of the Son of Man was impossibly abhorrent. They found the problem set by his strange language more impenetrable, and more scandalous, than ever.

In verse 54 and the following verses the verb 'to eat' is not *phagein*, which has been used hitherto, but *trōgein*, a coarser word, 'to munch' or 'to chew', used in classical Greek of animals eating. (The distinction could be well conveyed in German by using the verbs *essen* and *fressen* respectively.) It is doubtful, however, if much significance can be read into the use of the one verb or the other in the present context; it may be a further instance of the Evangelist's predilection for ringing the changes on synonyms.

In verse 54 it is the person who eats the flesh of the Son of Man and drinks his blood that will be raised up by him at the last day; in verse 40 the same promise is held out to 'every one who sees the Son and believes in him'. So, those who 'eat his flesh' and 'drink his blood' are those who see him and believe in him: it is they who have eternal life; it is they whom he will raise up at the last day. In his strange words, then, we recognize a powerful and vivid metaphor to denote coming to him, believing in him (cf. verse 35), appropriating him by faith.

Augustine of Hippo explains our Lord's language here as 'a figure, bidding us communicate in our Lord's passion, and secretly and profitably treasure in our memories the fact that for our sakes he was crucified and pierced'.[20] Elsewhere he sums up the truth in an immortal epigram: *Crede, et manducasti* ('Believe, and thou hast eaten').[21] Later, Bernard of Clairvaux expounds the words 'He who eats my flesh . . .' as meaning: 'He who reflects upon my death, and after my example mortifies his members which are upon earth, has eternal life – in other words, "If you suffer with me, you will also reign with me".'[22] Bernard's exposition is quoted simply to show that a twelfth-century mystic and (like Augustine) a doctor of the church saw no need to take the words in a literal or 'corporeal' sense; it is Augustine who penetrates more surely to their true meaning. Appropriating Christ by faith not only assures his people of life in the age to come when he raises them up at the last day; it makes that life of the age to come their heritage to be enjoyed by anticipation here and now. Moreover, this life is secured to them by the death of Christ, for the terms in which he describes their appropriation of him by faith imply that the one whom they so appropriate has yielded up his life in sacrifice.

The true sustenance and refreshment of our spiritual life are to be found only in him who died that we might live. In all ways in which his people feed on him by faith – not only at the Holy Table, but in reading and hearing the Word of God, or in private or united prayer and meditation (to mention no more) – they may fulfil the conditions which he lays down here, and receive the promised blessing.

6:56 'Whoever eats my flesh and drinks my blood, he remains in me and I in him.'

In effect, if not in form, Jesus here defines what is meant by eating his flesh and drinking his blood. This language denotes that faith-union by which a mutual indwelling, a 'coinherence,' of Jesus and his people is established. In the writings of John this experience is repeatedly expressed by means of the verb, *menō*, 'abide', 'remain' or 'dwell' (cf. John 15:4). Paul expresses the same mutuality of indwelling, without using this verb, when he uses such phrases as 'in Christ' and 'Christ in me'. A good Johannine instance, without the highly figurative language of the synagogue discourse in Capernaum, appears in 1 John 2:24: 'All who keep his commandments remain in him, and he in them.' For believing in Christ and keeping his commandments are two things which cannot be separated; there is no true faith without obedience, no true obedience without faith. Moreover, there can be neither true faith nor true obedience without true love, as appears especially in the upper-room discourses later in this Gospel (13:31–16:33), where the implications of the mutual indwelling of Christ and believers are further developed.

6:57 'As the living Father has sent me and I live because of the Father, he also who eats me will live because of me.'

The Son's dependence on the Father for 'life in himself', as well
as for every function which he exercises, has been emphasized in
John 5:19-30, especially in 5:26. Here it is stated briefly. The Son
who derives his own life from the Father has authority to impart
that life to those who believe in him, with this distinction: what he
receives is 'life in himself'; what they receive is life in him. 'At
every point the unity of Father and Son is reproduced in the unity
of Christ and believers'.[23] Here again is a theme which is to be fully
developed in the upper-room discourses and prayer (cf. John 15:9
f.; 17:18; 20:21).

**6:58 'This is the bread which came down from heaven, not like
(the bread which) your fathers ate and died; whoever eats this
bread will live for ever.'**

It is by contrast with the manna that the bread of heaven is true
bread. The manna fed men and women's bodies for a time, but the
true bread feeds their souls eternally. The manna was in a sense
'spiritual food', as Paul puts it (1 Cor. 10:3) – 'supernatural food'
(RSV) – but it was 'spiritual' by virtue of the spiritual reality to
which it pointed, not because of any inherent quality of its own.

This raises the question of the relation of the present discourse
to the Lord's Supper, in which the communicants participate by
faith in the blood and body of Christ (1 Cor. 10:16). The Fourth
Evangelist has no record of the institution of the Lord's Supper in
the upper room. Where the other Evangelists record the institution,
he gives us the account of the footwashing (John 13:2 ff.). But if
he gives no record of the institution, he does give us in this discourse of Jesus something which fills the Lord's Supper with a
deep wealth of meaning for the believer. Our Lord in this discourse
is not indeed speaking directly of the Lord's Supper, but he does
expound the truth which the Lord's Supper conveys. That truth is
well summed up in the words which accompany the handing of the
bread to the communicant in the Anglican *Book of Common
Prayer*: 'Take and eat this in remembrance that Christ died for
thee, and feed on him in thy heart by faith with thanksgiving.'

**6:59 These things were spoken to him as he was teaching in
the synagogue in Capernaum.**

'These things' should probably be understood to comprise the
discourse of verses 27-58. It deals in three stages with the true
bread of life – a theme which was doubly apposite in view of the
recent feeding of the multitude and in view of the time of year,
when the OT references to the manna were fresh in the minds of

many, especially if the relevant section of the Pentateuch formed
part of the synagogue lessons that day.

The ruined synagogue of white limestone discovered at Tell Ḥum
(commonly identified with Capernaum) by German archaeologists
early in the twentieth century and partially restored by the Fran-
ciscans on whose property it stands, is a structure of the third
century AD, but it may have been built on the same site as the
earlier synagogue in which Jesus spoke these words.

(d) Appendix (6:60–71)

**6:60 Many of his disciples, then, on hearing this, said, 'This
language is hard (to take). Who can listen to it?'**

The remaining verses of chapter 6 form an appendix to the
discourse, describing how many of Jesus's hearers, even of those
who had hitherto been well disposed to him and had been reckoned
among his adherents, were scandalized at his teaching. Although
they knew that he must be speaking figuratively when he talked
about eating his flesh and drinking his blood, yet such language
was more than they could endure. This was not simply because
they thought the metaphor outrageous but because the whole tenor
of his argument implied a claim to be greater than Moses – to be,
in fact, uniquely associated with God. His language was hard to
take not merely because it was difficult to grasp but because they
found it offensive. The NEB paraphrase tries (with doubtful success)
to catch the nuance: 'This is more than we can stomach! Why listen
to such talk?'

But were people who reacted in this way *disciples*? It is implied
that they had been disciples up to this point, although they were
so no longer. In John 8:31 Jesus tells his hearers how they may be
truly his disciples – by remaining in his word. This is precisely
what the people mentioned here declined to do. Instead of remaining in his word, they dismissed it as intolerable. They had been
disciples in name; they were far from being disciples in truth.

**6:61–64 Knowing in himself that his disciples were grumbling
about this, Jesus said to them, 'Do you take offence at this?
(What will you do) then if you see the Son of Man ascending
where he was before? It is the Spirit that gives life; the flesh is
of no use. The words that I have spoken to you – they are spirit;
they are life.' (For Jesus knew from the first who they were that
did not believe and who it was that would betray him.)**

As always, Jesus can read his hearers' unspoken thoughts (cf.
John 2:24 f.). So he goes farther in his endeavour to make his

meaning plain to them, so that they can appreciate the spiritual import of his discourse.

Hitherto he has spoken to them of the Son of Man's descent from heaven (verse 38). If they were stumbled by the claim which such words implied, what would they think if one day they saw the Son of man ascending back to heaven? Would they believe then? That would surely provide confirmation that his implied claim was justified. He had already said, 'The Son of Man must be lifted up, so that every one who believes may have eternal life in him' (John 3:14 f.). As we have seen, his being 'lifted up' on the cross is viewed in this Gospel as the first stage in his 'ascending where he was before'. What is, from one perspective, the lowest stage in the Servant's humiliation is, from another, the first stage in his being 'exalted and lifted up and made very high' (Isa. 52:13). To see Jesus lifted up, to look beyond the surface appearance and appreciate the inner significance of the exaltation of the Crucified One – that is true believing in him; that is the way to eternal life.

To try to take his words in a material sense, without attempting to penetrate beneath their surface meaning, is to miss their point. Eating the flesh of the Son of Man and drinking his blood must be understood as an attitude and activity of the spiritual realm. Eating material food cannot impart spiritual life; that much was evident from the fact that the Israelites who ate the manna died nevertheless. The distinction between spirit and flesh is as sharp here as it is in the conversation with Nicodemus (John 3:5–12).

One way of feeding on Christ is to cherish and obey his words; they are spiritual, life-giving food. Jeremiah found the words of God to have this property: 'Thy words were found, and I ate them, and thy words became to me a joy and the delight of my heart' (Jer. 15:16). Jesus claims for his own words what Jeremiah claims for the words of God. To believe Jesus' words is part of believing in Jesus himself. This is made plain in his challenge to the Jerusalem leaders: 'If you believed Moses, you would *believe me* . . . But if you do not believe his writings, how will you *believe my words*?' (John 5:46 f.). The history not only of the apostolic age but of the whole Christian era shows what regenerative power resides in the words of him who spoke as no other ever did. But if his words do not 'meet with faith in the hearers' (Heb. 4:2), they cannot do them the good they otherwise would; and so it was with those 'disciples'.

The Evangelist once more (in verse 64b) emphasizes Jesus' foresight and insight into the human heart. He was not taken by surprise when many turned away from him. But among his followers none turned away so far as did Judas, who carried his desertion to the point of treachery. Judas's defection still lay in the future, but Jesus foresaw it already, as his language in verse 70 indicates.

6:65 He went on to say, 'This is why I have told you that no one can come to me unless it is given to him by my Father (to do so).'

These words echo what has been said in verses 37 and 44. None can come to Christ in faith but those who are persuaded and enabled to do so by the Spirit; but all these will come, drawn by the irresistible grace of heavenly love, and none who comes is rejected.

6:66 After this, then, many of his disciples went back and accompanied him no longer.

Those disciples had already been scandalized by his 'hard' sayings, and his additional words did nothing to appease them. Until his refusal to be made their king, they had heard him gladly, but when he put them off by his insistence on the superiority of the bread of eternal life and his identification of that bread with his flesh, they lost interest. What they wanted, he would not give; what he offered, they would not receive. So, like many of his Jerusalem followers earlier (John 2:23–25), many of his Galilaean followers now failed to stand the test of unreserved allegiance. To be attracted by the signs is one thing, to appreciate and embrace their inward significance is another; and it is only those who do the latter who can be counted as true disciples. The disciples who now 'went back' showed by their doing so that they were only temporary disciples, and therefore no true disciples. Perseverance is the criterion of reality where discipleship to Jesus is concerned. In saying that they 'accompanied him no longer' (literally, 'no longer walked with him'), John does not simply mean that they no longer followed him in his itinerant ministry (some of them, probably, had never done that); he means that they were no longer with him in spirit. If they had once been disposed to look on him as their Master, leader and teacher, 'after this' (which may also imply 'as a result of this') they abandoned any such idea.

6:67 So Jesus said to the twelve, Do you want to go away too?'

We might almost infer that on this occasion the twelve were the only disciples who remained when all the others went back. Or perhaps he did not put this question to the twelve until he was alone with them. Had they, too, found his sayings too hard to take? Were there unspoken misgivings and resentments in their hearts too because of words which had caused offence to so many others? As John phrases our Lord's question in Greek, he implies that it was not asked in a mood of despair; the use of the Greek negative *mē* in a question indicates that the answer 'No' is expected. '*You* don't want to go away too, do you?'

6:68, 69 Simon Peter answered him, 'Lord, to whom shall we go? You have words of eternal life; and *we* have believed and recognized that you are the Holy One of God.'

John regularly uses the double name 'Simon Peter' in his narrative – in the other Gospels it occurs only infrequently (Matt. 16:16; Luke 5:8).

The advantage of Peter's constant willingness to act as spokesman of the twelve was his utter lack of sophistication, his inability to say anything but what was uppermost in his mind. When he spoke, he said what he thought. Another might have used words which masked his real thoughts from a desire not to hurt his Master's feelings; not so Peter. His reply therefore showed that he had indeed grasped what his Master had tried to make plain to all his hearers – that by believing in him they might have eternal life. Had Jesus just said, 'The words that I have spoken to you – they are spirit, they are life' (verse 63)? Then Peter would accept this as the plain truth; perhaps he had already begun to experience their life-giving properties. If the words of Jesus were words of life, as the words of no other were, how could Peter or any one like-minded ever wish to leave this Master to follow someone else? Others might be disillusioned because Jesus, instead of fulfilling the expected messianic programme and leading a war of national liberation (verse 15), insisted on the spiritual character of his kingdom. But Peter and his companions had begun to prove for themselves that Jesus could supply them with spiritual food which brought much more enduring satisfaction than material bread.

One who could speak as Jesus had done must be the Messiah, whatever might be said about his failure to come up to popular expectation. 'The Holy One of God' appears as a messianic designation in Mark 1:24 (on the lips of a demon-possessed person, significantly enough). The 'received text' here (cf. AV) reads 'the Christ, the Son of the living God' under the influence of Matt. 16:16. This is a Johannine counterpart to the Caesarea Philippi incident in the Synoptic accounts (Mark 8:27–30 and parallels). It is a remarkable point of contact between the Synoptic and Johannine outlines of the ministry, that the turning-point in both is

marked by a momentous confession on the lips of Peter, not long
after the miraculous feeding of the multitude.

Others had been prepared to acknowledge Jesus as the second
Moses, providing his people with food, but had no time for the
living bread which was offered for the life of the world. Peter and
his companions refused to be thus put off, but believed what he
said and drew the logical inference. He was more than the prophet
like Moses; he was the Holy One of God. Their earliest impression,
formed when they first met him by the banks of Jordan, had not
been mistaken: Andrew had been more right than he could have
realized at the time when he found his brother Simon and told him,
'We have found the Messiah!' (John 1:41). This was in truth the
one 'of whom Moses in the law, and the prophets wrote' (John
1:45).

**6:70 Jesus answered them, 'Have I not chosen all twelve of
you? Yet one of you is an adversary.'**

This episode is the only place where John refers to 'the twelve'
as such (apart from the incidental reference in 20:24 to Thomas as
'one of the twelve'). John knows that his readers will be aware that
Jesus made special choice of twelve, but he does not record their
appointment, as the other Evangelists do. Nor does he anywhere
call them 'apostles'.[24]

Here, however, it is plain that the twelve constituted the inner
circle, men whom Jesus had hand-picked. From them, if from any
of his disciples, might be expected such understanding as Peter had
shown. And yet even in that inner circle he could discern the spirit
of defection. One of them was a *diabolos* – the Greek word means
a 'slanderer' or 'calumniator' or 'false accuser', but it is probably
used here as the counterpart to Heb. *sāṭān*, 'adversary'. On the
occasion at Caesarea Philippi one of the twelve proved to be,
although unintentionally, an 'adversary' in the sense that he tried
to turn his Master's mind away from the path of suffering and
death, which was the way of the Father's will (Mark 8:33). That
one was Peter himself, who a moment before had confessed Jesus
to be the Messiah. But it is another member of the group who is
now in view, as John recognized in the light of the sequel.

**6:71 He meant Judas, son of Simon Iscariot. It was he who
was to betray him, one of the twelve as he was.**

Jesus' foreknowledge of the traitor's identity has been mentioned
in verse 64. This is the first occasion on which he is named. Each
of the other evangelists, when he mentions Judas for the first time,

identifies him as the one who was to turn traitor (Matt. 10:4; Mark 3:19; Luke 6:16), and so does John here. Thus, a year before the last Passover, that 'dark betrayal night' casts its shadow before. 'Iscariot' is probably the Hebrew *'ish qᵉriyyôth*, 'the man of Kerioth' (a Judaean locality mentioned in Josh. 15:25).[25] Such a territorial designation would be applicable both to Judas and (as here) to his father Simon.

NOTES

1. See comment on John 7:1 (p. 169).
2. The same word is used (in the singular) for the fish which the risen Lord prepared for his disciples in John 21:9–13 (see p. 401).
3. Hilary of Poitiers, in the 4th century AD (*Commentary on Matthew* 15.7, on Matt. 15:32–38), and other early commentators reckoned that the feeding of the 5,000 symbolizes the Lord's self-communication to the Jews, as his feeding of the 4,000 symbolizes his self-communication to the Gentiles. Later commentators have pointed out in this connexion that the word translated 'basket' (*kophinos*) in all four accounts of the feeding of the 5,000 is one which has Jewish associations; a different word (*spyris*, 'creel') is used in the two places where the feeding of the 4,000 is narrated (Matt. 15:37; Mark 8:8). Cf. A. E. J. Rawlinson, *The Gospel according to St. Mark* (London, 1925), pp. 87 (for the suggestion that the twelve *kophinoi* correspond to the twelve apostles), 104 (for the query whether or not the seven *spyrides* might correspond to the seven 'deacons' of Acts 6:3–6); also A. Richardson, *The Miracle Stories of the Gospels* (London, 1941), pp. 94–99.
4. See comment on John 1:21 (p. 48).
5. Rabbi Isaac (c. AD 300), quoted in *Ecclesiastes Rabba* (rabbinical commentary) 1.9.1, on Eccl. 1:9.
6. See p. 65, n. 34.
7. Cf. T. W. Manson, *The Servant-Messiah* (Cambridge, 1953), p. 70.
8. G. A. Smith, *Historical Geography of the Holy Land* (London, ²⁵1931), pp. 441 f.
9. Cf. I. Abrahams, *Studies in Pharisaism and the Gospels*, I (Cambridge, 1917), pp. 1–17.
10. See P. Borgen, *Bread from Heaven* (Leiden, 1965).
11. See comment on John 1:51 (p. 63).
12. Cf. A. Guilding, *The Fourth Gospel and Jewish Worship*, pp. 61–65.
13. This is implied in the petition of the Lord's Prayer: 'Give us this day our daily bread' (Matt. 6:11; Luke 11:3 has 'each day'). There the phrase *artos epiousios* may mean 'our bread for the morrow' (RSV margin), i.e. 'Help us to earn enough today to buy tomorrow's bread' (like the labourers in the vineyard of Matt. 20:2, 9 f.). It is unlikely that the petition meant 'Give us our bread for the age to come', although Jerome had something of the sort in mind when he translated *epiousios* by *supersubstantialis* (whence 'our supersubstantial bread' of the Douai-Rheims version, commonly understood as a reference to the eucharistic bread or to Christ as the bread of life).
14. B. Lindars, *Behind the Fourth Gospel*, p. 37.
15. B. Lindars (*Behind the Fourth Gospel*, p. 72) thinks that most of the 'I am' sayings, like the Prologue, reflect the Wisdom Christology at which the Evangelist had arrived. Here, against the background of such wisdom sayings as Prov. 9:5 ('Come, eat of my bread'), Jesus speaks of the lasting satisfaction which he brings to the souls into which he enters. In Sir. 24:21 Wisdom says, 'Those who eat me will hunger for more, and those who drink me will thirst

for more'; but Jesus says, 'he who comes to me shall not hunger, and he who believes in me shall never thirst' (cf. Lindars, *op. cit.*, p. 48).

16. C. H. Dodd, *The Interpretation of the Fourth Gospel*, p. 342.

17. The ordinary Greek verb meaning 'see' (*horaō*) tends to be replaced in NT Greek by one of its synonyms, such as *theōreō*.

18. Cf. A. Guilding, *The Fourth Gospel and Jewish Worship*, p. 63.

19. Cf. R. A. Henderson, *The Gospel of Fulfilment: A Study of St. John's Gospel* (London, 1936).

20. Augustine, *On Christian Doctrine*, 3.16.

21. Augustine, *Homilies on John*, 26.1.

22. Bernard, *The Love of God*, 4.11.

23. C. H. Dodd, *The Interpretation of the Fourth Gospel*, p. 195.

24. The word *apostolos* in John 13:16 has the quite general sense 'one who is sent'.

25. Attempts to relate the word to *sicarius* ('assassin') are anachronistic and philologically unsatisfactory.

CHAPTER 7

VI. Ministry in Jerusalem (7:1–10:39)

1. FEAST OF TABERNACLES (7:1–8:59)

(a) Jesus and his brothers (7:1–9)

7:1 After this Jesus went about in Galilee. He would not go about in Judaea because the Judaeans were seeking to kill him.

If we take the sequence of the chapters as they stand, 'after this' will mean 'after the feeding of the multitude and the discourse on the bread of life'. The verb 'walked' will then have the full force of its imperfect tense: 'Jesus continued to go about in Galilee'. Arguments have been put forward for the transposition of chapters 5 and 6, so that the beginning of chapter 7 would follow immediately after the end of chapter 5. Such arguments must, however, remain problematical in the absence of any supporting textual evidence. Certainly the reference here to the attempt to kill Jesus recalls the sequel to the healing of the cripple at the pool of Bethesda: 'the Jews', we are told in John 5:18, 'sought all the more to put him to death, because he not only broke the sabbath but also called God his own Father, making himself equal to God'. Later in this chapter we shall find further references to the healing at Bethesda and to the hostility which it provoked (verses 19–25). Because of this hostility, Jesus left Judaea for Galilee, where he spent the ensuing twelve months – 'the acceptable year of the Lord' (Luke 4:19) which witnessed the Galilean ministry, recorded in detail by the Synoptic Evangelists. These twelve months had now expired.

'Judaeans' is the preferable rendering of *Ioudaioi* here, because Judaea is contrasted with Galilee; 'Jews' would be less appropriate, because there were Jews in Galilee as well as in Judaea (cf. 6:41). It is, in any case, the religious establishment in Jerusalem that is meant (as in 5:10, 15, etc.).

7:2 The festival of the Jews known as Tabernacles was near at hand.

The festival of Tabernacles was celebrated on the 15th day of Tishri and the following week.[1] Since the Jewish months were lunar (the first day of each coinciding with the new moon), they cannot be exactly correlated with our calendar months (which begin and

169

end without reference to the phases of the moon); Tishri in general
covers part of September and part of October. If the year in question was AD 29, then the 15th of Tishri fell on October 12, six
Jewish months exactly before the last Passover.

By this time of year all the harvests had been safely gathered in
– not only the barley and wheat harvests, which were reaped
between April and June, but the grape and olive harvests too. This
'feast of ingathering at the end of the (agricultural) year' (Ex. 23:16;
cf. Ex. 34:22) was an occasion for great rejoicing. The Hebrews
called it the festival of booths (*sukkôth*), because for the full week
that it lasted people lived in makeshift booths of branches and
leaves (cf. Lev. 23:40–43); town-dwellers erected them in their
courtyards or on their flat housetops. Many Jews from outlying
parts of Palestine and from the Dispersion went to Jerusalem for
the festival, for this was one of the three great pilgrimages of the
Jewish year.

**7:3, 4 So his brothers said to him, 'Get away from here and
go to Judaea, so that your disciples also may behold your works
which you do. For no one works in secret and seeks to be in the
public eye himself. If you do these things, show yourself to the
world.'**

Jesus' 'brothers' here are most probably the members of his own
family, as elsewhere in the NT (cf. John 2:12). They are certainly
not his 'brothers' in the spiritual sense (as in John 20:17), for it is
plainly stated in verse 5 that they did not believe in him.

One explanation of their advice to Jesus is that there was a spirit
of revolt in the air, in Galilee as well as in Jerusalem. The brothers
were aware of it, and expected that it would manifest itself at
Jerusalem during the festival. They therefore urged Jesus to go to
Jerusalem to take charge of the revolt and turn it into a liberation
movement. If he was indeed the Messiah, that was the kind of
action which was popularly expected from the Messiah.[2] But there
is insufficient support for this idea in the present context. Such an
idea was certainly present in the minds of the men whom he fed in
the wilderness east of the lake of Galilee, but there it came to open
expression (John 6:15). What is meant here seems to be, more
generally: 'If you are indeed the Messiah, go to Jerusalem, for that
is the appropriate place to manifest yourself publicly to Israel as
the Messiah and invite them to recognize you.' It was widely
believed that when the Messiah came he would make himself publicly known in some spectacular way. According to one rabbinic
tradition, 'he will come and stand on the roof of the holy place;
then he will announce to the Israelites, "Ye poor, the time of your

redemption has arrived".".[3] (But others suggested that he would come unobtrusively and unrecognized except by those who had eyes to see.) Jesus did indeed proclaim at the outset of his ministry that the appointed time was now fulfilled and the year of release had come (Mark 1:15; Luke 4:18). But the suggestion that this proclamation should be attended by some impressively spectacular action which would strike the people's imagination was one which he rejected (it was an element indeed in the temptations which he repudiated in the weeks following his baptism). His 'disciples' mentioned by the brothers are those people who had been disposed to believe in him on his earlier visits to Jerusalem (cf. John 2:23); surely, it is implied, their incipient faith required to be strengthened by the sight of greater wonders than Jesus had thus far done in Jerusalem – wonders such as marked his recent Galilaean ministry. What the brothers did not realize was that those disciples' faith was imperfect precisely because it was based on the outward signs without proper appreciation of the inward truth they were intended to convey; that kind of faith would not be strengthened by the sight of greater or more numerous wonders.

It seemed incredible to the brothers that any one who believed himself to be the Messiah should deliberately avoid publicity. No one who aims at being a public figure will remain in the obscurity of a regional backwater, as Jesus (to the brothers' way of thinking) had now done for a year. He had certainly performed wonderful works in Galilee, but why not repeat them in Jerusalem, at the heart of the Jewish world? When they said, 'show yourself to the world', they meant 'to everyone' (using the phrase rather in the sense of French *tout le monde*). Everyone who mattered in Israel, at home or abroad, was likely to be found in Jerusalem during the great harvest-home celebrations. But John, after his fashion, probably sees a deeper meaning in the brothers' language. By going to Jerusalem, Jesus will indeed show himself to 'the world' in the widest sense; Jerusalem is the place where he must be 'lifted up' so that all without distinction may be drawn to him (John 2:14f.; 12:32).

7:5 For not even his brothers believed in him.

This is the impression that we get from the Synoptic Gospels also. Those who went to restrain him at Capernaum because people thought he was out of his senses, according to Mark 3:21, were his relatives ('his family', NEB). And it appears that, when his mother and brothers called for him around the same time (Mark 3:31), they did so because they failed to understand the nature and motives of the work in which he was engaged. It is not until after his

resurrection that his brothers are found among his followers (Acts
1:14), and this is no doubt due to his having appeared in resurrection to James (1 Cor. 15:7). At this stage, however, his brothers
did not believe in him because he failed so utterly to live up to their
preconception of the kind of person the Messiah would be and the
kind of things he would do.

7:6–8 So Jesus says to them, 'My time is not yet present; but
your time is always ready. The world cannot hate you, but it
hates me, because I bear witness about it, to the effect that its
works are wicked. Go up to the festival yourselves; I am not
going up to this festival, because my time has not yet been
fulfilled.'

As to his mother in Cana of Galilee Jesus had said, 'My hour
has not yet come' (John 2:4), so now he makes a similar reply to
his brothers. (The noun there was *hōra*; here it is *kairos*, 'appointed
time'.) When the time appointed for him by the Father came, to
go up to Jerusalem and be 'shown to the world' in a more profound
sense than they had any conception of, then he would go, but not
until then. But for people who had no such awareness of living
from moment to moment in sensitive rapport with God's directing
will, one time was as good as another: 'your time is always ready.'

The brothers had urged him to show himself to 'the world', but
Jesus now speaks of the world in another sense – the sense given
to the term in the prologue to this Gospel, where 'the world' failed
to recognize the eternal Word when he came into the world (John
1:10). This failure to give him the recognition and welcome to
which he was entitled was not a matter of mere indifference but of
positive antipathy. This antipathy was directed not only against
himself but also against any who did believe in him, thus demonstrating that they were not 'of the world' (see John 15:18–25).
Those who, like his brothers, did not believe in him did not experience the world's hostility. How could they? They belonged to
the world. He explains the world's hostility to him in language
reminiscent of John 3:19 f.: the entry of the true light into the
world exposed the world's evil for what it was, and those who
preferred their wicked works to the life-giving light hated the light
for its exposure of them.

Let the brothers go up to Jerusalem, then: those whose time is
always ready can go anywhere any time. But he whose will was
regulated by the Father's will would not move until that will was
shown. The textual evidence is divided between 'I am not (*ouk*)
going up' and 'I am not yet (*oupō*) going up'. On the whole, it is
easier to understand why an original 'not' should have been re-

placed by 'not yet' than *vice versa*. The reading ~~'I am not going up'~~ in any case implies the proviso: ~~'until the Father's will is shown'~~. Until then, Jesus' time was not 'fulfilled'.

7:9 Having said this, he himself stayed on in Galilee.

The third-century Neoplatonist Porphyry, who wrote a work *Against the Christians* in fifteen books, argued that it was a mark of irresoluteness for Jesus to stay in Galilee, and then go to Jerusalem after all a few days later.[4] The Evangelist's point is rather that the whole incident marks his steadfast resolution not to run before the Father's guidance nor yet to lag behind it.

(b) Excitement at the festival (7:10–13)

7:10 But when his brothers had gone up to the festival, then he himself also went up, not publicly but as it were in secret.

The Father's signal was given after the brothers had left for Judaea. Jesus' going up to Jerusalem 'as it were in secret' is in marked contrast to his brothers' insistence that he should court publicity. The time when it would be proper for him to make a public entry into Jerusalem had not yet come; six months later it came (cf. John 12:12 ff.). But now he bade farewell to Galilee, never to see it again before his death. That he was accompanied by at least some of the disciples on this secret journey to Judaea is highly probable, although they are not expressly mentioned here.

7:11 The Jews, then, were looking for him at the festival and saying, 'Where is that man?'

Meanwhile the scene shifts to Jerusalem. The 'Jews' who were looking out for him were members of the Sanhedrin, who hoped that, if he came to the festival, they might have an opportunity to arrest him this time. So they said, 'Where is that man (*ekeinos*)?' Galilee, where he had spent the past year, was ruled by the tetrarch Herod Antipas and was not under their jurisdiction, but in Jerusalem they held the chief executive power in Jewish affairs, subject to the overriding authority of the Roman governor.

7:12, 13 There was also much murmuring about him about the crowds. Some of them said, 'He is a good man'; others said, 'No; he leads the crowd astray.' However, no one spoke freely about him through fear of the Jews.

The distinction is clear between 'the crowds' and 'the Jews', of whom the crowds were afraid. The 'murmuring' about Jesus took the form of *sotto voce* discussion and disagreement; even in his absence, he provided a talking point. What he had done on his previous visit to the capital, and perhaps news of what he had been doing since then in Galilee, formed the topic of excited conversation. What were they to think of him? As some thought of the help and blessing which his works and words had brought to many, they were compelled to the conclusion that here was no public enemy, as the rulers maintained, but a good man. But others maintained that his deeds of mercy and power were simply a smokescreen to cover his real intentions: he was actually an impostor, claiming to be what he was not, and thus misleading the common people. This was the view that gained official currency in orthodox Jewish circles later on: an early tradition quoted in the Talmud says that he was executed on Passover Eve because he was a beguiler who led Israel astray.[5] But, whether they approved or disapproved of him, they did not voice their opinions too loudly or too publicly. The authorities did not wish him to be discussed at all, and any one who disregarded their wishes was liable to feel their displeasure.

(c) *Jesus at the festival* (7:14–8:59)

i. Moses and Christ (7:14–24)

7:14, 15 When it was now half-way through the festival, Jesus went up into the temple and began teaching. So the Jews were filled with wonder and said, 'How does this man know letters? He has never been trained.'

If Jesus had gone up with the pilgrims in time for the beginning of the festival, there might have been an attempt to give him such a triumphal entry as he was given six months later. A premature demonstration of this kind would have been specially embarrassing if this was shortly after the Galilaean massacre in the temple courts mentioned in Luke 13:1. But he went up quietly, arriving in the city half-way through the festival week, and the people who had been discussing him suddenly realized that he was there among them, teaching in the outer court of the temple (where a number of rabbis had their 'teaching pitches').

As the people, and especially the temple authorities and religious leaders, listened to his teaching, they were amazed. His mastery of the Scriptures and his power of persuasive exposition were undeniable, and yet he had been trained in none of the great rabbinical schools of the day. How could a man who had not sat at the feet of any of the masters in Israel hold his own so ably with the most gifted teachers of that time? A similar difficulty was experienced a year or so later, when the Sanhedrin, struck by the boldness with which 'unlearned (*agrammatoi*) and ignorant men' like Peter and John argued their case, put it down to the fact that they had been companions of Jesus (Acts 4:13). Peter and John spoke in Jesus' name, but Jesus invoked the authority of no teacher. The scribes always felt happier when they could quote the precedent of some past teacher but Jesus, now in Jerusalem as formerly in Galilee, 'taught as one who had authority and not as their scribes' (Matt. 7:29). Whence then did he derive his authority?

His knowledge of 'letters' does not mean his ability to read and write; that was no rare accomplishment among Jews. It means his command of sacred learning. The word here rendered 'letters' (*grammata*) was used in John 5:47 of the 'writings' of Moses. The Jews' question here, however, is not a direct reference back to the saying of Jesus recorded there (as has sometimes been suggested) but has to do rather with the substance of his temple discourses on the present occasion.

7:16-19 Jesus said to them in answer. 'My teaching is not my own; it comes from him who sent me. If any one is willing to do his will, he will know about the teaching, whether it comes from God or whether I speak on my own initiative. He who speaks on his own initiative seeks his own glory, but the one who is true is the one who seeks the glory of him who sent him; there is no wrong in him. Has not Moses given you the law? Yet none of you practises the law. Why do you seek to kill me?'

All the prophets, as the spokesmen of God, delivered a message that was not their own, but God's. So it was with the greatest prophet of all, who came to 'declare' the Father. As the works which he did were those which the Father had given him to do (John 5:36), so the words which he spoke were those which the Father had given him to speak (cf. John 3:34). Yet whereas the prophets said 'Thus says the LORD', Jesus, exercising the authority given to him by the Father, said 'I say to you' – 'Indeed and in truth I tell you'. The form of words in which he makes a distinction between 'me' and 'him who sent me' is found in the Synoptic Gospels (cf. Mark 9:37 with its parallels Matt. 10:40; Luke 9:48), but it is more frequent in this Gospel.

As then, so now it is not simply intellectual penetration that will determine truly whether Jesus' claim to impart the Father's teaching is well founded or not; an attitude of heart is also important. If there be a readiness to *do* the will of God, the capacity for dis-

cerning God's message will follow. Whoever has that readiness of
heart will recognize in the teaching of Jesus a message which au-
thenticates itself to spiritual perception and conscience as the truth.
Truth must ultimately be self-authenticating; it cannot appeal to
any authority external to itself: 'great is truth and mighty above all
things'. A faithful messenger seeks no credit for himself but for the
one with whose message he has been entrusted. Jesus' whole desire
is that those who hear what he has to say should glorify God by
believing it, since it is God who has commissioned him.

Having laid down these general principles, with their particular
application to his own ministry, Jesus now takes up the threads of
debate from his last visit to Jerusalem.[6] On that occasion the authorities tried to bring him to court on a capital charge because of
his attitude towards the sabbath law and because of the terms in
which he spoke of God as his Father. He defended himself then
against their charge of law-breaking by invoking Moses as a witness
against them. Moses spoke of him in advance as the coming
prophet, yet they gave no credence to Moses' testimony regarding
him (John 5:45–47). Now he invokes Moses again as a witness
against them because, for all their professed veneration for Moses'
law, they themselves were guilty of breaking it. Moses' law said
'Thou shalt not kill', yet they were trying to have him put to death.

**7:20 The crowd answered, 'You are demon-possessed; who is
seeking to kill you?'**

By 'the crowd' here we are doubtless to understand those elements in it which were hostile to him – those that accused him of
leading people astray (verse 12). Perhaps they did not catch the
reference to his previous visit; it seemed plain to them that he was
right now speaking publicly in the temple court and that no one
was trying to molest him. Hence their surprised comment. He was
surely demon-possessed, they suggested, a victim to persecution
delusions.

**7:21–24 Jesus replied to them, 'I did one work and you are all
amazed because of it. Moses has given you circumcision – not
that it comes from Moses but from the patriarchs – and you
circumcise a child on the sabbath day. If someone receives circumcision on the sabbath in order that Moses' law should not
be broken, are you angry with me because I made a whole man
well on the sabbath? Do not judge by outward appearance; let
your judgment be righteous judgment.'**

Jesus explains himself by reminding them of the healing of the cripple at the pool of Bethesda. They might well be amazed at the cure of a man who had been disabled for thirty-eight years, but their amazement was largely mixed with indignation because the cure had been performed on the sabbath. Jesus, however, argues that such an action was specially appropriate for the sabbath day.

The words *dia touto*, 'because of this', come in most versions at the beginning of verse 22, as though the meaning were 'Because of this Moses has given you circumcision' – but this raises the question 'Because of what?' and no answer is forthcoming in the context. It is better to attach them to the end of verse 21, where they make better sense (cf. RSV). The verb 'has given' (*dedōken*) is in the perfect tense because, although circumcision had been 'given' centuries before, it was still validly in being.

The rite of circumcision was instituted in Abraham's time (Gen. 17:10 ff.) and re-enacted in the law (Exod. 12:44 ff.). Each male infant in Israel was to be circumcised at eight days old, and if the eighth day coincided with the sabbath, the law of circumcision took precedence over the sabbath law: the child was circumcised, sabbath day or no sabbath day.[7] Jesus argues that if the sabbath law may rightly be suspended for the removal of a small piece of tissue from one part of the body, it cannot be wrong to heal a man's whole body on the sabbath day. This type of argument, in fact, was used by some rabbis to justify medical treatment in a case of urgency on the sabbath, but Jesus uses it to justify an act of healing whether the case is urgent or not.

It was a very superficial judgment which condemned him for performing such a good deed on the sabbath. Righteous judgment would penetrate beneath surface appearances and judge according to the spirit and purpose of the law.

ii. Jesus' messianic claims (7:25–31)

7:25–27 So some of the Jerusalemites said, 'Is this not the man that they are seeking to kill? But see, he speaks freely and they say nothing to him. Can it be that our rulers have really recognized that this is the Messiah? But we know where this man comes from. When the Messiah comes no one knows where he is from.'

The debate now moves away from the question of the sabbath law and concerns itself with Jesus' messianic claims. Various opinions are ventilated in the crowd, and there is a good deal of talking at cross purposes. Some might dismiss as madness his charge that an attempt was being made on his life; others knew that the charge was not baseless. But if his life was indeed being sought, that made his boldness the more remarkable, and not only his boldness but also the slowness of the authorities to arrest him or even to prevent him from speaking as he did in public. Why were they so reluctant to intervene? Perhaps (said some) since his last visit to Jerusalem the authorities had received evidence which proved that he really was the Messiah. (This is the first occasion in this Gospel where the idea of his being the Messiah is ventilated in Jerusalem.)

But the suggestion that he could be the Messiah, and especially that the authorities has been convinced that he was the Messiah, is immediately scouted. In the discussion which follows, three popularly held criteria of Messiahship are mentioned. The first of these is mentioned in verse 27, and Jesus did not appear to conform to it. It was widely believed that the Messiah, after coming into the world, would remain hidden in some unsuspected place until the divinely appointed time for his public manifestation came.[8] But (said they) this man obviously has not remained hidden until now; every one knows where he comes from.[9] This is an instance of 'Johannine irony'. They were thinking of Jesus' Galilaean home; to them he was 'Jesus of Nazareth'. But the Evangelist has in mind a profounder answer to the question whence Jesus came – an answer which comes to expression in Jesus' next words.

7:28, 29 So Jesus called out in the temple as he was teaching: 'You know me', he said, 'and you know where I am from? I have not come of my own accord, but he who sent me is true, and him you do not know. *I* know him, because I come from him and it is he who sent me.'

To their debate, which was carried on in small groups of disputants, Jesus gave a public answer as he continued to teach in the outer court 'You know me and you know where I come from? You may think you do, but in fact you do not know. I did not come on my own initiative, I was sent by God. I have come from him who is altogether true, the very source of truth; and when I speak the words which he has given me to speak, I speak the truth. But you do not know him, and therefore you do not really know where I come from.' So the coming of Jesus among men confronts them with the issue of the true knowledge of God. God cannot be known unless heed is paid to the one who is his *Word*.

This claim of Jesus echoes that preserved in the Synoptic record: 'no one knows the Father except the Son' (Matt. 11:27; cf. Luke 10:22). Jesus is sent by the Father, he proceeds from the Father; he knows the Father. The language is simple and unambiguous; the claim is august. Jesus asserts afresh his unique relation to the Father, and his hearers cannot miss the implication of his words.

7:30, 31 So they sought to arrest him, but no one laid a hand on him, because his hour had not yet come. Many members of the crowd believed in him: 'When the Messiah comes', they said, 'will he do more signs than this man has done?'

The attempt made to arrest Jesus may be that which is more fully described in verses 32, 45 f. It came to nothing, for in the purpose of God the hour for his arrest and passion had not yet arrived (cf. John 8:20; 12: 23, 27; 13:1; 17:1).

If the prophets of old gave proof that they were God's messengers by the signs which they performed, it was natural to believe that the Messiah would be accredited by even greater signs, which would provide conclusive evidence of his office and mission. But would the signs which the Messiah might be expected to perform be greater than those which Jesus was actually performing before their eyes? Such considerations moved many of his hearers to believe in him; these might include Galilaean pilgrims who had witnessed the feeding of the multitude six months previously, as well as natives of Jerusalem who remembered the healing of the cripple at the pool of Bethesda.

iii. Interlude: Attempt to arrest Jesus (7:32–36)

7:32 The Pharisees heard the crowd murmuring like this about him, and the chief priests and Pharisees sent officers to arrest him.

Those members of the crowd who wondered how the Messiah, when he came, could possibly perform greater signs than those being performed by Jesus in their midst, did not dare voice their thoughts aloud, but exchanged them under their breath with one another. But the religious authorities knew what they were thinking and saying *sotto voce*. If then, in spite of the authorities' refusal to recognize him as a teacher sent from God, so many of the common people were convinced that he was not only a teacher, but the Messiah in person, more drastic steps must be taken. The Sanhedrin (for so we should understand 'the chief priests and Pharisees') sent members of the temple police to arrest him. The chief priests (Gk. *archiereis*) were the members of the most wealthy and powerful priestly families, from whose ranks the high priest was regularly selected. They were the dominant figures in the party of the Sadducees, the majority party in the Sanhedrin. The temple police were responsible for the maintenance of law and order within the temple precincts. They were a picked body of Levites, and their commander (the 'captain of the temple') was an official wielding high authority, next only to the high priest, and he too was usually drawn from one or another of the leading chief-priestly families.[10]

7:33, 34 So Jesus said, 'For a short time I am still with you; then I am going to him who sent me. You will search for me, but you will not find me, and where I am you cannot come.'

After being told about the sending of the police to arrest Jesus, the readers are left in suspense regarding the outcome of their mission. Before John tells how they fared, he relates further words spoken by Jesus at the festival. These words plainly refer to the fact that Jesus had but a short time left before the completion of his earthly mission and his return to the Father. But they are (as so often) misunderstood by his hearers. We, of course, understand them better because we know the sequel, as the people in the temple court naturally could not. If those who looked for him before he arrived halfway through the festival week had such difficulty in finding him, and if his opponents had such difficulty in arresting him before his 'hour' had come, they would have even less chance of finding him when once he had returned to the Father.

7:35, 36 So the Jews said one to another, 'Where does this man plan to go that we shall not find him? Does he plan to go to the dispersion among the Greeks and teach the Greeks? What is the meaning of his saying, "You will search for me and not find me, and where I am you cannot come"?'

Jesus' hearers, and more particularly their leaders ('the Jews') failed to grasp his meaning, and talked (rather scornfully) as if he contemplated leaving Judaea for the lands of the dispersion north and west, where Jewish colonies were planted in a Greek environment. Was he planning a period of ministry among the Jews dispersed in those lands? Or was he conceivably thinking of a mission among the pagan Greeks themselves? In recording this remark, the Evangelist probably anticipates deliberately the implied invitation conveyed to Jesus by the Greeks who attended the Passover celebrations in Jerusalem six months later (John 12:20 ff.). Little did the speakers know that, while Jesus was not to go in person among the Greeks, his followers would be numbered in tens of thousands in the Greek lands in a few years' time. We may certainly trace here a further instance of 'Johannine irony'.

When his hearers repeat his words and wonder what they mean, there may be a hint of the implication which is more evident in John 8:21 ff., that it is sin (and especially the sin of refusing to believe in him) that will make it impossible for them to come where he is going. With regard to those who did believe in him he said on a later occasion, 'where I am, there my servant will also be' (John 12:26).

iv. The living water: further messianic debate (7:37–44)

7:37–39 On the last day, the great day of the feast, Jesus stood and called aloud, 'If any one is thirsty, let him come to me, and let him drink who believes in me. As the scripture has said, "Rivers of living water shall flow from his inmost being".' He said this with regard to the Spirit whom those who believed in him were going to receive; for the Spirit was not yet (present) because Jesus had not yet been glorified.

The festival lasted eight days, and on the eighth day was 'a holy convocation . . . a solemn assembly' (Lev. 23:36; cf. Num. 29:35 ff.; Neh. 8:18). When the people thanked God at the celebration of Tabernacles for all the fruits of the past year – vine and olive as well as barley and wheat – they did not forget his gift of rain, apart from which none of those crops would have grown. An association of this festival with adequate rainfall is implied in Zech. 14:16 f., and although the ceremony of water-pouring, well attested in connexion with Tabernacles for the two centuries preceding AD 70, is not mentioned in the OT (with the doubtful exception of 1 Sam. 7:6), it was probably of very considerable antiquity. This ceremony, which was intended to acknowledge God's goodness in sending rain and to ensure a plentiful supply for the following season, was enacted at dawn on the first seven days of the festival. A procession led by a priest went down to the pool of Siloam, where a golden pitcher was filled with water, and returned to the temple as the morning sacrifice was being offered. The water was then poured into a funnel at the west side of the altar, and the temple choir began to sing the Great Hallel (Pss. 113–118).[11]

It appears that the ceremony was not enacted on the eighth day, although a prayer for rain was recited then. If so, there is the more significance in John's statement that it was on the eighth day that Jesus made his proclamation. If no material water was poured then, spiritual and life-giving water was available to all who would receive it from him. The offer of this water had gone forth centuries before in the words of the prophet, 'Ho, every one who thirsts, come to the waters' (Isa. 55:1); but now it is repeated with a personal reference: 'If any one is thirsty, let him come to *me*.'

There are good reasons for revising the traditional punctuation of Jesus' invitation, so that it runs:

> If any one is thirsty, let him come to me;
> And let him drink who believes in me.

Both the rhythm and the rhyme of the resultant couplet echo with remarkable faithfulness the rhythm and rhyme of the original

Aramaic utterance so far as it can be reconstructed from the Greek text. Jesus had already told the Samaritan woman of the superior properties of the living water: 'Whoever drinks from the water that I shall give him will thirst no more: the water that I shall give him will become a spring of water within him, bubbling up to eternal life' (John 4:14). It is now suggested that this upspringing well not only refreshes one's own soul but flows out to refresh the lives of others. 'As the scripture has said, "Rivers of living water shall flow from his inmost being".' But where exactly does scripture say this? In the context of the book of Zechariah to which reference has just been made, we are told that in the day of the LORD 'living waters shall flow out from Jerusalem' (Zech. 14:8).[12] Ezekiel, giving further details about these waters, adds that 'everything will live where the river goes' (Ezek. 47:9). The fulfilment of these and similar prophecies (cf. Joel 3:18; Isa. 33:21) is not to be sought in twentieth-century schemes to cut a canal through Israeli territory to rival the Suez Canal or anything of that sort; it lies plain for all to read in John's description of 'the river of the water of life, bright as crystal, flowing from the throne of God and of the Lamb' (Rev. 22:1). It is from no earthly Jerusalem that the living waters go forth; it is from the dwelling-place of God in lives that are consecrated to him, in believing hearts where Christ has taken up his abode. And lest there should be any failure to grasp Jesus' meaning, the Evangelist adds an explicit note for the guidance of his readers: 'He said this with regard to the Spirit.'

Some Jewish teachers, it is interesting to note, connected the water-pouring ceremony with the promised outpouring of the Spirit. So, according to one rabbinical interpretation, the ceremony was called the 'water-drawing', and why? 'Because from there they draw the inspiration of the Holy Spirit, as it is written, "With joy you will draw water from the wells of salvation"' (Isa. 12:3).[13] It is here made plain that the living water promised by Jesus was the gift of the Spirit – a gift that could not be imparted in its fullness until Jesus was 'glorified'. This is the first of several references in this Gospel to the glorification of Jesus; from some of the later references it becomes clear that his glorification was his crucifixion – his being 'lifted up', to use another characteristic expression of this Evangelist. In the upper-room discourses Jesus emphasizes that the Paraclete cannot come to his disciples until he himself takes his departure: 'If I go', he says, 'I will send him to you' (John 16:7). The first fulfilment of this promise is recorded in John 20:22.

The best attested reading of the second-last clause of verse 39 is simply 'Spirit was not yet'. This does not mean that the Spirit did not yet exist; we have seen him active already (e.g. in John 1:32). It means that the Spirit was not yet present in the form which Jesus promised, or (as RSV has it) 'as yet the Spirit had not been given' – i.e. to the followers of Jesus.

7:40–42 So some of the crowd, hearing these words, said, 'This is surely the prophet.' Others said, 'This is the Messiah.' But the other side said, 'Why, is it out of Galilee that the Messiah is to come? Has not the scripture said that the Messiah is to come from the descendants of David, and from Bethlehem, the village where David was?'

Just as Jesus' feeding the multitude in the wilderness suggested to the people that he was the second Moses, the coming prophet of Deut. 18:15 (cf. John 6:14), so now his offer of living water suggested the same identification afresh, for many remembered how Moses had brought water out of the rock for their forefathers to drink (Exod. 17:6; Num. 20:11). The rabbi quoted above in our note on John 6:14 to the effect that 'as the first redeemer caused manna to descend . . . so will the last redeemer cause manna to descend', went on to say, 'As the first redeemer caused the well to gush forth, so will the last redeemer bring up water'.[14]

As appears in the attempts made to identify John the Baptist with some figure of eschatological expectation (John 1:20 f.), so here the Messiah is evidently distinguished in the popular mind from the prophet like Moses. They were clearly distinguished in the expectation of the Qumran community, which looked for a great prophet to arise at the end of the current age alongside the lay and priestly Messiahs. The early Christians may have been the first to identify the prophet like Moses with the Messiah of David's line, and they did so because they recognized in Jesus the one who fulfilled what was written of both these expected figures. But those Jerusalemites who on the present occasion identified Jesus with the Messiah were different from those who identified him with the coming prophet. Others, however, could not entertain the idea that the Messiah could be a Galilean; such an idea was revolutionary, clean contrary to all that they had been brought up to believe. It was generally accepted that the messianic King for whose advent they longed would be a descendant of David. This was implied in the promise of God communicated to David by Nathan in 2 Sam. 7:12–16, and it was confirmed in such prophetic oracles as Isa. 9:7. The 'sure mercies of David' (Isa. 55:3) could not be realized except in a prince of the house of David. Moreover, there was the express declaration in Micah 5:2 that Bethlehem in Judah would be the birthplace of the coming 'ruler in Israel'; it was most appropriate that great David's greater Son should be born in David's own native town. Here we have a signal instance of Johannine irony. John knew well enough, and so did many of his readers, that Jesus was indeed 'born of the seed of David according to the flesh' (Rom. 1:3), and that Judaean Bethlehem, not Galilaean Nazareth, was his birthplace. The fallacy inherent in this objection to the possibility of his being the Messiah was plain; no need to point it out in so many words. If we infer from this passage that the Fourth Evangelist either did not know or did not accept Jesus' Davidic descent or nativity in Bethlehem, we expose our own failure to appreciate his delicate handling of this situation.

7:43, 44 So a division took place in the crowd because of him. And some of them wanted to arrest him, but no one laid hands on him.

From now on the division (*schisma*) in the crowd on Jesus' account becomes a recurring note in the narrative (cf. 9:16; 10:19); people range themselves inevitably on this side or that according to their estimate of him. As in verse 30, the renewed attempt to arrest or restrain him comes to nothing.

v. Unbelief in high places (7:45–52)

7:45, 46 So the officers came to the chief priests and Pharisees, who said to them, 'Why have you not brought him?' The officers replied, 'No human being ever spoke as he does.'

The attempt to lay hands on Jesus, mentioned in verse 44, reminds the readers that a detachment of temple police had already been sent by the Sanhedrin to place him under restraint (verse 32). John knows how to use the device of suspense effectively; he now returns to those members of the police force and tells how they came back to the authorities empty-handed. The authorities naturally demand an explanation.

Although the actual terminology of witness is not used here, these police officers add their contribution to the cumulative witness borne to Jesus and recorded in this Gospel. The words which they heard him speak made such an impression on them that they could not bring themselves to execute their commission and arrest him. 'No one ever spoke like him.' Such authority (cf. Matt. 7:29), such grace (cf. Luke 4:22), they had never found in any other speaker. Their testimony was expressed in few and simple words, but it has stood the test of nineteen centuries.

7:47–49 So the Pharisees answered them, 'Have you also been led astray? Has any one of the rulers or of the Pharisees believed in him? But this crowd does not know the law; it is accursed.'

The rank and file of the populace might be carried away by Jesus' persuasive speech, the Pharisees implied, but it was surprising that disciplined police officers, whose duty was simply to carry out their orders, should also succumb to the persuasiveness of his words.

The question, 'Has any one of the rulers or of the Pharisees believed in him?' was intended to be a telling argument. As with the previous question, so with this, the form in which it is cast implies that the only reasonable answer is 'No'. Surely, if Jesus were indeed the Messiah, or even a genuine prophet of God, some of the rulers of the people would have acknowledged his claims, some of the religious experts would have recognized his true character. As it was, the argument suggested, only ignorant people could suppose that his claims had any substance. The argument was not so sound as they imagined: for one thing, Nicodemus was there to testify that at least one of the rulers, a Pharisee to boot, was well-disposed to Jesus; and for another thing, Jesus himself declared that the truth about his person and mission had been concealed from the wise and understanding and revealed to babes (Matt. 11:25; Luke 10:21). God habitually chooses the weak and foolish to confound the wise and mighty.

The disparaging judgment pronounced on the crowd expresses a characteristic attitude of many Pharisees towards the common people. The common people – 'the people of the land', as they called them – simply could not be expected to master the details of the oral law, the 'tradition of the elders', and therefore they were always liable to infringe it. Even the liberal Rabbi Hillel, of the generation before Christ, summed up this attitude when he said, 'No member of the common people is pious'.[15] From the Pharisees' point of view, the common people could easily be misled by any plausible teacher, because of their shocking ignorance of the true interpretation of the law.

7:50–52 Nicodemus – he who came to Jesus on a former occasion, and was one of their number – said to them, 'Does our law pass judgment on any one before it first hears from him and learns what he is doing?' They said to him in answer, 'Are you from Galilee too? Search and see: no prophet arises from Galilee.'

Nicodemus, introduced in John 3:1 (on the occasion when he came to Jesus by night) as 'a man of the Pharisees, a ruler of the

Jews', now speaks up and protests against this condemnation of Jesus in his absence. Whatever might be said of the ignorance of the common people, here was a man who knew the law and could cite it authoritatively, as befitted 'the teacher of Israel'.

The rule to which Nicodemus appealed is formulated thus in rabbinic literature: 'Flesh and blood may pass judgment on a man if it hears his words; if it does not hear them, it cannot establish its judgment.'[16] Roman law agreed with Jewish law on this point, as is evident from the words of Festus in Acts 25:16. In both codes, the accused must have the opportunity to speak in his own defence before the verdict of the court is reached.

But even Nicodemus's protest could only call forth from the angry majority the contemptuous suggestion that he too had become a Galilaean. No prophet could be expected from Galilee, they argued, because no prophet had ever come from there. Even if they were right on the point of historical fact, they might now be faced with an exception to the rule. But there had been exceptions to the rule before: no less a prophet than Elijah came from Gilead (Galilee beyond Jordan). But it was generally felt in the south that only in Judaea could pure religion be looked for – a heritage from the days immediately following the return from the Babylonian exile. The fact that Jesus was actually born in Judaea (cf. verses 41, 42) may not have been known to them.

The first hand of Papyrus 66 reads 'out of Galilee the prophet does not arise': that is to say, it was not from Galilee that the prophet like Moses of Deut. 18:15 would come. Not that there was any definite indication where he would come from, but they felt sure that, whatever region gave him birth, it would not be Galilee.[17]

NOTES

1. Cf. G. W. MacRae, 'The Meaning and Evolution of the Feast of Tabernacles', *CBQ* 22 (1960), pp. 251–276.
2. Cf. J. Pickl, *The Messias* (St. Louis, 1946), pp. 64, 88.
3. *Pesiqta Rabbati* (late rabbinical collection of homilies) 162a.
4. According to Jerome, *Dialogues against the Pelagians* 2.17.
5. Babylonian Talmud, tractate *Sanhedrîn* 43a.
6. B. Lindars regards verses 16–24 as 'an item of the discourse of chapter 5 which has been deliberately held over to form the starting-point for the complex debates which occupy chapters 7 and 8' (*Behind the Fourth Gospel*, p. 51).
7. 'They may perform on the sabbath all things that are needful for circumcision' (Mishnah, tractate *Shabbāth* 18.1; 19.2); 'Great is circumcision, which over-rides even the rigour of the sabbath' (Rabbi Jose, quoted in Mishnah, tractate *Neḏārîm* 3.11). With Jesus' present argument cf. the saying of Rabbi Eleazar ben Azariah (*c.* AD 100) in *Mekhilta* (rabbinical commentary) on Exod. 31:13: 'If in performing the rite of circumcision, which affects only one member of the body, one should set aside the sabbath laws, how much more should one do so for the whole body when it is in danger!' A parallel argument in Matt.

12:5 appeals to the fact that priests incur no guilt for carrying out their sacrificial duties in the temple on the sabbath.

8. According to Justin's Jewish interlocutor Trypho, the Messiah remains unknown, even to himself, until Elijah comes to anoint him and make him manifest to all (Justin, *Dialogue with Trypho* 8.7). One later fancy pictured him as engaged incognito at the gate of Rome in binding up the wounds of sufferers (Babylonian Talmud, tractate *Sanhedrin* 98a).

9. In verse 27 there is an instance of John's fondness for using synonyms in the same context: 'we know (*oidamen*) where this man comes from . . . no one knows (*ginōskei*) where he [the Messiah] is from.' In some places there may be a difference in nuance between *oida* and *ginōskō*, but not here. Cf. John 8:55.

10. See E. Schürer, *The History of the Jewish People in the Age of Jesus Christ*, II (Edinburgh, 1979), pp. 277 f.

11. Mishnah, tractate *Sukkāh* 4.9.

12. Zechariah 14 was the reading from the Prophets prescribed for the first day of Tabernacles (Babylonian Talmud, tractate *Mᵉgillāh* 31a).

13. Jerusalem Talmud, tractate *Sukkāh* 5.1, 55a; *Ruth Rabba* (rabbinical commentary) 4.8 (on Ruth 2:9). From the verb *shā'ab* ('draw') in Isa. 12:3 the temple court in which the ceremony took place was sometimes called *bêth ha-shᵉ'û-bāh*, 'the house of the water-drawing' (cf. p. 206, n. 1).

14. *Ecclesiastes Rabba* 1.9.1 on Eccl. 1:9 (see p. 146).

15. *Pirqê 'Abôth* 2.6.

16. Rabbi Eleazar ben Pedath (*c.* AD 300), quoted in *Exodus Rabba* (rabbinical commentary) 21.3 (on Exod. 14:15).

17. For John 7:53–8:11 (the incident of the adulterous woman) and comment see pp. 413–418.

CHAPTER 8

vi. The light of the world (8:12–20)

8:12 Then Jesus spoke to them again: 'I am the light of the world. Whoever follows me will not walk in the darkness, but will have the light of life.'

As the ceremony of the water-pouring provides an effective setting for Jesus' proclamation about the living water in verses 37 and 38, so the setting for his further claim to be the light of the world may be provided by another feature of the festival of Tabernacles: the temple precincts were brightly illuminated.[1]

In the OT God is his people's light (Ps. 27:1); in the light of his presence they enjoy grace and peace (Num. 6:24–26). The Servant of the LORD is appointed as a light to the nations, that God's salvation may extend to the end of the earth (Isa. 49:6). The word or law of God is also described as a light to guide the path of the obedient (Ps. 119:105; Prov. 6:23). So Jesus, as the Son of the Father, the Servant of the LORD and the Word incarnate, embodies this OT language. Even before the Word became incarnate, the life which he eternally possessed, says John, 'was the light of men' (John 1:4); now by his incarnation the true light has come into the world, providing illumination for all (John 1:9; 3:19).

The two realms, of darkness and of light, are clearly distinguished. It has already been shown how the sons of light and the sons of darkness inevitably declare themselves for what they respectively are with the coming of the true light into the world (John 3:19, 21). The sons of light come to the light and follow the light; those who will not do this must remain in the darkness, because there is no other light than the light of the world. The light which he imparts is the 'light of life' because it is life-giving. 'With thee is the fountain of life', says the psalmist to God; 'in thy light do we see light' (Ps. 36:9). In the Qumran *Rule of the Community* it is said that 'by the spirit of God's true counsel the ways of man, even all his iniquities, are atoned for, so that he can behold the light of life'.[2] Our Evangelist would have agreed with this, but would have insisted that the language, to have any effective meaning, must be understood personally, in relation to the living and life-giving 'light of the world'.

8:13 The Pharisees said to him, 'You are bearing testimony to yourself; your testimony is not true.'

The Pharisees' objection harks back to Jesus' own words in John 5:31, 'If I bear witness about myself, my witness is not true.' Ostensibly, their present objection had a point.

8:14–16 Jesus said in reply to them, 'Even if I do bear testimony to myself, my testimony is true, because I know where I came from and where I am going. As for you, you do not know where I came from or where I am going. You judge according to outward appearance; I judge no one. And if I do judge, my judgment is true, for I am not alone; along with me there is the one who sent me.'

If Jesus makes a statement about himself, such as 'I am the light of the world', that statement is not necessarily unsupported. Evidence given in a court of law must be confirmed by more than one, but the Son of the Father always speaks by the Father's authority, whether the Father's authority is expressly invoked or not. Jesus knows where he has come from – from the Father (cf. John 5:36 f.; 16:28) – and where he is going – to the Father (cf. John 13:1; 16:28). Meanwhile, by an eternal 'coinherence', he is in the Father and the Father in him (cf. John 14:11). Therefore if, by the formal letter of the law, his testimony need not be admitted if he seems to be speaking for himself, in fact it is always substantiated by the Father and so always to be admitted – and accepted. To the Pharisees he is at best 'a teacher come from God' (John 3:1) and therefore not entitled to speak in his own name. They did not know his true origin or destiny; they could judge only 'according to the flesh' – by outward appearance (cf. John 7:24) – and so their judgment about him was misguided. He was indeed the one to whom all judgment was committed by the Father (John 5:22), even if at present he did not exercise his prerogative of judgment; he had come to bring salvation, not to pronounce judgment (John 3:17; 12:47).

The verb 'to judge (*krinō*) is used here in two senses – the judicial sense ('I judge no one') and the sense of coming to a well-informed decision. In the latter sense their judgment was wrong, because it was superficial (cf. 1 Sam. 16:7); his judgment was right, because he reached it in fellowship with the Father. There is the implication here that, while they were sitting in judgment on him and his claims and reaching an adverse verdict it was in reality he who was judging them, and judging them beyond the possibility of error because of his oneness of mind with the one who had sent him.

8:17, 18 'Moreover, in your law it is written that the testimony of two men is true. I am one who bears testimony about myself, and the Father who sent me also bears testimony about me.'

Jesus reverts to the argument of John 5:37. The principle of the law which he invokes is laid down in Deut. 19:15: 'only on the evidence of two witnesses, or of three witnesses, shall a charge be sustained' (cf. Deut. 17:6). The law is called 'your law' because they acknowledged its authority and were bound to admit the force of an argument based on it. Indeed, it was on the basis of the principle now quoted by Jesus that they had refused to admit his testimony when he (as they said) bore witness about himself (verse 13). But, Jesus insists, there is a second witness to the truth of his claims, and that is the Father who had sent him: the Father's testimony carries absolute authority.

8:19 So they said to him, 'Where is your Father?' Jesus answered: 'You know neither me nor my Father. If you knew me, you would know my Father also.'

On the earlier occasion in Jerusalem when Jesus had appealed to his Father's testimony, he told those who were debating with him that they had never heard the Father's voice nor seen his form (John 5:37). Now, in response to their question, 'Where is your Father?' he makes a similar statement. They might claim to know where Jesus came from, thinking on an earthly level (John 7:27), but they were incapable of conceiving his eternal origin. If they knew him as he truly was, they would know his Father also, for he had come to reveal the Father (cf. John 14:9).

8:20 He spoke these words in the treasury while he was teaching in the temple. No one arrested him, because his hour had not yet come.

The 'treasury' was that part of the Court of the Women where thirteen-trumpet shaped containers were placed for the reception of various dues, six of them being for voluntary offerings.[3] It was in this neighbourhood, 'opposite the treasury', that Jesus sat on the occasion during Holy Week when he saw the widow put her two 'mites' into one of the containers (Mark 12:41–44).

John does not say whether or not an attempt was made to arrest him on this occasion, as had been done a short time before (John 7:32, 45 f.). He does say that no one in fact arrested him because (as was said in John 7:30) 'his hour had not yet come' – not simply the 'hour' of his arrest, trial and execution, but the 'hour of his departure from this world to the Father' (John 13:1). The arrest, trial and execution, when at last their time came, were but stages on his return journey to the one who had sent him into the world.

vii. 'I am He' (8:21–30)

8:21 So he said to them again, 'I am going, and you will look for me, but you will die in your sin. Where I am going you cannot come.'

Again Jesus makes a statement which his hearers cannot quite grasp. Their uncomprehending response to it then provides him with an opportunity to explain it and apply it to their condition. The incarnate Word is to be on earth in a visible form for a limited period only. This limited period is their opportunity: if they accept him for what he is, then they will receive the right to become God's children; eternal life will be theirs. But if they let the opportunity slip, it will not recur. The time of his visible presence with them will have passed, and they will seek him after that in vain. Instead of enjoying eternal life through faith in him, they will die in their sin – without having their sin removed. The 'sin' (singular) is preeminently their failure to believe in him (cf. John 16:9), their refusal to come to the light while it is available (cf. John 3:19–21).

The language here is in large part a repetition of John 7:33f.; it also anticipates in measure Jesus' words to the disciples in John 13:33–14:4. They too are told that he is leaving them, that they will look for him but not be able to follow him – not yet, at least, for in fact he is going to prepare a place for them so that they may be where he is.

8:22–24 So the Jews said, 'Will he kill himself, that he says, "Where I am going you cannot come"?' He said to them, 'You belong to the lower realm; I belong to the upper realm. You belong to this world; I do not belong to this world. That is why I told you that you will die in your sins. Unless you believe that I am He, you will die in your sins.'

On the former occasion when Jesus used such language, his hearers wondered if he was meditating a mission to the Greeks in the lands of the Dispersion (John 7:35). On this occasion some of them wonder if he is meditating something more drastic – suicide, no less. John's readers can savour the irony of this because they know that Jesus did indeed meeet a violent death, but at his enemies' hands, not at his own.

Jesus once again cuts into their debate with a peremptory declaration. He and they belong to two different realms, as is shown by the different presuppositions and perspectives of their very thought and language. They were 'from those below' (*ek tōn katō*), he said; he himself was 'from those above' (*ek tōn anō*). The genitive plural *tōn* may be either masculine or neuter; which is it here? Is he relating his hearers to 'the persons below' (*hoi katō*) or to 'the things below' (*ta katō*)? And is he relating himself to 'those above' (*hoi anō*) or to 'the things above' (*ta anō*)? Elsewhere in this Gospel, when Jesus' origin is designated by means of the preposition *ek* or *apo* followed by a personal noun, the personal noun is always singular, denoting God or the Father (cf. John 13:3; 16:28). It is more probable, then, that he speaks of himself here as coming from 'the things above' – the upper realm. And if this is so, his opponents will similarly be described as coming from 'the things below' – the lower realm. This indeed is confirmed by the words immediately following, where 'the lower realm' is replaced by 'this world' and 'the upper realm' is said to be 'not . . . this world' (but rather the heavenly world). 'This world' is the *kosmos* of John 1:10, which gave the divine Word no recognition when he came to it, the *kosmos* of which Jesus said to his brothers, 'it hates me, because I bear witness concerning it that its deeds are evil' (John 7:7). Jesus has described himself as 'the light of the *kosmos*', but it is only those who follow him that have the 'light of life' and avoid walking in darkness (verse 12). By following him they show that they, like him, are 'not of this world'. The others choose darkness and accordingly die in their sins. The plural 'sins' is used in verse 24, as against the singular 'sin' in verse 21; if the singular expresses the root sin of unbelief, the plural expresses those particular attitudes, words and actions which make up its fruit.

Those who belong to the lower realm cannot by themselves make the journey to the upper realm; they cannot even grasp the language of the upper realm. 'What is born of the flesh is flesh, and what is born of the Spirit is spirit' (John 3:6). The only possibility for those of the lower realm to be transferred to the upper realm is if someone descends from the upper to the lower realm and then 'ascends back where he was before' (John 6:62), opening up a way – indeed, himself constituting the way – by which others may ascend there too (John 14:6).

But has someone in fact descended in such a manner that others may ascend with him? The answer of this Gospel is that Jesus, 'the Son of Man whose home is in heaven', has done so (John 3:13). But only those who recognize him to be what he is, and commit themselves to him in faith, can make the ascent to life through him. The others go on living on the lower plane, and there, in due course, they die. As Jesus' words are rendered in the NEB; 'If you do not believe that I am what I am, you will die in your sins.'

The words, *egō eimi*, which NEB renders 'I am what I am', are capable of a wide range of meaning in this Gospel. On the most pedestrian level, they mean 'It is I', as when Jesus identifies himself to the disciples on the lake (John 6:20).[4] But when Jesus uses these words in this Gospel one wonders whether the Evangelist's thought is moving on two planes simultaneously. In the present context, at any rate, there is no question of simple self-identification: Jesus is saying something important about his person.

The NEB rendering is reminiscent of the revelation to Moses at the burning bush: when God commissioned him to go back to Egypt and tell his people that the God of their fathers was about to deliver them, Moses said, 'What name shall I give you when they ask for one?' and God said, ' "I am who I am"; tell them that "I am" has sent you' (Ex. 3:13 f.). In the Septuagint of Ex. 3:14 God's reply to Moses is, ' "*Egō eimi ho ōn* (I am the one who is)"; tell them that "*ho ōn* (The one who is)" has sent you'. If a direct reference had been intended to Ex. 3:14 in the present passage, one might have expected *ho ōn* rather than *egō eimi*. It is more probable here that *egō eimi* echoes 'I am He' (*'ănî hû*), used repeatedly as a divine affirmation in Isa. 40–55 and translated *egō eimi* in the LXX (e.g. Isa. 41:4; 43:10, 13, 25; 46:4; 48:12). This affirmation *'ănî hû* may be the origin of the unusual divine name *'ănî wᵉhû* (literally 'I and He') which was used in later days as a substitute for the ineffable name *Yahweh*, especially in the processional singing of Ps. 118:25 at the feast of Tabernacles.[5] The conjunction *wᵉ* ('and') was taken to convey the close association, amounting almost to identification, of the God of Israel and his people. It may well be that *egō eimi* here and in verse 28 below suggests that Jesus embodies the link binding God and his people together.[6]

8:25, 26 So they said to him, 'Who are you?' Jesus said to them, 'I am what I have been telling you all along. I have many things to say about you, many things to pass judgment on, but he who sent me is true, and what I say to the world is what I have heard from him.'

The question 'Who?' is the natural response to the claim 'I am He' if the meaning of the claim is not properly understood. And we have seen that *egō eimi* is an ambiguous utterance in itself.

Jesus' reply to his questioners' 'Who are you?' is perhaps the most difficult clause to translate in this whole Gospel. The translation 'Why should I speak to you at all?' (NEB) conveys the mean-

ing put upon the words by most of the Greek writers who dealt
with them in the early centuries AD, who might be expected to
know their own language. The phrase translated 'at all' is *tēn
archēn*; it is usually in negative clauses that it has this meaning,
but the negative idea may inhere in the sense ('Why should I speak
to you at all?' is equivalent to 'I should not speak to you at all').
The phrase *tēn archēn* literally means 'the beginning', in the accusative case. The accusative cannot well denote the object of the
clause here; it must be taken as an adverbial accusative. It is so
taken by those who translate it 'at all'; it is so taken, also, by those
who translate it 'from the beginning', as in RSV. ('Even what I have
told you from the beginning'). The accusative is hardly the case to
express *'from* the beginning' (which in Johannine Greek is *ap'
archēs*, as in 1 John 1:1); it might mean 'at first', as though Jesus'
reply to the question 'Who are you?' were 'Precisely what I tell
you (or "have been telling you") at first' (cf. NEB mg.: 'What I
have told you all along'). The Latin version makes Jesus claim to
be 'The Beginning' (cf. Col. 1:18). This is possible in Latin, where
the word for 'beginning' (*principium*) is neuter and so makes no
distinction between nominative and accusative; the Greek cannot
be made to yield this sense. A correction in Papyrus 66 inserts
before *tēn archēn* the two words *eipon hymin*, so that the sense
is: 'I told you at the beginning that which also I am speaking to
you (now').' This quite probably expresses the original sense, even
if the wording has been amplified to make the construction more
clear. Certainly in this Gospel Jesus has not been reticent in Jerusalem about his relation to the Father, ever since the controversy
precipitated by his action at the pool of Bethesda.

The difficulty about the rendering preferred by the Greek fathers
('Why should I speak to you at all?') is that it does not fit the
context. Far from being reluctant to speak to them 'at all', Jesus
assures them that he has much to say to them and about them –
much to say by way of judgment. The judgment here consists in
his declaration of the truth, so that the deficiencies of their beliefs
and practices may be exposed by its light. The truth which he
declares is not something that he himself has thought up; it has
been entrusted to him by the one who sent him. As the Son can do
nothing on his own initiative, but only what he sees the Father
doing (John 5:19), so the Son can teach nothing on his own initiative, but only what he is told by the Father. The Evangelist himself
has already borne testimony to this effect: 'He whom God has sent
speaks the words of God' (John 3:34). As God is true, the message
which he delivers to the world by the agency of his Son is the
truth, whether those who hear it find it palatable or not.

8:27–29 **They did not recognize that he was speaking to them about the Father. So Jesus said, 'When you have lifted up the Son of Man, then you will recognize that I am He, and that I do nothing on my own initiative, but as the Father has taught me, so I speak. And he who sent me is with me; he has not left me alone, because I always do the things that are pleasing to him.'**

It is strange that Jesus' hearers did not recognize that, when he spoke of the one who had sent him, he was referring to the Father. It might have been thought that this was sufficiently clear from the words which he had spoken to them on his previous visit to the capital, when he said, for example, 'The Father who sent me has borne witness concerning me' (John 5:37). John may wish to emphasize a spiritual obtuseness which arose from their unwillingness to admit his claims as valid. The first hand in Codex Sinaiticus and some western witnesses to the text have an addition to the wording which yields the sense: 'They did not recognize that he was saying that God was his Father'. Such a claim from him had enraged them on the former occasion (John 5:18); perhaps because this time he used the periphrasis 'he who sent me', instead of saying 'my Father', the claim was not so explicit. But John's readers have learned enough by this time to know very well what Jesus means.

To the question 'Who are you?' no adequate answer will be given until the Son of Man has been 'lifted up'; that will be the definitive answer. The cross is the complete revelation of the divine glory manifested in the Son. Jesus had told the first disciples of the coming time when they would see heaven opened and the angels of God ascending and descending on the Son of Man; they could see no greater vision than that (John 1:50 f.). 'The Son of Man must be lifted up', he said to Nicodemus, 'in order that every one who believes may have eternal life in him' (John 3:15). As we have seen before, his being 'lifted up' on the cross is not only pictured as the first stage of his journey back to the Father: it is in itself his exaltation, the occasion of his being glorified (cf. John 12:23, 31–33). Mark, the earliest Evangelist, expresses the same truth when he tells how, at the moment of Jesus' death, the temple curtain which concealed the divine glory was torn in two from top to bottom, while the centurion in charge of the execution confessed, 'Truly this man was God's Son' (Mark 15:38 f.).

Jesus came into the world to reveal the Father, and he revealed him most fully in his death on the cross. There, if anywhere, the scales fall from the eyes and the acknowledgement is constrained: 'lo, this is our God; we have waited for him; . . . let us be glad and rejoice in his salvation' (Isa. 25:9). Of course, even the cross and resurrection would not convince them all that the crucified one was the revealer of the Father, but if that would not convince them, nothing would.

His 'lifting up' would be his vindication: then it would be manifest that he had acted and spoken throughout by the Father's authority. 'As the Father has taught me, so I speak . . . I always do the things that are pleasing to him.' Even now, the ever-present awareness of this vindication gave him confidence; more than that, he had the assurance of the Father's constant presence and approval. In all that he did, the Father was with him: 'it is not I alone that judge', he has just said, 'but I and the one who sent me' (verse 16). So, on the eve of the cross, with the imminent prospect of desertion by his companions, he retained this assurance: 'You will all leave me alone; but I am not alone, because the Father is with me' (John 16:32).

8:30 **While he was saying this, many put their faith in him.**

Such was the power with which he spoke that many of his hearers were convinced by his words without waiting for the final evidence of his 'lifting up'. On an earlier occasion in Jerusalem many believed because of the signs which he performed (John 2:23); the faith which was called forth by his words may well have been more firmly founded than that which was based on the signs.

viii. Abraham's children (8:31–59)

8:31, 32 **So Jesus said to the Jews who had believed in him, 'If you remain in my word, you will truly be my disciples, and you will come to know the truth, and the truth will set you free.'**

To 'remain' in Jesus' 'word' is to adhere to his teaching – to direct their lives by it. The power of what he said had already moved some of his hearers to believe in him, but discipleship is something continuous; it is a way of life.[7] A true disciple has an affinity for his teacher's instruction and accepts it, not blindly but intelligently. The teacher's instruction becomes the disciple's rule of faith and practice. What Jesus taught was the truth; his disciples, by paying heed to him, received the truth. False belief holds the minds of men and women in bondage; truth liberates them. Truth by its very nature cannot be imposed by external compulsion, nor can it be validated by anything other than itself. One either sees the truth for what it is, or one does not. When we bear in mind the meaning of 'truth' in this Gospel, where the concept finds its embodiment in Jesus himself, it follows that for his disciples to know the truth 'they must not only hear his words: they must in some sort be united with him who is the truth'.[8]

8:33 They answered him, 'We are Abraham's offspring and have never been enslaved to any one. How can you say, "You will become free"?'

The polemical tone of the exchange which now follows between Jesus and his hearers makes it difficult to think of those hearers as confined to the Jews who had newly believed in him. At some point early in the exchange the circle of his interlocutors widens; by the time verse 37 is reached, it is unbelieving Jews who are addressed. The present question calls for elucidation of Jesus' words: 'the truth will set you free'. People who need to be set free are bound or enslaved, but the speakers have no consciousness of bondage. They repudiate the suggestion: they are Abraham's free-born descendants, and have never been held in slavery. True, their ancestors had been set to forced labour in Egypt and (later) carried captive to Babylon; but these experiences were temporary chastisements.[9] The ancient blessing pronounced through Abraham and through his offspring (Gen. 12:3; 22:18, etc.) would have been pointless if Abraham's offspring were a race of slaves. The promise to Abraham spoke of blessing for his descendants, and freedom was an essential element in that blessing.[10]

8:34–36 Jesus answered, 'Indeed and in truth I tell you: every one who practises sin is a slave of sin. He who is a slave does not remain permanently in the house; it is the son who remains there permanently. So, if the Son sets you free, you will be really free.'

Jesus reminds them that there is another kind of slavery than social or economic slavery. Sin is a slave-master, and it is possible even for people who think of themselves as free to be enslaved to sin. The words 'of sin' may not be part of the original text,[11] but the context makes it clear that 'a slave of sin' is what is meant. The teaching here is quite similar to Paul's in Rom. 6:12–23.

Verse 35 is probably a parenthetical parable.[12] A slave, no matter to whom he belongs, has no permanent standing in his master's house. He can very easily be sold to someone else; he is then in bondage to his new owner. But it is different with a son. He has a place in his father's house as of right: once a son, always a son. Verse 36 has a closer relation to verse 34: the sinner is enslaved, but he can be liberated. His liberator is the Son – not the son of his slavemaster, but the Son in the sense in which this designation is used throughout the Gospel of John. The son in a free household, when once he comes of age, can act with authority because of his status in that household: the Son of God acts with supreme authority because 'the Father loves the Son and has given everything into his hand' (John 3:35). If, acting by the authority with which the Father has invested him, the Son emancipates a slave, that slave henceforth is 'really free'.

8:37, 38 'I know that you are Abraham's offspring. But you are seeking to kill me, because my word has no place in you. I, for my part, speak the things which I have seen with my Father; you do what you have heard from your father.'

Jesus agrees that they are Abraham's descendants in the natural sense. But, he goes on to point out, moral relationship is more important than natural relationship, and Abraham's true children are those who follow Abraham's example. The charge that those whom he is addressing are still looking for an opportunity to put him to death rules out the possibility that they are the Jews who had believed in him. They are rather those who are described in John 5:18 as plotting to kill him soon after the healing incident at the pool of Bethesda. In them his teaching found no room, no acceptance; to those who believed in him, on the other hand, he spoke encouragingly about 'remaining' in his word (verse 31).

Jesus' claim to speak the things which he had 'seen' in the Father's presence (verse 38) echoes his language in John 6:46: 'he who comes from God, he has seen the Father'. The truth which he teaches is heavenly truth, although it is presented for acceptance by men and women on earth. But no one can speak of heavenly realities except one who has come down from heaven and imparts to his hearers on earth what he has seen and heard in that transcendent realm (cf. John 3:11–13).

It is possible to treat the verb 'do' in the second half of verse 38 as imperative: 'as for you, do the things which you have heard from the Father' (the possessive pronoun 'your' is absent from several witnesses to the text, including Papyrus 66 and Codex Vaticanus). In that case the things which they had heard from the Father would include the things which Jesus taught with the Father's authority. This, however, is not what they understood Jesus to mean. That does not prove that it was not what he meant: in this Gospel Jesus is quite frequently misunderstood. But on the whole it seems more probable that he means that, while his own works are in keeping with his Father's character, their works are in keeping with *their* father's character.

8:39–41a They said to him in answer, 'Our father is Abraham.' Jesus says to them, 'If you are Abraham's children, you would do Abraham's works. But as it is, you are seeking to kill me, a man who has told you the truth which I have heard from God. This is not what Abraham did. You do your father's works.'

They may have failed to grasp immediately what Jesus meant by his reference to their father: they claim, however, as any Jew would do, that Abraham is their father *par excellence.* 'Abraham our father' is the regular Jewish way of referring to Abraham (compare 'Moses our teacher' and 'David our king'). But Jesus insists explicitly now that moral kinship is the only kinship that matters: to cherish murderous intentions against someone who has imparted the truth of God to them is not the mark of children of Abraham. Abraham welcomed the word of God and obeyed his commandments. God himself testified: 'Abraham obeyed my voice and kept my charge, my commandments, my statutes and my laws' (Gen. 26:5). No; their father, the one whose works they perform, is a very different person from Abraham.

8:41b So they said to him, 'We have not been illegitimately born; we have one father – namely, God.'

If Jesus would not allow their claim that Abraham was their father, he could not surely disallow their claim to be children of the heavenly Father. It was God himself who said, 'Israel is my firstborn son' (Ex. 4:22), 'I am a father to Israel' (Jer. 31:9). But they protested against Jesus' denial that they were children of Abraham in any true sense: this implied the taint of illegitimacy in their lineage, and they resented any suggestion that they were born 'of fornication'.

Light may be thrown on this remark by their later charge (verse 48) that Jesus was a 'Samaritan'. The Jews and the Samaritans each disputed the others' right to be regarded as genuine Israelites. The Jews had their account of the mixed origin of the Samaritans. We cannot speak with certainty of the details of the Samaritans' account of Jewish origins. But there is evidence of a legend that viewed Cain as the fruit of the devil's seduction of Eve, and if some Samaritans charged the Jews with being descendants of Cain, not of Seth (the only son of Adam whom he is said, according to Gen. 5:3, to have begotten 'in his own likeness'), several allusions in the present exchange between Jesus and the unbelieving Jerusalemites could be explained. Their protest that they were not born 'of fornication', for example, might be due to a suspicion that Jesus was referring to a calumny which was current among Samaritans; this in truth, was far from being Jesus' intention.[13]

8:42, 43 Jesus said to them, 'If God were your father, you would love me, for I came forth and have come from God. I have not come on my own account; it was he who sent me. Why do you not recognize what I say? It is because you do not hear my word.'

Jesus insists on using the terms 'father' and 'children' in an ethical sense: the children are those who reproduce the father's qualities. Those with whom he engages in debate have claimed to be children of Abraham (by natural descent) and children of God (by adoption). He has already told them that Abraham's children might be expected to do Abraham's works; now he denies their claim to be children of God because nothing of the heavenly Father's character is to be seen in them. In particular, he is the unique Son of God; those who call themselves children of God might be expected to recognize him, and indeed to love him, for a family feeling would bind them to him in affection. 'Every one who loves the parent loves the child', John puts it elsewhere (1 John 5:1), whether the 'child' be the Son *par excellence* or any other member of the family of God. In saying 'I came forth and have come from God', Jesus may mean, 'I came forth (*exēlthon*, aorist) from God (by my incarnation into the world) and I have come (*hēkō*, present form with perfect meaning) from God to be his messenger to you right here and now. But Westcott, followed by Dodd, sees more in the words 'I came forth from God' than a reference to the incarnation. Pointing out that the preposition rendered 'from' is *ek* ('out of'), Westcott concludes that 'the words can only be interpreted of the true divinity of the Son, of which the Father is the source and fountain'. He finds the same sense in John 16:28, where Jesus says, 'I came forth from the Father and have come into the world' (where 'from' renders Gk. *para* with the genitive), and contrasts John 13:3 and 16:30, where his coming forth from God is expressed by means of the preposition *apo* and refers to the incarnation. We can no longer treat the theology of Greek prepositions as an exact science in the way that Westcott did; yet the meaning of the clause at present under consideration could well be, as Dodd puts it, that 'He had his origin in the being of the Father'.[14] This does not imply that there was a point at which he began to exist:[15] the aorist here refers to eternity, not to time. But whether the words point to his eternal generation or to his becoming flesh, it is as the one sent by the Father that he has come to those whom he now addresses.

As the one sent by the Father, he delivers the Father's message. Those who were truly children of God would recognize their Father's message on the lips of Jesus. But these people were manifestly incapable of such recognition; this showed that they did not know him whom they claimed as their Father (cf. John 7:28). 'They could not perceive the meaning or the source of His *speech*', says Westcott,' . . . because they could not grasp the purport of His Word, the one revelation of the Incarnate Son in which all else was included.' They did not understand his outward speech (*lalia*), which the ear could pick up, because they did not hear the word (*logos*), the message it expressed, which could be apprehended only by the enlightened mind.

8:44, 45 **'You are (the offspring) of your father the devil, and you are resolved to carry out your father's desires. He was a murderer from the beginning; he never stood in the truth, because there is no truth in him. When he utters what is false, he speaks from his own resources, for he is a liar and the father of lying. But because I speak the truth, you do not believe me.'**

Grammatically, the opening words of verse 44 could be translated 'You are from the father of the devil.' This mistranslation could lead to unprofitable speculation of a gnostic type,[16] and probably did so at one time; hence a couple of witnesses (Codex K and the Sinaitic Syriac) rule it out by omitting the words 'your father', so that the statement simply runs: 'You are (the offspring) of the devil.' But there is no need to abridge the text: 'father' and 'devil' are in apposition to each other.

As before, it is an ethical relationship that is implied. Jesus' enemies had tried to bring about his death; they showed themselves incapable of accepting the truth which he brought. In both respects they made it plain that they were children not of God but of the devil. God is the life-giver and the fountain of truth; the devil is the life-destroyer and the father of lies.

What is meant by the statement that 'he was a murderer, a man-slayer (*anthrōpoktonos*), from the beginning'? Probably that by his deceiving our first parents he 'brought death into the world, and all our woe'. 'Through the devil's envy death entered the world, and those who belong to his party experience it' (Wisdom 2:24). And as for his being the archetypal liar, his first recorded utterance not only calls in question, but flatly contradicts, what God has said. 'You shall surely die,' said God (Gen. 2:17); 'You shall not "surely die",' said the serpent (Gen. 3:4), which is viewed in the NT, and indeed earlier, as the mouthpiece of the devil. What God says is 'the truth'; what the devil says is 'the lie', because it contradicts 'the truth'. So Paul speaks of idolaters as 'exchanging the truth of God for the lie' (Rom. 1:25); elsewhere he says of those who refused to receive 'the love of the truth', that 'God sends on them a working of delusion, to make them believe "the lie" '

(2 Thess. 2:11). The devil utters falsehood as naturally and spontaneously as God utters truth: if 'it is impossible for God to lie' (Heb. 6:18), equally it is impossible for the devil to speak the truth – even when he chooses to 'quote scripture for his purpose'. The children of God, then, will be characterized by their love of the truth; the children of the devil by their refusal to accept the truth. Jesus does not say, '*although* I speak the truth, you do not believe me', but '*because* I speak the truth, you do not believe me'; in view of the spiritual lineage of his opponents, the fact that what he said was the truth was sufficient reason for them to reject it.

8:46, 47 **'Who among you convicts me of sin? If I speak truth, why do you not believe me? Whoever is (a child) of God hears the words of God. This is why you do not hear (them): you are not (children) of God.'**

They had supposed that Jesus was guilty of a double sin: sabbath-breaking and blasphemy (John 5:18). But would this accusation procure a conviction against him in the one court that finally mattered – the heavenly court? When he defended himself against the double accusation, his defence served only to add fuel to the fire of their hostility, but he was confident that it would be admitted in the presence of God.

Again he tells them that the reason for their refusal to accept the truth which he declares is that they are not children of the God of truth. If 'he whom God sent speaks the words of God' (John 3:34), so whoever is a child of God will give evidence of that fact by hearing – and recognizing – the words of God. Jesus' present words anticipate what he was to say later to Pilate: 'Everyone who is on the side of the truth listens to my voice' (John 18:37).

8:48 **The Jews said to him in reply, 'Are we not right in saying that you are a Samaritan, and demon-possessed at that?'**

As was suggested in the comment on verse 41, Jesus' denial that they were children of God reminded them of the aspersions cast by the Samaritans on the Jews and their origin. But in using such language Jesus did not even have the excuse of being Samaritan by race; for a Jew, as he was, to speak like this about his fellow-Jews was sheer madness, a token of demon-possession (cf. 7:20).

8:49–51 **Jesus answered, 'I am not demon-possessed; I honour my Father, and you dishonour me. I seek no glory for myself;**

there is one who seeks it, and judges (rightly). Indeed and in truth I tell you: whoever keeps my words will never see death.'

Jesus' words are far from being the product of demon-possession; they are the words which his Father has given him to utter (cf. John 3:34; 17:8, 14), and in uttering them Jesus glorifies his Father, just as in refusing them his hearers dishonour him – and, through him, his Father (cf. 5:23). It is his Father's glory that Jesus seeks to promote by obediently delivering his message; he is not concerned for his own reputation. He can trust his Father to take care of that, and in fact he, above all others, receives 'the glory that comes from the only God' (John 5:44). He need not be disturbed by the adverse judgment of those who cannot judge righteously because they judge 'according to outward appearance' (John 7:24); so long as he enjoys his Father's approval, he is well content.

In the synagogue at Capernaum, on the morrow of the feeding of the multitude, Jesus said of the words that he spoke, 'they are spirit; they are life' (John 6:63). Now he emphasizes again, with his double 'Amen', the life-giving potency of what he says: 'Any one who keeps my word will never see death.'[17] To 'see' death, like 'seeing the kingdom of God' (John 3:3), means to enter into it, to experience it. As Peter had already confessed, Jesus has 'words of eternal life' (John 6:68). The message which he brings delivers those who hear and keep it from eternal death.

8:52, 53 The Jews then said to him, 'Now we know that you are demon-possessed. Abraham has died, and so have the prophets, yet you say, "Whoever keeps my word will never taste death." Are you greater than our father Abraham, who has died? The prophets also have died. Whom do you make yourself out to be?'

Jesus' opponents in the debate continue to display what the readers are intended to recognize as crass literal-mindedness. While the readers know that death of the body (a matter of small importance in Johannine thinking) is not what is meant, the opponents suppose that it is. Abraham heard the word of God and obeyed it; yet Abraham died. The word of God came to the prophets of Israel, and they delivered it faithfully to their contemporaries; yet the prophets also died. If the word of God did not preserve from dying those who heard it and kept it, how can the word of this man serve as medicine against death? If he believes that, they reasoned, he is the victim of an illusion, and a demonic illusion at that.

To 'taste death' (cf. Mark 9:1; Heb. 2:9), like to 'see death' in verse 51, means 'to experience death'.

8:54–56 Jesus answered, 'If I glorify myself, my glory is of no
account. It is my Father who glorifies me – the one of whom
you say, "He is our God". You do not know him, but I know
him. If I say that I do not know him, I shall be a liar, like you.
But I know him, and I keep his word. Abraham your father
looked forward with exultation to see my day, and he saw it and
rejoiced.'

As a testimonial to oneself is no testimonial (John 5:31), so praise
of oneself is no praise, and even in a community of mutual admirers
one may wonder if the admiration is entirely unprejudiced (John
5:44). The only glory that matters in Jesus' eyes is the 'glory that
comes from the only God'. Jesus' opponents in the present debate
acknowledge this God, for they claim him as theirs – is he not the
God of Israel? But perhaps he is more particularly the God of those
in Israel who, like Nathanael, are Israelites indeed (cf. John 1:47).
To Jesus, indeed, he is more than the God of Israel; Jesus knows
him as 'my Father' – a designation to which, because of what it
seemed to imply on his lips, his opponents took special exception
(cf. John 5:17, 18). They took the greater exception to his use of
it during the present debate, because he denied it to them. When
they said 'We have one Father, even God', he told them that their
actions belied that claim (John 8:41, 42).

When Jesus says to them, 'You say, "He is our God", and yet
you do not know him', he echoes the insistence of the great
prophets of earlier days, that their contemporaries' claim to be the
people of God, and indeed the children of God, was an empty
claim, because they had rejected the knowledge of God (cf. Hosea
4:1; 6:6). There is probably no distinction in sense between the
two verbs for 'know' in verse 55: 'you do not know him (egnōkate,
perfect of ginōskō), but I know him (oida).' (Cf. John 7:27.)

Jesus's claim to know God is founded not only on his being
from eternity the Son of the Father, but also on his perfect obedience to the Father's will. Disobedience is a bar to the knowledge
of God, 'in knowledge of whom standeth our eternal life'. 'I know
him, and I keep his word' are two correlative clauses, but there is
the underlying implication: 'I know him, because I keep his word.'
If eternal life is to know God (John 17:3), it is made equally plain
here that to keep his word (as communicated through his Son) is
the way to eternal life. What does Jesus make himself out to be?
That which he essentially is: the living and lifegiving Word.

'Abraham your father exulted in order to see my day' (paraphrased here 'Abraham your father looked forward with exultation
to see my day') seems to point to a particular experience in the life
of Abraham. But which experience was it?

Various rabbis, toying with the statement in Gen. 24:1 that Abraham 'was advanced in years' – literally, 'entered into the days' – suggested that Abraham foresaw outstanding days in the history of Israel, such as the crossing of the Red Sea, the giving of the law, and so on into the age to come.[18] So the idea that he foresaw the messianic age would not be unacceptable to Jews. But when did he 'exult' (aorist of *agalliaomai*) to see the day of Christ? Perhaps when he said to Isaac, on their way to the place of sacifice, 'God will provide himself with a lamb for the burnt-offering' (Gen. 22:8).[19] The incident of the 'binding of Isaac' played a prominent part in Jewish religious thinking, especially where the doctrine of atonement was in view. But Jesus did not say that Abraham saw 'the day of Christ' or 'the messianic age'; he spoke of him as seeing 'my day', and it was this personal way of putting it that caused offence and excited ridicule.

8:57, 58 So the Jews said to him, 'You are not yet fifty years old. Have you seen Abraham?' Jesus said to them, 'Indeed and in truth I tell you, Before Abraham was born, I am He.'

They chose to understand Jesus' words as though they meant that he and Abraham were contemporaries. Such a claim was too absurd to be treated seriously. He had not said that he had seen Abraham, but that Abraham looked forward and saw his day, and that the sight filled Abraham with joy. But, said Jesus' opponents, he was born only the day before yesterday (so to speak); he was younger than many of themselves were: how could Abraham have seen him, or he Abraham?[20] (A few witnesses, including Papyrus 75 and Sinaiticus, actually read 'Has Abraham seen you?')

The 'fifty years' estimate of his age is a round number. True, he was much less than fifty years old, but in comparison with the antiquity of Abraham the difference between thirty and fifty was negligible. In the comment on the 'forty-six years' of John 2:20 mention has already been made of the far-fetched idea that the life of Christ on earth covered forty-nine years in which case 'not yet fifty years old' would mean 'not quite fifty years old'.[21]

Jesus' reply to their protest repeats the affirmation 'I am He' (*egō eimi*), used twice already in this chapter (verses 24, 28), and does so in a way which underlines the magnitude of the claim which it expresses. He echoes the language of the God of Israel, who remains the same from everlasting to everlasting: 'I, the LORD, the first, and with the last, I am He' (Isa. 41:4). How can a man who is 'not yet fifty years old' speak like that? Only if he speaks as the Word that had been with God in the beginning and was now incarnate on earth. Abraham looked forward to the time of his

incarnation, but he himself existed before his incarnation, before
Abraham was born (*genesthai*), before the worlds were made. The
Word of the eternal God cannot be other than eternal. So much,
in this context, is conveyed by *egō eimi*. And if we suppose that
the conversation was carried on in Aramaic or even in Hebrew,
then Jesus could have uttered the very words *'ănî hû*, as though
he were applying them to himself.[22]

**8:59 Therefore they took up stones to throw them at him, but
Jesus hid himself and went out of the temple.**

If Jesus' claim was not well founded, then his words were openly
blasphemous: he was using language which only God could use.
His hearers were horrified: their natural reaction was to inflict on
him summarily (though informally) the penalty prescribed for the
blasphemer: 'all the congregation shall stone him' (Lev. 24:16). The
verb 'hid himself' is literally 'was hidden' (*ekrybē*, passive), as also
in John 12:36. The passive of *kryptō* is repeatedly used in a re-
flexive sense, as in Gen. 3:8 LXX, where Adam and his wife 'hid
themselves' (*ekrybēsan*). A variant reading says that Jesus 'went
through the midst of them and (so) passed by' (*parēgen*) – which
prepares the reader for the opening words of chapter 9: 'and as he
passed by' (*kai paragōn*).

NOTES

1. 'There was not a courtyard in Jerusalem that did not reflect the light of the
   "house of water-drawing" ' (Mishnah, tractate *Sukkāh* 5.3).
2. 1QS 3.6 f.
3. Mishnah, tractate *Shᵉqālîm* 6.5.
4. See p. 148; also John 9:9 (p. 210), 18:5–8 (p. 341).
5. Mishnah, tractate *Sukkāh* 4.5. One view is that *'ănî wᵉ–hû* is a modification
   of the words *'annā YHWH*, 'we pray thee, O LORD!' in Ps. 118.25.
6. Cf. C. H. Dodd *The Interpretation of the Fourth Gospel*, pp. 349 f.
7. See John 6:60, with comment (p. 162).
8. C. H. Dodd *The Interpretation of the Fourth Gospel*, p. 178.
9. Although their land was now under Roman occupation, their resultant situation
   was scarcely one of bondage: at the time of Jesus' ministry they retained internal
   autonomy, and even when this Gospel was written (after the abolition of their
   commonwealth in AD 70), they still enjoyed religious independence.
10. For the suggestion that John has in mind Jewish Christians who continued to
    claim special privileges as descendants of Abraham and therefore 'birthright
    members' of the messianic community, in distinction from Gentile believers',
    see C. H. Dodd *Historical Tradition in the Fourth Gospel*, p. 379; also R. E.
    Brown *The Gospel according to John* (Garden City, N.Y. 1966), pp. 362 f.
11. They are omitted in Codex Bezae, the Sinaitic Syriac and the Old Latin Codex
    Veronensis.
12. Cf. C. H. Dodd *Historical Tradition in the Fourth Gospel*, pp. 379–382; J.
    Jeremias *The Parables of Jesus* (London 1954), pp. 69, 148; B. Lindars *Behind
    the Fourth Gospel*, p. 44.

13. Cf. J. Bowman, 'Samaritan Studies' *BJRL* 40 (1957–58), pp. 306–308.
14. C. H. Dodd *The Interpretation of the Fourth Gospel*, p. 259.
15. Cf. the quotation from Arius on p. 31 (on John 1:1).
16. According to the gnostic sect of Ophites, Ialdabaoth, whom the Jews allegedly worshipped, was the father of Mind (*nous*), which had the form of a serpent (*ophis*), venerated by the Ophites (Irenaeus *Against Heresies* 1.30.5) – but this fantasy is irrelevant to John 8:44. Cf. rather 1 John 3:8, 'he who practises sin is (a child) of the devil'.
17. The utterance of verse 51 entered in various forms into the oral tradition of later generations. The *Gospel of Thomas*, for example (a compilation of 114 sayings ascribed to Jesus), opens with the words: 'These are the secret words which Jesus the living one spoke and Didymus Judas Thomas wrote down; and he said: "Whoever finds the interpretation of these words will never taste death".' (For 'taste death' see verse 52.)
18. Cf. *Genesis Rabba* (rabbinical commentary) 59.6 on Gen. 24:1.
19. In the *Testament of Levi* 18:6 Levi foretells the coming of a 'new priest' for whom 'the heavens shall be opened, and from the temple of glory shall come upon him sanctification, with the Father's voice as from Abraham to Isaac' (presumably a reference to Gen. 22:8, the only words spoken by Abraham to Isaac anywhere in the Bible).
20. The ten references to Abraham (who is not mentioned elsewhere in this Gospel) hold together the dialogue of verses 31–58, on which see C. H. Dodd, 'Behind a Johannine Dialogue' in *More New Testament Studies* (Manchester 1968), pp. 41–57.
21. See pp. 76 f.
22. See comment on verse 24 (p. 193). B. Lindars (*Behind the Fourth Gospel*, p. 46) thinks rather of 'the self-predication of the Wisdom of God' – e.g. in Prov. 8:27, 'When he established the heavens, I was there' (Heb. *shām 'ānî*, 'there am I').

CHAPTER 9

2. THE HEALING OF THE BLIND MAN (9:1–41)

(a) The Pool of Siloam (9:1–12)

9:1-5 Then, passing by, he saw a man who was blind from birth. His disciples asked him, 'Rabbi, was it he or his parents who sinned, that he should be born blind?' Jesus replied, 'It was neither he nor his parents who sinned; it was that the works of God might be manifested in him. We must do the works of him who sent me while it is day. The night is coming, when no one can work. While I am in the world, I am the light of the world.'

As the healing of the cripple at the pool of Bethesda in chapter 5 introduces the presentation of Jesus as the one who executes judgment and imparts life, so the healing of the blind man at the pool of Siloam illustrates Jesus' claim (made already in John 8:12) to be the light of the world. In the lively account of the present healing (by contrast with the earlier one) the man who has been healed plays an active part. The cut and thrust of animated debate in this chapter, preceded and followed by the monologues of chapters 8 and 10, bears witness to the evangelist's versatility of style.

How the disciples knew that the man's blindness was congenital is not said, but it was this knowledge that dictated the form of their question. In their thinking about divine retribution they had not advanced far beyond the position of Job's friends. Blindness, they imagined, was a punishment for sin – but for whose sin? Did God punish the parents for some sin previously committed by causing their son to be born blind? The very idea is an aspersion on the character of God, but before we condemn the disciples let us reflect that even today one meets Christians whose thinking about God runs along very similar lines to theirs.[1]

Or, if his blindness was not due to his parents' sin, might it be due to his own? It does sometimes happen that men and women are themselves responsible in part for physical ailments that beset them; it may be implied in John 5:14 that the condition from which the cripple was healed at the pool of Bethesda was something for which he himself was to blame. But it is not usually so, and it seems particularly inept to suggest that congenital blindness could be due to the infant's own sin. The idea that an infant might sin while still in the womb, however, appears to have been entertained by some rabbis, and the disciples may have thought it possible.[2]

208

(It is less likely that they thought he might have sinned in a previous existence.)

The clause 'that he should be born blind' has in Greek the form of a purpose clause (*hina* with the subjunctive) but the sense requires us to take it as a clause of result. On the other hand, the clause in Jesus' reply, 'that the works of God might be manifested . . .' (again *hina* with the subjunctive) is a clause of purpose in meaning as well as in form. Jesus bids the disciples have done with their talk of the man's blindness being caused by somebody's sin. The purpose of his blindness was that a divine work should be wrought in him and the divine glory be revealed (as it is revealed in all the 'signs' of this Gospel). This does not mean that God deliberately caused the child to be born blind in order that, after many years, his glory should be displayed in the removal of the blindness; to think so would again be an aspersion on the character of God. It does mean that God overruled the disaster of the child's blindness so that, when the child grew to manhood, he might, by recovering his sight, see the glory of God in the face of Christ, and others, seeing this work of God, might turn to the true Light of the World.

'We must do the works of him who sent me', said Jesus, referring primarily to himself. At the time of the earlier healing he had said, 'My Father keeps on working until now, and I also work' (John 5:17) – doing the things he saw his Father doing. 'I have come down from heaven', he said in Galilee, 'not to do my own will but the will of him who sent me' (John 6:38). If his disciples were minded to be disciples indeed, then these were the works which they also must do, in fellowship with their Master (cf. also John 14:12).

Moreover, the Father's works must be done 'while it is day' – which meant, so far as Jesus himself was concerned, 'while I am in the world' (verse 5). The coming night was the period of his withdrawal from the world: so in John 13:30, Judas went out into the 'night', while the other disciples remained in the circle of the true light while the true light was with them (cf. John 12:35 f.). To the same effect Jesus, when he was about to raise Lazarus from the tomb (another 'sign' in which the glory of God was shown), said, 'Are there not twelve hours in the day? If one walks about in day-time, he does not stumble, because he sees the light of this world' (John 11:9), with the implication of an analogous truth where the light of the heavenly world is concerned.

The true light was not totally removed when the time came for Jesus 'to depart from this world to the Father' (John 13:1), for it was then mediated through others; but Jesus is here concerned with the existing situation, which would not last more than a few months now. The clause 'I am the light of the world' echoes the affirmation of John 8:12, but it does not carry the same emphasis here. The independent pronoun *egō* is absent here, so that this statement does not rank (as that of John 8:12 does) among the 'I am' affirmations of the Fourth Gospel. The incident introduced in these opening verses of chapter 9 is an acted parable setting forth Jesus' ministry as 'the light of the world'.

9:6, 7 Having said this, he spat on the ground and made mud with the saliva; then he smeared the mud on the man's eyes and said to him, 'Go to the pool of Siloam and wash.' (The word means 'Sent'.) So he went off and washed, and came back with his sight restored.

The application of saliva in healing is attested in Mark's record of the deaf and dumb man in the Decapolis (Mark 7:33) and of the blind man at Bethsaida (Mark 8:23), but there is no word there of its being mixed with earth to form a paste or poultice as here. When his sightless eyes had been covered with this paste, the man was told to wash it off in the pool of Siloam. The pool of Siloam may have been the nearest convenient water-supply, but the Evangelist points out a further significance. Siloam, he says, meant 'sent' – the Hebrew form *shilôaḥ* (as in 'the waters of Shiloah that flow gently' of Isa. 8:6) is patently derived from the verb *shālaḥ* 'send' – and it speaks of Jesus, the sent one (Gk. *apestalmenos*) of God, who alone is qualified to impart inward illumination. Without question, the man did as he was told: he went and washed the paste off his eyes in the pool of Siloam, and found himself able to see for the first time in his life.

The pool of Siloam, south-west of Ophel (the city of David) near the junction of the Tyropoeon Valley and the Valley of Hinnom, received the water which was carried, or 'sent', through a channel from the spring of Gihon (later called the Virgin's Fountain) in the Kidron Valley. It is called the 'Pool of Shelah' in Neh. 3:15, and is to be identified probably with the 'lower pool' or 'old pool' (Isa. 22:9, 11), today's *Birket el-Ḥamra*, lying a little way to the south-east of what is now known as the Pool of Siloam.[3]

9:8, 9 So his neighbours and those who were formerly used to seeing him (and knew) that he was a beggar started to say, 'Is not this the man who used to sit and beg?' Others said, 'Yes, it is he'; others again said, 'No, but he looks like him'. But the man himself said, 'I am he.'

The blind man had been a familiar sight in his neighbourhood.

The only way in which a person so handicapped could get a little money or anything else was by begging; people had been accustomed to seeing him begging (the present participle *theōrountes* in verse 8 has imperfect force). The man whom they now saw obviously seeing his way around was very like the well-known blind man; but it could not be he, could it? John characteristically reports the interplay of uninformed opinion (just as he has done in 7:12, 25–27, 31 when describing the variety of opinions expressed about Jesus at the feast of Tabernacles); it is cut short by the man's assurance that he is the selfsame person.

9:10–12 So they said to him, 'Well, how were your eyes opened?' He replied, 'The man called Jesus made mud and smeared my eyes with it; then he told me to go to Siloam and wash, so I went off and washed and received my sight.' 'Where is he?' they asked him. 'I do not know', said he.

Naturally they wanted to know what had happened to him. He gave them a brief factual account. It may be possible to trace a gradation in his estimate of Jesus in his successive references to him throughout the narrative. To begin with, he is 'the man called Jesus'; at the end, he is the object of his faith and veneration (verse 38). Unlike the cripple at the pool of Bethesda (John 5:13), the once-blind man knows his benefactor's identity and gives credit where credit is due. The question 'Where is he?' suggests that those who questioned the man would have liked to question Jesus too, to see if the two accounts tallied. But Jesus was not available to abide their question.

(b) Interrogation by the Pharisees (9:13–17)

9:13 They took the man who had formerly been blind to the Pharisees.

Why to the Pharisees? Because they felt that a religious issue was involved, and they respected the Pharisees as authorities on the law and its interpretation. Unlike the Synoptic Evangelists, John does not explicitly mention the scribes. In Jesus' day there were scribes attached to the Pharisaic party (Mark 2:16) and scribes attached to other parties, although it is the Pharisaic scribes who normally feature in the Synoptic Gospels. The scribes were the experts in the law, teaching their interpretations to the people in synagogue and elsewhere. By the time John's Gospel was written, there were no Jewish scribes except those in the Pharisaic tradition; he therefore can refer to all scribes as 'Pharisees' without fear of confusion. There were few areas of life which had no religious bearing, and it was natural to consult legal experts rather than medical men about this strange case of healing. Moreover, as now appears for the first time, there was one factor in the situation which made it very much a matter for legal inquiry.

9:14 Now it was a sabbath on the day when Jesus made the mud and opened the man's eyes.

So, Jesus had repeated the offence which led to so much trouble on the occasion of an earlier visit to Jerusalem: he had performed an act of healing on the sabbath. Not that an act of healing as such infringed the sabbath law, but an act of healing was very likely to involve something else which did infringe the law. On the former occasion Jesus encouraged a man to carry a burden through the streets on the sabbath; on this occasion he made a mud poultice with earth and saliva. What was wrong with that? Simply this: one of the categories of work specifically forbidden on the sabbath in the traditional interpretation of the law was kneading,[4] and the making of mud or clay with such simple ingredients as earth and saliva was construed as a form of kneading.

9:15 So they asked him again – the Pharisees this time – how he had received his sight. He told them, 'He put mud on my eyes, and I washed, and I can see.'

The man may well have told them his story in some detail, but the readers now need only the bare outline; they know what happened. The Pharisees are described as launching a serious inquiry; the man is interrogated as first witness, and when his witness proves inconclusive (from their point of view) they summon other witnesses (verse 18).

9:16 So some of the Pharisees said, 'This man is not from God; he does not keep the sabbath.' Others said, 'How can a man who is a sinner perform such signs?' There was a division among them.

Two opposed points of view are expressed, and two opposed conclusions are reached. The one viewpoint was based on the major premise: 'A man who breaks the sabbath law is not a man of God.' Few would have been found to quarrel with that premise. The minor premise was: 'Jesus has broken the sabbath law.' (The sabbath law forbids the doing of any work on the seventh day, and Jesus, according to the accepted interpretation of the law, had 'worked' on that day by making a mud-paste to smear on the blind man's eyes.) The conclusion seemed inevitable: 'Jesus is not a man of God'. The expression *para theou* ('from God') has no metaphysical significance: it is used in the sense in which it is used of John the Baptist in John 1:6. John, as a man 'sent from God', declared the word of God: he was a prophet. Jesus was held by many to be a prophet of God, but (it was argued) since he was guilty of sabbath-breaking, this could not be so.

The other viewpoint was based on the major premise: 'Anyone who cures a man of his blindness – especially a man *born* blind – is a man of God.' This premise would not have been universally admitted: in Deut. 13:1–5 the case is envisaged of a 'prophet' who by means of signs and wonders tries to gain a following and lead people astray from their allegiance to the true God. But some would have argued (and their argument would probably have been valid) that Jesus had not performed a sign or a wonder at random: this 'sign' involved a work of mercy, a work of healing, and such a work is so completely in accordance with the character of God that anyone who performs it must be in the way of God's will. So they framed their major premise, already expressed. The minor premise was: 'Jesus has cured a man of his blindness – a man, moreover, who was born blind.' The conclusion followed: 'Jesus is a man of God – he cannot be a sinner.' (A further conclusion might follow from that: the accepted interpretation of the sabbath law called for re-examination.)

As the crowd was divided in John 7:43, so the Pharisees are now divided over Jesus' credentials. Adolf Schlatter, who was no mean authority in rabbinical scholarship, thought that the division followed the tendencies attributed respectively to the schools of Shammai and Hillel.[5] The school of Shammai tended to argue from first principles (so here: anyone who breaks the law is a sinner); the school of Hillel tended to have regard to the established facts of a case (so here: Jesus has performed a good work). In a case like this, their conclusions were bound to conflict with each other.

9:17 So they say to the blind man again, 'What have *you* to say about him? It was your eyes he opened.' He said, 'He is a prophet.'

The blind man – the man who had been blind until recently – was no authority on law or religion. Still, he had had direct dealings with Jesus; it would be interesting to know his opinion of him. Since they themselves were divided in their judgment, they might do worse than appeal to a third party. He gave his considered opinion: 'he is a prophet'.

The Samaritan woman had perceived Jesus to be a prophet because her life-story was an open book to him. The crowd that had been fed with loaves and fishes and the Jerusalemites who heard his call to come and receive 'living water' identified him with 'the prophet' because in action and word he seemed to be the expected second Moses. The man who had received his sight may have thought of this work of healing as putting Jesus in the succession of Elijah and Elisha. What the Jordan had done for Naaman's leprosy the pool of Siloam had done for his blindness. But perhaps he simply used 'prophet' as a synonym for 'man of God'. In any case, he now gave an assessment much more positive than 'the man called Jesus' (verse 11).

(c) Interrogation of the parents (9:18–23)

9:18, 19 So the Jews refused to believe that he was blind and had recovered his sight until they had called the parents of the man who had recovered his sight. Then they asked them, 'Is this your son, who you say was born blind? In that case, how can he see now?'

'The Jews' of verse 18 are presumably the Pharisees of verse 13. The claim that the man had been *born* blind was a material factor in the incident which they were investigating; but obviously this was something on which his own testimony was not available. Even if he could not remember having ever seen, he might have lost his sight through some illness or accident in early infancy. The people who could testify acceptably whether he was born blind or not were his parents, so they were summoned. They obeyed the summons, but were very ill at ease. It was plain that the authorities were annoyed at what had happened and, although the parents were naturally glad that their son was no longer blind, they were unhappy that he should be mixed up with someone who was in disfavour with the authorities. But here they were, in a subordinate court of inquiry, and they had to give evidence. Wisely, they confined their evidence to what they actually knew; they gave plain answers to the first part of the question – 'Is this your son, who you say was born blind?' – but refused to indulge in speculation about his cure.

9:20, 21 So his parents replied, 'We know that this is our son, and that he was born blind. But we do not know how he can see now or who opened his eyes. Ask him; he is of age; he will speak for himself.'

'Yes', they said, 'he is our son' (of that they had no doubt). 'Yes', they said again, 'he was born blind' (they were equally sure of that). 'You ask, "How come he is able to see now?" We don't know. Nor do we know who restored his sight. You must ask himself: he is old enough to bear competent testimony in court.' (To be admissible as a witness in court he had to be at least thirteen; this man was certainly older than that.) But, limited to matters of known fact as the parents' testimony was, it made unpalatable hearing for the interrogators: they confirmed that their son had been born blind, and since he had plainly recovered his sight, it was difficult to avoid the conclusion that a miracle had been performed.

9:22, 23 His parents said this because they were afraid of the Jews; for they had already agreed that if any one confessed Jesus to be the Messiah he should be expelled from the synagogue. It was for this reason that his parents said, 'He is of age; ask him.'

Jesus' presence and activity in Jerusalem since he arrived halfway through the week of Tabernacles were well known through the city; and the man's parents were well aware that the healing of their son's blindness was due to Jesus. But anything they might say about Jesus was liable to be displeasing to the authorities; therefore they would say nothing at all about him. After all, they were not present when Jesus accosted their son and sent him to the Pool of Siloam, so they could reasonably plead ignorance of the cause and nature of his healing.

It is commonly suggested today that John, writing towards the end of the nineties, was influenced by a decision that had been taken by the reconstituted Sanhedrin a few years before. The Sanhedrin reconstituted with Roman permission in the period after AD 70 consisted exclusively of doctors of the law. One of these, Samuel the Less, reworded one of the blessings recited daily in the synagogues so as to make it impossible for 'Nazarenes' (Jewish Christians) to take part in synagogue worship. This blessing, which traditionally included a curse on the enemies of God ('let all wickedness perish as in a moment'), was revised so that the curse ran: 'let Nazarenes and heretics perish as in a moment; let them be blotted out of the book of life and not be enrolled with the righteous.'[6] The revision was approved by the Sanhedrin and adopted in synagogues, so that Nazarenes, being forced to keep silence when the new form of words were recited by the congregation, would give themselves away. John probably does allude to this situation when he reports Jesus as saying to the disciples in the upper room, 'They will put you out of the synagogues' (John 16:2). The same adjective, *aposynagōgos* (meaning 'excluded from the synagogue'), is used there as here in 9:22. But here (as in 12:42) the reference is to a situation in the context of Jesus' ministry, restricted perhaps to Jerusalem. It is uncertain whether we are to understand temporary expulsion or permanent excommunication here. The most solemn form of excommunication was to put some-one under the ban (Heb. *ḥērem*; Gk. *anathema*); that seems to have been involved in the new ordinance of AD 90, but it would probably be anachronistic to envisage it at this stage. Even so, the man's parents were sufficiently intimidated to keep their mouths shut and say nothing about Jesus, either good or bad.

(d) Second interrogation of the man (9:24–34)

9:24, 25 So they summoned back the man who had been blind and said to him, 'Give glory to God. We know that this man is a sinner.' He replied, 'I do not know if he is a sinner. I know one thing: I was blind and now I see.'

There was no way of getting around the evidence that the man had been born blind. Neither was there any way of getting around the evidence of their senses, that he was now able to see. The natural conclusion was that a miracle of healing had been wrought, but since the evidence also pointed unambiguously to Jesus as the one responsible for the cure, the further conclusion would be that the power of God had manifested itself through Jesus in an excep-tional degree – that he was indeed, as the man had said, a prophet. But this further conclusion was inadmissible: in their eyes he was no prophet, but a sinner, because he had broken the sabbath law. Therefore some factor in the situation must be eluding them; per-haps it was being deliberately concealed from them. Hence their charge to the man when he was summoned before them again: 'Own up; tell the truth.' 'Give glory to God' has the same force here as in the story of Achan: when the lot pointed to Achan as the man who had brought disaster on Israel, Joshua said to him, 'Give glory to the LORD God of Israel' – i.e. 'Own up; tell the truth' (Josh. 7:19). (It may well be that John plays characteristically on the double meaning of the words – the healing of the blind man did indeed reveal the glory of God – but our present concern is with what the interrogators meant.) 'Own up', they meant; 'what-ever *you* say, *we* know that this man Jesus is a sinner, and therefore cannot have performed such a miracle of healing as you pretend. Tell the truth; what are you hiding?'

In his first reply the man is as circumspect as his parents: he confines himself strictly to what he knows, which is the duty of a witness. '*You* know that he is a sinner; well, you are the authorities whose business it is to know that sort of thing. You wouldn't expect *me* to know anything about that. But here is what I do know: I was blind, and now I see.' It was frustrating for his interrogators that neither of those statements could be refuted: the former statement was confirmed by the evidence of the parents; the truth of the latter they could see for themselves. Why not admit the conclusion to which these two facts pointed?

The man's testimony has been repeated innumerable times by men and women who have found in his words the means of communicating their own experience of deliverance from spiritual blindness through the in-shining of the light of the world: 'I know one thing: I was blind and now I see.'

9:26, 27 So they said to him, 'What did he do to you? How did he open your eyes?' He answered them, 'I have told you already and you paid no need. Why do you want to hear it again? Do you also want to become his disciples?'

Thus far the man has given straight factual answers to the questions put to him by the authorities. But now that they begin to ask the same questions all over again, he suspects that it is not the plain truth that they want: they are trying to trip him up, so as to nullify his positive witness in favour of Jesus. He now displays a hitherto unsuspected capacity for ironical repartee. Some authorities (including, it appears, Papyrus 66) omit the negative from the clause 'you paid no heed', as though the man meant, 'You heard me the first time; why do you want me to tell you again?' He knows very well that his interrogators have no thought of becoming Jesus' disciples, but his ironical question is used by the Evangelist as a means of introducing again the subject of true discipleship, touched upon in John 8:31.

9:28, 29 Then they addressed him abusively, saying, 'You are that man's disciple; we are disciples of Moses. We know that God spoke to Moses; we have no idea where this fellow comes from.'

Naturally they do not appreciate the man's irony; it is too evident that he has seen through their plan to trip him up. They therefore have recourse to abuse. Who would be a disciple of someone whose origin was unknown and whose authority was disallowed by those in a position to judge such matters? An ignoramus like the man who stood before them might know no better than to take such a person seriously; they were better informed. Moses was their teacher; they were his disciples.[7] The tradition of oral law transmitted in the rabbinical schools was held to stem from Moses, who (they believed) had received it on Sinai together with the written law.[8] No one could doubt that God spoke to Moses: of him God himself had said, 'With him I speak mouth to mouth, clearly, and not in dark speech' (Num. 12:8). Moses was the pre-eminent prophet of the Lord; the claim to be disciples of his was a claim worth making. The disciples of this nobody from Nazareth were worthy of him whom they chose as their teacher. In all this, indeed, the Evangelist practises his own brand of irony: he and his readers know of Jesus' true origin; they know, moreover, that while 'the law was given through Moses', the full revelation of God came through Jesus Christ (John 1:17).

9:30–33 'Why', said the man in reply, 'this I find surprising. You do not know where he comes from; yet he has opened my eyes. We know that God does not listen to sinners, but if any one worships God and does his will, he listens to them. No one has ever heard of any one who opened the eyes of one who was born blind. If this man were not from God, he would not be able to do anything.'

The man continues to use the language of plain common sense. The authorities had previously argued among themselves, one group saying, 'This man is a sinner and therefore God cannot have performed a miracle through him', and another group saying, 'This man has worked a miracle which could not be performed without divine aid; therefore he is no sinner.' The man repeats and underlines the second of these lines of argument; he brought an unprejudiced mind to the problem (except in so far as the fact that it was *his* eyes that were opened prejudiced him in favour of Jesus). The restoration of sight to the blind was not unknown: Tobit was given back his sight in the apocryphal book which bears his name, but he was not *born* blind.[9] So far as memory and experience could say, congenital blindness was invariably incurable. Yet now, for once, congenital blindness had been cured. In the Synoptic Gospels the restoring of sight to the blind is a token that the new age has dawned, with such signs as the prophets foretold (Isa. 35:5; 42:7); here the emphasis is rather on the authority and character of the one who performs the cure. Without knowing it, the man anticipates a rabbinical maxim later expressed in the form: 'Every one in whom is the fear of heaven, his words are heard.'[10] A miracle of this magnitude must be recognized as an answer to prayer; the man who received this answer to prayer must be no ordinary man. The wonder is that the authorities disclaim all knowledge of him. The man can put two and two together; he has already concluded that Jesus must be a 'prophet' (verse 17), and now he reiterates his conviction by saying that he must have come 'from God'. This does not necessarily express faith in Jesus' divine origin in the sense in which that is taught by the Evangelist; it does at least mean that Jesus is acknowledged as 'a man sent from God' (*para theou*), as John was (John 1:6). In this sense Jesus must have come from God; otherwise he could never have wrought such a miracle. 'Does the All-merciful perform a miracle for *liars*?' a later rabbi was asked: the answer implied was an emphatic No.[11]

9:34 **They said in reply, 'You were altogether born in sins: are** *you* **teaching** *us*?' **So they drove him out.**

Their angry rejoinder shows that they realized they were getting the worst of the argument. On their own principles there was no answer to his argument. The context suggests that they not only pushed him out of the place where the interrogation was held, but expelled him from synagogue membership, as his parents had feared might be done to them (verse 22). 'You were altogether born in sins' implies that (as Jesus' disciples had supposed) his congenital blindness was due either to his parents' sins or his own. In any case it was an impertinence for such an untrained member of the common people to argue with the acknowledged interpreters of the law.

(e) Confession of faith (9:35-38)

9:35-38 **When Jesus heard that they had driven him out, he found him and said, 'Do you believe in the Son of Man?' 'And who is he, sir,' said the man in reply, 'that I might believe in him?' 'You have seen him', Jesus told him, 'and he is the person who is talking to you.' 'Lord, I believe', said he, and prostrated himself before him in reverence.**

The once-blind man now appears as a sample of those who, as the opening words of chapter 10 go on to indicate, are called out of the Jewish fold to become members of the flock of the good shepherd. Evicted from the synagogue, he is found by Jesus (whom he had not met since he went off at his bidding to wash in the Pool of Siloam) and is enrolled as one of his disciples. In Jesus' question our textual witnesses disagree about the self-designation used by Jesus – 'Son of Man' (as the oldest manuscripts have it, including Papyri 66 and 75) or 'Son of God'. The fact that the latter is the commoner designation in this Gospel makes it more likely that it has replaced an original 'Son of Man' than vice versa. 'Son of Man', as John 5:27 shows, is a designation associated with the rôle of judgment which the Father has committed to the Son, and prepares the reader for the language about judgment in verses 39-41. There may also be a link here with the rôle of advocacy assigned to the Son of Man in the Synoptic tradition, where those who acknowledge Jesus on earth are acknowledged by the Son of Man in the presence of the angels of God (Luke 12:8). On this occasion the Son of Man acknowledges his faithful confessor on the spot.

Naturally, the man does not know who the Son of man is, but he is very willing to learn, so he asks. Jesus replies in terms similar to those which he used when the Samaritan woman spoke of the coming Messiah: 'It is I, the person talking to you' (John 4:26). The man has no further hesitation. On whom would he more readily believe than on the man who had restored his sight? He had already called him a prophet; now he confesses him as more than a prophet. If the vocative *kyrie* in verse 36 has the courtesy sense of 'sir', in verse 38 it is more than a courtesy title; it implies that Jesus is a fit person to receive worship: 'Lord, I believe', he said, and bowed low in reverence before him. So quickly has an honest and good heart progressed from recognizing the benefactor as 'the man called Jesus' (verse 11) to confessing him as Lord.

(f) Judicial blindness (9:39–41)

9:39–41 **Then Jesus said, 'It is for judgment that I have come into this world, so that those who do not see may see and those who see may become blind'. Some of the Pharisees who were with him heard this and said to him, 'Are we blind too?' Jesus said to them, 'If you were blind, you would not have incurred sin. As it is, you say "We see"; your sin remains.'**

There is a *prima facie* discrepancy between this passage and those in which Jesus says that he did not come to judge the world (John 3:17; 12:47).[12] But there is no real discrepancy. Jesus is not saying here that he has come to execute judgment; rather, his presence and activity in the world themselves constitute a judgment as they compel men and women to declare themselves for or against him, as they range themselves on the one side or the other. Those who range themselves against him are 'judged already' (John 3:18), not because he has passed judgment on them but because they have passed it on themselves. The 'judgment' (*krima*) here is practically equivalent to the 'division' (*schisma*) which more than once developed among his hearers as they took sides over his claims.

The healing of the blind man is presented as a parable of spiritual illumination. Thanks to the coming of the true light of the world, many who were formerly in darkness have been enlightened; this is not only the effect but the purpose of his coming. But on the other hand some who thought they had no need of the enlightenment he brought, because they could see perfectly well already, turned their backs on him and, without realizing it, moved into deeper darkness. The lesson of John 3:19–21 was exemplified in them. Had they acknowledged their spiritual blindness and allowed him to remove it, they would have been blessed. Had they lived in darkness and found no way out into the light, their plight would have been sad but no blame would have attached to them. Blame did attach to those who, while living in darkness, claimed to be able to see, like those religious leaders who were present and heard Jesus' pronouncement about the effect of his coming. To be so self-deceived as to shut one's eyes to the light is a desperate state to be in: the light is there, but if people refuse to avail themselves of it but rather deliberately reject it, how can they be enlightened? As Jesus said, their sin remains.

NOTES

1. Despite what has sometimes been thought in more recent times, there is no suggestion here of the son's blindness being due to venereal disease contracted by one or other of the parents; to suppose otherwise is to credit the disciples with a degree of medical knowledge which they would not have possessed.

2. In the rabbinical commentary *Genesis Rabba* 63.6 there is a curious discussion of Esau and Jacob's pre-natal conduct (Gen. 25:22), in which Ps. 58:3 ('The wicked go astray from the womb') is variously interpreted so as to show how Esau's sinful propensity was manifested while he was still in the womb.

3. What is now known as the Pool of Siloam (and has been so known since Constantine's time) occupies the site of the 'upper pool' (Isa. 7:3; 36:2) and receives the water from Gihon through the tunnel constructed by King Hezekiah's engineers shortly before 701 BC (cf. Isa. 22:11; 2 Kings 20:20; 2 Chron. 32:4, 30). Before this tunnel was constructed the water flowed into the lower pool through a channel dug along the east and south side of the hill Ophel. See J. Wilkinson, *Jerusalem as Jesus knew it*, pp. 104–108; 'The Pool of Siloam', *Levant* 10 (1978), pp. 116–125.

4. Mishnah, tractate *Shabbāth* 7.2. In the Babylonian Talmud, tractate *'Abôdāh Zārāh* 28b, there is a discussion on whether, or how far, it is permissible to anoint sore eyes on the sabbath.

5. A. Schlatter, *Der Evangelist Johannes* (Stuttgart, 1930), p. 227.

6. The Hebrew text of this rewording was discovered among the fragments from the Cairo *genizah*; cf. S. Schechter, 'Geniza Specimens: Liturgy', *JQR* 10 (1898–99), p. 657. It is attested also in an early fifteenth-century Bodleian MS. But, having been devised to deal with a temporary situation, the rewording was allowed to lapse when that situation passed. See further K. L. Carroll, 'The Fourth Gospel and the Exclusion of Christians from the Synagogue', *BJRL* 40 (1957–58), pp. 19–32 and (for a different point of view) R. Kimelman, '*Birkat Ha-Minim* and the Lack of Evidence for an anti-Christian Jewish Prayer in Late Antiquity', in *Jewish and Christian Self-Definition*, ed. E. P. Sanders, II (London, 1981), pp. 226–244. See also W. Horbury, 'The Benediction of the *Minim* and Early Jewish-Christian Controversy', *JTS* n.s. 33 (1982), pp. 19–61.

7. Since Moses was the original teacher of the law (being called to this day *Mōsheh rabbēnû*, 'Moses our teacher'), rabbis as a class are known in the tradition as *talmîdâw shel Mōsheh*, 'disciples of Moses' (e.g. in Babylonian Talmud, tractate *Yōmā* 4a, where Sadducees are expressly excluded from those so designated).

8. Cf. *Pirqê 'Abôth* 1.1: 'Moses received the law [i.e. the oral law] from Sinai and delivered it to Joshua, and Joshua to the elders, and the elders to the prophets, and the prophets delivered it to the men of the great synagogue' – and so it was transmitted to one generation of teachers after another.

9. Tobit 2:10; 11:10–13.

10. Babylonian Talmud, tractate *Bᵉrākhôth* 6b, quoting Rabbi Huni (died AD 297).

11. *Bᵉrākhôth* 58a, in a debate with Rabbi Shila (early 3rd century).

12. See also John 5:22, 30; 8:15 f., with comments.

CHAPTER 10

3. THE SHEPHERD AND THE FLOCK (10:1–39)

(a) Parable of the good shepherd (10:1–21)

10:1, 2 'Indeed and in truth I tell you, if any one does not enter into the sheepfold through the door but climbs up some other way, he is a thief and a robber. He who enters in through the door is the shepherd of the sheep.'

These words follow on directly from the preceding narrative. The double 'Amen' of verse 1 ('indeed and in truth') marks the transition from dialogue to monologue. As becomes clear from the course of the parable, the blind man who was healed is a member of the flock of the good shepherd; what was true of him is true of the whole flock.

Who are the shepherds of God's flock? The religious leaders in Israel would no doubt have claimed the title. But it was they who were the most determined opponents of Jesus and his message. The man cured of his blindness looked in vain to them for the care that shepherds should give; in fact, they expelled him from the flock for which they were responsible. But, having been expelled by them, he found a true shepherd in Jesus. In this context, it is difficult to avoid identifying them with the thieves and robbers, the false shepherds, who sought by some unauthorized means to 'creep and intrude and climb into the fold'.

This parable should be read against the background of Ezekiel 34. There the God of Israel speaks as the chief shepherd of his people, who appoints under-shepherds to look after them. But those shepherds (like the 'worthless shepherd' of Zech. 11:17) are denounced for being more concerned to feed themselves than to feed the sheep entrusted to their care. Instead of looking after the sheep they neglected them, slaughtering the fatlings to gorge themselves on their flesh and using the wool to clothe themselves. Those unworthy shepherds will therefore be removed; God himself will seek his scattered sheep and gather them back into one flock from the distant places to which they have been allowed to stray. He will tend all those that need special care, and he will commit them to one who is worthy of the trust reposed in him: 'I will set up over them one shepherd, my servant David, and he shall feed them' (Ezek. 34:23). 'My servant David', as elsewhere in this section of the book of Ezekiel (cf. 37:24, 25), is clearly the Messiah of David's line. One who makes the claim voiced in Jesus' parable of the good shepherd is making a tacit claim to be the Davidic Messiah.

10:3-5 'The doorkeeper opens to him and the sheep hear his voice; he calls his own sheep by name and leads them out. When he lets all his own sheep out he goes in front of them and the sheep follow him, because they recognize his voice. They will not follow a stranger, but will run away from him, because they do not recognize the voice of strangers.'

These details were familiar to many of Jesus' hearers; even today they are aptly illustrated by the way of a shepherd with his sheep in the Holy Land. The fold would be a stone enclosure, roughly square in shape, with an entrance on one side. This entrance was guarded by a doorkeeper or watchman whose business it was to admit authorized persons and keep out intruders. If any one were seen climbing into the fold on one of the other sides, it was safe to assume that he was an intruder, up to no good. To discourage such persons the top of the wall might be protected by briars.

More flocks than one might be accommodated in the same enclosure; but all that was necessary was for the shepherd to stand at the entrance and call; his own sheep would recognize his voice and come to him. Not only so: the flock would be small enough for him to know each of his sheep individually and distinguish them by name. The name might be based on some special mark or feature. In my youth some shepherds in the Scottish Highlands not only called their individual sheep by name, but claimed that an individual sheep would recognize its own name and respond to it. In the picture here drawn by Jesus it is the personal bond between the shepherd and his sheep that keeps them together as they follow his guidance; unlike a modern shepherd, the shepherd of Bible days did not have the assistance of a sheepdog.

10:6 Jesus told them this parable, but they did not understand what his words meant.

The word 'parable' represents not *parabolē* (the term regularly used for the Synoptic parables) but *paroimia*, meaning a proverb (as in the OT book of Proverbs) or a cryptic saying.[1] A cryptic saying it remained to Jesus' hearers; in the light of the context it may be possible for us to understand it a little better than they were able to do.

The shepherd is Jesus himself: he is pictured as coming to the Jewish fold and calling his disciples out. One of them, indeed, had just been pushed out; others had come out already and yet others would come out before long. The members of the religious establishment could not communicate with the man who had been blind any more than he could communicate with them; to him their voice was 'the voice of strangers'. But when the true shepherd of Israel found him and spoke to him, he responded to him at once.

The sheep in the fold were protected by the walls. But when the shepherd summoned his own sheep out of the fold, what protection had they then? None, except what he provided. So long as they kept close to him, however, all was well: it is the mark of a good shepherd that he defends his sheep, even at the risk of his life. This good shepherd is not only revealed as the true King of Israel; he is also the obedient Servant of the Lord, fulfilling the first part of his commission – 'to bring Jacob back to him, and that Israel might be gathered to him' (Isa. 49:5).

10:7–9 Jesus said to them again, 'Indeed and in truth I tell you, I am the door of the sheep. All who came before me are thieves and robbers, but the sheep did not listen to them. I am the door: if any one enters in through me he will be safe; he will go in and out and find pasture.'

There is a patent problem in these words, placed as they are in their present context. In the preceding and following verses Jesus speaks of himself as the shepherd who calls his sheep and leads them out of the fold to the fields where they may safely graze; here he speaks of himself as the door through which they enter and leave the fold. It will not help to invoke the possibility that the shepherd himself lay by night across the entrance to the fold, making himself a sort of living door, so that no one could go in or out without his being aware of it: the parable speaks of a porter or doorkeeper whose business it was to guard the entrance and prevent any unauthorized person from getting in (verse 3). Nor can we take seriously C. C. Torrey's suggestion that the Aramaic word for 'shepherd' was misread as the word for 'door' and wrongly translated into Greek.[2]

It appears that we have a short parable, in which Jesus is compared to the door, inserted into the longer parable in which he is compared to the shepherd.[3] 'I am the door' is not unlike 'I am the way' (John 14:6): Jesus is naturally referred to as the door or the way to salvation. That he did indeed speak of himself as the door is indicated by the story of the martyrdom of his brother James, preserved by the second-century Palestinian writer Hegesippus. James, it is said, was challenged with the question, 'What is the door of Jesus?' (meaning 'the door of which Jesus spoke' or possibly 'the door of salvation'), and was put to death because his answer was construed as blasphemy.[4]

Although Jesus calls himself the door in verses 7 and 9, it is more probably in his rôle of shepherd that he speaks in verse 8. In verses 1 and 2 the rightful shepherd is contrasted with the thief or the robber, and it is evidently the same contrast that is made in verse 8. The 'thieves and robbers' may be the members of the establishment who had shown themselves such unworthy shepherds to needy members of the flock of Israel like the man whose blindness had been cured. We might think also of false Messiahs, insurgent leaders and the like, who gathered followers around them and led them to disaster, as Theudas and Judas the Galilaean did (Acts 5:36, 37). The warning of John 5:43, 'if another comes in his own name, you will accept him', is relevant here, even if he is to come in the future and the 'thieves and robbers' mentioned here came 'before' Jesus. (There is some textual doubt about the phrase 'before me', but its sense is implied if not expressed.[5])

10:10–13 'The thief comes only to steal, to kill, to destroy. I came in order that they might have life and have it in abundance. I am the good shepherd. The good shepherd lays down his life for the sheep. He who is a hireling and no true shepherd, who does not own the sheep, sees the wolf coming and leaves the sheep and takes to flight; and the wolf seizes them and scatters them. He behaves in this way because he is a hireling and has no concern for the sheep.'

The thief's designs on the sheep are wholly malicious; the good shepherd's plans for them are entirely benevolent. He desires and promotes their wellbeing: he is not content that they should eke out a bare and miserable existence; he wants them to live life to the full, to have plenty of good pasturage and enjoy good health. (It is difficult to translate *kalos* in *kalos poimēn* by any other English adjective than 'good'; there is a fairly obvious contrast with the 'worthless shepherd, who deserts the flock', of Zech. 11:17.) The 'good' shepherd shows himself to be a good shepherd because the welfare of the sheep, not his own, is his primary care. He even risks his life to save theirs: that is probably the sense of the verb *tithēsin* ('lays it on the line') as against the variant *didōsin* ('gives his life').[6] But then, they are his own sheep; he looks after them for their own sake.

The hireling is not malicious, as the thief or robber is, but he has not the personal care for the sheep that the true shepherd has. He looks after them for the wages he is paid; he does his duty well enough in normal times, but when danger draws near he is more concerned for his own safety than for theirs. He will not risk his life to defend them against the marauding wolf, as the true shepherd will. It cannot be said certainly if the hireling or the wolf correspond to figures in the contemporary situation: perhaps the hearers drew their own conclusions about this. But there is no doubt who is meant by the true shepherd.

10:14–16 'I am the good shepherd. I know my own (sheep) and my own (sheep) know me, just as the Father knows me and I know the Father; and I lay down my life for the sheep. And I have other sheep which do not belong to this fold: I must bring them also, and they will listen to my voice, and they will become one flock (under) one shepherd.'

It is the mark of a true shepherd to know his own sheep. The verb 'know' occurs four times in verses 14 and 15, and each time it is the present tense of *ginōskō* that is used, the present here having 'gnomic' or timeless force. The special knowledge which the Father and the Son have of each other in the eternal order (cf. Matt. 11:27 and Luke 10:22) is extended to embrace those whom the Son calls his 'own' (cf. the mutual and inclusive love of John 14:21, 23; 15:9). In the parable, the gender of 'my own' (*ta ema*) is neuter, referring to 'sheep' (*probata*); in reality, the reference is to those who are elsewhere (e.g. John 13:1) called 'his own' (*hoi idioi*). There may be an echo here of the LXX wording of Num. 16:5, 'the Lord knows those who are his' (quoted verbatim in 2 Tim. 2:19). The good shepherd's readiness to expose himself to the danger of death for his sheep is now predicated directly by Jesus himself (again there is a variant *didōmi*, 'I give', for *tithēmi*, 'I lay down').[7] Readers of the Gospel knew that Jesus did not merely expose himself to the danger of death for his people, but actually 'stood between them and the foe, and willingly died in their stead.' Indeed, this is made plain by the words of Jesus in verses 17 and 18.

His sheep who belonged to 'this fold' were of Jewish stock, but he had other sheep who must be brought to him who never belonged to that fold and indeed could not be accommodated within it. It is they who are described later in the Gospel as 'the children of God who are scattered abroad', to be gathered 'into one' by Jesus along with those belonging to 'the nation' of Israel (John 11:51, 52). The AV 'one fold' is an error going back to the Vulgate *unum ovile*, but King James's revisers had the less excuse in that William Tyndale had got it right ('one flock') in his versions of 1526 and 1534 (some pre-Vulgate forms of the Latin Bible had also done better than Jerome, so that he too was without excuse.)

These words of Jesus, then, point to the Gentile mission and to the formation of the community, comprising believing Jews and believing Gentiles, in which there is 'neither Jew nor Greek' (Gal. 3:28; Col. 3:11). The Jewish 'sheep' had to be led out of the 'fold' (*aulē*) before they could be united with the 'other sheep' to form one new flock (*poimnē*). What was to hold this enlarged flock together and supply the necessary protection from external enemies? Not enclosing walls but the person and power of the shepherd. The unity and safety of the people of Christ depend on their proximity to him. When they have forgotten this and tried to secure unity or safety by building walls round themselves, the results have not been encouraging. The walls have either been so comprehensive as to enclose a number of wolves along with the sheep (with disastrous consequences for the sheep), or they have been so restrictive as to exclude more sheep than they enclose.

10:17 'This is why my Father loves me – because I lay down my life, in order to receive it again.'

The Father loves the Son (cf. John 3:35; 5:20) because of the Son's utter self-dedication to do the Father's will, even when this involves the laying down of his life. The Father would indeed glorify him with the glory which he had with the Father before the world existed (John 17:5), but the laying down of his life was not only the necessary precondition of his receiving that glory: it was the first stage in his being glorified (John 12:23). If he was to impart resurrection life to others, he must receive resurrection life himself, and to receive resurrection life he must first pass through death. Only by falling into the ground and dying could the grain of wheat 'yield much fruit' (John 12:24). Only by laying down his life and receiving it again could the shepherd bring his 'other sheep' together with the sheep from the original fold into his 'one flock'.

10:18 'No one takes it away from me, but I lay it down of my own accord. I have authority to lay it down, and I have authority to receive it again. This is the commandment which I have received from my Father.'

In this Gospel one side of a complex truth is frequently emphasized to the point where it appears to be the whole truth – the particular aspect of the truth which the Evangelist wishes to bring out. Elsewhere in the NT our Lord's enemies are said to have 'killed' him – as of course they did. But at the same time he submitted to being violently taken and put to death; in the hour of death he seized the initiative and offered himself as a willing sacrifice to God. While at one level his enemies killed him, at a deeper level he laid down his life of his own volition. This he accepted as the Father's will; this he acknowledged obediently as the Father's commandment – and with the Father's commandment he received authority from the Father to fulfil it, both by dying (cf. John 19:11) and by rising again. Similarly, he is repeatedly said elsewhere in the New Testament to have been raised from the dead by God (cf. Acts 2:32; Rom. 6:4; Heb. 13:20; 1 Pet. 1:21, etc.), but here he rises of his own volition. John does not contradict the testimony of other NT writers; the difference is one of emphasis. If Jesus by his own choice resumes the life that he laid down, his choice is (in this respect as in all others) to do his Father's will, to obey his Father's commands. It is by the Father's authority that the Son acts as a free agent (John 5:19–30). This is no doubt a paradox, but it is a paradox inherent in the unique relationship subsisting between the Father and the Son.

10:19–21 **A division broke out again among the Jews because of these words. Many of them said, 'He is demon-possessed; he is mad. Why listen to him?' But others said, 'These are not the utterances of a demon-possessed person. Can a demon open blind people's eyes?'**

As earlier during the week of the festival of Tabernacles (John 7:43), so now Jesus' words precipitate a division among his hearers, as they take sides for or against him. (His words are called *logoi* in verse 19 and *rhēmata* in verse 21, but in using these two terms John is probably indulging his fondness for synonyms.)

The charge of demon-possession is raised once again, as in John 7:20; 8:48. But it is easily exploded: it is not by the power of a demon that a work of mercy, such as the restoring of a blind man's sight, is performed. That particular work of mercy had occasioned another division, between those who argued that one who disregarded sabbath restrictions was a sinner and those who argued that a sinner could not make a blind man see (John 9:16). Now the unprejudiced members of Jesus' audience argue that words of such sanity and grace as he spoke were not compatible with the charge of demon-possession.

(b) Encounter in the temple (10:22–30)

10:22, 23 **Then came the festival of Dedication at Jerusalem. It was winter, and Jesus was walking in the temple in Solomon's colonnade.**

The festival of Dedication was of relatively recent institution.

After the temple had been defiled for three years (167–164 BC) by the installation of a pagan cult under Antiochus Epiphanes, and the idolatrous altar, the 'abomination of desolation' (a mocking pun on the pagan divinity's name),[8] had been erected on top of the altar of Israel's God, the sacred site was recaptured by Judas Maccabaeus and his followers and the temple was reconsecrated to its proper use on 25 Kislev (= 14 December), 164 BC. The festival of Dedication (*Hanukkah*) commemorating this event, may have had a prehistory as a festival of the winter solstice, but from then on it was given a place in Israel's religious calendar, and to this day it is celebrated as the Feast of Lights (so called from the lighting of lamps or candles in Jewish homes to honour the occasion).

Jesus evidently had spent the two months since Tabernacles in or near Jerusalem (he is not said to have 'gone up' to Jerusalem for this festival). The note that 'it was winter' may be intended to explain why he was in a covered part of the temple precincts. Solomon's colonnade was the name given to the portico which ran along the east side of the outer court of Herod's temple. It is mentioned in Acts as the place where Peter addressed the crowd that congregated to see the man who had been cured of his lifelong lameness at the Beautiful Gate, and again as the place where the Jerusalem believers regularly gathered for their public witness to Jesus as the Christ (Acts 3:11; 5:12).

10:24 So the Jews came around him and said to him, 'How long do you keep us in suspense? If you are the Christ, tell us plainly.'

Jesus had not so far said outright in Jerusalem that he was the Messiah. His description of himself as the good shepherd was as near to such a claim as made little difference, but he had not used the actual designation 'Messiah'. It was one thing for him to tell the woman at the well of Sychar who he was (John 4:26); to her the term 'Messiah' (or its Samaritan equivalent) had purely religious connotations. But among the Jews it had political and military implications, which Jesus was careful to avoid. In this Gospel indeed he never makes an explicit messianic claim before the Jewish authorities – not even at his trial (as he does in the Synoptic record, Mark 14:62 and parallels).

The adverb 'plainly' represents Gk. *parrhēsia* which has been used three times in chapter 7 to denote Jesus' speaking out publicly (verses 4, 13, 26). But the authorities would not have been any more inclined to believe in him as the Messiah if he had made the claim 'plainly'. If his works and teaching did not convey their proper message, no words from him would have been any more convincing. The Evangelist reckons that, quite apart from any express claim from Jesus' lips, the record of his ministry should suffice to bring readers to believe in him as 'the Christ, the Son of God and, believing, to have life in his name' (John 20:31). If *readers* were expected to be led to faith by the written record, those who saw his works and heard his teaching might have been expected to recognize him even more promptly for who he was, but too many of them had their eyes blinded (John 12:40).

10:25 Jesus answered them, 'I told you and you do not believe. The works which I do in my Father's name themselves bear testimony concerning me.'

Jesus had appealed to the testimony of his works after the healing of the cripple at the pool of Bethesda (John 5:36). Now he makes the same appeal after the restoration of sight to the blind man. Such works were those which the Father gave him to do; he did them in his Father's name (that is, by his Father's authority), and they should have been sufficient to show those who saw them that the Father had sent him. The restoration of health, the restoration of sight, and the forthcoming restoration of life (in the Lazarus incident) were all works declaring the character as well as the power of God to those whose hearts were not totally insensitive. But where the heart of the spectator was insensitive, each successive work served but to harden it the more: it was the raising of Lazarus that made Jesus' enemies finally resolve to encompass his death (John 11:53).

10:26–28 'But *you* do not believe, because you do not belong to my sheep. My sheep hear my voice, and I know them and they follow me. Moreover, I give them eternal life and they will never perish; no one will snatch them out of my hand.'

In the prologue to the Gospel, when the eternal Word came to his own home, his own people (or those who might have been expected to be his own people) gave him no welcome. Some, however, did welcome him, and thus proved to be his own people in deed and not merely in word. By virtue of their faith in him they became members of the family of God, children of the second birth (John 1:11–13). Here they are described as the good shepherd's own sheep, who instinctively recognize his voice and follow him. Those who neither believe nor follow him show by that very fact that they do not belong to his own sheep. Not only do his own sheep recognize his voice; he for his part knows them – knows them individually, calls them by name (verse 3).

Jesus has already said that, by contrast with the thieves and robbers who seek to destroy the sheep (*apollymi*, active), he has come to give them life in abundance; now this abundant life is called eternal life (*zōē aiōnios*), promised earlier in the Gospel to those who believe in the Son (3:15, 16, 36; 6:40, 47). To have eternal life is to live for ever (6:51, 58); negatively expressed, those who have it 'will never see death' (8:51), 'will never taste death' (8:52), 'will never die' (11:26) or, as here, 'will never perish' (*apollymi*, passive). Physical life may be destroyed, but those who are united by faith to the Son of God, those who belong to the flock of the true Shepherd, can never lose real life, for he keeps it secure. 'No one', he says, 'will snatch them out of my hand.'

10:29, 30 'My Father, who has given them to me, is greater than all, and no one can snatch (them) out of my Father's hand. I and my Father are one.'

This translation of verse 29 does not follow the latest Nestle text, which must be rendered: 'What my Father has given me is greater than all.' It follows the Byzantine text, and is now known to have the early support of Papyrus 66. It makes such excellent sense that the only argument in favour of the other reading is that no scribe would have perpetrated it if he had found 'My Father, who has given them to me, is greater than all' in his master-copy. In what sense could it be said that what the Father has given to the Son is greater than all? 'It would mean either (*a*) that Christ's flock is greater than all forces that oppose it . . . – which I think John would never have said – or (*b*) that the authority God gave Christ is supreme (cf. 13:3), which is Johannine, but not obviously appropriate here.' So C. H. Dodd comments; he adds that the reading 'My Father, who has given them to me . . .', which is 'more widely if less weightily supported, is probably to be adopted'.[9]

Paul expresses the security of those who have died and been raised with Christ in the words: 'your life is hid with Christ in God' (Col. 3:3). The sense of our present passage is quite similar: God and Christ are together engaged to protect believers. Whom Christ protects, God protects; whom Christ keeps in his hand, God keeps in his, and even if it were (mistakenly) thought possible to snatch one of Christ's people from his hand, it is self-evident that no one is powerful enough to snatch any one or anything (no object is expressed) from the hand of God.

The 'shattering statement'[10] in verse 30, 'I and the Father are one', taken in isolation, could bear a wider meaning than it has in its present context, and a meaning quite consistent with the general teaching of this Gospel. Here we have a particular application of the statements in John 5:19-23. So responsive is the Son to the Father that he is one in mind, one in purpose, one in action with him. Where the eternal wellbeing of true believers is concerned, the Son's determination and pledge to guard them from harm is endorsed by the Father's word and confirmed by the Father's all-powerful act. 'This is the will of him who sent me,' Jesus has already said, 'that I should lose nothing of all that he has given me, but raise it up at the last day' (John 6:39; cf. 17:12). In guarding his people, he is obedient to the Father's will; what wonder, then, if they are simultaneously guarded by the Father himself?

(c) Renewed conflict (10:31-39)

10:31, 32 **The Jews again picked up stones to stone him. Jesus' reply to their action was: 'I have shown you many good works done on the Father's initiative. For which of these works are you stoning me?'**

The previous occasion of his enemies' trying to stone him in the temple precincts was when he made the declaration, 'Before Abraham was born, I am' (John 8:58, 59). The claim implicit in that declaration was similar to that made more expressly in the words, 'I and the Father are one.' It was a claim which, in their eyes, merited the penalty prescribed in the law for one who blasphemed the divine name. Now indeed he had 'told them plainly' (cf. verse 24), but the plainness was intolerable. They found Jesus' words even more provocative than his works. It was bad enough that he should make a cripple carry his pallet or smear clay on a blind man's eyes on the sabbath day, thus committing or abetting a technical breach of the sabbath law, but the arguments by which he justified these actions were, they thought, much worse. The attempt to take his life after the incident at the pool of Bethesda (presumably then also by stoning, though this is not said in so many words) was prompted by the fact that 'he not only broke the sabbath, but also called God his own Father, making himself equal with God' (John 5:18).

Jesus, however, asks them for which of his good works they are stoning him. All his works were done by the Father's direction (John 5:19); they were 'good works' (*erga kala*, 'beautiful works') not only because they were acts of obedience to the Father but also because they were acts of blessing to men. His works bore witness to his divine mission (John 5:36); his words were in perfect harmony with his works.

10:33 The Jews replied, 'It is not for a good work that we are stoning you but for blasphemy – namely, because you, human being as you are, make yourself God.'

On his works, apart from his words, they might have been able to put a different interpretation, but his words were unambiguous. While he subordinated himself to God, as the Son to the Father, yet he claimed to be one with the Father, placing himself on the other side of the chasm that separated God from man, the Creator from the creature. The logic of their argument seemed incapable of refutation: this was blasphemy, an offence that involved the whole community in serious guilt, unless the perpetrator were put away from among his people, 'cut off from Israel'. Readers of this Gospel, however, know better: they can follow its record of the sayings and actions of Jesus in the light of the prologue, from which they have already learned that Jesus is the incarnate Word, that Word which in the beginning was with God and was God. They have learned, too, that Jesus is uniquely the Son who has his being in the Father's bosom and has come forth from God to make him known in the world. High as his claims are, then, they are grounded in the truth of his being and his mission: his works are the works of God; his words are the words of God. He is not 'making himself God'; he is not 'making himself' anything, but in word and work he is showing himself to be what he truly is – the Son sent by the Father to bring light and life to mankind.

10:34–36 Jesus answered them, 'Is it not written in your law, "I have said, 'You are gods' "? If those to whom the word of God came were called gods by him (and scripture cannot be annulled), do you say, "You are a blasphemer" to the one whom the Father sanctified and sent into the world because I said, "I am God's Son"?'

Jesus rebuts their charge of blasphemy by means of an argument from scripture, of a kind with which they themselves were quite familiar. In Psalm 82 the supreme God rises in the divine council to pronounce judgment on beings called 'gods' (*'ĕlōhîm*).[11] His charge against them is that they administer justice unjustly, showing favour to the wicked instead of upholding the right of the helpless and oppressed; the sentence which he passes on them is death:

> I have said, 'You are gods.
>   sons of the Most High, all of you;
> nevertheless, you shall die like men,
>   and fall like any prince.'

Jewish interpreters were divided (as other interpreters have been divided since then) on the question whether those addressed in these terms by God are celestial beings or human judges. For our present purpose this question is not of the first relevance: what is relevant is that they are manifestly inferior beings to the supreme God, and yet he calls them 'gods' (verse 6) – *theoi* in Greek. If God himself calls them 'gods' (and 'sons of the Most High' at that), why should it be counted a capital offence in the sent one of the Father if he calls himself the Son of God? The argument is conducted thus far on the level of Jesus' opponents: his question would have made an interesting issue for rabbinical debate. The fact that the beings addressed in the psalm were called 'gods', they might have said, did not prove that he was right in speaking of himself as the Son of God; it simply proved that some created beings were properly called 'gods'.[12]

More than that must be said however: the beings addressed in the psalm were unjust judges, whether of human or angelic rank, divinely sentenced to death. But Jesus was 'the one whom the Father sanctified and sent into the world'. Before he was sent he was sanctified, i.e. set apart for his special mission in the world. We may compare the inaugural word of the Lord to Jeremiah: 'Before you were born I sanctified you (the verb in LXX is *hagiazō*, as here); I appointed you a prophet to the nations' (Jer. 1:5). 'He whom God has sent utters the words of God' (John 3:34); if he says 'I am the Son of God', his words must be treated seriously. He had not in the immediately preceding context used these precise words, but they were logically involved in what he said about his Father (verses 29, 30), just as they were involved in what he said about the Father and the Son in the sequel to the incident at Bethesda (John 5:17-27).

'Your law' (verse 34) is here a comprehensive term for the Hebrew Bible. They acknowledged its authority, and should therefore accept the implications of what it said. 'Scripture cannot be annulled' or 'made void' (Mark 7:13); it cannot be set aside when its teaching is inconvenient. What is written remains written.

10:37–39 **'If the works which I do are not my Father's, do not believe me; but if they are, then, even if you do not believe me, believe the works, so that you may recognize and know that the Father is in me and I am in the Father.' They endeavoured to seize him again, and he escaped their hands.**

Jesus appeals again to the evidence of his works (as he will do later in the upper room in John 14:10f.). The works which the Father gave him to do testify that he is the Son who does nothing on his own initiative, but only what he sees the Father doing (5:19), and they testify more than that. In the discourse on the good shepherd he has spoken of the mutual knowledge of the Father and himself, and has extended that knowledge to embrace the mutual knowledge of the shepherd and his own sheep (verses 14, 15). This mutual knowledge is now said to be based in a mutual indwelling. The claim is repeated in John 14:10; Jesus there goes on to make it plain that this 'coinherence' is a coinherence of love, which is extended to embrace his love for his people and theirs for him (14:20–24). Indeed, as the upper room discourse shows, such is Jesus' oneness with the Father that those who love him are brought into the sphere of the life of God, which is the life of perfect love.

Such teaching was meat and drink to those who listened to it in the upper room, but it was anathema to those who heard it on the present occasion. Their conviction that Jesus was a blasphemer was strengthened, and again they tried to arrest him, as they had done at the feast of Tabernacles (7:30), but again they failed. That 'his hour had not yet come' is not given as the explicit reason for their failure here, as it is there, but it is no doubt implied.

VII. Final Phase of Jesus' Ministry in the World
(10:40–12:50)

1. BEYOND JORDAN (10:40–42)

10:40–42 Then he went back across the Jordan to the place where John had been baptizing at first, and there he stayed. Many came to him, and they said, 'John performed no sign, but all the things that John said about this man were true.' And many believed in him there.

Jesus now left Jerusalem, which he was not to visit again until Palm Sunday, between three and four months later. He went to Bethany beyond Jordan, where John had borne witness to him in the early days, before the beginning of Jesus' public ministry. The phrase 'at first' may refer to the first part of the Evangelist's narrative, where John's testimony is related (John 1:19–36); or it may mean that this is where John's baptismal ministry was first carried out, before he went to Aenon near Salim (John 3:23).

The people who lived there remembered him, and they came to hear him. As they listened to his words and watched the things he did, they recalled John's testimony to him and were compelled to acknowledge its truth. 'John (unlike Jesus) performed no sign', they said repeatedly, 'but all the things that John said about this man were true.' This is one respect in which John did not manifest the power of Elijah: in none of our sources of information about him are any mighty works credited to him. None, indeed, were needed. In this Gospel John is presented from first to last as the ideal witness, and it is as such that he is presented here. John had long since been imprisoned and put to death, but his words lived on. No one called to be a witness could ask for any better encomium than that all the things he said were true. If John's disciples, on burying him (Mark 6:29), had tried to think of a suitable epitaph for him, no more suitable wording could have been devised than the testimonial of these former hearers of his at Bethany beyond Jordan. To be sure, some of the things John said about Jesus had not yet come true: he had not yet taken away the sin of the world or begun to baptize with the Holy Spirit, because he was 'not yet glorified' (John 7:39). But John's witness was so amply confirmed by the evidence of their eyes and ears during this short time that Jesus spent among them that many believed in Jesus. So John's witness remained effective after John himself was removed.

It has been pointed out that the successive references to John in this Gospel are progressively shorter, from the first chapter to this – a curious illustration of John's own words regarding Jesus: 'He must increase, but I must decrease' (John 3:30).

NOTES

1. Nowhere in this Gospel is *parabolē* found; for *paroimia* cf. John 16:25, 29.
2. C. C. Torrey, *Our Translated Gospels* (London, 1936), pp. 108, 111–113. The second-century Papyrus 75 and some Coptic witnesses read 'shepherd' for 'door' in verse 7, but this is a patent attempt to ease the sudden change of metaphor.
3. Cf. J. A. T. Robinson, 'The Parable of the Shepherd (John 10.1–5)' *Twelve New Testament Studies* (London, 1962), pp. 67–75, for some suggestions on the structure and setting of this parable.
4. Eusebius, *Hist. Eccl.* 2.23.12.
5. Among the witnesses which omit the phrase are Papyri 45 (apparently) and 75 and the first hand in Sinaiticus.
6. The main witnesses for *didōsin* ('gives') are Papyrus 45, the first hand in Sinaiticus and Codex Bezae.
7. For *didōmi* ('I give') the chief witnesses are Papyri 45 and 66 and the Sinaiticus (first hand), Bezan and Washington codices.
8. Actually, on the divinity's Aramaic name, *Ba'al Shāmēn* ('lord of heaven'), the Syrian counterpart to the Greek deity Olympian Zeus, of whom Antiochus claimed to be the earthly manifestation (hence his surname Epiphanes, 'manifest').
9. *The Interpretation of the Fourth Gospel*, p. 433. (It is just possible that the reading 'What my Father has given me . . . .' reflects a misunderstanding of an Aramaic stage in the course of transmission.) See also J. Whittaker, 'A Hellenistic Context for John 10, 29', *Vigiliae Christianae* 24 (1970), pp. 241–260, where it is pointed out further that the phrase 'greater than all' (*meizon pantōn*) appears to have been current as a Hellenistic invocation formula.
10. B. Lindars, *Behind the Fourth Gospel*, p. 52. It forms the climax to this discourse as 'Before Abraham was born, I am He' (John 8:58) forms the climax to an earlier one.

11. In a remarkable document from Cave 11 at Qumran (11Q Melchizedek), the word *'ĕlohîm* ('God') at the beginning of Psalm 82 is actually applied to Melchizedek, divinely installed as heavenly judge.
12. See E. D. Freed, *Old Testament Quotations in the Gospel of John* (Leiden, 1965), pp. 60–65.

CHAPTER 11

2. RAISING OF LAZARUS (11:1–46)

(a) Lazarus falls ill (11:1–5)

11:1, 2 There was a man who was ill, Lazarus by name, of Bethany, the village of Mary and her sister Martha. (It was that Mary who anointed the Lord with myrrh and wiped his feet with her hair, whose brother Lazarus was ill.)

The signal for Jesus to leave his retreat in Transjordan and return to the main scene of action in Judaea was not long in coming. It took the form of a message from Bethany, letting him know that Lazarus, a friend of his, was ill.

This is the first time that the family of Bethany finds mention in this Gospel, but the Evangelist knows that some of his readers have heard of at least one member of the family. Mary, one of the two sisters of Lazarus, on a memorable occasion poured myrrh over Jesus's feet and wiped them with her hair. This was such an extraordinary thing to do that those who heard of it were never likely to forget it. The Evangelist, who records the incident later (John 12:3), had presumably told the story already (no doubt with other stories to be written down eventually in his Gospel) in the companies of Christians among whom he moved. So, on mentioning Lazarus for the first time, he says, in effect, 'You will know whom I mean if I tell you that he was the brother of that Mary who anointed the Lord.'

Bethany near Jerusalem, on the other side of Olivet, less than two miles along the road to Jericho, has not been mentioned in John's record before this.

11:3–5 So Lazarus's sisters sent a message to Jesus: 'You should know, Lord, that the one whom you love is ill.' When Jesus heard it, he said, 'This illness is not mortal; it has come for the glory of God, so that the Son of God may be glorified by it.' (Now Jesus loved Martha and her sister and Lazarus.)

This family in Bethany, though unmentioned earlier in this Gospel, was evidently well known to Jesus and well loved by him. It was natural, then, that when Lazarus fell ill, his sisters should get in touch with Jesus at once.

The vocative *kyrie* ('Lord') was so widely current as a courteous mode of address that it is doubtful if it should be translated here by any stronger term than 'sir'. If (as is probable) the sisters spoke in Aramaic, then the natural mode of address would have been *Rabbi* (see note on verse 28).

Jesus' reaction to the news must strike the reader as strange, but the explanation of it can be read, if at all, only between the lines of John's record. This is the last of the signs preceding the passion of Jesus in which the divine glory was manifested through him, and it is this aspect of the incident that is uppermost in the Evangelist's account throughout. To say that the illness was not mortal (literally, 'not unto death'), when in fact Lazarus must have died shortly after the message was despatched, and Jesus knew that he had died, makes the reader pause and think. The disciples at first could take the words only *au pied de la lettre*, but the reader is better informed. One might take the meaning to be: This illness is not so much one that will terminate in death as one which will demonstrate the glory of God. There is ample evidence for the biblical idiom in which 'not . . . but' means 'not only . . . but also'. But the words mean more than that: the glory of God was to be demonstrated in the raising of Lazarus from death, so that while the illness resulted in temporary death, it resulted more impressively in resurrection and life.

The parenthetic statement that Jesus loved all three members of the family is intended to show that it was not lack of love or concern for them that made him react to the news as he did. (The verb rendered 'love' in verse 5 is *agapaō*, whereas in verse 3 it is *phileō* – sufficient evidence that, as we have seen already, John makes no distinction between the two verbs.)

It is an interesting coincidence, though no more than a coincidence, that the three names (Mary, Martha, Lazarus) were found in 1873 in ossuary inscriptions in one tomb near Bethany.[1]

(b) Going back to Judaea (11:6–16)

11:6, 7 So when Jesus heard that Lazarus was ill, he stayed for two days in the place where he was. Then, after that, he said to the disciples, 'Let us go back to Judaea.'

Jesus' remaining where he was for two days after receiving the news of Lazarus's illness presents another problem. The problem was felt by both the sisters, whose first words on meeting Jesus, one after the other, were, 'If you had been here, my brother would not have died.' It may be said that the record of this delay brought reassurance to Christians of a later generation, who were disappointed because they and their friends had to pass through death before experiencing the expected entrance into resurrection life; but this does not account for the delay in the historical situation. If the problem were put to the Evangelist, he might well have replied (in words which he uses elsewhere), 'He himself knew what he was going to do' (John 6:6). When the two days were past, then Jesus proposed to the disciples' astonishment that they should go back to Judaea.

11:8 The disciples said to him, 'Rabbi, only the other day the Judaeans were trying to stone you. Are you going back there?'

The reference to the attempt to stone him is to the incident at the festival of Dedication, recorded in John 10:31, when Jesus' claim, 'I and the Father are one', provoked this hostile reaction on the part of 'the Jews'. (But the mention of Judaea in verse 7 suggests the translation 'the Judaeans' here, as in 7:1.) Why, the disciples asked, should he venture into the lions' den again? Could he not cure Lazarus from a distance?

11:9, 10 Jesus answered, 'Are there not twelve hours in the day? If one walks about in daytime, he does not stumble, because he sees the light of this world. If one walks about by night, he stumbles, because he has no light.'

Jesus' answer is remarkably similar to his words in John 9:4, in relation to the blind man and his impending cure: 'We must work the works of him who sent me while it is day; the night is coming, when no one can work.' The blindness then and the illness now were means for the display of God's glory. The present words have an obvious surface meaning: those who walk in the daytime do not stumble against obstacles because the light of the sun shows them where they are going; people who go out in the dark are liable to stumble because they cannot see obstacles in their path. But there is a deeper meaning, where the true light of the world and not the light of this world is involved: one who shuts his eyes to the true light not only 'has no light' but 'the light is not in him'. The light of the sun shines from the sky; the true light shines within (cf. 1 John 2:8). In the present context, Jesus must follow the path of the Father's will while life lasts; it may be the eleventh hour of daylight, but that is no reason for staying in retirement.

11:11–13 These were his words, and then he said to them, 'Our friend Lazarus has fallen asleep; but I am going to wake him up.' The disciples said to him, 'If he has fallen asleep, Lord, he

will recover.' (Jesus had spoken of his death, but they supposed that he was speaking about resting in sleep.)

The use of sleep as a metaphor for death became, and remains, a common Christian locution, so common, indeed, that we may think that the disciples were unusually obtuse not to grasp what Jesus meant. But perhaps the locution was not so familiar to them; we may recall the bystanders' incredulous scorn when Jesus said that Jairus's daughter was 'not dead, but asleep' (Mark 5:39; that a different word for 'asleep' is used there from that found here is immaterial).[2] That the man who was ill should have fallen asleep seemed to the disciples to be a promising sign.

11:14-16 Then Jesus said to them plainly, 'Lazarus has died; and I am glad for your sakes that I was not there, so that you may believe. But let us go to him.' Then Thomas (that is, the 'Twin') said to his fellow-disciples, 'Let us go too, so that we may die with him.'

Jesus implies that, if he had been present in Bethany, Lazarus would not have died. As it is, however, the disciples will see such a manifestation of the glory of God as will kindle their faith, and for that he is glad. So, he said, 'let us go to him.'

Thomas's permission and loyalty are both expressed in his words to the others. Thomas (*t'ōmā*) is the Aramaic word for 'twin'; *didymos* is the Greek word (cf. 20:24; 21:2)[3]. The wording here and elsewhere suggests that in Greek-speaking circles Thomas was called Didymos (Didymus), just as Cephas was called Petros (Peter.)[4] Judaea is the place where the final manifestation of the divine glory in the incarnate Word is to be given; by the same token it is the place of Jesus' death. From the place of withdrawal from the world Jesus goes back to manifest himself to the world, and to do so more fully than when he went up to Jerusalem for the festival of Tabernacles (John 7:4). Thomas betrays some inkling of this truth, but if his Master is to die, he has no wish to survive him.

(c) Arrival at Bethany (11:17-27)

11:17-19) So Jesus came and found that he had already been four days in the tomb. (Bethany was near Jerusalem, about fifteen furlongs distant.) Many of the Jews had come to Martha and Mary to console them over their brother.

Perhaps on this occasion too Jesus waited until his 'hour' had come (cf. John 2:4; 7:6) – in this case the 'hour' when one of those in the tombs would hear his voice and come forth (John 5:28f.).

The belief is attributed to rabbis of a later date that the dead person's soul revisited the tomb during the first three days but left it permanently from the fourth day onwards; death was then irreversible.[5] It is possible that such a belief is implied in the further reference to Lazarus's four days' entombment in verse 39.

A 'furlong' (Gk. *stadion*) was about 202 yards 9 inches in length; 15 'furlongs' would thus be equivalent to rather less than a mile and three quarters. This is the exact distance between Jerusalem and Bethany. If Jesus came up the Jericho road from his Transjordanian retreat, he would arrive at Bethany shortly before the road reached its terminus in Jerusalem.

The 'Jews' who had come to visit Lazarus's sisters and condole with them were their Judaean friends and neighbours: the word is used here with no theological overtones.

11:20 **So, when Martha heard that Jesus was coming, she went to meet him; but Mary sat still at home.**

The portrayal of the two sisters' character and temperament in this Gospel agrees in general with that in Luke's record, where Mary sits at Jesus' feet while Martha is busily engaged with housework (Luke 10:38–42).[6]

11:21, 22 **So Martha said to Jesus, 'If you had been here, Lord, my brother would not have died. But even now I know that, whatever you ask from God, God will give it to you.'**

Martha uses the language of faith. If Jesus had been there at the time, Lazarus would not have died: this is not a complaint; it is an expression of her faith in Jesus' power. It is the same faith that finds voice in her assurance that God will grant Jesus whatever request he makes. She does not say, 'If you ask God to restore my brother to life, he will grant your request'; but it is implied that she had this in her mind. Her assurance in this respect has been compared to the assurance underlying the order given to the servants at Cana by Jesus' mother: 'Do whatever he tells you' (John 2:5).

11:23–26 **Jesus said to her, 'Your brother will rise again.' 'I know', said Martha to him, 'that he will rise in the resurrection on the last day.' Jesus said to her, 'I am the resurrection and the life. Whoever believes in me will live even if he dies, and no one who lives and believes in me will ever die. Do you believe this?'**

Martha takes Jesus' assurance, 'Your brother will rise again', to be a conventional word of comfort and hope such as was current among Jews who believed in the resurrection of the dead. Thanks to the influence of the Pharisees and those who followed their line, this was now the general belief among Jews, in spite of Sadducean resistance to it; and it has remained an article of Jewish orthodoxy to this day. Jesus, of course, fully shared and proclaimed the belief in resurrection, as is shown by the Synoptic account of his encounter with the Sadducees in the temple precincts (Mark 12:18–27). The resurrection hope was shared by Martha, as is seen from her answer; 'I know that he will rise in the resurrection on the last day.' The resurrection on the last day has been mentioned repeatedly by Jesus in earlier discourses in this Gospel, with this addition: he himself is the one who will raise the dead then, for the Father has authorized him to do so (John 5:21, 25–29; 6:39f.). Martha's answer was one of intelligence and faith, and it called forth from Jesus a further assurance, which went beyond the accepted belief in the resurrection of the dead.

The death of Lazarus, with its impending sequel of resurrection, is to be a paradigm of the grant of eternal life to all believers in Jesus. In the discourse following the healing of the cripple at the pool of Bethesda, Jesus claimed the authority, given to him by the Father, not only to recall to resurrection on a coming day those who lie in their tombs, but here and now to give life to the dead who 'hear the voice of the Son of God' (John 5:25). So here there is a further reference to the twofold aspect of the raising of the dead. But now Jesus is not only the one who effects the resurrection and bestows life; he is himself the resurrection and the life;[7] just as in the Capernaum discourse following the feeding of the multitude he not only gives the bread from heaven; he is himself that living bread (John 6:27, 35).

It seems that the two statements made by Jesus after his claim to be the resurrection and the life, while parallel, are not synonymous. Moreover, C. H. Dodd has made the attractive suggestion that the former of the two elucidates the claim 'I am the resurrection', while the latter elucidates the claim 'I am the life', thus: 'I am the resurrection: he who has faith in me, even if he dies, will live again. I am the life: he who is alive and has faith in me will never die.'[8] The believer in Jesus who undergoes physical death will nevertheless live. This is more than an announcement of the general resurrection on the last day; this looks forward to Jesus' own rising from the dead and affirms that believers in him, being united to him by faith, will share his risen life even though they experience bodily death. More than that, so far as this sharing his risen life, this possession of eternal life, is concerned, it is a life which knows no death. As Jesus has already said, 'any one who keeps my word will never see death' (John 8:51). Mortal life must come to an end; the life that is life indeed endures for ever. Here is an anticipation of the promise to be given in the upper room: 'because I live, you will live also' (John 14:19).

11:27 'Yes, Lord', she said to him, 'I assuredly believe that you are the Messiah, the Son of God, the one who was to come into the world.'

Did Martha believe what he told her? She could accept it by faith, but she could not understand it, any more than any other disciple of his could understand it before he rose from the dead. But, asked about her faith, she confessed her faith in the person who was speaking to her. Like Andrew, she confessed him as the Messiah (John 1:41); like Nathanael, she confessed him as the Son of God (John 1:49). He was the one whose coming Moses and the prophets foretold (John 1:45); now he had come. The perfect tense (*pepisteuka*) differs but little in force from the present (*pisteuō*): 'I have come to believe', she means, 'and now, as a settled attitude of soul, I believe.'

(d) On the way to the tomb (11:28–37)

11:28–31 With these words she went off and called her sister Mary secretly, saying, 'The Teacher has come; he is calling for you.' When Mary heard this, she rose up quickly and made her way to him. Jesus had not yet come into the village, but was still at the place where Martha had met him. So the Jews who were with Mary in the house, consoling her, seeing that she rose up quickly and went out, followed her; they supposed that she was going to the tomb to weep there.

Evidently Jesus' arrival was not yet generally known, and Martha did not want the crowd of sympathizing visitors to know that he had come. Hence the secrecy with which she told Mary that he had arrived and wanted to see her. ('The Teacher', i.e. 'the Rabbi', was the way in which they normally spoke of him and addressed him; see note on verse 3.) But Martha's attempt to keep his arrival secret was frustrated, for the visitors thought that Mary was setting out for the tomb and went after her, no doubt with the intention of continuing their consolation there.

11:32 So, when Mary came where Jesus was and saw him, she fell at his feet and said to him, 'If you had been here, Lord, my brother would not have died.'

Mary uses the same words as Martha had used not long before. It is likely that they had said this to each other several times since Lazarus died: 'if the Teacher had been here, our brother would not have died.' Martha had gone on to make an even more positive declaration of faith; Mary says nothing more, but it would be precarious to draw conclusions about the two sisters' varying state of mind. On each occasion where Mary of Bethany appears in the Gospels, she is at Jesus' feet (cf. Luke 10:39; John 12:3).

11:33–37 **So, when Jesus saw her weeping, and the Jews who had come with her weeping, he became deeply agitated in spirit and shook with emotion. 'Where have you laid him?' he said. 'Lord, come and see', they said to him. Jesus burst into tears. So the Jews said, 'Look, how he loved him!' But some of them said, 'Could not this man, who opened the blind man's eyes, have prevented him from dying?'**

The verb *embrimaomai*, translated here 'became deeply agitated', means literally 'snort (with indignation)' and regularly indicates displeasure of some kind. (In Mark 14:4 it expresses the spectators' indignation at the 'waste' of the precious ointment in Simon the leper's house in Bethany.) Here it points to Jesus' inward reaction ('in spirit'); but what was the cause of his displeasure? Most probably it was the presence of sickness and death, and the havoc they wrought in human life.[9] On this occasion, no doubt, their effect was to be overruled by God for his glory (see verses 4, 40); but their effect was plainly to be seen in the grief of Mary and her friends. So powerful was Jesus' emotional reaction to the spectacle that he 'shook' (literally, 'troubled himself') under the force of it. Not only did he shake, but when he was shown (in response to his question) where the body of Lazarus was, he burst into tears (this seems to be the 'ingressive' sense of the aorist).

Some commentators have found it difficult to suppose that he who is presented in this Gospel as the incarnate Word, knowing what he was going to do, should be genuinely moved by sorrow and sympathy (as others might at the graveside), and have put his tears down to some other cause – anger and frustration, perhaps, at the blindness and lack of faith which he saw in those who were around at the time. But the friends and neighbours who were there had no doubt about the cause of his tears: he was weeping for a dearly loved friend. 'Look, how he loved him!' they said. Some indeed thought, and not unnaturally, that such a healer as he had already shown himself to be might have done something to prevent his friend from dying. In truth, the reader may feel some surprise that Jesus, who was so completely in command of the situation, and knew that the glory of God was about to be manifested in a signal manner, should nevertheless shed tears of grief for a departed friend and his mourning relatives as any one else might do. But in him the eternal Word became truly *incarnate* and shared the common lot of mankind: our Evangelist would have agreed completely with the writer to the Hebrews that Jesus is well able to sympathize with his people's weaknesses, having been tested himself in the school of suffering. It was in sympathy with those who wept that he also wept. Here is no automaton, but a real human being.

(e) *The quickening shout* (11:38–44)

11:38 So Jesus, again deeply agitated within himself, came to the tomb. It was a cave, and a stone had been placed over it.

The tomb was a hollow in the rock, the entrance to which was blocked by a stone of suitable size and shape, fitting into it more or less like a cork. The description is quite like that of the tomb in which the body of Jesus himself was later laid. In the fourth century a church was built over the crypt which was believed to be the tomb of Lazarus; it was called the Lazareion (from which is derived the Muslim name of the village, El-Azariyeh). The opening in the hillside which is shown to visitors today as the tomb may or may not be authentic, but if it is, its present condition tells us little about its appearance or arrangement in AD 30.[10]

11:39–42 'Take away the stone', said Jesus. 'Lord', said Martha (sister of the dead man), 'by this time there will be a stench; he has been dead for four days.' Jesus said to her, 'Did I not tell you that, if you would believe, you would see the glory of God?' So they took away the stone. Then Jesus lifted up his eyes and said, 'Father, I thank thee that thou hast heard me. For my part, I knew that thou hearest me always, but I have spoken because of the crowd standing around, so that they may believe that thou hast sent me.'

Martha, practical as ever, points out that the effect of removing the stone, as Jesus had directed, will be unpleasant. Jesus reminds her of his promise. The actual words he uses now are more reminiscent of what he had said to the disciples earlier (verse 4), but they sum up the substance of the assurance he had given to Martha (verses 23–26). Evidently Martha now gives her consent to the removal of the stone, and it is removed.

Jesus does not pray that Lazarus may be raised from death at his word; it is implied that he has already prayed for this, and that he is assured of the granting of his prayer. He has no need to pray aloud to God; he does so now for the benefit of the bystanders, 'so that they may believe that thou hast sent me' (cf. John 17:21). Some commentators have seen a certain artificiality in such a prayer; however, 'if prayer is a form of union with God, then the Johannine Jesus is always praying, for he and the Father are one.'[11] The raising of the dead is a divine prerogative which the Father shares with the Son (cf. John 5:21, 25–29), and it is important that the bystanders should understand this. So, in their hearing, he thanks God for having heard him.

11:43, 44 **Saying this, he called with a loud voice, 'Lazarus, come out here!' The dead man came out, his feet and hands bound in winding sheets and his face wrapped round in a napkin. Jesus said to them, 'Unbind him, and let him go free.'**

The shout which calls Lazarus back to life is a parable of that coming day when all who are in the tombs will hear the same quickening shout and come out. It is only a parable, because Lazarus is called out to a renewal and continuation of mortal life, whereas those who hear the shout on the last day are called out to resurrection life. But before resurrection life could be imparted to others, Jesus himself must be raised from the dead. The different may be indicated by the fact that, when Jesus was raised, the graveclothes were left behind in the tomb (John 20:5–7). The body of Lazarus, like the body of Jesus later, had been swathed in winding sheets (Gk. *keiriai*, not used elsewhere in NT) and a napkin (*soudarion*, a loanword from Latin *sudarium*, 'sweatrag') had been wrapped round his head. He was still impeded by these as he made his way blindly out of the cave in the direction of the voice that had called him. Much need, then, that helping hands should unwind the cerements and the napkin, so that Lazarus could see and walk about freely. (This liberation has been used as a parable of moral and spiritual liberation, and not improperly, although the Evangelist does not make this point.)

(f) The spectators' reaction (11:45, 46)

11:45, 46 **So many of the Jews who had come to Mary and had seen what he did believed in him. But some of them went off to the Pharisees and told them what Jesus had done.**

The account of the raising of Lazarus raises a number of questions to which no answer is given. Some of those questions have been given memorable expression by one of our own poets:

> When Lazarus left his charnel-cave,
>   And home to Mary's house return'd,
>   Was this demanded – if he yearn'd
> To hear her weeping by his grave?
>
> 'Where were thou, brother, those four days?'
>   There lives no record of reply,
>   Which telling what it is to die
> Had surely added praise to praise.
>
> From every house the neighbours met,
>   The streets were fill'd with joyful sound,
>   A solemn gladness even crown'd
> The purple brows of Olivet.
>
> Behold a man raised up by Christ!
>   The rest remaineth unreveal'd;
>   He told it not; or something seal'd
> The lips of that Evangelist.[12]

The raising of Lazarus is the climax of the series of 'signs' which characterize John's record of Jesus' public ministry, serving as manifestations of the divine glory which is resided in the incarnate Word. At the same time it precipitates the series of events which culminate in the passion narrative.

At such a revelation of the glory of God (cf. verses 4, 40), it was not surprising that many believed in Jesus: whatever doubts they might have had before, it was now plain that he was the Sent One of God. 'The Jews who had come to Mary' are presumably those who left the house and followed her, 'supposing that she was going to the tomb to weep there' (verse 31). Even if we read, with other authorities, 'the Jews who had come with Mary', it is the same persons that are meant. But some went off and told the Pharisees what Jesus had done; it is implied that they did so with no friendly intention (the more so as they are set in contrast with the many who believed).

3. THE FATEFUL COUNCIL (11:47–53)

11:47, 48 So the chief priests and the Pharisees convened a meeting of the Sanhedrin. They were speaking like this: 'What are we to do? This man is performing many signs. If we let him go on like this, everybody will believe in him, and the Romans will come and take away both our place and our nation.'

The Sanhedrin, the supreme court of the Jewish nation, comprised seventy-one members, including the high priest, who presided over it by virtue of his office. The chief priests (the high priest, the captain of the temple and the members of the leading priestly families), together with the party of the Sadducees, to which most of them belonged, formed a majority of the court; the Pharisees constituted an influential minority.

It is plain that the members of the court were desperately afraid that Jesus' presence and activity in and around Jerusalem would attract a large following and, whether with or without his approval, spark off a popular rising. This would inevitably bring down the heavy hand of Rome and might lead to the abolition of the internal autonomy and temple-constitution of Judaea. 'Our place' which, they feared, would be taken away was the temple ('this holy place' of Acts 6:13 f.; 21:28). By the time this Gospel was written, the catastrophe which they dreaded had taken place, but not because of the presence and activity of Jesus.

11:49, 50 **But one of them, Caiaphas, who was high priest that year, said to them, 'You know nothing at all; you do not consider that it is to your advantage that one man should die for the people, rather than that the whole nation should perish.'**

Caiaphas, whose personal name was Joseph, had been high priest since AD 18, when he was appointed to that office by the Roman prefect Valerius Gratus.[13] He was son-in-law to Annas (cf. John 18:13), who had been high priest AD 6–15 and for many years thereafter retained considerable authority as the power behind the throne. Matthew is the only other Evangelist who names Caiaphas as the high priest in the passion narrative (Matt. 26:57); Luke mentions him twice in other contexts (Luke 3:2; Acts 4:6). It has been inferred from the phrase 'high priest that year' (cf. verse 51; 18:13) that the Evangelist, being imperfectly informed about the Jewish high-priesthood, imagined that, like some other high offices in the Graeco-Roman world, it was an annual appointment.[14] What the Evangelist means, however (as is indicated by his repetition of the words), is that in that momentous year Caiaphas was high priest. (His high-priesthood, in fact, lasted for the unusually long period of eighteen years.)

Like most members of the chief-priestly group, Caiaphas belonged to the party of the Sadducees. According to Josephus,[15] Sadducees had a reputation for rudeness, even among one another, and evidence of this has been seen in the abruptness with which Caiaphas now broke in on his colleagues' agitated chatter: 'You know nothing at all' (or, more freely, 'you don't know what you are talking about'). You ought to consider, he went on, that it is better that one man should die than that the whole nation should be destroyed. If the safety of the nation could be secured by one man's death, it was a matter of prudential calculation that that one man should die. In such a situation, he would die 'for the people'. (In this sentence the Jewish community is referred to both as the *laos*, the people, and the *ethnos*, the nation.) Justice took second place to prudence: it was a pity that a man should die unjustly, but if the choice lay between the death of one and the destruction of a nation, then the Sanhedrin should be in no doubt which decision to take. The high priest may not have intended to use language which could be interpreted in a sacrificial sense, but his words could very well mean that Jesus was to be 'devoted' to death as a scapegoat, an apotropaic offering, to ward off disaster from the people.

11:51, 52 In saying this he did not speak on his own initiative but, being high priest that year, he prophesied that Jesus was about to die for the nation – and not for the nation only, but also in order to gather into one the dispersed children of God.

Whatever the high priest's intention was, John views his words as overruled to express a nobler purpose than he himself had in mind. He implies that Caiaphas prophesied involuntarily by virtue of his office. In earlier days the high priest of Israel declared the will of God by the operation of the Urim and Thummim; and there is some evidence that even later the occasional gift of prophecy was believed to attach to the office, So John treats his words as a prophecy of the vicarious character of Jesus' death, and adds something not implicit in the high priest's language – that Jesus' death would be endured not only for the Jewish nation but for all mankind (cf. John 6:51, 'for the life of the world'). In particular, Jesus' death would effect the bringing together into a unity, into a united community, of the widely dispersed 'children of God'. The 'children of God' (according to John 1:12) are those who believe in Jesus' name, children of the new birth; John here repeats in different language what Jesus said in his discourse about the good shepherd: that he was to bring his 'other sheep' who did not belong to the Jewish fold and join them (with their fellow-believers of Jewish birth) into 'one flock', under one shepherd (John 10:16). Once again, the Gentile mission is foreshadowed (see also John 12:32).

11:53 So, from that day, they decided to put him to death.

Jesus' death was resolved upon at that meeting of the supreme court; it remained only to give effect to the resolution as promptly as was compatible with discretion.

4. JESUS' WILDERNESS RETREAT (11:54)

11:54 **So Jesus no longer walked openly among the Jews; instead, he went away from there into the territory near the wilderness, to a city called Ephraim, and he stayed there with the disciples.**

The Sanhedrin's resolution was not unknown to Jesus. He left the vicinity of Jerusalem and took his disciples to an out-of-the-way spot. Ephraim is mentioned by Josephus as a small town (*polichnion*) near Bethel;[16] it is probably the place called 'Ephron' in 2 Chron. 13:19. It is commonly identified with the modern et-Tayibeh, about 4 miles N.E. of Bethel.

5. LAST DAYS IN JERUSALEM (11:55–12:50)

(a) The pilgrims go up to the Passover (11:55–57)

11:55 **The Jews' Passover was near and many had gone up from the country to Jerusalem before the Passover, to purify themselves.**

This is the third Passover mentioned in John's Gospel. The first (2:13 ff.) was early in Jesus' ministry, before the arrest of John the Baptist (cf. 3:24). It was Jesus' first visit to Jerusalem after his baptism, and during it he performed certain 'signs' which brought forth a limited measure of faith on the part of many and encouraged Nicodemus to pay his famous visit to him by night. The second Passover recorded by John (6:4) fell in the course of Jesus' Galilaean ministry; he did not go up to Jerusalem on this occasion, but his discourse on the bread of life reproduced in this context (6:26 ff.) is based on Old Testament themes which were prominent in the synagogue service at this time of year. Now comes the third Passover; its approach found Jesus no longer in Galilee, but back in Judaea, where he had been since the Feast of Tabernacles of the previous autumn. During these six months he had visited Jerusalem for the festivals – Tabernacles in October (7:1 ff.) and Dedication in December (10:22ff.). Otherwise he stayed in more remote parts – first in the Jordan valley (10:40), from which he went to Bethany to raise Lazarus from the dead, and now at Ephraim.

If the first of the three Passovers fell in AD 28, 'forty-six years' after Herod began the rebuilding of the Jerusalem temple (2:20), this third Passover would be that of AD 30. John's repeated designation of the Passover as 'the Jews' Passover' – a form of words which he uses for other festivals too – suggests that he envisaged Gentiles as making up a substantial proportion of his reading public.

The necessity of ceremonial purification (e.g. after contact with a corpse) before keeping the Passover is laid down in Num. 9:6ff. Josephus confirms that pilgrims came up about a week before Passover[17] and indicates that they spent the days in Jerusalem before the feast undergoing the appropriate purificatory rites.[18]

11:56 So they were looking out for Jesus and saying to one another as they stood in the temple, 'What do you think? He will not come to the festival, will he?'

As earlier, at the Tabernacles festival in the autumn (7:11), so now the people wondered if Jesus would come to Jerusalem. The danger was greater this time; they knew that the authorities had decided on his arrest.

11:57 Now the chief priests and the Pharisees had issued orders that any one who knew where Jesus was should inform them, so that they might arrest him.

The publication of these orders was sufficient to let the residents in Jerusalem know the intentions of the Sanhedrin – 'the chief priests and the Pharisees'.[19] But the rulers' further intention, to procure his death when once they had him in their power, was probably not a matter of general knowledge.

NOTES

1. Also Simon (cf. Mark 14:3). See C. S. Clermont-Ganneau, 'Sarcophagi', *PEQ* 6 (1874), pp. 7–10; C. H. Kraeling, 'Christian Burial Urns', *Biblical Archaeologist* 9 (1946), p. 18. The bearing of these inscriptions on the Gospel narrative is simply that these were very common names at that period.
2. The verb here is *koimaomai* (in the perfect tense); in Mark 5:39 it is *katheudō* (in the present). Both verbs can be used figuratively of death.
3. The question naturally arises: whose twin was he? To this no answer is given; see, however, comment and note on John 14:22, 'Judas not Iscariot' (p. 307, n. 13).
4. See comment on John 1:42 (p. 58).
5. Cf. *Leviticus Rabba* (rabbinical commentary) 18.1 (on Lev. 15:1), where the soul is said to hover over the body for three days after death but to take its departure on the fourth day, when decomposition becomes evident.
6. A striking study of John's characterization of two sisters (as distinct from Luke's) is given by T. E. Pollard, 'The Raising of Lazarus (John xi)', *Studia Evangelica* 6 = *Texte und Untersuchungen* 102 (Berlin, 1973), pp. 434–443.
7. The words 'and the life' are absent from Papyrus 45, from the Sinaitic Syriac and from Cyprian's quotation of the text in his treatise *On Mortality* (21).

8. C. H. Dodd, *The Interpretation of the Fourth Gospel*, p. 365.

9. In an earlier phase of transmission 'it may perhaps have expressed the energy required for performing the miracle' (B. Lindars, *Behind the Fourth Gospel*, p. 59, with a reference to C. Bonner, 'Traces of Thaumaturgic Technique in the Miracles', *HTR* 20 [1927], pp. 171–180).

10. See J. Wilkinson, *Jerusalem as Jesus knew it*, p. 110, for a drawing of the original layout of the tomb.

11. R. E. Brown, *The Gospel according to John*, p. 436.

12. A. Tennyson, *In Memoriam*, canto 31.

13. Josephus, *Antiquities* 18.35, 95.

14. Cf. R. Bultmann, *The Gospel of John* (Oxford, 1971), p. 410.

15. Josephus, *Jewish War* 2.166.

16. Josephus, *Jewish War* 4.551.

17. *Jewish War*, 6.290.

18. *Jewish War* 1.229.

19. Cf. John 7:32, with comment (p. 179).

(b) *Supper and anointing at Bethany* (12:1–11)

12:1 Six days before the Passover, then, Jesus came to Bethany, where Lazarus was – Lazarus, whom Jesus had raised from the dead.

On the Sunday before Passover Jesus and his disciples left their temporary abode near the wilderness of Judaea and came to Bethany, on the slopes of Mount Olivet, rather less than two miles along the Jericho road from Jerusalem. It was here that, a few weeks before, he had called Lazarus from the tomb – a 'sign' so striking that it greatly increased his following in the Jerusalem district and precipitated the authorities' decision to adopt drastic measures to get rid of him. In Bethany, and especially in the home of Lazarus and his sisters, he had for long been a welcome and honoured guest; now, naturally, he was more welcome and honoured than ever.

12:2 So they prepared a supper for him there, and Martha was waiting at table, but Lazarus was one of those who were reclining with him.

The meal may well have been intended in part to celebrate the recent recovery of Lazarus from death, so Lazarus was treated as one of the guests of honour, alongside the Lord to whom he owed his new life. The depiction of Lazarus' two sisters – Martha serving and Mary worshipping – is once again remarkably consistent with Luke's portrayal of the two in the one paragraph where he mentions them (Luke 10:38–42).

12:3 Mary then took a pound of spikenard, very expensive ointment, and anointed Jesus' feet with it and wiped his feet with her hair. The house was filled with the fragrance of the ointment.

The 'pound' (Gk. *litra*) was slightly less than 12 oz. avoirdupois ('half a litre' in GNB) – a lavish expenditure of perfume for such a purpose, the more so in view of the costliness of the perfume. John calls it 'pistic nard' – probably a technical expression (found also in Mark 14:3). What 'pistic' (Gk. *pistikos*) means in this context is uncertain – the meaning 'faithful', which the adjective has in later

Greek, is hardly appropriate here, and 'potable', another suggested meaning, is even less appropriate. Nard, an oriental perfume, is mentioned in the Song of Songs (1:12; 4:13 f.), and the adjective 'pistic' may be a loanword from the east; we might think, for example, of the Indian *piçita*, the plant known to botanists as *Nardostachys jatamansi*. 'The house was filled with the fragrance of the ointment' may well be an eyewitness's reminiscence. Mary's action seemed doubly extravagant. The outpouring of all this expensive perfume was extravagant enough, but for a woman to let down her hair and wipe a man's feet with it would have been at least as extraordinary in the eyes of that company as it would be for us on a comparable occasion, and probably more so.[1] The shock of what they had seen must have caused a brief embarrassed silence, which was broken by one voice giving expression to the sentiments of many.

12:4, 5 Judas Iscariot, one of his disciples (the one who was about to betray him), says, 'Why was this ointment not sold for 300 denarii and given to the poor?'

Among the disciples who were present at the supper was Judas Iscariot, now mentioned for the second time in this Gospel (cf. 6:71).[2] After Judas's betrayal of Jesus, this action of his stood out so clearly in the mind of his former companions that they could not remember anything he had said or done in the earlier days of their discipleship without at the same time remembering that it was he who in due course played the traitor; all his previous words and actions are viewed in the light of that. So, wherever he is mentioned in the earlier narrative of the Gospels, he is always distinguished at the betrayer.

On this occasion he voiced what were probably the feelings of many as they saw with stupefaction what Mary was doing. 'Might not this have been sold for much and given to the poor?' is a sentiment not infrequently voiced by people who imagine that they are quoting Holy Writ, whereas in fact they are echoing a criticism which was rebuked by our Lord. Devotion cannot be measured in terms of pounds and pence, although some people think it can. And yet it is easy to sympathize with Judas's point of view. To judge by the Matthaean parable of the labourers in the vineyard, in which casual labourers are hired at a *denarius* a day, 300 *denarii* would have kept a working man and his family at subsistence level for a year (no wage would be earned, of course, on sabbaths and holy days).[3] Yet all this wealth had been wasted, it appeared, in one impulsive gesture!

12:6 **But he said this not because he was concerned about the poor but because he was a thief; it was he who had the money-box and he used to pilfer what was put into it.**

So, we are told, it was a mercenary spirit rather than an altruistic solicitude for the poor that underlay Judas's words. This is the only place in the New Testament where something is said to Judas's discredit apart from the record of his ultimate treachery. The 'money-box' (Gk. *glōssokomon*) was the receptacle for gifts made to Jesus and the disciples by well-disposed people like the women of Luke 8: 2, 3 who 'provided for them out of their means'. The Greek word was originally used for the case in which the mouth-piece or reed of a flute was kept, and then for a container for anything. The verb *bastazō* is used primarily of taking up or carrying anything (e.g. stones in John 10:31, the cross in 19:17, the Lord's body in 20:15), but like the English verb 'lift' it can have a more sinister meaning where the context so indicates. Here Judas is said not only to have carried the money-box but to have appropriated its contents. Unlike Mark, John does not directly associate Judas's treachery with his reaction to the lavish 'waste' of ointment and Jesus' acceptance of it, but what he says of Judas in this context prepares the reader in some degree for the sequel.

12:7, 8 **Then Jesus said, 'Leave her alone; let her keep it for the day of my burial. You have the poor with you all the time; you do not have me all the time.'**

Jesus' reply suggests that the outpouring of the ointment should be regarded as an anticipation of what might have been reserved for his burial. Unusual expense at a funeral was not regarded as unseemly; why should anyone object if the ointment which would otherwise have been used to anoint his dead body in due course was poured over him while he was still alive and able to appreciate the love which prompted the action? The construction here is not so clear as in Mark 14:8, where the same idea is expressed, but the general sense is plain: 'Let her keep the credit of having performed the last rites for me here and now, against the day of my burial.'[4] Concern for the poor was good and praiseworthy, but the poor would still be there to receive their charity (cf. Deut. 15:11) long after he had been taken away from them.[5]

12:9 **A multitude of the Jews, many in number, got to know that he was there, and they came not only because of Jesus but also to see Lazarus, whom he had raised from the dead.**

The crowd of Jews probably came out from Jerusalem, less than two miles away. Jesus had not remained in Bethany when he came from the Jordan valley to raise Lazarus, but withdrew immediately to the wilderness. Apart from the mourners, few people had seen him on that occasion. But the news of the raising of Lazarus spread quickly and aroused great excitement, so next time he came to Bethany a great crowd came to see him, and to seize the opportunity of seeing Lazarus too. Lazarus was perhaps shielded by his sisters from vulgar curiosity after he was restored to them, but this supper would have been something of a public occasion.

12:10, 11 But the chief priests planned to kill Lazarus also, because on his account many of the Jews were going and believing in Jesus.

The chief priests, led by Caiaphas, had already made plans to procure Jesus' death, 'to prevent the destruction of the whole nation' (11:50–53). Now it looked as if it might be expedient to have Lazarus put to death as well, because he was a living witness to the power of Jesus; so long as he was around, people would remember the 'sign' that had been performed for him, and acknowledge Jesus as the resurrection and the life. The expression 'were going and believing in Jesus' may be a Semitism, meaning 'were increasingly believing in Jesus'.

(c) Entry into Jerusalem (12:12–19)

12:12, 13 Next day the crowd, a large one, that had come for the festival, hearing that Jesus was coming to Jerusalem, took their palm branches and went out to meet him. They kept on shouting:
'Hosanna!
Blessed in the Lord's name be he who comes,
Even the King of Israel.'

This crowd consisted of pilgrims who, as we have been told in 11:55, had come up for the passover in advance, to purify themselves so as to be fit to celebrate it. Some of them were Galilaeans, who were excited at the arrival of the Galilaean prophet; others welcomed the opportunity, which they had not previously had, to give a fitting salutation to him who had so recently raised Lazarus from the dead.

The palm branches which they carried have given their name to the anniversary of this event in the Christian calendar: Palm Sunday (though the day does not appear to have been a Sunday by John's chronology). But the palm branches themselves raise one or two questions.[6] There was no difficulty in procuring them; date-palms grew (and still grow) in and around Jerusalem, even if dates do not ripen on them as they do down in Jericho. But what did they signify? Palm branches played no prescribed part at Passover; it was at Tabernacles that the people were commanded to rejoice before the LORD seven days with 'branches of palm trees' (Lev. 23:40). It has been suggested on this account that the triumphal entry has perhaps been transferred from an original Tabernacles setting to its present Passover setting.[7] But there is no need to adopt such a hypothesis. From the time of the Maccabees palms or palm-branches had been used as a national symbol. Palm-branches figured in the procession which celebrated the rededication of the temple in 164 BC (2 Macc. 10:7) and again when the winning of full political independence was celebrated under Simon in 141 BC (1 Macc. 13:51). Later, palms appeared as national symbols on the coins struck by the Judaean insurgents during the first and second revolts against Rome (AD 66–70 and 132–135). So well established was the use of the palm or palm-branch as a symbol for the Jewish nation that the Romans in their turn used it on the coins which they struck to celebrate the crushing of the Jewish revolts.[8] On this occasion, then, the palm-branches may have signified the people's expectation of imminent national liberation, and this is supported by the words with which they greeted our Lord.

The words of greeting are an elaboration of Ps. 118:25 f., from a psalm of thanksgiving to the God of Israel for a victory granted to his people.[9] 'Hosanna' represents Heb. *hôshî'āh-nnâ*, 'give salvation now' or 'give victory now'. 'Blessed be he who comes' (Heb. *bārûkh habbâ*) is the Jewish idiom for welcome: 'Welcome in the Lord's name' is what they say. But the person who is welcomed is hailed here as the King of Israel. In the psalm the welcome and victory congratulations may well have been expressed to a prince of the house of David, but this is not said explicitly. The crowd, however, spelt out plainly what the psalmist meant, and what they meant.[10] They had their own clear ideas of what the King of Israel would do; Jesus, without repudiating the title which they gave him, repudiated the military and political ideas which they associated with it by his following action.

12:14, 15 **Jesus found a donkey and sat on it, as it is written:**
'Fear not, daughter of Zion:
See, your King is coming,
Seated on an ass's colt.'

Jesus' riding into Jerusalem on a donkey was an acted parable, designed to correct the misguided expectations of the pilgrim crowds and to show the city its true way of peace. The Greek noun which John uses for 'donkey' is diminutive in form (*onarion*, diminutive of *onos*, the word rendered 'ass' in the abbreviated quotation from Zech. 9:9); the diminutive form does not necessarily imply the diminutive sense. Matthew and John expressly quote the oracle of Zech. 9:9 as finding its fulfilment in this incident, and Mark and Luke probably had the oracle in their minds, even if they do not quote it. Moreover, it is probable to the point of certainty that our Lord himself had the oracle in mind, and deliberately arranged to fulfil it. Like some other OT passages cited as 'testimonies' in the NT, this one carries its context with it – not only the full text of the oracle which Matthew and John variously abridge,[11]

> Rejoice greatly, O daughter of Zion!
>   Shout aloud, O daughter of Jerusalem!
> Lo, your king comes to you,
>   triumphant and victorious is he,
> humble and riding on an ass,
>   on a colt the foal of an ass,

but the divine promise which follows (Zech. 9:10):

> I will cut off the chariot from Ephraim
>   and the war horse from Jerusalem;
> and the battle bow shall be cut off,
>   and he shall command peace to the nations;
> his dominion shall be from sea to sea,
>   and from the River to the ends of the earth.

These last words, presaging worldwide sovereignty for Zion's king, are borrowed from Ps. 72:8, where they refer to the son of David. His reign establishes peace on earth; it is inaugurated with a disarmament programme. The choice of an ass as the royal mount, both in the oracle and in its historical fulfilment, underlines this king's peaceful policy; had a war-horse been preferred, a militant policy would have been equally clearly indicated, but no one would have thought in that case of quoting Zech. 9:9 f., where the war-horse is 'cut off' from Jerusalem. The establishment of peace and independence as a sequel to successful resistance would have been an attractive prospect to many, and now in Jerusalem, as earlier by the sea of Galilee (John 6:15), Jesus could have commanded a ready following had he been disposed to adopt this course of action. But he offered Jerusalem the policy of quiet and patient submission as the right one to follow, and the city did not recognize the things that made for peace, with disastrous consequences. Whether the pilgrims appreciated the meaning of his action is doubtful; even the disciples' comprehension was slow in dawning. The authorities thought they understood what was involved only too well.

12:16 **His disciples did not recognize this at first, but when Jesus had been glorified, then they remembered that these things had been written with reference to him and that they had done this to him.**

A similar remark to this comes in John 2:22 after the narrative of the temple cleansing and Jesus' following words about the temple which he would raise up in three days: 'So, when he had been raised from the dead, his disciples remembered that he said this, and they believed the scripture and the word that Jesus had spoken'.[12] In both places, the Evangelist's remark is probably to be understood in the light of Jesus' promise in 14:26 that the Spirit, when he came, would bring to their remembrance all that he himself had told them – which means that he would not only bring the Lord's words to their remembrance but enable them to understand them as they had not understood them at the time. Although the reference in our present passage is not to words of Jesus but to his entering Jerusalem in fulfilment of Scripture, here too it was the Spirit who enabled them to remember and understand all this, 'when Jesus had been glorified' – for, as has been said already in 7:39, the Spirit was not available to them so long as 'Jesus was not yet glorified'. His being 'glorified' is not confined to his being raised from the dead; it is one continuous movement of which his crucifixion (his being 'lifted up'), resurrection and ascension are phases.

12:17, 18 **So the crowd which was with him when he called Lazarus out of the tomb and raised him from the dead bore witness (to what he had done). This indeed was the reason the crowd went to meet him, because they had heard that he had performed this sign.**

Two crowds are distinguished: the crowd that had witnessed the raising of Lazarus (John 11:45) and the crowd of pilgrims that had reached Jerusalem earlier and now came out to meet Jesus with palm branches and escort him on the remainder of his way to the city (12:12). The former crowd bore loud testimony to what they had seen and heard, and the others voiced their appreciative response. One who could summon a dead man back to life would certainly be able to deliver the holy city from the yoke of Caesar.

12:19 **So the Pharisees said to one another, 'You see, you cannot do anything about it. See, the world has gone off after him!'**

The Pharisees, not meeting formally as members of the Sanhedrin, but viewing the enthusiastic procession and passing comment on it, had reason for what they said. Had Jesus so wished, he could there and then have led a band of willing freedom fighters against the Roman citadel. How their enthusiasm would have fared in face of Roman armour is another question. But the Pharisees' qualms were groundless: Jesus had no intention of doing what they feared he would do. Most of the Pharisees took the view that the Roman occupation, oppressive as it might be, was God's will and must be endured until he removed it. The Zealots, who in general adopted the same theological principles as the Pharisees, differed from them in this: pagan occupation of Israel's land was an insult to Israel's God, and any recognition given to the occupying power constituted high treason against God (this was a new doctrine, not held under earlier Gentile occupations of the holy land); the occupation, they held, must not be endured but violently resisted. The Sadducean establishment, on the other hand, thought the path of wisdom lay in co-operation with the occupying power.

By 'the world' (*kosmos*) these Pharisees meant 'everyone' (cf. John 7:4), i.e. everyone in Jerusalem – a natural exaggeration. But John sees a deeper and fuller meaning in their words: the *kosmos* for him is the world of humanity which God loved and Jesus came to save (John 3:16, 17). The crowd which acclaims Jesus as King anticipates all mankind which is to be united under his sovereignty.[13]

(d) The Greeks at the festival (12:20–33)

12:20–22 **Now among those who went up to worship at the festival were some Greeks. These men, then, approached Philip, who was from Bethsaida in Galilee, with the request: 'Sir, we wish to see Jesus'. Philip comes and tells Andrew; Andrew and Philip come and tell Jesus.**

These Greeks may have come from any part of the Greek-speaking world, possibly from a Greek city in Palestine itself. As elsewhere in the NT, the word is used of Greek-speaking Gentiles. These were no doubt God-fearing Gentiles, like Cornelius of Caesarea (Acts 10) or that other centurion of Capernaum who loved the Jewish people and built them a synagogue (Luke 7:5); they belonged, that is, to the class of Gentiles who attached themselves to the Jewish way of life and synagogue worship without becoming full proselytes or converts to Judaism. Such people occasionally went up to Jerusalem to worship at the festivals (like the Ethiopian eunuch in Acts 8:27); they were admitted to the outer court of the temple, which accordingly was called 'the court of the Gentiles'. Penetration into the inner courts was forbidden to Gentiles on pain of death, and warning notices were attached to the barrier – 'the middle wall of partition' – separating the inner courts from the outer court so that they might know to keep their distance. Seven years later a very distinguished Gentile came to Jerusalem in company with Herod Antipas 'to sacrifice to God' at the Passover season; this was Vitellius, the Roman governor of Syria. Josephus has occasion to mention this because halfway through the festal week news arrived of the death of the Emperor Tiberius (on 16 March, AD 37).[14] But even Vitellius had to content himself with worshipping in the outer court.

On this occasion the Greeks' curiosity about Jesus may have been stirred simply because everyone was talking about him. But there could have been a more special reason. Between verses 19 and 20 a day or two had elapsed: Jesus was no longer on the road to Jerusalem, but teaching daily in the temple precincts. And in the meantime, according to Mark 11:15-17, he had expelled the traders and moneychangers from the precincts – that is, more precisely, from the outer court – in order that the place might fulfil its divinely ordained purpose of being 'a house of prayer *for all the nations*' (Isa. 56:7).[15] Did these Greeks recognize his action as having been undertaken in the interests of Gentiles like themselves who, when they came up to worship the true God, had to confine themselves to the outer court? If that court was cluttered up with trade and traffic, their privilege was diminished thereby.

However that may be, they approached Philip (who, like Andrew, was Greek by name though not by nationality) and asked if they might be granted an interview with Jesus. They may have approached him because he spoke Greek, or because they came from the region to which he himself belonged.[16] Philip, unsure of what his Master's reaction to this unusual request would be, enlisted the aid of the resourceful Andrew, and both of them approached Jesus.

12:23, 24 **Jesus answered them: 'The hour has come for the Son of Man to be glorified. Indeed and in truth I tell you: unless a grain of wheat falls into the ground and dies, it remains alone; but if it dies, it yields much fruit.'**

Jesus' reply to Andrew and Philip merges into the general observations of verses 25 and 26, followed by the expression of soul-trouble and its sequel in verses 27–31, and is caught up again in verse 32. The essence of his reply is that the time is fast approaching when not only these Greeks but many others will come to enjoy the new life he imparts, but first he must die. Whether or not these Greeks did receive an opportunity to see him on this occasion is not recorded: their request is used by the Evangelist as a peg on which to hang the promise of widespread blessing to accrue from Jesus' death.

In verses 23 and 24, his death is spoken of in two ways: first, as the glorifying of the Son of Man, and then, under the figure of the seed being sown in the earth to produce a plentiful harvest.

As in the Synoptic record, so in this Gospel the designation 'the Son of Man' is used by Jesus in connection both with suffering and with coming in glory. But whereas in the Synoptic record the suffering and the glory are set in contrast, John brings them so closely together that the Son of Man's suffering becomes the first stage in his receiving of glory (cf. verse 16) and can indeed (as here) be spoken of absolutely as his being glorified (cf. 13:31).[17]

On earlier occasions in the Gospel his 'hour' (*hōra*) or 'appointed time' (*kairos*) had not yet come (cf. 2:4; 7:30; 8:20 for the former; 7:6, 8 for the latter); now, with his arrival in Jerusalem for the last Passover, it has come.

Jesus' being glorified is closely bound up with his refusal to seek his own glory (John 8:50, 54); far from seeking this, he is willing to be utterly expended that God's purpose may be fulfilled, to disappear from sight as completely as the grain of wheat when the earth covers it over, to die in order that new life may spring up. Some appreciation of this principle, manifested in the recurring sequence of seed-time and harvest, underlies the fertility cults of the dying and rising god, so familiar in the ancient Near East and elsewhere. But there is more contrast than resemblance between the repeated process of nature, mythologized and enacted year by year in a ritual designed to ensure its perpetuation, and the Son of Man's historical self-dedication, accomplished once for all and eternal in its efficacy.

The saying about the grain of wheat is emphasized by the double 'Amen' with which it is introduced. In an earlier discourse Jesus spoke of himself as the bread of life that came down from heaven to give life to mankind, indicating clearly, if figuratively, that his own life must be sacrificed before new life could be imparted to others (6:33–58); here, varying the figure a little, he speaks of himself as the seed whose sowing must precede the harvest of grain and provision of bread:

The corn that makes the holy bread
By which the soul of man is fed –
The holy bread, the food unpriced,
Thine everlasting mercy, Christ.[18]

12:25, 26 'He who loves his life will lose it, and he who hates his life in this world will keep it for life eternal. If anyone serves me, let him follow me, and where I am, there my servant will also be. If anyone serves me, the Father will honour him.'

The principle stated in verse 24 is of wide application; in particular, if it is true of Jesus, it must be true of his followers. They too must be prepared to renounce present interests for the sake of a future inheritance. This is a Johannine counterpart to the Synoptic saying about the disciple's obligation to take up his cross and follow his Master (cf. Mark 8:34–38). To love one's life here means to give it priority over the interests of God's kingdom; similarly to hate one's life is to give priority over it to the interests of God's kingdom. The kingdom of God and 'eternal life' are in practice interchangeable terms, since eternal life is the life of the age to come, when God's kingdom is established on earth, but in this Gospel especially eternal life is something that can be received and enjoyed here and now through faith-union with Christ. Nevertheless the Jewish idiom of this saying is preserved more faithfully in John 12:25 than in the various Synoptic parallels: it is here that the antithesis between 'this world' and the coming one is most clearly expressed. For the servant to follow the Master means to share the Master's suffering, but it also means to share the Master's glory: the Father, who glorifies the Son (8:54), will honour those who serve the Son and give them a share in his glory (cf. 14:3).

12:27, 28 'Now my soul is troubled, and what shall I say? Father, save me from this hour. But it was on this account that I came to this hour. Father, glorify thy name.' A voice then came from heaven: 'I have indeed glorified it; I will also glorify it again.'

This passage may be regarded as to some extent John's counterpart to the Synoptic narrative of the agony in Gethsemane (cf. also John 18:11). The Johannine Jesus is no docetic actor in a drama, about to play a part which he can contemplate dispassionately because it does not really involve himself. 'The hour has come for the Son of Man to be glorified', it is true, but for the Son of Man this involves arrest, binding, striking on the face, scourging, mocking, crucifixion and death – all to be endured in grim earnest.

Hence his inward disquiet; hence his spontaneous prayer to be saved from 'this hour'. But scarcely has the prayer left his lips than it is retracted. All that must be endured was the very reason for his coming to this hour; he must go through with it. An alternative punctuation puts a question-mark after 'Father, save me from this hour' – as though the meaning were: 'What shall I say? Shall I say, "Father, save me from this hour"? No; I came to this hour for the very purpose of enduring all that lies before me.' But this construction (cf. RSV) imparts to Jesus' words something of studied (not to say histrionic) artifice; the other is more natural. If the prayer to be saved from 'this hour' is retracted, however, it is immediately replaced by another prayer: that in the Son's endurance of all that 'this hour' brings, the Father's name may be glorified. The glorifying (or, in the language of the Lord's Prayer, the 'hallowing') of God's name is achieved in the doing of his will, and never so fully as in the Son's present self-dedication in obedience to the Father.

His prayer was acknowledged by a heavenly voice – the phenomenon which the rabbis knew as the *bath qôl*, the 'daughter (or echo) of the voice' of God.[19] To him it was articulate and intelligible; the others heard the sound, but could not distinguish the sense. God had glorified his name already, the voice declared – presumably in the ministry thus far of the incarnate Word and in the signs which manifested the divine glory to those who had eyes to penetrate beneath the surface. He would glorify his name again – presumably in the glorifying of the Son, in his impending passion.

12:29–33 The crowd, then, that stood and heard said that there had been a thunderclap. Others said, 'An angel has spoken to him'. Jesus answered: 'It was not on my account that this voice came, but on yours. Now is this world's judgment-day; now the ruler of this world is to be cast out. As for me, if I am lifted up from the earth, I will draw all people to myself.' In saying this he indicated in what manner he was going to die.

The bystanders in the temple court did not know what to make of the sound they had heard. The report of their varying attempts to account for it may be recognized as an instance of 'Johannine irony'. And yet Jesus assures them that what they had heard came for their benefit, not for his. He did not need audible confirmation of the Father's purpose, but for them this was intended as a token that the nodal point of all time was upon them, the judgment (*krisis*) of the present world-order. Repeatedly in the course of Jesus' ministry in the temple area there had been a division because of him (cf. 7:43; 10:19); now the decisive division was at hand. In its final reaction to him, the world would pass judgment on itself and reveal its true character: who then would stand for him and who would be against him? But the world's judgment on Jesus, directed by the sinister spirit-ruler (*archōn*) of the present order, would be overruled in a higher court; that spirit-ruler himself would be dislodged, for universal authority and judgment have been vested by the Father in the Son (John 3:35; 5:19–29), and the present order is about to be replaced by the eternal dominion of life and truth (17:2; 18:37 f.). If is from the cross of Jesus that the true light shines brightest: men declare themselves to be sons of light or sons of darkness according as they come to that light or avoid it, and this is the *krisis* (cf. 3:19–21; 12:45 f.). The *archōn* of this world is the adversary of the Son, but finds no accusation to bring against him (cf. 14:30). He is the adversary also of those who believe in the Son, but against his accusations they are to receive the powerful aid of the Paraclete, whose presence will be to them the evidence that 'the ruler of this world has been judged' (16:11). That ruler's dethronement, then, is effected by the death and resurrection of the Son and confirmed by the coming of the Spirit. It is expressed in apocalyptic language in Rev. 12:9, while in the early Christian compilation called the *Odes of Solomon* (to be dated not much later than the Gospel of John) Christ speaks of the Father as 'the one who otherthrew by my hands the seven-headed dragon, and set me over his roots that I might destroy his seed'.[20]

Through this impending victory Jesus would bring blessing to many more than had received blessing at his hands thus far. The 'lifting up' (*hypsōthēnai*) of the Son of Man is primarily his crucifixion; the expression has already been used in this sense in John 3:14 and 8:28. But a verb of double meaning is deliberately chosen; it can signify not only literal elevation (as on a cross) but also exaltation (in rank or honour).[21] It is used in this latter sense in the Septuagint of Isa. 52:13, where 'he (the Servant) shall be exalted' is rendered *hypsōthēsetai* in Greek. (Paul uses the same verb in Phil. 2:9 with the superlative prefix *hyper-* when he says that God has 'highly exalted' Jesus.) The appended note in verse 33 makes it plain that Jesus' death on the cross is meant here, in the first instance (and his hearers evidently understood his words in some such sense, to judge by their response in verse 34). But, as before, his being lifted up on the cross is the first stage in his re-ascent to the glory which he had with the Father before the world's foundation (cf. 17:5, 24). His being glorified is not a reward or recompense for his crucifixion; it inheres in his crucifixion. And when he has thus been lifted up, exalted and glorified, he will (like a spiritual magnet) draw to himself Gentiles as well as Jews, all without distinction. This has been alluded to previously in the 'other sheep'

who are to be brought to join those whom the Shepherd of Israel
has called out from the Jewish fold (John 10:16) and in the 'children
of God who are scattered abroad' whom Jesus by his death will
'gather together into one' (11:52). This, then, is his answer to the
request of the Greeks: in a short time, they may come to him as
freely as (at present) his Jewish disciples do. His death will oblit-
erate all racial and religious barriers. In the language of Luke 12:
50, he was limited until his appointed baptism was undergone; once
that ordeal was past, all limits would disappear.

(e) The Son of Man and the Sons of Light (12:34–36a)

12:34 **The crowd then answered him, 'We have heard from the
law that the Messiah remains for ever. How can you say, "The
Son of Man must be lifted up"? Who is this Son of Man?'**

In the immediate context Jesus has not spoken expressly of the
Son of Man's being 'lifted up' (so far as the Evangelist's wording
goes). In his reply to Andrew and Philip he had spoken of the Son
of Man's being 'glorified' (12:23); in his later words to the crowd
he said, 'If I am lifted up from the earth' (12:32). But the two
modes of expression are practically synonymous; the crowd had
not mistaken his meaning. Earlier in the Gospel he has said, 'The
Son of Man must be lifted up' (to Nicodemus, 3:14), and 'When
you have lifted up the Son of Man, then you will recognize that I
am He' (to his hearers in the temple court at the end of the Feast
of Booths, 8:28). But while the crowd here understood that he
referred to himself by the designation 'Son of Man', and that his
being 'lifted up' referred to his removal from earth in some sense,
they were still puzzled. Evidently by this time they had reached
the conclusion that his self-designation as Son of Man betokened
a messianic claim. This was not an inevitable conclusion; for all his
mention of the Son of Man, the authorities had come to him as
recently as the Feast of Dedication, less than four months previously, urging him to tell them plainly whether he claimed to be
the Messiah or not (John 10:24). But the general public did not
make careful distinctions between this and that figure of eschatological expectation (cf. 6:14 f., where the prophet and king seem
to be identified in the popular mind, by contrast with 7:40 f.,
where they are apparently distinguished).

The 'law' from which they had heard that the Messiah, when he
came, would remain for ever, is here the whole Hebrew Bible
rather than the Pentateuch, the Torah in the stricter sense of the
term (cf. John 10:34, where a passage from Psalm 82 is said to be
'written in your law'). Here we may think of such passages as Isa.
9:7, where the kingdom of the promised Prince of the house of

David is to be established for ever; Ezek. 37:35, where 'David my servant', as God calls him, will be Israel's prince for ever; and Psalm 72:17, where Messiah's name endures for ever. The speakers were right in accepting what they had been taught from the law, as they were right in their inference from Jesus' words; they were wrong in supposing that his words, as they understood them, contradicted the teaching of Scripture, and they were wrong because they failed to grasp that the Son of Man's being 'lifted up' would be the decisive inauguration of Messiah's endless reign. Their use of the designation 'the Son of Man' is no real exception to the rule that in the Gospels this designation is found only on the lips of Jesus: they are self-evidently quoting his words. Their question 'Who is this Son of Man?' is still repeatedly asked (it provides a title for many a lecture or essay and a question for many an examination-paper); the mystery which invested the designation as Jesus used it has not yet been completely dispelled.[22]

12:35, 36a So Jesus said to them, 'For a little time the light is still among you. Walk while you have the light, lest darkness overtake you. He who walks in the darkness does not know where he is going. While you have the light, believe in the light, so that you may become sons of light.'

The light-darkness antithesis, though not confined to the Johannine writings of the New Testament (cf. Rom. 13:12; Eph. 5:8f.; Col. 1:12 f.; 1 Thess. 5:4 ff.), supplies one of their most characteristic figures of thought and speech. In the prologue to the Gospel, the Logos is the light which, coming into the world, provides illumination for all, the light which shines in the midst of darkness and is not overcome by it (John 1:4–9). Later in the Gospel Jesus is 'the light of the world' by following whom men will enjoy 'the light of life' instead of walking in darkness (John 8:12; 9:1 ff.); it is by welcoming or avoiding this light that men show the quality of their lives and deeds (John 3:19–21). Similarly, in the First Epistle, God is said to be light, and those who are truly his children will 'walk in the light' (1 John 1:5 ff.). That is to say, God is the fountain of all holiness and righteousness, goodness and truth, and his children's lives are marked by these qualities.

Here, as his ministry to the 'world' is almost at an end, Jesus warns his hearers to avail themselves of the light while they have the opportunity. In daylight men see clearly and can walk about safely; when darkness overtakes them they stumble and lose their way. Now is their opportunity to believe in him who is the true light; if they do so, they will themselves become 'sons of light' – an instance of the idiomatic Hebraic use of 'son' to denote the ethical qualities of the person or persons thus described. The same expression occurs in 1 Thess. 5:5 (*hyioi phōtos*); in Eph. 5:8 another word is used for 'sons' or 'children' (*tekna phōtos*), but there is no difference in meaning. Those who refuse the light while it is present may find too late that it has withdrawn itself.

(f) Ministry in the world summarized (12:36b–50)

12:36b–38 **When Jesus had spoken thus, he went away and hid from them. But although he had performed so many signs in their presence, they would not believe in him: this brought about the fulfilment of what the prophet Isaiah said:**
'Lord, who believed our message?
And to whom was the Lord's arm revealed?'

Between Jesus' revelation of himself to the world (which began in ch. 2) and his revelation of himself to 'his own people' (which begins in ch. 13) John presents this epilogue, in which he summarizes the main themes of the foregoing ministry (verses 44–50) and reflects on the lack of positive response with which it met. If Jesus now left the temple precincts and hid from the crowd, he did not go far away – no farther, probably, than the slopes of Olivet – but he withdrew from public view in order to devote the short time left before his passion to the inner circle of those who did believe in him. As for the majority, the Evangelist has prepared us for their unbelief in the words of the prologue, where the divine Logos, the true light, 'came to his own place, and his own people gave him no welcome' (John 1:11). From the 'beginning of signs' which he performed in Cana (2:11) to the display of the glory of God in the raising of Lazarus (11:4, 40) he had revealed the Father in a succession of significant acts (not to speak of the discourses which provide an interpretation of the signs); yet he received no general credence. This reluctance to come to the light, shown by the very people who had been prepared over the centuries for the coming of the light, is a problem which demands an explanation. John, like Paul (Rom. 10:16), finds an explanation in OT prophecy. The people's unbelief had been foreseen and foretold. Perhaps we should not press the conjunction *hina* so as to make it yield its full classical sense of purpose ('*in order that* the saying of Isaiah might be fulfilled'); here the meaning may be no more than that their unbelief fulfilled the prophet's saying. The words of Isa. 53:1, from the fourth Servant Song, are quoted in their LXX form (as in Rom. 10:16), in which the vocative 'Lord' is prefaced to the question, and the question is treated as the prophet's astonished appeal to God at the rejection of his message. John (unlike Paul) quotes both the parallel questions: the 'arm of the Lord' is his power exerted, as it had been in Jesus' performance of 'so many signs'. The 'arm of the Lord' had indeed been revealed in those signs, but effectively only to those who had eyes to see.

12:39–41 **This is the reason they were unable to believe, because Isaiah said again:**
'He has blinded their eyes
   and made their heart obtuse,
lest they should see with their eyes
   and understand with their heart,
      and turn back, and I should heal them.'
Isaiah said these things because he saw his glory, and spoke about him.

These words from Isa. 6:10 constitute one of the most primitive Christian 'testimonies' from the OT, adduced at an early date to account for the problem of Jewish unresponsiveness to the gospel. In Mark 4:12 and the two Synoptic parallels the passage is associated with our Lord's choice of the parabolic method in teaching; in Acts 28:26 f. it is quoted by Paul to the leaders of the Jewish colony in Rome, while its thought (and possibly its language) underlies Paul's exposition in Rome. 11:7–25 of the partial and temporary 'hardening' which has befallen Israel. (Paul there uses the same word for 'hardening' or 'making obtuse' – Gk. *pōroō* – as John uses here to render Heb. *hashmēn*, strictly 'make fat', which is rendered more literally in the LXX.

When Isaiah was commissioned to undertake his prophetic ministry, he was warned in advance that the people to whom he was sent would pay no attention to him – that indeed all his words would be counter-productive and make them close their ears the more decisively. This would be the effect of his ministry, but it was not its purpose (its purpose was that they might 'turn and be healed'); it is expressed, however, as though God were actually sending him *in order that* his hearers would not listen to him. This Hebraic fashion of expressing result as though it were purpose has influenced John's wording – both in the introductory formula 'in order that the saying of Isaiah might be fulfilled' in verse 38 and again in the words 'This is the reason they were unable to believe' in verse 39. Not one of them was fated to be incapable of belief; it is made plain below (verse 42) that some did in fact believe. But the OT prediction had to be fulfilled, and fulfilled it was in those who, as a matter of fact, did not believe. From the NT writers' point of view, the unreceptive hearing which Isaiah was promised was not exhausted in the circumstances of his personal ministry: it was experienced by one prophet after another and found its definitive fulfilment in the unreceptive hearing given to him of whom the prophets spoke. As in Isa. 6:10 the prophet is commanded to make his hearers' minds obtuse and to dull their ears and close their eyes, so here, as though the command had been transferred to Jesus for him to fulfil it in *his* ministry, he is said to have done so. For verse 41 suggests that the one who 'has blinded their eyes and made their heart obtuse' is Jesus.[23] It was of him, says John, that Isaiah spoke on this occasion, 'because he saw his glory'. The reference is to Isa. 6:1, where the prophet says 'I saw the Lord'. In the Aramaic Targum to the Prophets (the 'Targum of Jonathan') this is paraphrased 'I saw the glory of the Lord'; and while the Targum as we have it is much later than John's time, many of the interpretations it preserves were traditional, going back for many generations. 'The glory' or 'the glory of God' is a targumic circum-locution for the name of God, but John gives the word its full force and says that the Lord whose 'glory' Isaiah saw was Jesus: Isaiah, like Abraham before him, rejoiced to see the day of Christ (John 8:56), for, like John and his fellow-disciples in the fulness of time, he too was permitted to behold his glory (cf. John 1:14). (It is of some interest that, when Isa. 6:10 is alluded to in Mark 4:12, the wording of the Targum is reflected there too.)[24]

12:42, 43 Nevertheless many even of the rulers believed in him, but because of the Pharisees they did not confess him, in case they should be banned from the synagogue; for they loved the glory of men more than the glory of God.

In various places throughout his Gospel John speaks of believing in Jesus or believing in his name in a sense that falls short of full commitment. An early instance is in John 2:23–25, where the 'signs' which he performed during an earlier Passover visit to Je-rusalem caused many to believe in his name, but he saw that their belief was superficial and not to be depended on; a later instance is in 8:31 ff., where 'the Jews who had believed in him' are told how they may be 'truly' his disciples. Among the 'rulers' who are now said to have 'believed in him' Joseph of Arimathaea and Nicodemus are to be reckoned (cf. 19:38 f.); their secret belief manifested itself in words and deeds of good will, but not in open confession. They are accordingly not included in the inner circle of 'his own people' to whom Jesus communicates himself specially in 13:1 ff. John probably knew of men at the time when his Gospel was being composed, who appreciated the teaching of Christ and wished his cause well, going so far perhaps as to demand for his followers fair treatment in the law-courts or, failing that, to secure them decent burial afterwards. But in his eyes this attitude is not good enough, and he wishes his readers to understand clearly that the belief which brings with it the birthright of the children of God (1:12) is the belief which shows itself in public and irrevocable commitment to Jesus, acknowledged as Messiah and Son of God. The fear of the secret believers mentioned here was not fear of judicial proceedings, which the Sadducean chief priests might have initiated, but fear of being banned from the worship and fellowship of the synagogue, where the influence of the Pharisees was dominant. This excommunication had already been incurred by the man whom Jesus cured of his blindness (9:22, 34).[25] The secret believers among the members of the Sanhedrin showed less outspoken courage than he did. But they were exposed to temptations from which he was immune: he had no reputation to lose, whereas they had come to value the 'glory' or praise which others gave them for their piety and learning, and were reluctant to exchange it for the obloquy which open confession of Jesus would have meant for them. So they aligned themselves with the men rebuked by Jesus in 5:44 as those 'who receive glory from one another and do not seek the glory which comes from the only God', and excluded themselves from the blessing which he held out in 12:26: 'If any one serves me, the Father will honour him.'

12:44, 45 **Jesus said, raising his voice aloud: 'Whoever believes in me believes not in me but in him who sent me; and whoever sees me sees him who sent me.'**

The final paragraph of John 12 (verses 44–50) sums up the main themes of Jesus' ministry to the world. Throughout his ministry, he insists, the initiative has not been his own. He has accomplished the works appointed for him by the Father and delivered the teaching given him by the Father: in deeds and words alike he has revealed the Father. Therefore the response which is made to him is made not so much to him as to the Father who commissioned him. The form of words used here belongs to the Synoptic as well as to the Johannine vocabulary: 'He who receives me receives him who sent me' he had told his disciples earlier (Matt. 10:40; Luke 9:48); 'he who rejects me rejects him who sent me' (Luke 10:16). (The two verbs for sending, *apostellō* and *pempō*, are used interchangeably in this kind of context.) To believe in the Son, then, is to believe in the Father who sent him; to see the Son is to see the Father (cf. 14:9). This emphasis has not been expressed in quite this way earlier in the Gospel, although it will recur with variations in the upper-room discourses; its substance, however, has been repeatedly implied.

12:46 'I have come as light into the world, so that no one who believes in me may remain in the darkness.'

On the *résumé* of the burden of the preceding discourses presented in these verses C. H. Dodd says: 'No new theme is introduced; yet the passage is no mere *cento* of phrases from the earlier chapters. It rings the changes afresh upon the themes of life, light and judgment, re-stating the central purport of what has already been said on these themes, in a series of concise, epigrammatic propositions'.[26] First, then, the theme of light is taken up. We have dealt with this theme above in the exposition of verses 35 and 36, and need not elaborate it afresh. The light which has come into the world is the light for the whole world; while it shines, none need stay where it is dark. To believe in Jesus is to come to the light. It has already been asserted that men pass judgment on themselves by their response to the true light; hence the theme of light is followed here naturally by the theme of judgment.

12:47, 48 'If any one hears my words and does not keep them, it is not I who judge him; for it was not to judge the world but to save the world that I came. Whoever rejects me and refuses to receive my words has a judge appointed for him: the message I have uttered is the judge that will judge him at the last day.'

If Jesus did not come to judge the world, that means that he did not come to sit in judgment on men or to pass sentence on them. 'God did not send the Son into the world to judge the world', we have been told earlier, 'but that the world might be saved through him' (John 3:17). Nevertheless, his ministry in the world was the judgment of the world (cf. verse 31) in the sense of his words in John 9:39: 'For judgment I came into this world, that those who do not see may see, and that those who see may become blind'. (There too the correlation between light and judgment comes to expression; those who expelled from their society Jesus' most recent disciple, the once blind man whose sight had been restored, by their own action demonstrated their blindness and brought on themselves the judgment of expulsion from the society of the Son of Man.) The adverse judgment which men incur here and now through refusing him awaits its eschatological promulgation, and in this sense the Father has conferred on the Son 'authority to execute judgment, because he is Son of Man' (John 5:22, 27). How this judgment is to be executed is now declared. Earlier, Moses was named as the one who would accuse Jesus' opponents before the Father – Moses, 'on whom you set your hope. If you believed Moses, you would believe me, for it was of me that Moses wrote.

But if you do not believe his writings, how will you believe my words?' (John 5:45–47).[27] The 'words' (*rhēmata*) of Jesus are summed up in his 'message' (*logos*), and with this message, the sum and substance of eternal truth, the final word of adjudication would lie.

Again, what is said here is not peculiar to the Fourth Gospel; the Sermon on the Mount ends with the affirmation that those who hear Jesus' words and put them into practice have provided a secure foundation for life, while those who hear them without translating them into action expose themselves to irremediable catastrophe (Matt. 7:24 ff.; Luke 6:47 ff.). 'If any one keeps my word (*logos*)', Jesus has already said in this Gospel, 'he will never see death' (8:51); the corollary is that those who refuse to keep his word will never see life (cf. John 3:36). The word of judgment on the last day, therefore, is not different from the word of life already sounded forth. The message which proclaims life to the believer is the message which proclaims judgment to the disobedient. To bestow life, not to execute judgment, was the purpose of the Son's coming into the world; nevertheless, judgment is the inevitable effect of his coming for those who turn their backs on life.

12:49, 50 'For I have not spoken on my own authority; the Father who sent me has himself given me commandment what to say and what to speak. I know that his commandment is eternal life. What I speak, therefore, I speak as the Father has bidden me.'

The Son's subordination to the Father, which has been elaborated in the discourse of John 5:19–30, is now affirmed summarily. The Son's message is not his own, but the Father's; he is the *logos*, the self-expression, of God. The Son's message conforms to the Father's commandment; as the Father's commandment is the commandment of eternal life, so the Son's message is the message of eternal life. To obey the Father's commandment, to believe the Son's message, is to have eternal life; conversely, to disobey the Father's commandment, to refuse credence to the Son's message, is to forfeit life and enter into judgment. The light of life has as its counterpart the darkness of judgment.

In the literature of the Qumran community, as has been said above, all mankind is apportioned between two dominions – that of the prince of light and that of the angel of darkness – and it is the latter who controls the great majority. But whereas in the Qumran texts this apportionment is largely independent of the choice of the human beings concerned, being fixed by a design formed before their coming into existence, in the Gospel of John the apportionment, while it reflects an eternal design, is based in time on the free and responsible reception given to the Son by those to whom he came with his message of life. If, when he 'came to his own place', he received no welcome from 'his own people', as the prologue says (John 1:11), it was not because they had no opportunity of giving him the welcome which was his due. They had every opportunity and indeed incentive: they searched the Scriptures which bore him witness, but would not come to him for the life which he alone could impart (John 5:39 f.); 'although he had performed so many signs in their presence, they would not believe in him' (12:37).

This paragraph, then, which summarizes the message of Jesus delivered in many discourses in the earlier part of the Gospel, forms an appropriate transition to the following division of the Gospel, in which Jesus turns from the unbelieving 'world' to reveal the Father's love to the inner circle of those who open their hearts to him and his revelation.

NOTES

1. In Mark 14:3 (followed in Matt. 26:6) it is over Jesus' head that the ointment is poured. In the incident recorded in Luke 7:36–50 the penitent woman in an unnamed city anoints his feet with ointment and wipes them with her hair – two details in common with this Johannine narrative. (Luke's narrative, like Mark's, mentions that the ointment was brought in an alabaster container.) The literary, or preliterary, relationship between the different narratives provides material for an interesting study in tradition and redaction. See I. H. Marshall, *The Gospel of Luke* (Exeter, 1978), pp. 304–307 (he finds it 'apparent' that Luke's story 'is originally quite separate' from the story of the anointing at Bethany).

2. If his sobriquet does indeed indicate an ancestral connexion with the Kerioth of Josh. 15:25, then he was probably the only Judaean among the twelve. The attempt by J. N. Sanders to make him another brother of the Bethany family (' "Those whom Jesus loved": St. John xi. 5', *NTS* 1 [1954–55], pp. 29–41) belongs rather to historical fiction than to straight history, as indeed Sanders himself conceded.

3. Cf. NIV: 'It was worth a year's wages.'

4. It is unlikely that G. Bertram is right in suggesting that 'Mary was to keep the broken container to put by the body of Jesus as His burial' (*TDNT* 7, p. 925, n. 41, *s.v. syntribō*). John, unlike Mark (14:3), makes no mention of the container or the breaking of it.

5. Verse 8 is absent from the Western text, and the last clause ('you do not have me all the time') from a few other witnesses; but the great weight of evidence favours the retention of the whole verse.

6. Cf. W. R. Farmer 'The Palm Branches in John 12:13', *JTS*, n.s. 3 (1952), pp. 62–66.

7. Cf. T. W. Manson, 'The Cleansing of the Temple', *BJRL* 33 (1950–51), pp. 271–282.

8. Cf. H. St. J. Hart, 'Judaea and Rome – The Official Commentary', *JTS*, n.s. 3 (1952), pp. 172–198.

9. The processional character of Ps. 118 finds expression in verse 27b: 'Bind the

festal procession with branches, up to the horns of the altar!' For the association of this psalm (the concluding part of the Great Hallel) with Tabernacles see comment on John 7:37 (p. 181); it played an important part at Passover also (cf. Mishnah, tractate *P^esāḥîm* 5.7; 9.3; 10.7).

10. Cf. E. D. Freed, *Old Testament Quotations in the Gospel of John* (Leiden, 1965), pp. 66–81.

11. In John's abridgement of Zech. 9:9 the words 'fear not' are perhaps derived from Isa. 40:9, where they are addressed to the bringer of good tidings to Zion. Cf. F. F. Bruce, *This is That* (Exeter, 1968), pp. 106 f.

12. See p. 77.

13. Cf. C. H. Dodd, *The Interpretation of the Fourth Gospel*, p. 371.

14. Josephus, *Antiquities*, 18.122.

15. Cf. John 2:14–22 for a different (programmatic) locating of this incident (see pp. 73–77).

16. Cf. John 1:44 (pp. 58 f.).

17. So, on the first occurrence of the title 'the Son of Man' in this Gospel, his cross is the ladder of ascent both for himself and (through him) for his followers, while the reference to attendant angels bespeaks the glory with which his passion is invested (1:51). See pp. 62 f.

18. J. Masefield, *The Everlasting Mercy*.

19. In rabbinical thought this form of direct divine communication was introduced after the Spirit of prophecy was withdrawn from Israel.

20. *Ode* 22.5. On the title 'the ruler of this world' see A. F. Segal, 'Ruler of this World: Attitudes about Mediator Figures and the Importance of Sociology for Self-Definition', in *Jewish and Christian Self-Definition*, ed. E. P. Sanders, II (London, 1981), pp. 245–268.

21. M. Black discerns behind Gk. *hypsōthēnai* the Aramaic *'izd^eqēph*, 'to be elevated', which in appropriate contexts can mean, 'to be hanged' (*An Aramaic Approach to the Gospels and Acts* [Oxford, ³1967], p. 141).

22. See pp. 67 with nn. 71, 73, 74, 75. Recent studies of the subject include M. Casey, *Son of Man: The Interpretation and Influence of Daniel 7* (London, 1979); A. J. B. Higgins, *The Son of Man in the Teaching of Jesus* (Cambridge, 1980); B. Lindars, *Jesus Son of Man* (London, 1983).

23. But according to J. Painter ('Eschatological Faith in the Gospel of John', in *Reconciliation and Hope*, ed. R. Banks [Exeter, 1974], p. 46), 'he' who 'has blinded their eyes' is the devil (cf. 2 Cor. 4:4), in distinction from 'me', who would otherwise 'heal them'.

24. The reading 'and be forgiven' in Mark 4:12 follows the Targum and not the Masoretic text or LXX.

25. See pp. 215 f., 219.

26. C. H. Dodd, *The Interpretation of the Fourth Gospel*, p. 380.

27. See pp. 138 f.

CHAPTER 13

C. JESUS REVEALS THE FATHER TO HIS DISCIPLES
(John 13:1–17:26)

I. The Last Supper (13:1–30)

1. THE FOOT WASHING (13:1–17)

13:1 It was before the festival of the Passover. Jesus knew that his hour had come, for him to leave this world and go to the Father. He had set his love on his own people who were in the world, and he loved them to the uttermost.

The upper room ministry of chapters 13–17 is directed to the inner circle of disciples, whereas the ministry of the earlier chapters had been directed to the general populace of Jerusalem or Galilee – 'the world' at large. If our Lord's 'own people' did not give him the reception and recognition which might have been expected, he would, for the few remaining hours, concentrate on the few who did recognize and receive him; it is they who are now called 'his own people' (*hoi idioi*). On them he had set his love in a special degree, and in the ministry of the upper room that love is poured out in action and word, as in the sequel it is poured out in suffering and death. 'No one has greater love than this', he said, 'to lay down one's life for one's friends' (John 15:13), and it is as his friends that he addresses his companions in the upper room. He loved them 'to the uttermost' (*eis telos*) – a phrase which combines the senses 'to the end' and 'absolutely'. God's wider love for 'the world' (3:16) is not displaced by this concentrated love of Jesus for his friends, but it is they who experience it in its fulness:

> The love of Jesus, what it is,
> None but his loved ones know.

In a very short time the visible presence on earth of the Word made flesh would come to an end; he whom the Father had sent into the world would complete his mission and return to the Father. On earlier occasions he had spoken of this 'hour' as something which was still to come; now it is here. The way back to the Father was the way of the cross; by going this way he would both fulfil his Father's purpose in sending him into the world and seal his love to 'his own people who were in the world'.

The opening time-note, 'It was before the festival of the Passover', refers not simply to the words immediately following but to the upper room narrative as a whole and indeed to the record of the crucifixion which follows, as is made plain from John 18:28. To relate John's passion chronology with that of the Synoptists, who quite clearly describe the Last Supper as a Passover meal, would require a separate excursus; suffice it to say here that while John times his passion narrative with reference to the official temple date of the Passover, our Lord and his disciples, following (it may be) another calendar, observed the festival earlier. Our present concern is with the exegesis of what John does say, but this exegesis, from time to time, will bring out points of relevance to this long-standing problem.

13:2 **Supper was now in progress. The devil had already resolved that Judas Iscariot, Simon's son, should betray Jesus.**

'Supper was now in progress' (*deipnou ginomenou*) is a preferable reading to the variant 'Supper having ended' (*deipnou genomenou*), chiefly because the sequel (verses 12:30) makes it plain that supper had not ended.[1] The point is that supper had already begun when Jesus rose from the table and began to wash the disciples' feet. First, however it is mentioned parenthetically that Judas Iscariot's treacherous policy had already been conceived. But conceived by whom? The construction is curious: 'the devil already having put it into the heart that Judas Iscariot, Simon's son, should betray him' – into whose heart? At first blush, we think of Judas's heart; the Western and Byzantine authorities, with some others, make this explicit by putting Judas Iscariot in the genitive. But this is certainly an occasion where the more difficult reading is to be preferred.[2] With the more difficult reading it is natural (C. K. Barrett goes so far as to hold that it is imperative) to take the heart to be the devil's own: 'the devil had already made up his mind that Judas Iscariot, Simon's son, should betray him' (the execution of the devil's plan is then recorded in verse 27a). John does not make Judas's teacherous resolution the immediate sequel to the anointing at Bethany, as Mark does (Mark 14:10), but since he (alone among the Evangelists) makes Judas voice the objection to the anointing (John 12:4), some connexion between that objection and Judas's ensuing course of action may be implied.

13:3–5 **Jesus knew that the Father had given all things into his hands, and that he had come forth from God and was going to God, so he got up from supper, put his outer garments aside, took a towel, and tied it round his waist. Then he put water in**

**the basin and began to wash the disciples' feet and wipe them
with the towel which was tied round him.**

The solemn language of verse 3 prepares us for some act of divine
majesty. Jesus, conscious of the universal sovereignty conferred on
him by his Father, fully aware of his heavenly origin and destiny,
does something which will strike home to the disciples' hearts an
indelible impression of that sovereignty, origin and destiny. So he
dresses himself like a household servant and performs a servant's
task. Any one of the disciples would have gladly performed this
service for him, but to perform it for the other disciples would
have been regarded as an admission of inferiority, not to be tolerated when there was such competition among them for the chief
place in their Master's kingdom. Luke supplies an interesting parallel when he tells how their disputing about this very matter at the
supper table drew forth from Jesus some words about the true
standards of greatness and an appeal to his own example: 'I am
among you as one who serves' (Luke 22:24–27).[3]

John's graphic description illustrates the statement of Phil. 2:6
f., that he who subsisted 'in the form of God' took 'the form of a
servant' – and by doing so manifested the form of God on earth
more perfectly than would otherwise have been possible. The form
of God was not *exchanged for* the form of a servant; it was *revealed
in* the form of a servant. In the washing of their feet the disciples,
though they did not understand it at the time, saw a rare unfolding
of the authority and glory of the incarnate Word, and a rare declaration of the character of the Father himself.

> Nearest the throne of God must be
> The footstool of humility.

Gordon Rupp, describing Thomas Cranmer's degradation from his
sacred office, says:

> And when at last he stood unfrocked, dressed in the clothes of a poor
> bargeman – *in servitutem et ignominiam habitus* – Bonner cried out,
> 'Now are you Lord no more.' Cranmer once said that he 'never set
> more by any title, name or style, that I write than by the paring of an
> apple', but he must have deeply felt this humiliation . . . And we may
> wonder whether even the Quakers ever put a more ironic question mark
> against Ecclesiastical Man than the fact that when all the layers had been
> removed, an Archbishop had been at last revealed 'in the FORM OF A
> SERVANT' – i.e. the only holy garments ever assumed by the Lord and
> Maker of the Church.[4]

Certainly no vestment is so becoming to a Christian minister as the 'apron of humility' (1 Pet. 5:5) – an expression in which one may detect the vivid reminiscence of an unforgettable occasion.[5]

13:6, 7 So he came to Simon Peter. He said to him, 'Lord, are you washing *my* feet?' Jesus answered: 'You do not know now what I am doing, but you will understand afterwards.'

The other disciples were probably as embarrassed as Peter was that their Master should take it upon himself to perform this humble service for them, but he (true to his nature) gave voice to what the others felt. It was bad enough to see his Master washing the feet of the others, but he could not allow him to wash his. But Jesus hinted that there was a deeper significance in what he was doing – a significance that Peter could not grasp there and then, but which would be made plain to him one day. 'Afterwards' means 'after my death and resurrection'; but not until his death and resurrection had taken place could Peter and his companions realize that this was what was meant.

13:8, 9 Peter said to him, 'You shall never wash my feet.' Jesus answered him: 'Unless I wash you, you have no part with me.' Simon Peter said to him, 'Lord, not only my feet; my hands and head too.'

Peter's sense of the unfitness of this situation finds peremptory expression in his refusal to let his Master wash his feet. But as soon as he hears that he will be sadly impoverished unless his Master performs this service for him, he changes his tune: 'In that case, don't wash my feet only; wash my hands and face too.'

Prepositions should not be treated as interchangeable. When the RSV makes Jesus say to Peter, 'you have no part in me' (verse 8), it uses the preposition which denotes life in Christ, but what is meant is fellowship with Christ in his ministry: 'you are not in fellowship with me' is the NEB rendering. In his impetuous reply, Peter shows that he has not grasped the deeper import of his Master's action; the external washing symbolizes something inward, and the washing of the feet alone can symbolize it just as well as the additional washing of the hands and face would do. The deeper import is indicated by Jesus' further reply to Peter (verse 10), but our understanding of that import is made more difficult by a variation in the text, which makes a substantial difference to the sense.

13:10, 11 Jesus said to him, 'He who has bathed has no need

to wash [except for his feet]; he is clean all over. Now you (disciples) are clean, but not all of you.' He knew who was going to betray him; that is why he said, 'Not all of you are clean'.

The phrase in square brackets, 'except for his feet'; is present in some of the most important early manuscripts and in the bulk of the later ones; it is absent from Codex Sinaiticus, from a number of Old Latin texts and the Vulgate, and from the Greek text known to Origen. Codex Bezae, our principal Western witness, has the erratic reading: 'He who has bathed has no need to wash his head, but only his feet'. This reading need not detain us, but as for the other two, the decision whether to retain or to omit the phrase 'except for his feet' tends to be made not so much on the bare textual evidence (which is inconclusive one way or the other) but on one's understanding of the whole passage.

If the phrase be retained (as it almost certainly should be), then it suggests that in addition to a once-for-all cleansing ('bathing') there is need for a repeated washing of the feet. In the literal sense this is quite intelligible: a man might have washed all over at the beginning of the day, but if he walked outside he would need to wash his feet on entering a house. But what would the spiritual significance be? One popular interpretation throughout the centuries has been a sacramental one: the once-for-all bathing is the initiatory washing of baptism (the inward and spiritual grace, of course, as well as the outward and visible sign), which is unrepeatable;[6] the repeated washing of the feet is another sacrament – penance, according to some expositors; the Lord's Supper, according to others. This last suggestion has sometimes been felt to be the more attractive in that John has otherwise no reference to the institution of the Lord's Supper in the upper room. Even so, it is a far-fetched interpretation. Others prefer a non-sacramental understanding of the once-for-all bathing as the initial cancellation of sin and cleansing from guilt which is received in regeneration, while the repeated washing of the feet corresponds to the regular removal of incidental defilement of conscience by confession to God and the guarding of one's way according to his word (cf. Ps. 119:9).

If the words 'except for his feet' are an addition to the original text, the addition must have been made at an early date, as it is present in Papyrus 66 (in the fuller form 'except for his feet only'). What would the text mean without these words? In their absence, no particular significance would attach to the use of two different verbs of washing, *louō* ('bathe') and *niptō*. John likes to vary his use of synonyms, as when he uses *oida* and *ginōskō* for knowing, or *phileō* and *agapaō* for loving. The meaning would then be: when once a man has received the cleansing benefits of Christ's passion, he cannot receive them all over again. The salvation effected by his death is complete, and no supplementation is either necessary or possible. This salvation, these cleansing benefits, the disciples have received – prospectively? – by faith, with the exception of that one of their number whose treachery was to reveal his lack of faith. The foot-washing is thus seen as a parabolic action pointing to the sacrifice of the cross. Whereas in common belief crucifixion and Messiahship were utterly incompatible, Jesus' words to Peter show his crucifixion, symbolized by the servile ministry of foot-washing, to be not only his uniquely saving act but by the same token to be the conclusive proof of his Messiahship.

If this last significance is present, it is present whether 'except for his feet' be retained or omitted. But the case for the retention of these words is apparently clinched by Jesus' insistence (verse 8) that the washing of the feet is indispensable for fellowship with him.

13:12 So, when he had washed their feet and taken his outer garments and reclined at table again, he said to them, 'Do you know what I have done to you?'

According to John, the Lord gave the disciples two explanations of his washing of their feet – one while he was engaged in washing them, and the other after he had taken his place with them at the supper table again. The former, as we have seen, is theological in character: the foot-washing symbolizes Jesus' humbling himself to endure the death of the cross and the cleansing efficacy of his death for the believer. The latter, unfolded in verses 12–17, is practical in character: Jesus has washed their feet in order that from his example they may learn to perform similar service one for another. There is no incongruity between the two explanations; it is quite unnecessary to suppose that they must be due to two different authors.[7] The second explanation is very much in line with Luke's account of the conversation which took place between the Lord and the disciples at the Last Supper (Luke 22:24–27), in which he drew their attention to his own example; but in Mark's counterpart to that conversation, which appears in an earlier context (Mark 10:35–45), Jesus' example of lowly service is brought into the closest association with the sacrifice of the cross: if any one of their number wants to be first, he 'must be slave of all' – because 'the Son of man also came not to be served but to serve, and to give his life as a ransom for many'. The close association of the two themes in this Johannine context, accordingly, is perfectly natural; it is one of a number of 'undesigned coincidences' between the Synoptic tradition and the independent record of the Fourth Gospel.

13:13–15 'You call me "Teacher" and "Lord", and rightly so; that is what I am. Therefore if I, your "Lord" and your "teacher", have washed your feet, you in your turn ought to wash one another's feet. I have given you an example that you should do as I have done to you.'

Answering his own question, Jesus reminds them of the implication of the titles by which they called him. 'Teacher' (Gk. *didaskalos*) is the equivalent of *Rabbi*, the Hebrew and Aramaic term by which Jewish disciples regularly addressed their masters (cf. John's disciples in John 3:26), and which in this Gospel Jesus frequently receives from his disciples and others (cf. John 1:39, 50; 3:2; 4:31; 6:25; 9:2; 11:8). 'Lord' (Gk. *kyrios*) is most probably the equivalent of *mar*, a title which continued to be given to Jesus after his resurrection by Aramaic-speaking believers as in the invocation *Marana tha* ('our Lord, come!'), and was even taken over into a Greek-speaking situation, as the NT (1 Cor. 16:22) and the *Didache* (10.6) bear witness.[8] But if, during his ministry, the title 'Lord' was given to him as a token of esteem, it was later raised to the highest power as 'the name which is above every name' designating him as the One whom God had exalted above the universe (cf. Phil. 2:9–11; Acts 2:36).

Here a personal argument is based on their use of these two titles. If they acknowledged him to be their Teacher and Lord, let them accept his direction and follow his example; his instruction was imparted by precept and practice alike. The reproachful words in the Synoptic record, 'Why do you call me "Lord, Lord", and not do what I tell you?' (Luke 6:46), might have as their counterpart here: 'Why do you call me "Teacher" and "Lord" and not do what I show you?' His washing their feet involved no diminution of his dignity, however much it embarrassed them to let him do it. 'When a man stands on his dignity', said William Temple, 'he usually succeeds in squashing it flat'; our Lord was the last person on earth to stand on his dignity, although his followers are too often prone to stand on theirs. His unself-conscious act of service was an involuntary enhancing of his dignity – a further manifestation of the divine glory which resided in the Word made flesh (cf. John 1:14). The studied formality of the *pedilavium* on Maundy Thursday, when bishops, abbots and sovereigns have traditionally washed the feet of paupers, may commemorate our Lord's action but in the nature of the case it can scarcely fulfil its spirit. It might be asked if the same consideration applies to those Christian communities which have practised the regular washing of one another's feet at their meetings as a sacrament of fellowship.

As with other sacramental acts, this one achieves its end if it promotes the inward and spiritual grace of which it is the outward and visible sign; but that Jesus' words in verses 14 and 15 should be understood as the institution of a recurring sacramental act is (to say the least) doubtful. It has indeed been argued by some expositors[9] on the present passage that there must have been such a sacrament in the circle of churches within which this Gospel appeared, and that the Evangelist recorded this incident in order to provide dominical authority for it; but there is no independent evidence for its existence at that time and place. In the regulations for admission to the register of widows in 1 Tim. 5:10, one qualification is that the candidate should have 'washed the feet of the saints', but this is included along with showing hospitality and relieving the afflicted as one among several aspects of 'doing good in every way'. Perhaps as good a commentary as any on our passage is supplied by the following paragraph from the biography of Robert Cleaver Chapman:

> No task was too lowly for Chapman. Visitors were particularly impressed by his habit of cleaning the boots and shoes of his guests. Indeed, it was on this point he met with most resistance, for those who stayed with him were conscious that despite the simplicity of his house he was a man of good breeding, and when they had heard him minister the Word with gracious authority, they were extremely sensitive about allowing him to perform so menial a task for them. But he was not to be resisted. On one occasion a gentleman, having regard no doubt to his host's gentle birth and high spiritual standing, refused at first to let him take away his boots. 'I insist', was the firm reply. 'In former days it was the practice to wash the saints' feet. Now that this is no longer the custom, I do the nearest thing, and clean their shoes.'[10]

A friend of mine, who as a matter of course cleaned the shoes of an elderly missionary, the late A. F. Eoll, who was a guest in his home, liked to think that he followed in R. C. Chapman's footsteps because Mr. Eoll, as a young man, stayed in Chapman's home and had his shoes cleaned by the patriarch of Barnstaple. It was certainly a worthy instance of apostolic succession. And the 'gracious authority' of Chapman's ministry of the Word was no doubt due in large measure to the fact that, like Chaucer's parson,

> Cristes lore, and his apostles twelve,
> He taughte, and first he folwed it himselve.

13:16 '**Indeed and in truth I tell you; a slave is not greater** than his lord, nor one who is sent greater than the one who sent him.'

This saying, or one quite similar to it, occurs elsewhere in the Gospels in different contexts (cf. Matt. 10:24 f.; Luke 6:40); in each place where it appears its exact force is dictated by its context. Here the point is unmistakable: if their Lord had not thought it beneath his dignity to perform a menial service for them, why should they think it beneath theirs to do the like for one another? The disciples are later reminded of the same saying in John 15:20 where, however, the point is different; if they incur the world's hostility, let them not be surprised; why should they expect more lenient treatment than their Lord received?

This occurrence of the noun translated 'one who is sent' (Gk. *apostolos*) is the only one in this Gospel, and it is used in no official sense. John does not specifically refer to the twelve as 'apostles'.[11] One who is sent derives his authority from the one who sends him (Gk. *apostellō*), to whom therefore he stands in a subordinate relationship. In this Gospel it is not until later that the disciples are 'sent' into the world by Jesus as he himself had been sent into the world by the Father (John 17:18; 20:21; cf. verse 20 below).

13:17 'If you know this, you are blessed if you do it.'

This beatitude relates to one particular aspect of a principle which Jesus repeatedly underlines in his ministry: it is not enough to hear, understand and approve what is right; one must *do* it. 'Not every one who says to me, "Lord, Lord", shall enter the kingdom of heaven, but he who does the will of my Father who is in heaven' (Matt. 7:21). It is the man 'who hears these words of mine and does them' who is compared to the wise man who built his house on a durable foundation (Matt. 7:24; cf. Luke 6:47 f.). Those who do the will of God are counted by the Lord as members of his family (Mark 3:35); those who continue in his Word are truly his disciples (John 8:31). This note in Jesus' ministry is amply attested by all four Evangelists.

2. THE TRAITOR IN THE CAMP (13:18–30)

13:18, 19 'I am not speaking of you all; I know those whom I have chosen. The scripture must be fulfilled: "He who eats my bread has raised his heel against me." I tell you this now before it happens, so that when it happens you may believe that I am He.'

The lesson on humble service merges almost imperceptibly into the warning that there was one among them for whom such a lesson had ceased to have any meaning. The warning took the disciples by surprise. John has more than once prepared his readers for the treachery of Judas (cf. 6:71; 12:4; 13:2); and Jesus has already hinted at it on the present occasion by saying 'Not all of you are clean' (verses 10 f.); but now he begins to be more explicit. It was because he knew the men he had chosen that he could read their hearts and distinguish the man who was cherishing a treacherous inclination from those who, for all their slowness of comprehension, were essentially and irrevocably loyal to him. It is difficult to suppose that Judas is here excluded from the number of the chosen ones, when we recall Jesus' words in John 6:70: 'Have I not chosen all twelve of you? Yet one of you is an adversary.'

That Judas's treachery was foretold in OT prophecy is affirmed by a number of NT writers. In Acts 1:16 ff. Peter expresses his conviction that 'the scripture had to be fulfilled, which the Holy Spirit spoke beforehand by the mouth of David, concerning Judas', and he adduces two passages from the Psalter (Ps. 69:25; 109:8) in confirmation of his words. Matthew (26:15; 27:3–10) sees in the payment and return of the 'thirty pieces of silver' (an exact sum of money specified by him alone among the Evangelists) the interpretation of Zech. 11:12 f.[12] Here the Lord himself states that the scripture had to be fulfilled in Judas's action.[13] This does not mean that Judas in particular was driven to his act of treachery by a decree of fate against which it would have been fruitless to struggle. Even if Jesus' betrayal by one of his intimate companions was foreseen, it was by Judas's personal choice that he, rather than any one else, eventually filled that rôle. The passage here quoted from Ps. 41:9 comes from a context in which a man of God is assailed and mocked by his enemies, but that is endurable as compared with the worst experience of all:

> Even my bosom friend in whom I trusted,
> who ate of my bread, has lifted his heel against me.

The Hebrew expression means literally 'has made his heel great against me' – i.e. 'has given me a great fall' or 'has taken a cruel advantage of me.'[14] The present setting of the supper table makes the citation of this text specially apt. That such citations do not always carry their entire contexts with them by implication is evident when we consider the inappropriateness to the present occasion of the words immediately following in Ps. 41:10 ('raise me up, that I may requite them!').

Jesus tells them this now so that, when they see it happen, they may not only be prepared for it but may also realize more fully who their Teacher is. The Greek words *egō eimi* ('I am'), which are here rendered 'I am what I am' in NEB, are sometimes used in the most everyday sense, 'it is I' (as in John 6:20; 9:9), but in this Gospel especially (cf. John 8:24, 28) they tend to be used with overtones of the Ineffable Name of Ex. 3:14 or even more, of the affirmation 'I am He' of Isa. 41:4, 43:10, 13, etc. (*'ănî hû*, rendered *egō eimi* in the LXX), in such a way as to hint at the speaker's oneness with the Father.[15]

13:20 'Indeed and in truth I tell you, he who receives any one whom I send, receives me; and he who receives me, receives the one who sent me.'

This is another saying common in various forms and contexts to all strands of the gospel story. Its closest parallel is Matt. 10:40 (cf. also Mark 9:37; Luke 10:16). Here it looks forward to the commissioning of the disciples in John 20:21 (cf. the comments on verse 16 above). Particular attention should be paid to the recurrent designation of the Father as 'the one who sent me'. The words bring encouragement not only to the disciples, as they remember whose ambassadors they are, but also to those who give them a welcome (cf. Matt. 25:40 for the general principle). In this verse the verb for sending is *pempō* twice over, but a comparison with parallel passages (cf. John 17:18; 20:21) will show that *pempō* and *apostellō* are for John completely interchangeable, with no distinctive nuances.

13:21, 22 Having said this, Jesus was troubled in spirit and spoke in solemn assurance: 'Indeed and in truth I tell you, one of you is going to betray me.' The disciples looked at one another, unable to think which of them he meant.

From his words thus far the disciples had not gathered the gravity of the situation. That their Master was not completely happy about all of them was evident; that one of their present company was going to turn traitor came as a shock to them when he told them so expressly.[16] Which of them could it be? Had one of them by some inadvertent action or word endangered his safety, or was he speaking of something more serious still – of a deliberate plan to put him into his enemies' hands? They looked round in bewildered silence.

13:23–26 **One of his disciples, the one whom Jesus loved, was reclining in Jesus' bosom. So Simon Peter made a sign to this disciple, as much as to say, 'Ask him whom he means.' That disciple, leaning back against Jesus' breast as he was reclining, asked him, 'Who is it, Lord?' 'It is he', Jesus answered, 'to whom I give the piece of bread when I have dipped it in the dish.' So he took the piece of bread, dipped it and gave it to Judas, son of Simon Iscariot.**

This is our first introduction to the disciple whom this Evangelist singles out as the one 'whom Jesus loved'. He figures on four occasions in the closing chapters of this Gospel: (i) here, in the upper room; (ii) at the cross of Jesus (19:26 f.); (iii) at the empty tomb (20:2 ff.); (iv) by the lake of Tiberias, when the risen Lord appeared to seven of his disciples (21:20 ff.). After the account of that appearance, a note is added making this disciple the authority for the narrative. In the present passage, if in fact none apart from the twelve was present with Jesus in the upper room, a process of elimination points to John the son of Zebedee as the disciple whom Jesus loved. (It may be added that when this disciple is so described, the verb *agapaō* and *phileō* seem to be used indiscriminately – the latter in chapter 20, the former in the other places.) A few expositors, on the strength of John 11:3, 5, 36 (where also *agapaō* and *phileō* are used interchangeably), have identified the beloved disciple with Lazarus, but there is a studied anonymity in the references to the beloved disciple which is inappropriate for Lazarus.

The verbs for 'reclining' (*anakeimai* in verse 23 and *anapiptō* in verse 25, as earlier in verse 12) suggest that, although this meal fell 'before the (official) festival of the passover' (verse 1), it was nevertheless treated by the participants as a passover meal.[17] The normal posture at table was sitting, as rabbinical sources indicate clearly enough; reclining was the posture reserved for special meals, such as parties, wedding feasts and the like – apart from meals taken in the open air, where seats were not available (cf. 6:10 f., where both *anakeimai* and *anapiptō* also occur). The passover supper ranked as a special meal where reclining was *de rigueur*; it was to be enjoyed in a relaxed and unhurried manner, in deliberate contrast to the haste with which their ancestors ate it in Egypt, staff in hand and ready for the road (Ex. 12:11). The participants reclined on the left side, leaving their right arms and hands fee. The beloved disciple therefore appears to have reclined next to Jesus, on the right, so that by leaning back against his bosom[18] he could whisper his question into his ear. Peter evidently was some distance away, so that it was necessary for him to communicate with the beloved disciple by a gesture. So the beloved disciple leaned back to ask

Jesus whom he meant, addressing him by one of the two titles
mentioned in verses 13 and 14. Jesus' answer was given so that the
beloved disciple alone could hear: the narrative goes on to make it
plain that even when Judas slipped out of the room the others did
not realize that he was the traitor. The word translated 'piece of
bread' ('morsel' or 'sop') is Gk. *psōmion*, which is not used elsewhere in the New Testament (it is a diminutive of *psōmos*, which
is used in the LXX of Ruth 2:14, where Boaz invites Ruth to dip her
cereal in his wine). For the host or master of the feast (as Jesus was
on this occasion) to offer one of the guests a particularly appetizing
morsel was a mark of special favour. The 'dish' or bowl (understood
in John's record but mentioned expressly in Mark 14:20) may have
contained the *harōseth*, the sauce of dates, raisins and sour wine
which was a regular feature of the passover table. Jesus, then,
dipping a piece of bread into it, reached it to Judas, who presumably was sitting conveniently near him – possibly on his left. The
sobriquet Iscariot is here given to Judas's father Simon (as in 6:71).

**13:27–30 It was when he had received the piece of bread that
Satan entered into him. So Jesus said to him. 'Get your business
done quickly.' But none of those who were reclining at the table
knew why he said this to him. Some supposed that, since Judas
had the money-box, Jesus meant 'Buy what we need for the
festival' or 'Give something to the poor'. So, when he had taken
the piece of bread, he went out immediately. It was night.**

Jesus' action, in singling Judas out for a mark of special favour,
may have been intended as a final appeal to him to abandon his
treacherous plan and play the part of a true disciple. Up to that
moment, the die had not been irrevocably cast. If Judas wavered
for a second, it was only to steel himself to carry out his fatal
resolution, to become the willing instrument of Satan whereas he
might have been the free follower and messenger of his Master.
Satan could not have entered into him had he not granted him
admission. Had he been willing to say 'No' to the adversary, all of
his Master's intercessory power was available to him there and then
to strengthen him. But when a disciple's will turns traitor, when
the spiritual aid of Christ is refused, that person's condition is
desperate indeed.
Seeing that Judas had made his 'wretched choice', Jesus bade
him complete his business as quickly as possible. None of the
others knew what he meant; not even the beloved disciple, to
whom the secret sign had been given, realized that the 'business'
regarding which Judas was being instructed was the business of
betrayal. The 'festival', for which some supposed that Judas was

sent to make some purchase, would be the *ḥagigah*, the feast of unleavened bread, which began on the night of Passover and lasted for seven days.

Various writers in recent years have tried to read between the lines of these few sentences, but what they have read there has usually been the reflection of a presupposition which they brought to the text. One, for example, presupposing that Judas suspected Jesus of having yielded to the policy of insurgent activism, argues that he thought he was being dismissed from the upper room to give Jesus and the other disciples an opportunity of completing their plans for a revolt without his unsympathetic presence.[19] Another, considering that the celebration of Passover otherwise than on the official date would have been treated by the chief-priestly authorities as a serious offence, suggests that Judas took the savoury morsel he had just received and produced it before them as evidence that this offence had been committed.[20] But such suggestions find no support in the context. Our records throw so little light on Judas's inward motives that the most contrary theories about them have been confidently propounded. But when the Evangelist remarks that 'it was night' when Judas went out, he not only reproduces the vivid reminiscence of an eyewitness but probably implies that the literal darkness into which he disappeared from the upper room was a symbol of the spiritual darkness which enveloped him as he left the others in order to carry out his plan to lead Jesus' enemies to the place where he would be found (cf. John 18:2).

II. The Upper Room Discourses (13:31–16:33)

More than once in the earlier section of this Gospel, the narrative of a 'sign' performed by Jesus is followed by a discourse in which the meaning of the sign is fully brought out. We may think of the discourse on life and judgment which follows the act of healing at the pool of Bethesda in chapter 5, or of the discourse on the heavenly bread which follows the feeding of the multitude in chapter 6. In this section of the Gospel, the upper room discourses (13:31–16:33), caught up and brought to their conclusion in the prayer of consecration (chapter 17), bring out the meaning of the final sign which they *precede* – that final sign being the cross and resurrection viewed as one continuous movement of glorification. Already (12:23) Jesus has spoken of his imminent passion as the hour 'for the Son of Man to be glorified'. Now, talking unreservedly and confidentially to 'his own people' in the intimacy of the upper room, he shows more fully what is involved in this. The passion of Jesus is as truly a revelation of the glory of God as any of the signs recorded earlier; indeed, it is the crowning revelation of his glory. Never has God been so glorified, never has his glory been so fully unfolded, as in the self-offering of Christ.

> But in the grace that rescued man
>   His brightest form of glory shines;
> Here on the cross 'tis fairest drawn
>   In precious blood and crimson lines.

And this is the perspective from which John wishes his readers to view the passion narrative.

The upper room discourses appear to fall into two main divisions: 13:31 to 14:31 and 15:1 to 16:33, the former being a dialogue on Christ's departure from his disciples and subsequent reunion with them, the latter being a dialogue on the loving relationship between Christ and his people. One recent writer finds a close affinity between the former dialogue and the interpretation of the foot-washing given in 13:8–11, and between the latter dialogue and the interpretation of the foot-washing given in 13:12–17.[21] Several expositors have suggested a dislocation of the text in the course of transmission, holding that 15:1–16:33 should follow immediately on 'So, when he had gone out, Jesus said' (13:31a), and that the remainder of chapter 13 and the whole of chapter 14 should follow the end of chapter 16. This rearrangement is familiar to many readers from its adoption in Moffatt's translation. It is urged that it has a number of advantages – e.g. our Lord's remark, 'None of you asks me, "Where are you going?" ' (16:5) no longer follows 13:36, where Peter has asked this very question; and the discourses end appropriately with the words, 'Arise, let us go hence' (14:31). But there is no objective textual evidence for the rearrangement, and we need not suppose that the Evangelist was greatly concerned about those principles of logical sequence which commend themselves to us.

1. DEPARTURE AND REUNION (13:31–14:31)

(a) The Son of Man glorified (13:31, 32)

13:31, 32 So, when Judas had gone out, Jesus said, 'Now the Son of Man has been glorified, and God has been glorified in him. If God has been glorified in him, God will also glorify him in himself, and he will glorify him immediately.'

A few days previously, while teaching in the temple precincts, Jesus had said, 'The hour has come for the Son of Man to be glorified' (John 12:23). We saw then that he was speaking of his impending passion. Now, with the departure of Judas from the

upper room, bent upon his work of betrayal, the passion narrative
is set in train, and with it, from the perspective of this Gospel, the
climax of the glory revealed in the Son of Man.

If Judas's mind has been made up, the Lord's mind has also been
made up. He has accepted the suffering and death which lie ahead
(had he not accepted them, he might even at this late hour have
taken evasive action), and therefore he can refer to the passion and
the glory in the past tense; they are as good as accomplished. 'The
Son of Man has been glorified, and God has been glorified in him'
(*edoxasthē*, aorist passive, in both clauses). God is glorified by the
Son's fulfilling of the Father's will; cf. John 17:4, 'I have glorified
thee on earth by finishing the work thou gavest me to do' (where
edoxasa, aorist active, is used).

The opening if-clause of verse 32 ('If God has been glorified in
him') is omitted by Papyrus 66 and a number of early and reliable
witnesses; even if it is not expressed, it is implied. (Even so, it is
more probable that the clause was omitted inadvertently than that
it was added intentionally.)

The words, 'God will also glorify him in himself', appear to have
much the same meaning as Jesus' petition, 'And now, Father,
glorify me with thyself[22] . . .' in John 17:5. This presupposes that
'in himself' here means 'in God the Father himself'; as the Father
is glorified in the Son, so the Son is to be glorified in the Father.
The alternative is to take 'in himself' as meaning 'in the Son himself', but this is less natural. Westcott sees here an affirmation 'that
God would glorify the Son of Man . . . by taking up His glorified
humanity to fellowship with Himself.' Moreover, he would do so
'immediately'; the course of events had already been set in motion
and would quickly be accomplished.

(b) The new commandment (13:33–35)

**13:33 'Children, I am still with you for a little while. You will
seek me and, as I said to the Jews, "Where I am, you cannot
come," so now I say also to you.'**

This is the only place in the Gospel where the diminutive *teknia*,
'little children' ('my dear children') is used; it is used seven times
in the First Epistle by the author addressing his readers (its one
other NT occurrence is in Gal. 4:19, in a particularly tender appeal
by Paul to his Galatian converts). At the Last Supper especially
Jesus filled the rôle of head of the family, the disciples being the
'children' whose function it was to ask him questions designed to
bring out the significance of the occasion.

Jesus now begins to prepare the disciples for his departure from
them. The short time during which he will still be with them will

be over in a few hours. Then, as he had already said to the Jewish leaders (John 7:33, 34), they will look for him and not be able to find him. (Since the disciples were themselves Jews, it is plain that 'the Jews' here, as so often in this Gospel, are Jews of a special category.)

13:34, 35 'I give you a new commandment, to love another: as I have loved you, so do you love one another. This is how all will recognize that you are disciples of mine, if you have love among one another.'

He is about to leave them, but he will bequeath spiritual treasures to them before he does so; his love, his joy (John 15:11) and his peace (John 14:27). The 'new commandment' (*mandatum novum* in the Vulgate) has given its name to the anniversary of the Last Supper: Maundy Thursday. And, while John does not record the institution of the holy communion, its association with the 'new commandment' is commemorated to this day in the introduction to the Nicene Creed in the Greek liturgy; 'Let us love one another, that with one mind we may confess Father, Son and Holy Spirit, Trinity one in essence and undivided.'

The standard of the love which the disciples are to have one for another is the love which their Lord has lavished on them: 'he had set his love on his own people who were in the world, and he loved them to the uttermost (verse 1). The commandment of love was not entirely new: all the law and the prophets were summed up in the twin commandments 'You shall love the LORD your God . . .' and 'You shall love your neighbour as yourself' (Deut. 6:5; Lev. 19:18; Mark 12:28–33; cf. Gal. 5:14); but by his teaching and still more by his example (cf. verses 14, 15 above) Jesus imparted a new depth of meaning to it. When the commandment is taken up and repeated in 1 John 2:7, 8, it is called 'no new commandment, but an old commandment which you had from the beginning', but at the same time 'a new commandment, as it has come to be truly in him and in you, because the darkness is passing away and the true light is already shining.'

If the Christian fellowship is marked by such love ('love among one another'), then it will be recognized as the fellowship of Christ's followers; it will bear the unmistakable stamp of his love. So Tertullian reports the pagans of his day (a century after this Gospel was published) as saying of Christians, 'See how they love one another!' And it was no merely superficial love that they spoke of, for they went on: 'How ready they are to die for one another!'[23] (cf. John 15:13; 1 John 3:16).

(c) Peter's confidence and the Lord's warning (13:36–38)

13:36–38 Simon Peter said to him, 'Where are you going, Lord?' Jesus answered, 'You cannot now follow me where I am going, but you will follow me later.' 'Lord,' said Peter, 'why can I not follow you now? I will lay down my life for you.' Jesus answered, 'Will you lay down your life for me? Indeed and in truth I tell you: the cock will not crow until you have denied me three times.'

This division of the upper room discourses (13:31b–14:31) contains more dialogue than the second division (15:1–16:33). Four named disciples break into Jesus' words of farewell: Peter (here), Thomas (14:5), Philip (14:8) and Judas (14:22). But it would be far-fetched to compare their interpositions to the questions traditionally asked on Passover Eve by four sons – the wise, the foolish, the simple, and the one who does not know how to ask.[24]

Peter's question and subsequent response are completely in character. Wherever his Master is going he will need company and support; Peter proposes to go with him and supply whatever attendance and help may be necessary. Peter, naturally, has no conception of what lies immediately ahead for his Master. Nor has he reached the state of heart in which he can take up his cross and follow him. One day things will be different. 'You cannot now follow me where I am going', said the Lord, 'but you will follow me later.' A new phase of discipleship would shortly begin, and then, restored and recommissioned, Peter would follow his Master, until he crowned his discipleship by following him in death (cf. John 21:15–19).

Peter would understand these words after Jesus' death and resurrection; for the present their meaning is obscure to him. Wherever his Master is going right now, he insists, he is prepared to follow him. He is utterly devoted to his Master; he will even die for him if necessary. So he said, and said so sincerely. There, in the upper room, it was not too difficult to believe himself prepared to die for his Master; later, in the uncongenial and intimidating environment of the high priest's palace, his resolution would weaken. That very night, before cockcrow, he would deny his Master three times. (Cockcrow was the third of the four Roman night-watches, halfway between midnight and dawn; cf. Mark 13:35.)

NOTES

1. So far as textual evidence goes, the two readings are rather evenly balanced: *deipnou genomenou* is attested over a wide range of authorities, from Papyrus

66 to the majority of mediaeval manuscripts. But the context is decisive in support of *deipnou ginomenou*.

2. Those authorities, including the Bezan and Koridethi codices and the majority of Byzantine witnesses, which read *Iouda* (genitive) instead of *Ioudas* (nominative), avoid what many commentators and translators have felt to be a difficulty and give the sense 'the devil having already put it into the heart of Judas'.

3. Cf. J. A. T. Robinson, 'The Significance of the Foot-Washing', in *Neotestamentica et Patristica*, ed. W. C. van Unnik (Leiden, 1962), pp. 144–147, for the view that this incident is 'the Johannine equivalent of the incident of Mark 10:32–45'. As Jesus then told James and John that they would drink his cup and share his baptism, so here his words to Peter in verse 8 might express 'a bid for . . . solidarity with him as he goes to his death'.

4. E. G. Rupp, *Six Makers of English Religion* (London, 1964), p. 49.

5. This is not the only point of contact between 1 Peter 5:1–5 and the Fourth Gospel (cf., e.g., 1 Pet. 5:2, 'shepherd the flock of God', with John 21:15–17).

6. That the foot-washing itself should represent baptism, as some highly reputable theologians have held, seems to me to be impossible.

7. As is argued by G. Richter, *Die Fusswaschung im Johannesevangelium* (Regensburg, 1967), pp. 314–320.

8. See comment on John 20:19, 20 (p. 391).

9. They are listed by G. Richter, *Die Fusswaschung im Johannesevangelium*, pp. 269 f.

10. F. Holmes, *Brother Indeed* (London, 1956), p. 39.

11. Only in John 6:67, 70 and 20:24 does he even refer to them as 'the twelve'.

12. This is discussed more fully in F. F. Bruce, *This is That* (Exeter, 1968), pp. 108–110.

13. See also John 17:12 (p. 332).

14. Or 'has walked out on me' (A. R. Millard).

15. See p. 206, with nn. 5, 6.

16. Cf. M. Wilcox, 'The Composition of John 13:21–30', in *Neotestamentica et Semitica*, ed. E. E. Ellis and M. Wilcox (Edinburgh, 1969), pp. 143–156.

17. See J. Jeremias. *The Eucharistic Words of Jesus* (Oxford, 1955), pp. 1–60, for a thorough discussion of the question 'Was the Last Supper a Passover Meal?'

18. The two words for 'bosom' (*kolpos* in verse 23 and *stēthos* in verse 25) illustrate John's fondness for the use of interchangeable synonyms.

19. J. Pickl, *The Messias* (St. Louis, 1946), pp. 114 f.; cf. D. L. Sayers, *The Man Born to be King* (London, 1943), pp. 30 f., 228–231, 239 f., 247–249.

20. M. Black, *The Scrolls and Christian Origins* (London, 1961), p. 201.

21. G. Richter, *Die Fusswaschung im Johannesevangelium*, p. 312.

22. B. F. Westcott makes a distinction between the two prepositions: 'in himself' marks unity of being, whereas 'with thyself' marks simply unity of position.

23. Tertullian, *Apology*, 39.7.

24. *Service for the First Nights of Passover*, ed. A. P. Mendes (London, 1878), p. 9.

CHAPTER 14

(d) The Father's house and the way there (14:1-7)

14:1 'Do not go on being troubled at heart: believe in God, believe in me also.'

It was not surprising that their hearts should be troubled. A short time before, as they reclined at table, Jesus himself had been 'troubled in spirit' as he spoke of the presence of a traitor in their midst (John 13:21). That was enough to fill them with unease, and there was also the distress which arose from his words about going away where they could not follow him (13:33, 36). Now he bids them be troubled no more: 'set your troubled hearts at rest' (NEB). Let them maintain their faith in God; let them maintain their faith in Jesus also.[1] They had never known him to let them down; he would not do so now, whatever appearances might suggest.

14:2-4 'In my Father's house there are many rooms; if there were not, would I have told you that I am going to get a place ready for you? And if I go and get a place ready for you, I am coming back again and will take you to myself, so that you also may be in the place where I am. And you know the way where I am going.'

The noun *monē* (allied to *menō*, 'stay', 'remain') occurs twice in the NT – here and in verse 23. It means 'a place to stay', and when it is said that there are many such places in a house, 'rooms' is the most natural rendering.

The Father's house has been mentioned by Jesus already in another sense: in John 2:16 'my Father's house' (*oikos*) is the Jerusalem temple. Here, however, 'my Father's house' (*oikia*) is plainly not on earth: it is the heavenly home to which Jesus is going and in which his people are also promised a place. Earlier during that week Jesus had said, 'where I am, there my servant will also be' (John 12:26); now he adds to that promise by saying that he will take his followers there personally. They had been dismayed when he spoke of going away; now they are assured that his going away is for their advantage. He is going to get a place ready for them and, having done that, he will come back and take them there.

John does not touch on the cosmic dimensions of the Lord's return; it is introduced here as the consummation of the personal

fellowship between him and his disciples. In the Pauline writings
we may compare the personal note of 1 Thess. 4:13–18, where
believers are comforted with the assurance 'so we shall always be
with the Lord',[2] over against the 'world-historical' setting in which
the great event is placed in 2 Thess. 2:3–8. It would, indeed, be
interesting to explore the relation between the 'word of the Lord'
reported by Paul in 1 Thess. 4:15–17 and the word of the Lord
here recorded by John.

Moreover, in these upper-room discourses quite similar language
is used in connexion with (a) the coming of the Paraclete (verse 18
below) and (b) Jesus' appearance to his disciples after his rising
from the dead (verse 19 below; 16:22). The distinction between
Jesus' predictions of his resurrection and his predictions of his
coming again, which is quite clear in the Synoptic Gospels, 'is a
vanishing distinction in John'.[3]

Jesus' words in verse 4, 'you know the way (to the place) where
I am going', are amplified in many witnesses to 'you know where
I am going, and you know the way' (cf. AV). The witnesses attesting
this fuller reading (which may represent an attempt to pave the way
more precisely for Thomas's reply in verse 5) include the majority
of later manuscripts, but they also include the first hand in Papyrus
66 (a second hand in that papyrus has corrected it to the shorter
reading).

**14:5–7 Thomas said to him, 'Lord, we do not know where you
are going; how can we know the way?' Jesus said to him, 'I am
the way, the truth and the life; no one comes to the Father
except through me. If you have come to know me, you will
know my Father also. From now on you know him; indeed, you
have seen him.'**

Thomas's bewildered question, like many questions in the Fourth
Gospel, provides Jesus with the opportunity of expanding and
elucidating what he has just said. Jesus is going to the Father, and
his disciples are to follow him; for them he is himself the way to
the Father.[4] He is, in fact, the only way by which men and women
may come to the Father; there is no other way. If this seems
offensively exclusive, let it be borne in mind that the one who
makes this claim is the incarnate Word, the revealer of the Father.
If God has no avenue of communication with mankind apart from
his Word (incarnate or otherwise), mankind has no avenue of
approach to God apart from that same Word, who became flesh
and dwelt among us in order to supply such an avenue of approach.
Jesus' claim, understood in the light of the prologue to the Gospel,

is inclusive, not exclusive. All truth is God's truth, as all life is God's life; but God's truth and God's life are incarnate in Jesus.

It has been suggested that, in the Semitic language which Jesus spoke, the nouns 'truth' and 'life' were governed by 'the way', as though he said, 'I am the way of truth and life' – 'I am the true and living way.' This is no doubt an attractive suggestion (cf. the mention in Heb. 10:20 of 'the new and living way which he opened for us . . . through his flesh'); but that is not how our Evangelist understood the words. For him the three nouns are co-ordinate, and are best understood by us as they were by him: 'I am the way and the truth and the life.' Jesus is not only the way to God; he is the truth of God – how could he be otherwise, since he is the embodiment of God's self-revelation? – and he is the life of God, 'the true God and eternal life' (1 John 5:20), manifested on earth to give his flesh 'for the life of the world' (John 6:51).

No further comment on Jesus' claim need be made than that of Thomas à Kempis:

> Follow thou me. I am the way and the truth and the life. Without the way there is no going; without the truth there is no knowing; without the life there is no living. I am the way which thou must follow; the truth which thou must believe; the life for which thou must hope. I am the inviolable way; the infallible truth; the never-ending life. I am the straightest way; the sovereign truth; life true, life blessed, life uncreated. If thou remain in my way thou shalt know the truth, and the truth shall make thee free, and thou shalt lay hold on eternal life.[5]

To come to God by this way is to know him. The disciples have already begun to know the Father because they have come to know the Son;[6] in fact (although they do not realize it yet) in the Son they have seen the Father.

(e) Seeing the Father in the Son (14:8–11)

14:8–11 Philip said to him, 'Lord, show us the Father, and we are satisfied.' Jesus said to him, 'Have I been with you all[7] for such a long time and you, Philip, have not come to know me? Whoever has seen me has seen the Father. How can you say, "Show us the Father"? Do you not believe that I am in the Father and the Father in me? The words which I speak to you all I do not speak on my own initiative; it is the Father who dwells within me who does his works. Believe me that I am in the Father and the Father in me; otherwise, believe because of the works themselves.'

Philip's request betrays ignorance of the truth that the Son came into the world to reveal the Father, and has been doing so throughout his ministry. To know the Son is to know the Father; to see the Son is to see in him the otherwise invisible God. As the prologue to the Gospel has put it, 'No one has ever seen God; the only-begotten, (himself) God, who has his being in the Father's bosom, is the one who has declared him' (John 1:18).

Jesus now emphasizes afresh the mutual indwelling of the Father and the Son (cf. John 10:38); he claims that the words he speaks are those given him by the Father to speak (cf. John 12:49) and that the works he does are those given him by the Father to do (cf. John 5:19 f.). The oscillation between the words and the works in verse 10 is anticipated in John 8:28: 'I do nothing on my own initiative, but as the Father has taught me, so I speak.' The appeal to the testimony of the works themselves has been made in John 5:36; 10:37 f. But whereas formerly these things were said to the incredulous 'world', now they are repeated to disciples who, however uncomprehending they may be, are most willing to believe.

(f) Work and prayer (14:12–14)

14:12 'Indeed and in truth I tell you: if any one believes in me, that person will do the works that I do and will do greater works than these, because I am going to the Father.'

When, after the healing at the pool of Bethesda, Jesus affirmed that the works he did were those which the Father showed him, he added, 'he will show him greater works than these, to give you cause for marvel' (John 5:20). Now he tells his disciples that they in turn would do the works that he did. That must have been surprising enough. But what were they to think when he went on to say that, because he was going to the Father, they would do even greater works than they had seen him do? His promise indeed came true: in the first few months after his death and resurrection many more men and women became his followers through their witness than had done so during his personal ministry in Galilee and Judaea. The disciples knew that in themselves they were quite incapable of any such achievement, but he went on to tell them of the coming of the Paraclete, who would empower them and make their witness effective. The 'greater works' of which he now spoke to them would still be his own works, accomplished no longer by his visible presence among them but by his Spirit within them. And it was only by his going to the Father that the Paraclete would come to them (John 16:7).

14:13, 14 'And whatever you ask in my name, this I will do, in order that the Father may be glorified in the Son. If you ask [me] for anything in my name, I will do it.'

If something is asked for in Jesus' name, the request is probably viewed as addressed to the Father. The Father denies nothing to the Son, and a request made in the Son's name is treated as if the Son made it. The textual evidence in verse 14 is fairly evenly divided between the omission and retention of 'me'; but the logic and the thought here favour its omission, which indeed seems to be demanded by the plain sense of 16:23a. Such is the reality of the mutual indwelling between the Father and the Son, however, that a request addressed to either in the Son's name is assured of an answer in the Son's name (cf. John 15:16; 16:23b). This promise is a Johannine counterpart to the Synoptic promise of Matt. 18:19.

(g) *First Paraclete Saying: The Spirit as Helper* (14:15–17)

14:15 'If you love me you will keep my commandments.'

Hitherto Jesus has spoken of his love for his disciples and of their obligation to love one another; now for the first time in this Gospel he speaks of their love for him.[8] The vital link between their love for him and their obedience to him (cf. verses 21, 23; 15:14) is a recurring theme in the Johannine writings. 'This is the love of God, that we keep his commandments' (1 John 5:3), and chief among these is the commandment that the followers of Jesus should love one another; indeed, 'we know that we love the children of God, when we love God and obey his commandments' (1 John 5:2). To love the Father is to love his children; to love the Son is to love his followers; for them to love one another is to love the Father and the Son. In such love the keeping of the divine commandments realizes its perfection. And in such a setting of love the first promise of the Paraclete is made.

14:16, 17 'And I will make a request to the Father, and he will give you another Paraclete, to be with you for ever – the Spirit of truth. The world cannot receive him, because it neither sees him nor knows him. You know him, because he remains[9] with you and will be in you.'

The word *paraklētos*[10] is best understood as a verbal adjective with passive force, denoting one who is called alongside as a helper or defender, a friend at court. Jesus' mention of 'another' Paraclete implies that they already have one, and this can only be himself. In 1 John 2:1, indeed, Jesus is called 'our "Paraclete" with the

Father'; the word is there aptly rendered 'Advocate', from Latin *advocatus*, which is the exact equivalent of Greek *paraklētos*. But in 1 John 2:1 Jesus' advocacy is exercised in the heavenly court; in our present passage it is implied that he had been his disciples' advocate or paraclete on earth. So indeed he had been while he was with them; he had been their champion and helper, the one on whose guidance and support they could rely; but now he was about to leave them. He had been with them for a short time, but the 'other paraclete', his *alter ego*, would be with them permanently, and not only with them but in them.

What is involved in the Paraclete's being called 'the Spirit of truth' will appear clearly in later sayings about him (especially in 16:12–15). His help as Jesus' *alter ego* will be available specifically to the disciples, to compensate them for the loss of Jesus' visible presence. In this capacity he will have nothing to offer the 'world' – the sum-total of unbelievers, who are incapable of appreciating or recognizing him. He will indeed have a ministry to the 'world', as appears from John 16:8–11, but a ministry of quite a different kind.

The Spirit has been mentioned occasionally in the earlier part of the Gospel – notably in his descent on Jesus 'like a dove', marking him out as the one who would baptize with the Holy Spirit (John 1:32 f.), in the instruction to Nicodemus about being born of the Spirit (John 3:5–8), in the words to the Samaritan woman about worship 'in spirit' (John 4:23 f.), in the reference at Capernaum to the quickening power of the Spirit (John 6:63), and in the Evangelist's explanation of Jesus' announcement in the temple court at Tabernacles: 'He said this with regard to the Spirit whom those who believed in him were going to receive; for the Spirit was not yet present because Jesus had not yet been glorified' (John 7:39). But the fullest teaching about the Spirit and his ministry in this Gospel is given in five passages in these upper-room discourses: (i) John 14:15–17; (ii) 14:25 f.; (iii) 15:26 f.; (iv) 16:4b–11; (v) 16:12–15. In these the Spirit is presented successively as helper, interpreter, witness, prosecutor and revealer.

These five passages have sometimes been treated as detachable from their context. They do indeed form a self-consistent unity when taken together; but they are also consistent not only with other references to the Spirit in this Gospel but with references to him in the Synoptic Gospels, not least the references to the aid he will give to disciples as they bear witness to Jesus and make their defence in court (cf. Matt. 10:20; Mark 13:11).[11]

(h) Jesus' promised reappearance to the disciples (14:18–24)

14:18, 19 'I will not leave you orphans; I am coming to you. Only a little while now, and the world sees me no more, but you will see me. Because I live, you also will live.'

'Orphans' (*orphanoi*) are bereft of their natural supporter. That is how the disciples would feel when Jesus was no longer with them in the form to which they had grown accustomed. But they need not feel like that; he would come back to them.

But which aspect of his coming is signified here? If the reference is to his resurrection appearances, they were brief and temporary – although they did bring the glad assurance that he was no longer dead but alive for evermore. If the reference is to their realization of his presence through the Spirit, that would fit well with his promise that they would not be bereft of support, for the Spirit would be their supporter, their *paraklētos*. But we must see a reference also to his words in verse 3: 'I am coming back again and will take you to myself.' Indeed, his present words illustrate what was said in the comment on verse 3, that in this Gospel the distinction between various phases of Jesus' promised coming to his disciples is a 'vanishing distinction'. Every phase of his promised coming is embraced in this assurance: 'I am coming to you.'

As for 'the world', it had seen him during his public ministry and it would see him again for a short time during his trial and crucifixion, but not after that. After that he would be visible to faith alone. His disciples would go on seeing him by faith (the present tense 'you see me' implies continuity stretching indefinitely into the future); more than that, his resurrection life guaranteed unending life to them, because by faith they were united to the Living One, and would draw their life from him. Although the Spirit is not explicitly mentioned here, it is through him, as the Lord and life-giver, that they will draw their life from the ever-living Christ.

14:20, 21 'In that day you will know that I am in my Father and you in me and I in you. The one who loves me is the one who holds my commandments and keeps them. Yes, and the one who loves me will be loved by my Father, and I will love him and will manifest myself to him.'

'That day' is the day when Jesus will have returned to the Father and sent the Spirit to be with and in his disciples. Then they will learn in a new way the truth of his mutual oneness with the Father of which they had so often heard him speak. They will know in their own experience that as he is in the Father they are in their living Lord and their living Lord in them. This threefold coinherence is a coinherence of love; those who are admitted to it are those who love their living Lord, showing their love by their obedience. The Father who loves the Son (John 3:35; 5:20) loves those who are united to the Son, and they, thus loved by the Father, have the assurance that the Son loves them and will reveal himself to them.

Augustine carried the present thought a stage farther by combining the teaching of the Paraclete sections with that of their context. The Spirit, according to him, is the bond of love (*vinculum caritatis*) who binds the Father and the Son together and is the full expression of the love which flows between the Lover and the Beloved.[12] The disciples, already loved by the Father and by the Son, now have the same Spirit imparted to them and, being introduced by him into the circle of the divine love, are enabled not only to reciprocate that love but also to manifest it to one another and to all mankind (cf. Rom. 5:5; 15:30; Col. 1:8).

14:22–24 **Judas (the other Judas, not Iscariot) said to him, 'Lord, what has happened that you will manifest yourself to us and not to the world?' Jesus said to him in reply, 'If any one loves me, he will keep my word, and my Father will love him, and we will come to him and make our home with him. Whoever does not love me does not keep my words. And the word which you hear is not mine; it is the word of the Father who sent me.'**

This Judas[13] is probably identical with Judas the son of James, listed as the eleventh apostle in Luke 6:16 and Acts 1:13. But the question which he asks (as spokesman, no doubt, for his fellow-disciples) is one which must have occurred to many who heard or read these words of Jesus as recorded by the Evangelist. If 'all the tribes of the earth . . . will see the Son of man coming on the clouds of heaven with power and great glory' (Matt. 24:30), what kind of private revelation is this of which Jesus speaks?

It is not a revelation from outside which strikes terror into the beholders; it is a revelation within the family of love. Where love and obedience are shown, the presence of God and of Christ is realized; Father and Son together make their home with each of the children. (The word rendered 'home', *monē*, is that rendered 'room' in verse 2.) No such revelation is possible where love and obedience are absent. (There is a remarkable similarity between the promise here and that to the obedient Laodicean in Rev. 3:20.)

(i) Second Paraclete Saying: The Spirit as Interpreter (14:25, 26)

14:25, 26 **'I have said these things to you while I remained with you. But the Paraclete, the Holy Spirit, whom the Father**

will send in my name, he will teach you everything and remind you of everything that I said to you.'

It is repeatedly indicated in this Gospel (and not only in this Gospel) that the disciples failed to understand much that Jesus said and did during his earthly ministry (cf. John 2:22; 12:16). Now they are told that when the Paraclete comes, he will enable them to recall and understand what Jesus taught: he will serve them, in other words, as remembrancer and interpreter. The Father's sending him in Jesus' name is another way of saying that the Father will send him in response to Jesus' request (verse 16; see further the comment on John 15:26).

(j) Jesus' bequest of peace (14:27–31)

14:27 **'Peace I leave you; my peace I give you. What I give you is not the kind the world gives. Do not go on being troubled at heart; do not be fearful.'**

'Peace (*shālôm*) be with you' was (and is) the usual Jewish greeting when friends met and parted. Jesus' farewell word of peace was different from that which was current in the world.[14] What he called 'my peace' was something deeper and more lasting, peace at heart which would banish anxiety and fear. Paul speaks to the same effect of the 'peace of Christ' which arbitrates in the hearts of his people, maintaining harmony among them (Col. 3:15), and of the 'peace of God' which stands sentry over their hearts and minds, preventing anxiety from gaining an entrance (Phil. 4:7). In these farewell discourses Jesus not only imparts to the disciples 'my peace' but also 'my love' (15:9, 10) and 'my joy' (15:11). When we recall that love, joy and peace are the first three graces in the fruit of the Spirit in Gal. 5:22, we may wonder if these three did not form a triad in primitive Christian thought comparable to faith, hope and love.

14:28, 29 **'You have heard what I said to you: "I am going and I am coming to you." If you loved me, you would have rejoiced that I am on my way to the Father, because the Father is greater than I. And now I have told you before it happens, in order that, when it happens, you may believe.'**

When Jesus first spoke about his impending departure (John 13:33 ff.)., their hearts were troubled, and not even his words about coming back to them (14:3) relieved their anxiety. Now he tells them that he is going to the Father, and that they would be glad rather than sorrowful if they knew what that meant. The words 'if you loved me' in this context imply that love involves some insight into the heart and mind of the person loved and some sympathy with him in hope and purpose. That the Father's authority is greater than the Son's, even if the Son is one with the Father (10:30) is plain: the one who is sent is not greater than the one who sent him (13:16).[15] But now the purpose for which the Son was sent is about to be accomplished. The disciples are told about its imminent accomplishment in order that, when it takes place, they may recognize in it the fulfilment of Jesus' words and believe that he is the person that he claims to be (cf. 13:19).

14:30, 31 'I will not talk much with you any longer, for the ruler of the world is coming. He has nothing (to lay hold of) in me; but the world must know that I love the Father and that I do as the Father has commanded me. Rise up; let us be on our way from here.'

The 'ruler of the world' is about to meet his downfall, as Jesus said a few days earlier (John 12:31). He does not know this: his plan is to overthrow the sent one of God; but there is nothing in Jesus that he can lay hold of so as to gain an advantage over him. The outcome of the impending spiritual conflict will be Jesus' vindication, as the one whose love for the Father is exhibited in perfect obedience to his will. The Son's vindication in the sight of the universe is in accordance with the Father's purpose; the whole course of events is overruled to his end. His vindication involves the discrediting of 'the ruler of the world' (John 16:11). To the Father's good pleasure, then, Jesus confidently commits himself.

It would be easy to believe that the words, 'Rise up; let us be on our way from here', marked the end of the upper-room discourses, as they do in Moffatt's rearrangement, if any textual support for this rearrangement were forthcoming.

NOTES

1. It is impossible to be sure whether the first occurrence of *pisteuete* is indicative, 'you believe', or imperative, 'believe'; but it is more likely to be imperative, as it certainly is in its second occurrence: 'believe in me also.'
2. Compare also the personal note in Paul's words about being 'at home with the Lord' (2 Cor. 5:8), 'with Christ, which is far better' (Phil. 1:23), where Paul's death, not the Lord's advent, is in view.
3. C. H. Dodd, *The Interpretation of the Fourth Gospel*, p. 395.
4. 'What Jesus is saying is, "You know the way; you do not need to know where it leads." Thomas objects, "If we do not know the destination, how can we know the way?" which is the voice of common sense. But Jesus replies, "I am the way" ' (C. H. Dodd, *The Interpretation of the Fourth Gospel*, p. 412, n. 1).
5. *The Imitation of Christ* 56.1

6. There is a well attested variant in verse 7 which reads: 'If you knew (had known) me, you would know (would have known) my Father also.'

7. The first 'you' is plural (hence 'you all' in the above translation). The second 'you' is singular (hence translated 'you, Philip'). In 'How can you say . . . ?' and 'Do you not believe . . . ?' the pronoun is singular again; then the plural is resumed: 'The words which I speak to you (all) . . . Believe me . . . '

8. In John 8:42 he speaks of the *absence* of love for him in those whom he addresses.

9. The present tense 'remains' presupposes the accentuation *ménei*; the accentuation *meneî* would denote the future tense: 'will remain'.

10. Gk. *paraklētos* was taken over into Hebrew and Aramaic as a loanword (*pᵉraqlît*), together with its synonym *synēgoros* (*sanêgôr*) and its antonym *katēgoros* (*qatêgôr*). While *katēgoros* ('accuser', 'prosecutor') is not found in this Gospel, the activity which it denotes is ascribed to the Spirit in John 16:8. In later rabbinical commentaries the function of a *sanêgôr* ('advocate', 'intercessor'), especially on Israel's behalf, is ascribed to the Holy Spirit (e.g. *Leviticus Rabba* 6.1 on Lev. 5:1, where the Holy Spirit pleads for Israel in the divine lawcourt). See p. 326, n. 6.

11. Cf. H. Windisch, 'The Five Johannine Paraclete Sayings' (1927) in *The Spirit-Paraclete in the Fourth Gospel* (Philadelphia, 1968), pp. 1–26; W. F. Howard, *Christianity according to St. John* (London, 1943), pp. 71–80.

12. Augustine, *On the Trinity* 15.27. The way had been prepared for Augustine a generation or two earlier by Marius Victorinus, the first theologian to speak of the Spirit as the principle of unity in the Godhead, the *copula* of the eternal Trinity, completing the perfect circle of the Divine Being (*Against Arius* 1.60; *Hymns on the Trinity* 1, lines 3, 74; 3, lines 17, 18).

13. The Curetonian Syriac reads 'Judas Thomas' for 'Judas not Iscariot' (the Sinaitic Syriac reads simply 'Thomas'). Syriac Christians seem regularly to have called the apostle Thomas 'Judas Thomas'; he is so called in the Gnostic Acts of Thomas and in the *Doctrine of Addai* (whence he is introduced as 'Judas who is also Thomas' in Eusebius, *Hist. Eccl.* 1.13.11), and Ephrem the Syrian quotes John 20:24 in the form: 'But Judas Thomas . . .'. (The reading 'Judas the Cananaean' here for 'Judas not Iscariot' in a couple of Coptic versions is due to confusion with Simon the Cananaean, who is listed as eleventh apostle in Mark 3:18 and Matt. 10:4.)

14. Some commentators point out that the world can only *wish* peace; Jesus *gives* it.

15. Both 'I and my Father are one' (John 10:30) and 'the Father is greater than I' have been detached from their contexts and misused as proof-texts in the arsenal of christological controversy. In their contexts the two sayings are appropriate and readily intelligible. The conjunction 'because' before 'the Father is greater than I' attaches the clause to that immediately preceding: Jesus is on his way back to the Father who sent him, having completed the mission with which he was entrusted, *because* 'one who is sent is not greater than the one who sent him' (John 13:16) and must therefore render to him an account of his commission. See C. K. Barrett, ' "The Father is greater than I", John 14:28: Subordinationist Christology in the NT', *Essays on John* (London, 1982), pp. 19–36.

CHAPTER 15

2. THE LORD AND HIS PEOPLE

(a) The Vine and the Branches (15:1–11)

15:1–3 'I am the true vine and my Father is the vinedresser. He removes every branch in me that does not produce fruit, and he prunes every branch that does produce fruit, to make it produce more fruit. You are clean already because of the word that I have spoken to you.'

The vine is one of the OT figures used to illustrate the people of Israel.[1] In Ps. 80:8–19 Israel is the vine which God brought out of Egypt and planted in the ground which he had cleared to make room for it. The psalmist bewails the fact that it flourishes no longer, that its defences are demolished and it is ravaged by marauders; he prays:

> Look down from heaven, and see;
> have regard for this vine,
>   the stock which thy right hand planted . . .
> let thy hand be upon the man of thy right hand,
>   the son of man whom thou hast
>   made strong for thyself!

Jesus is here presented as the true Israel, the genuine vine, the man of God's right hand. As in the psalm, God is both the planter and cultivator of the vine. The noun translated 'vinedresser' is the ordinary Greek word for 'farmer' (*geōrgos*), but in English 'farmer' is not used in connexion with the vine.

The thought of the mutual indwelling, the coinherence, of Christ and his people has found repeated expression in Chapter 14; here it is conveyed in the parable of the vine and the branches. If Jesus is the vine, his disciples are the branches, deriving their life and fruit-producing strength from him. The Father tends the vine with loving care, making it as fruitful as possible: he removes unfruitful branches and prunes those that are fruitful, clearing away superfluous wood so that they may be even more fruitful. There are plays on words in the Greek that cannot easily be reproduced in English'; 'he removes' is *airei* and 'he prunes' is *kathairei*. Moreover, *kathairei* can also mean 'he cleanses' and is linked with 'clean' in verse 3: 'you are *katharoi*'. Here is an echo of John 13:10, 'you are clean (*katharoi*), but not all'. Judas was the exception then; in terms of the present parable, he is an unfruitful branch that has to be removed. The disciples who keep Jesus' word (cf. John 14:23), in whom his word has found a lodging place (cf. verse 7 below), are 'clean' on that account; it may be implied that his word is the means used by the Father to perform his work of pruning.

15:4–6 'Remain in me, as I remain in you. As the branch cannot produce fruit on its own account, unless it remains in the vine, so you also cannot produce fruit unless you remain in me. I am the vine; you are the branches. The one who produces fruit is the one who remains in me, as I remain in him; for apart from me you cannot do anything. If any one does not remain in me, he is thrown out like a branch and withers away; then people gather them and throw them into the fire and they are burned.'

A vine-branch is lifeless and useless unless it remains attached to the vine. The living sap from the stock flowing into it enables it to produce grapes; otherwise it is fruitless. So with Jesus' disciples: only as they remain in union with him and derive their life from him can they produce the fruit of the Spirit.[2] Paul does not use Johannine idiom but he expresses the same truth when he says, 'It is no longer I who live, but Christ who lives in me' (Gal. 2:20), and 'I can do all things in him who strengthens me' (Phil. 4:13).

In another OT passage where Israel is compared to a vine, it is stressed that the wood of the vine is useless except for the fulfilling of the vine's proper function – the production of grapes. The wood of a dead vine branch cannot be used to make a piece of furniture or a utensil of any kind: it will not even serve as a peg to hang something on. A vine branch that does not produce grapes is good only for fuel (Ezek. 15:1–8). The moral of the parable should have spoken for itself in Ezekiel's day; it speaks for itself in the new setting and application given to it by Jesus.

15:7, 8 'If you remain in me, and my words remain in you, ask what you will, and it shall be done for you. My Father is glorified in this, that you should produce abundant fruit and so be (truly) disciples of mine.'

There is no practical difference between Jesus' personal indwelling in his disciples and his words' remaining in them. The 'words' (plural) here are *rhēmata*; the 'word' (singular) of verse 3 is *logos*. The *logos* is his teaching in its entirety; the *rhēmata* are the individual utterances which make it up. He himself is the living embodiment of all his teaching. In John 14:13 f. the promise of answered prayer is made to the one who believes in Jesus; the same promise is made here to the one who remains in him and in whose heart his words have a permanent residence. Faith in Jesus, acceptance of his words, inaugurates a union with him through which his eternal life and power become for ever available to the believer.

Receiving an answer to the prayer of faith appears to be one form of spiritual fruitbearing. In John 14:13 the Father is glorified in the answering of such a prayer; here he is glorified in the producing of abundant fruit in the life of the true disciple. As the Father is supremely glorified in the obedience of Jesus (John 13:31 f.; 17:1, 4), so he is glorified in those whose lives reproduce the obedient life of Jesus. The 'fruit' of which this parable speaks is, in effect, likeness to Jesus (the same may be said of the ninefold 'fruit of the Spirit' in Gal. 5:22 f.). Those who manifest such likeness show conclusively that they are truly disciples of his. The same truth has been set forth already, without the explicit emphasis on fruitbearing, in John 8:31 f., 'If you remain in my word (*logos*), you will truly be my disciples, and you will come to know the truth, and the truth will set you free.' Those words were addressed to people whose faith and discipleship were doubtful; the faith that leads to union with Christ is the faith that manifests itself in true discipleship, a discipleship of obedience, love and joy.

15:9, 10 'As the Father has loved me, so I have loved you. Remain in my love. If you keep my commandments, you will remain in my love, as I have kept my Father's commandments and remain in his love.'

As we have seen in John 14:20–24, the mutual indwelling of the Father and the Son, and of Jesus and his disciples, and of the disciples with their heavenly Father as his children, is a mutuality of love, a love in which obedience is a spontaneous joy and not a painful duty. 'My love' in which Jesus bids his disciples remain is, in the context, the love with which (as he says) 'I have loved you' – although it goes without saying that it evokes a responsive love from them. The Father's love for the Son has been declared in John 3:35; 5:20 (see also 17:23, 24 below).

Jesus' love for the Father was shown in his obedience to him, and was requited in his constant awareness of the Father's loving approval: 'he has not left me alone', he said, 'because I always do the things that are pleasing to him' (John 8:29). So the disciples' love for their Master should be shown in their obedience to him, and their requital will be the constant awareness of their Master's loving approval; thus they will remain in the love of him who remains in the Father's love.

15:11 'I have told you this so that my joy may be in you and your joy may be fulfilled.'

In verses 10 and 11 Jesus adds 'my love' and 'my joy' to 'my peace' which he has already bequeathed to the disciples (John 14:27). The assurance of an eternal relationship of mutual love with the Father and himself was well calculated to banish the misgivings which had filled their hearts at the thought of his departure, and to fill them with his own joy. There is an echo of these words in 1 John 1:4.

(b) The friends of Jesus (15:12–17)

15:12–14 'This is my commandment, that you love one another, as I have loved you. No one has greater love than this, to lay down one's life for one's friends. You are my friends if you do what I command you.'

This paragraph (verses 12–17) is an expansion of the new commandment of John 13:34 f.; it begins and ends with the injunction to love one another. The measure of the love enjoined by Jesus – 'as I have loved you' – is beyond measuring. 'In this we come to know love, in that *he* laid down his life for us; and *we* ought to lay down our lives for our brothers' (1 John 3:16). The greatest love that any one can show for friends is to die for them. To try to set these words over against Rom. 5:8–10, where Paul speaks of *enemies* as reconciled to God by the death of his Son, is to risk missing the point of both passages. Jesus is speaking to his friends, for whom he is about to give his life, thus showing that they are truly his *philoi*, the objects of his love. (In this context the words for 'love' are the noun *agapē* and the verb *agapaō*, while the word for 'friend' is *philos*: in John's vocabulary there is no difference in meaning between the two roots.) The interpenetration between love and obedience appears again in the statement that Jesus' friends are those who do whatever he commands them.

15:15 'I no longer call you slaves, because the slave does not know what his master is doing. I have called you friends, because I have made known to you all that I have heard from my Father.'

We should not infer from 'no longer' that Jesus had formerly called his disciples 'slaves' (*douloi*), or treated them as such. The point is rather that now, in the upper room, he is admitting them to the inner motives of his ministry and impending sacrifice. It is not for the slave to know why his master says, 'Do this'; it is for the slave to do it: his not to reason why. But with a friend one shares one's hopes and plans. The contrast between the slave and the friend here is not unlike the contrast between the slave and the son in Gal. 4:7. John Wesley, looking back on his conversion in later years, described it as the time when he exchanged the faith of a servant for the faith of a son.[3] Had he expressed himself in Johannine rather than Pauline language, he might have said that he then exchanged the obedience of a slave for the obedience of a friend.

To his friends, then, Jesus has disclosed all that he himself has learned from the Father. True, there is much that they are not yet able to grasp (John 16:12), but the limitation lies with their capacity for comprehension, not with his willingness to impart the full truth.

15:16, 17 'It was not you who chose me, it was I who chose you and appointed you to go and produce fruit. Your fruit is destined to remain, so that whatever you ask the Father in my name, he will give it to you. This is my commandment to you: love one another.'

Jesus now harks back for a moment to the figure of the vine and its fruit. On the day that he first met his disciples and conscripted them into his service with the command 'Follow me!' he chose them that they might share his ministry. The fruit produced by the branches is the fruit of the vine itself. This is no Dead Sea fruit, which turns to dust and ashes at a touch; this is the enduring fruit of lives in union with the ever-living Christ, bearing witness to his abiding grace. Again (as in verse 7) the promise of answered prayer is made to the disciple who remains united to Jesus as the fruit-bearing branch is united to the vine. United to Jesus, that disciple can plead his prevailing name with confidence in the Father's presence. Jesus lives in his disciples' lives and prays with their hearts and through their lips.

With the repetition of the command to love one another the paragraph ends.

(c) Warning of persecution (15:18–25)

15:18, 19 'If the world hates you, you know that it hated me before it hated you. If you belonged to the world, the world would love that which is its own. But because you do not belong to the world, but I have chosen you out of the world – for this reason the world hates you.'

From recommending the cultivation of the mutual love within

the fellowship of his followers, Jesus turns to warn them against hostility from those who are outside.[4] As so often in the Johannine writings, 'the world' is the godless world, the world organized in opposition to God, and therefore opposed to his people. At the moment, Jesus himself was the target for their opposition; in a few hours he would be the victim of their hostility. It was inevitable that his associates should incur the world's hatred as he himself had done. It is an odd fact that the world soon justified its hostility to them by imputing to them the initiative in hatred. The earliest extant reference to Christians in pagan literature charges them with 'hatred of the human race'.[5]

Jesus' followers have been described in John 13:1 as 'his own people who were in the world', on whom he set his love. He chose them 'out of the world' to be 'his own people', and therefore they no longer belonged to the world. The world looked on them as aliens, and treated them accordingly.

15:20, 21 **'Remember the word that I spoke to you: "A servant is not greater than his master." If they persecuted me, they will persecute you also; if they kept my word, they will keep yours also. Indeed, they will do all this to you for my name's sake, because they do not know the one who sent me.'**

The statement that 'a servant is not greater than his master' is repeated from John 13:16. It appears also in Matt. 10:24, in a context not unlike the present one. In Matt. 10:16–25 (as also, more briefly, in Mark 13:9–13) Jesus forewarns his disciples against the persecution which they will have to endure on his account: 'you will be hated by all for my name's sake' (Matt. 10:22; Mark 13:13). Those who appreciated Jesus' teaching will appreciate the teaching which the disciples impart in his name; they will acknowledge that the disciples have been commissioned by Jesus as Jesus himself was commissioned by God. But those who repudiated his teaching, refusing to recognize him as the sent one of God, will repudiate the disciples when they come teaching in their Master's name. The close association between his persecution and theirs finds expression in the voice from heaven which Saul of Tarsus heard on the Damascus road: 'why do you persecute me?' (Acts 9:4; 22:7; 26:14). The Lord who was personally persecuted on earth continued to be persecuted, even in his exaltation, in the person of his persecuted followers. Their being persecuted for his sake was a sign that they belonged to him, as it was a token of coming judgment on their persecutors (cf. Phil. 1:28; 2 Thess. 1:5–10).

15:22-25 'If I had not come and spoken to them, they would not have (incurred) sin; but as it is, they have no excuse for their sin. Whoever hates me hates my Father also. If I had not done the works among them which no one else ever did, they would not have (incurred) sin; but as it is, they have both seen and hated me and my Father. This has happened to fulfil the saying that is written in their law: "They hated me without a cause." '

It is emphasized repeatedly in the Synoptic Gospels that the generation to which Jesus came bore a greater responsibility than any previous generation, because men and women of earlier days had not heard his teaching or seen his mighty works, as his own contemporaries did. His own contemporaries for the most part rejected his teaching and refused to admit the evidence of his works; therefore they compared unfavourably with pagans like the queen of Sheba who was impressed by Solomon's wisdom or the people of Nineveh who repented at Jonah's preaching (Luke 11:31 f.). Indeed, the cities which had been the centres of his ministry would receive severer judgment on the great day than the sinners of Sodom (Matt. 11:23 f.).

The Evangelist has noted earlier that, although Jesus had performed so many signs in full view of his hearers (especially in Jerusalem), yet 'they would not believe in him' (John 12:37); here a similar judgment is expressed on Jesus' own lips. The greater the privilege, the greater the responsibility; and no greater privilege could have been enjoyed than that of hearing Jesus' teaching and seeing his works. If the hatred which his disciples were to receive from 'the world' was due to its hatred of him (verses 18, 19), the hatred which he himself received is traced back by him to hatred of God: 'they have both seen and hated me and my Father.' They saw the Father in the Son (cf. John 14:9) but did not realize that this was so. Had they recognized Jesus as the Son of God, they would have recognized the Father in him; as it was, in repudiating the Son they repudiated the Father also (cf. John 5:23b). He had come to show them the love of God, but they reacted to his love with hatred, just as, when he came to them as the light of the world, they chose darkness rather than light (John 3:19). They thus passed judgment on themselves: if they rejected the giver of true life, they shut themselves up to the only alternative – death.

'Their law' here (like 'your law' in John 10:34) refers to their own acknowledged scriptures, whose authority they were bound to recognize. The fact that Jesus quotes this 'law' as authoritative indicates that it was not exclusively *their* law; the Evangelist, like his Master, accepted it as the word of God. Here (as in John 10:34) it is the Psalter that is quoted. 'They hated me without a cause' might be taken either from Ps. 35:19 or Ps. 69:4 but in view of the currency of Ps. 69 as a source of messianic 'testimonies', especially in relation to the passion of Jesus (cf. John 2:17), it is Ps. 69:4 that is probably in view here.[6]

(d) Third Paraclete Saying: The Spirit as Witness (15:26, 27)

15:26, 27 'When the Paraclete comes, the one whom I will send to you from the Father – the Spirit of truth who proceeds from the Father – he will bear witness to me. And do you bear witness also, because you have been with me from the first.'

The witness which Jesus had borne, by his words and works, to the grace and truth of God would not come to an end when he was no longer in the world. The Spirit would take up this ministry of witness and carry it on, and he would do so not least through the disciples. It is not surprising that this aspect of the Spirit's work is foretold in a persecution context. In the related Synoptic contexts the Spirit enables the persecuted disciples to bear their witness boldly: 'When they deliver you up, do not be anxious how you are to speak or what you are to say; for what you are to say will be given to you in that hour; for it is not you who speak, but the Spirit of your Father speaking through you' (Matt. 10:19 f., cf. Mark 13:11). There is, moreover, a remarkable instance of the fulfilment of this promise in Acts 5:32, where Peter and his colleagues, making their defence before the high priest and council, proclaim the resurrection and enthronement of Jesus and say, 'And we are witnesses to these things, and so is the Holy Spirit whom God has given to those who obey him.' So here, the witness borne by the Spirit and that borne by the disciples are one and the same witness. Since the disciples' witness is mentioned in the present tense, whereas the Spirit's witness is foretold in the future tense, the present *martyreite* may be imperative (as it has been rendered above) rather than indicative ('you bear witness').

Neither the witness of the Spirit nor the witness of the disciples is confined to the forensic setting, of course, but it is plain that in this Johannine text and in its counterpart in Acts such a setting is implied. A wider relevance for the Spirit's witness is indicated in 1 John 5:6, 'it is the Spirit that bears witness, because the Spirit is truth' (cf. his designation here and in 14:17 as 'the Spirit of truth').[7] The witness of the disciples takes many forms in Acts, but it cannot begin until the Holy Spirit comes on them with power (Acts 1:8). Whereas in John 14:26 it is the Father who sends the Paraclete in the Son's name, here it is the Son who sends him. Similarly in Acts 2:23 the Son receives 'the promise of the Holy Spirit' from the

Father and 'pours it out' on the disciples. The statement that the Spirit 'proceeds from the Father' has probably no metaphysical significance; it is another way of saying that the Spirit is sent by the Father. The clause is quoted in the Nicene-Constantinopolitan Creed. The western expansion of the clause, 'who proceeds from the Father and the Son' (*filioque*), could be justified by the fact that the Son as well as the Father is said to send the Spirit; the basic objection to it is that it was unwarranted for one part of the church to make such an alteration in the wording of the ecumenical creed without reference to the rest of the church.[8]

The disciples are said to have been with Jesus 'from the first' (*ap' archēs*, 'from the beginning') in the sense that they had been with him from the beginning of his ministry, the period following his recognition by John the Baptist (John 1:35 ff.).

NOTES

1. It has sometimes been supposed that after 'Rise up; let us be on our way' at the end of chapter 14 Jesus and the disciples were now moving towards the Kidron valley and Olivet, and that the words about the vine were suggested by the sight of the great golden vine overhanging the main entrance to the sanctuary proper (Josephus, *Jewish War* 5.210; *Antiquities* 15.395; Tacitus, *Histories* 5.5; Mishnah, tractate *Middoth* 3.8). This supposition (made, e.g., by J. Pickl, *The Messias*, p. 180) is, however, quite improbable.

2. It is a matter of historical interest that one of the earliest literary works of Karl Marx was a graduation essay written at the age of seventeen on 'The union of believers with Christ according to John 15:1-14, showing its basis and essence, its absolute necessity, and its effects' (K. Marx/F. Engels, *Collected Works*, I [London, 1975], pp. 636-639). It was approved as 'a thoughtful, copious and powerful presentation of the theme' (E. H. Carr, *Karl Marx: A Study in Fanaticism* [London, 1934], p. 5; cf. H. P. Adams, *Karl Marx in his Earlier Writings* [London, 1940], pp. 15 f.).

3. J. Wesley, *Journal*, I (London, 1872), pp. 76 f., footnotes.

4. For the structure of John 15:18-16:4a and its relation to similar passages in the Synoptic Gospels see B. Lindars, 'The Persecution of Christians in John 15:18-16:4a' in *Suffering and Martyrdom in the New Testament*, ed. W. Horbury and B. McNeil (Cambridge, 1981), pp. 48-69.

5. Tacitus, *Annals* 15.44.5.

6. See comment on p. 75.

7. In *Testament of Judah* 20:5 'the Spirit of truth testifies (*martyrei*) all and accuses (*katēgorei*) all' (for the latter rôle cf. John 16:8).

8. See G. Bray, 'The *Filioque* Clause in History and Theology', *Tyndale Bulletin* 34 (1983).

CHAPTER 16

(e) Further warning of persecution (16:1–4a)

16:1, 2 'I have told you this so that you may not take offence. They will expel you from the synagogue; indeed, the time is coming when any one who kills you will think he is offering worship to God.'

If the troubles predicted by the Lord were to come on the disciples unawares, they might feel resentfully that they should have been forewarned and conclude that he had let them down. The verb (*skandalizō*) has been used in John 6:61 of the people of Capernaum who were put off by Jesus' unacceptable discourse in the synagogue. In Mark 14:27 the same word is used in Jesus' warning about the disciples' reaction to his unresisting submission to arrest in Gethsemane later in the same evening.[1]

Expulsion from the synagogue of those who confessed Jesus to be the Messiah has been mentioned in John 9:22; 12:42. At the time when the Gospel was written these words had acquired a special relevance from the inclusion in the synagogue prayers of a curse on the Nazarenes, which was intended to ensure that the followers of Jesus could take no part in the service.[2]

As for the idea that the killing of Jesus' followers was pleasing to God, we may recall how Paul's unenlightened 'zeal for the law' was shown in his persecution of the church (Phil. 3:6). There were some militant Zealots who regarded the killing of an apostate as an acceptable sacrifice to God.[3]

16:3, 4a 'They will do this because they have not come to know the Father or me. I have told you this so that, when the hour for these things comes, you may remember what I said.'

As in John 14:7, to know Jesus (as the one sent by the Father) is to know the Father (as the one who sent him). Such knowledge Jesus came to impart; to possess it is to have eternal life (John 17:3). Hostility to Jesus and his followers springs from lack of his life-giving knowledge (cf. verse 21 above). Once more Jesus impresses on the disciples that he is telling them this so that, when it happens, they may not be taken by surprise but may remember his words (cf. John 13:19; 14:29).

(f) Fourth Paraclete Saying: The Spirit as Prosecutor (16:4b–11)

16:4b–7 'I did not tell you this earlier, because I was with you. But now I am going to him who sent me, yet none of you asks me, "Where are you going?" But your hearts are filled with sorrow because I have told you this. Yet I tell you the truth: it is to your advantage that I should go away. If I do not go away, the Paraclete will not come to you; but if I go, I will send him to you.'

While Jesus was with them, he was their protector and could deflect to himself attacks aimed at them; in fact, he continued to do so to the moment of his arrest (cf. John 18:8, 9). It was therefore not necessary to warn them of impending persecution earlier – literally, 'from the beginning' (*ex archēs*, as in 6:64, meaning from the beginning of their association with him; cf. *ap' archēs* in 15:27). Now, however, things would be different: he himself would no longer be with them in the way to which they had grown accustomed, and they would be direct targets for the attacks of their opponents.[4]

'I am going to him who sent me' is another way of saying 'I am going to the Father' (as in verse 10); cf. John 4:34; 5:23; etc.

The formal contradiction between 'none of you asks me, "Where are you going?" ' and Peter's question 'Where are you going, Lord?' (13:36) has been used as an argument for rearranging the discourses so that 15:1–16:33 precedes 13:31b–14:31; but this presupposes a greater degree of logical sequence in the discourses than may be warranted.

It is no wonder that the disciples were dismayed by Jesus' warning of persecution to come. But even so, he assures them, it is better for them that he should leave them, even if his departure does signal the onset of persecution. The coming of the Paraclete[5] will compensate them for the loss of his own visible presence, and will in addition equip them with all the resources they will need in the new way of life on which they are about to enter.

16:8–11 'And he, when he comes, will expose the world's error with regard to sin and to righteousness and to judgment: with regard to sin, because they do not believe in me; with regard to righteousness, because I am going to the Father and you see me no more; with regard to judgment, because the ruler of this world has been judged.'

The Spirit is the 'advocate' or helper of those who believe in Jesus, their counsel for the defence. But in relation to unbelievers, to the godless world, he acts as counsel for the prosecution.[6] In both respects he duplicates the work of Jesus: Jesus had been his disciples' helper while he was with them, and at the same time his presence and witness in the world had served as an indictment of those who closed their minds to his message.

The Spirit's prosecuting ministry is here expressed by the verb *elenchō*, meaning (according to the context) expose, refute, convince or convict.[7] His very presence will be a demonstration to the world which condemned Jesus that he was in the right and they were in the wrong. In the paraphrastic wording of the NEB, he will 'show where wrong and right and judgement lie' and thus 'confute the world'. This is not quite the same as what is often called the Spirit's 'convicting' work in the heart, leading to repentance and faith. One stanza of an old gospel song runs:

> I know not how God's Spirit moves,
>   Convincing men of sin,
> Revealing Jesus through the Word,
>   Creating faith in him –

but while this is an admirable summary of the Spirit's inward work which results in true conversion, it is not the aspect of his activity which is in view here. The Spirit bears witness to the world (not least through the witness of Jesus' followers, as was affirmed in John 15:26 f.) that Jesus, rejected, condemned and put to death by the world, has been vindicated and exalted by God. His rejection, condemnation and execution expressed in violent clarity the world's refusal to believe in him; that unbelief is now exposed as sin. His condemnation, promulgated after due process of law, is now shown to have been utterly unrighteous; his return to the Father is the demonstration of his righteousness – and at the same time the vindication of the Father's righteousness (in John 17:25 Jesus addresses him as 'righteous Father'). The relevance of the clause 'you see me no more' seems to be that Jesus' departure is the condition of the Spirit's presence. His disciples see him no longer as they formerly did because he has gone to the Father and the Spirit has come to perform his ministry of witness and confutation.

Behind the men who acted as Jesus' prosecutors and judges stood the adversary-in-chief, 'the ruler of this world' who, as Jesus said, 'is coming' but 'has nothing to lay hold of in me' (John 14:30). Jesus had foretold his imminent expulsion as the Jerusalem ministry drew to a close: 'Now it is this world's judgment', he said; 'now the ruler of this world is to be cast out' (John 12:31). The presence of the Spirit is the token that this prediction has been fulfilled: judgment in the supreme court has been given for the Son of Man and against the world; and the world's spirit-ruler, in consequence of that adverse judgment, has been deposed. 'Our great foe is baffled; Christ Jesus is King!'

(g) Fifth Paraclete Saying: The Spirit as Revealer (16:12–15)

16:12, 13 **'I have still many things to tell you, but you are not yet able to bear them. But when he comes who is the Spirit of truth, he will guide you in (the way of) all truth. He will not speak on his own initiative: whatever he will hear, that he will speak, and he will declare to you the things that are to come.'**

Jesus had come to earth as the revealer of the Father, but the limited period of his ministry was too brief for the disciples to take in all that he had to reveal. His ministry of revelation would, however, be carried on after his departure by the Spirit. As in John 14:16f., the Spirit is called 'the Spirit of truth' – here, with reference to the truth which he would disclose to the disciples. Jesus himself is the embodiment of truth (John 14:6); the truth which the Spirit will disclose is not truth additional to 'the truth as it is in Jesus' (Eph. 4:21); it is the further unfolding of that truth. It is not that he will guide them 'into' all truth; they had already been introduced to the way of truth by Jesus, and the Spirit would guide them further along that way.

Jesus had insisted more than once that he did not speak or act on his own initiative; his words were those which the Father gave him to utter (John 5:19, 30; 8:28; 12:49). So, when the Paraclete comes, he will not speak on his own initiative. He has no message over and above that which is implicit in the incarnate Word; it is his function to make that message explicit. We are no doubt intended to infer that the Gospel of John provides a prime example of the fulfilment of this promise.

As for 'the things that are to come', the Spirit's declaration of these may be understood as exercised through the gift of prophecy in the church. But the verb 'declare' is the same as that used in John 4:25, where the Samaritan woman says that when the Messiah comes, 'he will declare (*anangelei*) all things to us'. As the Messiah was expected to bring out plainly the fuller implications of the revelation that had preceded his coming, so the Paraclete will bring out plainly the fuller implications of the revelation embodied in the Messiah and apply them relevantly to each succeeding generation.

16:14, 15 **'He it is who will glorify me, because he will take from what is mine and declare it to you. Everything that the Father has is mine; that is why I have said that he will take from what is mine and declare it to you.'**

For the fifth and last time in these Paraclete sayings the emphatic demonstrative *ekeinos* (masculine, in agreement with *paraklētos*) is used of the Spirit. He and no other will teach the disciples everything (14:26), will bear witness to Christ (15:26), will expose the world's error (16:8), will guide the disciples in the way of all truth (16:13), and (now) it is he who has as his supreme mission the glorifying of Jesus. As the Son has glorified the Father by his work on earth (John 7:18; 17:4), so the Spirit by his coming will glorify the Son. One might amplify this statement by reference to teaching about the Spirit in other NT writings (especially the letters of Paul), but in the present context the Spirit glorifies the Son by unfolding clearly the meaning of his person and work. 'What is mine' includes his teaching and general activity. Since it has already been emphasized that all Jesus' words were spoken and all his deeds performed by the Father's authority (so that his words were the Father's words and his deeds the Father's deeds), 'what is mine' on Jesus' lips means 'all that the Father has given me'. And since the Father has given him 'all things' (John 13:3), what the Spirit discloses to the disciples is 'everything that the Father has'. In making known the Son, the Spirit at the same time makes known the Father who is revealed in the Son.

(h) 'A little while' (16:16–18)

16:16–18 **'For a little while you see me no more, and again a little while and you will see me.' So some of his disciples said one to another, 'What does this mean that he says to us – "For a little while you do not see me, and again a little while and you will see me", and "Because I am going to the Father"?' So they were saying, 'What is this "little while" of which he speaks? We do not understand what he is saying.'**

We should not imagine too quickly that we understand what was so unintelligible to the disciples. It is easy to suppose that Jesus meant, 'In a little while you will not see me, because I am about to die; but in a little while after that you will see me again, because I am going to rise on the third day and appear to you once more.' Certainly he was going to be taken from them in 'a little while' – in a few hours' time – but 'you see me no more' (cf. verse 10) seems to indicate a longer interval than that between Jesus' arrest and the resurrection appearances. Perhaps, then it is that 'coming again' promised in John 14:3 that is in view in the words: 'again a little while and you will see me.' But in saying this we must recall what was said in the comments on John 14:3, 18 about the 'vanishing distinction' in the upper room discourses between Jesus'

coming in the resurrection appearances, in the Spirit's abiding presence, and at his final advent.[8]

When the disciples, wondering aloud what Jesus can mean, add
to his words quoted from verse 16 the clause 'Because I am going
to the Father', they hark back to what he has said in verse 10: 'I
am going to the Father and you see me no more.'[9]

(i) Joy instead of Sorrow (16:19–24)

16:19–22 Jesus knew that they were reluctant to ask him, and
he said to them, 'Is this what you are inquiring about one with
another – because I said, "In a little while you will see me no
more, and again a little while and you will see me?" Indeed and
in truth I tell you: you will weep and wail, but the world will
rejoice; you will suffer pain, but your pain will be turned into
joy. When a woman is in labour she is in pain, because her time
has come; but when she has given birth to her child, she re-
members her anguish no more for joy that a human being has
been born into the world. So then, you are in pain now, but I
will see you again, and your heart will rejoice, and no one takes
your joy away from you.'

Even if Jesus does not explain his strange language to them in
such terms as they might have hoped for, he does assure them that
their present bewilderment and their imminent grief will be
short-lived; soon they will be given assurance and joy. Their sense
of bereavement at this departure and the anguish and apprehension
caused by his crucifixion will be dispelled when he comes to them
again, imparting the joy of uninterrupted fellowship with him
henceforth through the Spirit. The inbreaking of that new joy, of
which none can ever deprive them,[10] will make them forget the
nightmare of the hours which are lying immediately ahead of them.
A mother's delight in her newborn child, following her labour
pains,[11] provides an apt analogy. (It is unlikely that there is any
allusion here to the rabbinical teaching about the 'messianic birthpangs',[12] the time of distress which will precede and herald the
dawn of the new age.)

Whereas Jesus has said above, 'you will see me' (verse 16), now
he says, 'I will see you again', but it is difficult to see any real
distinction of emphasis in this variation of wording. He means 'I
will come and see you again', with the implication that they would
see him. The initiative in reunion would be entirely his.

The 'world' that would rejoice at his disappearance would be
restricted to those who could not rest until they had got him out
of the way (cf. John 11:50) and felt relief and satisfaction when
they thought they had accomplished their purpose. His return

would fill them with dismay, but it would fill his friends with gladness. So it is recorded later, in fulfilment of his promise to them: 'Seeing the Lord, then, the disciples rejoiced' (John 20:20).

16:23, 24 'On that day you will ask me for nothing. Indeed and in truth I tell you: if you ask the Father for anything in my name, he will give it to you. Up to the present you have asked for nothing in my name: ask and you will receive, so that your joy may be complete.'

The first sentence in verse 23 is ambiguous. Does Jesus mean 'you will ask me no question' or 'you will ask me for nothing'? While the verb *erōtaō* in classical Greek means 'ask a question', it is used repeatedly in the NT (and not least in this Gospel) in the sense of asking someone for something, and the context makes it clear that this is the sense here. 'On that day' – i.e. when I have come back from death and you have the assurance of my abiding presence with you through the Spirit – then you will not ask me for anything; you will address your requests direct to the Father in my name, and you shall have what you ask for. In John 14:13 f. Jesus tells them that he will do whatever they ask in his name, 'in order that the Father may be glorified in the Son'; here he tells them that the Father will give them whatever they ask for in his (Jesus') name – and the clause of purpose might equally well have been added here: 'in order that the Father may be glorified in the Son'. Whether it be in the bestowal of the Spirit (compare John 14:16 with 16:7), or in the granting of any other boon, the Father and the Son act as one, so that either of them can be the subject of the verb.

When the disciples are encouraged to make their requests to the Father in Jesus' name, this is based on their close relationship with Jesus – their dwelling in him and his dwelling in them. One might think that there is a suggestion of his interceding with the Father on their behalf, but this seems to be excluded (so far as the answering of prayer is concerned) by Jesus' words in verses 26 f. They had prayed to the Father before – Jesus indeed had taught them to do so[13] – but hitherto they had not prayed to him in Jesus' name. To pray in Jesus' name was a privilege belonging to the new order on which they were about to enter with Jesus' departure and return. Access to the Father in Jesus' name was part of the joy which was promised in place of their present sorrow; it would, indeed, bring that joy to completion.

(j) Tribulation and victory (16:25–33)

16:25–28 'I have told you these things in parables. The hour is coming when I will no longer speak to you in parables, but tell you plainly about the Father. On that day you will ask in my name, and I do not say to you that I will make request to the Father for you, for the Father himself loves you, because you have come to love me and believe that I came forth from God. I came forth from the Father and have come into the world; now I leave the world and am on my way back to the Father.'

According to Mark 4:33 f., Jesus did not speak to the multitudes 'without a parable, but privately to his own disciples he explained everything.' Here the situation is somewhat different: he has been speaking to his disciples in 'parables' (*paroimiai*, as against the Synoptic *parabolai*) but henceforth he will speak to them 'plainly' (*parrhēsia*). Since his instruction to them has almost ended, we might suppose that the non-parabolic teaching which he promises to give them henceforth is that further teaching which he will give them through the Spirit (cf. verses 12–15); but the disciples' response in verse 29 suggests that what he now says (verses 26–28) is the plain, non-parabolic teaching. The noun *parrhēsia* (in the dative case) has been used before of Jesus' public appearance and teaching (cf. John 7:4, 26; 11:54), but also of plain speech as opposed to figurative language (cf. John 10:24; 11:14). In the upper room Jesus had used the figure of the vine (John 15:1–8) and the analogy of a woman in childbirth (verse 21 above) to illustrate his meaning; now, in summing up, he dispenses with such illustrative devices.

Earlier Jesus had told them that he would request the Father to send them 'another Paraclete' (John 14:16). But now he does not promise to make similar requests to the Father on their behalf. They must not be led to think that he has to persuade the Father to answer their prayers: the Father is only too ready to do so because, as Jesus has assured them of his own love, so they may be assured of the Father's direct and personal love for them. This is not simply a matter of their sharing in his general love for the world (John 3:16); it is a token of the Father's appreciation of their love for his Son and their belief in him as the one whom the Father has sent.[14] Thanks to their loving and believing reception of him, they have received 'authority to become God's children' (John 1:12), and as children they have direct access to the Father with the confidence that he welcomes them and gladly attends to their requests.

Jesus is returning to the Father who sent him, having fulfilled his mission in the world; but he remains the revealer of the Father to those of whom he now takes his leave – with this difference, that he now reveals him through the Spirit.

16:29, 30 **His disciples say, 'Now at last you do speak plainly; this is no parable that you are telling. Now we know that you know everything and have no need to be asked questions: because of this we believe that you have come forth from God.'**

As Jesus has continued talking to them, the perplexity with which they received his earlier words about going away has begun to give place to clearer understanding: now they do not feel that he is talking in riddles. Their belief in him as the revealer whom God has sent has been confirmed because he not only answers their questions with convincing authority; he even anticipates their questions. There may be an allusion to the unvoiced uncertainties which could only with difficulty be framed as articulate questions: Jesus shows the ability to read them and answer them without their having first to be put into words. The verb *erōtaō* is ambiguous here as in verse 23 above, but whereas there it more probably denotes asking for things, here it more probably refers to the asking of questions.

16:31, 32 **'Do you now believe?' Jesus answered them. 'Mark this: the hour is coming – indeed it has come – for you to be scattered, each one to his home,**[15] **and leave me alone. But I am not alone, because the Father is with me.'**

Jesus read their hearts better than they knew. Not only could he answer their unspoken questions: he could assess the strength of their belief in him. It was sincere and genuine, bound up with their love for him, but it was about to be exposed to a test such as they had not imagined. For all their faith and love, they would abandon him in the hour of his greatest need. Peter had already been warned of the impending collapse of his resolution (John 13:38), but they would all prove unequal to the coming test. If their support was all that their Lord had to rely on, it would prove a broken reed. But the Father's presence and support were assured to him (cf. John 8:29); confident of these, he would go forward.

The oracle in Zech. 13:7 about the smitten shepherd and the scattered sheep is not quoted here, as it is in the corresponding passage in Mark 14:27, but there is an implied allusion to it. In Mark 14:27 the quotation is preceded by the words 'You will all take offence'; in this Gospel the mention of scattering is separated from that of taking offence (verse 1: 'I have told you this so that you may not take offence'), but the logical link between the two is not broken.

16:33 'I have told you this so that you may have peace in me. In the world you have tribulation, but take courage! I have overcome the world.'

There are two spheres of existence: 'in me' and 'in the world'. That those who are in Christ inevitably suffer tribulation in the world is the consistent witness of the NT writers. They are encouraged, indeed, to welcome such tribulation as a token of their Lord's approval and a harbinger of eternal bliss (cf. Rom. 8:17; Phil. 1:28). With this assurance they may well enjoy inward peace. A comparison of verse 33 with verse 1 suggests that to have peace in Jesus is the antithesis to taking offence at him.

The peace which his people have in him is not only the peace which he gives (cf. John 14:27); it is the peace which he himself enjoys and which he shares with them. It is theirs as they remain in him, participating in his life. The world which inflicts tribulation on them is his enemy as well as theirs (cf. John 15:18–25). But it is a beaten enemy: the cross which the Lord in spirit has already embraced marked his triumph and the world's downfall. His triumph, like his peace, is shared by his people. The 'victory that overcomes the world', it is affirmed in 1 John 5:4 f., is 'our faith' – the faith that 'believes that Jesus is the Son of God'. It is this faith that unites his people to him, so that his victory becomes theirs also.

> As surely as he overcame,
>   And triumphed once for you,
> So surely you that love his name
>   Shall triumph in him too.

NOTES

1. In Mark 14:27 RSV translates 'you will all fall away'; what is meant is indicated clearly in John 16:32 ('you will be scattered').
2. See comment on John 9:22 (p. 221, with n. 6).
3. With reference to what is said of Phinehas in Num. 25:13 the rabbinical commentary *Numbers Rabba* 21.4 asks: 'Did he then bring an offering, that power to make atonement should be attributed to him? By this you may learn that every one who sheds the blood of the godless is like one who brings an offering.' But this inference was by no means universally admitted among the rabbis.
4. The supper-table conversation of Luke 22:35–38 presents a noteworthy parallel to this warning.
5. 'I will send' (Gk. *pempsō*), as in 15:26.
6. A correlation between 'advocate' and 'accuser' appears in the saying of Rabbi Eliezer ben Jacob in *Pirqê Abôt* 4:11: 'He who does one precept has acquired

for himself one advocate (p'raqlit, loanword from Gk. paraklētos), and he who commits one transgression has acquired for himself one accuser' (qaṭēgôr, loanword from Gk. katēgôr or katēgoros). See pp. 307, n. 10.

7. Cf. the two earlier instances of elenchō in this Gospel: in 3:20 (meaning 'expose') and in 8:46 (meaning 'convict').

8. In verses 16 and 17 'you see' is theōreite, while 'you will see' is opsesthe; this is evidence enough that John intends no distinction in meaning between theōreō and horaō (of which opsomai is used as the future). These two occurrences of the present theōreite have really a future reference: Jesus' departure is so imminent that the present tense is used.

9. The Alexandrine codex and the majority of later witnesses add 'because I am going to the Father' at the end of verse 16, supplying the clause from verse 17.

10. In the last clause of verse 22 the textual witnesses vary between the present airei, 'takes away', and the future arei, 'will take away'.

11. In verse 21 both tiktō and gennaō are used of the mother's role in giving birth (for gennaō cf. 1:13; 3:3–8).

12. Heb. ḥeblô shel māshiaḥ (Babylonian Talmud, tractate Sanhedrin 98b). There is probably an allusion to this concept in 'the beginning of the sufferings' (lit. 'birthpangs') in Mark 13:8.

13. Cf. Matt. 6:9; 7:7–11; Luke 11:2, 9–13.

14. In the last clause of verse 27 our witnesses vary between 'from God' and 'from the Father'; the latter reading may have been influenced by the first clause of verse 28. The preposition rendered 'from' in both clauses is para; in the similar clause ('from God') at the end of verse 30 it is apo. There is no difference in meaning.

15. Gk. eis ta idia, as in 1:11; 19:27.

CHAPTER 17

III. The Prayer of Consecration (17:1–26)

The theme of the upper-room discourses finds its conclusion in the prayer of chapter 17, commonly called our Lord's high-priestly prayer – a designation which it is said to have first received from the Lutheran theologian David Chytraeus (1530–1600).[1] It is a fitting designation, for our Lord in this prayer consecrates himself for the sacrifice in which he is simultaneously both priest and victim. At the same time it is a prayer of consecration on behalf of those for whom the sacrifice is offered – the disciples who were present in the upper room and those who would subsequently come to faith through their testimony. Comparing the part it plays in the Gospel with similar literary compositions elsewhere Ernst Käsemann has called this prayer 'the testament of Jesus'.[2] This description may be applicable in terms of form criticism but, if content is to be considered, his 'testament' should rather be recognized in the preceding discourses, addressed directly to the disciples.

John Knox, on his death-bed in 1572, asked his wife to read to him John 17, 'where', he said, 'I cast my first anchor.'[3] And almost his last words show how much his mind dwelt on this chapter, with its implications for 'the troubled church of God, the spouse of Jesus Christ, despised of the world but precious in his sight'.[4] He clearly appreciated that the church's true life is lived on a higher plane than the turbulent political stage in which he had been so much involved and with which he was by now so thoroughly disillusioned.

1. JESUS ASKS THE FATHER TO GLORIFY HIM (17:1–5)

17:1, 2 Having spoken thus, Jesus raised his eyes heavenwards and said, 'Father, the hour has come. Glorify thy Son, so that thy Son may glorify thee, since thou hast given him authority over all flesh, in order that he may give eternal life to all that thou hast given to him.'

Jesus now turns from holding communion with his disciples to hold communion with his Father on their behalf. While this is his prayer of consecration in view of the impending sacrifice of the cross, yet in some ways it presupposes the presentation and acceptance of that sacrifice and becomes the prototype of the perpetual intercession in which, as his people's ascended high priest, he is engaged on their behalf at the Father's right hand.[5]

On repeated occasions throughout the Gospel we have been told that his 'hour had not yet come' (the first of these occasions being at John 2:4). Now, by his own testimony, it 'has come'. Anticipating its arrival, he had said a short time before, 'The hour has come for the Son of Man to be glorified' (John 12:23); now he prays that he may indeed be glorified. None can glorify him but the Father: unlike others, he seeks 'the glory which comes from the only God' (John 5:44). The cross, as he knows full well, is to be the vehicle of that glory, and he prays that he may so accept it as to bring glory to his Father in turn.

He will glorify his Father by doing his will, even by enduring the cross, and fulfilling the Father's purpose of blessing for many by means of that cross. His acceptance of the cross, indeed, is an exercise of that authority which the Father has given him 'over all flesh' – i.e. over all the human race.[6] It is on the cross that his kingship is proclaimed (cf. 19:19); it is through the cross that he will discharge his Father's commission to him to bless his people with eternal life. His people are here described (as earlier in John 6:37, 39) as the sum total of those whom the Father has given him. If the predestinarian note seems here to be absolute, it is modified below in verse 12. Jesus has previously spoken of himself as giving his flesh 'for the life of the world' (John 6:51) and has made it plain that faith in him is the condition for receiving this life (John 6:40). Now that life is defined more precisely.

17:3 'And this is eternal life: to know thee, the only true God, and the one whom thou hast sent – Jesus Christ.'

Eternal life, then, consists in the knowledge of God. Since the knowledge of God is mediated through the revealer whom God has sent, and is indeed embodied in that revealer, the knowledge of the revealer is one with the knowledge of the God who is revealed. Nor is this knowledge a matter simply of intellectual apprehension: it involves a personal relationship. The Father and the Son know each other in a mutuality of love, and by the knowledge of God men and woman are admitted to the mystery of this divine love, being loved by God and loving him – and one another – in return. This is the basis of the unity for which Jesus prays in verses 20–23 below.

17:4, 5 'I have glorified thee on earth by fulfilling the work which thou gavest me to do; and now, Father, do thou glorify

me with thyself with the glory which I had with thee before the world existed.'

Up to the present moment, he had glorified his Father on earth by obediently carrying out his will. One act of obedience remained to be performed – one, moreover, in which the Father would be supremely glorified – but this act is not excluded from Jesus' present thought. On the eve of the sacrifice of the cross, as he consecrates himself for it, he is so totally committed to it that he speaks of it as already accomplished. Any mention of his 'finished work' would be unthinkable if it did not embrace that greatest work of all.

The glory which he would receive from the Father would be the glory which he enjoyed in his presence before creation, in that 'beginning' in which the Word was eternally with the Father (John 1:2). Yet, since the resumption of that glory would be attained by way of the cross, it would inevitably have a new dimension which was absent from it 'before the world existed'. John, unlike Paul, does not set Jesus' coming exaltation in contrast to the disgrace of the cross (cf. Phil. 2:6–11), but he thinks of the cross as the essential stage towards that glory which will be enhanced for Jesus because it will now be shared with those who have believed in him. Of this new dimension of glory Jesus has already spoken to his disciples: 'If God has been glorified in him (the Son), God will also glorify him in himself' (John 13:32).

2. REVELATION TO THE DISCIPLES (17:6–8)

17:6–8 **'I have manifested thy name to the people whom thou gavest me out of the world. They were thine, and thou gavest them to me, and they have kept thy word. Now they have come to know that all that thou hast given me comes from thee. I have given them the words which thou gavest to me, and they have received them and have learned in truth that I came forth from thee, and they have believed that thou didst send me.'**

Jesus speaks as the revealer of the Father. The Father's name is his character, which Jesus has manifested to his disciples, pre-eminently in his actions and words there in the upper room (13:1–16:33). The 'world' as a whole had failed to recognize Jesus as the revealer of the Father (cf. 12:37), but a select company of men and woman (*anthrōpoi*) was given to him 'out of the world' – those who are called 'his own people' in John 13:1. They showed themselves to be truly 'his own people' by believing in him, acknowledging that his teaching came from God and accepting it accordingly. They 'kept' the word of God which he communicated to them by laying it up in their hearts and obeying it in their lives. They thus proved in experience the truth of his promise: 'If any one is willing to do the will of God, he will know whether my teaching comes from God or whether I speak on my own initiative' (John 7:17). In recognizing that Jesus' teaching came from God they recognized at the same time that he himself came from God, as the Father's 'sent one'.

3. PRAYER FOR THE DISCIPLES (17:9–18)

17:9, 10 'I pray for them. I do not pray for the world, but for those whom thou hast given me, because they are thine. All that is mine is thine, and what is thine is mine; and I have been glorified in them.'

For his disciples, then, Jesus prays. If he does not pray for the world, it is not because he had no concern for the world; he is, indeed, the Saviour of the world (John 4:42; cf. 3:17; 12:47). But the salvation of the world depends on the witness of those whom the Father has given him 'out of the world' (see verses 21, 23), and it is they who need his intercession at this junction. If it is the Father who has given them to him, they belong originally to the Father; because the Father has given them to the Son, they belong equally to the Son. In the reciprocal love which unites the Father and the Son, the Father withholds nothing from the Son: 'all that is mine is thine', says Jesus, 'and what is thine is mine.' But had he truly been 'glorified' in his disciples? He had warned them that they would soon be scattered and leave him alone (John 16:32); he had warned their most vocal member that before cockcrow he would have denied him three times (13:38). Apart from that, their unintelligent questions and interruptions as he talked to them in the upper room showed how far they still were from appreciating thier Master's purpose or the seriousness of the hour which had now come for him – and for them. But he looked at them with the insight of faith, hope and love, and realized their present devotion and their potential for the future. In themselves they were weak indeed, but with the Father's enabling grace and the guidance and illumination of his Spirit, they would fulfil the mission with which they were now being entrusted and bring glory to their Master in fulfilling it. So confident of this is he that he speaks in the perfect tense: 'I have been glorified in them.'

17:11, 12 'Now I am no longer in the world, but they are in

the world, while I am on my way to thee. Holy Father, keep them in thy name which thou hast given to me, that they may be one as we are. When I was with them, I kept them in thy name which thou hast given to me: yes, I have guarded them, and not one of them has been lost, except for him who was destined to be lost, in order that the scripture might be fulfilled.

Jesus was on his way to the Father, and would no longer be with his disciples 'in the world' to guard[7] them as he had done hitherto, but the Father would guard them by his name, that is, by his power. The name of God in the OT denotes not only his character (as in verse 6 above), but also his power; cf. Ps. 20:1 ('the name of the God of Jacob protect you!'); Ps. 54:1 ('Save me, O God, by thy name', where 'by thy name' stands in synonymous parallelism with 'by thy might'); Prov. 18:10 ('The name of the LORD is a strong tower'). By the Father's power, imparted to Jesus, Jesus himself had guarded them as a treasure entrusted to him by the Father, and now he gives an account of his stewardship. All of them were safe but one, and that was the one to whose defection the scripture pointed forward, as Jesus had said before when he announced to his disciples that there was a traitor among them (John 13:18–30). The reference to one 'who was destined to be lost' (literally, 'the son of perdition') is paralleled in 2 Thess. 2:3 where the 'man of lawlessness' is so described, but the expression does not have quite the same force in the two passages.[8] Despite the predestinarian flavour of the language, Judas was not lost against his will but with his consent. He might have responded to Jesus' last appeal to him in his gesture of fellowship at the supper table, but he chose to respond instead to the great adversary. Jesus has no responsibility for Judas' fatal decision. Judas, like the other disciples, had been given by the Father to the Son, but even among those so given apostasy is a solemn possibility.

17:13 'Now I am on my way to thee, but I say this (while I am still) in the world so that they may have my joy fulfilled in themselves.'

Earlier that evening Jesus had said to his disciples, 'I have told you this so that my joy may be in you and your joy may be fulfilled' (John 15:11). 'This' was the assurance that they were being welcomed into the mutual relationship of love that had already existed from the beginning between the Father and himself. Now, so to speak, he reports to the Father what he has said to them. If they hear him as he now prays, the assurance he had given them will be confirmed in their minds; moreover, not only does he state the purpose of his giving to them this assurance but he prays that the Father may fulfil that purpose within them: that the joy which he himself finds in the Father's love may be fully reproduced in their hearts. The example of his intercession for them may further encourage them to approach the Father in his name: 'ask, and you will receive', he had told them, 'so that your joy may be complete' (John 16:24).

17:14–16 'I have given them thy word and the world has hated them, because they do not belong to the world just as I do not belong to the world. I ask thee, not to take them out of the world, but to keep them from the evil one. They do not belong to the world just as I do not belong to the world.'

The teaching they have received from Jesus comprises all that God delivered to him to impart to them: 'thy word'. The singular 'word' here is the sum-total of all the 'words' of verse 8. The unresponsive 'world' had not believed him when he delivered his Father's message in person (John 5:47; 12:37–50); it was unlikely to give it any more credence when it came from the lips of the disciples. Had this 'world' embraced their prospective hearers in their entirety, the outlook for their witness would have been bleak indeed; as it is, this is the godless 'world', devoid of any appreci- ation of heavenly truth[9] – a world to which they belong no more than their Master himself does. (This is emphasized by repetition – in verses 14b and 16.) As this world had not only rejected what he said but manifested hostility to himself personally, so it would manifest hostility to his followers. He had just warned them that it would be so (John 15:18–25); now, again, he reports to his Father what he had said to them.

Hostile as the world is, however, they are not to be removed from it. 'The whole world lies in the power of the evil one' who dominates it as a usurper (1 John 5:19; cf. 1 John 2:13 f.; 3:12; 5:18); Jesus prays that they may be delivered from him, just as he had already taught them to pray for such deliverance (Matt. 6:13). The genitive *ponērou* might indeed be construed as neuter ('keep them from evil') rather than masculine ('from the evil one'); but the reference is more probably to the being who has been thrice mentioned already as 'the ruler of this world' (John 12:31; 14:30; 16:11).

17:17, 18 'Sanctify them by means of the truth; thy word is truth. As thou didst send me into the world, so also I have sent them into the world.'

The statement 'I have sent them' is perhaps proleptic: his actual sending of them is recorded later, after his return from the dead (John 20:21). Since they are to be sent into hostile territory, to reclaim it for its rightful owner, they must be given spiritual protection. Negatively, they must be preserved from the power of the usurper, whose occupied domain they have invaded; positively, they must be 'sanctified'. This involves their consecration for the task now entrusted to them; it involves further their inward purification and endowment with all the spiritual resources necessary for carrying out that task. This purification and endowment are the work of the Spirit, but here Jesus declares the instrument of that work to be 'the truth' – the truth embodied in the Father's 'word' which Jesus had given to the disciples as he himself had received it from the Father (verses 8, 14). The very message which they are to proclaim in his name will exercise its sanctifying effect on them: that message is the continuation of his message, just as their mission in the world is the extension of his mission.

So, the disciples were given to Christ by the Father 'out of the world' (verse 6), they therefore no longer 'belong to the world' (verses 14, 16), although they remain 'in the world' (verse 11) and are not immediately to be taken out of it (verse 15). They not merely remain in it because they can do nothing else: they are positively sent into it as their Master's agents and messengers. If Jesus does not pray explicitly for the world at this time (verse 9), yet his prayer for the disciples involves hope for the world. God's electing grace is not exercised in such a way that the non-elect are lost, but rather with the purpose that through the elect the non-elect may receive his blessing.[10]

4. THE SON'S CONSECRATION OF HIMSELF (17:19)

17:19 'And for their sake I sanctify myself, so that they themselves also may be sanctified in truth.'

If the disciples are to be effectively set apart for the work which they must do, the Son must first set himself apart for the work which *he* must do. He therefore consecrates himself to God on their behalf: Chrysostom paraphrases 'I sanctify myself' as 'I offer myself in sacrifice'. Here is a Johannine counterpart to the Gethsemane prayer (for other counterparts see John 12:27f.; 18:11).

It was not what Jesus' executioners did to him, but what he did himself in his self-offering, that makes his death a prevailing sacrifice 'for the life of the world' (John 6:51; cf. 1:29). Here, then, the priest dedicates the sacrificial victim: it is because priest and victim are one that the sacrifice is not only completely voluntary but uniquely efficacious.[11]

3. PRAYER FOR THE CHURCH TO COME (17:20–23)

17:20, 21 'Nor is it only for these that I pray, but also for those who believe in me through their word, that they may all be one, as thou, Father, art in me and I in thee, that they in their turn may be (one) in us, so that the world may believe that thou didst send me.'

The disciples are the nucleus of the community of the new age. As a result of their being sent into the world with the message of life, others will believe in Jesus through their testimony. For those others also Jesus prays, and specifically that they may all be one.[12] The unity for which he prays is a unity of love; it is, in fact, their participation in the unity of love which subsists eternally between the Father and the Son. 'All will recognize that you are disciples of mine', Jesus had said to the eleven, 'if you have love among one another' (John 13:35). Their manifest oneness in love would give public confirmation both of their relationship with Jesus and of his with the Father. The world, which thus far has not recognized him, will learn from the witness of the disciples' love that he is indeed the sent one of God; it will accept their testimony 'that the Father has sent his Son as the Saviour of the world' (1 John 4:14). Then the usurper's control will be thrown off and the world, at last acknowledging its rightful Lord, will respond in faith to his love for it.

17:22, 23 'I have given them the glory which thou hast given me, that they may be one as we are one – I in them and thou in me, so that they may be made perfect in one – in order that the world may know that thou hast sent me and hast loved them just as thou hast loved me.'

Earlier, the Evangelist has observed that Jesus, by his death, would 'gather into one the dispersed children of God' (John 11:52). It is this same unity for which Jesus now prays, and his language makes it plain that it is a unity of love – a unity which has its root within the soul but is manifested in outward action. Otherwise the world could not see it and be convinced by its witness to the divine revelation in Christ. It is no invisible unity that is prayed for here. 'I in them', says Jesus – but they are also in him (John 15:4). 'Thou in me' – but he is also in the Father (John 14:10). If the Father is in him and he is in them, then the Father is in them: they are drawn into the very life of God, and the life of God is perfect love.[13] That this vital unity through Christ with God is maintained and attested by the indwelling Spirit is clear, even if this aspect of the Spirit's ministry is not spelled out expressly in these chapters as it is elsewhere in the NT (cf. 1 John 4:13, 'By this we know that we abide in him and he in us, because he has given us of his own Spirit'). If Christ is in his people and the Father is in him, it follows that they share in the eternal love which the Father has for the Son.

6. The glorified church (17:24)

17:24 'Father, as for (all) that thou hast given me, my desire is that, where I am, they also may be with me, so that they may behold my glory which thou hast given me, for thou didst love me before the world's foundation.'

The clause 'as for what thou hast given me' at the beginning of the sentence refers more naturally to the sum-total of believers (as in verse 2) than to the eternal glory; hence 'all' is added in the translation above to make the sense plain.

Jesus has prayed to be reinvested with the glory which he had with the Father before the world existed (verse 5). (He enjoyed the Father's love together with the glory before all worlds,[14] but he has no need to pray to be reinvested with the love; that he enjoyed in fullness throughout his life on earth.) Now he prays that his followers may behold this glory[15] and, by implication, have a share in it.[16] If the gift of glory to the Son is the token of the Father's love for him, those who share that love will naturally share the glory. The disciples had seen the divine glory in the incarnate Word on earth (John 1:14); they will see it more fully when they live in the presence of the glorified Lord – not, perhaps, because he will then be endowed with more of that glory but because they will be better able to behold it.[17]

Jesus, then, has prayed first for the original disciples (verses 9–18), then for the church on earth throughout the ages (verses 20–23), and now for the glorified church of the future, united with him in the place which he is going to prepare for it (verse 24; cf. John 14:3).

7. Conclusion (17:25, 26)

17:25, 26 'Righteous Father, the world has not known thee, but I have known thee, and these have come to know that thou didst send me. I have made known thy name to them and will

continue to make it known, so that the love with which thou hast loved me may be in them, and I myself may be in them.'

In these closing words the prayer is summed up.

By worldly standards of success Jesus had little to show for his mission. He had come to make the Father known, but the vast majority of his hearers refused the knowledge which he offered them. The merest handful of men and women – a very unimpressive company at that – had recognized him as the sent one of God and had come to know the Father in him. Yet to them his mission on earth was confidently entrusted, as he dedicated them to the Father to this end. One further revelation of the divine glory remained to be given to them: the impartation of the knowledge of God would be consummated in his self-sacrifice. The Father's name, already declared[18] to the disciples by the Son, would be declared in the Son's death on the cross more eloquently than in any other way.

For the rest, his prayer is that the Father's love, which he himself enjoys in perfection, may remain within and among them, as he himself does. Is he not the embodiment of the love of God? 'I am with you' is good indeed (Matt. 28:20); 'I am in you' is better still.[19]

Now, then, he goes forth to his final and fullest manifestation of the Father's love and glory.

NOTES

1. '*Precatio summi sacerdotis*' was his phrase.
2. *The Testament of Jesus* is the title of the English translation of Käsemann's monograph on John 17 (London, 1968).
3. Cf. Richard Bannatyne's account of Knox's last illness and death in John Knox, *Works*, ed. D. Laing, vi (Edinburgh, 1895), p. 643.
4. *Ibid.*, p. 641.
5. Cf. Heb. 7:25.
6. Cf. Matt. 11:25 with its parallel Luke 11:22; Matt. 28:18. For 'all flesh' see Luke 3:6 (from Isa. 40:5); Acts 2:17 (from Joel 2:28).
7. John's characteristic interchange of synonyms is illustrated by his use of two verbs meaning 'keep' or 'guard' in verses 11 and 12: *tēreō* in verse 11 and both *tēreō* (in the imperfect tense *etēroun*) and *phylassō* (in the aorist *ephylaxa*) in verse 12.
8. However, R. H. Lightfoot (acknowledging indebtedness to R. W. H. Phillips), observes that 'in this gospel the day of the Lord is regarded as realized in the life, the work, and, above all, the death of Jesus Christ', and concludes that therefore 'St. John invites those who welcome his interpretation of the Gospel to see in Judas "the man of sin, the son of perdition" ' (*St. John's Gospel*, p. 301). This I find quite improbable, despite the designation of Judas as a *diabolos* in John 6:70 f. (see p. 166).
9. Cf. John 1:10c; 7:7; 8:23; 12:31; 15:18, 19; 16:20, 33.
10. Thus Abraham, the paradigm of divine election, was chosen not only for blessing on himself and his posterity, but for blessing to 'all the families of the earth' (Gen. 12:2, 3; Gal. 3:6–9, 14). The Servant of the LORD, who is the Elect

One *par excellence*, brings blessing to many because of his election (Isa. 42:1; 53:11, 12).

11. This is brought out fully in the letter to the Hebrews where, in contrast to involuntary animal sacrifices which can never take away sins, Christ's spontaneous offering of himself to do the will of God effects the sanctifying and 'perfecting' of his people (Heb. 10:1–14).

12. On this see ch. 7 ('Will the church ever be one?') in R. P. Martin, *The Family and the Fellowship* (Exeter, 1979), pp. 86–96.

13. The classic treatment of this theme is Henry Scougal's *The Life of God in the Soul of Man*, first published in 1677 (London: Inter-Varsity Press, 1961).

14. The *katabolē* of the world (cf. Matt. 13:35; 25:34; Luke 11:50; Eph. 1:4; Heb. 4:3; 9:26; 1 Pet. 1:20; Rev. 13:8 17:8) is the 'laying down' of its foundation.

15. Cf. Stephen's experience (Acts 7:55, 56).

16. Cf. 2 Cor. 4:18.

17. Cf. 1 Cor. 13:12.

18. In verse 6 the verb 'declare' in *phaneroō*; here (verse 26) it is *gnōrizō* – a further example of John's variation of synonyms. 'I will continue to make it known' could be an echo of Ps. 22:22, quoted in Heb. 2:12 (where the verb used is *apangellō*).

19. This indwelling cannot be separated from the Spirit's indwelling, promised in 14:17. Cf. 1 John 3:24.

CHAPTER 18

D. PASSION AND TRIUMPH (John 18:1–20:31)

I. The Passion Narrative (18:1–19:42)

1. ARREST IN THE GARDEN (18:1–11)

18:1, 2 **Having said this, Jesus with his disciples went out across the Kedron ravine, (to a place) where there was a garden, into which he and his disciples entered. Judas, his betrayer, also knew the place, because Jesus had often met with his disciples there.**

The phrase 'having said this' refers to the words spoken in the upper room, and more particularly to the prayer of consecration in chapter 17. In the narrative which follows Jesus puts his self-consecration into effect.

Jesus now leaves the upper room and leads his disciples out of the city eastwards down into the Kidron valley and up the other side. *Kidron* reproduces the Hebrew spelling and pronunciation; the word is derived from a root meaning 'dark' (from which comes also OT *Kedar*, an Arab community so called from their black tents, mentioned in Cant. 1:5). *Kedron* here as in the LXX (2 Sam. 15:23, etc.), represents the Greek spelling and pronunciation. Some copyists or editors of the NT text misunderstood it here to be related to Gk. *kedros* ('cedar') and changed the form of the definite article before it so as to yield the sense 'the ravine of the cedars' – which is quite inappropriate. The word translated 'ravine' is Gk. *cheimarrhous*, meaning literally a stream that flows in winter; here it denotes a wadi, dry for the greater part of the year but a torrent in rainy seasons. The Kidron valley (*Wadi en-Nar*) pursues a long winding course south-east to the Dead Sea, down which Ezekiel in his vision saw the river flowing which rose under the sanctuary threshold (Ezek. 47:1 ff.; cf. Zech. 14:8).[1] Opposite the temple area the bottom of the valley is over 200 feet below the platform of the outer court. East of the valley rises the Mount of Olives, on the lower slopes of which was the 'garden' to which Jesus and his disciples went. Mark (14:32) and Matthew (26:36) call it Gethsemane, '(the place of) the oil-press'. This was no doubt the place to which Jesus went night by night during Holy Week (Luke 21:37), but John may mean that it had served as a rendezvous for him and his disciples during earlier visits to Jerusalem also. It is plain that, having consecrated himself for the impending sacrifice, he now made no attempt to hide from his enemies, but went to the place where Judas would normally expect to find him.

18:3 So Judas, taking the cohort, and officers from the chief priests and the Pharisees, comes there with lanterns and torches and weapons.

Nowhere is John's independence of the Synoptic narrative more apparent than in his unambiguous statement that Roman soldiers, in addition to temple police, were involved in the arrest of Jesus.[2] Unfortunately many of our standard translations do not bring this out clearly enough. In the AV and (surprisingly) RSV the reader would naturally suppose that the 'band of soldiers' as well as the 'officers' were procured from the chief priests and Pharisees. The distinction between the two is made a little clearer in the RV because of its precise punctuation, but the retention of the colourless word 'band (of soldiers)' to represent Gk. *speira*, which is the technical equivalent of Lat. *cohors*, obscures the fact that Roman soldiers are meant. The NEB is more explicit, although it prefers 'detachment' to the technical term 'cohort': 'So Judas took a detachment of soldiers, and police provided by the chief priests and the Pharisees, equipped with lanterns, torches and weapons, and made his way to the garden.' Here the 'detachment' of soldiers is clearly distinguished from the police (members of the temple guard, as in 7:32) provided by the Sanhedrin (called 'the chief priests and the Pharisees' as in 11:57, etc.). An auxiliary cohort, such as garrisoned the Antonia fortress north-west of the temple area, comprised a paper strength of 1,000 men (760 infantry and 240 cavalry); it was commanded by a military tribune (Gk. *chiliarchos*, lit. 'commander of a thousand'), like Claudius Lysias, who occupied this post twenty-seven years later, at the time of Paul's arrest (Acts 21:31 ff.). We need not suppose that every member of the cohort was called out on the present occasion, but evidently a sufficiently large detachment was sent to warrant the presence of the officer commanding the whole garrison (verse 12). The fact that Roman troops were there as well as temple police implies that the Jewish authorities had already approached the military command, probably indicating that they expected armed resistance to be offered. That it was the Jewish authorities and not the Romans who took the initiative is shown by the fact that, after the arrest, the Jewish authorities were allowed to take Jesus into their custody. When Judas is described as 'taking' the cohort and the police to the place, all that is meant is that he acted as their guide.

18:4–9 So Jesus, knowing everything that was about to happen to him, went out and said to them, 'Whom do you seek?' They answered him, 'Jesus the Nazarene.' He said to them, 'I am he'. (Judas, his betrayer, was also standing with them.) So, when he had said to them 'I am he', they went back and fell to the ground. So he asked them again, 'Whom do you seek?' They said, 'Jesus the Nazarene'. Jesus answered, 'I have told you I am he. If I am the one whom you seek, then, let these men begone.' This was to fulfil his previous saying: 'Of those whom thou has given me I have lost none.'

The narrative proceeds in such a way as to show how Jesus took command of the situation. As the soldiers and police, led by Judas, approached the garden, Jesus came out to meet them and asked whom they were looking for. 'Jesus the Nazarene (Nazoraean)', said they – an expression which for our Evangelist, as for the other NT writers who use it, is synonymous with 'Jesus of Nazareth' (1:45), the designation by which he was commonly known. His reply, 'I am he' (Gk. *egō eimi*), can be understood on two levels, and this is probably the Evangelist's intention. On one level, it simply means 'I am he' in the ordinary sense, such as any man might use in similar circumstances. But in an appropriate setting *egō eimi* is more than that; it is a word of power, the equivalent of the God of Israel's self-identifying affirmation 'I am He'.[3] On the lips of Jesus it has already had something approaching this force in the Gospel of John (cf. 8:24, 28); and that it has this force here is plain from the retreat and prostration of those addressed. Twice they fall back, and when at last Jesus permits them to take him away, it is on condition that they let his disciples depart unmolested.

Thus in a sense he authorized the fulfilment of his prediction in John 16:32: 'The hour is coming – indeed it has come – for you to be scattered, each one to his home, and leave me alone.' But it is not these words that John quotes as being fulfilled on this occasion, but the words in the high-priestly prayer (John 17:12), where Jesus claims that he has kept all those whom the Father gave him. Since Judas the betrayer was standing there, John had no need here to repeat the exceptive words in the prayer: 'none of them has been lost, except for him who was destined to be lost' – the prodigal whose defection was not only the subject of prophetic foresight but also the result of his own deliberate choice. Otherwise Jesus accomplished 'the will of him who sent me, that I should lose nothing of all that he has given me, but raise it up (i.e. the whole community of faith) at the last day' (John 6:39; cf. 10:27–30). Since in the words of Jesus' prayer here quoted by John, as in similar passages elsewhere in the Gospel, the preservation referred to is spiritual, relating to eternal life, it has sometimes been thought that John's present comment is inappropriate, since it is preservation from physical harm that is in view here. But this is a superficial objection, betraying (as C. H. Dodd says) 'a failure to appreciate the way the evangelist's mind works'.[4] The Evangelist's thought moves on two levels, and in the Lord's intervention to save his disciples from physical harm he sees a parable of his saving them from eternal death.

One further point: John employs the same form of words to introduce a saying of Jesus as he employs elsewhere to introduce 'testimonies' from the prophetic scriptures (cf. verse 32). The words of Jesus could not have *less* validity than the words of the prophets.

18:10, 11 **Simon Peter, then, having a sword, drew it, struck the high priest's servant and cut off his right ear. (The servant's name was Malchus.) So Jesus said to Peter, 'Put your sword back in its sheath. Shall I not drink the cup which my Father has given me?'**

There was some attempt at resistance, but it was amateurish and ineffective, and Jesus immediately checked it. John agrees with Luke in saying that it was the man's *right* ear that Peter cut off; he agrees with Matthew in telling how Jesus ordered his well-meaning but misguided disciple to replace his sword. He alone of the Evangelists gives the man's name – not (if one may mention a far-fetched explanation) because he saw in the incident a fulfilment of Zech. 11:6, where 'his king' is Heb. *malkō*,[5] but (much more probably) because his record is based on first-hand acquaintance with the high priest's household (cf. verse 16). (Malchus was a common enough name in the Near East of that day.) The Lord's words 'Shall I not drink the cup which my Father has given me?' are reminiscent of his words of entreaty to his Father in Gethsemane, as reported in the Synoptic Gospels (see 12:27 for another Johannine parallel to the Gethsemane narrative). Peter's impulsive action was more likely to get himself and his companions into serious trouble than to do his Master any good, but even if it had a better chance of success, Jesus would now allow nothing to stand in the way of his bringing to completion the work which his Father had given him to do; any other course would have rendered his prayer of consecration meaningless. Provided his disciples' safety was assured, he would not seek his own.

Possibly, had this rash attempt at armed resistance not taken place, the Roman troops would have stood back and let the temple police make the arrest; as it was, they now came forward to lend a helping hand, and the only surprising element in the story is that, even so, the disciples were able to get clean away.

2. CHIEF-PRIESTLY INQUISITION (18:12–24)

18:12–14 **So the cohort and the military tribune, and the officers of the Jews, arrested Jesus and bound him, and led him first to Annas. He was father-in-law to Caiaphas, who was high priest that year. It was Caiaphas who had advised the Jews that it was expedient that one man should die for the people.**

As in verse 3 the two companies that had come to arrest Jesus – the Roman and the Jewish – are distinguished. With the 'cohort' its commanding officer (Gk. *chiliarchos*) is mentioned this time; as was said above, whatever the size of the Roman detachment was, it was large enough – or the situation was deemed serious enough – to warrant his presence. Whereas in verse 3 the temple police are said to have been sent by 'the chief priests and the Pharisees', here they are called 'the officers of the Jews'; in verse 12 and verse 14 'the Jews' are the Sanhedrin, the supreme council of seventy-one elders, over whom the reigning high priest presided by virtue of his office.

Annas had been high priest from AD 6 to 15; he was appointed to the office by Quirinius, governor of Syria, about the time when Judaea was reduced to the status of a minor Roman province, and was deposed nine years later by Valerius Gratus, prefect of Judaea.[6] But even after his removal he retained great power and prestige as senior ex-high priest. Several members of his family occupied the high-priesthood at various times throughout the half century following his deposition – five sons, one grandson and (as we are told here) one son-in-law, Caiaphas. John is our only authority (but a sufficient authority) for the information that the two men were related in this way. According to Josephus, Caiaphas's personal name was Joseph.[7] He was appointed to the high-priesthood in AD 18 by Valerius Gratus and held the office for eighteen years – a longer period than any other high priest in New Testament times. The fact that Pilate, Gratus's successor as prefect of Judaea, did not replace him when he came to the province in AD 26, may suggest that Caiaphas made it worth Pilate's while to leave him in office, or that prefect and high priest were able to establish a mutually advantageous understanding. Both were removed from their respective offices in AD 36 by Lucius Vitellius, governor of Syria.[8]

Caiaphas's advice that it was expedient that one man should die for the people has been recorded in John 11:49 f.[9]

The men who arrested Jesus, says John, 'led him first to Annas'.
Of this preliminary and informal inquiry in the house of Annas the
Synoptic evangelists say nothing; they concentrate on the more
official session of the court over which the reigning high priest
presided. John, for his part, makes but cursory mention of the role
of Caiaphas in his trial narrative. Anyone undertaking to write a
full account of the trial of Jesus would have to do equal justice to
the evidence of John and the Synoptists; here we are concerned
with the exegesis of John's account, and only incidental reference
to Synoptic parallels is called for. The editor of one of our more
important non-Greek witnesses to the text, the Sinaitic Syriac version of the Gospels, was so concerned about the harmonization of
the Johannine and Synoptic accounts that he changed John's order
to make it appear that Jesus was taken immediately from Annas to
Caiaphas and that all that is recorded from verse 15 to verse 27
took place in the house of Caiaphas. After verse 13 this edition
exhibits the following sequence: verses 24, 14, 15, 19–23, 16–18
and then 25 ff.[10] (This sequence has the incidental effect of making
the story of Peter's denial run on consecutively, without interrup-
tion – which is not an improvement on John's original sequence.)
A more unobtrusive attempt at harmonization appears in the AV at
verse 24.

18:15, 16 **Simon Peter was following Jesus and so was another
disciple. That disciple was known to the high priest and went in
with Jesus into the high priest's courtyard, but Peter was (left)
standing at the door outside. So the other disciple, who was
known to the high priest, went out and spoke to the doorkeeper,
and brought Peter in.**

Two questions of identification arise here: who is the 'high priest'
mentioned in these verses, and who was the 'other disciple'? As
John's narrative proceeds, it is natural to think that the high priest
was Annas. True, he was no longer reigning high priest, but once
a man had occupied the office, the title would continue to be given
to him in an 'emeritus' sense. Luke similarly gives Annas the title
'high priest' in Luke 3:2 (in association with Caiaphas) and Acts
4:6. (Moreover, the word in the plural, commonly translated 'chief
priests', is used of members of the high-priestly families and temple
establishment in general, but no single member would be called
'the high priest' unless he had actually served in this capacity.)
More interesting is the question of the identity of the 'other
disciple', to whom the Evangelist probably owes his knowledge of
the course of events at this point.[11] We should not too readily
conclude that he was the beloved disciple whom we have met in

the upper room; in that case the Evangelist would probably have made the identification explicitly. He may have been a Jerusalem disciple who had the entrée into top society. The word 'known' (Gk. *gnōstos*) suggests something more intimate than the knowledge an archbishop or prime minister might have of his fishmonger; it means an acquaintance, sometimes even a relative (like 'friend' in the Scots sense); in Luke 2:44 it is used in close conjunction with kinsfolk. Whoever he was, he was able to walk in unquestioned; then, when he found that Peter, not presuming to enter, had stayed outside, a word from him to the servant-girl who was attending to the door was sufficient to gain admission for Peter too.

18:17, 18 **So the servant-girl who was acting as door-keeper said to Peter, 'You are not one of this man's disciples too, are you?' He said, 'I am not.' The servants and officers had lit a charcoal fire, because it was cold, and were standing and warming themselves.**

The servant-girl presumably knew the 'other disciple' to be a follower of Jesus, and when she saw him bringing in Peter, she said, in effect: 'Oh no, not another!' Her question to Peter is cast in the form expecting the answer 'No', and Peter seizes the cue and gives that answer. Unlike the 'other disciple', he was was not accustomed to entering the headquarters of persons in high society, and the unfamiliarity of these surroundings added to the general sense of uneasiness that made him lose his nerve. For all the confidence with which, in the upper room, he had declared his readiness to lay down his life for his Master (13:37), the event was to prove that his Master knew Peter better than Peter knew himself (13:38).

The charcoal fire, burning in a brazier in the courtyard, reappears in verse 25, where Peter has joined the group of palace servants and temple police warming themselves at it. In itself it is of little significance, but it seems to have burned itself into someone's memory, for Mark (14:54) and Luke (22:55 f.) both mention it in their account of Peter's denial. Moreover, it confirms, against the opinion of those who try to reconstruct the course of events in accordance with their conception of what 'more probably' took place, that there was indeed a nocturnal examination of Jesus. (This was necessary if they were to bring him before Pilate during business hours next day; Pilate, like any other Roman official of the time, would begin his duties at dawn and hope to have them over by 10 or 11 a.m.) The Jewish authorities, 'because of the festival, were in a hurry. Hence there was every reason to hold the unusual night session if they were to catch the Procurator at the right

moment. The quite unessential detail of the fire . . . supports the
Marcan version. Why light a fire – an act of some extravagance –
if anyone was sleeping through the night?'[12]

18:19–21 So the high priest asked Jesus about his disciples and
about his teaching. Jesus answered him: 'I have spoken openly
to the world. I always taught in synagogue and in the temple,
where all the Jews come together; I said nothing in secret. Why
do you ask me? Ask those who have heard what I said to them.
See, these people know what I said.'

If Annas suspected Jesus of subversive speech and action, he
wanted to know how many people were implicated in the subver-
sion, and what its nature was. Hence he interrogated Jesus about
his disciples and about the substance of his teaching. About his
disciples Jesus said nothing – wishing perhaps, as shortly before,
when he was arrested (verse 8), to distract the authorities' attention
from them. But even if that motive for saying nothing about them
had not been present, what could he have said? Not much to their
credit – certainly nothing that would have encouraged his inquisi-
tors to suppose that they need be taken as a serious threat. But he
had no reason to conceal the substance of his teaching, although at
the same time he had no need to repeat it. Since the beginning of
Holy Week he had been teaching daily in the temple court, not to
speak of earlier occasions when he had visited Jerusalem and taught
there. Elsewhere, as in Capernaum (John 6:59), he had taught in
synagogues, with equal publicity. 'The world', as in 7:4 and 12:19,
means 'everybody'. It was not in accordance with the best judicial
procedure in Israel to make an accused person incriminate himself,
and in this particular instance it was not necessary. His teaching
had been given in public, and many of his hearers were available
as witnesses; perhaps some of them were actually present in the
building, if that is the force of his words, 'See, these people know
what I said.' There was, of course, his instruction to the disciples
in the upper room, but that was hardly the kind of thing of which
the law would have taken cognizance, and it would have been lost
on Annas even if it had been repeated to him. Jesus therefore
claimed that, if his teaching was in question, evidence should be
heard in the normal way.

18:22, 23 When he said this, one of the officers standing by
gave Jesus a slap on the face, saying, 'Is that the way to answer
the high priest?' Jesus answered him: 'If I spoke wrongly, bear
witness to the wrong; if rightly, why do you strike me?'

The incident is quite similar to that recorded in Acts 23:2–5, where Paul appears before the Sanhedrin; in both places the correct way to address the high priest is brought up. Paul apologized (to the official, if not to the man) for calling Ananias a 'white-washed wall', admitting that his language contravened the law which forbade insulting words towards a judge or ruler (Exod. 22:28). But Jesus had used no insulting language in addressing the emeritus high priest; he had made a straightforward declaration of right. Hence, instead of apologizing, he protests against the temple policeman's rude action. If he had spoken amiss, then a formal charge of contempt of court should have been lodged against him; if there was nothing wrong with what he said, then the slap in the face which he had received was an unjustified assault.

18:24 So Annas sent him, (still) bound, to Caiaphas the high priest.

The AV rendering, 'Now Annas had sent him bound unto Caiaphas the high priest', which has an antecedent in the Geneva version, cannot be sustained. There are occasions when the context requires the aorist to be construed in a pluperfect sense (cf. 'had cut off' in verse 26), but this is not one. The pluperfect is completely ruled out by the conjunction *oun* ('so', 'therefore'), which is amply attested as part of the authentic beginning of the sentence; but it is an unnatural way to render the verb even if one retains the received text, in which no conjunction appears. (A few witnesses have the conjunction *de*, 'and', 'but', instead of *oun*.) The pluperfect rendering was calculated to harmonize John's narrative with that of the Synoptists; but it is best, as we have seen, to realize that John omits all the details of Jesus' appearance before Caiaphas. Plainly Annas's attempt to find incriminating evidence in the contents of Jesus' teaching or the identity of his disciples was unfruitful, so the preliminary inquiry before him came to an end. If Jesus was to be accused before the Roman governor, this had to be done by the reigning high priest as leader of the nation and president of the supreme court; to Caiaphas therefore he was sent.

3. PETER'S FINAL DENIAL (18:25–27)

18:25–27 Now Simon Peter was standing and warming himself. So they said to him, 'You are not one of his disciples too, are you?' He denied it: 'I am not', said he. One of the high priest's servants, a kinsman of the man whose ear Peter had cut off, said, 'Did I not see you in the garden with him?' So Peter denied it again, and immediately the cock crew.

There is considerable literary skill in the way the stages of Peter's denial are dovetailed into the narrative of Jesus' interrogation before the high priest; the twofold element of suspense thus introduced heightens the interest.

We are brought back to the charcoal fire, burning in a brazier in the palace courtyard (cf. verse 18). As Peter stood and warmed himself there with the members of the high-priestly household and the temple police, one of them repeated the question which had been put to him by the girl at the door when the 'other disciple' brought him in: as then, so now the question is framed in a form expecting the answer 'No', and this is the answer Peter gives again (cf. verse 17). He was already feeling uncomfortable when another of his companions, looking at his face in the firelight, recognized him as having been with Jesus when the police came to arrest him in the garden. Peter, losing his nerve altogether, repeats his denial once more. The crowing of the cock which immediately followed brought to his mind Jesus' reply in the upper room to his confident assertion that he was prepared to die for him: 'Will you lay down your life for me? Indeed and in truth I tell you: Before the cock crows you will deny me three times' (13:38).

4. TRIAL BEFORE PILATE (18:28–19:16a)

(a) *Pilate interrogates the prosecutors* (18:28–32)

18:28 **So they bring Jesus from Caiaphas into the praetorium. It was early morning. They themselves did not enter into the praetorium, in order that they might not contract defilement but might eat the passover.**

While John gives no details of Jesus' appearance before Caiaphas, something of what took place may be inferred from the following account of his appearance before Pilate. The term 'praetorium' denotes the headquarters of a Roman military governor (as the governor of Judaea was). In a Roman camp, the praetorium was the commander's headquarters in the centre of the camp. The Roman governor of Judaea normally resided in Caesarea, where the palace built by Herod the Great for himself was available as the praetorium (cf. Acts 23:35). When the requirements of public order brought him to Jerusalem (e.g. when the city was overflowing with visitors at the great pilgrimage festivals), the building where he took up temporary residence would be his praetorium for the time being. The question then arises whether we can identify the place which served as the praetorium on the present occasion (cf. Mark 15:16). Two buildings in particular come up for consideration.[13] One of these is Herod's palace on the western wall. (The tower Phasael, which was incorporated into this palace, survives as the north-eastern tower of the present Citadel, south of the Jaffa gate.) The other is the Antonia fortress north-west of the temple area, connected with the outer court of the temple by the 'steps' of Acts 21:35, 40. This was Herod's reconstruction of an earlier Hasmonaean fortress known as Baris, which he renamed in honour of his patron Mark Antony. On the site of part of this fortress the Convent of Our Lady of Zion now stands. This is the traditional location of Pilate's praetorium; here, at the Ecce Homo arch, the Via Dolorosa begins its course which ends in the Church of the Holy Sepulchre.

'It was early morning'; a Roman official, as we have seen, liked to begin his work at dawn and get it over as early as possible in the day. The chief priests and their associates did not want to annoy the governor by keeping him waiting, especially if they had already made an appointment with him for early morning.

However, ritual considerations prevented them from entering the pagan precincts on this occasion. Whatever was the nature of the supper which Jesus had shared with his disciples in the upper room on the previous evening, the official Passover (for which the lambs had to be slaughtered in the temple during the afternoon of the day which had just dawned) was yet to be eaten (immediately after sunset), and those who were in a state of ceremonial purity in readiness to eat it could not now afford to contract defilement and be excluded from the Passover. It appears that entering a Gentile house at this time would have conveyed defilement, perhaps because of the presence of leaven,[14] but remaining outside in the colonnade did not. There is, of course, characteristic Johannine irony in this reference to the chief priests' scrupulousness in the matter of ceremonial defilement, when all the time they were incurring incomparably greater moral defilement by their proceedings against Jesus.

Pontius Pilate, who was at this time governor of Judaea, had received his appointment from the Emperor Tiberius in AD 26 (some four years earlier than the events we are discussing) and held it practically until that emperor's death in March, AD 37. A Latin inscription in the Herodian theatre of Caesarea, discovered in 1961, gives Pilate the title 'prefect (*praefectus*) of Judaea'. Tacitus gives him the title 'procurator',[15] although it has been suggested of late that the Roman governors of Judaea did not receive this latter title until AD 44. He was a weak man who tried to cover up his weakness by a show of obstinacy and violence. His tactlessness involved him in actions which repeatedly offended Jewish public opinion; his period of office was marked by several savage outbreaks of bloodshed (cf. Luke 13:1). In addition to the NT writers and Tacitus, the Jewish authors Philo and (more especially) Josephus provide information about his governorship.[16]

18:29, 30 So Pilate went out to them and said, 'What accusation do you bring against this man?' They answered him: 'If this man were not a criminal, we should not have handed him over to you.'

Since Jesus' accusers would not enter the praetorium, Pilate went out to hear what they had to say. Presumably, as they remained by the outer colonnade of the courtyard, he had his movable *bēma* or tribunal (cf. 19:13) brought out into the courtyard so that he could judge the case there. Then he opened the judicial proceedings (*cognitio*), as was his duty, by asking them to state their charge against the man whom they had brought before him. But they, instead of playing their part straightforwardly as *delatores*, demurred at the terms of Pilate's question, regular though it was according to Roman practice. It was evident that Pilate was in effect opening a new trial, instead of simply confirming the death penalty which, as they had maintained, Jesus had incurred in terms of Jewish law. An outline of the case had probably been conveyed to Pilate in advance, and they hoped that he would be satisfied with this and conduct no further inquiry. But a Roman governor had complete discretion in deciding how to exercise his *imperium*, and if Pilate decided to investigate the case *de novo*, they had to accept his decision. It was necessary, therefore, that they should state their charge formally, and the terms in which they did so are made clear in the sequel: Pilate's question in verse 33 implies that they charged Jesus with claiming to be 'king of the Jews'. Before they formulated their charge, however, Pilate and they engaged in a little further fencing.

18:31, 32 So Pilate said to them 'You take him, and pass judgment on him according to your law.' The Jews said to him, 'We are not allowed to put any one to death.' (This was to fulfil the word that Jesus had spoken, indicating by what kind of death he was to die.)

Pilate knew very well that they were bringing a capital charge against Jesus, but they had not said so formally thus far, and he pretended not to know this. Since they had found this man to be a criminal, a law-breaker, then, said Pilate, they should pass judgment on him as their law provided. But they protested that they were unable to do so, since their law provided for capital punish-

ment in a case like this, and the right to inflict the death penalty
had been taken away from them.

Their statement, 'We are not allowed to put any one to death',
is certainly in accordance with Roman provincial practice, in which
capital jurisdiction was the governor's prerogative. When Judaea
became a Roman province in AD 6 and a Roman prefect was
appointed by the emperor to govern it, this prerogative was expressly reserved to him.[17] Such exceptions as may be adduced (so
far as Judaea is concerned) are the exceptions that prove the rule.
As a special concession the Jewish authorities were allowed to
execute sentence of death against violators of the sanctity of the
temple, even if the violators were Roman citizens.[18] This may
explain why, according to Mark's narrative, an abortive attempt
was first made before the Sanhedrin to fasten on Jesus a charge of
uttering threats or insults against the temple (Mark 14:57–59). A
few years later a conviction on comparable grounds was procured
against Stephen (Acts 6:13 ff.), and there was no need to have the
death sentence against *him* ratified by the Roman governor. But
normally 'the capital power was the most jealously guarded of all
the attributes of government'.[19]

The evidence of John is confirmed by a second-century rabbinical
tradition preserved in the Jerusalem Talmud, to the effect that
'forty years before the destruction of the temple the right to inflict
the death penalty was taken away from Israel'.[20] It is curious that
the tradition should specify *forty* years before AD 70, and not
sixty-four years; it may be that the remembrance persisted of a
situation around AD 30 when the deprivation of this right was of
special significance.

John sees a special significance of another kind in the deprivation
of this right. He does not mean that the chief priests and their
associates ('the Jews' of verse 31) pleaded their inability to execute
the death sentence with the deliberate intention of fulfilling Jesus'
words about his death – still less that the Romans had deprived
them of this right with any such intention. He means that the
whole situation was providentially overruled by God to bring about
this result. John has already stated that Jesus' saying about his
being 'lifted up from the earth' presaged the manner of his death
(John 12:32 f.) – presaged, in other words, death by crucifixion.
If the Jews had not lost the right of capital jurisdiction, their rulers
could have carried out the death sentence in accordance with precedent, which would have been (as later in Stephen's case) by
stoning, the penalty prescribed for blasphemy. Among the forms
of execution known to Jewish law hanging did not normally figure;[21] what Jewish law did know in this regard was the hanging up
(not beyond sundown) of the dead body of an executed criminal

(Deut. 21:22 f.). In Jewish eyes, as is confirmed by a well-known Qumran text, 'hanging men alive' was an abomination: 'it was not so done in Israel.'[22] But 'hanging men alive' was an accurate description of crucifixion, a common Roman form of execution, especially for sedition. And the charge brought against Jesus before Pilate was, in Roman law, tantamount to sedition. What John means, then, is that the obligatory referring of Jesus' case to Pilate's jurisdiction made it possible for sentence of death by crucifixion to be passed on him; by the execution of this sentence he would be literally 'lifted up from the earth'.

(b) Pilate interrogates Jesus (18:33–38a)

18:33 So Pilate went back into the praetorium, called Jesus and said to him, 'Are you the king of the Jews?'

Pilate decided to investigate the charge more closely, so he had Jesus brought into the praetorium for interrogation. Pilate's question, 'Are you the king of the Jews?' shows that Jesus' accusers had by now formulated their charge against him. The accused man was now asked, in effect, whether he pleaded Guilty or Not Guilty. It was alleged that he claimed to be king of the Jews (cf. 19:21). Was the allegation true or false? And if it was true, in what sense had he made this claim? When Pilate, after interrogating Jesus, let it be known that he found little substance in the charge of sedition, the chief priests reformulated their charge in a theological rather than a political sense: 'he made himself Son of God' (19:7). Could Jesus have used language which could be interpreted equally as a claim to be 'king of the Jews' and as a claim to be 'Son of God'? He could indeed, if he claimed to be Messiah. John, who preserves no details of Jesus' appearance before Caiaphas, has nothing to say here of his affirmative answer (safeguarded by necessary qualifications) to Caiaphas's question: 'Are you the Messiah, the Son of the Blessed One?' (Mark 14:61 f.).[23] But John's narrative plainly implies what the Synoptists explicitly record: that Jesus did give such an answer. Perhaps it was the added qualifications, rather than the claim to be Messiah in itself, that was adjudged blasphemous; but there was no doubt how the messianic claim could be most effectively represented to Pilate. The Messiah was, by definition, the king of Israel (cf. John 1:49); and any one who claimed kingship in a Roman province denied the sovereignty of Caesar and was guilty of sedition against him.

18:34, 35 Jesus answered: 'Do you say this on your own initiative, or was it others who told you this about me?' Pilate

answered: 'Am *I* a Jew? It is your own nation – the chief priests – that handed you over to me. What have you done?'

The other Evangelists record no such interchange between Jesus and Pilate as John now reports. But John reports it for a purpose of his own. That Jesus was executed as 'king of the Jews' was the best-known fact about him to people living in the Hellenistic world nearly two generations after the event. But if they knew nothing more than that about him, it cannot have appeared to be a matter of great importance who was or was not king of the Jews in AD 30. If that was the charge on which Jesus was put to death, how could his death have significance for them? This interchange with Pilate brings out the true character of Jesus' kingship and underscores its abiding relevance. The identity of the rightful king of the Jews in AD 30 may be a matter of historical interest to a few; the nature of ultimate truth must be a matter of personal concern to serious people of all times and races.

18:36–38a Jesus answered: 'My kingship does not proceed from this world. If my kingship did proceed from this world, my servants would have fought to prevent my being handed over to the Jews; but as it is, my kingship proceeds from another source.' So Pilate said to him, 'You *are* a king, then?' Jesus answered: 'It is you who say that I am a king. The purpose of my birth, the purpose of my coming into the world, is that I should bear witness to the truth. Everyone who belongs to the cause of truth listens to my voice.' 'What is truth?' said Pilate to him.

Pilate disclaimed responsibility for the expression 'king of the Jews'; that was how the charge against Jesus had been formulated to him. If Jesus demurred, let him choose his own form of words. So Jesus explained that the kingship which he claimed was nothing like the forms of kingship – whether sacral or secular – which were current in the world; it was not the sort of kingship of which Roman law took cognizance. Speaking of the anarchy in Judaea which followed Herod's death in 4 BC, Josephus says: 'Any one might make himself king by putting himself at the head of a band of rebels whom he fell in with.'[24] Had Jesus been a king in that sense, there would have been a real battle when the soldiers and police came to arrest him in the garden. The fact that he was taken so easily showed that his was a different sort of kingship.

All that Pilate was concerned with was that he did seem to be claiming some kind of kingship: 'You *are* a king, then?' 'King', said Jesus, 'is your word. But if that is the word to be used, then the kingdom of which I am speaking is the kingdom of truth; the citizens of that kingdom are those who love truth; and they listen to me because they recognize in me their true king.' Here it is the incarnate Logos who is speaking, the embodiment of eternal truth, now revealed on earth at a particular time and place. Roman law took many situations within its purview, but not the nature of eternal truth. Pilate knew his business, and to discuss the nature of truth formed no part of it. So he broke off the interrogation with the curt dismissal 'What is truth?' Whatever this man might have said or done, he constituted no threat to imperial authority. But if 'the kingship of Jesus consists in His witness to the truth, and the allegiance He claims is that of obedience to the truth',[25] then his Messiahship cannot be confined to Jewish particularism; it has permanent and universal validity, and confers genuine liberation on those who acknowledge it (cf. John 8:31 f.). Jesus' words might be lost on Pilate, but John hopes and believes that many of his readers will take them to heart, and come to know him who is not only 'a witness to the truth' but the truth in person – the truth that makes men and women free.

(c) 'We want Barabbas!' (18:38b–40)

18:38b Having said this, Pilate went out to the Jews again, and said to them, 'I find him guilty of no crime.'

The response to Pilate's question 'You *are* a king, then?' – 'It is you who say that I am a king' (verse 37) – might in certain circumstances have been construed as an admission of the charge brought against the accused. If it was tantamount to 'Yes', it was sufficient in Roman law for conviction, for Roman law, unlike Jewish law, could convict on a plea of guilty without confirmation from witnesses. But it was evident to Pilate that Jesus' response to his question was not tantamount to 'Yes' – that whatever the nature of his claims might be, he had committed no offence against the law which it was Pilate's duty to administer.[26] Hence, leaving Jesus under guard inside the praetorium, he went out to speak to his accusers, and told them that, so far as he was concerned, Jesus was not guilty of any crime. Here John shows independent agreement with Luke, who evidently had his own sources of information about the course of the trial: according to Luke (23:14), Pilate says to Jesus' accusers, 'You brought me this man as one who was perverting the people; and after examining him before you, I tell you, I found him not guilty of any of your charges against him.'

18:39, 40 'But you have a custom that I should release one man to you at the Passover. Do you want me to release to you the "King of the Jews"?' They shouted back: 'Not him; we want Barabbas!' (Barabbas was a bandit.)

The Barabbas episode is recorded by all four evangelists. Whereas John and Matthew seem to make Pilate take the initiative in offering to release a prisoner under the customary paschal amnesty, Mark and Luke suggest that the accusers and bystanders first ask Pilate to observe the annual practice. Perhaps a request had already been made for the release of Barabbas; now Pilate offers to release Jesus instead. In doing so, he cannot refrain from annoying the Jewish leaders by calling Jesus 'the King of the Jews' – a title which, as their accusation made plain, they repudiated.

The practice of releasing a prisoner at Passovertide is unattested outside the New Testament. The testimony of the Evangelists is evidence enough for the historicity of the practice, but it is strange that no express reference to it can be found elsewhere – not even in Josephus. It was presumably a custom which the Roman governors took over from their Herodian and Hasmonaean predecessors. It may originally have been intended to commemorate the theme of release in the paschal commemoration; but in the absence of clear evidence its origin and purpose must remain matters of speculation. At a later date, as the Theodosian code shows, Roman law made provision for amnesties at Eastertide, but this was introduced after the Christianization of the Empire to celebrate the Christian significance of the season, and offers no analogy to the custom referred to here.

A possible allusion to the custom has been traced by some scholars in a passage in the Mishnah,[27] where it is laid down that the paschal lamb may be killed for certain persons who may or may not be able to eat it, but not killed for them by name, since if it proved impossible for them to eat it after all, the sacrifice would in that case become invalid. The list of such persons includes 'one whom they have promised to bring out of prison'. The 'prison' would naturally be a Gentile prison, since provision would normally be made for Jewish inmates of a Jewish prison in Jerusalem to eat the Passover. It is conceivable that the custom under consideration is alluded to, but this is not a necessary inference from the Mishnaic passage, for it might envisage the situation in which a prisoner was due for release shortly in the normal course, and might be released in time to take the paschal supper, although there could be no certainty of this.

As it was, however, the people demanded Barabbas, and the sacrosanctity of the custom can be inferred from the fact that Pilate had no option but to liberate a man whom Roman law would normally have been most unwilling to set free. For when John says that 'Barabbas was a bandit' (Gk. *lēstēs*, 'brigand'), he uses the term almost certainly to denote (as Josephus habitually does) a Zealot insurgent. In Mark 15:27 (cf. Matt. 27:38) the same word is used of the two men who were crucified along with Jesus. Our interpretation of the word as used by John here is confirmed by the more circumstantial statement in Mark 15:7, that Barabbas was 'among the rebels in prison, those who had committed murder in the insurrection'. (We have no further account of this particular 'insurrection', but the reference is probably to some recent outbreak of militant resistance against the Roman occupation.) A variant reading in John's text calls Barabbas a 'bandit leader' (Gk. *archilēstēs*); we may compare the description of him as 'notorious' (Gk. *episēmos*) in Matt. 27:16. There is no little irony in the fact that the man whose release was granted had been convicted of the same kind of offence as that with which Jesus was now charged; the irony, we may be sure, was not lost on Pilate. But he was still left with Jesus on his hands; what steps should he now take with him?

NOTES

1. Another reference to this river has been made in the comment on John 7:37–39 (p. 182).
2. The historical probability of the participation of Roman soldiers has been variously assessed – negatively, by T. Mommsen, *Römisches Strafrecht* (Leipzig, 1899), p. 240, n. 2; positively, by M. Goguel, *The Life of Jesus* (London, 1933), pp. 468 f., and P. Winter, *On the Trial of Jesus* (Berlin, 1961), p. 44. It runs counter to the later increasing tendency to make the Jewish authorities exclusively responsible for the proceedings against Jesus and to exonerate the Romans.
3. See pp. 193, 195.
4. Cf. C. H. Dodd, *The Interpretation of the Fourth Gospel*, pp. 432 f.
5. Cf. A. Guilding, *The Fourth Gospel and Jewish Worship*, pp. 165 f.
6. Josephus, *Antiquities*, 18.26, 34, 95.
7. Josephus, *Antiquities* 18.35, 95.
8. Josephus, *Antiquities*, 18.89, 95.
9. See comment on pp. 250 f., (as also for his designation as 'high priest that year' (John 11:49, 51).
10. Codex 225 of the Greek Gospels, written in 1192, displays a different rearrangement: verses 13a, 24, 13b, 14–23 and then 25 ff.
11. See F. Neirynck, 'The "Other Disciple" in Jn 18, 15–16', in *Evangelica* (Leuven, 1982), pp. 335–364.
12. A. N. Sherwin-White, *Roman Society and Roman Law in the New Testament* (Oxford, 1963), p. 45.
13. These two identifications have been defended outstandingly by two French Dominican scholars: that with the Antonia fortress by L. H. Vincent, *Jérusalem de l'Ancient Testament*, I (Paris, 1954), pp. 216–221; that with Herod's palace by P. Benoit, 'Praetorium, Lithostroton and Gabbatha', *Jesus and the Gospel*, I (New York, 1973), pp. 167–188; 'L'Antonia d'Hérode le Grand et le Forum

Oriental d'Aelia Capitolina', *HTR* 64 (1971), pp. 135–167. See further comments on John 19:5, 13 (pp. 363 f., 380, n. 3).

14. For the obligatory removal of leaven before the Passover meal see Exod. 12:19; 13:7; Mishnah, tractate *Pᵉsāḥîm* 1.1; 2.1, etc.

15. Tacitus, *Annals* 15.44.4.

16. Philo, *Legation to Gaius* 299–305; Josephus, *Jewish War* 2.169–177; *Antiquities* 18.35–89. See also J.-P. Lémonon, *Pilate et le Gouvernement de la Judée* (Paris, 1981).

17. Josephus, *Jewish War* 2.117.

18. Josephus, *Jewish War* 6.124–126. Thus, when Paul was charged with an offence against the sanctity of the temple, the Sanhedrin, through their spokesman Tertullus, complained to the procurator Felix that the officer commanding the Roman garrison in the Antonia fortress had forcibly taken him out of their hands when they were going to judge him 'according to our law' (Acts 24:6 f., Western text).

19. A. N. Sherwin-White, *Roman Society and Roman Law in the New Testament*, p. 36.

20. Jerusalem Talmud, tractate *Sanhedrin* 1.1; 7.2.

21. The mode of execution sometimes rendered 'hanging' in the Mishnaic tractate *Sanhedrîn* 7.1; 11.1 was actually strangulation.

22. 4QpNah. col. 1, lines 6–8 (commentary on Nah. 2:12). The Qumran commentator interprets Nahum's 'lion' of Alexander Jannaeus, who in 88 BC crucified 800 of his rebel subjects (Josephus, *Jewish War* 1.97; *Antiquities* 13.380). See comment on John 19:6 (p. 360).

23. In this Gospel, however, there is a running debate between Jesus and the Jerusalem authorities from 5:17 to 10:39 over his claim to be the Son of God.

24. Josephus, *Antiquities*, 17.285.

25. C. H. Dodd, *The Interpretation of the Fourth Gospel*, p. 427. This exposition of the interchange between Jesus and Pilate in verses 33–38 is greatly indebted to Professor Dodd's discussion.

26. L. Janssen, ' "Superstitio" and Persecution', *Vigiliae Christianae* 33 (1979), p. 155, taking John 18:33–38a as a factual report, considers that Pilate understood what was being said to him better than is commonly supposed.

27. Mishnah, tractate *Pᵉsāḥîm* 8.6. The relevance of this passage to the Barabbas question is maintained by J. Blinzler, *The Trial of Jesus* (Cork, 1959), pp. 218–221, and denied by P. Winter, *On the Trial of Jesus*, pp. 91–99.

CHAPTER 19

(d) 'Here is your king!' (19:1–16a)

19:1–3 Then Pilate took Jesus and had him flogged. The soldiers, for their part, plaited a garland of thorns and put it on his head, they dressed him up in a purple cloak and began to come up to him saying 'All hail, King of the Jews!' – striking his face as they did so.

Since Pilate had decided that Jesus was not guilty of the sedition with which he had been charged, he hoped that his accusers would be content if he inflicted a lighter punishment. The infliction of any punishment on one who had been convicted of no crime was an act of injustice, but ordinary provincials did not enjoy the legal protection extended to Roman citizens. Pilate probably reckoned that Jesus had been indiscreet in his public utterances and needed to be taught a lesson. Here again John's narrative is in line with that of Luke, according to whom Pilate said to Jesus' accusers: 'nothing deserving death has been done by him; I will therefore chastise him and release him' (Luke 23.15f.).

The severest form of beating was not normally inflicted as a punishment by itself but as a prelude to crucifixion or the like; thus in Mark's passion narrative (15:15; cf. Matt. 27:26) Jesus is sentenced to be scourged and crucified. This latter scourging (*phragelloō*) was a murderous form of torture; the whips with which it was carried out were reinforced with sharp pieces of metal or bone with left the victim's body a bloody pulp, and it is not surprising that this treatment was sometimes sufficient in itself to cause death. If the flogging (*mastigoō*) of John 19:1 was designed to teach Jesus a lesson, it may have been less severe than that, but any beating carried out by Roman soldiers was brutal enough.[1]

When they had carried it out, they engaged in a bit of barrack-room sport with their victim. His accusers had alleged that he claimed to be king of the Jews; let him be treated as a king, then. So they dressed him up in a military cloak to serve as a royal robe, placed a makeshift crown on his head and queued up to pay him mock homage, each one giving him a blow on the face as he did so. (The Greek word for such a blow, *rhapisma*, has already been used in 18:22.) If the praetorium where this took place was the Antonia fortress (see above on 18:28 and below on 19:13), it is at least a coincidence to recall that part of the Roman pavement or courtyard on that site can still be seen marked out for the 'king

358

game' (Gk. *basilinda*); it has been conjectured (but precariously) that this was an appropriate spot for the mock coronation ceremony.

The 'thorns' (Gk. *akanthai*) of which the makeshift crown was plaited have been identified with various species, but a strong case has been made out for seeing in them the 'thorns' of the *Phoenix dactylifera* or date-palm (see above on 12:13), which were well adapted for the imitation of a 'radiate crown' such as oriental god-kings were depicted on coins as wearing. Jesus would then have been acclaimed as *divus Iesus radiatus*.[2] Even if the primary intention of the crown was mockery, the 'fierce and formidable thorns' of *Phoenix dactylifera* (as H. St. J. Hart calls them) could also have caused acute pain.

19:4, 5 **Pilate came out again and said to the Jews, 'See, I am bringing him out to you, to let you see that I find him guilty of no crime.' So Jesus came out, wearing the crown of thorns and the purple cloak. Pilate said to them, 'See, here is the man!'**

Pilate evidently hoped that the sorry spectacle of a man disabled and disfigured by a severe flogging and dressed up in mockery would satisfy Jesus' accusers that he had learned his lesson and was no longer likely to do any harm. The implication of the words, 'to let you see that I find him guilty of no crime', was that in Pilate's eyes Jesus' claims, such as they were, were more fit for ridicule than for serious legal action. 'See, here is the man!' might mean, so far as Pilate's intention was concerned, 'Here he is, poor fellow!' But the Evangelist discerns a deeper significance, which is well conveyed by a more hieratic rendering 'Behold the Man' (NEB, following AV).[3] (We may compare John's discerning a deeper significance in the words of Caiaphas in 11:49–52, and Mark's discerning in the centurion's words in Mark 15:39 a confirmation of his own basic emphasis on Jesus as the Son of God.)

19:6 **So, when the chief priests and the officers saw him, they shouted: 'Crucify! crucify!' 'Take him and crucify him yourselves', said Pilate to them; 'I find him guilty of no crime.'**

But the chief priests and their associates were in no mood to be pacified. The sight of Jesus dressed up as a pantomime king enraged them the more, for they were being exposed to ridicule even more than he. When, some years later, a king of the Jews (Agrippa the elder) made a public procession through Alexandria and the Greek populace of the city parodied the occasion by dressing a local idiot up in royal robes and paying him homage in the gymnasium, it was not the instrument of their sport who took offence but the Jewish community and the Jewish king.[4] The Roman soldiers had expressed their contempt for the Jews by their treatment of Jesus, and the Jewish authorities were further exasperated. They knew quite well what the outcome would be if Pilate found Jesus guilty of the charge which they preferred against him. For a non-Roman the penalty for sedition was almost bound to be crucifixion – and during the generation that had elapsed since the death of Herod they had seen ample evidence of this in Judaea and the adjoining regions. This was the penalty they sought for Jesus, and now they demanded it outright.

In saying, 'Take him and crucify him yourselves' Pilate was teasing them again, he knew very well that they could execute no capital sentence against him, and even if they could, crucifixion was not a form of execution normally authorized by Jewish law.[5]

19:7 The Jews answered Pilate, 'We have a law, and according to the law he should be put to death, because he made himself (out to be) Son of God.'

It appeared to Jesus' accusers that their attempt to have him convicted and sentenced by Pilate on a charge of sedition was going to be unsuccessful. They therefore tried to gain their end by another route. The governors of Judaea not only had the duty of enforcing Roman law in the province; they also undertook the responsibility of respecting and (where necessary) enforcing Jewish religious law. The claim to be king of the Jews was a capital offence against Roman law; the claim to be Son of God was a capital offence against Jewish law. But if the governor would not grant a capital conviction in respect of the former offence, he might be persuaded to permit the execution of the capital sentence required by Jewish law in respect of the latter offence – a sentence which could not be carried out without his licence (cf. 18:31). As we have seen in the comment on 18:33 a claim to be the Messiah could be construed both as a claim to be king of the Jews and as a claim to be Son of God. When the one formulation (which might have been expected to procure immediate conviction from Pilate) seemed to fail in its purpose, the chief priests tried the other. Their language presupposes that a claim to be Son of God was *ipso facto* blasphemous and rendered the claimant liable to the death penalty prescribed in Lev. 24:16, as indeed is presupposed earlier in this Gospel (cf. 5:18; 10:33). In the OT the anointed king of Israel was son of God by adoption (cf. Ps. 2:7; 89:26 f.); but our Lord's contemporaries recognized (rightly) that much more than this official relationship was implied in the language he used. In the later and idealized codification of Jewish law in the Mishnah (published in written form *c.* AD 200) the express pronouncing of the Ineffable Name is a necessary element in blasphemy;[6] but in the time of the Second Commonwealth (which ended in AD 70) the offence was not so restricted. Despite our Lord's qualifications in his reply to the high priest's question – or perhaps all the more so because of these qualifications – the terms of the reply were adjudged blasphemous. If Pilate would not send Jesus to the cross for sedition, he might agree to his execution for blasphemy.

19:8, 9 So, when Pilate heard this statement, he took fright instead (of responding as they had hoped), and went back into the praetorium and said to Jesus, 'Where are you from?' But Jesus gave him no answer.

The usual translation 'he was the more afraid' (NEB: 'he was more afraid than ever') suggests that Pilate had already begun to be afraid, but there is no hint of this in John's narrative. It is preferable therefore to take *mallon ephobēthē* to mean 'he became afraid rather (than complied with their desire)'. Hard-bitten and down-to-earth as the average Roman official was, he was apt to have somewhere in his make-up a rich vein of superstition, which might be exposed without warning. If a man claimed to be son of God, that was no blasphemy to a Greek or a Roman; if the claim was true, the man was a *theios anēr*, a man with some quality of the divine about him. And, come to think of it, Pilate realized that this was exactly the impression that Jesus had been making on him throughout their confrontation. Pilate felt uneasy and tried to cover up his uneasiness by a display of authority. 'Here, you, where do you come from?' he asked, going back into the praetorium. The motif of Jesus' silence before Pilate, prominent in the Markan record, finds expression only at this point in John's account. What answer that he could have given would have meant anything to a pagan judge or conveyed any sense of what he had in mind when he spoke to others of having come forth from the Father?

19:10, 11 So Pilate said to him, 'Don't you speak to *me*? Don't you know that I have authority to release you and authority to crucify you?' Jesus answered, 'You would have no authority at all against me if it were not given to you from above. For this reason he who handed me over to you has greater sin.'

Pilate is annoyed by Jesus' silence. It borders on contempt of court; moreover, it is foolish, for Pilate is the one man who can be of any use to him in his present situation. 'No one who has power to condemn is without power to acquit', says a maxim of Roman law;[7] and it may be that by mentioning acquittal before condemnation Pilate implies that acquittal, if it be possible, is still his intention. Pilate's authority (Gk. *exousia*) was indeed delegated to him by the emperor, but so long as he retained the imperial commission it was, within the limits of his province, a very far-reaching authority indeed – *imperium*, as the Romans called it – which gave its holder great discretionary power.

But Jesus discerns behind Pilate's discretionary power a higher authority than the emperor's. The emperor himself, not to speak of his lieutenant, wields his authority by grace of God, by whose wisdom 'kings reign, and rulers decree what is just' (Prov. 8:15). The expression 'from above' (Gk. *anōthen*) denotes heavenly derivation here as it does in John 3:3, 7, 31. The corollary which Jesus draws from this assertion of the heavenly derivation of all earthly power gives one pause. Its meaning depends not only on the identity of the one who, as he says to Pilate, 'handed me over to you', but also on the force of the connecting phrase 'for this reason' (Gk. *dia touto*). The verb 'hand over' (Gk. *paradidōmi*) has been used repeatedly in the earlier part of the narrative to denote Judas's act of betrayal. Judas, however, is hardly in view here; for one thing, he did not betray Jesus *to Pilate*; for another, he has disappeared from the story in the episode of the arrest in the garden (18:5) and his reintroduction now would scarcely be relevant. Since then, the same verb has been used twice (18:30, 35) of the action of Jesus' accusers in handing him over to Pilate after the high-priestly inquiry, and the present reference is probably to this. Since the aorist participle is used in the singular, one person is indicated, and he must be the high priest Caiaphas, the head of the Jewish establishment. Since all authority is held by delegation from God, Caiaphas was as responsible to God for the way in which he exercised his authority as Pilate was in respect of his. But there was this difference: Pilate was acting in accordance with the terms of his divinely appointed authority in investigating a charge which was brought before him, whereas Caiaphas, who for reasons of political expediency handed Jesus over to him on a charge of sedition, for which he hoped a capital conviction would be forthcoming, was abusing the authority which attended his sacral office as high priest. *For this reason* Caiaphas's sin was greater – meaning perhaps not 'greater than Pilate's' but 'greater than it would have been if he had not received from God the privileges and responsibilities of the high-priesthood.'[8]

19:12 Thereupon Pilate sought (a way) to release him. But the

Jews raised a shout: 'If you release this man, you are no friend of Caesar's. Any one who sets himself up as king is a rebel against Caesar.'

If Pilate had found no substance in the charge of sedition, he certainly had no mind to take up the religious charge, and was about to pronounce formal acquittal, when a new and sinister note was introduced into the proceedings. On other occasions, when Pilate had offended his Jewish subjects, they had found means of conveying their complaints against him to his superiors, not without success. What would the emperor's reaction be, if it were reported to him that his governor in Judaea had acquitted a man brought before him on a charge of sedition – a well-founded charge, too, it would be emphasized? We may dismiss as mere court gossip some of the accounts that have come down to use of Tiberius's behaviour and character, but we are left in no doubt that he was naturally distrustful and morbidly suspicious. 'Caesar's friend' does not appear to have been an official title at this stage, as it became under Vespasian (AD 69–79). Nor need we see a reference here to Aelius Sejanus, prefect of the praetorian guard, who had been Tiberius's trusted friend until in AD 31 he fell catastrophically to disgrace and death.[9] The term is used non-technically, but with a clear political flavour: 'You are no true representative of Caesar if you acquit this man – and you know quite well that this will be Caesar's own judgment.' Pilate got the message; his mind was effectively made up for him. Sentence must be passed, and passed on the original charge of sedition.

19:13 Hearing these words, then, Pilate brought Jesus out and took his seat on the tribunal in a place called 'Pavement' (*Gabbatha* in Hebrew).

The tribunal was the raised platform (Gk. *bēma*) on which a Roman magistrate sat in the discharge of his judicial functions. Normally Pilate would have conducted the whole trial from this position; the Jewish leaders' unwillingness to contract defilement by entering the praetorium led to his moving back and forth between them, where they stood by the outer colonnade, and Jesus, whom he examined in the building itself. But it was necessary that sentence should be pronounced from his seat of office. 'Pavement' is the rendering of Gk. *lithostrōtos* ('paved with stones'); I should be disposed to render it by a term familiar in some Scottish towns – 'The Plainstones' – except that it would not be so familiar to the majority of readers. The place was known in Hebrew – or rather in Aramaic (which John includes under his blanket usage of 'He-

brew') – by a word apparently meaning 'The Ridge'. This has often
been identified with a magnificent Roman pavement excavated beneath the Ecce Homo arch and the convent of Our Lady of Zion,
originally measuring almost 3,000 square yards, which has further
been identified as the courtyard of the Antonia fortress (see notes
on 18:28; 19:2f., 5).[10]

It must be accounted a curiosity of translation and exegesis that
in a number of versions (e.g. those of Moffatt, Goodspeed and C.
B. Williams), Pilate is said to have made *Jesus* sit on the tribunal.
It is true that the first aorist active of the verb 'sit' (*ekathisen*) may
be transitive as well as intransitive (although, as in John 12:14, it
is regularly intransitive in NT); but the determinant point is simply
this: there are many things which a Roman judge might do, but
some things which he would not do, and to make the accused sit
in the judge's seat is one of the latter, whether the accused himself
or his accusers were to be the target of such mockery. Some of the
translators in question might agree that Pilate would never do such
a thing, but would maintain that John represented him as doing
so, for purposes of symbolism (as though to suggest that from a
higher point of view it was Pilate who was being judged and Jesus
who was the real judge). But John's intention is to record things
that really happened; if in some of the events he narrates he saw a
deeper significance, they were none the less historical events. Some
second-century writers indeed, like Justin Martyr and the author
of the apocryphal *Gospel of Peter*, might represent Jesus as being
placed in mockery on the judge's seat, but that merely indicates
their remoteness from historical fact, coupled with their capacity
for OT misinterpretation (they relate the supposed incident to Isa.
58:2, 'they ask of me righteous judgments').[11]

**19:14, 15 It was Passover Eve, about the sixth hour. He said
to the Jews, 'See, here is your king!' So they raised a shout:
'Take him away! Take him away! Crucify him!' 'What!' said
Pilate: 'crucify your *king*?' 'We have no king but Caesar,' said
the chief priests in reply.**

As John has recorded the place explicitly, so now he notes the
time. 'It was Passover Eve' he says – or, since *paraskeuē* acquired
in Jewish Greek the special sense of 'sabbath eve', i.e. Friday, we
might render his words, 'It was Friday of Passover Week'.[12] Since
on this occasion Passover fell on a sabbath, it was Friday whichever
way we take it. As for the time of day, it was getting on towards
noon. Despite Westcott's arguments, no evidence is forthcoming
that at this time, whether among Romans, Greeks or Jews, hours
were ever reckoned otherwise than from sunrise.[13]

When a British king is about to be crowned, immediately after his entrance into Westminster Abbey he is made to face the assembled company in four successive directions, while the Archbishop of Canterbury says, 'Sirs, I here present unto you King –, the undoubted king of this realm. Wherefore, all ye who are come this day to do your homage, are you willing to do the same?' To these words the reply comes in unison from the four successive directions: 'God save King –!' This part of the ceremony is called the Recognition. Something of the same sort, albeit in mockery, is suggested here. Pilate has been put on the spot by the chief priests, and sees no alternative to condemning Jesus to death, but he has his revenge on them by insisting that this bloodstained and dishevelled figure is their king, and inviting them to recognize him as such. Far from so recognizing him, they insist on his death – death by crucifixion. The idea that he could be their king they dismiss with indignation; Caesar is the only sovereign they acknowledge (Caesar was never called *rex* or 'king' by the Romans, but Gk. *basileus* did duty for both 'emperor' and 'king'). No doubt they were honest in saying that Caesar was the only *basileus* they knew; their status and privileges depended on their collaboration with the imperial power. But normally they would not have been so rash as to say so outright and thus scandalize true Jewish patriots even more than they already did: they were goaded into saying so by Pilate's insistence that Jesus was their king.

But, as with an earlier utterance of Pilate's (see comment on verse 5) John sees a deeper meaning in his words: 'See, here is your king!' Jesus, he implies, is the true king of the true Israel, of all the people of God who belong to the cause of truth and obey the voice of him who is truth incarnate (cf. 18:37). And in the fact that these words were spoken towards midday on Passover Eve he implies something else: Jesus is the true paschal lamb, about to suffer death at the appropriate hour of the appropriate day for the life of his people.[14]

19:16a So then, at their insistence, he handed him over to be crucified.

John may not say in so many words that Pilate pronounced the death sentence, but he implies that he did so: that was why he took his seat on the tribunal, and that he assumed full responsibility is evident not only from the fact that the sentence was executed by the soldiers under his command but also from his initiative in the matter of the 'title' affixed to the cross (verse 19). The expression 'at their insistence' is literally 'to them' (*autois*). If 'to them' denotes the persons to whom Jesus was literally handed over, it indicates the soldiers; but more probably it is to be taken as a 'dative of advantage' and rendered somewhat as NEB does: 'Then at last, to satisfy them, he handed Jesus over to be crucified.' Exactly the same sense is expressed in Luke 23:25, 'he handed Jesus over to their will' (tō thelēmati autōn).[15]

5. JESUS ON THE CROSS (19:16b–30)

(a) The executioners' work (19:16b–25a)

19:16b, 17 **So they took Jesus; and he went out, carrying his cross to the so-called 'Place of a Skull', the Hebrew name of which is Golgotha.**

Those who 'took' Jesus are the Roman soldiers detailed to act as executioners on this occasion: they 'took him along with them', if we are to press the full meaning out of the prefix *para* in the compound verb *parelabon*.[16] In stating that Jesus 'went out, carrying his cross' – literally 'carrying the cross for himself (*heautō*)' – John is not deliberately contradicting the Synoptic account of Simon of Cyrene, whose services were commandeered by the military to carry Jesus' cross after him; he is rather emphasizing that, as at his arrest in the garden, Jesus is still in command of the situation. He is 'taken' to the place of execution, it is true, but he is no reluctant victim, compelled to go whither he would not: he goes with his executioners of his own volition and carries the cross for himself.[17] The fathers saw in this the antitype of Isaac's carrying the wood for the sacrifice (Gen. 22:6) – carrying it, as one rabbinical commentary puts it, 'as one carries the cross on his shoulder'[18] – but John makes no express allusion to an OT precedent. It has further been suggested that John wishes to exclude one docetic account of the matter, in which Simon of Cyrene not only carried the cross to the place of execution but was actually crucified instead of Jesus;[19] but this is not very probable.

The traditional account, according to which Simon relieved Jesus of his burden at the fifth Station of the Cross on the Via Dolorosa, provides a simple harmonization of the Synoptic and Johannine accounts, and may approximate to the historical fact. But in the actual exegesis of John's narrative such harmonization is unnecessary and intrusive, for it tends to blunt the point that John is concerned to make both by what he says and by what he leaves unsaid.

It was normally the cross-piece (*patibulum*), and not the complete gibbet, that the condemned man carried into place of execution; the upright stakes were probably standing there already. From our Lord's words to his disciples about taking up their cross and following him,[20] we may judge that the sight of a man carrying the *patibulum* was common enough to be immediately understood; the words were not used metaphorically.

The verb 'went out' may mean that he went out from the precincts of Pilate's praetorium or that he went out of the city through one of the gates in the wall (cf. Heb. 13:12). 'Golgotha' is *gulgolta*, the Aramaic word for 'the skull', with the second *l* assimilated to the following *t* ('Hebrew' in this Gospel, as in verse 13, includes Aramaic; the Hebrew form of the word is *gulgoleth*). The familiar designation 'Calvary' is derived from Latin *calvaria* ('skull') and has come into Western European languages from the use of the Latin word in the Vulgate text of all four passion narratives. The origin of the name 'Skull-place' remains a matter of conjecture. As for its actual location, it lay outside the city wall, presumably outside the second north wall (the third north wall, farther to the north, was not begun until about twelve years later, under Herod Agrippa I). If the praetorium of the trial narrative is to be identified with the Antonia fortress, then the present Via Dolorosa probably marks the route to the cross with substantial accuracy, although it runs several feet above the first-century level. Until a few years ago it was uncertain whether the traditional site of Golgotha, covered by the Church of the Holy Sepulchre, was outside the line of the second north wall or not; that it actually was outside was indicated by excavations conducted in 1963 and later in the Muristan area, to the south of the site.[21]

19:18 There they crucified him, and two others with him on either side, Jesus being between them.

Crucifixion, 'the cruellest and foulest of punishments,' as Cicero called it,[22] was carried out in a variety of ways. The commonest way, which is implied in this narrative, was to fasten the victim's arms or hands to the cross-beam and then hoist it on to the upright post, to which his feet were then fastened; a piece of wood attached to the upright might serve as a sort of seat (*sedecula*) – not so much for the victim's relief as to prolong his life and his agony. The hands and feet might be fastened to the wood with thongs or nails. According to John (who is the only one of the evangelists to give this detail), nails were used in Jesus' crucifixion (cf. 20:25). A more eloquent commentary on crucifixion than any literary description from antiquity is provided by the study of the bones of a crucified man of this period found in an ossuary on Ammunition Hill (Giv'at ha-Mivtar) north of Jerusalem, in June 1968, and described in the *Israel Exploration Journal*, January 1970.[23] Anatomical examination

of the bones revealed that the victim – one John son of Ezekiel
(the father's name is not quite clear), about twenty-five years old
– had been fastened to his cross by one nail through each forearm
and a single nail through both heels together. The latter nail had
turned when it was being driven in, and could not be extricated
afterwards, so it remained *in situ*, with some of the wood still
adhering to it.[24]

John gives no details of the two men who were crucified along
with Jesus. Mark and Matthew call them 'bandits' (Gk. *lēstai*),
using the same word as John uses of Barabbas (18:40); they were
probably freedom fighters of his company. John is more concerned
to emphasize that Jesus was crucified between them (a fact which
the other Evangelists mention, but more incidentally), as though
to show how completely he was 'numbered with the transgressors'
(Isa. 53:12) – although indeed he says nothing about their being
lawbreakers.

19:19–22 **Pilate wrote a 'title' and put it on the cross. The
writing was: 'Jesus of Nazareth, the King of the Jews'. So this
'title' was read by many of the Jews, because the place where
Jesus was crucified was near the city. It was written in Hebrew,
Latin and Greek. So the chief priests of the Jews said to Pilate,
'Do not write "The King of the Jews"; make it plain that it was
he who said, "I am King of the Jews".' Pilate answered, 'What
I have written, I have written.'**

It was customary to write on a placard the crime of which a
condemned person had been found guilty and fix it above his head
(as here) or tie it round his neck. The Latin word for such an
inscribed placard was *titulus*, which appears here as the Greek
loanword *titlos*. All four of the canonical Gospels record the wording of this placard, with slight verbal variations which may not be
unconnected with the trilingual form of its text. Hebrew (or Aramaic) was the vernacular of the Palestinian Jews; Latin was the
official language of the Roman army; Greek was the common
medium of culture and conversation in the eastern provinces of the
Roman Empire. The statement that 'Pilate wrote' the inscription
does not mean that he formed the letters with his own hands but
that he personally chose and dictated the wording, with the deliberate purpose of annoying the chief priests. It was a calculated
insult to them, and to the nation which they led, to represent a
crucified man as 'The King of the Jews'. But to their protest he
gave no satisfying answer. According to this Evangelist, Pilate had
a natural turn for fashioning a memorable sentence (cf. 18:38; 19:5),
but it was not matched by resolution in act, where resolution was

called for. The obstinacy and insensitivity with which Pilate is credited by other first-century writers were tokens of weakness, not of strength.[25]

The wording of the 'title' makes it plain that the charge on which Jesus was sentenced to be crucified was the charge on which he was originally brought before Pilate (cf. 18:33); in any official record of his execution the crime would be set down as sedition. But, as previously with Pilate's presentation of Jesus as King immediately before passing sentence from his tribunal (19:13 f.), so now John sees a deeper meaning in the 'title' on the cross than either Pilate or the chief priests could appreciate. 'The hour has come for the Son of Man to be glorified.' The Crucified One is the true king, the kingliest king of all; because it is he who is stretched on the cross, he turns an obscene instrument of torture into a throne of glory and 'reigns from the tree'.[26] And the inward significance of his kingship for his true followers has been made plain in his interchange with Pilate recorded in 18:34–38.

The place of crucifixion, it appears, was just outside the city, by the roadside, so that the inscription could be read by all who passed by on their way out or in. This was a very public execution – intentionally so, as a warning to others.

19:23–25a **When the soldiers, then, had crucified Jesus, they took his outer garments and made four parts, one to each soldier. Then they took his tunic; but the tunic was seamless, woven in a whole piece from top to bottom. So they said to one another, 'Don't let us tear this up; let us throw dice for it, to decide who shall have it.' This was for the fulfilment of Scripture where it says:**
'They divided my garments among themselves,
And cast lots for my clothing.'
This, then, is what the soldiers did.

It would be easy to say that this incident (recorded also in the three Synoptic Gospels) was constructed out of the *testimonium* quoted from Ps. 22:18. But in fact the clothes of an executed man were the legal perquisite of his executioners, and the claim that this narrative is based on the report of an eyewitness (verse 35) is borne out by the addition here of a circumstantial detail not derived from the *testimonium*. True, as the Evangelist reflected on the incident, he recognized in it the fulfilment of prophecy, but that is another matter. His reference to the fulfilment of Ps. 22:18 does not mean, of course, that the soldiers were knowingly fulfilling it, but that their action, carried out as a matter of course, was overruled to this end. The work of crucifixion, it appears, had been entrusted to a quaternion of soldiers (cf. Acts 12:4).

There were two main garments – the cloak (*himation*) or outer garment and the tunic (*chitōn*) or inner garment. The cloak was divided into four parts, perhaps along the seams. But the tunic, consisting of one complete piece of material, was worth much more if left entire than if it were cut into four parts. So they decided to throw dice for it, and the man whose number turned up had it to himself. This detail is not derived from the wording of Ps. 22:18; for in the Hebrew and Greek texts alike the two words used for clothing are synonymous, the two clauses making the same state-ment in different language, according to the rules of Hebrew par-allelism.[27] But in John's narrative the two words *himation* (used in its plural form *himatia* in verses 23 and 24) and *chitōn* are not synonymous; they denote the cloak and the tunic respectively, and are used by John because of what actually took place.

The cue for the liberal use made of Psalm 22 in the recording of the passion narratives and in other New Testament references to the death and exaltation of Christ was provided by his own appro-priation of verse 1 in his cry of dereliction. John does not mention the cry of dereliction, which would not have consorted well with his perspective, but he is familiar with the primitive employment of Psalm 22 as a *testimonium* of the passion, and draws upon it in his own way.

The 'seamless robe' has often been treated allegorically – with reference, e.g., to the 'one' community created by the death and exaltation of Christ (cf. John 10:16; 11:52; 17:11, 21, 23) – but it is doubtful if John had any allegorical intention. If he had, he may have thought of our Lord as his people's high priest; Josephus[28] says that the high priest's *chitōn* was woven in one piece, and Philo[29] treats it as a symbol of the Logos who binds all things into a unity. But if John had similar thoughts, he did not express them, and it is unlikely that he could reasonably have expected his readers to infer them.

(b) Last words from the cross (19:25b–30)

19:25b But standing by the cross of Jesus were his mother and his mother's sister, Mary the wife of Clopas and Mary of Magdala.

The first clause of verse 25 refers back to the dividing of Jesus' garments; in contrast to the conduct of the soldiers attention is now focused on the group of women standing by the cross. John is the only evangelist to introduce the mother of Jesus here; it is his narrative that underlies the words of the thirteenth-century hymn *Stabat Mater* ('At the cross, her station keeping'). If we take John's language by itself, it is uncertain whether he mentions three women or four; Mary the wife of Clopas might be the sister of Jesus' mother or might be a separate person. If, however, we correlate John's information with that about the women who were 'looking on from afar' in Mark 15:40 f. and Matt. 27:55 f., we might conclude that the sister was Salome (mother of the sons of Zebedee), while Mary the wife of Clopas was Mary the mother of James the younger and of Joses (Joseph).[30] John nowhere refers to the mother of Jesus by name, possibly to avoid confusion with other women named Mary. According to the second-century Palestinian writer Hegesippus, Clopas was the brother of Joseph the carpenter and father of that Simeon who became leader of the Jerusalem church after the stoning of James the Just.[31] Mary of Magdala (a town on the west shore of the Lake of Galilee, two or three miles north of Tiberias) figures in the passion narratives of all four Gospels.

19:26, 27 **So, when Jesus saw his mother, and the disciple whom he loved standing by her, he said to his mother, 'See, my lady, there is your son.' Then he said to the disciple, 'See, there is your mother.' And from that time the disciple took her to his own home.**

The beloved disciple, whom we have met previously at the supper table in the upper room (John 13:23 ff.), now appears by the cross, standing beside the mother of Jesus, possibly supporting her. None of the other Gospel narratives mentions a male disciple in this connexion. To his care Jesus now commits his mother: henceforth the beloved disciple (possibly her nephew by natural relationship) is to be a son to her, and to treat her as his mother. The phrase 'to his own home' (*eis ta idia*) at the end of verse 27 is identical with that at the beginning of John 1:11, 'he came to his own home' (cf. 16:32). The brothers of Jesus were still too unsympathetic to him to be entrusted with her care in this sad hour; in any case, they may not have been in Jerusalem at the time.[32]

As in John 2:4, it is difficult to decide on the best English equivalent of the vocative *gynai* in Jesus' address to his mother. In both places the NEB rendering is 'mother', but this obscures the probably significant fact that Jesus did not address her as 'mother', which he could easily have done had he wished to do so.

It is natural to wonder if John wishes to suggest some symbolic meaning beneath the historical fact of Mary's being entrusted to the care of the beloved disciple, but even if he does, we have no means of knowing certainly what that meaning might be. Taken

separately, the beloved disciple has often been taken to represent
the ideal follower of Jesus, and his mother to represent the faithful
remnant of Israel in the midst of which he was born; but in what
sense was that faithful remnant entrusted to the care of the ideal
disciple or disciples? Rudolf Bultmann interprets the symbolism
otherwise: 'The mother of Jesus, who tarries by the cross, represents Jewish Christianity that overcomes the offence of the cross.
The beloved disciple represents Gentile Christianity, which is
charged to honour the former as the mother from whom it has
come, even as Jewish Christianity is charged to recognize itself as
"at home" within Gentile Christianity, i.e. included in the membership of the one great fellowship of the Church.'[33] C. H. Dodd,
on the other hand, describes attempts to give the incident a symbolic meaning as 'singularly unconvincing'.[34] It is difficult not to
agree with him.

19:28 **After this, knowing that all things had now been accomplished, Jesus, in order that the scripture might be fulfilled, said,
'I am thirsty'.**

In the course of this narrative, various things are said to have
taken place in order that this or that scripture might be fulfilled –
the soldiers' dividing of Jesus' garments, for example (verses 23 f.).
But the agents who did those things had no idea that they were
fulfilling scripture: their actions were providentially overruled for
its fulfilment. When Jesus is the agent, the situation is different. It
goes without saying that he was actually thirsty and craved something to drink: exposure on a cross to the afternoon Judean sun
must have caused rapid and exhausting dehydration. But, as he
uttered the words, 'I am thirsty', he knew that in doing so he was
fulfilling scripture. The scripture in question may have been Ps.
69:21 ('for my thirst they gave me vinegar to drink') or Ps. 22:15
('my tongue cleaves to my jaws'). John does not want to give a
histrionic impression of our Lord's utterance: his words were unreservedly spontaneous – indeed, the more spontaneous they were,
the more truly was scripture fulfilled.

19:29, 30 **There was placed there a jar filled with vinegar. So
they soaked a sponge in the vinegar, put it on hyssop and
reached it to his mouth. So, when Jesus had taken the vinegar,
he said 'It is accomplished!', and he reclined his head and committed his spirit (to God).**

The 'vinegar' in the jar was probably sour wine, placed conveniently there for the soldiers to drink from time to time as they

guarded the three crosses. In soldiers' Latin it was called *posca*; John uses the same Greek word for 'vinegar' (*oxos*) as is used in the LXX of Ps. 69:21 (quoted above). It is not to be confused with the 'wine mingled with myrrh' which, according to Mark 15:23, Jesus refused when it was offered to him on his arrival at the place of execution. That was a sedative provided by charitable people in Jerusalem to dull the senses of the victims and to relieve something of their agony; Jesus resolved to die with unclouded mind. The present incident in John's narrative has its parallel in Mark 15:36, where the vinegar, far from dulling the senses, may be intended to preserve or revive full consciousness. Whereas Mark says that the sponge was put on a reed, John says it was placed on 'hyssop', meaning perhaps a sprig of hyssop (NEB mg. 'marjoram'). A sprig of hyssop seems an unsuitable instrument for the purpose, but John's wording may be influenced by the symbolic use of hyssop in the Old Testament, e.g. in the Passover ceremony (Exod. 12:22) and in purificatory ritual (Num. 19:6, 18; Ps. 51:7). The death of Jesus is the true Passover and the effective means of inward cleansing. Another possibility is that the sponge soaked in sour wine, with some hyssop thrust into it, was stretched to Jesus' mouth on the end of a reed or the like, in order that the cooling effect of the hyssop leaves might enhance the refreshing property of the sour wine.

Mention must be made, however, of the textual variant *hyssō* ('on a javelin') which is adopted in the NEB text, in preference to *hyssōpō* ('on hyssop). The reading *hyssō* was first suggested in the sixteenth century by Joachim Camerarius as a conjectural emendation; more recently it has been identified in the first hand of an eleventh-century Greek manuscript of the Gospels (minuscule 476), where a later hand has changed it to *hyssōpō* in conformity with the general text. For all its attractiveness, says G. D. Kilpatrick, 'this plausible conjecture lands us in improbabilities and difficulties greater than those of the text of our manuscripts'.[35] His main reason for saying so is that Gk. *hyssos* was the equivalent not of any kind of javelin but of one particular weapon, the Latin *pilum*, with which Roman legionary troops, not auxiliary troops, were armed. But during the six decades before AD 66 it was auxiliary troops, not legionary troops, that were stationed in Judaea; therefore no *hyssos* would have been available when our Lord was crucified for stretching the sponge to his lips. It could, of course, be urged that John used the word in a looser sense than do other Greek writers who use it in reference to the Roman army, but its attestation is so slender that it scarcely merits consideration (despite its adoption not only by the NEB but also by Moffatt, Goodspeed, Rieu, Phillips, the Basic Bible, and Kingsley Williams).[36]

Jesus' cry 'It is accomplished!' (*tetelestai*, perfect passive of *teleō*) confirms the Evangelist's preceding statement in verse 28 that he knew 'that all things had now been accomplished' (*tetelestai*). All scripture that was due to be accomplished in his passion had now been accomplished; the entire purpose for which the Father had sent the Son into the world was now assured of fulfilment, and since that purpose included the salvation of the world and the procuring of eternal life for all believers (John 3:14–17), salvation and eternal life were henceforth freely available. In John 17:4 the Son could say to the Father in anticipation, 'I have fulfilled the work which thou gavest me to do' (where 'fulfilled' represents the verb *teleioō*, used also of the fulfilment of scripture in verse 28); now, no longer in anticipation but in the consummating moment of death, he declares this work to be finished.

Elsewhere in the Gospels the same phrase as is here used of Jesus' reclining his head in death is used of reclining one's head in sleep (Matt. 8:20; Luke 9:28, 'the Son of Man has nowhere to lay his head'); the implication here may be that he voluntarily reclines his head, ready now to sleep the sleep of death. This is reinforced by the words 'he committed his spirit' (that is, to God), for these words are John's counterpart to Luke's report that his last words were, 'Father, into thy hands I commit my spirit' (Luke 23:46). These words from Ps. 31:5 have for centuries formed part of the evening prayer of pious Jews, and may well have done so for Jesus. If, then, he was accustomed to repeat these words before going to sleep, so he repeated them now for the last time.

6. CRURIFRAGIUM, DEPOSITION AND BURIAL (19:31–42)

19:31 So, since it was the eve of the sabbath, the Jews requested Pilate that the men's legs should be broken and that they should be taken down. The object of this request was that their bodies should not remain on the crosses on the sabbath, for that sabbath day was a great day.

In verse 14 *paraskeuē* ('preparation') was translated 'Passover Eve' because there it is linked with the noun *pascha*. Here it stands alone, and therefore more probably means 'Sabbath Eve' or Friday. It makes no practical difference, because in that year the Passover coincided with the weekly sabbath: that is why John says 'that sabbath day was a great day'. Such a conjunction of weekly sabbath and annual passover still occurs from time to time in the Jewish calendar.

According to Jewish law, bodies might not be left exposed on gibbets after sundown (Deut. 21:22f.). The Roman administration, of course, would not consider itself bound by Deuteronomic law, but urgent representations were made to Pilate by the Jewish authorities on this occasion, because the continued exposure of the bodies would be exceptionally offensive on a day when sabbath and passover coincided. They asked, therefore, that the men's legs might be broken and their bodies removed.

The breaking of the legs (*crurifragium*) was an established custom when it was desired to hasten the death of a crucified person. The young man whose bones, recently discovered, gave clear evidence of crucifixion (see comment on verse 18) was apparently subjected to this treatment: one of his legs had sustained a clean fracture from a single blow which also cracked the other, but the other had in addition suffered comminution. The common view today seems to be that the breaking of the legs hastened death by asphyxiation. The weight of the body fixed the thoracic cage so that the lungs could not expel the air which was breathed in, but breathing by diaphragmatic action could continue for a long time so long as the legs, fastened to the cross, provided a point of leverage.[37] When the legs were broken this leverage was no longer available and total asphyxia followed rapidly.

19:32–34 So the soldiers came and broke the legs of the first man and of the other who was crucified with him. Then they came to Jesus, but when they saw that he was dead already, they did not break his legs; but one of the soldiers pierced his side with a lance, and immediately blood and water came out.

Since Jesus was crucified between the two others (verse 18), the fact that they were dealt with first implies that one or two soldiers worked from either side; having broken the legs of the other two, they came together where the body of Jesus was hanging and said, 'No need to do it to *him*!' Just to make sure, however, one of them pushed the point of his lance into Jesus' side; but there was no sign of life.

Attempts have been made by medical experts to diagnose the cause of Jesus' death from the effusion of blood and water which followed the piercing of his side. Not surprisingly, the diagnoses have varied: for one thing, John does not say which side was pierced (an early tradition specifies the right side); for another, we have no idea whether the blood and water came from just beneath the skin or from a deeper source (such as the pericardial sac). The physiological significance of John's statement is uncertain (and perhaps it should be added that to call in the marks on the Holy Shroud of Turin as evidence is not really helpful); but it was with the fact of death, not with the cause of death, that John was concerned. For John it was important that the reality of Jesus' death (and therewith the reality of his manhood) was so objectively established; this was sufficient answer to those forms of docetism current when he wrote which held that the Christ did not really die. The persistence of this view is reflected in the statement in the Qur'ān that 'they did not kill him, neither did they crucify him; it only seemed to be so'.[38] John refutes it in his epistles as well as in the Gospel, but it is doubtful whether there is any direct correlation between the 'water and blood' of 1 John 5:6, 8, and the 'blood and water' mentioned here.[39]

19:35 And he who has seen it has borne testimony, and his testimony is true, and *he* knows that he is telling the truth, in order that you also may believe.

These words are plainly designed to emphasize in the most solemn manner that what has just been recorded is the testimony of a reliable witness. What the eyewitness saw kindled faith in him, and his testimony is set down here in order that by it similar faith may be kindled in the readers. We may compare the declared purpose of the whole record in 20:31: 'These have been written in order that you may believe that Jesus is the Christ, the Son of God, and that believing you may have life in his name.' The eyewitness has (not unnaturally) been identified with the beloved disciple (cf. verse 26), of whom it is said in 21:24, 'This is the disciple who testifies of these things and who wrote these things.'[40]

The further testimonial which is immediately added there, 'and we know that his testimony is true' (probably appended by the persons responsible for publishing the Gospel) is of the same character as the present testimonial, 'and his testimony is true' (which may be given by the same group). But it is more difficult to interpret the further words, 'and *he* knows that he is telling the truth', with the emphatic pronoun *ekeinos* as the subject of 'knows'. Who is it who knows that the eyewitness is telling the truth? One suggestion is that appeal is being made to the testimony of the now ascended Christ; in 1 John the pronoun *ekeinos*, whenever it is used personally, always denotes Christ. But in the occurrences in 1 John the context makes it plain that the pronoun refers to Christ; it is not so plain here.

If the beloved disciple's associates, who may have been responsible for the publication of his record, affirmed their belief in his veracity, they could have added that that disciple himself vouched for the truth of what he said – if that disciple was still alive at the time of writing, as seems to be indicated.[41]

That eternal life is received through faith in the Son of God is repeatedly emphasized in this Gospel, but this faith must be exercised in him not only as the one who truly became flesh but as the one who truly died. The testimony of verse 35 is thus an aid to saving faith.

19:36, 37 For these things took place in order that the scripture might be fulfilled: 'No bone of him shall be broken.' Again, there is another scripture which says: 'They will see the one whom they pierced.'

As with the fulfilment of scripture by the partition of Jesus' clothes, so here there is no suggestion that the soldiers had any inkling that their actions were giving effect to what had been written long before. Rather, their actions were providentially overruled by God for the accomplishment of his purpose.

For the first quotation there are two OT passages that call for consideration. One is Ps. 34:20 where God is portrayed as the deliverer of the righteous man: 'He keeps all his bones (i.e. God guards all the bones of the righteous man); not one of them is broken.' If this scripture were in the Evangelist's mind here, his reference to it would underline Jesus' righteousness or innocence, much in the spirit of Luke's version of the centurion's testimony: 'Certainly this man was innocent (righteous)!' (Luke 23:47). But, while some exegetes consider this reference 'more likely' than a reference to the paschal lamb,[42] there would be much more point here if John had in mind the prescription with regard to the paschal lamb: 'you shall not break a bone of it' (Ex. 12:46; cf. Num. 9:12). Jesus, in John's eyes, is the antitypical paschal lamb, and his death on the cross coincides with the sacrificing of the lambs in the temple precincts. R. C. Chapman penetrated to the heart of the Evangelist's intention in the opening lines of his communion hymn:

> No bone of Thee was broken,
> Thou spotless Paschal Lamb!

Whereas in Ps. 34:20 the guarding of the righteous man's bones means the preservation of his general well-being, the literal sense of the term in John's narrative consorts better with its literal sense in the prescription regarding the passover lamb.[43]

If John sees one scripture fulfilled in the non-breaking of Jesus' legs, he sees another fulfilled in the positive act of the piercing of his side. This time no question arises about the identity of the scripture: it is Zech. 12:10, where, after the defeat of the nations who lay siege to Jerusalem at the end-time, the God of Israel says: 'I will pour out on the house of David and the inhabitants of

Jerusalem a spirit of compassion and supplication, so that, when they look on me whom they have pierced, they shall mourn for him, as one mourns for an only child . . .' In Rev. 1:7 these words are applied to the parousia of Christ (cf. Matt. 24:30). The original life-setting of the words in Zechariah, with the curious oscillation (in the Massoretic text) between the pronouns 'me' and 'him', may belong to the national liturgy of Israel, where the king, the Lord's anointed, is (symbolically) pierced.

Since the king is God's representative, the treatment he receives is reckoned by God as meted out to himself; hence the divine oracle runs (in the NEB rendering of Zech. 12:10, which does justice to both pronouns at once): 'They shall look on me, on him whom they have pierced.' But John recognizes the fulfilment of the oracle in no merely symbolical piercing, but in the literal piercing of the side of him who endured a real passion, historical and not simply dramatic, as 'The King of the Jews'. The oracles of Zech. 9–14 have profoundly influenced all four passion narratives in the NT, but nowhere more impressively than here.[44]

19:38 After this Joseph of Arimathaea, a disciple of Jesus (but a secret one, for fear of the Jews), asked Pilate for permission to remove Jesus' body. Pilate gave him permission.

Joseph of Arimathaea (perhaps identical with Ramathaim-Zophim of 1 Sam. 1:1) receives honourable mention from all four Evangelists, but only in connexion with his rendering this last service to the body of Jesus. According to Mark and Luke, he was a member of the Sanhedrin. It is noteworthy, but not psychologically incredible, that after having so cautiously concealed his adherence to Jesus' cause from his fellow-councillors thus far, he should now throw caution to the winds and reveal his true colours. A member of the Sanhedrin, indeed, would have readier access to the governor than Jesus' humbler friends and followers could venture to seek. Roman law normally handed over the bodies of executed criminals to their next of kin, but not if they had been executed for sedition. Why then did Pilate hand over the body of Jesus to Joseph, who was not related to him, when Jesus had in fact been executed for sedition? Perhaps because Pilate was convinced that Jesus was not really guilty of the crime alleged against him.

19:39, 40 Nicodemus too (who on a former occasion had come to Jesus by night) came with a mixture of myrrh and aloes, about a hundred pounds in weight. So they took the body of

Jesus and wrapped it in strips of linen cloth with the spices, according to the Jews' burial custom.

If all four Evangelists mention Joseph, only John mentions Nicodemus, another member of the Sanhedrin. Nicodemus has appeared on two earlier occasions in this Gospel: when he sought Jesus out by night during one of Jesus' previous visits to Jerusalem (3:1 ff.) – the occasion to which John makes reference here – and when he challenged his fellow-councillors' right to pass judgment on Jesus unheard, six months before the events now being recorded (7:50 ff). Now he appears again, bringing a hundredweight of mixed spices for the burial (to bring such a quantity he must, of course, have had the aid of servants).[45]

Even if his mixture of myrrh and aloes was not so costly an ointment as Mary of Bethany's 'pistic nard' (John 12:3–5), so great a weight of it must have represented an outlay which only an exceptionally wealthy man could afford. But why so great a weight of aromatic spices to prepare one man's body for burial? One would not be surprised if it were for a royal burial – but that is precisely what Jesus' burial was in the eyes of Nicodemus, and probably of Joseph too. To them he was in fact what the inscription on the cross had proclaimed him to be in mockery – 'The King of the Jews'. The spices in powdered form were spread on the lengths of linen cloth (*othonia*) which were used as winding sheets, so that grave-clothes and body alike were impregnated with them. This procedure was not the Egyptian practice of embalming: the Jews did not first remove various internal organs from the body and fill the cavities with sweet spices, as the Egyptians did.

19:41, 42 Now in the place where he was crucified there was a garden, and in the garden there was a new tomb, in which no one had yet been laid. So, since the tomb was near at hand, they laid Jesus there, because it was the eve of the Jewish sabbath.

The 'place where he was crucified' recalls the previous occurrences of the word 'place' (*topos*) in this connexion (verses 17, 20); it is so used, in fact, by all four Evangelists. The concluding phrase (literally 'because of the Jews' preparation') contains the word *paraskeuē* without qualification, as in verse 31, and what was said there applies here. Time was short, because sundown would bring on the sabbath, when work would have to stop, so because of the proximity of the garden tomb the body was placed in it. A rock-hewn tomb is to be understood, as is made explicit in the Synoptic narratives.

Eusebius, in his contemporary account of the uncovering of the traditional tomb by Constantine (c. AD 325), describes it as a 'cave'.[46] (It is commonly referred to as the 'edicule'.) To locate it, Constantine had to demolish and remove the temple of Venus which Hadrian had erected there when he built his new city of Aelia Capitolina on the site of Jerusalem in AD 135 and the following years. On the site so uncovered Constantine built his 'Church of the Resurrection'; it has been occupied since Crusading times by the Church of the Holy Sepulchre.[47] (The site now called the Garden Tomb probably presents the visitor with a general picture of what the original site looked like in AD 30, even if the tomb seen there is of a style two or three centuries later than that date.)

NOTES

1. On more and less severe beatings in Roman penal law see A. N. Sherwin-White, *Roman Society and Roman Law in the New Testament*, pp. 27 f.
2. See H. St. J. Hart, 'The Crown of Thorns in John 19.2–5' *JTS* n.s. 3 (1952), pp. 66–75.
3. In the Latin Bible, *Ecce homo*. Hence the name given to the 'Ecce Homo arch', the traditional site of this incident, at the beginning of the Via Dolorosa. The arch actually belongs to the Emperor Hadrian's rebuilding of Jerusalem (AD 135), but may approximately cover the actual site (eight feet beneath the present street level) if the trial took place in the precincts of the Antonia fortress.
4. Philo, *Flaccus*, 36–39.
5. See comment and note on John 18:32. The 'Temple Scroll' from Qumran makes provision for 'hanging a man on a tree, that he may die', in specific situations where the Israelite covenant-bond has been violated (11Q Temple 64.6–13); but it is not clear that this relates to current penal practice. Cf. J. A. Fitzmyer, 'Crucifixion in Ancient Palestine, Qumran Literature, and the New Testament', *CBQ* 40 (1978), pp. 493–513.
6. Mishnah, tractate *Sanhedrin*, 7.5.
7. Justinian, *Digest* 50.17.37.
8. Although Caiaphas owed his appointment as high priest to a Roman governor, this is not taken into the reckoning here. The high priesthood was a divine institution and the fact that Caiaphas now occupied it imposed certain responsibilities on him.
9. Sejanus's downfall is recorded by Josephus, *Antiquities* 18.181 f.; Tacitus, *Annals* 5.6–9; Suetonius, *Tiberius* 61–65; Dio Cassius, *History* 58.4.1–16.7; 65.14.1 f.; cf. Juvenal, *Satire* 10.56–107. He is credited with a virulently anti-Jewish policy (Philo, *Legation to Gaius*, 159–161), but that Pilate was his nominee, charged with carrying out that policy in Judaea, is an uncertain inference from Philo. Those who draw this inference are disposed to the view that Pilate's ready capitulation to the chief priests' threat on the present occasion was due to the recent disgrace and death of his sponsor, which rendered his own position insecure, and that the trial and death of Jesus should therefore be dated after AD 31 (and accordingly in AD 33, a calendrically suitable year).
10. See L. H. Vincent, 'Le lithostrate évangélique', *RB* 59 (1952), pp. 513–530; for a contrary view, P. Benoit, 'Prétoire, Lithostroton and Gabbatha', *Jesus and the Gospel*, I (New York, 1973), pp. 167–188. Cf. also John 18:28, with comment and notes.
11. Justin, *First Apology* 35.6; *Gospel of Peter* 3:7 ('they . . . set him on the judgment seat and said, 'Judge righteously, O King of Israel!'' ').

12. But the first clear occurrence of Gk. *paraskeuē* in the sense of 'Friday' is in the *Martyrdom of Polycarp* 7.1 AD 156).

13. There is a useful discussion of this point (and of the relation of the present passage to the time-note in Mark 15:25) in L. Morris, *The Gospel according to John* (Grand Rapids, 1971), pp. 800 f., notes 34, 35. See also John 1:39 with comment and note (pp. 56, 66, n. 56).

14. According to Mishnah, tractate P^esāḥîm 5.1, when the Passover fell on the eve of a Sabbath, the evening burnt-offering was slaughtered at 12.30 p.m. and offered up at 1.30 (two hours earlier than usual), and after that the paschal lamb was slaughtered.

15. The verb used here by both John and Luke is *paradidōmi* (for which see comment on verse 11). Where Jesus is the object of this verb, the subject is variously Judas (John 6:71), Caiaphas (verse 11, by implication), Pilate (here) and indeed (though not in John) God (cf. Rom. 8:32, 'delivered him up for us all').

16. The verb *paralambanō* ('receive') is the regular correlative to *paradidōmi* ('deliver'), used in the earlier part of this verse: the latter action by the one party implies the former action by the other.

17. Cf. Plutarch, *The Divine Vengeance* 554 A/B: 'Each criminal as part of his punishment carries his cross on his back.'

18. *Genesis Rabba* 56.4 (on Gen. 22:6).

19. Irenaeus (*Against Heresies* 1.24.2) charges Basilides with this misrepresentation, but the validity of the charge is doubtful.

20. Mark 8:34 and parallels.

21. Cf. K. M. Kenyon, *Jerusalem: Excavating 3000 Years of History* (London, 1967), pp. 146–154; *Digging Up Jerusalem* (London, 1974), pp. 226–232, 261; U. Lux, 'Vorläufiger Bericht über die Ausgrabungen unter der Erlöserkirche im Muristan in der Altstadt von Jerusalem', *ZDPV* 88 (1972), pp. 185–201; 'Jerusalem: Quartier du Mauristan', *RB* 79 (1972), pp. 577 f.

22. Cicero, *Verrine Orations* 5.64. See P. Barbet, *The Passion of our Lord Jesus Christ* (Dublin, 1954), and especially M. Hengel, *Crucifixion* (London, 1977).

23. Cf. V. Tzaferis, 'Jewish Tombs at and near Giv'at ha-Mivtar, Jerusalem', *IEJ* 20 (1970), pp. 18–32; J. Naveh, 'The Ossuary Inscription from Giv'at ha-Mivtar', *ibid.*, pp. 33–37; N. Haas, 'Anthropological Observations on the Skeletal Remains from Giv'at ha-Mivtar', *ibid.*, pp. 38–59.

24. John does not expressly say that Jesus' feet were nailed to the cross; this may be implied in Luke 24:40 (a text absent from the Western witness and therefore double-bracketed by Westcott and Hort as a 'Western non-interpolation').

25. Cf. Philo, *Legation to Gaius* 301, where Pilate is described as 'naturally inflexible, a blend of obstinacy and relentlessness'.

26. A gloss on the LXX text of Ps. 96:10, much prized by some second-century Christians, read: 'Say among the nations, "The Lord reigned *from the tree*" ' (cf. Justin, *Dialogue with Trypho* 73).

27. In the LXX (as quoted here) the noun in the first clause is *himatia* (plural of *himation*) but that in the second clause is not *chitōn* but *himatismos*.

28. Josephus, *Antiquities* 3.161.

29. Philo, *On Flight and Finding*, 110–112.

30. Joses (Mark 15:40) is simply one of the Hellenized forms of Joseph (Matt. 27:56); cf. Joses in Mark 6:3 alongside Joseph in Matt. 13:55, and the variant readings Joses/Joseph in Acts 4:36.

31. Eusebius, *Hist. Eccl.* 3.11.

32. The striking change in attitude shown by our Lord's brothers who did not believe in him six months before his death (John 7:5) but are found (along with his mother) in the company of the apostles immediately after his ascension (Acts

1:14), would be inexplicable apart from Paul's information that in resurrection the Lord 'appeared to James' (1 Cor. 15:7).

33. R. Bultmann, *The Gospel of John* (Oxford. 1971), p. 673.

34. C. H. Dodd, *The Interpretation of the Fourth Gospel*, p. 428. See also F. Neirynck, '*Eis ta idia*: Jn 19, 27b (et 16, 32)', in *Evangelica* (Leuven, 1982), pp. 456–464; 'La traduction d'un verset johannique: Jn 19, 27b', *ibid.*, pp. 465–488.

35. G. D. Kilpatrick, 'The Transmission of the New Testament and its Reliability', *Journal of Transactions of the Victoria Institute* 89 (1957), pp. 98 f.

36. In a manuscript with no spacing between the words, *hyssōpō perithentes* ('putting it on hyssop') would have been written HYSSOPOPERITHENTES. The letters ŌP, which appear twice, could have been accidentally copied once only (by haplography); those who prefer the reading *hyssō* ('on a javelin') considers that they were accidentally copied twice (by dittography).

37. Where a *sedecula* was provided (see comment on verse 18), this afforded further support and deferred the welcome moment of death.

38. *Sura*, 4.156. Muhammad's knowledge of the gospel story seems to have been dependent on a 'docetic' source.

39. See F. F. Bruce, *The Epistles of John*, pp. 118–121. In an article entitled ' "Mingled" Blood from the Side of Christ', Dr. J. M. Ford argues, on the basis of rabbinical usage, that John's statement in verse 34 is intended to show that this passover victim completely satisfied levitical requirements (*NTS* 15 [1968–69] pp. 337 f.).

40. It might be inferred from the last clause of verse 27, however, that the beloved disciple took Jesus' mother home with him as soon as she had been committed to his care, and so would not have been present when Jesus' side was pierced. W. Temple assumes that he left Mary at home in order to return himself 'to hear the last words and to see the wondrous end' (*Readings in St. John's Gospel* [London, 1940], p. 367).

41. See pp. 408 f.

42. Cf. C. H. Dodd, *The Interpretation of the Fourth Gospel*, p. 428, n. 1.

43. Cf. also Paul's words, 'Christ, our paschal lamb, has been sacrificed' (1 Cor. 5:7); the same association is implied in 1 Peter 1:19.

44. For a fuller discussion see F. F. Bruce, *This is That* (Exeter, 1968), pp. 101–113. On the two OT quotations here see E. D. Freed, *Old Testament Quotations in the Gospel of John*, pp. 108–116.

45. Five hundred servants carrying spices took part in Herod the Great's funeral procession in 4 BC (Josephus, *Antiquities* 17.199). The natural inference from the present record is that Joseph and Nicodemus, with their servants, took Jesus' body down from the cross and saw to its embalming and burial.

46. Eusebius, *Life of Constantine* 3.26, 28. It was indeed a cave, albeit an artificial one.

47. Cf. J. Wilkinson, 'The Tomb of Christ', *Levant* 4 (1972), pp. 83–97; C. Coüasnon, *The Church of the Holy Sepulchre, Jerusalem* (Oxford, 1972).

CHAPTER 20

II. The Resurrection Narrative (20:1–29)

1. THE EMPTY TOMB (20:1–10)

'After the presentation of the death of Jesus as itself his "exaltation" and "glorification" ', a recent writer has remarked, 'the resurrection comes as something of a surprise in this Gospel.'[1] If John were concerned merely to provide his readers with a theological meditation on the significance of Jesus, there might be some substance in that remark. But John is concerned to relate events which really happened – and the resurrection really happened, so he could not leave it out. Otherwise he might have brought his narrative to a close with 'It is finished' (19:30) or with the solemn attestation of the eyewitness in 19:35 (where Vacher Burch, over half a century ago, argued that an original Aramaic draft of the Gospel ended).[2] The fact that John did not stop there, but went on to describe Jesus' burial in preparation for the resurrection narrative, is further testimony to his fidelity to the primitive apostolic message, in which crowning emphasis was laid on the fact of the risen Christ.

We can discern two cycles of resurrection appearances in the NT: a Galilaean cycle (presupposed by Mark and recorded by Matthew) and a Judaean cycle (recorded by Luke). (The appearances listed by Paul in 1 Cor. 15:5–7 are not geographically located by him, although we can locate some of them in the light of other evidence.) Both cycles find a place in this Gospel – the Judaean cycle in chapter 20 and the Galilaean cycle in chapter 21.

20:1, 2 On the first day of the week Mary of Magdala comes to the tomb early, while it was still dark, and sees the stone moved away from the tomb. So she runs and comes to Simon Peter and the other disciple, the disciple whom Jesus loved, and says to them. 'They have taken the Lord out of the tomb, and we do not know where they have put him.'

John's use of the present tense conveys the vividness of the events and Mary's excitement. Considering how little we know about Mary of Magdala, it is surprising what a vivid impression we get of her vital personality. Only one piece of information has been preserved about her before the passion narrative: Luke includes her in the number of the women who attended our Lord and the

disciples during the Galilaean ministry and 'provided for them out
of their means' (cf. Mark 15:41), mentioning that from her 'seven
demons had gone out' (Luke 8:2 f.), which suggests exceptionally
acute mental disturbance. Mark, with Matthew, agrees expressly
with John that she was one of the women who witnessed the
crucifixion, and Luke agrees by implication (cf. Luke 23:49, 55,
with 24:10); all four of the Evangelists make her one of the first
witnesses of the empty tomb.

It is from John's resurrection narrative, however, that we get the
clearest picture of her, and we are left wishing that we knew much
more about her, especially about her subsequent career, than we
do. Legend is very willing to fill the gap left by factual records,
but the only positive value of legend is its confirmation of the
impression of her devotion and enterprise which the Gospel narratives give. It is not surprising that she has been confused in
tradition with another Mary whose devotion to our Lord was
equally outstanding – Mary of Bethany – but John's narrative in
particular rules out any identification of the two.

Her words to Peter and John, 'we do not know where they have
put him', indicate that she was not unaccompanied when she went
to the tomb, but she so obviously took the lead that John does not
even say in so many words that there were other women with her,
let alone mention their names, as the other Evangelists do. But
when the others mention her companions' names, they agree in
putting hers first. This may reflect the early church's remembrance
that she was the first witness of the risen Christ, preceding even
Peter in this regard. If her witness nevertheless was not stressed
(as Peter's was) in the primitive preaching, this was probably because a woman's testimony was of little public account.[3] Celsus,
the anti-Christian polemicist of the later second century, dismisses
the resurrection narrative as based on the hallucination of a 'hys-
terical woman'.[4]

All that the removal of the stone (not previously mentioned by
John) and the untenanted tomb meant to Mary was that the body
of Jesus had been removed – by whom or whither she could not
think. But the news must be brought at once to the most responsible of Jesus' followers, so she ran to tell Peter and the beloved
disciple what she had found.

**20:3-5 So Peter and the other disciple set out and came to the
tomb. Both of them ran together, and the other disciple ran
ahead faster than Peter and came to the tomb first. He bent
down and looked in, and saw the lengths of linen cloth lying
there, but did not go in.**

If the beloved disciple got to the tomb before Peter, it was probably because he was younger and fleeter of foot; it is hazardous to seek some allegorical significance in John's statement. Until his companion caught up with him, the beloved disciple contented himself with peeping into the tomb from outside (which is what is meant by the verb *parakyptō* used here). He could see the grave-clothes lying unoccupied, which suggested that it was not just a simple removal of the body that was involved.

20:6, 7 Then hard on his heels Simon Peter came also, and he went into the tomb. There he saw the lengths of linen cloth lying, and the napkin too, which was over the Lord's head; it was not lying with the lengths of linen but rolled up separately in one place.

With characteristic impetuosity Peter went right into the tomb when he caught up with his companion. There he saw not only the graveclothes in which the Lord's body had been wrapped up, but also the napkin which had been round his head. The word for 'napkin' (*soudarion*) is a loanword from Latin (*sudarium*) and means literally 'sweat-rag' (cf. Luke 19:20; Acts 19:12), but it had a more general usage. Lazarus also had a *soudarion* tied round his head when he emerged from his tomb at Jesus' command (John 11:44). The phrase 'in one place' may mean 'in a place by itself' (RSV, NEB). This may mean that the napkin was 'separated by the brief space where the neck had been' from the other grave clothes, as William Temple suggests; but we cannot be sure. The glorified body may have passed through the winding sheets as later it appeared suddenly within closed doors (verse 19), but the description of the napkin suggests not that it retained the shape which it had when the Lord's head was inside it but rather that someone, having no further use for it, had rolled it up and laid it tidily aside. At any rate, 'it is extraordinarily vivid, and such as no invention would devise, no freak of imagination conjure up'.[5]

20:8, 9 So then the other disciple, the one who had arrived at the tomb first, entered in also, and he saw – and believed. For they did not yet know the scripture, (which said) that he must rise from the dead.

When the beloved disciple followed Peter into the tomb, he saw what Peter had seen, but with the eye of faith he saw more. Like a flash it came home to him what had happened: the Lord had risen from the dead and left the tomb. It is implied that Peter was only puzzled by what he saw, and could not fathom what it meant –

although Rudolf Bultmann draws the opposite inference: 'Clearly, it is presupposed that Peter before him was likewise brought to faith through the sight of the empty grave'.[6] In general, it is true that 'the early Christians did not believe in the resurrection of Christ because they could not find his dead body; they believed because they did find a living Christ'.[7] But there was one exception: the beloved disciple believed in his resurrection before he saw him alive again – not indeed because he saw the empty tomb but because the disposition of the grave-clothes suddenly made the truth clear to him.

But did they not expect the Lord to rise from the dead? Why did the beloved disciple have to wait until the mute witness of the grave-clothes convinced him? And why did even that witness not bring the truth home to Peter? The reason, says John, is that up to this point they did not know that his rising from the dead was foretold in prophetic scripture. It was only in the light of the events themselves that the testimony of scripture became luminous to them. At the cleansing of the temple court their Master had spoken of the raising up of 'the temple of his body'; but, says John as he records this incident, 'when he had been raised from the dead, his disciples remembered that he said this; and they believed the scripture and the word that Jesus had spoken' (John 2:19–22).

It is uncertain whether the singular 'scripture' (*graphē*) points to one particular text or refers to the general testimony of the Old Testament. Since John does not specify any scripture, we cannot be sure which he may have had in mind, but we might think of Hosea 6:2 ('on the third day he will raise us up') or Lev. 23:11 ('the morrow after the sabbath'). The 'must' (*dei*) is the 'must' of the divine decree. There is no need to see a tension between verse 9 and what goes before (Bultmann calls verse 9 'a gloss of the ecclesiastical redaction');[8] the fact that it is linked to what goes before by the conjunction 'for' (*gar*) indicates a causal connexion, and an attempt has been made to bring out this connexion in the foregoing paragraph.

20:10 So the disciples went back home again.

So ends John's narrative of the empty tomb. That the tomb was found empty is recorded as a matter of some importance by all four evangelists, but it is given no prominence in the apostolic preaching. In Paul's summary of that preaching in 1 Cor. 15:3–7 it is not mentioned, although it is implied by his mention of the Lord's burial between his death and his resurrection. The emptiness of the tomb in itself would suggest only the conclusion to which Mary came – that the body had been removed. But if the tomb had *not* been empty, or if the body of Jesus could have been produced, the apostles' proclamation that the Lord had risen indeed would never have got off the ground; it would have been refuted in their hearers' minds by the brute facts of the case. For to them resurrection meant bodily resurrection; the empty tomb, therefore, while by no means sufficient to confirm the resurrection message, was essential to its acceptance.

The Greek phrase rendered 'home' is *pros hautous* (=*heatous*), 'to themselves' (cf. *pros heauton*, 'to himself', with reference to Peter alone, in Luke 24:12), practically synonymous with *eis ta idia* (19:27, etc.).

2. Appearance to Mary of Magdala (20:11–18)

20:11–13 But Mary stood by the tomb, outside it, weeping. While she was weeping, she bent down and looked into the tomb, and saw two angels in white sitting, one at the head and one at the feet, where the body of Jesus had been lying. They said to her, 'Woman, why are you weeping?' She said to them, 'They have taken my Lord away, and I do not know where they have put him.'

Mary was determined to find out what had happened to the body of Jesus; she reckoned, probably, that if she stayed around someone might come along who could give her the information she wanted. As she stood there weeping, she bent down and looked into the tomb, as the beloved disciple had done (the same verb *parakyptō* is used here as was used of him in verse 5). The relation of the two angels whom she saw to the 'two men' whom, according to Luke 24:4, she and her companions saw, need not detain us here. It is one of the less important problems which arise when an attempt is made to correlate the various accounts of the visits to the tomb and the resurrection appearances.[9] Such attempts have an interest and, indeed, importance of their own, but they are not directly relevant to the straightforward exegesis of one writer's coherent narrative. Unlike the two men of Luke 24 (or the one 'young man' of Mark 16:5 ff.), these two angels do not tell Mary that Christ has risen from the dead. In answer to their question, she tells them why she is weeping, using language similar to that of her report to the two disciples in verse 2 but marked by a more personal note. They make no reply to her – nor, indeed (as the sequel showed), had they any need to do so.

The incident of the two angels is of special interest because of its possible bearing on the details of the tomb. The tomb itself had been recently hewn out of the rock,[10] and its entrance was normally

THE GOSPEL OF JOHN

sealed by a stone (what was commonly used for such a purpose
was a roughly squared stone fitting into the entrance like a stopper).
But what of the resting-place for the body? Various provisions for
such a resting place are known from that period: a *loculus* or burial
chamber hollowed out in the inner wall of the tomb (of a type
familiar in the Roman catacombs), a bench running round the inner
wall, a bench-arcosolium (a flat surface under a recessed arch in
the wall) or a trough-arcosolium (a sarcophagus hollowed out under
a recessed arch).[11] A *loculus* has been thought to be ruled out by
the description of the angels sitting at the head and feet; of the
other possibilities a bench or bench arcosolium would seem to be
more likely. The earliest Christian writers who describe the tomb
uncovered in the fourth century tend rather to imply a trough-
arcosolium. But angels would not require the same material support
as beings of flesh and blood, and even if it was a trough-arcosolium
they may have appeared to be seated on its edge or rim at either
end.

20:14, 15 **Having said this she turned back and saw Jesus
standing, but did not know that it was Jesus. Jesus said to her,
'Woman, why are you weeping? Who is it you are looking for?'
Supposing that he was the gardener she said to him, 'Sir, if it is
you who have removed him, tell me where you have put him,
and I will take him away.'**

In some of the resurrection narratives Jesus is not immediately
recognizable by his friends. In the story of the two disciples on the
Emmaus road, for example, 'their eyes were kept from recognizing
him' (Luke 24:16). Mary, however, may simply have been so
blinded by her tears that she could only make out the form of a
man standing behind her. But the kindly words in which the supposed gardener addressed her[12] encouraged her to think that now
at last she had found someone who could tell her what had happened to the body of her Lord. If that was so, he would know
why she was weeping and who it was she was looking for; hence
she does not repeat her sad tale, 'They have taken away my Lord',
but simply says, 'If it is you who have removed him, tell me where
you have put him.'

20:16 **Jesus said to her, 'Mary!' She turned and said to him in
Hebrew, 'Rabbuni!' (which means 'Teacher').**

Mary's willingness to make arrangements for the proper disposal
of the body show her to have been a woman of enterprise and
probably also of substance (as Luke 8:2 f. suggests); she was willing

to pay for the labour and other expenses involved. One may wonder why, when she found that the tomb had (as she thought) been
tampered with, she did not go straight to Joseph of Arimathaea
and enlist his aid. It can hardly have been because he was too
distinguished a personage to be disturbed. Perhaps he was inaccessible; in fact, he has been inaccessible to our knowledge ever since
he rendered the last services to the body of the crucified one, for
we have no further information about him.

If the sympathetic stranger's kindly enquiry was insufficient for
recognition, his calling her by name was all that was necessary.
Immediately her distress vanished; here was something far better
than she had dreamed possible. Instead of the dead body she had
hoped to recover, she found herself face to face with her living
Lord. The word with which she greeted him was probably her
regular designation for him. 'Rabbuni' (used also by Bartimaeus in
Mark 10:51) was an Aramaic form, more emphatic and perhaps
more honorific than the simpler 'Rabbi'.[13] (We have seen in John
19:13, 17 how this Evangelist uses 'Hebrew' to include Aramaic.)
That there was little essential difference in meaning between 'Rabbuni' and 'Rabbi' seems clear from John's use of the Greek vocative
didaskale to render both forms (cf. John 1:38).

20:17, 18 **Jesus said to her, 'Don't hold on to me, for I have
not yet ascended to the Father. Go to my brothers and tell them,
"I am ascending to my Father and your Father, to my God and
your God".' Mary of Magdala came with the news to the disciples, 'I have seen the Lord', and she told them that he had said
these things to her.**

The exact significance of Jesus' admonition, 'Don't hold on to
me', is uncertain; it depends in part on the force of the conjunction
'for' which links it to the following statement, 'I have not yet
ascended to the Father'. The use of the negative *mē* with the
present imperative indicates that Mary is being told to stop what
she is doing. The AV rendering 'Touch me not' is thus inadequate;
it might easily be taken to mean 'Don't lay a finger on me'. The
most natural interpretation is that Mary, in her delight at finding
her Lord alive, clutches him lest she should lose him again. His
words might mean, 'Let me go; I have not ascended to the Father
yet. Go and take this message to my brothers; I shall still be
available when you have done so.' But this is by no means certain.
The ascension referred to here may be an earlier occasion than that
described in Acts 1:9, when a cloud enveloped him and removed
him from the sight of his watching disciples. That brought an end
to the series of resurrection appearances to them over a period of

forty days; this has to do with a new phase of Jesus' personal relationship with the Father, apart from which he could not confirm his spiritual presence to his disciples in perpetuity. If so, his words may mean, 'Let me go; don't impede my ascending to the Father.' (We need not be detained by that curiosity of exegesis which supposes that he had still to enter the heavenly holy of holies to complete the antitype of the Day of Atonement initiated by his sacrifice on the cross.)[14] There is probably the further implication that Mary, like his other followers, would have to get used to a new situation in which it would no longer be possible to see him and touch him as formerly; this lesson is more emphatically taught in the Thomas episode which follows, and especially in verse 29.

That Jesus' words 'Go to my brothers' refer to his disciples is evident from verse 18; this was how Mary understood them.[15] We may compare his words to the women in Matt. 28:10, 'go and tell my brothers . . .', where the reference (according to verse 16) is to 'the eleven disciples'. Such coincidences between Matthew and John are sufficiently rare to be particularly noteworthy when they occur. He speaks of them thus because God is their Father as he is his Father. Some have discerned an allusion to Psalm 22:22, where the righteous sufferer, delivered from affliction, says to God, 'I will tell of thy name to my brothers' (cf. Heb. 2:11 f.). So, when Jesus goes on to speak of 'my Father and your Father' and 'my God and your God', he not merely distinguishes himself from them with regard to their respective relationship to God; by the same token he links them with himself. His words are reminiscent of Ruth's words to Naomi: 'your people shall be my people, and your God my God' (Ruth 1:16). 'I am ascending to my Father who is also yours, to my God who is also yours' – so we may understand the force of his words. This message, then, was taken to the disciples by Mary who, as she delivered it, bore her personal witness: 'I have seen the Lord!' John does not say how they reacted to her story, but we might suppose that they received it sceptically, even if we had not positive statements to this effect elsewhere (cf. Luke 24:10 f.).

Of the record of Jesus' appearance to Mary, C. H. Dodd speaks of his 'feeling' (cautiously he adds 'it can be no more than a feeling') that it 'has something indefinably first-hand about it. It stands in any case alone. There is nothing quite like it in the gospels. Is there anything quite like it in all ancient literature?'[16]

3. APPEARANCE TO THE DISCIPLES (20:19–23)

20:19, 20 **Late that day, the first day of the week, when the doors were closed where the disciples were, for fear of the Jews,**

Jesus came and stood in their midst, and said to them, 'Peace be to you.' Having said this, he showed them his hands and his side. Seeing the Lord, then, the disciples rejoiced.

It is scarcely to be doubted that the occasion described here is identical with that of Luke 24:36 ff., in spite of incidental differences in detail. The memory of this coming of the Lord to his disciples may well have something to do with the church's early practice of meeting together on the evening of the first day of the week and bespeaking his presence with them in the words *Marana tha*, 'Our Lord, come!'[17]

'The Jews' of whom the disciples were afraid are, as so often in this Gospel, the authorities, especially the chief-priestly establishment. Jesus' greeting was the regular one used when friend met friend, and is still used thus in Hebrew today: *Shālôm 'āleikhem* (cf. Arabic *Salaam 'alaikum*). But on this occasion it bore its literal meaning to the fullest extent. As they heard it, they would remember how recently he had said to them, 'Peace I leave with you; my peace I give to you' (John 14:27) – and yet it must have seemed years ago, because of what had happened since then. We are probably intended to understand that there was no need to unlock the doors to admit him (cf. verse 26 below): suddenly he was there in their presence. And yet it was in bodily form that he was there: the nail-pierced hands and the wounded side identified him unmistakably as the crucified one. Seeing and recognizing him, the disciples, no longer fearful, were filled with joy. 'I will see you again', he had said in the upper room, 'and your hearts will rejoice, and no one takes your joy away from you' (John 16:22). His promise was now fulfilled.

20:21–23 So Jesus spoke to them again: 'Peace be to you. As the Father has sent me, so I send you.' Having said this, he breathed into them and said to them, 'Receive (the) Holy Spirit. Whose sins you remit, they are remitted to them; whose sins you retain, they are retained.'

In prayer to his Father in the upper room, Jesus had said of his disciples, 'As thou didst send me into the world so also I have sent them into the world' (John 17:18). Now comes their actual sending. The technical term 'apostle' is avoided by John, but by the use of the cognate verb *apostellō* he indicates that the disciples now become effectively apostles in the sense of 'sent ones'. The Son's mission in the world is entrusted to them, since he is returning to the Father; but as the Son had received the Spirit in unrestricted fullness for the discharge of his own mission (John 1:32–34; 3:34), so they now receive the Spirit for the discharge of theirs.[18] At an earlier stage in Jesus' ministry the evangelist had said, 'the Spirit was not yet present, because Jesus had not yet been glorified' (John 7:39): now the time for imparting the Spirit has come.

The Spirit is imparted by the breath of Jesus. The verb used here (*emphysaō*) is that used in the LXX of Gen. 2:7 where, after fashioning the first man from dust, God 'breathed into his face the breath of life, and the man became a living soul', and again in the command to the *pneuma* in Ezek. 37:9, 'Come from the four winds and breathe into these corpses, and let them live.' But it is not the bestowal of life that is in view now, but empowerment for ministry. The absence of the definite article before 'Holy Spirit' here has led some commentators to suggest that it is not the personal Spirit that is in view here, but a spiritual gift or endowment. This is a precarious argument; the presence or absence of the article with *pneuma* (or *pneuma hagion*, as here) is not an infallible criterion for distinguishing between the Giver and his gifts. Since the Spirit is bestowed to empower them to fulfil the commission they have just received, the authority conveyed in the Lord's following words is probably also related to the fulfilment of their commission.

In the proclamation of the gospel remission of sins is assured to believers, with the corollary of retention of sins to unbelievers (cf. John 9:41, 'your sin remains'). The language is not unlike that of the twofold commission of Matt. 16:19 and 18:18, 'retaining' and 'remitting' corresponding respectively to 'binding' and 'loosing'; indeed, a common Semitic original has been suggested for both sayings, along the lines of Isa. 22:22 (cf. Rev. 3:7).[19] But whereas the Matthaean contexts point to an interpretation in terms of church discipline, the present context is related to the disciples' mission in the world. The two passives – 'they are remitted' and 'they are retained' – imply divine agency: the preachers' rôle is declaratory, but it is God who effectively remits or retains. The servants of Christ are given no authority independent of his, nor is any assurance of infallibility given to them. 'It is only the interpretation of the promise as a guarantee against error that is wrong. A certainty that the Holy Spirit will sustain the Church in responsible action as it cleaves to God in Christ is the certainty that the Church needs and on which it can rely.'[20]

4. APPEARANCE TO THOMAS (20:24–29)

20:24, 25 But Thomas (whose name means 'Twin'), one of the twelve, was not with them when Jesus came. So the other disciples told him, 'We have seen the Lord'. But he said to them, 'Unless I see the mark of the nails in his hands and put my finger

into the place where the nails were, and put my hand into his side, I will not believe.'

Thomas, like one or two of the other disciples who are only names in the Synoptic narrative, plays a more individual part in this Gospel. He has appeared in the story of the raising of Lazarus (John 11:16) and in the conversation in the upper room (14:5) as a loyal but rather pessimistic follower of Jesus. Here, as in John 11:16 and 21:2, his Aramaic and Greek names are given together.[21]

The expression 'one of the twelve' is interesting; it occurs in one other place in this Gospel, with reference to Judas Iscariot (John 6:71). The point here is that, although Thomas was one of the twelve, he was not with the others on the occasion just described. (Judas was also absent, but for a different reason.)

Some people, in times of great and desolating sorrow, find comfort in one another's company. Others prefer to creep into a corner and be alone with their grief. Thomas belonged to this latter category. When the others sought him out and told him their exciting news, he was not impressed. They might have succumbed to wishful thinking, but he was not to be taken in. Even when they told him how they had identified the Lord by the nail-prints in his hands and the spear-wound in his side, he would not be persuaded; he knew what imagination was capable of. Seeing would not be enough for him; only if he put his finger into the nail-prints and his hand into the spear-wound would he be convinced. Optical illusions were not unknown, but he reckoned that the evidence of touch would show whether there was solid flesh there or not. He has come to be known as 'doubting Thomas', but he was not really any more doubting than the others; had he been with them on the evening of that first Easter Day, his doubts would have been removed at the same time as theirs. As it was, he had to wait a further week.

20:26–28 **After eight days the disciples were again within, and Thomas was with them. Closed as the doors were, Jesus came and stood in their midst, and said, 'Peace be to you'. Then he said to Thomas, 'Reach your finger here and see my hands, reach out your hand and put it into my side. Don't be unbelieving any longer; believe!' Thomas said to him in answer, 'My Lord and my God!'**

The eight days are to be reckoned inclusively; it was the first day of a new week. The days of the festival of unleavened bread were over, and the disciples were probably preparing to return to Galilee, but held this rendezvous before they set out. The others were no doubt full of expectation this time, but Thomas, not having shared their experience a week before, was sceptical. The appearance of Jesus in front of them, together with his greeting, is recorded in much the same language as before. But now he has a special word for Thomas, inviting him to exploit his sense of touch as well as sight, and incidentally revealing that he knew what Thomas had said to the others. Thomas's resolute scepticism vanished: the evidence of eye and ear sufficed, and there was no need now to satisfy himself with probing fingers. Thomas might have been slower than his fellow-disciples to come to faith in the risen Christ, but when he did so, his faith was expressed in language which went beyond any that they had used.

It is probably a mistake to make a distinction between 'my Lord' and 'my God', as though Thomas meant, 'It is my Lord (as I knew him before his death) but now that I see him risen he is also my God' (an interpretation along these lines has been proposed by F. C. Burkitt and C. H. Dodd).[22] 'My Lord' should rather be taken as a divine ascription alongside 'my God'. The words are to be construed as nominative, not vocative. Thomas is affirming his new-found faith, 'with absolute conviction', according to the stage-direction of Dorothy Sayers, who renders his words as a statement: 'You are my Lord and my God.'[23] Thomas's confession thus corroborates the prologue to the Gospel: 'the Word was God'. In John's Gospel it plays the climacteric part that is played in Mark's record by the centurion's comment: 'Truly this man was the Son of God!' (Mark 15:39).

20:29 **Jesus said to him, 'Have you believed because you have seen me? Blessed are those who have believed without seeing.'**

This last beatitude had a special message for the readers of this Gospel when it was first published; it has the same message for readers of the Gospel today. They had not seen, and neither have we; yet they might believe, and so may we. Thomas was no different from the other disciples in this respect: they did not believe until they saw: if they believed a week earlier than Thomas, that was because they saw a week earlier than he. Even of the beloved disciple it is said that 'he saw – and believed' (verse 8), although the visible evidence that wrought faith in him was not the sight of the risen Lord but the disposition of the grave-clothes in the tomb. But since the apostolic generation passed from earth, all believers in the crucified and risen Lord have believed without seeing, and to them is assured the special blessing here pronounced by him. To us, faith comes not by seeing but (as Paul puts it) 'from what is heard, and what is heard comes by the preaching of Christ'

(Rom. 10:7). John knows this, and therefore he presents his readers with 'the preaching of Christ' – the story of Jesus – in written form, that faith may come to them.

III. Purpose of the record (20:30, 31)

20:30, 31 Now there are many other signs, not written in this book, which Jesus did in the presence of his disciples; but these have been written in order that you may believe that Jesus is the Christ, the Son of God, and that, believing, you may have life in his name.

Although the 'signs' recorded in chapters 2:12 were performed in the presence of more than the disciples, yet they cannot be excluded from those referred to here. They were performed in the presence of the 'world', but no resultant faith was manifested: 'though he had done so many signs before them, yet they did not believe in him' (John 12:37). But to those who did believe he made his glory known in the transcendent twofold sign of his passion and triumph interpreted in advance in the upper room discourse. From the much greater number of signs that the Evangelist might have recorded had he been so minded, he selected those which are actually 'written in this book' in order to produce and foster faith in his readers. Commentators have discussed whether John's purpose was to awaken faith for the first time or to maintain and strengthen faith already there: this question is further posed by the variation of reading between the aorist (NEB margin, 'that you may come to believe') and the present (NEB text, 'that you may hold the faith'). Probably we are not shut up to two mutually exclusive alternatives, regardless of the reading adopted: John's record has the power to awaken new faith and to revive faith already awakened. The substance of the faith is stated in propositional terms – 'that Jesus is the Christ, the Son of God' – but it is plain from the whole of this Gospel that more than propositional faith is intended: the faith in view is personal faith in Jesus as 'the Christ, the Son of God'. For John, 'the Christ' is still frequently a title rather than a name. 'The Christ' (i.e. the Messiah) and 'the Son of God' are synonymous terms, but some of John's readers (those particularly of Jewish antecedents) might find 'the Christ' more meaningful while to others 'the Son of God' would make more sense.

The one to whom John bears witness is the perfect revealer of the Father. And those whose faith in him is kindled by the testimony of the 'signs' and discourses here recorded receive *ipso facto* life through him (his 'name' is his person). As John has already testified, 'he who believes in the Son has eternal life' (John 3:36). In order that men and women might believe in the Son and live, he wrote his Gospel: nineteen centuries bear witness to the abundant degree in which his noble purpose has been achieved.

NOTES

1. C. F. Evans, 'The Gospel according to John' in *A Source-Book of the Bible for Teachers*, ed. R. C. Walton (London, 1970), p. 329; cf. his *Resurrection in the New Testament* (London, 1970), p. 116.
2. V. Burch, *The Structure and Message of St. John's Gospel* (London, 1928), pp. 130, 211, 222–228.
3. Mishnah, tractate *Rôsh ha-Shānāh* 1.8, implies that a woman's evidence was not normally admissible.
4. Origen, *Against Celsus*, 2.55.
5. W. Temple, *Readings in St. John's Gospel*, p. 378. This is the only Gospel to mention the napkin. In the Synoptic Gospels (Mark 15.46, with Matt. 27:59 and Luke 23:53) the body of Jesus is said to have been wrapped in a *sindōn*, a linen sheet (cf. Mark 14:51 f.). John speaks of *othonia* (used also in Luke 24:12), lengths of linen cloth which were wound round the body like a bandage (cf. Lazarus's *keiriai*, John 11:44).
6. R. Bultmann, *The Gospel of John*, p. 684.
7. C. T. Craig, *The Beginning of Christianity* (New York/Nashville, 1943), p. 135. In Luke 24:12 (a text which, although disputed, is probably genuine) Peter, on hearing the women's report, 'rose and ran to the tomb: stooping and looking in (*parakyptō*, as in John 20:5), he saw the linen cloths (*othonia*) by themselves; and he went home wondering at what had happened'. Here no one else is mentioned along with Peter, but it is implied in Luke 24:24 that he was not unaccompanied. See also F. Neirynck, '*Parakypsas blepei*. Lc 24, 12 et Jn 20,10', in *Evangelica* (Leuven, 1982), pp. 401–440; '*Apēlthen pros heauton*. Lc. 24, 12 et Jn 20, 10', *ibid.*, pp. 441–455.
8. R. Bultmann, *The Gospel of John*, p. 685. There is a parallel to verse 9 in Luke 24:25, where the risen Lord reproaches the Emmaus disciples for being so slow to believe 'all that the prophets have spoken'.
9. Cf. J. W. Wenham, *Easter Enigma* (Exeter, forthcoming).
10. See John 19:41 with comment (p. 379).
11. According to J. P. Kane ('Burial', *Illustrated Bible Dictionary*, Inter-Varsity Press, 1980), the trough-arcosolium is not found before the second century A.D., though Sanhedria Tomb VII in north Jerusalem (shortly before A.D. 70) shows the beginnings of it in a rock-cut sarcophagus beneath an arcosolium.
12. For 'woman' as a courteous mode of address on Jesus' lips cf. John 2:4; 19:26 (to his mother); 4:21 (to the Samaritan woman) – not to mention John 8:10 (to the adulterous woman).
13. In rabbinical Hebrew God is frequently addressed as *ribbônô shel 'ôlām*. 'Lord of the world'. (The title *Rabbān* was given to leading rabbis, like Gamaliel.)
14. Propounded by C. E. Stuart, *A Few Remarks as to Atonement, Propitiation, and the Priesthood of the Lord Jesus Christ* (London, 1888); cf. K. M. Monroe, 'Time Element in the Atonement', *EQ* 5 (1933), pp. 397–408, with refutation by T. Houghton, 'The Atonement', *EQ* 6 (1934), pp. 137–146.
15. It is not overlooked that his brothers appear as a distinct group of church leaders in the Acts and Epistles (cf. Acts 1:14; 1 Cor. 9:5). See p. 381, n. 32 (on 19:26, 27).
16. C. H. Dodd, 'The Appearances of the Risen Christ', *in More New Testament Studies* (Manchester, 1968), p. 115.
17. See comment on John 13:13 (p. 284).
18. The relation between this incident (the 'insufflation') and what happened at

Pentecost (Acts 2:1–21) is a question which naturally arises but which is not easily answered. What John records is no mere anticipation of Pentecost but a real impartation of the Spirit for the purpose specified. The Pentecostal out-pouring of the Spirit was more public, and involved the birth of the Spirit-indwelt community, the church of the new age.

19. See J. A. Emerton, 'Binding and Loosing – Forgiving and Retaining', *JTS*, n.s. 13 (1962), pp. 325–331.

20. H. Cunliffe-Jones, 'Two Questions Concerning the Holy Spirit', *Theology* 75 (1972), p. 289.

21. See John 11:16 and 14:22, with comments and notes (pp. 242, 307, n. 13).

22. C. H. Dodd (*The Interpretation of the Fourth Gospel*, p. 430, n. 1) mentions that F. C. Burkitt paraphrased Thomas's confession thus: 'Yes: it is Jesus! – and He is divine!'

23. D. L. Sayers, *The Man Born to be King*, p. 340.

CHAPTER 21

EPILOGUE (John 21:1–25)

1. THE CATCH OF FISH (21:1–11)

21:1–3 After this, Jesus manifested himself to the disciples again by the sea of Tiberias, and this is how he revealed himself. Simon Peter, Thomas (whose name means 'Twin') and Nathanael from Cana of Galilee were together with the sons of Zebedee and two more of his disciples. Simon Peter said to them, 'I am going out fishing.' They said to him, 'We are coming with you too.' So they set off and got aboard the boat, and caught nothing that night.

If we were reading this Gospel for the first time, we should be surprised to find another incident recorded after the conclusion of the work at the end of chapter 20. If chapter 21 makes on us the impression of being an addition to the original work, it must be said on the other hand that there is no evidence that the work ever circulated without this chapter. The Greek text of the chapter contains 28 words which do not appear elsewhere in the Gospel. Many of these, however, are due to the subject-matter of the opening narrative (verses 1–14), and we cannot fail to recognize the recurrence of a large number of characteristic Johannine features in the style of this chapter. We have, for example, the variation of synonyms (verses 15–17), the double 'Amen' (verse 18), the construction 'This he said, indicating . . .' (verse 19; cf. 12:33).

Only in this Gospel is the lake called 'the sea of Tiberias' (cf. 6:1), and most of the *dramatis personae* are familiar to those who have read the Gospel thus far. If the first eighteen verses of chapter 1 are called the prologue of the Gospel, chapter 21 is most appropriately called the epilogue: an epilogue is more integral to the main work than an 'appendix', for instance, would be. The actual circumstances of the composition of the Gospel are concealed from us, but we may picture the Evangelist entrusting his *magnum opus* to his associates (the 'we' of verse 24), who, before publishing it, added this epilogue which they had heard from his own lips, in the form in which he had narrated it.[1]

The story opens with several of the disciples back in Galilee; we last saw them in Jerusalem. Their movements between Easter and Pentecost, from Jerusalem to Galilee and back to Jerusalem, can be correlated with the sacred calendar; they had left Jerusalem after the week of unleavened bread – not immediately, with the main body of pilgrims, but quietly, two or three days later.[2] Here in Galilee, then, they found themselves together, in one of their old haunts by the lakeside.

On this occasion there were seven disciples in all. Simon Peter, as usual, is named as their leader; Thomas ('Twin') has already figured in the resurrection narrative (John 20:24 ff.), while the call of Nathanael was recorded in 1:45 ff. It is only here that Nathanael is said to have belonged to Cana, the scene of Jesus' first sign (2:1 ff.). The sons of Zebedee have not previously been mentioned in this Gospel – not, at least, as such. The omission from the body of the work of any explicit reference to two such outstanding members of the twelve is in itself significant. Perhaps the editors used this form of words here to help readers to reach some conclusion about the identity of the beloved disciple who, as the following narrative makes plain, was one of the company. However, by adding that two other, unnamed, disciples were present, they have avoided making the identification too easy.

Simon Peter has sometimes been rather oddly criticized for proposing a fishing expedition, as though his idea had been to abandon his commission and resume his career as a fisherman. It was better for him to employ his time usefully than to remain idle. In proposing to join him, some at least of his companions knew what they were about; they too had been fishermen by trade. But their expedition is fruitless; the story develops in a manner reminiscent of that occasion recorded by another Evangelist, when Simon and his companions 'toiled all night and took nothing' (Luke 5:5).

21:4–6 **When it was already early morning Jesus stood on the beach, but the disciples did not know that it was Jesus. So Jesus said to them, 'Boys, have you got anything to eat?' 'No', they answered. 'Shoot the net to starboard', he said, 'and you will find some.' They did so, and now they were unable to haul it in because of the large catch of fish.**

It may have been still too dark for them to recognize the figure standing on the beach, though they were within earshot as he called out to them. His question is framed so as to indicate that the answer 'No' was expected. The Greek word rendered 'anything to eat' is *prosphagion* (the prefix *pros* with the root of the verb *phagein*, 'eat'); what he had in mind was fish, and this is what they understood. There may be some deeper significance in his direction to 'shoot the net to starboard' (NEB). In popular belief the right was the side of good luck, but the disciples would know this in any case, and it would be trivializing Jesus' words to find this kind of meaning in them. We may take it that he knew there was an abundance of fish on their starboard side; as for the disciples, the old instinct of implicit obedience asserted itself almost before they became fully conscious of his identity. Their casting net immediately became so full of fish that they could not haul it into the boat; they had to let it drag along behind.

21:7, 8 So that disciple whom Jesus loved said to Peter, 'It is the Lord!' Hearing that it was the Lord, Simon Peter tied his outer garment round himself (for he had stripped) and jumped into the sea. The other disciples came in by boat (they were not far from land, only about a hundred yards), dragging the net full of fish behind them.

The insight which had led the beloved disciple to grasp what had happened when he looked inside the empty tomb now led him to grasp the identity of the figure on the beach. Memory of a not dissimilar occasion from earlier days would also have helped. At any rate it was in him that the subconscious awareness first rose above the surface and found expression in the ejaculation, 'It is the Lord!' It was equally characteristic of Peter that, on hearing this, he should impetuously hurl himself overboard and strike out for land in order to get there first. He was dressed only in his under garment, so first he donned his outer garment (*ependytēs*) out of respect for the Lord.

One might normally have expected a man to throw *off* his outer garment if he was planning to swim ashore, to give his limbs the freedom they required.[3] The verb translated 'tied round himself' is the middle of *diazōnnymi*, used earlier by John to describe Jesus' tying a towel round his waist when he was about to wash the disciple's feet (13:4, 5); so perhaps we are intended to picture Peter as tucking up the lower part of his outer garment into his belt or girdle, so as not to impede his legs. Whereas in the similar incident of Luke 5:1–11 the heavy nets were taken on board (lest they should break), so that they put the boats in danger of sinking, here the net is dragged along behind the boat.[4]

21:9–11 So, when they had come ashore, they saw a charcoal fire laid, and fish placed on it, and bread, Jesus said to them, 'Bring some of the fish which you have caught just now.' Simon Peter got up and hauled the net ashore, full of big fish, a hundred and fifty-three in all. Although there was so many, the net did not break.

The risen Lord had breakfast ready for his tired disciples, a meal of bread and fish such as they remembered from former times. But now they were invited to make their own contribution to the meal, by bringing some of the fish which they had just caught. It is possible that thus far only one fish was broiling on the charcoal fire: the Greek singular *opsarion* might have this meaning, or it might be collective, like our English word 'fish'.[5] The disciples were told to bring some of their *opsaria* (plural). The noun *opsarion* is peculiar to this Gospel in the New Testament; it has been used earlier of the two fish which were multiplied in the feeding of the five thousand (John 6:9, 11). The word means 'relish', anything that might be taken along with bread, but especially fish. When used of fish, it usually denotes salt or dried fish, but here it is used to cover the freshly caught fish.

Once the net was in shallow water, it was easier to haul it up on to dry land than it had been to drag it through the deeper water, but Peter's hauling it up single-handed is a tacit tribute to his physical strength; Lloyd Douglas's description of him as 'the big fisherman' was not mere guesswork.

What can be said of the number of the fish, apart from the observation that someone counted them and remembered how many there were? Is there any symbolism in the number? If so, it may point to the wide range and variety of converts, Jewish and Gentile alike, that were to be taken in the gospel net as the disciples fulfilled their commission. According to Jerome, Greek zoologists reckoned that there were 153 different kinds of fish in the world – but there is reason to suspect that Jerome has adapted their reckoning to John's total.[6] Dr. Aileen Guilding sees a reference to the 153,600 'proselytes' (as the LXX calls them) who were included among Solomon's subjects (2 Chron. 2:17; cf. 1 Kings 5:15 f.).[7] From early days it was noticed that 153 is the total of all the whole numbers from 1 to 17 inclusive (in other words, the triangular number of 17) and attention was directed to the symbolical properties of 17 – the number of law (10) with the number of grace (7) added to it (so, e.g., Augustine).[8] Others have pointed out that 153 is the sum of the squares of 12 (the number of the apostles) and 3 (representing the Trinity). But if there is any symbolism in the number (and the narrative does not indicate that there is), it must bear some relation to the subject-matter of the context.

The statement that 'although there were so many, the net did not break', seems unmistakably to point a contrast with the incident of Luke 5 where the disciples' 'nets were breaking' because of the great shoal of fish which they had enclosed (verse 6). If there is a symbolical significance in the unbroken net, it lies ready to hand. The gospel net will never break, no matter how many converts it catches; there is no limit to the number it will take. And if there is also symbolical significance in the fact that on this occasion the net was not hauled on board, it may simply be that no boat (not even the barque of St. Peter) is large enough to accommodate all the fish that are taken in the gospel net, just as no fold is large enough to accommodate all the sheep in the good shepherd's flock (John 10:3 f., 16).

The incident of the catch of fish (verse 1–11) is not expressly called a 'sign', but it has many of the features of a 'sign' in the Johannine sense. The reader is given the impression that there is more in it than meets the eye, and something of its inner significance is unfolded in the discourse that follows. The disciples' haul of fish is a parable of their missionary activity in the time that lies ahead. But this activity, with its pastoral sequel, will be attended by success only as they follow the directions of their risen Lord.

2. Breakfast by the lake (21:12–14)

21:12–13 Jesus said to them, 'Come and have breakfast.' None of the disciples dared to ask him, 'Who are you?' They knew it was the Lord. Jesus came and took the bread and gave it to them, and the fish likewise.

The disciples, it appears, were conscious of a certain uneasiness in the presence of their risen Lord. There was something quite familiar in having him with them by the lakeside, yet there was something quite unfamiliar in the company of one who had returned from the dead. Formerly they would not have thought of asking him 'Who are you?' – but now they felt as if they ought to ask him; yet they could not bring themselves to do so, because, after all, they *knew* who it was. Of our present experience of the risen Christ Albert Schweitzer wrote, in a well-known passage: 'He comes to us as One unknown, without a name, as of old.'[9] And those disciples, although they saw him then (as we do not now) with outward vision, experienced something of the same kind: they knew him quite well, and yet in a sense they saw him as a stranger, one who henceforth belonged to another order of existence. But he put them at their ease, inviting them to come and share the breakfast[10] which he had prepared for them. The bread and the fish represented the harvest of the earth and the harvest of the sea. In Luke's record of his Easter appearance to them in Jerusalem it was they who gave him 'a piece of broiled fish' (*ichthys*) but that was to strengthen their faith, not to supply his need; here it is he who feeds them, as he had fed the multitude by the lakeside during his earlier ministry. If he had not explicitly ordained the bread and the *cup* to be the memorials of his passion on the night in which he was betrayed, we could well envisage the emergence of a sacramental meal of bread and *fish* in the church. As it is, we may wonder how much the early Christian use of fish as a symbol both of Christ and of his people owes to the part played by fish in the feeding narratives of the Gospels. We know, of course, that the five letters of Gk. *ichthys* were treated as an acrostic of the title 'Jesus Christ, God's Son, Saviour' (*Iēsous CHristos THeou hYios Sōtēr*), but this may have been the rationalization of a practice already established on other grounds.[11]

21:14 This now is the third time that Jesus was manifested to the disciples after being raised from the dead.

This note is to be understood with exclusive reference to the Johannine resurrection narrative. In this narrative (apart from the appearance to Mary of Magdala, which was not an appearance to the *disciples*) the first resurrection appearance is recorded in 20:19–23 and the second (a week later) in 20:24–29; this is the third. The note may be an editorial one, contributed by one or more of those who were responsible for publishing this Gospel in its present form. It is difficult, if not impossible, to place this appearance in chronological relation to the appearances recorded by other NT writers. Some have surmised that this appearance may have been recorded earlier in the 'lost ending' of Mark's Gospel; this, of course, is incapable of proof, even if there ever was such a 'lost ending'. The statement that Jesus 'was manifested' (passive of *phaneroō*) is more emphatic than the commoner expression 'he appeared' (*ōphthē*), found in Luke 24:34; Acts 13:31; 1 Cor. 15:5–8. Like the active of the verb in verse 1, the passive here implies the disclosing of the risen one's identity. The intransitive active *anastēnai* ('rise'), as in 20:9, and the passive of *egeirō* ('be raised'), as here, are used interchangeably in this Gospel and throughout the NT of our Lord's resurrection from the dead.[12]

3. PETER'S NEW COMMISSION (21:15–19)

21:15–17 When they had taken breakfast, then, Jesus said to Simon Peter, 'Simon, son of John, do you love me more than these (do)?' 'Yes, Lord,' he said, 'you know I love you.' 'Feed my lambs', said he to him.

He said to him again, a second time, 'Simon, son of John, do you love me?' 'Yes, Lord', said he, 'you know I love you.' 'Shepherd my sheep', said he to him.

He said to him for the third time, 'Simon, son of John, do you love me?' Peter was hurt because he had said to him 'Do you love me?' a third time, and he said to him, 'You know

everything, Lord; you know I love you.' 'Feed my sheep', said Jesus to him.

We are probably to gather from the wording of verse 20 that after breakfast Jesus took Peter for a short walk, and held this conversation with him in private. In isolation, the question 'Do you love me more than these?' is ambiguous: it might mean 'Do you love me more than you love these people?' (meaning presumably his fellow-disciples) or even 'Do you love me more than you love these things?' – which might be a reference to his fishing activity. But in the context of the whole passion and resurrection narrative it is more natural to take it as meaning 'Do you love me more than these others do?' But how could Peter know how much the others loved their common Lord? Of course he could not know; but not long before he thought he did, and reckoned that his love could outdo theirs. Whatever the others might do, Peter asserted in the upper room, 'I will lay down my life for you' (John 13:37). But, however willing the spirit was, the flesh was weak, as Peter proved in the courtyard of the high priest's palace; and the reason Peter was hurt because Jesus asked him three times if he loved him was probably that he remembered how on three successive occasions during that terrible night he had denied all knowledge of him. Now, in answer to Jesus' question, Peter affirms his love for him, but he refuses to make any comparison between himself and others in this respect.

Stylistically, this interchange between the Lord and his disciple is interesting because of the use of synonyms. Two words for 'love' are used (*agapaō* and *phileō*), two words for tending the flock (*boskō* and *poimainō*),[13] two for the flock itself (*arnia* and *probatia*) and two for 'know' (*oida* and *ginōskō*). This interplay of synonyms is a feature of the writer's Greek; it can hardly represent a comparable variation of vocabulary in the language which Jesus and Peter probably spoke.

Of the four pairs of synonyms mentioned, it is the pair *agapaō* and *phileō* that commentators have generally found most interesting. The risen Lord uses *agapaō* in his first two questions and *phileō* in the third; Peter uses *phileō* in all three replies. But those who see a difference in force between the two verbs here are not agreed on the nature of the difference. According to R. C. Trench. Peter finds the word on his Lord's lips (*agapaō*) 'far too cold' at a time when 'all the pulses in the heart of the now penitent Apostle are beating with a passionate affection' towards him. He himself uses a word (*phileō*) which more adequately conveys the warmth of that affection, and triumphs when on the third occasion the Lord consents to use that word.[14] B. F. Westcott, on the other hand, takes *agapaō*, the word used by the Lord in his first two questions, to denote 'that higher love which was to be the spring of the Christian life', whereas Peter, by using *phileō*, affirms only the natural love of personal attachment. When, on the third occasion, the Lord uses *phileō*, Peter is the more hurt because the Lord now seems to be questioning even 'that modified love which he had professed'.[15]

When two such distinguished Greek scholars (both, moreover, tending to argue from the standards of classical Greek) see the significance of the synonyms so differently, we may wonder if indeed we are intended to see such distinct significance. Let us consider these facts: (i) The verbs *agapaō* and *phileō* are used interchangeably in the Septuagint to render one and the same Hebrew word (e.g. in Gen. 37:3 Jacob's preferential love for Joseph is expressed by *agapaō* but in the following verse by *phileō*). (ii) The verb *agapaō* in itself does not necessarily imply a loftier love; it does so when the context makes this clear (on the other hand, in 2 Tim. 4:10 Demas's regrettable love for 'the present age' is expressed by *agapaō*). (iii) More important still for our present purpose is the fact that John himself uses the two verbs interchangeably elsewhere in his Gospel, e.g. in the statement that 'the Father loves the Son' (*agapaō* in 3:35; *phileō* in 5:20) and in references to 'the disciple whom Jesus loved' (*agapaō* in 13:23; 19:26; 21:7, 20; *phileō* in 20:2). It is precarious, then, to press a distinction between the two synonyms here.

What is important is that Peter reaffirms his love for the Lord, and is rehabilitated and recommissioned. The commission is a pastoral one. When first he was called from his occupation of catching fish to be a follower of Jesus, he was told that thenceforth he would catch men (Luke 5:10; cf. Mark 1:17). Now to the evangelist's hook there is added the pastor's crook, so that, as had often been said, Peter proceeded to fulfil his double commission 'by hook and by crook'. How seriously he took this second commission may be gathered from 1 Peter 5:1–4 where, speaking towards the end of his life as an elder to fellow-elders, he urges them to 'shepherd the flock of God' so faithfully that they would receive an unfading garland of glory at the manifestation of the chief shepherd. The chief shepherd, whose voice has been heard in chapter 10, delegates his responsibility to under-shepherds, among whom Peter is first to be so commissioned.

21:18, 19 '**Indeed and in truth I tell you: When you were younger, you would gird on your own clothes and go where you wanted; but when you have grown old, you will stretch out**

your hands and someone else will gird you and bring you where you do not want (to go).' In saying this he indicated the kind of death by which Peter would bring glory to God. And having spoken thus he said to him, 'Follow me.'

The further words addressed to Peter in verse 18 might seem cryptic; in themselves they could point to the weakness of old age, when he would no longer be able to dress himself or go around of his own accord. But the Evangelist's comment in verse 19 gives them a more sinister meaning: they indicate the manner of his death (the comment is remarkably similar to that in John 12:33, which brings out the meaning of an utterance of Jesus regarding his own death). But the disciple's death, like his Master's, would be for the glory of God.

By the time the Gospel was written, Peter had glorified God in martyrdom. Knowing what form Peter's martyrdom took, the Evangelist could see a precise reference to it in the words of Jesus, such as could not have been seen at the time.[16] The stretching out of his hands could have been for the fitting of handcuffs, and there might be the further picture of his being led off in chains to the place of execution. Clement of Rome (c. AD 96) speaks of Peter's martyrdom but does not indicate what form it took[17]; for this we have to wait until Tertullian (c. AD 212), who says, with evident reference to our present text, that it was 'when Peter was bound to the cross that he was girt by someone else'.[18] The stretching out of his hands would then be understood in retrospect to be their stretching out on the cross-beam of the cross. (We need not take too seriously the later embellishment, found in the apocryphal *Acts of Peter* and in Eusebius, according to which he was crucified head downwards at his own insistence.)[19]

Then, in words which echo the first call of the disciples by the bank of Jordan (cf. 1:43), Jesus concludes Peter's commission with the command 'Follow me'. 'Follow me as my disciple; follow me also in death.' So Peter's protestation, though deferred, will yet be fulfilled: 'I will lay down my life for you' (13:37).

4. THE BELOVED DISCIPLE (21:20–23)

21:20, 21 Peter turned and saw the disciple whom Jesus loved following. (It was he who leant back against Jesus' breast at the supper and said 'Lord, who is it that is going to betray you?') Seeing him, then, Peter said to Jesus, 'And what about this man, Lord?'

It has been suggested that the Lord took Peter for a short walk along the lakeshore, so that their conversation could be private; we may then envisage the beloved disciple also detaching himself from the others and following the Lord and Peter along the shore. Since this is the first mention of the beloved disciple in the epilogue, his identity with the beloved disciple who figures in the main body of the Gospel is established by a reference back to the first occasion on which he makes an appearance in the narrative – at table in the upper room (John 13:23 ff.). Now that Peter has received his fresh commission, he turns round and sees his friend following, and naturally wonders what commission their Lord has for *him*. Hence his question, concisely phrased with no verb expressed, so that we may understand 'what shall this man do?' (AV, RV) or 'what will happen to him?' (NEB).[20] For 'the disciple whom Jesus loved' some special ministry must surely be reserved, some special martyrdom may even be in store.

21:22 Jesus said to him, 'If I want him to remain till I come, what concern is that of yours? You follow me.'

Peter is told that his business is to follow the Lord and be faithful to his own commission; the Lord has his own plans for the beloved disciple, but it is not necessary that Peter should know them. The beloved disciple may, like Peter, have to suffer a martyr's death; he may, on the other hand, live on until the Lord's coming, but there can be no advance certainty of this even for the beloved disciple himself, still less for Peter. The verb 'remain' in this sentence simply means 'remain alive on earth'; it does not have the fuller force of 'abiding' in Christ which it has in the upper room discourses (still less does it mean, as one writer has preposterously suggested, 'remain in the tomb').[21] The clause 'till I come' (or 'while I am coming') implies a future event, together with the possibility (no more) that this event could take place within the beloved disciple's lifetime. There is no adequate ground for saying that the future eschatology of the epilogue, expressed in this clause, is at variance with the realized eschatology of the main body of the Gospel; in the main body of the Gospel we find realized and future eschatology side by side (compare John 5:24 f. with 28 f.). On the one hand, Jesus does not leave his disciples orphans; he comes to them during their earthly life and manifests his presence with them by his Spirit (John 14:18–23), while on the other hand, having prepared their place in the Father's house, he will come and take them so that they may be there with him (John 14:3). It is this latter coming that is in view in his present saying about the beloved disciple, and its introduction here is no innovation; the reader of the Gospel is already familiar with the idea.

21:23 So the report spread among the brotherhood that that
disciple was not going to die. But what Jesus said to Peter was
not 'He is not going to die' but 'If I want him to remain till I
come, what concern is that of yours?'

Some witnesses to the text (including Codex Sinaiticus and the
Sinaitic Syriac) omit the clause 'what concern is that of yours?'
from verse 23.

From the contents of this verse it may be confidently inferred
that the beloved disciple was an actual individual, not a personali-
zation of the ideal follower or the embodiment of some group in
the church. Rudolf Bultmann, who views him elsewhere as a symbol of Gentile Christianity,[22] agrees that he is a real individual in
chapter 21, but this, he thinks, is because the author of chapter 21
did not understand the true significance of the beloved disciple in
the main body of the Gospel – an arbitrary conclusion indeed![23]

Was the beloved disciple dead at the time when verse 23 was
penned? Perhaps not. If he had died by then, it would have been
easy to refute the unfounded report by showing how it had been
falsified by the event. As it is, the argument against the report is
simply that it is unfounded because Jesus did not say what the
report alleged him to have said. That the beloved disciple did in
due course die we may be sure – although there is evidence that
even his death did not put an end to the 'report'. At the beginning
of the fifth century Augustine refers with disapproval to some who
asserted in his day 'that the apostle John is still living, lying asleep
rather than dead in his tomb at Ephesus'.[24] Rumour had it that the
earth above his tomb was manifestly in a state of constant disturbance, heaving up and down; and what, it was asked, could be the
cause of this if not John's continued breathing, as he still waited
for the Lord to come before he saw death?

But it is a reasonable inference from the growth of the 'report'
that the beloved disciple lived on to an advanced age, probably
surviving Peter by many years. One disciple may bear his witness
in martyrdom, another by reaching old age in relative peace; both
may be equally faithful disciples. So, in Heb. 11:34, 37, some by
faith 'escaped the edge of the sword' while others by faith 'were
killed with the sword'.[25] But reports like the one mentioned here
tend to grow with advancing years. I recall a Bible teacher in
Scotland, highly esteemed and venerated in his own select following, who lived and maintained his ministry into his nineties. Some
of his followers expressed their conviction that he was being preserved into extreme old age as a witness to the truth ('the truth' in
this case being a special aspect of church doctrine which he had
defended for some seventy years); others added, confidentially,

'. . . and I shouldn't wonder if he is being kept alive until the Lord comes.' (He himself, more wisely, said, 'I believe that the Lord is keeping me alive for a purpose of his own. My prayer is that I may rise to his purpose.')

Another view, however, is that the saying reflects the crisis occasioned in the early church by the death of the last eyewitness.[26] It can well be imagined that the death of the last member of the generation contemporary with Jesus – more particularly of the last of his closest associates – necessitated a reappraisal in the thinking of those who had expected his return while some, or at least one, of those associates survived to see it. It can well be imagined, too, that those who cherished such an expectation found some basis for it in the 'report' to which reference is made here. But it is more likely, as had been said above, that the beloved disciple was still alive when these words were penned, in which case the passage cannot reflect a crisis which had not yet occurred.

5. First postscript (21:24)

21:24 This is the disciple who bears witness concerning these things and who wrote these things, and we know that his testimony is true.

Here we have a plain statement that the beloved disciple is the real author of the Gospel. Even if the words 'who wrote these things' do not mean that his hand held the pen, any more than the language of John 19:19 means that Pilate with his own hand wrote the inscription which was fixed to the cross, they do point to him as the guarantor of the record. 'These things' cannot be confined to the narrative of chapter 21; indeed, since chapter 21 has the nature of an epilogue, they may refer more directly to the preceding chapters than to this. The claim, then, is that the witness to the truth of this Gospel is one who was in close touch with all that is described in it. The words of 1 John 1:3, 'what we have seen and heard we declare to you also', are as applicable to the Gospel as to the Epistle which they actually introduce. Indeed, as Dorothy Sayers used to remind us, 'of the four Evangels, St. John's is the only one that claims to be the direct report of an eye-witness' – adding: 'And to any one accustomed to the imaginative handling of documents, the internal evidence bears out this claim.'[27] It is not only that 'he who has seen has borne testimony', as the passion narrative assures us (19:35); this eyewitness has also a rare appreciation of the inner significance of what he has seen and heard. The spiritual sensitivity which enabled him to see and believe when, with Peter, he visited the empty tomb (20:8) was greatly quickened and deepened when, with his fellow-disciples, he received the promised endowment with the Spirit of truth to bring to his memory the words of Christ and make plain to him the things of Christ (14:26; 16:14 f.). Many years of communion with the risen Lord and reflection on his words and works made clear to his mind what had formerly been obscure.

> What once were guessed as points, I now knew stars,
> And named them in the Gospel I have writ.[28]

We cannot be sure who the people are who add their testimonial: 'we know that his testimony is true.' They may have been the group of John's disciples who preserved his record and gave it to a wider public. But how did they know that his testimony was true? Not because they were present at the events which he describes: they were not. They are giving expression rather to the inward testimony of the Holy Spirit. The Spirit whom they, equally with John, had received produced within them the assurance that his witness to Christ was true: that witness had begun to validate itself in their personal experience, and thus they knew it to be true. In that same sense many readers of the Gospel today, as they consider the Evangelist's record, are impelled to say from their own experience, 'we know that his testimony is true.' For that record still comes home to us with the self-authenticating quality of eternal truth. He to whom this witness is borne is the revelation of God in human life, and when he is received, God dwells in us and we in God.

6. Second postscript (21:25)

21:25 There are also many other things that Jesus did; if they were written one by one, I suppose that not even the world itself would contain the books that would be written.

The authorship of this final postscript is uncertain; we cannot be sure how the 'I' in 'I suppose' is related to the preceding 'we' in 'we know'. The words seem to be an echo of the Evangelist's own conclusion to his work in 20:30 f. Perhaps it is not only the factual recording of the story of Jesus that is in view, but the unfolding of its significance; in that case the sentiment is similar to that of the well-known lines beginning 'Could we with ink the ocean fill'.[29]

The scribe of Codex Sinaiticus brought the Gospel to an end with verse 24, and followed it with a flourish and a subscription. But later he washed out the flourish and subscription and added verse 25, repeating the flourish and subscription lower down. Presumably he copied his manuscript from an earlier one in which the Gospel ended with verse 24, and then corrected it on the basis of another one which contained verse 25.

Whatever the historical implications of this fact may be, it would be inappropriate to conclude an exposition of the Fourth Gospel on a minor note of textual criticism.

The Evangelist's desire is to help his readers to penetrate behind the surface appearance of the incidents recorded so as to recognize in the One to whom he bears witness the Eternal Word of God, made man for man's salvation. 'We beheld his glory, . . . full of grace and truth' (John 1:14) is his own testimony, with which he associates his fellow-disciples; and he tells his story in such a way that his readers may see that glory too. The passion and resurrection narratives form the climax of the story; it is here, above all, that to the believer the divine glory shines forth. No study of this Gospel could promote the purpose for which it was composed if it did not enable the reader more clearly to see that divine glory in the crucified and risen Jesus, and to hail him, like Thomas, as 'my Lord and my God'.[30]

NOTES

1. On this epilogue see S. S. Smalley, 'The Sign in John XXI', *NTS* 20 (1973-74), pp. 275-288.
2. C. F. D. Moule, 'The Post-Resurrection Appearances in the Light of Festival Pilgrimages'. *NTS* 4 (1957-58), pp. 58-61; cf. also J. Carmignac, 'Les apparitions de Jésus ressuscité et le calendrier biblico-qumrânien', *Revue de Qumran* 7 (1969-71), pp. 483-504.
3. R. E. Brown (*ad loc.*) suggests that Peter had nothing on under his outer garment, i.e. that *gymnos* here means 'naked' in the total sense, and that it was for this reason that he put on his outer garment, although it was inconvenient for swimming.
4. On the relation between the two incidents see I. H. Marshall, *The Gospel of Luke* (Exeter, 1978), pp. 199-201.
5. It is collective in verse 13 below.
6. Jerome (*Commentary on Ezekiel* 47:6-12) appeals to the testimony of Oppian, but Oppian (in his poem *On Fishing*) lists 157 varieties.
7. A. Guilding, *The Fourth Gospel and Jewish Worship*, p. 226.
8. Augustine, *Homilies on John*, tractate 122. 'This is a great mystery', says Augustine; he sees further significance in the fact that 153 is thrice 50 (the number of Pentecost) plus 3 (the number of the Trinity) while 50 can be broken down further as the square of 7 with the addition of 1. Others have had recourse to gematria: in reference to Ezek. 47:10 it has been pointed out that the numerical value of Gedi in Hebrew letters is 17 and of Eglaim 153, or that the numerical value of the Greek letters of Engedi plus Eneglaim is 153 – and so on, and so forth!
9. A. Schweitzer, *The Quest of the Historical Jesus* (London, 1910), p. 401.
10. This is the classical sense of the verb *aristaō* and is self-evidently demanded by the context here. In Luke 11:37 it is used in the more general Hellenistic sense of the main meal of the day.

11. The noun used in verse 13 is not *ichthys* but *opsarion* (see comment on verses 9, 10, p. 411, n. 5); but *ichthys* is used in the phrase 'big fish' in verse 11.

12. Paul has a marked preference for *egeirō*.

13. Dr. Aileen Guilding points out that the same alternation between *boskō* ('feed') and *poimainō* ('tend like a shepherd') is found in the LXX of the shepherd-oracle of Ezek. 34 (on which see p. 223). There the two synonyms render one and the same Hebrew word (*The Fourth Gospel and Jewish Worship*, p. 226).

14. R. C. Trench, *Synonyms of the New Testament* (London, ⁹1880), §xii, p. 40.

15. B. F. Westcott, *The Gospel according to St. John*, p. 303. Some translations endeavour to bring out the variation. For example, despite the limited vocabulary of Basic English, *The Bible in Basic English* renders our Lord's first two questions 'is your love for me greater than the love of these others?' and 'have you any love for me?' but the third: 'am I dear to you?' To the first two Peter answers 'you have knowledge (*oidas*) that you are dear to me' but to the third: 'you see (*ginōskeis*) that you are dear to me.'

16. When reference back to the Lord's prediction is made in 2 Pet. 1:14, quite a different figure for death is used: 'the putting off of my tabernacle.'

17. 1 Clement 5.4

18. Tertullian, *Scorpiace* 15.

19. *Acts of Peter* 37–39. Eusebius (*Hist. Eccl.* 3.1) summarizes traditions about the careers and martyrdoms of various apostles, and expresses indebtedness to Origen's lost commentary on Genesis, but it is not clear that his reference to Peter's being crucified head downwards was derived from Origen. The description given in the *Acts of Peter* is full of legendary embellishments. That people were sometimes crucified in this position, however, is independently attested by Seneca (*Consolation to Marcia*, 20).

20. Literally: 'and this man – what?'

21. E. Schwartz, 'Noch einmal der Tod der Söhne Zebedaei', *ZNW* 11 (1910), pp. 89–104 (especially 96–98). See F. F. Bruce, *Men and Movements in the Primitive Church* (Exeter, 1979), pp. 137 f.

22. See comment on John 19:26 f. (pp. 371 f.).

23. R. Bultmann, *The Gospel of John*, pp. 483, 715 with n. 5.

24. Augustine, *Homilies on the Gospel of John* 124. R. Eisler, *The Enigma of the Fourth Gospel* (London, 1938), p. 122 argued that the phenomenon was caused by gusts of air from an underground ventilator beneath the high altar of St. John's basilica.

25. For example, in Acts 12:2, 11 James was so killed while Peter escaped.

26. Cf. R. E. Brown, *The Gospel according to John*, II (Garden City, N.Y., 1966), pp. 1117–1119, 1142.

27. D. L. Sayers, *The Man Born to be King*, p. 33. As a literary critic C. S. Lewis classed John's Gospel as 'reportage', comparable to Boswell's *Johnson* ('Modern Theology and Biblical Criticism', in *Christian Reflections* [London, 1967], p. 155).

28. R. Browning, *A Death in the Desert*.

29. Could we with ink the ocean fill
    And were the skies of parchment made,
Were every blade of grass a quill
    And every man a scribe by trade,
To write abroad the love of God
    Would drain the ocean dry,
Nor could the scroll contain the whole
    Though stretched from sky to sky.

30. See C. K. Barrett, 'John 21.15–25' *Essays on John* pp. 159–167.

APPENDIX

The woman taken in adultery (John 7:53–8:11)

These twelve verses are ruled off from the preceding and following context in NIV, they are relegated to a footnote in RSV and printed on a separate page after the Gospel in NEB, under the heading 'An incident in the temple'. They are missing from a wide variety of early Greek manuscripts from the earliest forms of the Syriac and Coptic Gospels, from several Armenian, Old Georgian and Old Latin manuscripts, and from the Gothic Bible. They constitute, in fact, a fragment of authentic gospel material not originally included in any of the four Gospels. Its preservation (for which we should be thankful) is due to the fact that it was inserted at what seemed to be a not inappropriate place in the Gospel of John or of Luke. Among the manuscripts of John which include it, the majority place it between 7:52 and 8:12; others place it after 7:36, after 7:44, or after 21:25. One family of manuscripts (family 13) places it after Luke 21:38. Many of the witnesses which do contain it mark it with asterisks or daggers, to indicate the uncertainty of its textual attestation.[1] In style it has closer affinities with the Synoptic Gospels than with John. One reason for its being placed in this context in John may have been the idea that it served as an illustration of Jesus' words in 8:15, 'I judge no one'.

7:53–8:1 And every one went to his home, but Jesus went to the Mount of Olives.

This is closely parallel to Luke's account of Jesus' procedure during Holy Week: 'He spent the days teaching in the temple, and at night he went out and camped on the Mount of Olives.' Holy Week, in fact, provides a suitable setting for this incident.

8:2 Early in the morning he came into the temple again, and all the people came to him, and he sat down and began to teach them.

Again, Luke 21:38 provides a close parallel: 'And all the people came to him early in the morning in the temple to hear him.' Many scribes had teaching-pitches in the outer court, where they sat and expounded the law to their pupils; Jesus did the same – but with a difference.

8:3-5 Then the scribes and Pharisees brought a woman taken in adultery. Making her stand in the midst, they said to him, 'Teacher, this woman has been caught in the very act of committing adultery. Now in the law Moses has commanded us that such women should be stoned. What do you say, then?'

The expression 'scribes and Pharisees' is common in the Synoptic Gospels, but it is not Johannine; indeed, the very word 'scribe' is absent from John's Gospel. The scribes were the official students and expositors of the Scriptures; many, though not all, of them were attached to the party of the Pharisees. Possibly some of the Pharisees present were members of the Sanhedrin, whose responsibility it was to deal with such a serious breach of the law.

'Teacher' (Greek *didaskale*, vocative) no doubt translates Heb. *Rabbi* (cf. John 1:38, 49; 3:2).

There is something highly suspicious about the accusation. Adultery is not the kind of offence that can be committed by one person in solitude; if she was caught red-handed, how was her guilty partner allowed to escape? Probably he was the more agile of the two, and was able to get away, ungallantly leaving her in the lurch. Was no attempt made to give him chase and catch him? The impression we get is that the woman's accusers were not so much concerned with seeing that justice was done as with putting Jesus in an embarrassing situation.

From the reference to stoning it has sometimes been supposed that the woman was betrothed but not yet married; in Deut. 22:23 f. stoning is prescribed as the punishment for a betrothed virgin who is unfaithful to her bridegroom, as well as for her paramour. But in Deut. 22:22 as in Lev. 20:10, the death penalty is laid down for all unfaithful wives and their paramours, and although stoning is not explicitly mentioned, it is probably implied as the means of execution. In fact, it appears that by the first century AD the full rigour of the law was no longer applied as a general rule, in urban communities at any rate. But the ancient law prevails in all its severity in less sophisticated parts of the Near East to our own day. Thus the Vatican periodical *Oriente Moderno* reported a number of years ago: 'Two Muslim pilgrims returning from Mecca, found *in flagranti* guilty of adultery on July 11, 1957, were taken to the judge in Mecca and sentenced to death by stoning. The sentence was executed on July 12, the Mufti himself casting the first stone.'[2] And it is a matter of common knowledge that in 1980 the dramatic treatment of a similar offence and penalty, involving a member of a royal family in that part of the world, came near to precipitating an 'international incident'.

'What do *you* say?' they asked Jesus. Moses' ruling was unambiguous; would Jesus rule differently? They probably suspected that he would, and hoped that by setting himself against Moses he would forfeit public esteem and perhaps render himself liable to prosecution before the Sanhedrin.

8:6 In saying this they were putting him to the test, with the hope of bringing a charge against him. But Jesus bent down and wrote on the ground with his finger.

There is a similarity between the question now put to Jesus and the question about the tribute money recorded in the Synoptic Gospels. Both questions were calculated to impale Jesus on the horns of a dilemma: if he answered one way, he would forfeit popular good will; if he answered the other way, he could be charged with sedition before the Roman governor. If he gave an independent ruling on the point of issue, and especially if he said that the death penalty should be carried out, he could be accused of usurping the governor's jurisdiction, or of usurping jurisdiction which the Roman administration had expressly reserved to the Sanhedrin. The Sanhedrin retained the right to *pronounce* the death sentence for capital offences against Jewish law, although they could not *execute* it without the governor's authorization (see 18:31). These were matters with which a layman would be well advised not to meddle; but Jesus was now challenged to speak his mind on such a matter.

Why did he stoop down and trace letters on the ground? T. W. Manson suggested that he was imitating the action of a Roman magistrate, who wrote down his sentence and then read it out aloud.[3] If that is so, the words which he wrote would be those which he utters in verse 7. This is the only occasion on which Jesus is recorded to have written anything, and what he wrote must remain a matter of conjecture. It would soon have been obliterated in any case. Some manuscripts add *mē prospoioumenos*, 'pretending not (to hear)', i.e. 'taking no notice', which may be the origin of the AV addition, *'as though he heard them not'* – but AV indicates the poor attestation of this clause by printing it in italics.

8:7, 8 When they kept on questioning him, he straightened up and said to them, 'Let him who is sinless among you be the first to throw a stone at her.' Then he bent down and wrote on the ground again.

In cases of execution by stoning, the ancient prescription ran: 'The hand of the witnesses shall be against him first to put him to death, and afterwards the hand of all the people' (Deut. 17:7; cf.

13:9; also Lev. 24:14). (That is why it was necessary for someone to hold the outer garments of the witnesses against Stephen, as recorded in Acts 7:58.) Jesus makes no modification in the Mosaic law which demanded death by stoning for the type of offence which this woman had committed. He simply rules that only those who were guiltless themselves (guiltless, presumably, with respect to this particular category of sin) could with any propriety take the responsibility of carrying out the sentence. No exception could be taken to this ruling, but in practice it made it impossible for the execution to take place.

We may recall Jesus' own words about the lustful look which constitutes adultery in the heart (Matt. 5:28), but more was involved in his ruling than that. The law dealt more severely with women than with men. For a betrothed or married woman to have sexual relations with a man other than her bridegroom or husband was a capital offence; for a married man to have such relations with another woman than his wife was relatively venial, provided the woman was not betrothed or married to another man. It was possible for men to maintain public respectability in spite of certain irregular incidents in their lives; Jesus' ruling therefore came as a challenge to the conscience of each man who heard him. The embarrassment was no longer his, but theirs. His ruling about adultery, like his ruling elsewhere about divorce, amounts to a redressing of the unfavourable balance in favour of the underprivileged sex. But by his appeal to the consciences of the witnesses, he takes the question off the judicial plane altogether and raises it to the moral level where it properly belongs, in accordance with his regular attitude and teaching.

Some manuscripts amplify verse 8 by stating that what he wrote on the ground was 'the sins of each one of them' (one manuscript, indeed, inserts this in verse 6). The addition was no doubt designed to gratify a natural curiosity about what he actually wrote.

8:9 When they heard that, they went out one by one, beginning with the oldest, and he was left alone, with the woman still in the midst.

The 'received text' and the AV say that they were 'convicted by their own conscience', which is no doubt true, even if it is not part of the original text of the passage. The description of their departure implies that the oldest went out first, and so on till the youngest. Some witnesses to the text make this more explicit by adding 'even unto the last'. The omission of this phrase makes it possible to suppose that those of them who were 'elders' (*presbyteroi*), i.e. members of the Sanhedrin, went out first; but this is unlikely.

Verse 3 probably means that they formed a ring around the woman; if she is still said to be 'in the midst' after they were all gone, all that is meant is that she remained where they had set her.

8:10, 11 Then Jesus straightened himself up again, and said to her, 'Woman, where are they? Has no one condemned you?' She said, 'No one, sir.' Then said Jesus, 'Neither do I condemn you. Be on your way: from now on do not sin any more.'

Not until all the woman's accusers had departed did Jesus look up from his writing on the ground. His ruling on who was entitled to take action against her was sufficient to convict them: he would not embarrass them further by looking them in the eye. There is nothing discourteous in his addressing her as 'Woman'; he addresses his mother thus in John 2:4 and 19:26, Mary of Magdala in 20:13, and the woman of Sychar in John 4:21. She addresses him as *kyrie* (vocative of *kyrios*), which may as readily be translated 'Sir' as 'Lord'; there is no hint that she had any idea who he was. Evidently he accepts her accusers' charge against her as true; his refusal to condemn her does not mean that she was not guilty of adultery, but he 'came not to judge the world, but to save the world' (John 12:47; cf. 3:17). He discharges the sinner without condoning her sin. With his command to her not to go on sinning we may compare his similar command to the man who was cured at the pool of Bethesda (John 5:14).

Whatever textual problems are raised by this passage, 'the account has all the earmarks of historical veracity'.[4] We may safely recognize the incident as taking place in the temple precincts during Holy Week, a companion piece to those which are related in Mark 12:13–34, and especially to the incident of the tribute money.

NOTES

1. The textual evidence is set out in detail in B. M. Metzger, *A Textual Commentary on the Greek New Testament* (London/New York, 1971), pp. 219–223. The case for continuing to treat the passage as integral to the Gospel of John is presented by Z. C. Hodges, 'The Woman Taken in Adultery (John 7:53–8:11): The Text', *Bibliotheca Sacra* 136 (1979), pp. 318–332; 'The Woman Taken in Adultery (John 7:53–811): Exposition', *Bibliotheca Sacra* 137 (1980), pp. 41–53.
2. *Oriente Moderno* 37 (1957), p. 593, quoted in *CBQ* 20 (1958), p. 224.
3. T. W. Manson, 'The Pericope de Adultera (Joh 7.53–8.11)', *ZNW*, 44 (1952–53), pp. 255 f.
4. B. M. Metzger, *A Textual Commentary on the Greek New Testament*, p. 220. It has sometimes been thought that the incident may have been derived from the *Gospel according to the Hebrews* – a Jewish-Christian work current in the early centuries AD – largely on the strength of a statement by Eusebius (*Hist. Eccl.* 3.39.17) that Papias (bishop of Hierapolis c. AD 130), in his *Exegesis of the*

Dominical Logia 'sets forth another narrative, concerning a woman accused before the Lord of many sins – a narrative contained in the *Gospel according to the Hebrews*'. But the identification of the two incidents is precarious; the woman of John 7:53–8:11 was not accused of *many* sins.

Persons, places and subjects mentioned in the text of the Gospel are discussed in the accompanying exposition and are therefore, for the most part, not included in the Index.

THE EPISTLES OF JOHN

THE EPISTLES
OF JOHN

Introduction, Exposition and Notes

BY

F. F. BRUCE

WILLIAM B. EERDMANS PUBLISHING COMPANY
GRAND RAPIDS, MICHIGAN

First published 1970 by Pickering & Inglis Ltd. This
American edition published 1979 through special ar-
rangement with Pickering & Inglis by Wm. B. Eerdmans
Publishing Company, Grand Rapids, Michigan.

Library of Congress Cataloging in Publication Data

Bruce, Frederick Fyvie, 1910-
   The Epistles of John

   "The Bible text . . . is the Revised version of 1881."
   "The substance of this commentary appeared in
twenty-four installments in the Witness during 1967
and 1968."
   Bibliography: p. 20.
   Includes index.
   1. Bible. N.T. Epistles of John — Commentaries.
I. Bible. N.T. Epistles of John. English. Revised. 1979.
II. Title.
BS2805.3.B77 1979   227'.94'077   78-22069

PREFACE

THE substance of this commentary appeared in twenty-four instalments in *The Witness* during 1967 and 1968. It is mainly due to the friendly insistence of the Editor of *The Witness*, Mr. G. C. D. Howley, that the work was undertaken in the first instance.

Like my exposition of Ephesians, published in 1961, these studies are intended chiefly for the general Christian reader who is interested in serious Bible study, not for the professional or specialist student. Textual, linguistic and other critical questions have been touched on lightly; the main aim has been to bring out the meaning and message of the three Epistles. The professional student may, however, find some help in a number of the notes which have been added for the publication of the work in book form, especially in those which provide bibliographical information on matters of exegetical importance.

The Bible text on which the exposition is based is the Revised Version of 1881, since that is the most literal of all the standard renderings of the Greek text. Other versions, however, have been freely utilized.

August, 1970   F.F.B.

CONTENTS

ABBREVIATIONS

AV   Authorized (King James) Version
BJRL   *Bulletin of the John Rylands Library* (Manchester)
CSEL   *Corpus Scriptorum Ecclesiasticorum Latinorum*
Hist. Eccl.   *Ecclesiastical History* (Eusebius)
JBL   *Journal of Biblical Literature*
JTS   *Journal of Theological Studies*
LXX   Septuagint (Greek Old Testament)
NEB   New English Bible
NT   New Testament
NTS   *New Testament Studies*
OT   Old Testament
RSV   Revised Standard Version
RV   Revised Version
TDNT   *Theological Dictionary of the New Testament*, edited by
       G. Kittel and G. Friedrich, English translation by
       G. W. Bromiley (Eerdmans, Grand Rapids, 1964–)
TEV   Today's English Version (Good News for Modern Man)
TU   *Texte und Untersuchungen*
ZTK   *Zeitschrift für Theologie und Kirche*

GENERAL INTRODUCTION

I BACKGROUND AND OCCASION OF THE THREE EPISTLES

The Roman province of Asia occupied roughly the western third of the peninsula which we call Asia Minor. The Romans gave it the name of Asia because it was the first territory on the continent of Asia to come under the direct control of the Roman state. For a century and a half before its incorporation in the Roman Empire, this territory had constituted the kingdom of Pergamum, whose rulers were friends and allies of Rome. When the last king of Pergamum died, in 133 BC, he bequeathed his realm to the Roman senate and people, and after deliberation they decided to accept the bequest. After reorganization as a Roman province, it was governed by a senior ex-magistrate called a proconsul, who was appointed by the senate, normally for one year. The province is therefore referred to sometimes as 'proconsular Asia'. To begin with, the proconsul's seat of government was at Pergamum, the capital of the former kingdom, but later it was moved to Ephesus, and there it remained throughout New Testament times. Asia was regarded as the wealthiest of the Roman provinces; its cities had been centres of Greek culture for many centuries.

Christianity may have been introduced to the province of Asia by individuals before the middle of the first century AD, but it was effectively established in the province during Paul's Ephesian ministry, to be dated probably from the late summer of AD 52 to the spring of 55. So thoroughly did Paul and his colleagues prosecute the work of evangelization during those years that not only the people of Ephesus but 'all the residents of Asia heard the word of the Lord, both Jews and Greeks' (Acts 19. 10). The seven churches of Revelation, and other churches besides, were founded at that time, and the continuous history of Christianity in that territory can be traced from then until the Graeco-Turkish exchange of populations in 1923.

13

The intellectual activity of the cities of Asia could not leave the gospel unaffected. Among the Jews of the province – especially in Asian Phrygia, its most easterly region – there is ample contemporary evidence of syncretism in life and thought, of the fusion of their ancestral beliefs and practices with features from the older ethnic religions of Asia Minor and from more recent mystery cults and philosophical trends. The same sort of thing was not long in making its appearance among the Christians of the province. There is an ominous note in Paul's Miletus address to the elders of the Ephesian church, when they are warned that from their own ranks 'will arise men speaking perverse things, to draw away the disciples after them' (Acts 20. 30). An outstanding example of the threat presented by syncretistic tendencies to the unique essence of Christianity is the 'Colossian heresy' which, only a few years after Paul's Ephesian ministry, was rife in the church of Colossae and other cities of the Lycus valley (in Asian Phrygia) and which is refuted in the Epistle to the Colossians (*c*. AD 61). Worse was to follow: a landslide away from apostolic teaching[1] is implied in the words of 2 Tim. 1. 15, 'You are aware that all who are in Asia turned away from me'.

The sixties of the first century, however, saw a welcome revitalizing of apostolic Christianity in proconsular Asia. This was due to the immigration of a number of Christians from Palestine shortly before the outbreak of the Jewish War in AD 66. These were not the more Judaistic members of the Jerusalem church who around the same time migrated to Transjordan, but outward-looking members of the church of Caesarea and other churches in the tradition of those Hellenistic believers who were dispersed after the martyrdom of Stephen and inaugurated the Gentile mission in Syrian Antioch and elsewhere. Those who migrated to proconsular Asia included some very eminent Christians – Philip the evangelist and his daughters, for example, whose tombs were pointed out some generations later in Hierapolis in Asian Phrygia, and 'John the disciple of the Lord', who is associated mainly with Ephesus.[2] The identity of this John has been much discussed. Those writers who mention him regard him as a companion of our

Lord and an eyewitness of His ministry. More important for our purpose is his relation to the unnamed author of the three Epistles of John; suffice it to say that here it is accepted that the Epistles were written by this 'John the disciple of the Lord', and also that he is the Fourth Evangelist.[3]

John lived to a great age, until the time came when he was the sole survivor of those who had been in close contact with Jesus before His death and resurrection. It needs little imagination to understand how eagerly he would be sought out and listened to by people who valued first-hand information about the deeds and words of his Master and theirs. We know of two leaders in the Asian churches in the first half of the second century who never forgot what they had heard from John – Polycarp, bishop of Smyrna, who told his own young disciples in turn 'of his intercourse with John and the others who had seen the Lord',[4] and Papias, bishop of Hierapolis, who thought that what he could get from books would not help him so much as what came from 'a living and abiding voice'.[5]

These men, and others before them, attached special importance to the testimony of a man like John when teachers came along presenting a new brand of doctrine with the claim that it was the original and authentic doctrine of Christ – perhaps secretly committed by Him to chosen vessels and transmitted orally by them until the time was ripe for wider publicity. What were Christians to do or say when claims like these were put before them? A decision on their validity was not so easy to reach in days before the New Testament documents were collected and in general circulation. It was not altogether satisfactory to reply, 'This is quite different from what we have always been taught' – such a reply might betoken an excessively conservative clinging to tradition, and the new teachers might say that the doctrine which they brought was part of 'all the truth' into which Jesus said the Holy Spirit would lead His followers. Moreover, the new brand of doctrine would probably be so completely in accordance with the prevailing climate of opinion that in the eyes of many thinking people this was manifestly the way in which the gospel was to be 're-stated' for their day if it was to have any chance of acceptance and indeed survival.

One form of 're-stating' the gospel which was very much in keeping with the current climate of opinion at the end of the first Christian century was that which its critics called 'Docetism'.[6] It sprang from a dualistic interpretation of the world, widely accepted in those days, which viewed matter as essentially evil and spirit as essentially good. There could be no peaceful co-existence between the two; in particular, it was unthinkable that there could be any direct relation between the supreme God, who was pure spirit and essentially good, and the material universe, which by definition was essentially evil. The biblical doctrine of creation must therefore be jettisoned; the material universe must be regarded as the work of some inferior power or 'demiurge'.[7] The biblical doctrine of resurrection must also be jettisoned; it was unacceptable to the Greek mind in any case, as reactions to Paul's teaching in Athens and Corinth showed (Acts 17. 32; 1 Cor. 15. 12 ff.), but it was logically excluded by the dualistic world-view, which thought of the climax of redemption as the final liberation of the soul from its bodily shackles, not the receiving of a new (albeit 'spiritual') body as its vehicle of communication with a new environment.

It is in special relation to the person of Christ that this dualistic outlook gave rise to Docetism. The first disciples of Christ knew their Master to be a real human being; they also confessed him to be the Son of God, their Divine Lord. When this confession was understood, as it was by many Greek Christians, in metaphysical terms, it raised problems which were hotly debated in the great Christological controversies of the following centuries. To thorough-going dualists the problem was simply this: How could the true God indwell a human body of flesh and blood? The general Docetic answer to this problem was that, since such an indwelling was plainly impossible, the human body of flesh and blood was not a real one but an imaginary one; it only *seemed* to be so.[8] One special variety of Docetism is associated with the name of Cerinthus, who flourished in the nineties of the first century, and who is traditionally represented as the *bête noire* of John the disciple of the Lord.[9] Cerinthus, a man trained in Egypt but resident in the province of Asia, accepted the general dualistic world-view (including the creation of matter by an inferior power), but propounded a novel Christology. He distinguished the man Jesus (the son of Joseph and Mary, endowed with greater virtue and wisdom than other men), from 'the Christ', who descended on Jesus in the form of a dove after He was baptized, empowering Him to perform miracles and proclaim 'the unknown Father', but who left Him before He died, so that 'Jesus suffered and rose again, while the Christ remained immune from suffering, since He was a spiritual being'.[10] In spite of second-century tradition, however, it is not certain that it is his views exclusively that are controverted in 1 and 2 John.[11]

John writes with conscious authority, whether he is refuting the claims of those whose teaching denies that 'Jesus Christ has come in the flesh' or directing churches to welcome visitors who bring the true gospel but to give no countenance to any doctrine which is inconsistent with it. If in some places there is a tendency to disregard his authority, as there was in the church ruled by Diotrephes, he is confident that a personal visit will suffice to re-establish his authority; Diotrephes will be cut down to size. John's authority in this circle of churches is comparable to Paul's in his Gentile mission-field: 'I will come to you soon, if the Lord wills', writes Paul to the Corinthians, 'and I will find out not the talk of these arrogant people but their power' (1 Cor. 4. 19). But whereas Paul invokes the *apostolic* authority committed to him by the Lord, John does not argue in these terms; the word 'apostle' is absent from his Epistles, and in the Gospel it occurs only once, and that in the general sense of 'messenger' (John 13. 16, 'he who is sent'). John is the bearer and representative of what we should call 'apostolic tradition' (although he does not describe it as 'apostolic'); indeed, because of his personal association with the earliest days of Christianity, he is the embodiment of that tradition[12] – more particularly, the tradition as it is set forth in his Gospel.[13] This tradition, together with him who embodies it, is vested with the authority of the Lord Himself – not only because it stems from

Him as a matter of history but also because it is continuously validated by Him as the exalted and ever-living One, who is still active in the world by His Spirit in His servants.[14] This is the authority by which John acts and writes, and of those who repudiated his authority he might well say, like Paul, 'if I come again I will not spare them – since you desire proof that Christ is speaking in me' (2 Cor. 13. 2 f.).

II   THE THREE EPISTLES IN THE EARLY CHURCH

The first epistle of John was known in the province of Asia quite early in the second century. Ignatius, bishop of Antioch (martyred *c.* AD 110), has one or two *possible* allusions to it, especially in a passage in his letter to the Ephesian church where he speaks of the incarnation as 'God having become in flesh',[15] which could be a typically Ignatian paraphrase of 1 John 4. 2, 3. A telescoped quotation of these same two verses appears in Polycarp's letter to the Philippian church (*c.* AD 120),[16] and Polycarp's contemporary Papias is said by Eusebius to have 'made use of testimonies from the former epistle of John'.[17] Other second-century writers in whom traces of this epistle have been recognized are the Gnostic Valentinus,[18] Justin Martyr in Rome,[19] and the anonymous author of the *Letter to Diognetus*.[20]

Later in the century Irenaeus of Lyons[21] and Tertullian of Carthage[22] quote it explicitly and repeatedly, ascribing it to John the apostle and according it therefore unquestioned authority.

Towards the end of the second century two, if not three, of the epistles were not only known in the Roman church but recognized as canonical. The Muratorian list of New Testament books, drawn up at Rome *c.* AD 190 and preserved in a single incomplete Latin manuscript of the seventh or eighth century, discovered and published in 1740 by Cardinal L. A. Muratori (whence its designation) and now in the Ambrosian Library at Milan, gives a free quotation from the opening words of 1 John in connection with its account of the Fourth Gospel. The author of the list, wishing to emphasize that this Gospel presents the evidence of an eyewitness, goes on to say:

What wonder, then, that John in his epistles also should lay such bold claim to the following experiences, one by one, saying of himself: 'What we have seen with our eyes and heard with our ears and our hands have handled, this is what we write to you.' For in these words he claims to be not only a spectator and hearer, but also a writer of all the Lord's wonderful works in order.[23]

Later in the list two epistles 'of the aforementioned John' are said to be included *in catholica*,[24] which presumably means that they were accepted in the Catholic Church. The identity of these two is uncertain. The compiler of the list may mean two in addition to the one already quoted (i.e. 2 and 3 John in addition to 1 John);[25] he may mean 1 John together with one of the others or, if 2 and 3 John were taken together as one (which is not very probable), he may mean 1 John together with 2 and 3 John. Most probably he means 1 and 2 John. There is evidence that 3 John was rendered into Latin by another (and later?) translator than 1 and 2 John;[26] this being so, the Muratorian author, and the church whose New Testament canon he recorded, may well have known only 1 and 2 John. This was the situation at the same time in Alexandria: Clement of Alexandria appears to have known 1 and 2 John only,[27] whereas one or two generations later, in that same city, Origen and Dionysius knew 3 John as well. An African list of New Testament books of *c.* AD 360 (the Cheltenham or Mommsenian Canon) indicates that when it was drawn up 'three epistles of John' were recognized in the church of Carthage, but the added words 'one only' suggest that some conservative spirits were none too sure about 2 and 3 John. The evidence points to the canonical recognition of 1, 2 and 3 John in stages, one at a time.

Origen (*c.* AD 231) says that John 'has left an epistle of a very few lines and, it may be, a second and a third, for not all say that these [i.e. the second and the third] are genuine'.[28] According to Eusebius, writing *c.* AD 325, 1 John in his days belonged to the 'acknowledged books' (*homologoumena*), while 2 and 3 John were 'disputed' (*antilegomena*), because 'they might be the work of the evangelist or of someone else with the same name'.[29] The authorized version of the Bible in Syriac (the Peshitta), published early in the fifth century, included 1 John but not 2 and 3 John. Not until the Philoxenian version of AD 508 were these two epistles (with 2 Peter, Jude and Revelation) included in an edition of the Syriac New Testament.

The first epistle belongs properly to the group of New Testament documents called Catholic (or General) Epistles, because they are not addressed to any one person or community. Origen applies the epithet 'catholic' to 1 John;[30] his disciple Dionysius, bishop of Alexandria, also speaks of 1 John as John's 'catholic epistle'[31] – perhaps in contrast to 2 and 3 John, which are addressed to specified persons.[32] Later, however, 2 and 3 John were also reckoned among the seven Catholic Epistles (James, 1 and 2 Peter, 1, 2 and 3 John, Jude);[33] in this broader sense the term 'catholic' meant more or less 'canonical'[34] – canonical, that is to say, in addition to the Pauline epistles.

All three epistles are included in Athanasius's list of twenty-seven New Testament books issued in AD 367, and in the similar lists approved by the Councils of Hippo (393) and Carthage (397).

III   BIBLIOGRAPHY

Among the numerous expositions of these Epistles there are seven which I have found outstandingly useful:

B. F. Westcott, *The Epistles of St. John* (London, first edition, 1883; fourth edition, 1902). This commentary, based on the Greek text, was reissued in 1966 by the Marcham Manor Press, Abingdon, Berkshire.

G. G. Findlay, *Fellowship in the Life Eternal* (London, 1909).

R. Law, *The Tests of Life* (Edinburgh, first edition, 1909; third edition, 1914). This study, described by A. M. Hunter as 'a liberal education in Biblical theology', was reissued in 1968 by the Baker Book House, Grand Rapids, Michigan, in their 'Limited Editions Library'.

A. E. Brooke, *The Johannine Epistles*. International Critical Commentary (Edinburgh, 1912). Based on the Greek text.

C. H. Dodd, *The Johannine Epistles*. Moffatt New Testament Commentary (London, 1946). Based, like all the volumes in the same series, on James Moffatt's translation.

R. Schnackenburg, *Die Johannesbriefe*. Herder's Theological Commentary on the NT (Freiburg, third edition, 1965).

R. Bultmann, *The Johannine Epistles*. Hermeneia (Philadelphia, 1973).

J. L. Houlden, *A Commentary on the Johannine Epistles*. Black's New Testament Commentaries (London, 1973).

Among shorter and more popular commentaries these are worthy of special mention:

N. Alexander, *The Epistles of John*, Torch Commentaries (London, 1962).

J. R. W. Stott, *The Epistles of John*, Tyndale NT Commentaries (London, 1964).

R. R. Williams, *The Letters of John and James*, Cambridge Bible Commentary on the New English Bible (Cambridge, 1965).

Other works containing material relevant to the study of the three Epistles are:

O. Cullmann, *The Early Church* (London, 1956).

W. F. Howard, *Christianity according to St. John* (London, 1943).

T. W. Manson, *On Paul and John* (London, 1963).

W. Nauck, *Die Tradition und der Charakter des ersten Johannesbriefes* (Tübingen, 1957).

Further important contributions to their study, especially in the form of periodical or occasional articles, are mentioned in footnotes.

NOTES

1. Although the apostles are not referred to as such in either the Gospel or the Epistles of John. this commentary uses the terminology 'the apostolic (*or* the apostles') teaching, fellowship *or* tradition' to denote what John prefers to call 'that was from the beginning' (see notes on 1. 1; 2. 7, 24).

2. Polycrates, bishop of Ephesus, writing to Victor, bishop of Rome *c.* AD 190, mentions among the 'great luminaries' who died and were buried in proconsular Asia Philip and two of his daughters (whose graves were in Hierapolis) and a third daughter (whose grave was in Ephesus), 'and John, who leaned on the Lord's breast, who was a priest wearing the *petalon*, a martyr and teacher; he also sleeps in Ephesus' (quoted by Eusebius, *Hist. Eccl.* iii. 31. 3; v. 24. 2). The *petalon* was the inscribed plate of gold attached to the high-priestly mitre or turban; Polycrates's language about it is best understood figuratively. Polycrates appears to have confused Philip the

apostle with Philip the evangelist; his contemporary, the Phrygian Montanist Proclus, points clearly to the Philip of Acts 21. 8 f. when he says in his correspondence with Gaius, a Roman presbyter, that 'the four daughters of Philip, who were prophetesses, were at Hierapolis in Asia; their grave is there and so is their father's' (quoted by Eusebius, *Hist. Eccl.* iii. 31. 4). About the same time Irenaeus, bishop of Lyons, states that 'John the disciple of the Lord, who leaned on His breast, himself also published the Gospel while he stayed at Ephesus in Asia' (*Against Heresies* iii. 1. 1). In the time of Dionysius, bishop of Alexandria (*c.* AD 270), two places were pointed out at Ephesus as the site of John's tomb (Eusebius, *Hist. Eccl.* vii. 25. 16).

3. Identified in John 21. 20–24 with 'the disciple whom Jesus loved'; cf. also John 13. 23 ff. (where this disciple is described as 'lying close to the breast of Jesus' at the Last Supper); 19. 26 f. (where he stands near the cross); 20. 2 ff., where he is convinced by the silent witness of the empty tomb); 21. 7 (where he recognizes the risen Lord). See also pp. 135 f.

4. From Irenaeus's letter to Florinus, in which he goes on to remind his former companion how Polycarp recalled 'the things concerning the Lord which he had heard from them, His miracles and His teaching, and how Polycarp had received them from eye-witnesses of the Word of life and reported all things in accordance with the Scriptures' (quoted by Eusebius, *Hist. Eccl.* v. 20. 6). Similarly, in his letter to Victor of Rome on the proper date of Easter, Irenaeus affirms that Polycarp had always followed the quartodeciman dating (i.e. he observed Passover on Nisan 14, after the Jewish precedent, irrespective of the weekday on which it fell) 'in company with John the disciple of our Lord and the other apostles with whom he associated' (quoted by Eusebius, *Hist. Eccl.* v. 24. 16). The absence of any reference to John in Pionius's later *Life of Polycarp* (*c.* AD 250) does not weaken the testimony of Irenaeus; Pionius's strong anti-quartodeciman convictions would be sufficient to dictate silence about John, who was regarded as the greatest authority for quartodeciman practice.

5. From his *Exegesis of the Dominical Oracles*, a work in five books now extant only in fragments quoted by later Christian writers, several of them by Eusebius, like the present one (*Hist. Eccl.* iii. 39. 4). Among those about whose testimony he sought information he mentions 'John' in a list of 'disciples of the Lord' in the past tense, and 'the elder John' as one of two 'disciples of the Lord' in the present tense (see the whole quotation on p. 136). If he means to distinguish two men called John, the former being presumably the apostle, the question arises whether 'John the disciple of the Lord' referred to by other Asian writers should be identified with the apostle or with 'the elder John'. This question remains unresolved; it was discussed by Dionysius of Alexandria in his day and by Eusebius fifty years later (*Hist. Eccl.* vii. 25. 6–27). The late fourth-century *Apostolic Constitutions* gives a list of bishops alleged to have been appointed to their sees by apostles, including 'in Ephesus, . . . John appointed by me John' (vii. 46). The independent value of this list is negligible, but it probably does bear witness to the tradition of two Johns at Ephesus, as does also a treatise (implausibly ascribed to Eusebius) found in some manuscripts of the Syriac Peshitta version, which mentions among three disciples of John the Evangelist 'John, to whom he committed the presbyterate and the episcopal see after him'.

Irenaeus had no doubt that Papias was 'a hearer of John and a companion of Polycarp' (*Against Heresies* v. 33. 4); Eusebius, on the other hand, thinks that Papias makes it plain that, while he had heard Aristion and the elder

John, 'he had by no means been a hearer and eyewitness of the holy apostles' (*Hist. Eccl.* iii. 39. 2, 7). But Eusebius was anxious that no suspicion of apostolic authority should attach to Papias's millenarian views, of which he disapproved. The anti-Marcionite prologue to the Fourth Gospel, extant only in a corrupt Latin translation of the Greek original (which may be dated *c.* AD 175), seems to confirm Irenaeus's testimony: 'The Gospel of John was published and given to the churches by John while he was yet in the body, as a man of Hierapolis, Papias by name, John's dear disciple, has related in his five exegetical books' (the adjective 'exegetical' is a highly probable emendation).

Several legends about John were preserved in Ephesus and its neighbourhood, including one about a former disciple of his who became a brigand chief and was sought out by John and restored to Christian fellowship (Clement of Alexandria, *Who is the rich man who is saved?* 42, quoted also by Eusebius, *Hist. Eccl.* iii. 23. 5–19), and another to the effect that in extreme old age, when he was taken to meet fellow-Christians, all he could do was to sum up the burden of his ministry by repeating the admonition: 'Little children, love one another' (Jerome, *Commentary on Galatians* 6. 10). No historical worth attaches to the apocryphal *Acts of John* (*c.* AD 160).

6. From Gr. *dokein*, 'to seem'. Cf. Ignatius, *To the Smyrnaeans* 2, where, after affirming his faith in Jesus incarnate, crucified and risen, he says: 'He suffered all these things for us that we might be saved; and he truly suffered, even as he truly raised himself – not, as some unbelievers say, that he *seemed* to have suffered' (where the repeated 'truly' is set in antithesis to mere *seeming*); similarly *To the Trallians* 10.

7. From Gr. *dēmiourgos*, literally 'public workman' (*dēmio-ergos*), 'artisan'; it is the word used of God in Heb. 11. 10 (but not in a dualistic or gnostic sense) and translated 'maker' in AV, RV and RSV (NEB 'builder').

8. The Christianity with which Muhammad became acquainted in his early days appears to have been docetic in outlook; hence the statement in the *Qur'ān* (4. 157): 'they did not kill him and did not crucify him, but he was counterfeited for them' (i.e. it was an effigy or simulacrum of Jesus that was fastened to the cross).

9. As in the legend about John's leaving the public baths at Ephesus in precipitate haste when he heard on one occasion that Cerinthus had entered: 'Let us flee, lest the baths fall in while Cerinthus, the enemy of the truth, is within' (related by Irenaeus, *Against Heresies* iii. 3. 4, as a story told by Polycarp).

10. Irenaeus, *Against Heresies* i. 26. 1. Gaius of Rome, contemporary with Irenaeus, charged Cerinthus with teaching that the marriage supper of the Lamb would last on earth for a thousand years, and indeed held that the Johannine Apocalypse was the work of Cerinthus. Dionysius of Alexandria also ascribed millenarian views to Cerinthus (both Gaius and Dionysius are quoted to this effect by Eusebius, *Hist. Eccl.* iii. 28. 1–5; cf. vii. 25. 1–3).

11. R. M. Grant (*A Historical Introduction to the NT*, London, 1963, p. 233) thinks that John might have in mind the views of Menander of Antioch, a follower (it is said) of Simon Magus (his views are summarized by Irenaeus, *Against Heresies* i. 23. 5).

12. 'John conducts himself with the independence and sovereignty of one who was in a position to say: *La tradition, c'est moi!*' (P. H. Menoud, *L'évangile de Jean d'après les recherches récentes*, Neuchatel & Paris, 1947, p. 77).

13. Cf. C. H. Dodd, *Historical Tradition in the Fourth Gospel* (Cambridge, 1963);

J. A. T. Robinson, 'The New Look on the Fourth Gospel', in *Twelve NT Studies*, London, 1962, pp. 94 ff., an essay which ends with the words: 'The decisive question is the status and origin of the Johannine tradition. Did this come out of the blue round about the year AD 100? Or is there a real continuity, not merely in the memory of one old man, but in the life of an on-going community, with the earliest days of Christianity? What, I think, fundamentally distinguishes the "new look" on the fourth Gospel is that it answers that question in the affirmative. But if we do assert this continuity, it is obviously going at one and the same time to reduce the necessity for making everything depend upon apostolic authorship *and* to make us very much more open to its possibility' (p. 106). The Johannine Epistles, it may be said, provide us with living evidence for the maintenance of the tradition both 'in the memory of one old man' (the Elder) and 'in the life of an on-going community' (the companies addressed and referred to as adhering to what they had heard 'from the beginning').

14. Cf. O. Cullmann, 'The Tradition', in *The Early Church* (London, 1956), pp. 59 ff.

15. *To the Ephesians* 7. 2. Cf. also John 1. 14; 2 John 7. Ignatius does not hesitate to speak of Jesus as God.

16. Every one who does not confess that Jesus Christ has come in the flesh is Antichrist' (*To the Philippians* 7. 1). Cf. 2 John 7. See p. 72.

17. Eusebius, *Hist. Eccl.* iii. 39. 17.

18. Possible traces in the Valentinian *Gospel of Truth* (*c.* AD 140) are 'the Father knows all things' (27. 24; cf. 1 John 3. 20) and 'he came forth in flesh' (31. 4 f.; cf. 1 John 4. 2 f.).

19. Justin's statement that 'we are called God's trueborn children, and so we are, if we keep his commandments' (*Dialogue with Trypho* 123. 9) looks very much like a reminiscence of 1 John 3. 1, coupled with 2. 3.

20. Compare, e.g., 'how greatly will you love Him who so loved you first?' (Diogn. 10. 3) with 1 John 4. 19.

21. E.g. *Against Heresies* iii. 16. 5.

22. E.g. *Against Marcion* v. 16.

23. Lines 26–34.

24. Lines 68 f. For practical purposes *in catholica* may be translated 'in the canon'.

25. So P. Katz, 'The Johannine Epistles in the Muratorian Canon', *JTS* n.s. 8 (1957), pp. 273 f.

26. Cf. A. Harnack, *Zur Revision der Prinzipien der neutestamentlichen Textkritik* (Leipzig, 1916), pp. 61 f.; T. W. Manson, 'The Johannine Epistles and the Canon of the NT', *JTS* 48 (1947), pp. 32 f.

27. *Miscellanies* ii. 15. 66; *Adumbrations* iv. 437, etc.

28. Quoted by Eusebius, *Hist. Eccl.* vi. 25. 10.

29. *Hist. Eccl.* iii. 24. 17 f.

30. *Commentary on Matthew*, xvii. 19.

31. Quoted by Eusebius, *Hist. Eccl.* vii. 25. 7, 10.

32. Cf. Eusebius, *Hist. Eccl.* vii. 25. 11.

33. Eusebius refers to the seven epistles 'called catholic' (*Hist. Eccl.* ii. 23. 25).

34. In this sense Jerome sometimes renders Gr. *katholikos* by Lat. *catholicus*, sometimes by *canonicus*.

THE FIRST EPISTLE OF JOHN

Introduction

1 *Character and Purpose*

The First Epistle of John neither begins nor ends like an epistle; it does not start with any indication of the identity of the writer or of the people whom he addresses,[1] nor does it end with personal greetings. In form and content it is a message of encouragement and reassurance, sent to a group of Christians who were perplexed and bewildered by recent happenings in their midst. We cannot be sure whether it was sent to a single church or to several churches in an area; what is reasonably certain is that the recipients lived in some district of the province of Asia, and that shortly before the sending of this message some of their most talented brethren had left them in order to form a new community or communities devoted to a specially attractive line of teaching which was represented as an advance on anything that Christians had been taught thus far. When we say it was specially attractive, we mean that it was specially attractive to people of some intellectual attainment. For the ordinary rank and file of Christians it had less appeal; indeed, it was not intended for them, but rather for an élite of spiritual initiates. It deviated from the teaching which had previously been current among the churches of Asia in theory and practice alike.

In its theory it closely resembled the docetic brand of Gnosticism; in particular, it denied that Jesus Christ had 'come in the flesh' (1 John 4. 2 f.). In the particular climate of opinion to which this teaching owed its existence, 'thoughtful men' could not be expected to believe in the 'crude' incarnationalism of the primitive message; it was a relief to have a re-statement of Christianity presented to them which did not compel them to be obscurantists or to keep different areas of knowledge in watertight compartments.

The re-stating of the gospel is a necessary task which must

engage the serious concern of those who wish to commend it to their fellows in each succeeding generation. In the first Christian century no one played a more conspicuous or successful part in re-stating the gospel than John himself did. A comparison of the Synoptic Gospels with the Fourth Gospel makes it plain that in the latter the message of the former has been transposed into a different key. Yet the message which John thus transposes or re-states is the same essential message as that of the earlier Evangelists, but presented in an idiom which was more intelligible to Hellenistic readers in the eastern Mediterranean two generations after the saving events had taken place – in an idiom which was calculated to bring out the eternal validity of those events, and which in fact continues even in our day to bring out their eternal validity. There can be a true re-statement of the gospel as there can be a false one; everything depends on whether the essence of the gospel is preserved or lost in the re-statement. Since the incarnation of the Son of God is of the abiding essence of the gospel, the Cerinthian re-statement or anything of the same general character could not be accepted as truly Christian.

On the practical level these new teachers claimed to have reached such an advanced stage in spiritual experience that they were 'beyond good and evil'. They maintained that they had no sin, not in the sense that they had attained moral perfection but in the sense that what might be sin for people at a less mature stage of inner development was no longer sin for the completely 'spiritual' man. For him ethical distinctions had ceased to be relevant. Perhaps he called them 'merely' ethical distinctions. (Christians stand on the brink of disaster when they begin to modify the adjective 'ethical' with the adverb 'merely'.) The new teaching thus combined a new theology with a new morality.

Neither theology nor morality is necessarily the worse for being 'new'. When our Lord began His public ministry in Galilee His hearers recognized that what He brought was 'a new teaching' (Mark 1. 27); and those who listened to the Sermon on the Mount were aware that they were being presented with a 'new morality', for all our Lord's claim that He was but reaffirming the essence of the law and the prophets, 'for he taught them as one who had authority, and not as their scribes' (Matt. 7. 29). The question to be asked of all teaching is not 'Is it new?' but 'Is it true?' When this latter question was put to the new teaching with which John takes issue, the answer was that it was not true. It could not be, for it was at variance with the truth incarnate in Jesus; far from bringing out the deeper implications of the gospel, it utterly subverted it. No appeal to the principle of complementarity could reconcile the one to the other.

In such a situation it was impossible for those who propagated and embraced the new teaching to continue with those who believed that the old was better. In doctrine and practice alike the two were so incompatible that their respective supporters had to part company. The new teachers led their followers out from the fellowship of those who refused to go along with their teaching; they probably accused those who adhered to the old ways of shutting their eyes to the light, if not of committing the sin against the Holy Spirit.

The Christians who remained in their former fellowship were hard hit and shaken by the secession of these others, and needed to be reassured. The others were so confident that they were right; they talked in such superior terms of their special initiation into the true knowledge that humbler believers might well wonder whether their foundation was so secure as they had thought. Where did the truth lie? Where was eternal life to be found? In their old fellowship, or with the seceders? The seceders probably said, 'We've got it; you haven't!' How could it be known which side was right? What were the criteria?

To Christians in this perplexity, then, the First Epistle of John was written. The writer was in the best possible position to state the criteria of truth and life, and to help his readers to see that they, and not the seceders, satisfied these criteria. 'I write this', he says, 'to you who believe in the name of the Son of God, that you may know that you have eternal life' (1 John 5. 13).

Here is a man who knows what he is talking about. He knows what the true gospel is, because he was there when it began. He had been a companion of the incarnate Word of Life – had seen Him, heard Him, touched Him. His readers had not had this experience, but he writes to share with them what he and his fellow-disciples experienced. Thus 'the Elder' (as he was called *par excellence* in his circle of friends) and his 'little children' would rejoice together in the certainty which he possessed already and which, imparted by him to them, would banish their bewilderment and doubt.

The doctrinal basis of the epistle is the common stock of apostolic Christianity, the *kērygma* ('preaching') and *didachē* ('teaching') of which appear here as 'the witness' and 'the commandment'. The 'witness' proclaims the love of God in the sacrifice of Christ; the 'commandment' applies the practical implication of the 'witness' to the lives of believers.[2]

Where is eternal life to be found? In the Son of God. 'God gave us eternal life, and this life is in His Son. He who has the Son has the life; he who has not the Son of God has not the life' (1 John 5. 11 f.). But the Son of God had become incarnate; those who denied His incarnation had not the Son, and therefore could not have that eternal life which was to be found only in Him. It was as simple as that.

John and his readers, who remained faithful to the original teaching and fellowship,[3] were in the sphere where eternal life might be enjoyed, because their fellowship was with the Father and with His Son Jesus Christ. Those who turned their backs on this fellowship turned their backs on eternal life. They might claim to possess it – indeed, they might claim to be in exclusive possession of it – but their claim was vain. They had abandoned the true foundation. So, John exhorts his readers, 'let what you heard from the beginning abide in you. If what you heard from the beginning abides in you, then you will abide in the Son and in the Father' (1 John 2. 24).

In these words, John makes a solemn affirmation of the permanent validity of the apostolic witness to Christ. For us, that witness is enshrined in the New Testament writings, our rule of faith and practice. We may transpose, re-state, re-translate as much as we will; only let us see to it that our transposition, re-statement and re-translation make the apostolic witness clearer than ever, rather than obscure it or dilute it or turn it into something else. 'For no other foundation can any one lay than that which is laid, which is Jesus Christ' (1 Cor. 3. 11). It is not for nothing that the heading of 1 John in the New English Bible is 'Recall to Fundamentals'.

2   Structure and Authorship

Attempts to trace a consecutive argument throughout 1 John have never succeeded. For the convenience of a commentator and his readers, it is possible to present such an analysis of the epistle as is given on pp. 31 f., but this does not imply that the author himself worked to an organized plan. At best we can distinguish three main courses of thought: the first (1. 5–2. 27), which has two main themes, ethical (walking in light) and Christological (confessing Jesus as the Christ); the second (2. 28–4. 6), which repeats the ethical and Christological themes with variations; the third (4. 7–5. 12), where the same two essential themes are presented as love and faith and shown to be inseparable and indispensable products of life in Christ.[4]

If attempts to trace a consecutive argument have not been successful, attempts to distinguish sources have been even less so. It is plain to the observant reader that we have here passages in homiletic style interspersed with epigrammatic theses, often grouped in antithetic pairs. We may think of the repeated 'If we say . . .' of 1. 6 ff., 'He who says . . .' of 2. 4 ff., or the four pairs of antitheses in 2. 28–3. 10.[5] Rudolf Bultmann has discerned twenty-six antithetical couplets (closely related in his mind to the 'revelation discourses' of the Fourth Gospel), which he regards as the core of the epistle, worked over in homiletic fashion by another author, to whom we owe the epistle in its present form.[6] Wolfgang Nauck similarly distinguishes the antithetical core from the revised and enlarged document, but ascribes both parts of the work to the same hand.[7] It is unlikely, however, that the antitheses ever existed as a separate document; the author may well have used them in his oral ministry to drive home his message, and incorporates them at appropriate points in this written homily. Source criticism is as barren an exercise in the study of this epistle as it is in the study of the Fourth Gospel.[8]

The main question of authorship raised by the study of 1 John is whether it is the work of the Fourth Evangelist. To some students of the two compositions no such question arises.[9] Thus T. W. Manson, lecturing on Johannine theology, pointed out that this cannot be deduced with certainty from the Fourth Gospel, because of the difficulty of distinguishing the teaching of Jesus from the interpretation of the Evangelist; if we are to 'examine the Johannine theology in its relatively pure state', then 'the proper method is to begin with the Epistle and there find what are the leading theological ideas of the author'.[10] Many years previously another English writer, John Chapman, went so far as to say that 'no sane critic will deny that the Gospel and the first Epistle are from the same pen'.[11] In expressing himself thus, he presumably meant to exclude from the category of 'sane' critics certain continental scholars who had denied identity of authorship, but his prediction (whether it was intended as such or not) was falsified twenty-six years later when C. H. Dodd – a 'sane critic' if ever there was one – presented an argument for diversity of authorship, based partly on vocabulary and style and partly on theological outlook. He found the Epistle to be less Hebraic and Jewish than the Gospel and freer in its adoption of Hellenistic thought-forms and expressions, and in its theology – its doctrine of the atonement and the Paraclete, and especially its eschatology – to be nearer to popular Christianity than is the Gospel. Accordingly he gave up what he acknowledged to be 'the unvarying tradition from early times'.[12]

No one disputes the remarkably close relation between the two compositions in language and outlook; they clearly come from the same circle or school if not from the same individual. It is not easy to speak dogmatically about the common authorship of two anonymous works which, while exhibiting this close relation, belong to different literary genres. This last fact may account in large measure for the differences in vocabulary and style; as for the theological differences, these have been exaggerated. There is futurist as well as realized eschatology in the Fourth Gospel (cf. John 5. 28 f.; 6. 39 f., 44; 12. 48) and realized as well as futurist eschatology in the Epistle (e.g. the recognition of false teachers as 'antichrists' already present in 1 John 2. 18). Moreover, the 'notable differences between the Gospel and the Epistle turn out to be differences not between the Epistle and the Gospel as a whole, but between the Epistle and certain sections of the Gospel'[13] – those sections, more specifically, which are characterized by Aramaisms. On the whole, it cannot be said that the arguments for diversity of authorship are sufficient to overthrow the evidence, both internal and external, for common authorship.[14]

A date towards the end of the first century is most probable.[15] This is indicated by the type of heretical teaching against which the readers are put on their guard, and is confirmed by the evidence that the Epistle was known early in the second century – possibly by Ignatius and certainly by Polycarp and Papias.[16]

3 *Analysis of 1 John*

1 Prologue (1. 1–4)

2 Walking in Light (1. 5–2. 2)
   (*a*) The character of God (1. 5)
   (*b*) Three antithetic tests of life (1. 6–2. 2)

3 The New Commandment (2. 3–17)
   (*a*) The test of obedience (2. 3–6)
   (*b*) The test of love (2. 7–11)
   (*c*) Encouragement to three age-groups (2. 12–14)
   (*d*) Warning against the world (2. 15–17)

4 The Teaching of Antichrist (2. 18–27)
   (*a*) Many antichrists (2. 18)
   (*b*) The test of perseverance (2. 19)
   (*c*) Distinguishing truth and error (2. 20–27)

5 Children of God (2. 28–3. 24)
   (*a*) The two families (2. 28–3. 10)

NOTES

1. Augustine (*Questions on the Gospels* ii. 39) gives 1 John the title 'To the Parthians'; this title was first (mistakenly) attached to 2 John, and then in the course of transmission transferred to the beginning of the group of three epistles. See p. 145, n. 13.

2. See especially C. H. Dodd, *The Johannine Epistles* (London, 1946), pp. xxvii ff.

3. A detailed examination of the beliefs held in common by John and the readers of his first epistle is made by O. A. Piper, 'I John and the Didache of the Primitive Church', *JBL* 66 (1947), pp. 437 ff.

4. Here I follow rather closely W. G. Kümmel, *Introduction to the New Testament* (London, 1966), pp. 306 f.

5. See p. 78.

6. 'Analyse des ersten Johannesbriefes', *Festgabe für A. Jülicher* (Tübingen, 1927), pp. 138 ff. Later Bultmann argued for the further activity of an ecclesiastical redactor, who added an appendix (5. 14–21) and a few other passages propounding the church's eschatology and doctrine of atonement through the blood of Christ ('Die kirchliche Redaktion des ersten Johannesbriefes', *In memoriam E. Lohmeyer*, Stuttgart, 1951, pp. 181 ff.). Most recently, in his commentary, he has confirmed his continued adherence to these views, but supplemented them with the suggestion that 1 John 1. 5–2. 27 was a preliminary draft, and that the same themes as are handled in it are treated again in the individual literary units making up 2. 28–5. 12, in a modified and amplified but unconnected fashion (*The Johannine Epistles*, Philadelphia, 1973, p. 2).

7. *Die Tradition und der Charakter des ersten Johannesbriefes* (Tübingen, 1957), pp. 1 ff.

8. In *The Puzzle of 1 John* (London, 1966), J. C. O'Neill argues that the author of the epistle was a member of a Jewish sectarian group who, in common with the majority of his fellow-members, came to acknowledge Jesus as the Messiah. The epistle comprises twelve poetic admonitions belonging to the traditional literature of the group which he enlarged to show that the ideals of the group had been realized in Jesus. Those people whose views are controverted in the epistle are the members of the group who had refused to join in recognizing Jesus as the Messiah. The prologue (1. 1–4) is omitted from Dr. O'Neill's purview for purposes of this analysis.

9. Cf. B. F. Westcott: 'The arguments which have been alleged to support the opinion that the Books [the Fourth Gospel and the First Epistle] were by different authors, do not seem to me to need serious examination. They could not be urged if the books were not detached from life and criticised without regard to their main characteristics' (*The Epistles of St. John*, London, 1902, p. xxx, n. 1).

10. *On Paul and John* (London, 1963), pp. 87 f.

11. *John the Presbyter and the Fourth Gospel* (Oxford, 1911), p. 72.

12. 'The First Epistle of John and the Fourth Gospel', *BJRL* 21 (1937), pp. 129 ff.; cf. also his *The Johannine Epistles* (London, 1946), pp. xlvii ff. In particular, his conclusions were influenced by the contrast he saw between the realized eschatology of the Gospel and the futurist eschatology of the Epistle.

13. T. W. Manson, *On Paul and John*, pp. 86 ff.; see also his *Studies in the Gospels and Epistles* (Manchester, 1962), pp. 116 f.

14. Detailed arguments for common authorship, marshalled with C. H. Dodd's arguments for diversity of authorship in mind, are most cogently presented by W. F. Howard in 'The Common Authorship of the Johannine Gospel and Epistles', *JTS* 48 (1947), pp. 12 ff., reprinted in *The Fourth Gospel in Recent Criticism and Interpretation*⁴ (London, 1955), pp. 282 ff.

15. The same approximate date is indicated for the Gospel, but which of the two was earlier or later cannot be determined.

16. See p. 18.

TEXT AND EXPOSITION

CHAPTER I

1 PROLOGUE (1. 1–4)

V. 1 That which was from the beginning, that which we have heard, that which we have seen with our eyes, that which we beheld, and our hands handled, concerning the ¹Word of life (v. 2 and the life was manifested, and we have seen, and bear witness, and declare unto you the life, the eternal *life*, which was with the Father, and was manifested unto us); v. 3 that which we have seen and heard declare we unto you also, that ye also may have fellowship with us:

¹ Or, *word*.

The structure of the sentence covering the first two and a half verses of chapter 1 (with the parenthesis in verse 2) is unusually complicated for the Johannine writings, and an English version will be more readily intelligible if it takes four sentences to say what the Greek text says in one:

> Our theme is that which was from the beginning, which we have heard, which we have seen with our eyes, which we beheld and our hands handled. Our theme, in short, concerns the word of Life – that Life which was made manifest. Yes, we have seen and we bear witness; we make known to you the Eternal Life which was with the Father and was made manifest to us. What we have seen and heard we make known to you also, in order that you in your turn may have fellowship with us.

The opening words of the epistle, 'that which was from the beginning (Gr. *ap' archēs*)', resemble the opening words of the Gospel of John, 'In the beginning (*en archē*) was the Word'. It is not necessary, however, to conclude that the two 'beginnings' are identical; more probably they are not. The 'beginning' of John 1. 1 is the beginning of time, the 'beginning' of Gen. 1. 1, in which God created the heaven and the earth. At that time, says the Evangelist, when the material universe came into being, the Word

34

already existed. The world had a beginning, but the Word had none.[1] The phrase 'from the beginning' in 1 John 1. 1 is best understood in the sense which it occasionally bears later in the epistle: for example, in 1 John 2. 7, where John reminds his readers of the 'old commandment which you had *from the beginning*', and in 1 John 2. 24, where he urges them to adhere to 'what you heard *from the beginning*'.[2] The 'beginning' in this sense is the beginning of the gospel – in 1 John 2. 7, 24, the beginning of the gospel so far as their acquaintance with it was concerned, while in 1 John 1. 1 it is the beginning of the gospel absolutely, the beginning as it was known to one who was present at the time and directly witnessed the saving events. The neuter gender of 'that which was from the beginning' points to the gospel rather than to the personal Christ, although indeed the gospel is so completely bound up with the personal Christ that what is primarily true of the one may be said of the other. It was the personal Christ who was heard, seen and touched by John and his fellow-disciples, and if it is maintained that, despite the neuter gender of the relative pronoun, He is the one who is said to have been 'from the beginning', an analogy to this use of the phrase could also be found in chapter 2, where mention is made of God or Christ as 'him who is from the beginning' (verses 13, 14).

John's authority to speak about 'that which was from the beginning' is the authority of first-hand knowledge. He could be described, in Luke's language, as one of 'those who from the beginning (Gr. *ap' archēs*, as here) were eyewitnesses and ministers of the word' (Luke 1. 2). This, he says (including his fellow-disciples along with himself), is the reality 'which we have heard, ... which we have seen with our eyes, ... which we beheld, and our hands handled'.[3] They were the men to whom Jesus said, 'blessed are your eyes, for they see, and your ears, for they hear. Truly, I say to you, many prophets and righteous men longed to see what you see, and did not see it, and to hear what you hear, and did not hear it' (Matt. 13. 16, 17; cf. Luke 10. 23, 24). The language John uses is the language of apostolic witness: 'we cannot but speak of what we have seen and heard' was the reply

of the apostles Peter and John to the Sanhedrin when they were
ordered to give up speaking or teaching in Jesus' name (Acts 4. 20).
If we ask *who* it was that they heard and saw, the answer is that
they heard and saw Jesus; if we ask *what* it was, the answer is that
they heard His words and saw His works.

But in addition to seeing with the eyes, John speaks of 'that
which we beheld'. Here the Greek verb (*theaomai*) is the one used
in John 1. 14, where the Evangelist tells how, when the Eternal
Word became flesh and tabernacled among men, he and his
companions '*beheld* his glory'. So in the present passage the
implication of this rather 'elevated' verb of seeing may be that
they penetrated beyond what was accessible to outward vision to
discern the inward glory. And as for the further statement that
'our hands handled' the reality of which he speaks, it can hardly be
overlooked that this verb (Gr. *psēlaphaō*) is used in reference to
the risen Christ, not indeed in the Gospel of John (although the
Thomas incident of John 20. 24–29 springs to mind in this
connexion), but in Luke 24. 39, where the disciples, frightened at
the sudden appearance of the Risen One, are bidden: 'handle me,
and see; for a spirit has not flesh and bones as you see that I have'.[4]

From the compiler of the Muratorian canon[5] onwards, many
commentators have treated the eyewitness claim of these verses as
a reference to the contents of the Fourth Gospel, as though this
epistle were a covering note sent out with the Gospel and certifying
the authenticity of its record. But there is nothing in the present
context to suggest this; it is better to understand the eyewitness
claim as the author's way of emphasizing the authority with which
he writes on 'that which was from the beginning'.

'Our theme, in short, concerns the word of life.' These two
terms, 'word' (Gr. *logos*) and 'life' (Gr. *zōē*), are keywords of the
Gospel of John. Of the Eternal Word the Evangelist says, 'In him
was life, and the life was the light of men' (John 1. 4). But whereas
in the Prologue to the Gospel it is the term 'Word' rather than
'life' that is used personally of the One who was in the beginning
with God, here it is the term 'Life' rather than 'word' that is so
used. The 'word of life' is the message of life (that is, the gospel);

but the life which forms the subject-matter of that message is 'the eternal life, which was with the Father and was manifested to us'. If the Gospel speaks of the incarnation of the Eternal Word, the Epistle speaks of the manifestation of the Eternal Life. 'The Word was God', says the Gospel; 'this is the true God and eternal life', says the Epistle (1 John 5. 20). When it is said that the Eternal Life was 'with the Father', the same preposition (Gr. *pros*) is used as in the repeated statement of John 1. 1, 2, that the Word was *'with* God'. There is no theologically profound significance in the preposition itself, except as it borrows some such significance from its context; the same preposition is similarly used in a quite non-theological context when the people of Nazareth, astonished at the power and wisdom of their fellow-townsman Jesus, say 'are not his sisters here *with* us?' (Mark 6. 3).

This epistle, then, is justly called 'the epistle of eternal life'.[6] It shows how and in whom that life was uniquely and perfectly manifested; it shows how the presence of that life in men and women may be recognized. John's own experience of that life entitles him to speak of it with assurance and communicate his assurance to others: this, he says, we have seen; to this we bear witness; this we make known to you.

It has been argued that this language is not necessarily to be understood as the language of an eyewitness. Christians of every generation have entered into the fellowship of the first Christian generation, and take the language of its witness on their own lips:

> What we have seen and heard
> With confidence we tell.

So here, it may be said, the 'we' is the corporate 'we', just as a twentieth-century Englishman (recalling the death of Joan of Arc in 1431) can speak of

> That old, undying sin we shared
> In Rouen market-place

or just as in Amos 2. 10, half a millennium after the Exodus, the corporate 'you' is used in God's words to the Israelites: 'I brought you up out of the land of Egypt, and led you forty years in the wilderness'.[7]

But the antithesis between 'we' and 'you' in 1 John 1. 3 makes this interpretation improbable. John tells his fellow-Christians to whom he writes of what he and his contemporaries had seen and heard, because his readers had *not* seen and heard it. We must sometimes distinguish between the *inclusive* 'we' (meaning 'you and I' or 'you and we') and the *exclusive* 'we' (meaning 'we and not you'); and in 1 John 1. 3 'we' is exclusive: *we* had this experience, *you* did not have it, but *we* are sharing it with *you* in order that *you* may share it with *us* – 'in order that you in your turn may have fellowship with us'. This language is most naturally understood if a surviving member of the first Christian generation is addressing members of a later Christian generation, who could not have that unmediated contact with the beginning of the gospel that he himself had. (We should compare the inclusion in the dominical petition of John 17. 20 of the next generation which will believe through the original disciples' witness.)

But the implications of their sharing what John had to impart to them were more far-reaching than they might have expected. They were called to follow the steps of their predecessors who, after the first Christian Pentecost, 'devoted themselves to the apostles' teaching and fellowship' (Acts 2. 42); and they were to learn that perseverance in the apostolic fellowship[8] involved fellowship with more than the apostles and their successors.

V. 3b yea, and our fellowship is with the Father, and with his Son Jesus Christ:

John desires his readers to have fellowship with himself and his associates by sharing their experience of the manifested life; but fellowship with John and his associates meant at the same time fellowship with the Father and with the Son. The word 'fellowship' (*koinōnia*) and its cognates are absent from the Gospel of John, but the idea which they express is not absent. It is present in Jesus' words to Peter, 'if I do not wash you, you have no part with me'

(John 13. 8);⁹ it is present in the parable of the Vine and the Branches (John 15. 1–16). It is present in Jesus' prayer for the disciples: 'as thou, Father, art in me, and I in thee, that they also may be in us, . . . I in them and thou in me, that they may become perfectly one' (John 17. 21, 23). It is present also in a form which comes quite close to what John says here in Jesus' answer to Judas (not Iscariot) in John 14. 23: 'If a man loves me, he will keep my words, and my Father will love him, and we will come to him and make our home with him'. True believers are those who dwell in Christ – that is to say, in the fellowship which embraces all the members of Christ. Since the apostles were the first to enter this fellowship, any one who adhered to the apostles' fellowship had, by that token, fellowship with Christ. And since Christ is the Son of God in whom the Father dwells (John 14. 10) and who in turn dwells in the Father's love (John 15. 10), so those who dwell in Him dwell in the Father (1 John 2. 24) – in other words, those who have fellowship with Him have fellowship with the Father through Him. There is nothing vague or merely sentimental about this fellowship; it involves obedience to the commandments of Christ and faithfulness to His teaching communicated through His apostles. Those who abandoned the apostolic teaching and fellowship severed themselves from fellowship with the Father and the Son.

Nothing is said here of the part played by the Spirit in this fellowship; but elsewhere in the epistle it is made plain that those to whom the Spirit of Christ has been given know by that fact that they dwell in Christ and He in them (1 John 3. 24; 4. 13). For Christian fellowship, in Paul's language, is the 'fellowship of the Spirit' (2 Cor. 13. 14; Phil. 2. 1); it is the fellowship into which believers are introduced and in which they are maintained by the indwelling Spirit of Christ.

V. 4 **and these things we write, that ¹our joy may be fulfilled.**
¹ Many ancient authorities read *your*.

There are two textual variants in this verse: the bulk of later manuscripts read 'to you' (*hymin*) in place of the emphatic 'we' (*hēmeis*) of the first clause (meaning 'we as distinct from you'), and 'your' (*hymōn*) in place of 'our' (*hēmōn*) in the second clause.[10] Neither of these variants is important. If 'to you' is not expressed in the first clause, it is in any case implied; and if 'our' is the possessive pronoun in the second clause, it is the inclusive 'our' (meaning 'our joy and yours together'), not the exclusive ('our joy, not yours'). John certainly sought his readers' joy, but their joy would be his, and that joy would be filled brimfull if they were firmly established in Christian faith and fellowship. The same theme of fulness of joy appears in the upper room discourses (John 15. 11; 16. 24).

2   WALKING IN LIGHT (1. 5–2. 2)

(a) *The Character of God* (1. 5)

If they are to have fellowship with the Father and with the Son, they must know the character of the God who has called them into fellowship with Himself.

V. 5   And this is the message which we have heard from him, and announce unto you, that God is light, and in him is no darkness at all.

Light in Gen. 1. 3 is the beginning of God's creation. In Ps. 104. 2 it is God's garment-like covering.[11] The light of God is frequently found as a metaphor for the life or salvation that He imparts: 'in thy light do we see light' (Ps. 36. 9) has as its parallel clause 'with thee is the fountain of life'. When, by a bolder use of metaphor, God Himself is described as light in the Old Testament, the intention is the same: 'The LORD is my light and my salvation' (Ps. 27. 1) stands in synonymous parallelism with 'The LORD is the stronghold of my life'. Similarly, when the Servant of the Lord is given 'as a light to the nations' in Isa. 49. 6, the purpose is, in God's words, 'that my salvation may reach to the end of the earth'.

So, in the prologue of John's Gospel the Eternal Word is 'the true light that enlightens every man' (John 1. 9); it is the life that resides in the Word that is 'the light of men' (John 1. 4). In the body of the Gospel Jesus accordingly says: 'I am the light of the world; he who follows me will not walk in darkness, but will have the light of life'[12] (John 8. 12). While life is the central thought in this use of 'light', however, there is in this Gospel the further thought of the spiritual illumination which comes when God reveals Himself in His Word, and this carries an ethical emphasis with it. If, despite the entry of the true light into the world, men love darkness rather than light, it is because their deeds are evil (John 3. 19-21); Jesus, in His final utterance to the Jewish public during Holy Week, urges them to believe in Him and so become 'sons of light', else the darkness will overtake them (John 12. 35 f., 46). This ethical sense of 'light' appears elsewhere in the New Testament, especially in Ephesians 5. 8-14, where the readers, who were once 'darkness' but are now 'light' in the Lord, are encouraged to live as 'children of light' and bring forth the 'fruit of light' rather than participate in the 'unfruitful works of darkness'. Outside the New Testament, the ethical use of the terms 'light' and 'darkness' is specially marked in the Qumran literature, where men are ruled either by the Prince of Light or by the Angel of Darkness, and practise truth and righteousness or falsehood and iniquity accordingly.[13] Such phraseology plays a prominent part in the series of affinities of concept and language which have been traced between the Qumran literature and the Johannine writings.

It is in the ethical sense that John here affirms that 'God is light, and in him is no darkness at all'. God, that is to say, is the source and essence of holiness and righteousness, goodness and truth; in Him there is nothing that is unholy or unrighteous, evil or false. He revealed Himself thus in the age of preparation before Christ came, and when the age of fulfilment dawned in Christ, this was the character of God as unveiled in the life that was the light of men. This being so, those whose 'fellowship is with the Father and with his Son Jesus Christ' will in their lives reflect the character of God; they will 'walk as children of light'.[14] Here, then, the first of a series of 'tests of life' is laid down.

(b) Three antithetic tests of life (1. 6–2. 2)

V. 6 If we say that we have fellowship with him, and walk in the darkness, we lie, and do not the truth:

Three tests are here laid down in the form of a false claim introduced by the clause 'if we say', each of these false claims being followed by the truth which is its antidote. The first of the three false claims is the claim to have fellowship with God at the same time as one's life is marked by unrighteousness. 'He who does what is true comes to the light, that it may be clearly seen that his deeds have been wrought in God' (John 3. 21); but 'every one who does evil hates the light, and does not come to the light, lest his deeds should be exposed' (John 3. 20). It may well be that the false teachers against whom John puts his readers on their guard were wide open to criticism in this respect, but it is equally necessary for those who adhere to the apostolic teaching and fellowship to be reminded that orthodoxy of doctrine is no substitute for righteousness of life. 'Truth in the inward being' (Ps. 51. 6) is what God desires in His people, and where that is present, it will manifest itself in all the ways of life.

This ethical use of the verb 'to walk' (*peripateō*) in the New Testament is particularly common in the Pauline letters but is also characteristic of these three Johannine letters, especially when we consider their brevity (cf., in addition to verses 6 and 7 here, 1 John 2. 6, 11; 2 John 4, 6; 3 John 3, 4). Similar language occurs in the Qumran texts; for example, the 'sons of righteousness' are said to 'walk in the ways of light' while the 'sons of wickedness' 'walk in the ways of darkness'.[15] In the Gospel of John there are a few passages which mark a transition from the literal sense of the verb to its denoting one's manner of life; Jesus says, for instance, 'If any one walks in the day, he does not stumble, because he sees the light of this world; but if any one walks in the night, he stumbles, because the light is not in him' (John 11. 9 f.); and again, 'Walk while you have the light, lest the darkness overtake you; he who walks in the darkness does not know where he goes. While you have the light, believe in the light, that you may become sons of light' (John 12. 35 f.).[16]

V. 7 but if we walk in the light, as he is in the light, we have fellowship one with another, and the blood of Jesus his Son cleanseth us from all sin.

Those who walk in the darkness do not know where they are going and cannot co-ordinate their courses; they stumble against one another and fall into confusion. On the other hand, those who walk in the light can see one another and avoid such clashes. Where spiritual light is concerned, much more than this can be said: those whose environment is that light in which God dwells are not only preserved from getting in one another's way, but actively and positively they enjoy fellowship one with another because each enjoys fellowship with God Himself.[17] This is the antithesis to the evil conduct and false claim which John has just exposed. The children of light are those whose behaviour reflects the character of God; they share with one another the fellowship which each enjoys 'with the Father and with his Son Jesus Christ'. By contrast, those who have opted out of this divine fellowship have abandoned the realm of light. Most serious of all the consequences of their apostasy is this: the blood of Jesus, which is constantly accessible for the cleansing[18] of those who remain within the fellowship, is not available for those who show a persistent preference for 'walking in darkness'.

The statement that 'the blood of Jesus . . . cleanseth us from all sin' (1. 7) is the subject of an 'Additional Note' in B. F. Westcott's commentary, entitled 'The idea of Christ's Blood in the New Testament', in which it is argued that the significance of blood in sacrifice is not restricted to the laying down of life but embraces 'the thought of the life preserved and active beyond death'.[19] Westcott expresses his indebtedness to an extended note in William Milligan's Croall Lectures for 1879–80, in which the classical passage on this subject, Lev. 17. 11, is taken to mean that the blood sprinkled on the altar is still 'a living thing, brought into the most intimate relation with the grace of God in its greatest potency'.[20] This interpretation of the shedding of the blood to mean the *release* of life rather than the sacrifice of life is open to criticism.[21] What John has in mind here is that cleansing of the conscience from guilt and moral defilement which is so insisted on in the Epistle to the Hebrews,[22] and which takes a leading place among the saving benefits of the redemptive self-sacrifice of Christ. These saving benefits are permanently available to those who are united to Christ, but not to those who sever themselves from Him. To be severed from the fellowship of Christ's people is to be severed from the fellowship of Christ Himself, so closely are He and His people joined.

V. 8   If we say that we have no sin, we deceive ourselves, and the truth is not in us.

But, say some of those against whom John's polemic is directed, what is it to us if the blood of Jesus is not available to cleanse us from sin? We have no sin! Here is the second false claim in the present series. If people claim – perhaps on the ground of their possession of the Spirit[23] – to have got beyond good and evil, to have reached a stage of spiritual development where moral principles are no longer relevant, they are self-deceived. The words 'the truth is not in us' are reminiscent of what is said of the devil in John 8. 44, 'there is no truth in him'. Those in whom the truth resides – and we may recall that in the Johannine writings the truth is embodied in Christ (John 14. 6) – will exhibit it in their lives; they will *practise* the truth (verse 6).

V. 9   If we confess our sins, he is faithful and righteous to forgive us our sins, and to cleanse us from all unrighteousness.

Here is the antidote to the second false claim: those who deny their sin will feel no need of recourse to the cleansing power of Christ; those who, conscious of their sins, confess them have in Christ a Saviour from whom forgiveness and cleansing from every sinful act may be freely received – not because He is indulgent and easy-going but because He is 'faithful and righteous'. He is *faithful* in that His promise is sure: those who put their trust in Him will not be let down; those who come to Him will not be cast out. The relevance in this connexion of His being *righteous* appears clearly in 2. 1, where His righteousness is associated with His advocacy. We need not press too fine a distinction between 'unrighteousness' and 'sin'; 'all unrighteousness is sin' (5. 17).

V. 10 **If we say that we have not sinned, we make him a liar, and his word is not in us.**

The third false claim is similar to the second but not identical with it. To assert that one has never sinned is to contradict the consistent witness of divine revelation and human experience. God makes provision for men as sinners; the acknowledgement of honest men confronted with the holiness of God takes the form, 'I have sinned'. 'He who does not believe God has made him a liar' (5. 10), whether the divine testimony to which he refuses credence concerns his own sin or the provision of life eternal in Christ. There is perhaps a slight difference between 'his word is not in us' at the end of verse 10 and 'the truth is not in us' at the end of verse 8; if John is moving to a climax, the situation described here is even more serious than that described in verse 8, but in the light of John 17. 17, 'thy word is truth', the distinction must be a fine one. In John 5. 38 Jesus says to His hearers in reference to the Father's witness, 'you do not have his word abiding in you, for you do not believe him whom he has sent'; again, in John 8. 37 He charges His opponents with seeking to kill Him 'because my word finds no place in you'. Such expressions in the Gospel indicate how the analogous language of the Epistle is to be understood.

NOTES

1. See A. Ehrhardt, *The Beginning* (Manchester, 1968), pp. 193 f.; he thinks it was pre-eminently Mic. 5. 2, LXX (*ap' archēs*), that was in John's mind.
2. Cf. Polycarp, *To the Philippians* 7. 2: 'let us turn back to the word which was delivered to us from the beginning (*ex archēs*)'.

3. It has been suggested that, in addition to stressing the eyewitness testimony on which the gospel was based, these words might be calculated to refute agnostic misuse of the saying quoted in 1 Cor. 2. 9 – perhaps in a form like that occurring in the *Gospel of Thomas* (Saying 17): 'I will give you what eye never saw, what ear never heard, what hand never touched . . .' (A. Ehrhardt, *The Framework of the New Testament Stories*, Manchester, 1964, pp. 28 ff.).

4. Cf. Ignatius: 'I know and believe that he was in the flesh even after the resurrection. And when he came to Peter and his companions he said to them: "Take, handle (*psēlaphaō*) me and see that I am not a bodiless phantom" ' (*To the Smyrnaeans* 3. 1 f.).

5. See pp. 18 f.

6. As in the title of G. Goodman, *The Epistle of Eternal Life* (Pickering and Inglis, 1936). On 'eternal life' see also note on 5. 11 (p. 122).

7. Cf. C. H. Dodd, *The Johannine Epistles* (London, 1946), pp. 9 ff.

8. See p. 21, n. 1, for the relevance of the term 'apostolic' in a commentary on documents from which it is absent.

9. Cf. NEB: 'you are not in fellowship with me'.

10. The principal witnesses for 'our' are Codices Sinaiticus and Vaticanus. This textual variation between the pronouns of the first and second persons plural is one of the commonest in NT because by the first century AD there was little, if any, difference in pronunciation between them.

11. If some places in OT speak of God as dwelling in 'thick darkness' (e.g. Ex. 20. 21; 1 Kings 8. 12; Psalm 97. 2), that is because His effulgent light is so unapproachable (cf. 1 Tim. 6. 16) that it must be hidden from men behind the cloud of the *shekinah*. Cf. E. R. Goodenough, *By Light, Light* (New Haven, 1935), p. 267.

12. For the phrase 'the light of life' cf. the Qumran *Rule of the Community* 3. 6 f.: 'Through the spirit of God's true counsel atonement is made for a man's ways, even for all his iniquities, so that he may see the light of life'.

13. *Rule of the Community* 3. 13 ff. Cf. note on 1 John 4. 1 (p. 104).

14. Cf. Eph. 5. 8. See also note on 1 John 2. 8 (p. 54).

15. *Rule of the Community* 3. 20 f.

16. Cf. John 8. 12 (quoted on pp. 40 f.); 12. 46; 1 John 2. 11.

17. The words 'one with another' may mean believers with fellow-believers or believers with God. It is unnecessary to insist on the one meaning as against the other, since the one implies the other.

18. In OT to be 'cleansed' from sin is synonymous with having one's sin 'atoned for'; cf. Lev. 16. 30, with reference to the Day of Atonement: 'on this day shall atonement be made for you, to cleanse you; from all your sins you shall be clean before the LORD' (LXX has the same verb for 'cleanse', *katharizō*, as John uses here). This is relevant to the NEB rendering of Gr. *hilasmos* in 1 John 2. 2 and 4. 10 as 'remedy for the defilement (of our sins)'. A. T. Hanson draws a parallel between Ps. 130 (LXX 129) and 1 John 1. 7–2. 5; he points in particular to verse 4 of the psalm, 'with thee is forgiveness (LXX *hilasmos*)', and verse 8, 'he will redeem Israel *from all its iniquities*'. His suggestion is that Psalm 130 'was considered in the early Church to refer to Christian baptism and that John had this psalm in mind as he wrote this passage in his First Epistle' (*Studies in the Pastoral Epistles*, London, 1968, pp. 91 ff.).

19. *The Epistles of St. John* (London, 1902), pp. 34 ff.

20. W. Milligan, *The Resurrection of our Lord* (London, 1894), p. 280. A similar

view of the significance of sacrificial blood-shedding in another context is presented in W. R. Smith, *The Religion of the Semites*[2] (London, 1894), pp. 269 ff., 317 ff., 338 ff.

21. Cf. A. M. Stibbs, *The Meaning of the Word 'Blood' in Scripture* (London, 1947); L. Morris, 'The Biblical Use of the Term "Blood"', *JTS* n.s. 3 (1952), pp. 216 ff.; *The Apostolic Preaching of the Cross* (London, 1955), pp. 108 ff.; F. J. Taylor, in *A Theological Word Book of the Bible*, ed. A. Richardson (London, 1950), pp. 33 f. (*s.v.* 'Blood'). 'The interest of the New Testament is not in the material blood of Christ, but in His shed blood as the life violently taken from Him. Like the cross, the "blood of Christ" is simply another and even more graphic phrase for the death of Christ in its soteriological significance' (J. Behm, in *TDNT* i, Grand Rapids, 1964, p. 174, *s.v.* αἷμα).

22. Cf. Heb. 9. 14; 10. 2, 22.

23. Cf. 1 John 4. 1 (pp. 103 f.).

CHAPTER II

V. 1 My little children, these things write I unto you, that ye may not sin. And if any man sin, we have an ¹Advocate with the Father, Jesus Christ the righteous: v. 2 and he is the propitiation for our sins; and not for ours only, but also for the whole world.

¹ Or, *Comforter* Or,*Helper* Gr. *Paraclete.*

John uses two different Greek words in this epistle when he addresses his readers as 'children'. That used here and six other places¹ is *teknia*, the plural of *teknion*. Jesus uses it in John 13. 33 when speaking to His disciples in the upper room; Paul uses it in a tender passage in Gal. 4. 19. The other is *paidia*, the plural of *paidion*; it is used only twice in this epistle (in verses 13 and 18 of this chapter),² although it is much commoner than *teknia* in the New Testament as a whole and indeed in general Greek usage. Since *teknia* retains something of its diminutive force (*teknion* being the diminutive form of *teknon*),³ it is properly translated 'little children'; *paidia*, on the other hand, while also a diminutive in form (*paidion* being the diminutive of *pais*), had lost its diminutive force by this time, so it might well be rendered 'children' (as in John 21. 5).

While insisting, against the false teachers, that it is wrong to say either that 'we have no sin' or that 'we have not sinned', John does not wish to give his readers the idea that sin may be regarded as a normal phenomenon in the Christian life. Far from it: the main purpose of his touching the subject at all is to put them on their guard against committing sin. Sin, indeed, is so thoroughly uncharacteristic of the Christian life that a life which is marked by sin cannot be called Christian; this is a point to which John returns in chapter 3. But instead of making false claims about sinlessness, a Christian should be grateful to know that, if he does

48

commit sin, his case is not hopeless. In the presence of God he has an Advocate, a powerful counsel for the defence. This Advocate does not need to resort to questionable devices to secure acquittal for his clients; he is a *righteous* Advocate. The designation 'The Righteous One' was used of the coming Messiah or Son of Man in pre-Christian times,[4] and in the New Testament it appears as a title of Jesus (cf. Acts 3. 14; 7. 52; 22. 14); but here the epithet (Gr. *dikaios*) has special reference to His advocacy on His people's behalf.

In the New Testament the word 'Advocate' (Gr. *paraklētos*) is found only five times, all in the Johannine writings; its four other occurrences are in the Gospel, on the lips of Jesus, in reference to the Holy Spirit as 'another Advocate' – or, as RSV has it, 'another Counsellor' (John 14. 16; cf. 14. 26; 15. 26; 16. 7).[5] The implication of the expression 'another Advocate' is that Jesus Himself is the primary Advocate. While the word itself does not appear outside the Johannine writings, the idea which it conveys is embedded in primitive Christian teaching. Paul speaks of the Spirit as one who 'intercedes for the saints' (Rom. 8. 26, 27) and describes Jesus as the one 'who is at the right hand of God, who indeed intercedes for us' (Rom. 8. 34). The promise of Luke 12. 8, 'every one who acknowledges me before men, the Son of Man also will acknowledge before the angels of God', found an early fulfilment in Stephen who, having witnessed a good confession before men, saw 'the Son of Man standing at the right hand of God' (Acts 7. 56) – in the posture of an advocate. In the Epistle to the Hebrews, too, advocacy forms part of our Lord's intercessory ministry as His people's high priest.[6]

This intercessory ministry is not a new activity on His part; we recall His promise to pray for Peter that his faith might not fail (Luke 22. 32) and in the upper room His high-priestly prayer, as it has been aptly called from the time of David Chytraeus in the sixteenth century, embraces in its intercession both His immediate disciples (John 17. 9–19) and their converts (John 17. 20 ff.). But now this ministry is reinforced by His perfect sacrifice.

There is no question of this Advocate's having to extort a favourable verdict from a reluctant Judge; His presence before the

Father is advocacy enough by itself, for He is there as the 'propitiation' for His people's sins. With the word *hilasmos* (used in the New Testament only here and in 1 John 4. 10) we may compare *hilastērion* (from the same root) in Rom. 3. 25. We need not stay to enquire whether 'expiation' (RSV) or 'remedy for defilement' (NEB)[7] would be a preferable rendering of *hilasmos*; 'propitiation' or 'atonement' will do well enough, if we use either word in its biblical sense – not as something which men must do to placate God,[8] but something which God has provided in His grace to bring men into His presence with the assurance that they are accepted by Him, since He has removed the barrier that kept them at a distance – guilt, with its attendant retribution, the 'punishment' which is banished by 'perfect love' (4. 18). 'Now in Christ Jesus', says another New Testament letter, 'you who once were far off have been brought near in the blood of Christ' (Eph. 2. 13); this is the truth that John states here in different language.[9] Nor will John let his readers think of their blessings in restrictive terms. The propitiation that has availed to wipe out their sins is sufficient to do the same for all. Jesus is 'the general Saviour of mankind' as well as the particular Saviour of each believer. According to the Fourth Gospel, He is 'the true light that enlightens every man' (John 1. 9) or, in the forerunner's language, He is 'the Lamb of God, who takes away the sin of the world' (John 1. 29).[10] Christians must not rest content with the assurance of their own salvation, but spread the joyful news world-wide. I know of no commentary on 1 John 2. 2 so apposite as Charles Wesley's hymn, 'Arise, my soul, arise':[11]

> He ever lives above
>   For me to intercede,
> His all-redeeming love,
>   His precious blood, to plead;
> His blood atoned for all our race,
> And sprinkles now the throne of grace.
>
> Five bleeding wounds He bears,
>   Received on Calvary;
> They pour effectual prayers,
>   They strongly speak for me;
> Forgive him, O forgive! they cry,
> Nor let that ransom'd sinner die!

3 THE NEW COMMANDMENT (2. 3–17)

(a) *The test of obedience* (2. 3–6)

V. 3 And hereby know we that we know him, if we keep his commandments.

The test of obedience is simple and can be applied to all kinds of religious profession. 'If you love me', says Jesus to His disciples in the upper room, 'you will keep my commandments' (John 14. 15). In our present passage the object 'him' probably denotes God, since the seceding teachers had so much to say about their knowledge of God, but since the knowledge of God is mediated through Christ, to know the Father is to know the Son. Those who boasted of their knowledge of God could give proof of their claim by their obedience to Him. The expression 'hereby we know' or something very similar occurs frequently in this epistle when a practical test of verbal profession is laid down (see 2. 5b; 3. 10, 16, 19, 24b; 4. 2, 13; 5. 2).

V. 4 He that saith, I know him, and keepeth not his commandments, is a liar, and the truth is not in him:

This sentence is the converse of the preceding one. The same damning indictment is pronounced against one who falsely claims to know God as is pronounced in 1. 8 against those who say they have no sin. Here we have the first of three statements introduced by 'he that saith', where the introductory words serve much the same purpose as 'if we say' in 1. 6, 8, 10; the two others come in verses 6 and 9 of this chapter. They all underline the importance of matching profession with practice.

V. 5a but whoso keepeth his word, in him verily hath the love of God been perfected.

'The love of God' here is 'our love for God' (in other words, 'of God' represents the objective genitive); as our *knowledge* of God is

to be tested by our obedience, so too is our *love* for Him – in fact,
obedience is the full flowering of our love for Him. 'This is the
love of God, that we keep his commandments' (1 John 5. 3). What
is involved in this perfection of love is spelt out in greater detail in
1 John 4. 12, 17 ff.; there too it is made plain that the love of believers
for God (and for one another) is the response to His love for them.

V. 5b Hereby know we that we are in him: v. 6 he that saith he abideth in him ought himself also to walk even as he walked.

A further test is introduced, as in verse 3, by the words 'hereby
know we'. It is easy for a man to claim that he is 'in God' – that
his life is bound up in the life of God, that he has fellowship with
God. (To distinguish between being in the Father and being in the
Son is to make a distinction without a difference; the one involves
the other.) But such a claim – introduced, as in verse 4, by 'he that
saith' – is to be verified by a searching practical test. As we have
been told already that no one who walks in darkness can have
fellowship with the God of light, so now it is emphasized that the
character of God will be displayed in those who abide in Him.
And the character of God is not something about which we are left
to speculate. God incarnate lived on earth; the character of God
has been manifested in the conduct of Christ. The emphatic
pronoun *ekeinos* occurs in a personal sense six times in this letter,
always with reference to Christ, and usually with reference to
Christ as His people's example; indeed, in four occurrences out of
the six (of which this is one) it appears in the phrase *kathōs ekeinos*,
'as *he*' (see also 3. 3, 7; 4. 17).[12] We know how Christ conducted
Himself; the glory which His disciples discerned in Him was 'full
of grace and truth', and something of these qualities will be evident
in anyone who truly 'abides'[13] in Him, which is another way of
denoting the experience of truly 'knowing' Him (verse 4). What is
meant by abiding in Him is illustrated at greater length in the
parable of the vine and the branches in John 15. 1–17; as it is the
life of the vine in the branches that enables them to produce the

fruit of the vine, so the life of Christ in His people will be manifested as their behaviour resembles His.

(b) The test of love (2. 7–11)

**V. 7 Beloved, no new commandment write I unto you,
but an old commandment which ye had from the beginning:
the old commandment is the word which ye heard.**

Love and obedience are inextricably interwoven because all the
commandments of God are summed up in the law of love. 'You
shall love the Lord your God' was the authoritative summary of
the Old Testament law (Deut. 6. 5), and when Jesus was asked
which was the greatest commandment of all, this was the one which
He quoted, coupling with it the similar commandment of Lev. 19.
18 enjoining love to one's neighbour (Mark 12. 28 ff.). These words
of Jesus were embedded from the earliest days in the apostles' witness: 'the whole law', says Paul, 'is fulfilled in one word, "You shall
love your neighbour as yourself" ' (Gal. 5. 14; cf. Rom. 13. 8–10).
So John, in underlining afresh the law of love, is not telling his
readers anything they did not already know; it is no innovation but
'an old commandment' which they had been taught 'from the beginning' – an expression which, as in the opening clause of the epistle,
denotes the beginning of the gospel. The apostolic witness which
they received at the commencement of their Christian experience included both the record of God's saving work in Christ and instruction (based on the teaching of Christ Himself) about the way of life
befitting the beneficiaries of this saving work. In this 'word' which
they 'heard' in those early days the commandment of love had a
foremost place; in this sense it was an 'old commandment'.

**V. 8 Again, a new commandment write I unto you, which
thing is true in him and in you; because the darkness is
passing away, and the true light already shineth.**

Yet, old as the commandment of love is in one sense, there is a
sense in which it is new. Jesus had summed it up in words from

the Old Testament law which were centuries old by His time, but when He laid it on His disciples afresh in the upper room, He called it 'a new commandment': 'A new commandment I give to you, that you love one another' (John 13. 34a). And it was new because by His own fulfilment of it He was giving it a depth of meaning which it had not possessed before: ' . . . even as I have loved you, that you also love one another. By this all men will know that you are my disciples, if you have love for one another' (John 13. 34b, 35). This aspect of the 'new commandment' will be insisted upon repeatedly in this epistle, and indeed it is implied here, where John tells his readers that the substance of this commandment has come 'true [perfectly] in him [i.e. in Christ] and [in measure] in you'. But here it is 'a new commandment' because it is the characteristic commandment of the new age. Christ, the Light of the world, came to dispel the darkness of sin and ignorance and to inaugurate the era of light and love. The language is not peculiar to the Johannine writings in the New Testament. In 1 Thess. 5. 5, for example, Paul says, 'you are all sons of the light and sons of the day; we are not of the night or of darkness'; in Col. 1. 12 f. God has qualified His people 'to share in the inheritance of the saints in light' and has delivered them 'from the dominion of darkness', while in Eph. 5. 8 believers in Christ are told: 'once you were darkness, but now you are light in the Lord'. But the terminology of light and darkness is specially characteristic of John,[14] and he uses it to describe the difference that Christ has made. Jewish eschatology distinguished 'this age' from 'that age', i.e. the resurrection age (cf. Luke 20. 34 f.), sometimes interposing 'the days of the Messiah' between the two. This general framework is adopted by the New Testament writers, but it is radically modified and re-interpreted in terms of the work of Christ. In His ministry the new age ('the kingdom of God') is in process of inauguration; when His ministry is crowned by His death and resurrection, it is fully inaugurated (the kingdom of God has 'come with power'). The 'days of the Messiah' have begun with His exaltation to the throne of God, from which He reigns until God has put all His enemies beneath His feet (1 Cor. 15. 25). For His people the new age has been anticipated; having died with Him they share His resurrection life and are already enthroned with Him in the heavenly realm, in the sense of Eph. 2. 6. Eternal life ('the life of the age to come') is theirs to possess and enjoy here and now. All this is made possible for them by the Spirit, who both makes effective in them what Christ did for them and enables them to realize the heritage of glory which will be theirs in fulness at the consummation. But as long as the new age is inaugurated but not yet consummated (as it will be by the *parousia* of Christ), the old age is still in being. Believers who belong spiritually to 'that age' live temporally in 'this age'. Although 'the true light' is already shining, the darkness has not passed completely away; it is in process of 'passing away'.[15] Thanks to the victory of Christ, the outcome of the conflict between light and darkness is a foregone conclusion, but the conflict is still going on. Hence the tension of Christian life in the present world, a tension reflected throughout this epistle, not to say throughout the whole New Testament. In the words of Lord Eustace Percy:

> Ever since Christianity was first preached the Christian citizen has been a puzzle both to himself and to his rulers. By the elementary necessities of his creed he has been a man living in two worlds. In one he has been a member of a national community, in the other of a community 'taken out of the nations'. In one he has been bound to obey and enforce the laws of his State, in the other to measure his conduct by standards not recognised by those laws and often inconsistent with them. This dualism has been made tolerable only by the prospect of a reconciliation. That prospect is, again, an elementary necessity of the Christian creed. Somehow, somewhere, the conflict of loyalties will end. The kingdom of this world will pass: the Kingdom of God will be established.[16]

V. 9 He that saith he is in the light, and hateth his brother, is in the darkness even until now. v. 10 He that loveth his brother abideth in the light, and there is none occasion of stumbling in him. v. 11 But he that hateth his brother is in the darkness, and walketh in the darkness, and knoweth not whither he goeth, because the darkness hath blinded his eyes.

Since the new commandment of love is the distinctive commandment of the new age, the test of obedience is pre-eminently a
test of love. The claim to be 'in the light' – once more introduced
by the phrase 'he that saith' – is a claim to have fellowship with
God. In 1. 6 John has insisted that such a claim is incompatible
with walking in darkness; here he insists that such a claim is
incompatible with loveless behaviour. No one is allowed to imagine
that he can get away with a claim to be a lover of God on the
ground that this is an inward attitude, invisible to other men. The
twin commandments of love to God and love to one's neighbour
are like two sides of a coin; the one is essential to the other. So
the claim to live 'in the light', to enjoy fellowship with the God of
light, must be tested by a man's treatment of his brother. The word
'treatment' should be emphasized because, as John makes clear
later, it is not a matter of sentimental feelings and language,
familiar in certain brands of pietism, but of loving 'in deed and in
truth' (3. 18).

That the rights of knowledge must be exercised in consistency
with the claims of love is emphasized in other parts of the New
Testament as well as in the Johannine writings, as Paul's teaching
about the obligations due to fellow-believers with weaker consciences illustrates (cf. Rom. 14. 15; 1 Cor. 8. 11). Paul, indeed,
insists that knowledge divorced from love is not true knowledge;
'but if one loves God, one is known by him' (1 Cor. 8. 3) and his
knowledge of God will manifest itself in his love towards others.
The two great affirmations about God in John's first epistle are
that 'God is light' (1. 5) and 'God is love' (4. 8, 16); the knowledge
of God will therefore produce holiness resembling His and acts
of love resembling His.

John characteristically sees life in terms of black and white;
intermediate greys have no existence for him. So there is no
middle course between love and hatred, and by hatred he does not
necessarily mean positive animosity but mere lack of love. Lack of
love (including that form of it which postpones an act of charity
to a more convenient season) can blind a man's spiritual vision as
effectively as the prejudice arising from hatred does, so that he is

tripped up by all kinds of moral obstacles that lie in life's way, and is disabled from forming ethical decisions which are crystal-clear to his brother whose love of heart and hand maintains him in fellow-ship with God, in whose light he sees light.[17] If it is possible, on the one hand, to over-simplify moral issues through one-sided pre-judice or inadequate appreciation of the relevant facts, it is pos-sible, on the other hand, to find them more complex than they really are through failure to assess them in the light of the love of God. This consideration applies not only to personal ethics but to issues of global scale.

John has more to say about divine love later in this epistle;[18] here he is content to anticipate his fuller exposition of the subject by insisting that religious profession must be tested by the presence or absence of love in action. Before he proceeds to a further stage of his argument, he rounds off his statement of the 'new command-ment' with two paragraphs of encouragement and warning.

(c) *Encouragement to three age-groups* (2. 12–14)

V. 12   **I write unto you, *my* little children, because your sins are forgiven you for his name's sake.**

V. 13a   **I write unto you, fathers, because ye know him which is from the beginning.**

V. 13b   **I write unto you, young men, because ye have over-come the evil one.**

V. 13c   **[1]I have written unto you, little children, because ye know the Father.**

V. 14a   **[1]I have written unto you, fathers, because ye know him which is from the beginning.**

V. 14b   **[1]I have written unto you, young men, because ye are strong, and the word of God abideth in you, and ye have overcome the evil one.**

[1] Or, *I wrote.*

No completely satisfying explanation has been given by com-mentators of the duplication of this threefold encouragement. The three sentences in verses 13c and 14a, b may represent a later and fuller re-writing of what is preserved as an earlier draft in verses 12 and 13a, b. The tense of the verb 'write' changes from the first to the second draft; in the former it is the present *graphō*, in the latter it is the aorist, *egrapsa*, but there is no material significance in the change, since the aorist 'I have written' is here probably the epistolary aorist, denoting the time-perspective of the readers rather than of the writer. Another minor distinction is that between '*my* little children' (*teknia*) in verse 12 and 'little children' (*paidia*) in verse 13c; as both nouns take their precise meanings from their correlation in the two contexts with 'fathers' and 'young men', they must be synonymous, indicating a more re-stricted group than the general 'my little children' (*teknia*) of verses 1 and 28 or 'little children' (*paidia*) of verse 18.

The threefold grouping relates to spiritual maturity, not years reckoned by the calendar. Even if, in the third Christian generation, there was a growing tendency for spiritual maturity and natural age to coincide (as we may find in many Christian churches today when we compare the elderhood with the Bible class), nevertheless it is spiritual experience that is emphasized. The younger believers have made a beginning by knowing their sins forgiven for Christ's sake. They have also started to appreciate their new status as children of God (cf. 3. 1) in that they have come to 'know the Father'. The senior believers, as is stated twice, have come to 'know him who is from the beginning'. This is the same God as the children have come to know, but whereas the children have come to recognize Him as their Father – demonstrating thereby, as Paul would say, that they have received the Spirit that makes them sons,[20] the Spirit of Christ Himself, since like Him they now call God 'Abba, Father!' (Rom. 8. 15 f.; Gal. 4. 6) – the fathers, through long experience of Him, have come to know Him in a fuller and deeper fashion. While it is to be hoped that all the children of God know Him as their Father and love spontaneously to address Him and speak of Him thus, there are some men and women whom we naturally describe as people who 'know God' because over the years they have sought, and been freely granted, such access to the heart of God that God knows them, as He knew Moses, 'face to face' (Deut. 34. 10).[21]

The *children*, then, have made a good beginning by knowing that through Christ their sins have been forgiven and that God is their Father, and with proper guidance and care they may advance from there; the fathers have attained a ripe and intimate acquaintance with the eternal God (whatever 'from the beginning'[22] may mean elsewhere in these epistles, it can denote nothing less than God's eternity here); but it is the *young men* who receive chief attention – as is indicated perhaps even by their being placed last in each of the two drafts. They are the believers who have reached a stage of spiritual development where they are expected to bear the burden and heat of the day; they are the church's first line of defence against attack, whether that attack takes the form of overt persecution or of subtle undermining of Christian faith and life. The young men whom John addresses have shown themselves worthy of his commendation; they 'have overcome the evil one', as he assures them twice, and thus they have proved that they 'are strong', endued with spiritual power, and that 'the word of God abides' in them. In all the main Johannine writings – Gospel,[23] First Epistle[24] and Revelation[25] alike – the theme of overcoming is present, and in all it is through Christ, the supreme Overcomer, that His people overcome. When in the wilderness He overcame 'the evil one',[26] it was by virtue of the word of God abiding in Him ('It is written', 'It is said', was His weapon); so His people, according to Paul, may not only 'quench all the flaming darts of the evil one' by means of 'the shield of faith', but may go over to the offensive against their spiritual foe with 'the sword of the Spirit, which is the word of God' (Eph. 6. 16 f.). (While *rhēma* is the noun rendered 'word' in Eph. 6. 17 and not *logos*, as in our present passage,[27] the point is that, for both Christ and Christians, 'the word He hath spoken shall surely prevail'.)

(d) Warning against the world (2. 15–17)
V. 15   **Love not the world, neither the things that are in the world. If any man love the world, the love of the Father is not**

in him. v. 16 For all that is in the world, the lust of the flesh, and the lust of the eyes, and the vainglory of life, is not of the Father, but is of the world. v. 17 And the world passeth away, and the lust thereof: but he that doeth the will of God abideth for ever.

The 'world' (Gr. *kosmos*) has a wide range of meaning in the Johannine writings, and the context must determine, from one place to another, which phase of its meaning is to be understood. On the one hand, the world was made by God through the agency of His 'Word' (John 1. 10); it was loved by God (John 3. 16); it is the object of God's saving purpose (John 3. 17). Christ is the Light of the world (John 1. 9; 8. 12; 9. 5), the Saviour of the world (John 4. 42; 1 John 4. 14), the propitiation for the whole world (1 John 2. 2), 'the Lamb of God, who takes away the sin of the world' (John 1. 29). On the other hand, the world at present lies in the grip of 'the evil one' (1 John 5. 19) and is therefore orientated against God;[28] accordingly, when He who is the Word and the Light came into the world, the world failed to recognize Him (John 1. 10; 1 John 3. 1) and similarly it does not recognize His followers (1 John 3. 1); indeed, it hates them (John 15. 18 f.; 17. 14; 1 John 3. 13), just as it hated Him (John 7. 7; 15. 18, 23, 24, 25). What John says about the world is similar to what Paul, in different language, says about the creation: it 'was subjected to futility, not of its own will but by the will of him who subjected it in hope; because the creation itself will be set free from its bondage to decay and obtain the glorious liberty of the children of God' (Rom. 8. 21).

What John warns his readers against in the present passage is the world orientated against God, 'the godless world', as the NEB paraphrases it. The spirit that dominates the world so orientated, 'the spirit that is now at work in the sons of disobedience', as it is put in Eph. 2. 2, is inimical to the love of God and to the uninhibited outflowing of His love in the lives of His people. Conformity to that spirit is wordliness. Worldliness, it must be emphasized in face of much superficial thought and language on the subject, does not lie in things we do or in places we frequent; it lies in the human heart, in the set of human affections and attitudes. It may manifest itself in petty but soul-stunting ambitions like 'keeping up with the Joneses'; it may manifest itself in unthinking acquiescence in current policies of monstrous malignity, as when too many Christians in Nazi Germany found it possible to go along with (or close their eyes to) their government's genocidal treatment of the Jews. Worldliness of the latter sort is not that which has usually been denounced by popular pietism; our Saviour's remark about the gnat and the camel may come to mind in this connection. If, in a world where the richer nations tend to become richer and the poorer to become poorer, the administration of a richer nation makes further increases in economic prosperity a major plank in its platform, the Christian – especially, perhaps, the Christian who prefers to remain as detached as possible from political responsibility – must be constantly vigilant lest his own life reflect the unadmitted assumptions underlying such a policy. To share political, social or economic presuppositions which are inconsistent with the Father's love is one form of worldliness.

Indeed, John's understanding of worldliness seems to be very much of this character, when we consider the three elements which he specifies as making up what is 'in the world'.[29] For the 'desire of the flesh' and the 'desire of the eyes'[30] and the 'pretentiousness of life', as it may be rendered,[31] comprise the outlook which is commonly designated materialism. Worldliness does not reside in 'things', but it does certainly reside in our concentration on 'things'. If our affections, instead of being set on what is of permanent importance, are set on passing things that the heart desires and the eye delights in, or things that encourage us to have a good conceit of ourselves, we are fearfully impoverished. If my reputation, my 'public image', matters more to me than the glory of God or the well-being of my fellows, the 'pretentiousness of life' has become the object of my idol-worship.

This 'pretentiousness of life' is equated in the lexicon of Bauer–Arndt–Gingrich with 'pride in one's possessions', and it can be a very subtle enemy of the soul. My house, my garden, my car, my

library or some other 'status symbol' – whatever it is I take most
pride in – can minister to this peril. One begins to understand why
R. C. Chapman, returning to live in the town where he used to
drive his carriage and pair, with coachman and footman, took a
working-class house in a back street: 'my pride never got over it',
he said.[32] But even such an action as that, on the part of a lesser
soul than Chapman, might simply be an inverted form of 'the
pretentiousness of life' – the exceptionally deadly 'pride that apes
humility'. The one effective antidote to worldliness is to have one's
heart so filled with the Father's love that it has no room for any
love that is incompatible with that.

Another form of worldliness, highly relevant to the situation in
which John wrote, is the adaptation of the gospel to some contemporary tendency or philosophy or spirit of the age. It used to be
said by acute foreign observers that Christians in this country had
difficulty in distinguishing the interests of the kingdom of God
from those of the British Empire; nowadays this tendency to
confuse the gospel with national or imperial ideals may be more
clearly manifested in equal and opposite degree in other parts
of the world. There are other Christians, more internationally
minded, who are prone to identify the rule of God in the world
with the advancement of the United Nations. Deplorable as these
forms of worldliness are, they are not so deplorable as the identification of the kingdom of God with this or that ecclesiastical
organization, whether it be the World Council of Churches or my
own particular 'Little Bethel'. Such an identification has too often
served as an excuse for all sorts of ethically dubious policies and
actions. Nothing that is unrighteous or uncharitable in itself is
ever truly done for the glory of God, however much we may
persuade ourselves that it is so.

Reference has already been made to that variety of worldliness
which consists in 're-stating' the gospel so thoroughly in terms of
the current climate of opinion that the 're-statement' bears no
relation to the original essence of the gospel.[33] John deals faithfully
with proponents of such a 're-statement' in his day; the same sort
of thing is perfectly familiar today. When we are told that 'thought-

ful men can no longer accept' one or another of the articles of the historic Christian faith, we need not be overmuch concerned; the way in which this affirmation is made begs the question at issue. Some 'thoughtful men' find no intellectual difficulty in believing what other 'thoughtful men' reject; so much depends on the axioms or premises on which one's thought is based. We may listen respectfully to a well-reasoned case for the acceptance or repudiation of some belief or other, but if the argument amounts to no more than that the belief is in conformity (or out of conformity) with the contemporary climate of opinion, it is wise to bear in mind the possibility that the contemporary climate of opinion may be wrong.

The prevalent secularism of western man has so influenced some Christian thinkers of our own day that they endeavour to 're-state' Christian doctrine or Christian ethics in terms which would be equally relevant whether one believed in the living God or not – sometimes, indeed, in terms which would make better sense if the living God were dismissed from our thinking. Whatever such a 're-statement' may properly be called, it cannot be called Christianity. As the Docetism which John attacked was one way in which worldliness was invading the church at the end of the first century, so the passing fashion of the 'death of God' theology (a contradiction in terms if ever there was one) is one way among many in which worldliness has invaded the church today. There may be something to be said for what has been called 'holy worldliness', if that means giving that place to the material order as God's creation which the Bible gives it, instead of dismissing all things temporal as evil; but a system of thought or way of life from which the Creator is deliberately excluded is a manifestation of *unholy* worldliness.

The world, as Paul said, is to be 'used' by the Christian as a means to the true end of his Christian living, not as an end in itself, 'for the form of this world is passing away' (1 Cor. 7. 31). So, says John, 'the world is passing away'³⁴ and so is all our desire for it – or, if desire (Gr. *epithymia*) can be taken here in a concrete sense, all the desirable things that it contains. Why should heirs of the eternal world concentrate their interests and ambitions on such a transient order? Why should they place all their eggs in such a perishable basket? Why does Christian practice so often fall short of Christian profession? If it is indeed in the ever-living God that we have placed our trust, if it is by His love that our lives are dominated, then His interests will be paramount with us. His kingdom, into which He has called His people, is the one unshakable order.

'Seek first his kingdom and his righteousness', said our Lord, 'and all these things [temporal necessities] shall be yours as well' (Matt. 6. 33). It was thought by some to be mildly blasphemous when, in recent years, an African ruler modified this wording in a public inscription to read: 'Seek ye first the political kingdom . . .' (and he soon discovered how mistaken he was). But without overtly modifying our Lord's words, many people who would regard themselves as better Christians than Dr. Nkrumah put their own private glosses on them (to be proved as mistaken in their turn as he was). Since all live *to* God (Luke 20. 38) it is well if all live *for* Him: 'he who does the will of God abides for ever'.

4 THE TEACHING OF ANTICHRIST (2. 18–27)

(a) *Many antichrists* (2. 18)

V. 18   Little children, it is the last hour: and as ye heard that antichrist cometh, even now have there arisen many antichrists; whereby we know that it is the last hour.

Here John addresses all his readers as his 'children' (*paidia*).[35]

The days between the first appearance of Christ and His coming advent in glory are the 'last days' in New Testament parlance – the days which witness the fulfilment of all that the Old Testament prophets foretold as destined to happen 'in the latter days'. The 'last hour' (*eschatē hōra*) might be regarded as an alternative expression for the 'last days', but more probably it denotes the terminal phase of the 'last days', like the 'last time' (*kairos eschatos*) of 1 Pet. 1. 5 at which the final salvation is to be revealed. According to Jude 18 the apostles of Christ foretold that scoffers would arise 'in the last time' (*ep' eschatou chronou*); Jude sees the fulfilment of their words in the emergence of the false teachers whom he denounces in his epistle. So John infers from the appearance of the false teachers against whom he warns his readers that the end-time Antichrist is now at hand and that his spirit is active in these teachers; that is how 'we know that it is the last hour'.

But in what sense was it 'the last hour'? John may have thought that in fact the last decade of the first century was five minutes to midnight on the clock of destiny: that he and his fellow-Christians were witnessing the onset of the great revolt which would immediately precede the *parousia*. Nothing that he knew precluded such an expectation; much that he knew encouraged it. But if 'the last hour' be understood thus in terms of common chronology, what validity could John's expectation and language have for his readers today, between eighteen and nineteen centuries later? If the last hour is to be dated between AD 90 and 100, what terminology can be applied to AD 1970? The truth is, as John Henry Newman put it last century, that:

> though time intervene between Christ's first and second coming, it is not *recognized* (as I may say) in the Gospel scheme, but is, as it were, an accident. For so it was, that up to Christ's coming in the flesh, the course of things ran straight towards that end, nearing it by every step; but now, under the Gospel, that course has (if I may so speak) altered its direction, as regards His second coming, and runs, not towards the end, but along it, and on the brink of it; and is at all times near that great event, which, did it run towards it, it would at once run into. Christ, then, is ever at our doors.[36]

In the Christian era it is always five minutes to midnight. But as 'the course of things' runs along the edge of the final consummation, that edge at times becomes a knife-edge, and at such times the sense of its being 'the last hour' is specially acute.

So it was with John. That Antichrist would come he and his readers knew, and in the false teachers he discerned the agents, or at least the forerunners, of Antichrist, sharing his nature so completely that they could be called 'many antichrists.' 'You have heard', he says, 'that Antichrist is coming'. But this is the first occasion in the New Testament – or indeed in the Greek Bible – where this term appears. John is the only biblical writer who uses it; he does so in this present context (verses 18, 22), in 1 John 4. 3 and in 2 John 7. It must not be inferred that his readers had heard something unknown to readers of the earlier New Testament letters or to those who listened to our Lord's teaching; the word 'Antichrist' may be peculiar to John's letters in biblical literature, but the idea expressed by the word is not.

If we ask where and when John's readers had heard of the coming of Antichrist, the answer probably is that they heard of it from their first instructors in the faith, but these instructors did not invent the doctrine; they delivered what they themselves had first received. One of the earlier New Testament letters includes a passage that is specially relevant in this regard: the passage is 2 Thess. 2. 1–12, where Paul warns his Thessalonian converts against unsettling forms of eschatological expectation which lack any foundation. The day of the Lord, he says, is not here yet –

> for that day will not come, unless the rebellion comes first, and the man of lawlessness is revealed, the son of perdition, who opposes and exalts himself against every so-called god or object of worship, so that he takes his seat in the temple of God, proclaiming himself to be God. Do you not remember that when I was still with you I told you this? And now[37] you know what is restraining him so that he may be revealed in his time. For the mystery of lawlessness is already at work; only he who now restrains it will do so until he is out of the way. And then the lawless one will be revealed, and the Lord Jesus will slay him with the breath of his mouth and destroy him by his appearing and his coming. The coming of the lawless one by the activity of Satan will be with all power and with pretended signs and wonders, and with all wicked deception for those who are to perish, because they refused to love the truth and so be saved.[38]

John's readers had no doubt received teaching to much the same effect as Paul gave to the Thessalonian Christians both while he was still with them and in the words just quoted from 2 Thessalonians. That is to say, a day would come when the restraint at present imposed on the forces of lawlessness and anarchy by the power of law and order would be removed, and lawlessness would break forth in all its malignity, incarnated in a sinister figure called 'the man of lawlessness' or 'the lawless one'. This 'lawless one' is appointed to final destruction by the brightness of the epiphany of the true Christ. But during the heyday of his reign he would claim divine honours, and so skilfully would he hoodwink men by impressive signs, performed by Satan's aid, that they would bow to his claims and follow him blindly to perdition. It is to this figure that John probably refers when he says, 'You have heard that Antichrist is coming'.

But even Paul was not the first to give such teaching, although he gave it to the Thessalonians, both by word of mouth and in writing, as early as AD 50. His description of 'the lawless one' setting himself up as God in the very temple of God recalls our Lord's words about 'the abomination of desolation standing where he ought not'[39] (Mark 13. 14, RV) – the reference being apparently to a person who embodies the principle of idolatrous outrage portrayed in similar terms in the book of Daniel.[40]

To the New Testament picture of Antichrist several historical figures and events have contributed: Antiochus Epiphanes banning the worship of Israel's God and turning the Jerusalem temple over to the cult of Olympian Zeus, of whom he himself claimed to be the manifestation on earth (167 BC);[41] the Emperor Gaius demanding that his image be set up in the temple at Jerusalem to show his Jewish subjects that they must offer sacrifice *to* him as well as *for* him (AD 40);[42] the Roman soldiers setting up their legionary standards in the temple court, opposite the east gate, and sacrificing to them in celebration of their victory (AD 70).[43] In the eyes of pious Jews these persons or incidents were blasphemous, inspired by a spirit hostile to God, variously called Belial (*Beliar* in Greek)[44] or Mastema[45] (we may compare the role of Satan in 2 Thess. 2. 9 or of the dragon in Rev. 13. 2, 4). But while they made their contribution to the New Testament picture of Antichrist, the New Testament picture is controlled by the fact that God has revealed Himself definitively and brought His salvation near in Jesus, His Son, the long-expected Christ; in the mind of the church, Antichrist is so called because he claims for himself the honour that

rightly belongs to Christ. The imperial beast of Rev. 13 is Antichrist (in fact, although it is not expressly so called in Revelation)
not simply because of its persecution of the church but because it
claims universal worship. When Christians were commanded to
acknowledge Caesar as Lord in the sense which was reserved for
Christ alone, they recognized Caesar as Antichrist and refused his
demand. In the same way their successors of more recent times
have recognized and resisted the spirit of Antichrist in modern
totalitarian systems which have endeavoured to enslave the souls
of men.

But the early Christians recognized Antichrist not only in the
enemy who attacked them from without but also in the enemy who
seduced them from within. In this sense *antichristos* is practically
synonymous with *pseudochristos*, the word used in Mark 13. 22
where our Lord warns His disciples that '*false Christs* and false
prophets will arise and show signs and wonders, to lead astray, if
possible, the elect'. It is people of this latter class – 'deceivers', as he
calls them in 2 John 7 (where the noun *planos* is related to the verb
apo–planaō rendered 'lead astray' in Mark 13. 22) – that John has
in mind when he warns his readers that 'many antichrists' have
already appeared. He is not the only New Testament writer to
think in this way of subverters of the apostolic teaching. Jude, for
example, describes other false teachers as 'loudmouthed boasters',
echoing the language used in Dan. 7. 8 of the 'little horn' with 'a
mouth speaking great things' and in Dan. 11. 36 of the 'wilful king'
who will 'speak astonishing things against the God of gods' (the
Theodotionic Greek version of Daniel[46] uses the same adjective,
hyperonka, in the latter passage as is used in Jude 16 and 2 Peter 2.
18, where RV renders 'great swelling words'). The little horn and
the wilful king of Daniel, two figures which were identical from the
start, are regularly interpreted of Antichrist in early Christian
literature.[47]

(b) The test of perseverance (2. 19)

**V. 19   They went out from us, but they were not of us; for
if they had been of us, they would have continued with us:**

but *they went out,* **that they might be made manifest ¹how that they all are not of us.**

¹ Or, *that not all are of us.*

To the tests already laid down – the test of obedience and the test of love – another, the test of perseverance or continuance, is now introduced. Steadfast persistence in the way of God, without turning aside from it, is inculcated and commended throughout the biblical record. As the parable of the sower teaches, to make a spectacular beginning is not the important thing; it is those who 'hear the word and accept it and bear fruit' (Mark 4. 20), not those who merely 'endure for a while' (Mark 4. 17), who show the genuineness of their profession. The perseverance of the saints is a biblical doctrine,[48] but it is not a doctrine designed to lull the indifferent into a sense of false security; it means that perseverance is an essential token of sanctity. Not that perseverance is the product of the saints' native resolution and energy; it is He who 'began a good work' in them who 'will bring it to completion at the day of Jesus Christ' (Phil. 1. 6). But the maintenance and completion of the good work provide the evidence that the good work was ever begun. When Paul, not without reason, says to the Corinthian church, 'Do you not realize that Jesus Christ is in you? – unless indeed you fail to meet the test!' (2 Cor. 13. 5), he implies that all those in whom the risen Christ is present by His Spirit will indeed meet the test, while those who fail to meet the test, who show themselves 'reprobate' (*adokimoi*), prove by that fact that the root of the matter was never in them, whatever appearance of genuineness they may once have presented. Continuance is the test of reality.

So in the present situation the fact that the dissenters had left the apostolic fellowship simply showed that at heart they had never belonged to it. Had they been securely built on the foundation of eternal life, they would not have been so easily shifted from it. John's words are not applicable (although they have sometimes been misapplied) to people who leave one Christian company for another; they are applicable only to people who deliberately abandon the ground of Christianity rightly so called – and one should be quite certain that this is what they have done before speaking or thinking of them in these terms. John, however, is concerned that his readers should not be shaken in their faith by the secession of their former associates. The situation was not one in which a group of true believers held a position at variance with that held by another group of true believers; the seceding group by their action had shown that they were not true believers at all.

The last clause of verse 19, introduced by the distinctive Johannine expression *all' hina* ('but ... that'),[49] is ambiguous. The two senses which it can bear are indicated in the text and footnote respectively of the NEB. 'They went out', says the NEB text, 'so that it might be clear that not all in our company truly belong to it'. But the variant rendering in the footnote runs: 'so that it might be clear that none of them truly belong to us'. The footnote rendering does little more than repeat what has just been said in the first part of the verse; the rendering in the text, which is probably to be preferred, discloses the general truth involved in a special situation. Membership in a Christian society does not always imply that one belongs to the persevering saints; enrolment in the register of a local church on earth does not necessarily carry with it enrolment in the heavenly book of life.

(c) Distinguishing truth and error (2.20–27)

V. 20 And ye have an anointing from the Holy One, [1]and ye know all things. v. 21 I have not written unto you because ye know not the truth, but because ye know it, and [2]because no lie is of the truth.

> [1] Some very ancient authorities read *and ye all know*.
> [2] Or, *that*.

The seceders claimed to have been initiated into an advanced grade of knowledge, and may have spoken disparagingly of those who remained content with 'elementary' teaching like those whom they left behind. C. S. Lewis has warned us of the seductiveness of 'the inner ring',[50] the temptation to gain admission at all costs to that exclusive élite of the people who really matter, who know what's what. The fascination of such an inner circle can be as powerful and dangerous in religion as in society. We are flattered by the idea that we are different from the rank and file, that we have access to deeper teaching, to more esoteric truth, even, it may be (and this is supremely soul-destroying), to a higher level of holiness than the majority. Our Lord crushed such pretensions when He thanked God for hiding from the wise and understanding things which were revealed to babes (Matt. 11. 25). Paul did the same when he told the Corinthian Christians who prided themselves on their intellectual attainments that he could impart the 'secret and hidden wisdom of God' only to those who were spiritually mature – that is, mature in *agapē* rather than in *gnōsis* – and to all of those (1 Cor. 2. 6–3. 3); or when he emphasized to the Colossians (who were being invited in their day to savour the attractions of a superior brand of wisdom) that his commission consisted in 'warning *every man* and teaching *every man* in all wisdom, that we may present *every man* mature in Christ' (Col. 1. 28). So John assures his readers at a later date that the 'anointing' they have received 'from the Holy One' admits them to the true knowledge. Paul had used the same term in relation to the gift of the Spirit: 'it is God', he writes to the Corinthians (coupling them with himself and his colleagues), 'who . . . has anointed us;[51] he has put his seal upon us and given us his Spirit in our hearts as a guarantee' (2. Cor. 1. 21, 22). Of these three terms by which the bestowal of the Spirit is described – *chrisma*, *sphragis* and *arrabōn* – John employs the first as most appropriate to his purpose[52] of assuring his readers that they suffer no disadvantage as compared with the 'inner ring': 'You, no less than they, are among the initiated; this is the gift of the Holy One, and by it you all have knowledge' (NEB).

NEB 'you all', like RV margin and RSV, follows the reading *pantes* (nominative plural masculine), whereas RV text, 'ye know all things', follows the reading *panta* (accusative plural neuter). The latter is the majority reading, but the former has the weighty support of the early witnesses to the Alexandrian text-type.[53] In favour of *pantes* is the fact that it is the more difficult reading (an

object is normally expected after the verb 'know') and therefore
more likely to be changed to *panta* than *vice versa*. Against this, it
has been suggested that the reading *pantes* may have been influenced by the occurrence of the same word in verse 19 ('*they all*
are not of us'). The reading *panta* ('all things') could be understood
in the same sense as verse 27, 'his anointing teaches you about
everything'.[54]

If we adopt the reading 'you all know' here, the point is that the
true knowledge is not confined to a favoured élite but is accessible to them all. What they all know is made clear by the words
that follow: they know the difference between truth and falsehood.
They know the difference between these not because they have
explored the mazes of falsehood but because they 'know the truth'.[55]
For believers this 'truth' is embodied in a person, in Him who
said 'I am . . . the truth' (John 14. 6). They know it because they
know Him, and this knowledge is theirs because they have received
'the Spirit of truth' (John 14. 17; 15. 26; 16. 13). When He comes,
said Jesus of the Spirit, 'he will guide you into all the truth' (John
16. 13), and to the same effect He prayed for His disciples: 'Sanctify
them in the truth; thy word is truth' (John 17. 17). Those who have
come to know the truth 'as the truth is in Jesus' (Eph. 4. 21) have, it
is implied, a built-in spiritual instinct which enables them to detect
and refuse whatever is basically incompatible with that truth, no
matter how speciously and eloquently it may be set before them.
They know that 'no lie is of the truth' – or, to quote the NEB
rendering again: 'lies, one and all, are alien to the truth'.

So contrary to the truth of the gospel, so subversive of the saving
message, is this 'lie' that it must be stamped as the teaching of
Antichrist. Some two decades later John's disciple Polycarp, bishop
of Smyrna, echoes his teacher's language: 'Every one who does not
confess that Jesus Christ has come in the flesh is Antichrist. And
whosoever does not confess the testimony of the cross is of the
devil; and whosoever perverts the oracles of the Lord to his own
lusts and says that there is neither resurrection nor judgment – he
is Satan's firstborn'[56] By 'the testimony of the cross' Polycarp
appears to mean the witness which our Lord's passion and death

bore to Him as the incarnate Son of God (cf. John 19. 35; 1 John 5. 8).

V. 22   Who is the liar but that he denieth that Jesus is the Christ? This is the antichrist, *even* he that denieth the Father and the Son. v. 23 Whosoever denieth the Son, the same hath not the Father: he that confesseth the Son hath the Father also.

'Lies, one and all, are alien to the truth'; but John, like Paul in 2 Thess. 2. 11,[57] is thinking of one fundamental Lie. Plato made a distinction between those lies which are errors of fact and the mortal disease of 'the lie in the soul';[58] to John the Lie *par excellence* is that which refuses to see the Godhead shine in the human life and death of Jesus, that which drives a wedge between 'the Christ' and the man Jesus of whom, according to Cerinthus, 'the Christ' took temporary possession.[59] To deny that Jesus is the Christ is to deny that He 'is the Son of God' (5. 5) or that He 'has come in the flesh' (4. 2). This denial is deadly, because only in the Christ, the Son of God, who came in the flesh is eternal life to be had (5. 11).

The false teachers who perverted the received teaching about Jesus as the Christ and Son of God probably did not expressly deny *the Father*. Indeed, 'the Father' was the designation that many of them reserved for the God who is above all, in contradistinction to the inferior deity whom they envisaged as creator of the world.[60] According to Cerinthus, it was after 'the Christ' descended on the man Jesus at His baptism in the form of a dove that 'He proclaimed the unknown Father'.[61] But words have value only in accordance with their meaning; the Cerinthians and those like-minded might speak of the 'Father' but they did not give the same meaning to the term as John does when he speaks of 'the Father'. To John, the Father is He who has revealed Himself uniquely and fully in the incarnate Jesus, not only in the ministry of word and work for which He was anointed by the Spirit at His baptism, but equally so – indeed, supremely so – in His death on the cross.

Those who denied the incarnation of the Son of God and saw no
revelatory element in His passion refused that revelation of the
Father which is imparted in the gospel. In denying the Son, they
denied the Father too, little as they may have intended to do so.
This is a corollary to the repeated assertion in the Gospel of John,
that the knowledge of the Father is inseparable from the knowledge
of the Son (John 8. 19; 14. 7), and to a passage like John 5. 23,
where the divine purpose in the committal of judgment to the Son
is said to be 'that all may honour the Son, even as they honour the
Father. He who does not honour the Son does not honour the
Father who sent him'. 'The only Son,[62] who is in the bosom of
the Father, he has made him known' (John 1. 18); to deny the Son
is to deny the knowledge of the Father which He unfolds, and so to
deny the Father Himself. This is not to exclude those prior and
preparatory forms of divine revelation implied in the prologue to
the Gospel of John;[63] it is to affirm that those earlier forms of
divine revelation were brought to perfection when the Eternal
Word became incarnate in the Son, so that it is no longer possible
to confess the Father except as He has made Himself known in the
Son, while it is impossible to believe in the Son without acknowledging the Father whom He has made known.[64] Whether Jesus
expressed Himself in the imperative or in the indicative mood when
He said, 'Believe in God, believe also in me'[65] (John 14. 1), He
spoke essentially of one form of belief, not two.

**V. 24 As for you, let that abide in you which ye heard
from the beginning. If that which ye heard from the beginning abide in you, ye also shall abide in the Son, and in
the Father.**

'What you heard from the beginning' is the apostolic message as
it was first delivered to them, as we have seen already in verse 7.
Like the Gospel of John (cf. John 5. 38; 15. 7), so the Epistles can
speak interchangeably of the word of God or of Christ 'abiding' in
men (1 John 2. 14; 2 John 2) and of their 'abiding' in it (2 John 9).
Either way, it is faithful adherence to the message that is intended,

and this carries with it faithful adherence to the Father and the Son to whom in that message the Spirit bears witness. This personal relation with the Godhead is similarly mutual: those who 'abide' in God have God 'abiding' in them (cf. 1 John 4. 12–16). But those who have abandoned the foundation of their faith in the original apostolic testimony have severed themselves from fellowship with the true God, for that is the true testimony to God (cf. 1 John 5. 9–11).

V. 25 **And this is the promise which he promised ¹us,** *even* **the life eternal.**

> ¹ Some ancient authorities read *you*.

Eternal life is the promise held out to believers by God in the message which makes Him known; it is embodied, as has been made plain in 1 John 1. 2, in the Son of God who is the centre and circumference of that message. The original force of the phrase, especially in the Hebrew or Aramaic expressions which underlie the Greek *zōē aiōnios*, relates to 'the life of the age to come', i.e. resurrection life. But for those who are united by faith to Him who by His triumph over death is 'the resurrection and the life' (John 11. 25), the promise of resurrection life is already realized; they enjoy it here and now. John's readers will do well if they hold fast to the message and remain in the fellowship, without which eternal life is unattainable. If eternal life consists in the knowledge of the only true God and Jesus Christ whom He has sent (John 17. 3), then it cannot be dissociated from the message which conveys that knowledge.

V. 26 **These things have I written unto you concerning them that would lead you astray. v. 27 And as for you, the anointing which ye received of him abideth in you, and ye need not that any one teach you; but as his anointing teacheth you concerning all things, ¹and is true, and is no lie, and even as it taught you, ²ye abide in him.**

> ¹ Or, *so it is true, and is no lie; and even as &c.*
> ² Or, *abide ye.*

'I have written' is the aorist tense (Gr. *egrapsa*), as in verses
13c–14 and 21. Once again we may recognize the 'epistolary aorist',
or perhaps the reference here is to what has just been written about
the 'many antichrists'. The most effective safeguard which the
readers have against these people and their teaching is that
'anointing from the Holy One' already mentioned in verse 20 which
enables them to recognize the truth and refuse falsehood. The fact
that they have not followed the teachers of error in their secession
is a token that this 'anointing' remains in them. The statement
that because of it they do not need any one to teach them is to be
understood in its context. It is not to be taken as absolute affirmation that the experience of the Spirit in personal life carries
with it independence of the ministry of teaching in the church.
The ministry of teaching is the Spirit's gift by which He provides
instruction for believers. What is John himself doing in this letter
if he is not 'teaching' his readers? But the ministry of teaching
must be exercised by men who themselves share the 'anointing' of
which John speaks, men who remain in the fellowship of the Spirit.
No one from outside that fellowship – and the false teachers had
placed themselves outside it – can provide teaching which will
either correct or supplement the truth of the Christian revelation.
The believers to whom John writes have not become so impoverished within their fellowship that they need any one from
outside it to teach them. It is within the fellowship that the Spirit
operates; it is there that He teaches the people of God. So Paul
prays that those who are inwardly strengthened by the Spirit of
Christ 'may have power to comprehend *with all the saints* what is
the breadth and length and height and depth' (Eph. 3. 18). In the
period before the canon of the New Testament began to circulate
as a documentary collection, oral ministry was even more necessary
than afterwards as the means by which the Spirit guided believers
'into all the truth'. They had their sacred scriptures in the books of
the Old Testament, but these books had to be understood in the
light of their fulfilment by Jesus, and a great part of early Christian
teaching consisted in the imparting of this understanding. The
Spirit by whom the prophets spoke was the Spirit by whose

illumination the words of the prophets were understood (1 Pet. 1. 10–12).

In assuring his readers that the Spirit's 'anointing' teaches them about 'all things', John echoes the promise to the disciples in John 14. 26: 'the Counsellor, the Holy Spirit, . . . will teach you all things'. The apostolic teaching which the readers have already received represents the fulfilment of this promise. Here is the truth; whatever contradicts it is falsehood. Those who have been taught it will do well to adhere to it, to 'abide' in the Spirit's anointing as that anointing 'abides' in them.

It is not completely clear whether we are to understand the anointing or the Spirit in the last two clauses of verse 27. RV text, following AV and followed by RSV, makes the anointing ('it') subject of 'taught' but takes *en autō* at the end of the verse to refer to the Spirit ('in him'), not to the anointing ('in it', which is also a permissible rendering). Since 'the anointing' is the subject of the earlier part of the sentence, we might well retain it throughout: 'as it has taught you, abide in it'. NEB, on the other hand, sees the Spirit in both of the two last clauses: 'As he taught you, then, dwell in him'. Certainty is not attainable; practically it makes no difference, since the anointing is the Spirit's anointing.

5   CHILDREN OF GOD (2. 28–3. 24)

When John in this epistle addresses his readers as his 'children', he uses the diminutive form *teknia* (except, as we have seen, for two places in Chapter 2 – verses 13 and 18 – where he calls them *paidia*), but when he calls them 'children of God' he uses the plural *tekna* (the form of which *teknia* is the diminutive). The phrase *tekna tou theou* occurs similarly for 'children of God' in the Gospel (John 1. 12; 11. 52). When speaking of believers' relationship to God, John never uses the noun *hyios* ('son'); he reserves it for Christ, as the unique (*monogenēs*) Son of God.[66] The words used to denote relationship to God carry with them also the connotation of likeness to God; the two ideas are inseparable, for likeness is the proof of relationship.

(a) The two families (2. 28–3. 10)

Some students of this epistle have discerned behind these verses
an earlier document consisting of a series of antitheses,[67] e.g.:

(i) Every one who does right is born of him/
   Every one who commits sin is guilty of lawlessness (2. 29/3.4)
(ii) No one who abides in him sins/
   No one who sins has either seen him or known him (3. 6a/b)
(iii) He who does right is righteous/
   He who commits sin is of the devil (3. 7/3. 8)
(iv) No one born of God commits sin/
   Whoever does not do right is not of God (3. 9/3. 10)

This identification of an earlier document, no longer extant, behind an existing document is a precarious exercise. But it is a
perfectly reasonable, and even probable, supposition that the
Elder, in his teaching, whether oral or written, was accustomed to
sum up the contrast between the true way and all others in pairs
of antitheses like these. As previously, so here he insists on the
ethical criteria of the true way; no amount of profession will
compensate for their absence.

**V. 28 And now, *my* little children, abide in him; that, if
he shall be manifested, we may have boldness, and not be
ashamed ¹before him at his ²coming.**

¹ Gr. *from him.*   ² Gr. *presence.*

The emphatic 'And now' (Gr. *kai nyn*) introduces a new
thought. Even if 'abide in it' were the right rendering at the end
of verse 27, the same clause at the beginning of verse 28 is certainly to be understood personally, 'abide in him'. There is no
material difference; those who 'abide' in the 'anointing' and in the
teaching which accompanies it are bound to 'abide' in Christ (cf.
John 15. 4). Those who 'abide in him' can look forward to His
coming with joy; they 'have confidence for the day of judgment'
(4. 17, RSV). This is the only place in the Johannine writings where
the word *parousia* ('advent') is used; but the idea that it expresses
is frequently conveyed by other terms, as in this very context by
the clause 'if he shall be manifested'. Neither here nor in the

repetition of the clause in 3.2 does 'if' suggest any uncertainty; it is the equivalent of 'when'. 'The life which was manifested' (1. 2) will be manifested again. The first person plural in 'we may have boldness' . . . is probably the inclusive 'we', meaning 'we and you together'. Attempts have been made to interpret the passage as though it meant '*You* must abide in Him, in order that *we* (your teachers) may have confidence and not be ashamed . . .' (a similar sentiment to Paul's in Phil. 2.16; 1 Thess. 2.19 f., etc.); but in that case we should have expected the contrast between the pronouns to be expressed more emphatically, as it is in 1.3. Here as elsewhere John takes away the ground from any antinomian perversion of the gospel; what else could an unfaithful servant do than 'shrink in shame'[68] (cf. RSV) from his Master's searching eye? 'Boldness' ('freedom of speech')[69] in the Lord's presence is the antithesis to such shame.

V. 29   If ye know that he is righteous, [1]ye know that every one also that doeth righteousness is begotten of him.

[1] Or, *know ye.*

That God is righteous is a biblical axiom: 'the LORD is righteous, he loves righteous deeds' (Ps. 11. 7). In Old Testament times He required righteousness in His people because they were called by His name: 'righteousness, righteousness you shall follow' (to give the literal rendering of Deut. 16. 20). In the teaching of our Lord, not least in the Sermon on the Mount, it is emphasized that the children[70] of the heavenly Father will reproduce His character (Matt. 5. 45, 48; Luke 6. 35 f.). So John makes it clear that membership in the family of God is to be recognized by the family likeness; since the Father of the family is righteous, the children will practise righteousness. If anyone claims to belong to His family and does not practise righteousness, his claim cannot be admitted; anyone who practises righteousness is known by that very fact to be a child of God, even if he makes no such claim in words. Actions speak louder than words.[71]

NOTES

1. In 1 John 2. 12, 28; 3. 7, 18; 4. 4; 5. 21. Where *teknia* is not accompanied by the possessive pronoun 'my' (Gr. *mou*), as it is in 2. 1, RV in this epistle distinguishes it by adding this pronoun in italics: '*my* little children'.
2. It appears as a variant reading to *teknia* in 1 John 3. 7.
3. In these epistles *teknon* occurs in 1 John 3. 1, 2, 10 (twice); 5. 2; 2 John 1, 4, 13; 3 John 4 (always in the plural).
4. E.g. in the *Similitudes of Enoch* (1 Enoch 38. 2, etc.).
5. The form *parakletos* is a verbal adjective from *parakaleo*. The AV and RV rendering 'Comforter' in the Gospel passages gives it an active force, relating it to the sense 'comfort' or 'encourage' which the verb frequently has (cf. Matt. 2. 18; 5. 4; Luke 16. 25; 2 Cor. 1. 4, 6). But its force is more probably passive (as is usual with such verbal adjectives), related to the sense 'call to one's side (as a helper)'; cf. Latin *ad-uocatus*, whence our 'advocate'. In this sense *parakletos* was taken over as a loanword into Mishnaic Hebrew, in the form *peraqlit*, 'advocate', 'intercessor'.
6. E.g. in Heb. 7. 25.
7. For the relevance of the NEB rendering see p. 46, n. 18.
8. This was the force of these words (associated with the verb *hilaskomai*, 'propitiate') in pagan Greek. But the NT force of this word-group is based on its use in the Septuagint to render the Hebrew word-group associated with the verb *kipper* ('atone'), in which God, far from being the object, takes the initiative. Cf. Rom. 3. 25, where it is God who has set Jesus forth as a propitiation by means of His blood – i.e. His sacrificial death (cf. pp. 43 f.); the word there rendered 'propitiation' (Gr. *hilasterion*) is the same as is used in the Septuagint (cf. Heb. 9. 5) to render Heb. *kapporeth*, 'mercy-seat', 'place (or means) of propitiation'. The object of the propitiatory action is men's sins, as in Heb. 2. 17, where 'sins' (Gr. *hamartias*) is in the accusative case after the infinitive *hilaskesthai* ('to make atonement for', 'to expiate').
9. Cf. Heb. 10. 19: 'we have confidence to enter the sanctuary by the blood of Jesus'.
10. For the world (*kosmos*) as the object of Christ's saving work cf. 1 John 4. 14; also John 3. 16, 17; 4. 42; 12. 47. John Calvin, in commenting on the present passage, agrees that 'Christ suffered sufficiently for the whole world but effectively only for the elect' but denies (no doubt rightly) that this is John's meaning here (*Commentary on John 11–21 and 1 John*, trans. T. H. L. Parker, Edinburgh, 1961, p. 244).
11. So magnificent a composition that for the sake of the rest of it I can even bring myself to sing 'My God is reconciled' – provided I may treat 'reconciled' as an adjective, describing God's attitude to mankind, and not as a participle, as though the sacrifice of Christ produced a change in His nature.
12. The other two occurrences are 1 John 3. 5 ('*he* was manifested . . .'), 16 ('*he* laid down his life . . .').
13. The verb 'abide' (Gr. *meno*), in addition to its ordinary usage, appears frequently in the Johannine Gospel and Epistles with a distinctive sense, setting forth the mutual coinherence of the believer in Christ (and in the Father) and of Christ (and the Father) in the believer. Paul does not use the verb in this sense, but occasionally expresses a similar idea by means of *oikeo, enoikeo, katoikeo*, 'dwell' (cf. Rom. 8. 9, 11; 1 Cor. 3. 16; 2 Cor. 6. 16; Eph. 3. 17), and in one well-known passage by means of *zao*, 'live' (Gal. 2. 20: 'it is no longer I who live, but Christ who lives in me'), but more

often without the use of any verb, in such phrases as 'in Christ', 'Christ in you'. The quotation from Epimenides in Acts 17. 28 ('In him we live and move and have our being') presents a formal parallel, but there it is physical life that is meant.

14. See note on 1 John 1. 5 (pp. 40f.). W. Dittenberger quotes a Greek inscription (dated AD 515/6) from the Church of St. George in Zorava, Syria (in allusion to its having been built where a pagan temple once stood): 'The saving light has shone, where darkness once concealed' (*Orientis Graeci Inscriptiones Selectae*, Leipzig, 1905, No. 610, 2).

15. This is the force of the present tense *paragetai* (used also of 'the world' in verse 17).

16. E. Percy, *John Knox* (London, 1937), pp. 73 f.

17. Cf. John 11. 9 f.; 12. 35 f., quoted in the note on 1 John 1. 6 (pp. 42 f.).

18. Cf. 1 John 3. 10 ff.; 4. 7 ff.

19. This is more probable than the view that these terms in verses 12 and 13c also apply to the whole body of John's readers, who are then subdivided into 'fathers' and 'young men'.

20. See p. 83, n. 66.

21. See p. 143 with p. 145, n. 29.

22. Gr. *ap' archēs*, as in Mic. 5. 2, LXX (see p. 45, n. 1).

23. Cf. John 16. 33.

24. Cf. 1 John 4. 4; 5. 4 f.

25. Cf. the promises to the 'overcomer' in the Letters to the Seven Churches (Rev. 2. 7, 11, 17, 26; 3. 5, 12, 21) and in Rev. 21. 7; also Rev. 5. 5; 12. 11; 15. 2.

26. 'The evil one' (Gr. *ho ponēros*) appears several times in NT as a designation of the devil or the tempter, especially in Matthew; e.g. in the Lord's Prayer (Matt. 6. 13) and in the interpretation of the parables of the Sower (Matt. 13. 19) and of the Tares (Matt. 13. 38). In John 17. 15 our Lord prays that His disciples may be kept 'from the evil one'. Cf. 1 John 3. 12; 5. 18 f.

27. The distinction between *logos* and *rhēma* should not be overpressed; cf. John 8. 31, 'if you abide (*menō*) in my word (*logos*), you are truly my disciples', and 15. 7 f., 'if . . . my words (*rhēmata*) abide in you, . . . so shall you be my disciples'.

28. The 'world' in this sense corresponds to the 'darkness' of verse 8 (see note on p. 55). Compare Paul's language about 'the present evil age (*aiōn*)' in Gal. 1. 4 and the Qumran description of the current era as 'the epoch of wickedness' (*Damascus Rule* 6. 10, etc.).

29. Cf. the NEB paraphrase: 'Everything the world affords, all that panders to the appetites, or entices the eyes, all the glamour of its life'.

30. In 2 Pet. 2. 14 the lust of the eyes has a sexual connotation (cf. Matt. 5. 29), but that is not necessarily so here.

31. On John's use here of Gr. *alazoneia* (RV 'vainglory') E. K. Simpson says: 'He is contemplating the unregenerate world as a Vanity Fair, and the full strength of his expression can be brought out only by some such translation as the *charlatanry* or *make-believe* of life' (*Words Worth Weighing in the Greek New Testament*, London, 1946, p. 18). Cf. the same word in Jas. 4. 16: 'you boast in your *arrogance*' (RSV).

32. F. Holmes, *Brother Indeed* (London, 1956), p. 37.

33. Cf. pp. 15 f., 25 f.

34. Gr. *paragetai*, as in verse 8. In 1 Cor. 7. 31 Paul uses the active voice *paragei*

intransitively in the same sense. Cf. 2 Cor. 4. 18: 'the things that are seen are transient'.

35. See note on 2. 1 (p. 48).

36. J. H. Newman, 'Waiting for Christ', *Parochial and Plain Sermons*, vi (London, 1896), p. 241.

37. The resumptive adverb 'now' is more naturally construed with 'you know' than (as in RSV) with 'what is restraining him'. W. Kelly stigmatizes the latter construction as a solecism (*The Epistles to the Thessalonians*,³ London, 1953, p. 146).

38. 2 Thess. 2. 3–10.

39. That the 'abomination' is personal in Mark 13. 14 is indicated by the choice of the masculine participle 'standing' (Gr. *hestēkota*) although the noun which it qualifies is in the neuter gender (*bdelygma*). Cf. NEB: 'when you see "the abomination of desolation" usurping a place which is not his'.

40. Dan. 9. 27; 11. 31; 12. 11.

41. 1 Macc. 1. 41–61 (especially verse 54: 'on the fifteenth day of Chislev, in the one hundred and forty-fifth year [i.e. of the Seleucid era, beginning 312 BC], they erected an "abomination of desolation" [i.e. a pagan altar] on the altar of burnt-offering').

42. Philo, *Embassy to Gaius*, 203 ff., Josephus, *War* ii. 184 ff., *Antiquities* xviii. 261 ff.

43. Josephus, *War* vi. 316.

44. 2 Cor. 6. 15; the word, used in the sense of 'death' or 'hell' in OT (cf. Ps. 18. 4 f., where it appears in synonymous parallelism with 'death' and 'Sheol'), is employed in this personal way in the Qumran texts and other Jewish and Christian literature of the late BC and early AD epoch.

45. Literally 'enmity', used personally (like Belial/Beliar) in the Qumran texts and other Jewish and Christian literature of this period.

46. Theodotion's Greek version of the OT, intended to replace the 'Septuagint' for Jewish use, appeared late in the second century AD; his version of Daniel was so far superior to the older, paraphrastic 'Septuagint' version that it was adopted by Greek-speaking Christians. It seems, however, to have been based on an earlier, non-Septuagintal, version with which some of the NT writers were acquainted.

47. They are thus interpreted in the earliest surviving full-scale exposition of the doctrine of Antichrist in Christian literature – Hippolytus's treatise *On Antichrist* (*c.* AD 200).

48. For a detailed exegetical study of this doctrine see I. H. Marshall, *Kept by the Power of God* (London, 1969); the evidence of the Epistles of John is examined on pp. 183 ff.

49. Cf. John 1. 8, 31; 3. 17; 9. 3; 11. 52; 12. 47; 13. 18; 14. 31; 15. 25.

50. 'The Inner Ring', in *Transposition and Other Addresses* (London, 1949), pp. 55 ff.; *Screwtape Proposes a Toast and Other Pieces* (London, 1965), pp. 28 ff.

51. Jesus Himself is said similarly to have been 'anointed . . . with the Holy Spirit' (Acts 10. 38; cf. Isa. 61. 1 in the light of 11. 2; 42. 1); this is probably a reference to the descent of the dove at His baptism (Mark 1. 10, etc.).

52. Perhaps because the seceders laid claim to a special 'anointing' (*chrisma*) which admitted them to esoteric 'knowledge' (*gnōsis*, a noun never used in the Johannine literature, surprisingly but no doubt designedly). In the following century the members of the gnostic sect of the Naassenes claimed: 'we alone of all men are Christians, for we complete the mystery at the third gate and are anointed there with unspeakable chrism' (Hippolytus,

Refutation of Heresies v. 9. 22). Cf. the anointing of Aseneth mentioned on p. 131, n. 11.

53. Especially Codices Sinaiticus and Vaticanus and the Sahidic Coptic version.

54. T. W. Manson, following A. Harnack, states his preference for 'all things', partly on the ground that *oida* ('I know') 'is not used absolutely in the Fourth Gospel or the Johannine Epistles', and refers to John 14. 26 ('Entry into Membership of the Early Church', *JTS* 48, 1947, p. 28, n. 1).

55. The tense of 'I have . . . written' in verse 21 is the epistolary aorist (*egrapsa*), as in verses 13c and 14.

56. *To the Philippians* 7. 1. The expression 'Satan's firstborn' seems to have been a favourite of Polycarp's: many years later (AD 154), when Polycarp was on a visit to Rome, the heresiarch Marcion is said to have sought an interview with him and asked the aged bishop if he recognized him, to which he received the answer, 'I recognize – Satan's firstborn!' (Irenaeus, *Against Heresies* iii. 3. 4).

57. Where God sends 'a strong delusion' on those who refused the love of the saving truth, so that instead they believe 'the Lie'. Cf. Rom. 1. 25, where disobedient mankind 'exchanged the truth about God for the Lie'. In the teaching of Zoroaster 'The Lie' (Avestan *druj*) denotes the whole system of evil.

58. *Republic* ii. 382 b–c.

59. See pp. 16 f.

60. This is plain, for example, in the later *Gospel of Thomas* (a compilation of sayings of Jesus with a gnosticizing tendency), where the supreme Being, proclaimed by Jesus, is called 'the Father', whereas the designation 'God' is reserved for an inferior power.

61. See p. 17.

62. So RSV text. But the reading which is relegated to the margin of RSV (as of RV, ARV and NEB), 'God only-begotten, who has his being in the Father's bosom . . .', has strong external and internal support.

63. The Divine Word was in the world in various ways before 'becoming flesh' and so communicating the fullness of God's glory (John 1. 9–14); cf. the 'many and various ways' in which God spoke to men before 'in these last days' He spoke His definitive word in the Son (Heb. 1. 1 f.).

64. There is no valid ground for the italicization in AV of the second part of verse 23; although these words 'he who confesses the Son has the Father also' are absent from later manuscripts and from the 'Received Text', they are well attested in our major authorities.

65. The repeated form *pisteuete* is identical in both moods.

66. Paul uses *tekna* ('children') and *hyioi* ('sons') indiscriminately to denote Christians' relationship to God, as an examination of Rom. 8. 14–21 shows, though he prefers *hyioi* (as in Gal. 3. 26–4. 7), perhaps because of its presence in the compound *hyiothesia*, 'adoption' (see note on 2. 12 ff., p. 58). A near exception in the Johannine usage is the phrase *hyioi phōtos*, 'sons of light', in John 12. 36, but this was probably a stereotyped phrase (cf. Luke 16. 8; 1 Thess. 5. 5, although Eph. 5. 8 has *tekna phōtos*).

67. Cf. W. Nauck, *Die Tradition und der Charakter des ersten Johannesbriefes* (Tübingen, 1957), pp. 1 ff. Somewhat similar is P. Carrington's working out of a primitive Christian catechism in 1 John 3 (*The Primitive Christian Catechism*, Cambridge, 1940, pp. 19 ff.).

68. Gr. *aischynomai apo*, a construction not found elsewhere in NT. It occurs five times in LXX, but never quite in the same sense as here (usually the noun

following *apo* denotes something or someone of which the subject of the verb is rightly ashamed). The nearest parallel is Sir. 21. 22: 'The foot of a fool rushes into a house, but a man of experience stands respectfully before it (*aischynthēsetai apo prosōpou*).'

69. Gr. *parrhēsia*; cf. 3. 21; 4. 17; 5. 14.
70. In Matt. 5. 45 and Luke 6. 35 the word used is *hyioi* ('sons'); those who press a distinction between this and *tekna* should reflect that in Hebrew or Aramaic no such distinction is possible; one and the same word (*bnê*, construct plural) must be envisaged behind either rendering.
71. As RV margin indicates, the verb *ginōskete* may be imperative as well as indicative. RSV ('you may be sure . . .') and NEB ('you must recognize . . .') probably present free renderings of the imperative.

CHAPTER III

V. 1 Behold what manner of love the Father hath bestowed upon us, that we should be called children of God: and *such* we are. For this cause the world knoweth us not, because it knew him not. v. 2 Beloved, now are we children of God, and it is not yet made manifest what we shall be. We know that, if ¹he shall be manifested, we shall be like him; for we shall see him even as he is.

¹ Or, *it*.

This language echoes that of the Prologue to the Gospel, where the Eternal Logos receives no welcome among those who should be first to acknowledge him: 'but to all who received him, who believed in his name, he gave power to become children of God; who were born . . . of God' (John 1. 12, 13). Here, however, God's calling believers His children is a token of the greatness of His love for them. A parallel statement in a Jewish context is ascribed to Rabbi Akiba (died AD 135): 'Beloved is man, for he was created in the image of God, but by a special love it was made known to him that he was created in the image of God, as it is said, "For in the image of God made he man" (Gen. 9. 6). Beloved are Israel, for they were called children of God, but by a special love it was made known to them that they were called children of God, as it is said, "You are children of the LORD your God" (Deut. 14. 1).'¹ The words 'and such we are', omitted in later manuscripts and in AV, remind us that when God calls, His call is effectual; people and things *are* what He calls them.

These first two verses of 1 John 3 celebrate the accomplishment of God's eternal purpose concerning man. This purpose finds expression in Gen. 1. 26, where God, about to bring into being the crown of creation, says: 'Let us make man in our image, after our likeness'. In other words, He declares His intention of bringing into existence beings like Himself, as like Himself as it is possible

85

for creatures to be like their Creator. In words which echo the language of Genesis 1, the status and function of man in the purpose of God are celebrated in Ps. 8. 5 ff.: 'thou hast made him little less than God, and dost crown him with glory and honour. Thou hast given him dominion over the works of thy hands; thou hast put all things under his feet'. But Genesis 3 tells how man, not content with the true likeness to God which was his by creation, grasped at the counterfeit likeness held out as the tempter's bait: 'you will be like God, knowing good and evil'. In consequence, things most *unlike* God manifested themselves in human life: hatred, darkness and death in place of love, light and life. The image of God in man was sadly defaced. Yet God's purpose was not frustrated; instead, the fall itself, with its entail of sin and death, was overruled by God and compelled to become an instrument in the furtherance of His purpose.

In the fullness of time the image of God, undefaced by disobedience to His will, reappeared on earth in the person of His Son. In Jesus the love, light and life of God were manifested in opposition to hatred, darkness and death. With His crucifixion it seemed that hatred, darkness and death had won the day, and that God's purpose, which had survived the fall, was now effectively thwarted. But instead, the cross of Jesus proved to be God's chosen instrument for the fulfilment of His purpose. 'To this end was the Son of God manifested, that he might destroy the works of the devil' (1 John 3. 8), and it was by His cross that He did so (cf. Col. 2. 14 f.). The last Adam by His obedience has restored what the first Adam by his disobedience forfeited and has ensured the triumph of God's purpose. This purpose is stated by Paul in terms which go back far beyond the act of creation in Genesis 1: 'those whom he foreknew he also predestined to be conformed to the image of his Son, in order that he might be the first-born among many brethren' (Rom. 8. 29). The children of God, who enter His family through faith in His Son, display their Father's likeness, because of their conformity to Him who is the perfect image of the invisible God. They display it in measure here and now; they will display it fully on a coming day, for 'we know that, if he shall be manifested, we shall be like him; for we shall see him even as he is'. The consummation of God's purpose in man coincides with the advent of Christ in glory: then those who 'have borne the image of the man of dust' will 'bear the image of the man of heaven' (1 Cor. 15. 49); the new man, who at present 'is being renewed in knowledge after the image of his Creator' (Col. 3. 10), will have come to full maturity. When Christ, His people's life, is manifested, they will be manifested with Him in glory (Col. 3. 4), so that the day of His appearing is also the day of 'the revealing of the sons of God' (Rom. 8. 19). Sonship is present, but vision is future.[2]

Referring to the present work of sanctification, Paul says that the people of Christ, beholding His glory and then reflecting it 'as in a mirror', are 'transfigured into his likeness' (2 Cor. 3. 18, NEB). If progressive assimilation to the likeness of their Lord results from their present beholding of Him through a glass darkly, to behold Him face to face, to 'see him even as he is', will result in their being perfectly like Him.

In the sentence, 'For this cause the world knoweth us not, because it knew him not', the pronoun 'him' probably refers to 'the Father', since He is the only one mentioned in the singular in the preceding sentence; otherwise we might think of the world's failure to recognize or welcome the Son of God when He came. But it is a matter of small moment; the reception given to the Son is reckoned as given to the Father too: 'If I had not done among them the works which no one else did, they would not have sin', says Jesus to His disciples in the upper room; 'but now they have seen and hated both me and my Father' (John 15. 24). Similarly our Lord forewarned His disciples that the reception given to Him would equally be given to them.[3]

Before moving on from verse 2, it may be well to make passing reference to the NEB rendering: 'what we shall be has not yet been disclosed, but we know that when it is disclosed we shall be like him, because we shall see him as he is'. Here the subject of the clause which RV renders 'if he shall be manifested' is taken to be not 'he' but 'it' (cf. RV margin), harking back to 'what we shall be'.[4]

This is a perfectly permissible rendering, but it is better to understand a personal subject, as in NEB margin, where 'when he appears' is given as an alternative rendering to 'when it is disclosed' of the text. NEB suggests yet another rendering in a further marginal note: 'we are God's children, though he has not yet appeared; what we shall be we know, for when he does appear we shall be like him'. This presupposes a different punctuation from the other renderings, but on the whole the familiar punctuation seems to be more satisfactory.

V. 3   And every one that hath this hope *set* on him purifieth himself, even as he is pure.

The use of the preposition 'on' (Gr. *epi*) after the noun 'hope' makes it sufficiently certain that 'him' means Christ, or God in Christ. The AV 'every man that hath this hope in him' is ambiguous; it might be taken to mean 'everyone who has this hope (implanted) in himself', whereas the pronoun following *epi* must denote the object of the hope.[5] As in 2. 6 and two other places in this letter,[6] 'he' in the phrase 'as he' represents Gr. *ekeinos* and denotes Christ. Christ Himself is pure – He is indeed the very norm of purity – and a hope that rests 'on him' cannot but have a purifying effect in the life of the one who so hopes. For to have one's hope set on Christ implies that He is a constant object of meditation and contemplation; when that is so, the words of Paul come true, that 'we all, with unveiled face, beholding the glory of the Lord, are being changed into his likeness from one degree of glory to another' (2 Cor. 3. 18). This is the proper preparation for the day when His people's conformity to His likeness will be consummated, when, at His appearing, they become completely 'like him', because then they will 'see him as he is'. Here and now they are urged 'to lead a life worthy of the calling' with which God has called them (Eph. 4. 1), and since that calling involves their ultimately being glorified with Christ (Rom. 8. 28–30), present likeness to Christ is indispensable to a life worthy of that calling. 'Blessed are the pure in heart, for they shall see God' (Matt. 5. 8).

V. 4   Every one that doeth sin doeth also lawlessness: and sin is lawlessness.

The practising of sin is the opposite of the practising of righteousness which, as John has said in 2. 29, characterizes those who have been born into God's family. Lest someone in the opposite camp should interrupt at this point in order to discuss theoretically what is and what is not the nature of sin, John cuts him short with a terse definition, which is adequate for his practical purpose: 'sin is lawlessness'. The seceders' 'new morality' took little account of divine law or of sin against it; John insists that sin, in the common sense of the term, is rebellion against God. The AV rendering, 'sin is the transgression of the law' (taken over from the Geneva Bible), is unfortunate, since it suggests the contravention of this or that specific law rather than a generally lawless attitude towards God. 'Sin is not transgression of law but lawlessness, and lawlessness is sin. It is a convertible or reciprocating proposition, the subject being identified with the predicate.'[7]

V. 5   And ye know that he was manifested to ¹take away sins; and in him is no sin. v. 6 Whosoever abideth in him sinneth not: whosoever sinneth hath not seen him, neither ²knoweth him.

¹ Or, *bear sins.*   ² Or, *hath known.*

The noun sins' is preceded in the original by the definite article. If we include the article in a literal translation, '*he* (the emphatic *ekeinos*[8]) was manifested to take away the sins', the question arises, 'What sins?' – to which the answer is 'Ours'. (In fact some manuscripts, including Codex Sinaiticus, with the Sahidic Coptic and Syriac Peshitta, add the pronoun, making '*our* sins' quite explicit.) In John 1. 29 Jesus is proclaimed by the Baptist to be 'the Lamb of God, who takes away the *sin* of the world' in the singular; here the plural 'sins' has in view the individual sins of His people,[9] as in 2. 2, where he is called 'the propitiation for our sins'. The taking away of sins can be accomplished only by one who is himself sinless; hence the reminder:

'in him is no sin'. This goes further than to say that He committed no sin; it denies the presence of indwelling sin in His heart, and approximates to Paul's designation of Him in 2 Cor. 5. 21 as the One 'who knew no sin' (i.e. had no consciousness of it in His personal experience). If, then, He appeared on earth to take away His people's sins and is Himself the sinless One, how can sin be cherished by anyone who 'abides' in Him? In saying that no one who 'abides' in him sins, John is not asserting that it is impossible for a believer to commit an occasional act of sin. He has already pointed to the provision made for such an emergency by means of confession (1. 9) and Christ's activity as His people's Advocate (2. 1 f.), and has warned his readers against unfounded claims to be sinless within or without (1. 8, 10). What he does assert is that a sinful life does not mark a child of God, so that anyone who leads such a life is shown thereby not to be a child of God. When a boy goes to a new school, he may inadvertently do something out of keeping with the school's tradition or good name, to be told immediately, 'That isn't done here'. A literalist might reply, 'But obviously it *is* done; this boy has just done it' – but he would be deliberately missing the point of the rebuke. The point of the rebuke is that such conduct is disapproved of in this school, so anyone who practises it can normally be assumed not to belong to the school. There may be odd exceptions, but that is the general rule, which has been verified by experience. Fellowship with the sinless One and indulgence in sin are a contradiction in terms. Whatever high claims may be made by one who indulges in sin, that indulgence is sufficient proof that he has no personal knowledge of Christ. So, in the Gospel of John, Jesus says to His disciples, 'If you had known me, you would have known my Father also; henceforth you know him and have seen him' (John 14. 7); to those who refused Him credence He says, 'His [the Father's] voice you have never heard, his form you have never seen; and you do not have his word abiding in you, for you do not believe in him whom he has sent . . . You know neither me nor my Father; if you knew me, you would know my Father also' (John 5. 37 f.; 8. 19). Similarly, in his letter to Gaius, John propounds the simple antithesis: 'He who does good is of God; he who does evil has not seen God' (3 John 11).

V. 7 *My* **little children, let no man lead you astray: he that doeth righteousness is righteous, even as he is righteous: v. 8 he that doeth sin is of the devil; for the devil sinneth from the beginning. To this end was the Son of God manifested, that he might destroy the works of the devil.**

The false teachers with their sophistry (cf. 2. 26) were capable not merely of condoning sin, but of making it seem virtuous. Against their arguments John's 'little children' (*teknia*) would be fortified if they remembered his plain, uncomplicated maxims. Behaviour is of unsurpassed importance in the Christian way. Believers are indeed justified before God by His grace, which they accept by faith; but those who have been justified thus will show it by their behaviour. Righteousness is as consonant with the character of Christ – since 'he (*ekeinos*) is righteous' – as sin is consonant with the character of the devil, who has been sinning, rebelling against God (this is the force of the Greek present here), ever since the beginning.[10] In the Gospel Jesus tells some people who boasted in their descent from Abraham that their behaviour proclaimed them to be children not of Abraham but of the devil, because the latter 'was a murderer from the beginning' (John 8. 44). Here the antithesis is between the family of God and the family of the devil; in either family the children may be known by their moral likeness to the head of the family. The very purpose of the Son of God's appearance on earth was 'to destroy the works of the devil' – 'destroy' renders Gr. *lyō*, here used in the same sense as it has in Eph. 2. 14, where Christ 'has broken down the middle wall of hostility'. Chief of the devil's works is sin, which the Son of God came to take away (cf. verse 5). How can one in whose life sin has manifestly not been destroyed or taken away claim to dwell in Christ? Is it not rather self-evident that he belongs to the family which is characterized by rebellion against God, and whose head is the arch-rebel?

V. 9 Whosoever is begotten of God doeth no sin, because his seed abideth in him: and he cannot sin, because he is begotten of God.

The first sentence of verse 9 repeats in substance the first sentence of verse 6: 'whosoever abides in him does not sin'. Once again, John emphasizes that the practice of sin is something that characterizes the children of him who 'has been sinning from the beginning' (v. 8), not the children of God. The reason the child of God does not practise sin is said to be that 'his seed abides in him' – a clause which can be understood in more than one way. That 'his seed' means God's seed is fairly certain. This may mean the divine nature implanted in the believer through the new birth; so RSV: 'God's nature abides in him' and thus prevents him from sinning (cf. NEB: 'the divine seed remains in him; he cannot be a sinner, because he is God's child').[11] But 'seed' is frequently used in the sense of 'offspring' (as, for example, in the discussion about Abraham's 'seed' in Gal. 3. 16–29); if that is the sense of the word here, then the meaning of the passage is not 'God's nature remains in the child of God' but 'God's child remains in God and cannot sin because he is *God's* offspring'. There is not much practical difference between the two constructions; the difference resides mainly in the precise force of the noun 'seed' and the reference of the pronoun 'him'. The latter construction might be regarded as an expansion of verse 6a.

One way or the other, the new birth involves a radical change in human nature; for those who have not experienced it, sin is natural, whereas for those who have experienced it, sin is unnatural – so unnatural, indeed, that its practice constitutes a powerful refutation of any claim to possess the divine life. John's antitheses are clear-cut. While they are to be understood in the context of his letter and of the situation which it presupposes, any attempt to weaken them, out of regard for human infirmity, or to make them less sharp and uncompromising than they are, is to misinterpret them. True interpretation must allow an author to mean what he says, even if that meaning is uncongenial to the interpreter.

V. 10 **In this the children of God are manifest, and the children of the devil: whosoever doeth not righteousness is not of God, neither he that loveth not his brother.**

In summing up the criteria which distinguish the two spiritual families one from the other, John adds love of one's brother to the practice of righteousness as a mark of the child of God, and the absence of such love, with the practice of unrighteousness, as a disqualification for membership in God's family. Righteousness by itself, while infinitely preferable to unrighteousness, might appear to be coldly judicial, but the addition of brotherly love (cf. 2. 9 f.) imparts a transforming warmth to John's exposition. For him, righteousness and love are inseparable; since they are inseparable in the character of God and in His revelation in Christ, so they must be inseparable in the lives of His people. If, slightly changing the lawyer's question in the Gospel story, we ask, 'And who is my brother?' the answer, especially in the light of verse 17 (p. 96), will be not unlike that which our Lord gave to 'Who is my neighbour?' – 'Any one who needs my love'.[12]

(b) The test of love (3. 11–18)

V. 11 **For this is the message which ye heard from the beginning, that we should love one another: v. 12 not as Cain was of the evil one, and slew his brother. And wherefore slew he him? Because his works were evil, and his brother's righteous.**

Love is an indispensable feature in the lives of the children of God, because it is the embodiment of the gospel message, and of the 'new commandment' which they received when first they were taught the Christian way. John has already emphasized this test in 2. 7–11; now he returns to emphasize it afresh. The family likeness is bound to appear; the love of the Father will be reproduced in His children. It was so in the earliest days of the human race; here John introduces the one Old Testament reference in his letters, and the only proper name (apart from designations of

Christ or God) in this particular letter.[13] Cain, who murdered his
brother (Gen. 4. 8), showed by that act that he hated him, and his
hatred indicated quite clearly to which spiritual family he belonged.
There is no ground for supposing that Cain is here said to have
been 'of the evil one' (*ek tou ponērou*) in a biological sense, as
though he were the fruit of the tempter's seduction of Eve sexually
understood – an idea current in some Jewish circles around this
time.[14] The statement that 'Cain was of the evil one' is to be
understood in the same sense as our Lord's words to those who
were trying to encompass His death: 'You are of (*ek*) your father
the devil' (John 8. 44). He said so because, in seeking His life,
they showed themselves to be spiritual children of him who 'was
a murderer from the beginning'. In the same way Cain, the first
murderer, showed his spiritual lineage. The verb used here for
'murder' (Gr. *sphazō*) is not found in the New Testament (apart
from this verse) outside Revelation, where it is used of the
slaughtered Lamb (5. 6, 9, 12; 13. 8), of the holy martyrs (6. 9;
18. 24), of the internecine slaughter of war (6. 4) and of the
beast's head that was 'wounded' to death (13. 3). It is a forceful
and vivid word, perhaps used here to bring out the malice afore-
thought with which Abel was murdered; but the fact that its
primary meaning is to cut the throat (as in slaughtering an animal)
hardly justifies K. S. Wuest's translation of it here as 'killed his
brother by severing his jugular vein'![15]

The reason for Cain's hatred, as stated here, is completely in
line with the Genesis narrative; it was 'because his works were
evil, but his brother's were righteous'. When Cain was angry
because his sacrifice was disregarded, God said to him: 'If you do
well, will you not be accepted?' (Gen. 4. 7). He was invited, in
other words, to learn the lesson that comes to such frequent
expression elsewhere in the Old Testament, that 'the sacrifice of
the wicked is an abomination to the LORD, but the prayer of the
upright is his delight' (Prov. 15. 8). Abel, on the other hand,
'received approval as righteous, God bearing witness by accepting
his gifts' (Heb. 11. 4).

The principle of the hostility of the wicked to the righteous is one which John sees operating in the environment of himself and his readers; hence he adds a word of encouragement:

V. 13   Marvel not, brethren, if the world hateth you.

This is a direct echo of the words of our Lord in the upper room: 'If the world hates you, know that it hated me before it hated you. If you were of the world, the world would love its own; but because you are not of the world, but I chose you out of the world, therefore the world hates you. Remember the word that I said to you, "A servant is not greater than his master" ' (John 15. 18–20). The Synoptic record is to the same effect: 'He who hears you hears me', says Jesus to the seventy, 'and he who rejects you rejects me, and he who rejects me rejects him who sent me' (Luke 10. 16), while He reminds the twelve that 'a disciple is not above his teacher, nor a servant above his master; it is enough for the disciple to be like his teacher, and the servant like his master' (Matt. 10. 24, 25).[16]

The world, orientated against God, is, as John has indicated already (1 John 2. 15–17), inherently inimical to the cause of God. Manifestations of its hostility, therefore, should not take the children of God by surprise. The warfare between the two sides continues, although the decisive victory has been won; this gives the children of God confidence that they can overcome the world by faith in Him who has already overcome it (1 John 4. 4; 5. 4 f.; cf. John 16. 33).

V. 14   We know that we have passed out of death into life, because we love the brethren. He that loveth not abideth in death. v. 15 Whosoever hateth his brother is a murderer: and ye know that no murderer hath eternal life abiding in him.

As the presence of murderous hatred is a token that one does not belong to the family of God, the presence of brotherly love is a sure sign that one does belong to it, that one has, through the new birth, 'passed out of death into life' (cf. John 5. 24). The pronoun 'we' in 'we know' is emphatic – *we*, in contrast to the world and all who bear the mark of Cain. The definite article before 'brethren' is equivalent, in the context, to an unemphatic possessive pronoun (cf. NEB: 'we love our brothers'). Love is the supreme manifestation of the new life, so much so that any one who fails to manifest it shows that he has never entered into the new life; he 'abides in death'. 'By this', said Jesus, 'all men will know that you are my disciples, if you have love for one another' (John 13. 35). These words were spoken immediately after the departure of Judas, who by his lack of love was self-excluded from the number of those who were disciples indeed. As with Cain, hatred is the root which, if unchecked, yields the fruit of murder. Hence our Lord's warning in the Sermon on the Mount that not just the man who commits murder, but 'every one who is angry with his brother[17] shall be liable to judgment' (Matt. 5. 22). If murder, the end-product of hatred, proves that eternal life is absent, so does the root principle of hatred itself.

V. 16 **Hereby know we love, because he laid down his life for us: and we ought to lay down our lives for the brethren.**

When John speaks of love (*agapē*), it is no sentimental emotion that he has in mind, but something intensely practical. Christians have one supreme example of love, the love shown by their Lord in that *He* (as before, John uses the emphatic pronoun *ekeinos*) 'laid down his life' for them. No Christian should speak readily of his love for others unless he is prepared, if need be, to show that love as Christ showed His, by giving up his life for them – indeed, by regarding it as his plain duty so to do. This is what is meant by showing the love of Christ in one's life.

V. 17 **But whoso hath the world's goods, and beholdeth his brother in need, and shutteth up his compassion from him, how doth the love of God abide in him?** v. 18 *My* **little children, let us not love in word, neither with the tongue; but in deed and truth.**

Frequently, however, a Christian will not be called upon to give his life, or even risk it, for his fellows. But he will have frequent opportunity of showing them his love in less exacting ways. Many of them suffer material hardship and privation; a Christian who is blessed with this world's goods will instinctively show 'the love of God'[18] by sharing what he has with others less fortunate.[19] If, on the contrary, he hardens his heart and refuses to show them compassion in such a practical way, what is the use of his talking about 'the love of God'? By paying it lip-service without exhibiting it in kindly and helpful action, he is simply bringing on himself and his associates the charge of hypocrisy. It is love 'in deed and truth' that is expected from a child of God, not the kind of pious talk that devalues the currency of heavenly love because it is unmatched by corresponding action. James says something very much to the same effect: 'If a brother or sister is ill-clad and in lack of daily food, and one of you says to them, "Go in peace, be warmed and filled", without giving them the things needed for the body, what does it profit?' (Jas. 2. 15 f.).

(c) Christian confidence (3. 19–24)

V. 19 Hereby shall we know that we are of the truth, and shall ¹assure our heart before him, v. 20 whereinsoever our heart condemn us; because God is greater than our heart, and knoweth all things.

¹ Gr. *persuade*.

The RV rendering of this sentence is followed by RSV: 'By this we shall know that we are of the truth, and reassure our hearts before him whenever our hearts condemn us; for God is greater than our hearts, and he knows everything' (cf. the former of two alternative renderings in NEB margin: ' . . . and reassure ourselves in his sight in matters where our conscience condemns us, because God is greater than our conscience . . .').[20] This involves taking *ho ti* (with which verse 20 begins) not as the conjunction *hoti* 'that' (translated 'for' in AV),[21] but as the neuter of the relative pronoun *hostis*, made indefinite by the addition of *ean* (lit. 'if'), and treated

as an accusative of respect: 'in respect of whatsoever'. If we
regard the first word of verse 20 as *hoti*, 'that', we find ourselves
faced with an unnecessary repetition of the same conjunction at
the beginning of the next clause ('that if our heart condemns us,
that God is greater than our heart'). NEB text recognizes just such
a repetition, and ignores one of the two occurrences of *hoti* in
its rendering: 'This is how we may know that we belong to the
realm of truth, and convince ourselves in his sight that even if our
conscience condemns us, God is greater than our conscience and
knows all'. 'The greatness of God, which is above both accusation
and Satan, to whom all accusations go back (cf. 1 John 4. 4),
consists in the forgiveness which remits guilt and in the power
which gives fulfilment of the commandments.'[22]

John has urged his readers to see to it that their love is exercised
not in word only but 'in deed and truth'. Such spontaneous,
practical and outgoing love is a token that one belongs to the
divine fellowship, to the realm of truth (cf. John 18. 37). When we
are thus united to the all-knowing God in the bond of love, 'that
fact assures us of His sovereign mercy',[23] no matter how hostile a
verdict our own conscience may pass upon us. John repeats in
effect here with regard to those who dwell in love what he has
said earlier about the availability of cleansing for those who walk
in the light (1 John 1. 7). The realm of light and the realm of love
are one and the same realm, the realm in which the children of
God are united in Christ to their heavenly Father.

V. 21 **Beloved, if our heart condemn us not, we have
boldness toward God;** v. 22 **and whatsoever we ask, we
receive of him, because we keep his commandments, and
do the things that are pleasing in his sight.**

When God, who is greater than our conscience and pronounces
a more authoritative verdict, one based on perfect knowledge of
us and of all the relevant circumstances, assures us of the forgiveness of our sins for Christ's sake, we enjoy peace of conscience.
The accusation of conscience must always be treated seriously;

only when it is overruled by the pardoning edict of God can its voice be properly hushed. The cleansing from every sin which the blood of Jesus' self-offering procures for us is, as the writer to the Hebrews insists, a cleansing of the *conscience* (Heb. 9. 9, 14; 10. 2, 22).[24] A sin-stained conscience is the most effective barrier between man and God; where the stain is blotted out, the barrier is removed, and instead of separation from God there is 'boldness toward God' – openness in His presence. The writer to the Hebrews, in terms of his special interest, speaks of 'confidence to enter the sanctuary by the blood of Jesus' (Heb. 10. 19). John who has already spoken of the believer's 'boldness' or 'confidence' (*parrhēsia*, lit. 'freedom of speech') in an eschatological sense, of the believer's attitude to Christ at His advent (2. 28; cf. 4. 17), uses it here in a sense not unrelated to its earlier occurrence:

> for the Christian the judgement is not only future, but present; love towards the brethren is the test for abiding in the love of Christ. If we have not a bad conscience in that respect ... because we love in deed and truth, we have 'freedom of speech' towards God and may ask Him everything ... This is again stressed in 5. 14 ... This free intercourse with God, which His children abiding in Christ enjoy, has an immediate practical consequence. It has its foundation in Christ, is here now, and will be in the final judgement: 'freedom of speech' in the children of God who are in His love and show forth love.[25]

In the Father's realm of love and light, the children gladly do His bidding and act so as to please Him: they do not find Him difficult to please nor are His commands burdensome to them (cf. 5. 3). It has not occurred to them that there could be any tension between love and obedience; they have learned their Master's lesson: 'If you keep my commandments, you will abide in my love, just as I have kept my Father's commandments and abide in his love' (John 15. 10). In such an atmosphere of love, confidence and obedience it is the most natural thing in the world for the children to 'ask' their Father for what they need, assured that He will give them what they ask. This too forms a part of their Master's teaching: 'if you ask anything of the Father, he will give it to you in my name' (John 16. 23).

**V. 23 And this is his commandment, that we should
¹believe in the name of his Son Jesus Christ, and love one
another, even as he gave us commandment.**

¹ Gr. *believe the name.*

The Father's commandment is the commandment of faith and
love. Here the faith is the initial act of believing which leads to
the life of faith; this is suggested by the use of the aorist tense
(*pisteusōmen*) which is here best regarded as the 'ingressive' aorist.
Here the construction following the verb 'believe' is not *eis* ('into')
with the accusative (used later in 5. 10, 13)[26] but the simple
dative; it is difficult to see a material distinction between the two
constructions. The 'name', as so often in biblical literature, is not
merely the label of identification attached to the person but the
person's character and indeed the person himself. Faith in Christ,
then, is the first step of life in the family of God, and this life is a
life of love as well as a life of faith. The 'commandment' to 'love
one another' has already been emphasized as the commandment
which is both new and old (2. 7, 8), the commandment given by
Christ to the disciples in the upper room (John 13. 34; 15. 12).

**V. 24 And he that keepeth his commandments abideth
in him, and he in him. And hereby we know that he abideth
in us, by the Spirit which he gave us.**

Obedience to the Lord's commandments is not the cause but
the proof of His people's dwelling in Him. Moreover, their
'abiding' in Him has as its correlative His 'abiding' in them (cf.
John 6. 56). It is by His Spirit that He 'abides' in them, and it is
equally by His Spirit that they learn of His 'abiding' in them.
This is the first mention of the Spirit in this letter;[27] He appears
again as the Spirit of truth in ch. 4 and as the Spirit of witness (as
here) in ch. 5. Whether He who 'abides' in us and has given us
His Spirit is the Father or the Son (cf. John 15. 4a) is not altogether
clear; but in the light of the foregoing clauses (and especially the
words 'his Son Jesus Christ' in verse 23) the Father is most

probably meant (as explicitly in 4. 12, 15, 16). In fact, however, the Father and the Son together make their home with the believer (John 14. 23) and bestow the gift of the Spirit (in John 14. 26 the Father sends Him in the Son's name; in John 15. 26 the Son sends Him from the Father).

NOTES

1. *Ethics of the Fathers (Pirqe Aboth)* 3. 18.
2. Cf. W. Michaelis in *TDNT* v (Grand Rapids, 1968), p. 366 (*s.v. ὁράω*).
3. Cf. John 15. 18–20 and Synoptic parallels quoted in the comment on 3. 13 (p. 95).
4. Cf. W. Michaelis in *TDNT* v (Grand Rapids, 1968), p. 366 (*s.v. ὁράω*).
5. NEB 'everyone who has this hope before him' is even more open to criticism than AV.
6. 1 John 3. 7; 4. 17.
7. W. Kelly, *The Epistles to the Thessalonians*[3] (London, 1953), p. 150 (on 2 Thess. 2. 7).
8. See note on 2. 6 (p. 52).
9. As in Isa. 53. 12, LXX.
10. Here the 'beginning' is the beginning of creation or the beginning of the Bible story.
11. For this use of seed J. C. O'Neill compares 1 Enoch 84. 6, 'establish the flesh of uprightness as a plant of the eternal seed' (*The Puzzle of 1 John*, London, 1966, p. 37). It is possible that John is countering an esoteric use of the concept 'divine seed' among the false teachers, such as we find in the second century among the Valentinians and Naassenes (cf. Irenaeus, *Against Heresies* ii. 19).
12. Cf. Luke 10. 25 ff.
13. It is difficult to find evidence for supposing that here or in Jude 11 there is a covert allusion to predecessors of those second-century Gnostics called Cainites, closely associated with the Naassenes or Ophites (cf. Irenaeus, *Against Heresies* i. 31).
14. The earliest allusion to it is probably in 4 Maccabees (an Alexandrian Jewish document of the first century BC), where the mother of the seven martyred brothers, after referring to the formation of Eve, says 'nor did the false beguiling serpent sully the purity of my maidenhood' (18. 8).
15. *Expanded Translation of the New Testament*, iii (Pickering and Inglis, 1959), p. 198.
16. Cf. Matt. 10. 22a; 24. 9: 'you will be hated by all (nations) for my name's sake'. See also verse 1b above (p. 85).
17. The attempt in later editions of the text to ease this 'hard saying' by the addition of 'without a cause' (cf. AV) is not supported by our earliest authorities.
18. The 'love of God' may be taken here either as our love for God (objective genitive) or God's love for man (subjective genitive). In favour of the former is such a parallel passage as 1 John 4. 20, where love for one's brother is the visible expression of one's love for God (see pp. 114 f.). At the same time such love for one's brother is a reflection of God's own love poured into His children's hearts (cf. Rom. 5. 5). So, in the upper room, Jesus tells His

disciples, 'As the Father has loved me, so have I loved you' (John 15. 9), and charges them 'even as I have loved you, that you also love one another' (John 13. 34).

19. The verb translated 'beholdeth' (RV) is Gr. *theōreō*, which John uses in preference to the present tense of *horaō* (never found in his Gospel or Epistles).

20. The second of the two alternative marginal renderings in NEB is: 'and yet we shall do well to convince ourselves that even if our own conscience condemns us, still more will God who is greater than conscience (condemn us)'. This is a possible way of taking the words by themselves, but is inconsistent with the context.

21. The conjunction *hoti* may mean either 'that' (introducing an indirect statement after a verb of saying or knowing) or 'because' (introducing a causal clause); AV takes it the latter way and translates it 'for'. The distinction in spelling between the conjunction *hoti* (as one word) and the pronoun *ho ti* (as two words) is merely a convention in printing, but a convenient one.

22. W. Grundmann, in *TDNT* iv (Grand Rapids, 1967), p. 538 (*s.v. μέγας*). In appropriate contexts the verb *peithō*, 'persuade' (here translated 'assure' in RV text), has the sense 'conciliate, pacify, set at ease *or* rest', so that peace of conscience in the sight of God appears to be in view here (cf. W. Bauer, W. F. Arndt, F. W. Gingrich, *Greek-English Lexicon of the NT* . . . , Cambridge, 1957, p. 645).

23. B. F. Westcott, *The Epistles of St. John*, p. 117. Westcott's whole comment on these two verses will repay careful study.

24. See comments on 1 John 1. 7 (pp. 43 f.); 2. 2 (pp. 49 f.).

25. W. C. van Unnik, 'The Christian's Freedom of Speech in the NT', *BJRL* 44 (1961–62), p. 486.

26. The construction *pisteuō eis* is the characteristic expression for 'believing in' in the Fourth Gospel, e.g. John 1. 12 ('who believed in his name'), 2. 11 ('his disciples believed in him'), etc.

27. That is to say, the first *explicit* mention; the Spirit is, of course, the 'Holy One' who imparts the 'anointing' of 2. 20, 27 (pp. 70 ff.).

CHAPTER IV

6 THE TWO SPIRITS (4. 1–6)

V. 1 Beloved, believe not every spirit, but prove the spirits, whether they are of God: because many false prophets are gone out into the world.

In the apostolic churches, as in ancient Israel, communications were made from time to time by 'prophets', men and women who spoke as the mouthpieces of a power beyond themselves. Every prophet claimed to be a spokesman of God, to be inspired by the Spirit of truth, but in Old and New Testament times alike it was necessary to test these claims. In Elijah's day we meet prophets of Baal and prophets of Asherah, spokesmen of Canaanite divinities (1 Kings 18. 19), as well as those who, like Elijah himself, were prophets of the God of Israel (1 Kings 18. 4, 13, 22). To distinguish between the former and the latter was no difficult task. It was different when contradictory utterances were made by men claiming to be prophets of the God of Israel. How could it be known for sure that Micaiah the son of Imlah was speaking the truth when he foretold catastrophe at Ramoth-gilead, as against Zedekiah the son of Chenaanah and his companions who so confidently predicted victory? True, the fact that the latter all told King Ahab so unanimously what he wanted to hear was suspicious in itself, and Micaiah had no doubt of the authenticity of his message of doom, having heard it pronounced in the heavenly council;[1] but his ultimate appeal could only be to the event: 'If you return in peace, the LORD has not spoken by me' (1 Kings 22. 28).

Jeremiah in his day stood almost alone as a messenger of doom, opposed by others who prophesied smooth things to the king and people in Jerusalem. How was it to be known whether he or they were right? 'In truth the LORD sent me to you to speak all these words in your ears', said Jeremiah (Jer. 26. 15), but if his hearers refused to accept his assurance, he could only appeal to the out-

come: 'As for the prophet who prophesies peace, when the word
of that prophet comes to pass, then it will be known that the LORD
has truly sent the prophet' (Jer. 28. 9). And in the event Jeremiah
was all too terribly proved to be the true prophet, and the others
to be false prophets.

In Deuteronomy two tests are laid down to determine whether
a prophet is truly a spokesman of God or not: (i) 'if the word does
not come to pass or come true, that is a word which the LORD has
not spoken; the prophet has spoken it presumptuously, you need
not be afraid of him' (Deut. 18. 22); (ii) even if the word which
the prophet speaks comes true, yet if he tries to lead his hearers
astray to serve other gods, he is a false prophet (Deut. 13. 1–5).

The presence of true prophets in the church of New Testament
days stimulated the activity of others who claimed to be prophets
but whose claims were unfounded – or, if they did speak by
inspiration, showed by the content of their utterances that the
spirit that spoke through them was not the Spirit of God. In
either case they were false prophets: men who falsely claimed to
speak by inspiration or men who were inspired by a spirit of
falsehood. To test the prophets then was in effect to test the
spirits by whose impulsion they spoke. John indeed envisages but
two spirits – the Spirit of God and the spirit of Antichrist. In this
he shows a striking affinity with a passage in the Qumran literature
which declares that God 'has appointed for man two spirits in
which to walk until the time of His visitation: the spirits of truth
and falsehood'.[2]

**V. 2 Hereby know ye the Spirit of God: every spirit
which confesseth that Jesus Christ is come in the flesh is of
God: v. 3 and every spirit which [1]confesseth not Jesus is not
of God: and this is the *spirit* of the antichrist, whereof ye have
heard that it cometh; and now it is in the world already.**

[1] Some ancient authorities read *annulleth Jesus*.

A few decades earlier Paul, writing to the Corinthian Christians
on the subject of prophetic utterances, laid down a simple criterion

by which true and false utterances might be distinguished. It was this: what testimony did any such utterance bear to Christ? 'No one speaking by the Spirit of God ever says "Jesus be cursed!" and no one can say "Jesus is Lord" except by the Holy Spirit' (1 Cor. 12. 3). John adopts essentially the same criterion, but rewords it with special reference to the Docetic denial of the Incarnation that was current when he wrote. Test the prophets: ask them if Jesus Christ has come in flesh or not. If they say Yes, then they are to be recognized as speaking by the Spirit of God; if not, then it is not the Spirit of God but the spirit of Antichrist that speaks through them. The words 'every spirit which confesseth not Jesus' could have a wider application than to a denial of His incarnation, although it is evidently this that John has primarily in mind. The variant reading 'annulleth Jesus'[3] may imply the severance of Jesus of Nazareth from the Christ or the Son of God, after the manner of Cerinthus (so R. A. Knox: 'no spirit which would disunite Jesus comes from God'), or it may denote a positive abjuration of His authority, like 'Jesus be cursed!' in 1 Cor. 12. 3. So O. A. Piper argues: 'The phrase *lyei ton Iēsoun*, as its contrast with 1 John 4. 2 and the parallel in 1 Cor. 12. 3 (*anathema Iēsous*) show, signifies a curse, whereby it is believed that Jesus will be deprived of his supernatural power'.[4] Such a denial has already (1 John 2. 18, 22) been branded as a sure sign of Antichrist: the spirit of the great Antichrist of the end-time is already present and operative through these 'many antichrists' who refuse to acknowledge Jesus. No matter how charming, how plausible, how eloquent the prophets in question may be, the test of their witness to Christ and His truth is the test by which they must be judged.

V. 4 Ye are of God, *my* little children, and have overcome them: because greater is he that is in you than he that is in the world.

John's readers were not more learned, more skilled in philosophical debate, than the false teachers; yet by refusing to be persuaded by the false teachers they had overcome them. This they were able to do because of the indwelling Holy Spirit, whose anointing had imparted to them the true knowledge – a 'built-in spiritual instinct', as it was called in the comment on 1 John 2. 20, enabling them to hold fast to truth and reject error. If 'he that is in you' is the Holy Spirit, 'he that is in the world' is the spirit of falsehood, called 'the spirit of antichrist' in verse 3 and 'the spirit of error' in verse 6.[5]

V. 5 They are of the world: therefore speak they *as* of the world, and the world heareth them. v. 6 We are of God: he that knoweth God heareth us; he who is not of God heareth us not. By this we know the spirit of truth, and the spirit of error.

But why should the leaders of the other party, with their followers, be said to be 'of the world'? Because the philosophy to which they endeavour to accommodate the gospel, depriving it of what makes it the gospel in the process, is current secular philosophy, the prevalent climate of opinion. We have already seen that there is no form of 'worldliness' so inimical to Christianity as this kind of 're-statement'. Such a re-statement is congenial to 'the world' because it is in line with contemporary fashion; nevertheless it is doomed to pass away because with a change in fashion it loses its appeal, which the gospel never does. The gospel, like its faithful preachers, is 'of God', and the people of God recognize it as such through the inward witness of the Spirit in their hearts (cf. 5. 7–11). They are thus in no danger of confusing 'the Spirit of truth' with 'the spirit of error', the spirit that leads men astray (cf. 2. 26).

7 WALKING IN LOVE (4. 7–21)
(a) In praise of love (4. 7–12)
Like Paul in 1 Corinthians 13, John in this section has his hymn in praise of heavenly love.

V. 7 Beloved, let us love one another: for love is of God; and every one that loveth is begotten of God, and knoweth

God. v. 8 He that loveth not knoweth not God; for God is love.

The love of which John, like Paul, speaks is self-giving love, not acquisitive love. It is sometimes suggested that the verb *agapaō* and the noun *agapē*, which are used here as so commonly in the New Testament, bear the former sense intrinsically as against *erōs*, which denotes possessive love; this is the implication of the title of Anders Nygren's great work *Agape and Eros*.[6] But it is not a question of the intrinsic sense of the words used (in the Septuagint of 2 Sam. 13. 1–15 both *agapē* and *agapaō* are used of Amnon's passion for Tamar) but of the sense placed on them by speakers or writers. The love which the New Testament enjoins involves a consuming passion for the well-being of others, and this love has its wellspring in God. Since 'love is of God', says John, 'let us love one another'; the children of God must reproduce their Father's nature. Those who show such love to one another give proof in doing so that they are God's children and that it is they (not those who say so much about the true *gnōsis* or knowledge of God without regard for the love of God) who really know Him. Those, on the other hand, from whose lives such love is absent give proof by that fact that they have never begun to know God, however confident their claims may be. To know the God of love means to manifest His love. 'God is love' is as compressed a statement of the gospel as is well imaginable; yet it is no more a reversible statement than is its counterpart in 1 John 1. 5, 'God is light'. 'Love is of God'; love is divine; but one can no more say that 'love is God' than one could say that 'light is God'. 'God is love' is an affirmation about God; while it is a compressed statement of the gospel, it is so in the sense which is spelt out in the following sentence, 'that God sent his only Son into the world, so that we might live through him'. It is this act of God that gives meaning to His love; indeed, it is this act that gives meaning to love absolutely, in the sense which it bears in the Johannine writings and in the New Testament generally.

The gospel gives no countenance to the facile and optimistic assertion that God is love as though, in the light of all the facts of life, this were the easiest of all things to believe. Bishop Gore, who is reported to have called it the hardest of all things to believe ('believe that, and you can believe everything else'), speaks of many

> who certainly have 'the will to believe', but who find the belief that God is love very difficult. The days seem to them far off when it was possible with any plausibility to contrast the 'simple doctrine' that God is love with the 'elaborate and difficult dogmas' of the Church. For they feel that it is only the dogmas that Jesus Christ is God, and His mind God's mind, and that God, the God of nature, really vindicated Him by raising Him from the dead, that do in fact sustain their tottering faith and hope in God.[7]

The Christian affirmation that God is love is not sustained by ignoring the cross, in all its stark obscenity, but by setting it in the forefront of the situation.

V. 9 Herein was the love of God manifested [1]in us, that God hath sent his only begotten Son into the world, that we might live through him. v. 10 Herein is love, not that we loved God, but that he loved us, and sent his Son *to be* the propitiation for our sins.

> [1] Or, *in our case.*

John has already pointed to Christ's laying down His life for His people as the perfect manifestation of love (3. 16). He returns to the sacrifice of Christ again, and presents it from the Father's point of view, in words similar to those of the Gospel (John 3. 16). The supreme act of God's love was His sending 'his only begotten Son into the world'. As in the Gospel, the adjective 'only be-gotten' (*monogenēs*) is used in a sense which combines the ideas of 'only-begotten' and 'well-loved' (like Heb. *yachid* in Gen. 22. 2, which is rendered *agapētos*, 'beloved', in the Septuagint, but *monogenēs* in Josephus, Aquila and Heb. 11. 17).[8] The purpose of His thus sending His Son is our blessing – 'that we should receive life through him', for thus the ingressive force of the aorist *zēsōmen* may be expressed. Here the initiative lies entirely with God; before there was any possibility of our exercising such love

He first manifested it when He 'loved us and sent his Son as a propitiation for our sins'. These last words are repeated from 2. 2, wherein the meaning of 'propitiation' (*hilasmos*) has been discussed.[9]

V. 11 **Beloved, if God so loved us, we also ought to love one another. v. 12 No man hath beheld God at any time: if we love one another, God abideth in us, and his love is perfected in us:**

God's love for us, then, supplies the motive power for His people's love for one another. The adverb 'so' (Gr. *houtōs*) has the emphatic force here that it has at the beginning of John 3. 16. 'We also ought to love one another', because we are His children. If the children of God must be holy because He is holy (Lev. 11. 44 f.; 1 Pet. 1. 15 f.) and merciful because He is merciful (Luke 6. 36), so they must be loving because He is loving – not with the 'must' of external compulsion but with the 'must' of inward constraint: God's love is poured into their hearts by the Holy Spirit whom they have received (Rom. 5. 5). They are, in fact, the witnesses on earth to God's love. 'No one has ever beheld God', but He may be seen in His children when they love one another. John has already made this statement (except for the variant 'seen', *heōraken*, instead of 'beheld', *tetheatai*) in the prologue to his Gospel, but there the invisible God has been made known on earth by His Son (John 1. 18). Now that the Son has returned to the Father, God is made known on earth by those who through faith in His Son have become His children – if they love one another. The love of God displayed in His people is the strongest apologetic that God has in the world. When His love is planted in their hearts, and He Himself thus dwells within them, His love is 'perfected' in the complementary response which it finds in them, towards Him and towards their fellows. It is in this way that they are not only holy and merciful as He is holy and merciful, but, as enjoined by their Lord in the Matthaean version of the Sermon on the Mount, 'perfect' as their 'heavenly Father is perfect' (Matt. 5. 48), and all through that

perfection of love poured out for them in the sacrifice of the cross.
'The only kind of personal union . . . with which we are acquainted',
says C. H. Dodd, 'is love'. John, he continues:

> makes use of the strongest expressions for union with God that con-
> temporary religious language provided, in order to assure his readers
> that he does seriously mean what he says: that through faith in
> Christ we may enter into a personal community of life with the
> eternal God, which has the character of *agapē*, which is essentially
> supernatural and not of this world, and yet plants its feet firmly in
> this world, not only because real *agapē* cannot but express itself in
> practical conduct, but also because the crucial act of *agapē* was
> actually performed in history, on an April day about AD 30, at a
> supper-table in Jerusalem, in a garden across the Kidron valley, in the
> headquarters of Pontius Pilate, and on a Roman cross at Golgotha.
> So concrete, so actual, is the nature of the divine *agapē*; yet none the
> less for that, by entering into the relation of *agapē* thus opened up for
> men, we may dwell in God and He in us.[10]

(b) *Perfect love and sound doctrine* (4. 13–21)

**V. 13   hereby know we that we abide in him, and he in
us, because he hath given us of his Spirit. v. 14 And we have
beheld and bear witness that the Father hath sent the Son
to be the Saviour of the world.**

Not only is God's love poured into His children's hearts through
the Holy Spirit; an appreciation of God's truth has been imparted
to them by the same Spirit. The Spirit of love is the Spirit of truth.
The Spirit persuades and enables us to believe in Jesus as the Son
of God; He communicates to us the new life which is ours as
members of God's regenerate family; it is through Him that we
remain in union with the ever-living Christ and He with us; it is
through His inward witness that we receive the power to bear our
witness in turn. Thus our Lord's promise in the upper room is
fulfilled: 'when the Counsellor comes, whom I shall send to you
from the Father, even the Spirit of truth, who proceeds from the
Father, he will bear witness to me; and you also are witnesses,
because you have been with me from the beginning' (John 15. 26,
27). While these words were primarily applicable to His com-

panions in His earthly ministry, they have become applicable to
later generations of disciples also who have heard the testimony of
the eyewitnesses and having thus had fellowship with them have
fellowship also with the Father and with His Son Jesus Christ
(1 John 1. 3). The substance of the witness of the Spirit and of
those whom He indwells is this: 'the Father has sent the Son as
Saviour of the world'. Here is another summary of the gospel,
expressed this time not in the form of a permanently valid proposition, like 'God is love', but in the form of a historical statement
in the light of which the validity of the proposition is seen. The
designation 'the Saviour of the world' is peculiar to the Johannine
writings in the New Testament; in addition to its single occurrence
in the First Epistle it occurs once in the Gospel (John 4. 42), on the
lips (significantly enough) of Samaritans, who had no interest in
promises which were attached to the tribe of Judah but great
interest in promises which spoke of a world-wide salvation. As
earlier, where he speaks of Christ as 'the propitiation . . . for all the
world' (1 John 2. 2), so here John ascribes the widest scope to the
saving purpose of God. The pronoun 'we' in 'we have beheld' is
emphatic;[11] John may be thinking in the first instance of himself
and his original associates, who delivered to others the testimony of
what they had 'beheld' (cf. 1 John 1. 1) so that others in turn might
bear the same testimony; but in the light of verse 16, where the
similarly emphatic 'we' can scarcely have this force, he more
probably thinks of himself and his readers, by contrast with those
who had left the fellowship, thus renouncing the bond of love and
the witness of the Spirit. This appears to be confirmed by the words
which immediately follow.

**V. 15 Whosoever shall confess that Jesus is the Son of
God, God abideth in him, and he in God.**

John has just said that if we love one another, God abides in us
(verse 12); now he says that God abides in us if we 'confess that
Jesus is the Son of God'. He seems to be conscious of no tension
at all between Christian love and Christian truth. The love of God

was manifested in the giving up of His Son; if Jesus is not the Son of God and if His death does not atone for the sins of men, then there is no Christian message and Christian love and truth fall together, as they stand together if that message is true. If none can acknowledge Jesus as the Son of God apart from the enlightenment and empowering of the Spirit, it is equally true that the mutual coinherence of God and His children is the Spirit's work, as is also the outflowing of the love of God through them to others. Mutual indwelling, perfect love and confession of the truth are bound up in one another; God has joined them together and they may not be put asunder.

V. 16 And we know and have believed the love which God hath ¹in us. God is love; and he that abideth in love abideth in God, and God abideth in him.

¹ Or, *in our case.*

What is here being said about love is no matter of mere theory; it is something which is proved in experience and faith. In speaking of 'the love which God has in us'¹² John may mean more than His love *for* us; that is included, indeed, but the love which God has for His children is poured into their hearts by His Spirit and flows out to others. The love which dwells in the community of God's children and which they show one to another is His love imparted to them. More than that: the God of love imparts Himself to His people, so dwelling within them that they, in their turn, dwell in His love and dwell in Him (cf. verse 12).

V. 17 Herein is love made perfect with us, that we may have boldness in the day of judgement; because as he is, even so are we in this world. v. 18 There is no fear in love: but perfect love casteth out fear, because fear hath punishment; and he that feareth is not made perfect in love.

The perfection of love, John has already said (verse 12), is realized when God dwells in His children and they love another. This perfection of love, he adds here, is specially manifested in the confidence with which they will face the day of judgment.[13] This is the advent day of 2. 28, where those who dwell in God are assured that they will have no need to shrink from His presence with shame on that great day. Christian confidence and Christian love go together; they find their antithesis in shame and fear. A sense of awe in face of the majesty and righteousness of God is proper; anything in the nature of unnerving fear at the coming of Him whose name is love denies the love 'which God has in us'. Here we have the last occurrence of the phrase *kathōs ekeinos*, 'as He', in reference to the risen Christ: 'as he is, so even are we in this world'. It was this revelation that replaced fear by confidence in John Bunyan's heart when the words of Rom. 3. 24, 'justified freely by his grace, through the redemption that is in Christ Jesus', were expounded to him thus as though by a voice from heaven:

> Sinner, thou thinkest that because of thy sins and infirmities I cannot save thy soul, but behold my Son is by me, and upon him I look, and not on thee, and will deal with thee according as I am pleased with him.[14]

The day of judgment need have no terror for anyone who has appropriated the assurance of John 5. 24: 'he who hears my word and believes him who sent me, has eternal life; he does not come into judgment, but has passed from death to life'. Nor can it have terror for anyone who knows himself united in faith and love to the Son of Man to whom all judgment has been entrusted by the Father (John 5. 22, 27). All such terror is banished by the 'perfect love' in which the members of God's family live. 'Fear has to do with punishment' (RSV),[15] but 'punishment' (*kolasis*) is the portion of those who through disobedience are 'condemned already', not of those who, believing in the Son of God, are 'not condemned' (John 3. 18). A believer who contemplates the judgment day with trepidation, says John, is one in whom divine love has not yet reached its full maturity, and one therefore who himself has not yet reached full spiritual maturity. Charles Wesley was right when he defined entire sanctification in terms of

> A heart in every thought renewed
> And full of love divine.

V. 19 We love, because he first loved us. v. 20 If a man say, I love God, and hateth his brother, he is a liar: for he that loveth not his brother whom he hath seen, ¹cannot love God whom he hath not seen. v. 21 And this commandment have we from him, that he who loveth God love his brother also.

¹ Many ancient authorities read *how can he love God whom he hath not seen?*

AV, following the Received Text, reads 'we love him' in verse 19, but the textual evidence makes it clear that 'him' is a later addition by scribes or editors who felt that an explicit object was necessary. (A few other scribes or editors from the same motive added 'God' as the object.) But in the context 'we love' is the more suitable reading as it is the better attested one. We love God, it is true, but in loving Him we inevitably love His children. In taking the initiative in loving us, He not only showed us how to love one another (cf. 3. 11) but He imparted the desire and the power to follow this example of His. Our Lord made it plain that the two great Old Testament commandments of love to God and love to one's neighbour are two sides of one coin (Mark 12. 29–31; cf. Luke 10. 27 f.), and when He said to His disciples in the upper room, 'If you love me, you will keep my commandments' (John 14. 15), He laid down as His new and chief commandment that they should love one another as He loved them, so that everyone would know that they were truly His disciples (John 13. 34 f.). Similarly in this letter John has already emphasized that brotherly love characterizes the children of God; to hate one's brother is to proclaim one's kinship with Cain (3. 10–18). Here the same lesson is emphasized afresh; once more the test of love is applied. Where God's love or our love for God is mentioned, John makes no distinction between the Father and the Son; alike in loving men and in being loved by them in return the Son and the Father are one (cf. John 10. 30). Peter speaks of Christ as the One 'whom, not having seen', His people love (1 Pet. 1. 8); John agrees, but adds that love for the unseen One will be attested by love for His people whom we do see. Much verbal expression of devotion for the person of Christ can co-exist with remarkably un-Christian attitudes towards the people of Christ; John's comment on this inconsistency is sharp and undisguised. In this he is at one with his Master, who declared that in the judgment behaviour towards His brethren will be counted as behaviour towards Himself (Matt. 25. 31–46). Those whose lives are marked by lack of love in this regard may well have a sense of trepidation as they look forward to the day of review.

NOTES

1. Cf. Jer. 23. 18, 22, where the false prophets of Jeremiah's day have no authentic message to deliver because none of them 'has stood in the council of the LORD'; if they had, says God, 'then they would have proclaimed my words to my people, and they would have turned them from their evil way'.
2. *Rule of the Community* 3. 18 f. These two spirits are otherwise called the Prince of Light and the Angel of Darkness (see note on 1 John 1. 5, p. 41).
3. This variant appears in the margin of the important codex 1739, was known to Irenaeus, Clement of Alexandria and Origen, and is attested by the Latin version.
4. 'I John and the Didache of the Primitive Church', *JBL* 66 (1947), pp. 443 f.
5. Cf. Eph. 2. 2: 'the spirit that is now at work in the sons of disobedience'.
6. Translated from Swedish (London, 1932–39).
7. C. Gore, *Belief in God* (Penguin edition, 1939), p. 150.
8. W. Bauer, W. F. Arndt and F. W. Gingrich, *Greek-English Lexicon of the NT* . . . (Cambridge, 1957), mention the further possible meaning 'begotten of the Only One' (*s.v. μονογενής*).
9. See p. 50.
10. C. H. Dodd, *The Interpretation of the Fourth Gospel* (Cambridge, 1953), pp. 199 f.
11. Gr. *hēmeis*, as in 3. 14, 16; 4. 6, 10, 11, 16, 17, 19 (inclusive), and 1. 4 (exclusive).
12. Gr. *en hēmin*, as in verse 9. Cf. the use of *en* in Acts 4. 2; Gal. 1. 16.
13. The RSV rendering 'confidence for the day of judgment' is scarcely adequate; the confidence is maintained when the day of judgment arrives – 'confidence on the day of judgement' (NEB).
14. *Grace Abounding*, §§ 257, 258.
15. Cf. NEB: 'fear brings with it the pains of judgement'. A verbal parallel to this clause is provided by Philo where, speaking of the effects of shame and fear in one who has broken the eighth commandment, he says: 'Fear is a sign that he considers himself worthy of punishment (*kolasis*), because it is punishments (*kolaseis*) that (in prospect) instil fear' (*Special Laws* iv. 6).

CHAPTER V

8   THE VICTORY OF FAITH (5. 1–5)

**V. 1   Whosoever believeth that Jesus is the Christ is be-
gotten of God: and whosoever loveth him that begat loveth
him also that is begotten of him.**

To love the Father (whom we have not seen) involves loving
His child (whom we can see): thus John sums up what has just
been said. And who is the child of God? Any one who believes that
Jesus is the Christ. In the Johannine writings this means more
than assenting to the proposition that Jesus is the promised
Messiah; it means personal faith in Him, personal union with Him,
who has been revealed 'in the flesh' (4. 2) as the Christ and Son of
God. In the Gospel it is to all who received the living Word, to
all 'who believed in his name', that God 'gave power to become
children of God' (John 1. 12); the Gospel in fact was written in
order that its readers might 'believe that Jesus is the Christ, the
Son of God' and thus 'have life in his name' (John 20. 31).

**V. 2   Hereby we know that we love the children of God,
when we love God, and do his commandments.** v. 3 **For this
is the love of God, that we keep his commandments:**

Love to God and love to His children, love to God and obedience
to God, are so completely involved in each other that any one of
them implies the other two. A man may say he loves God, but his
love to God can become manifest to himself and to others only in
so far as he obeys God's commandments and shows practical love
to God's children. It is easier to deceive ourselves in these matters
than it is to deceive others. If we tell them that 'we love God', they
will look for some visible evidence; we should look for some visible
evidence ourselves. If the visible evidence is forthcoming, it will
not be necessary to say that 'we love God'; the evidence will say so

more convincingly. Keeping the commandments of God includes first and foremost keeping the primary commandment of love. 'If love to men proves the truth of our love to God, love to God proves the worth of our love to men'.[1] There is indeed much genuine and practical philanthropy in the world which rests on a humanist basis; John insists that love to man finds its strongest and most enduring motive in love to God in whose image man was made and by whose grace man was redeemed. Again, the test of love and the test of obedience are seen to be not two tests, but one.

V. 3b and his commandments are not grievous. v. 4 For whatsoever is begotten of God overcometh the world: and this is the victory that hath overcome the world, *even* **our faith. v. 5 And who is he that overcometh the world, but he that believeth that Jesus is the Son of God?**

The punctuation of the clause 'and his commandments are not grievous' (RSV, NEB 'burdensome') is doubtful; it may go more closely with the foregoing or with the following words. The argument for taking them with the following words is that the following words explain why the commandments of God are not burdensome: it is because the new life imparted to members of the family of God carries with it a new desire to do His will and a new power to give effect to that desire. Not only so, this new power enables them to 'overcome the world' – everything that is opposed to God. This may be the world of current thought inimical to the 'teaching of Christ' which was communicated 'from the beginning'; it may be the world with its attractiveness and pretentiousness against which the readers of this letter are put on their guard in 2. 15–17; it may be the world in open hostility, meting out to the disciples of Christ the same kind of treatment as was meted out to their Master. In the Gospel, Jesus' last word to His disciples before His passion is, 'In the world you have tribulation; but be of good cheer, I have overcome the world' (John 16. 33). By their faith in Jesus as the Son of God[2] they are so united with Him that His victory becomes theirs; they conquer by His power. So John has already encouraged his readers: 'You are of God, little children, and you have overcome them, because he who is in you is greater than he who is in the world' (4. 4). In the Revelation, too, every kind of incentive is held out to the hard-pressed disciples to maintain their faith and so prove themselves 'overcomers'. When 'the deceiver of the whole world' launches his final and deadliest attack against them, they win the victory over him with the same weapons as their Master used: 'they have conquered him by the blood of the Lamb and by the word of their testimony, for they loved not their lives even unto death' (Rev. 12. 11). This victory over the world and every other hostile force was common Christian experience in the apostolic age: with the language of the Johannine writings we may compare Paul's assurance that 'in all these things we are more than conquerors through him who loved us' (Rom. 8. 37) and his thanksgiving to God 'who gives us the victory through our Lord Jesus Christ' (1 Cor. 15. 57).

9   THE GROUND OF ASSURANCE (5. 6–12)

V. 6   This is he that came by water and blood, even Jesus Christ; not ¹with the water only, but ¹with the water and ¹with the blood.

¹ Gr. *in.*

We are naturally reminded of the incident in the passion narrative of the Gospel of John, in which blood and water come out from our Lord's side after His dead body is pierced with the soldier's lance (John 19. 34).[3] In the narrative much importance is clearly attached to this phenomenon, emphatically supported as it is by trustworthy eyewitness testimony (John 19. 35): whatever else it may signify, it does (in the Evangelist's intention) signify our Lord's real humanity. Something of the same significance is present here, though the details are to be interpreted rather differently. The sequence 'water and blood' is not accidental, but corresponds to the historical sequence of our Lord's baptism and passion.[4] Cerinthus, we recall, taught that 'the Christ' (a spiritual being) came down on the man Jesus when He was baptized but left Him before He died. The Christ, that is to say, came through *water* (baptism) but not through *blood* (death).[5] To this misrepresentation of the truth John replies that the One whom believers acknowledge to be the Son of God (verse 5) came 'not with the water only but with the water and with the blood': the One who died on the cross was as truly the Christ, the Son of God, as the One who was baptized in Jordan. This is the primary force of John's words; if there is any substance in the sacramental significance which has been discerned in them (mentioned in the note on verse 8), it is at best secondary.[6]

V. 7 And it is the Spirit that beareth witness, because the Spirit is the truth.

John and his associates bear witness to the truth of what they have seen and heard (1. 2; 4. 14), but behind their witness lies the witness of the Spirit (cf. 3. 24; 4. 13). This is completely in line with the promise of our Lord in the Gospel: 'when the Counsellor comes, . . . the Spirit of truth, . . . he will bear witness to me; and you also are witnesses, because you have been with me from the beginning' (John 15. 26 f.). The fulfilment of this promise was realized early in apostolic history: 'we are witnesses to these things', said the apostles to the Sanhedrin when challenged for proclaiming the crucified and risen Jesus; 'and so is the Holy Spirit whom God has given to those who obey him' (Acts 5. 32). The Spirit witnesses in the believer's heart and in the believing community; their experience of His power and guidance confirms the truth of the gospel to which they have committed themselves. To this 'inward witness' must be added the 'outward witness' of the Spirit in Holy Scripture; while this aspect of the Spirit's witness does not come to the fore in this epistle, it is prominent in most of the New Testament documents: the Spirit who spoke through the prophets bore witness by their written words, interpreted in the light of their fulfilment in Christ, to the truth of the message which the apostles proclaimed.[7] Whatever form the witness of the Spirit takes, it can be implicitly trusted, for 'the Spirit of truth', as He is repeatedly called in the upper room discourse in the Gospel (John 14. 17; 15. 26; 16. 13), is Himself 'the truth'.[8]

V. 8   For there are three who bear witness, the Spirit, and the water, and the blood: and the three agree in one.

It is in the community who hold fast to what they were taught from the beginning, those who believe in Him who came by water and blood, that the Spirit is present to 'bear witness';[9] those who deny the truth conveyed by 'the water and the blood' cannot lay claim to the Spirit who bears witness by means of these. The Spirit's ministry in the world includes as one of its principal elements the bearing of witness to Christ; this He did as early as the baptism, when He descended like a dove and remained on Him (John 1. 32 f.). The Baptist saw and accepted this witness of the Spirit, and thereafter he himself bore witness 'that this is the Son of God' (John 1. 34). Again, when the death of Jesus was certified by means of the soldier's lance-thrust instead of the breaking of His legs, the witness of the Spirit of prophecy was doubly confirmed, as the Evangelist is at pains to underline (John 19. 36 f.), while true witness was further borne by one 'who saw it' (John 19. 35). The witness of the 'water' and the witness of the 'blood' are thus aspects of the Spirit's witness. The witness which all three bear is 'one' and the same:

> His Spirit answers to the blood,
> And tells me I am born of God.

Another account of 'the Spirit and the water and the blood' interprets them in terms of three stages of Christian initiation in certain areas of the early church – (*a*) the reception of the Spirit (with or without the laying on of hands); (*b*) baptism; (*c*) first communion. This sequence is attested for Syria, by contrast with the Christian West. This interpretation has been worked out in particular by Wolfgang Nauck,[10] who finds affinities between this primitive Christian order and the practice of certain Jewish communities, especially the procedure for admission to the covenant-community of Qumran and the procedure reflected by the treatise

Joseph and Aseneth[11] and the *Testament of Levi*.[12] That the mention of 'blood' alone without a companion mention of the body should denote the Eucharist is unlikely, and the context of John's argument implies a historical rather than a sacramental interpretation. The most that can be said is that Christian communities which observed this particular order of initiation (cf. Acts 10. 44 ff. for an apostolic precedent) may have appealed to the sequence of the three witnesses in our present text. There could be an allusion to the witness which the Spirit bears to and through believers as they identify themselves with Christ in baptism and declare their 'interest in the Saviour's blood' in communion, but any such allusion would be secondary to the main thrust of the psssage.

V. 9 If we receive the witness of men, the witness of God is greater: for the witness of God is this, that he hath borne witness concerning his Son. v. 10 He that believeth on the Son of God hath the witness in him: he that believeth not God hath made him a liar; because he hath not believed in the witness that God hath borne concerning his Son.

The witness of the Spirit and the witness of the Father are one: at our Lord's baptism, for example, the Spirit's descent and the Father's voice alike proclaimed Jesus to be the Son of God. This witness that God has 'borne concerning his Son' is amplified in the gospel narratives – we may recall that the Gospels of Mark and John alike, in their respective ways, are concerned to produce within their readers the conviction that Jesus is the Son of God (compare Mark 1. 1; 15. 39 with John 20. 31). Whoever, by accepting 'the witness of God', believes in the Son of God,[13] has the witness in himself:[14] the record is no longer simply something that he has heard from others, or reads in a book; it comes to life in his own experience, because the witness-bearing Spirit now resides within him. On the other hand, refusal to accept 'the witness of God' is tantamount to calling Him a liar (cf. 1. 10). So clearcut is the antithesis which John sees between belief and unbelief.

**V. 11 And the witness is this, that God gave unto us
eternal life, and this life is in his Son. v. 12 He that hath the
Son hath the life; he that hath not the Son of God hath not the
life.**

'Eternal life' (Gr. *zōē aiōnios*) means in the first instance 'the
life of the age to come', the life of the resurrection age. As such, it
is something to be experienced in the future. But in Jesus the
powers of the age to come have manifested themselves already; He
proclaims Himself to be 'the resurrection and the life' in such a
way that those who are united by faith to Him enjoy eternal life
here and now, whereas those who reject Him are 'condemned
already' without waiting for the sentence of the great day (compare
John 11. 25 f. with 3. 18). The Son of God who died and rose
again is the embodiment of 'the eternal life which was with the
Father and was made manifest to us' (1. 2), so that to have 'the
Son' is to have 'the life' and failure to have Him means forfeiture of
'the life'. Very much the same statement is made in the Gospel (cf.
especially John 3. 36); here probably John has in mind more particularly those false teachers, who, by denying that Jesus Christ
had come in the flesh (cf. 4. 2), showed that they had not 'the Son
of God' in the sense in which the apostolic message had proclaimed Him 'from the beginning', and showed by the same token
that they were outside the pale of eternal life.

10 Epilogue (5. 13–21)

**V. 13 These things have I written unto you, that ye may
know that ye have eternal life, *even* unto you that believe on
the name of the Son of God.**

Towards the end of the Gospel of John its readers are told that
the 'signs' recorded in it 'are written that you may believe[15] that
Jesus is the Christ, the Son of God, and that believing you may
have life in his name' (John 20. 31). The First Letter is written to
those, who do 'believe in[16] the name of the Son of God' to assure
them that it is they who, in virtue of this belief, possess eternal life.

The question where eternal life was to be found, as has been said above, had probably been the subject of animated debate, the seceders claiming that it was to be found in their circle by reason of the higher teaching which they had embraced. But John affirms that the seceders, by denying the incarnation of the Son of God, did not truly believe in His person (which is what is meant by 'the name' in such contexts as the present) and so had no claim on the eternal life which was to be had in Him alone. While this contemporary situation may have been uppermost in John's mind, however, his affirmation has a wider reference; because of its abiding validity it has remained a classic and effective text conveying the assurance of eternal life in all generations to those who believe in the name of the Son of God.

V. 14 And this is the boldness which we have toward him, that, if we ask anything according to his will, he heareth us: v. 15 and if we know that he heareth us whatsoever we ask, we know that we have the petitions which we have asked of him.

This is the fourth occurrence of 'boldness' or confidence (Gr. *parrhēsia*) in 1 John (cf. 2. 28; 3. 21; 4. 17 for the other occurrences). Here the confidence which is particularly in the writer's mind is related to the free access and freedom of speech which the children of God enjoy as they come to their Father to present their requests to Him. There is a close relation between these words and the promise of Jesus to the disciples in the upper room: 'Whatever you ask in my name, I will do it, that the Father may be glorified in the Son; if you ask anything in my name, I will do it' (John 14. 13 f.; cf. 15. 7, 16; 16. 23 f.). If in the Gospel and the Epistle alike it is not always clear whether the request is made to the Father or to the Son, this is because of the perfect unity subsisting between the Father and the Son. It is through the Son that the children approach the Father; it is in the Son that the Father's grace is conveyed to the children. With this confidence, the children know that the Father's hearing of their prayers is synonymous with His answering their prayers. 'Constantly', said C. H. Spurgeon, 'we

hear God addressed as "the hearer *and answerer* of prayer", a mere
vulgar and useless pleonasm, for the Scripture idea of God's
hearing prayer is just his answering it – "O thou that hearest
prayer, unto thee shall all flesh come".'[17]

**V. 16 If any man see his brother sinning a sin not unto
death, [1]he shall ask, and *God* will give him life for them that
sin not unto death. There is [2]a sin unto death: not concerning this do I say that he should make request. v. 17 All unrighteousness is sin: and there is [2]a sin not unto death.**

> [1] Or, *he shall ask and shall give him life,* even *to them &c.*   [2] Or, *sin.*

After the general assurance about the answering of prayer in
verses 14 and 15 comes this special encouragement to pray for a
fellow-Christian in spiritual need. The present participle 'sinning'
may denote engagement in a sinful course rather than committing
an isolated act of sin; we cannot be sure, and in the one case as in
the other the 'brother' could well be regarded as standing in the
need of prayer. The question arises what the distinction is between
'sin unto death' and sin which is 'not unto death' (since 'not'
represents the Greek negative *mē,* it is implied that the reference is
to the kind or class of sin which is 'not unto death'). We should not
think of the distinction between venial and mortal sin as this has
been traditionally elaborated in moral theology.[18] The distinction
is one which John's readers were expected to recognize. But it is
difficult to see how they could recognize the distinction except by
the result. Elsewhere in the New Testament instances occur of
sins which caused the death of the persons committing them, when
these persons were church members. Ananias and Sapphira come
to mind (Acts 5. 1–11); the incestuous man at Corinth is possibly
another example, if he suffered 'the destruction of the flesh' in the
literal sense (1. Cor. 5. 5), and those other Corinthian Christians
who are said to have 'fallen asleep' because of their profanation of
the Lord's Supper (1 Cor. 11. 30) certainly provide further examples. It may be, then, that by 'sin unto death' John means an
act or course of sin which has resulted in the death of the sinning

brother. If so, his words 'I do not say that one is to pray for that'[19] (RSV) amount to a deprecation of praying for the dead. Another possibility is that he has apostasy in mind.[20] In that case, he does not encourage prayer for the restoration of those who, like the false teachers of 2. 18–23, had manifested the spirit of Antichrist and shown where they properly belonged by quitting the fellowship in which alone eternal life was to be found. With regard to such men John may have felt much as the writer to the Hebrews did in another situation, that it was 'impossible to renew them to repentance';[21] renunciation of the apostolic witness to Christ and His saving power was indeed a 'sin unto death'.

Apart from such an exceptional case (whichever form it took), John gives his readers every encouragement to pray for their fellow-believers whom they see falling into sin. Such prayer is in line with the ministry of their Advocate with the Father. Foreseeing the certainty of Peter's fall, their Lord on the eve of His passion assured that self-confident apostle of His intercession: 'I have prayed for you that your faith may not fail; and when you have turned again, strengthen your brethren' (Luke 22. 32); this too was an example of a service which His disciples could perform for one another, with similar happy effects in those who were thus prayed for. 'All unrighteousness (RSV, NEB: 'all wrongdoing') is sin', but not every unrighteous act is irremediably mortal, if it be repented of; and the intercession of a fellow-Christian may be a most effective means of inducing repentance and reliance on the promise given earlier in this letter: 'If we confess our sins, he is faithful and righteous to forgive us our sins and cleanse us from all unrighteousness' (1 John 1. 9).

V. 18 **We know that whosoever is begotten of God sinneth not; but he that was begotten of God keepeth** [1]**him, and the evil one toucheth him not.** v. 19 **We know that we are of God, and the whole world lieth in the evil one.** v. 20 **And we know that the Son of God is come, and hath given us an understanding, that we know him that is true,**

[1] Or, *himself*.

As he draws his exhortation to a conclusion, John reminds his readers of some of the basic articles of the faith which they have held 'from the beginning'. He has already told them that their knowledge derives from the anointing they have received from 'the Holy One' (2. 20); now he mentions some of the most important things that they 'know'. It is significant that the first of these underlines the ethical implication of their faith: the child of God does not sin. Earlier in the letter John has said that the child of God does not sin because he abides in God (3. 6, 9); there we saw that he wants to make it quite clear that anyone who leads a life of sin is shown thereby not to belong to the family of God. Here the reason the child of God does not sin is expressed in different terms; it is because the Son of God keeps him, protecting him against the designs of the enemy of souls. The adjective clause 'whosoever is begotten of God' represents a Greek construction with the perfect participle passive *gegennēmenos*, and refers to every child of God; the expression 'he that was begotten of God' represents the construction with the aorist participle passive *gennētheis*, and denotes the one and only Son of God, as RSV indicates by (exceptionally) capitalizing the antecedent pronoun 'He'. (NEB makes the meaning equally clear by rendering more freely, 'We know that no child of God is a sinner; it is the Son of God who keeps him safe, and the evil one cannot touch him'.[22]) The Received Text obscures the sense by reading 'himself' (Gr. *heauton* or *hauton*) after 'keepeth' instead of 'him' (*auton*); hence the misleading rendering of AV, 'he that is begotten of God keepeth himself', as though the subject of 'keepeth' were the child of God (as at the beginning of the verse) and not (as in fact it is) the Son of God.

The second thing that 'we know' is more personal: 'we know that we are of God'; and the basis of this knowledge can only be that the tests of eternal life have been applied and the results have been positive. To claim to belong to the family of God is one thing; to exhibit the marks of His family, in the light of the criteria of obedience, love and perseverance, is another thing. In the case of John and his 'little children', these criteria have been satisfied. As for those not included in the family of God, they belong to the

godless 'world' (in the sense of 2. 15–17; 3. 1), which lies in the
grip of 'the evil one', called in the Gospel 'the ruler of this world'
(John 14. 30). As this ruler, on Jesus' own testimony, has no
authority over Him, so he has none over those who by faith share
in Jesus' victory over the world. But those who are still dominated
by the standards of the world organized without reference to God
are enslaved by its ruler and cannot share in the victory which has
overcome him. This passing world order and its ruler are on their
way out, to be superseded by the eternal order and *its* Ruler; the
subjects of the latter will abide for ever (cf. 2. 17).

In the world which God created man has been made in his
Creator's image to represent Him to the rest of the created world.
But man has abdicated his dominion over the world as God's
representative in favour of a dominion which he imagines is
autonomous, but which in fact has let in the powers of evil and
anarchy. Nevertheless the created world, as distinct from the
transient world order, remains God's world, and through the Son
whom the Father sent as Saviour of the world (4. 14) man's
rightful dominion under God is to be re-established and the
usurpation of 'the evil one' brought to an end.[23]

The third thing that 'we know' is that 'the Son of God has
come' – 'come in flesh', that is to say (4. 2), come moreover
'through water and blood' (5. 6) – and has given us spiritual intelligence, a faculty of perception or apprehension (Gr. *dianoia*)
which far surpasses the 'knowledge' cultivated by the Gnostic
seceders, for through it we come to the personal knowledge not
only of truth in the abstract (2. 21) but of 'the True One' Himself.
Whether, as 'fathers', they know Him as the One who is 'from the
beginning' or, as 'children', know Him as 'the Father' (2. 13 f.), it
is through the Son of God that they have acquired this knowledge:
He has made known the God whom no one has ever seen (John 1.
18).

V. 20b   **and we are in him that is true,** *even* **in his Son Jesus
Christ. This is the true God, and eternal life.** v. 21 *My* **little
children, guard yourselves from idols.**

Not only has the Son of God made the true God known; through faith-union with Him His people have their being in 'the True One'. To abide in the Father and to abide in the Son are two ways of stating the one experience: 'if what you heard from the beginning abides in you', John has already told them, 'then you will abide in the Son and in the Father' (2. 24). It may be that the seceders claimed a special part in the Father, but since they denied the Son His true status, their claim was disallowed, for it is only through the Son that men and women may dwell in God, just as it is only through the Son that God is pleased to dwell in men. 'If a man loves me', says Jesus in the Fourth Gospel, 'he will keep my word, and my Father will love him, and we will come to him and make our home (monē, cognate with menō, 'abide') with him' (John 14. 23). John, in closing, takes up the theme of his opening paragraph, where he assured his readers that the fellowship which he shared with them was fellowship 'with the Father and with his Son Jesus Christ'. As in the prologue to the letter Jesus Christ is described as 'the Eternal Life which was the Father and was made manifest to us', so here He is characterized as 'the true God and eternal life'. So fully is the Father expressed in His Son that what is predicated of the former can be predicated of the latter: 'what God was, the Word was' (John 1. 1, NEB). Our Lord is rightly acclaimed as 'true God of true God'; as C. K. Barrett says in commenting on the first verse of the Gospel of John: 'The deeds and words of Jesus are the deeds and words of God; if this be not true the book is blasphemous'.[24] Since, then, it is only in the true God and in His Son Jesus Christ that eternal life resides, it is urgently necessary to distinguish truth from error. The 'idols' or false appearances (Gr. eidōla) against which John warns his readers to be on their guard are not material images; they are false conceptions of God.[25] Any conception of Him that is at variance with His self-revelation in Christ is an idol. Hence, says John, since you have received the truth, have nothing to do with counterfeits; beware of imitations and refuse all substitutes.[26]

NOTE ON THE 'THREE HEAVENLY WITNESSES'

The sentence which appears in the AV as 1 John 5. 7 ('For there are three that bear record in heaven, the Father, the Word, and the Holy Ghost; and these three are one') is no part of the original text of the letter. It appears in a treatise written by Priscillian (a Spanish Christian executed on a charge of heresy in AD 385) or by one of his followers.[27] It may have originated as a comment on the authentic passage about the three witnesses (1 John 5. 8); at any rate in the course of the fifth century it was incorporated from the margin into the text of an Old Latin (pre-Vulgate) manuscript. It was not incorporated into the text of the Vulgate until about AD 800, but once incorporated it remained there securely, and the balancing words 'in earth' were added in the following sentence. When Erasmus published his first printed edition of the Greek New Testament (1516) he was attacked for omitting the 'three heavenly witnesses', but he replied reasonably enough that he found them in no Greek manuscript. Rather incautiously he added that, if a Greek manuscript could be produced which contained the passage, he would include it. In due course such a Greek manuscript was produced – by no means an ancient one, for it was written about 1520! Erasmus knew that this was no evidence at all – the passage had plainly been translated into Greek from the Latin Vulgate by the writer of this manuscript – but he had given his promise, and he was a man of peace, so in his next edition (the third edition, 1522) he included it, adding a footnote in which he complained that the manuscript had been written with the express purpose of putting him on the spot. From Erasmus's third edition the passage was translated into German (by Luther) and into English (by Tyndale); it was taken over into other early printed editions of the Greek New Testament, and hence appears in the 'Received Text' and in the Authorized Version.

The Greek manuscript which was produced for the discomfiture of Erasmus is now in the library of Trinity College, Dublin.[28] Today we know of three other Greek manuscripts which contain the passage: one of the fifteenth century,[29] one of the sixteenth,[30] and another in which it is added in a seventeenth-century hand in the margin of a twelfth-century manuscript.[31]

The official Sixto-Clementine edition of the Vulgate published in 1592 contained the passage, and therefore its authenticity was for long accepted *de rigueur* in the Roman Catholic Church. In 1897 the Holy Office issued a ruling, confirmed by Pope Leo XIII, that the genuineness of the passage could not be safely denied. The American 'Confraternity Edition' of the English New Testament (a revision of the Rheims-Challoner version), published in 1941, included it;[32] a footnote points out that 'according to the evidence of many manuscripts, and the majority of commentators', it does not belong to the true text, but adds: 'The Holy See reserves to itself the right to pass finally on the origin of the present reading' (i.e. the reading which preserves the reference to the three heavenly witnesses). As late as 1945, it was included in the translation of the New Testament prepared by R. A. Knox under archiepiscopal direction; a footnote was added: 'This verse does not occur in any good Greek manuscript. But the Latin manuscripts may have preserved the true text'. In fact, the best Latin manuscripts also lack the verse. It is perhaps a measure of the advance made in twenty years that the verse is absent both from the Catholic Edition of the RSV (1965) and from the Jerusalem Bible (1966). There are one or two Protestant quarters where rearguard actions in defence of the verse are still attempted, but evidence is evidence.

Although the verse came to be valued as a proof-text for the doctrine of the Trinity when once its place in the Vulgate and 'Received' texts was established, the validity of this doctrine is completely independent of it. The classic formulations of Nicaea (325), Constantinople (381) and Chalcedon (451) were the work of theologians who knew nothing of the 'three heavenly witnesses'.

NOTES

1. G. G. Findlay, *Fellowship in the Life Eternal* (London, 1909), p. 368.
2. Confessing Jesus to be the Son of God is tantamount to confessing Him to be the Christ (1 John 2. 22; 5. 1); the twofold formulation is brought together by the Evangelist in John 20. 31: 'that you may believe that Jesus is the Christ, the Son of God' – where the designation 'the Christ' may be

appropriate to Jewish readers (cf. W. C. van Unnik, 'The Purpose of St. John's Gospel', in *The Gospels Reconsidered*, Oxford, 1960, pp. 167 ff.) and the designation 'the Son of God' (i.e. the One in whom God is fully revealed) for Gentile readers.

3. Cf. Augustine, *Against Maximin* ii. 22. 3. J. Massingberd Ford (' "Mingled Blood" from the Side of Christ', *NTS* 15, 1968–69, pp. 337 f.) sees in John 19. 34 a reference to Jesus as the Passover Lamb, and 'cannot correlate this interpretation to any other references to water and blood in the Johannine corpus' (namely those in 1 John 5. 6, 8).

4. So Tertullian, *On Baptism*, 16. Several authorities, including Codices Sinaiticus and Alexandrinus, with a few minuscules and some editions of the Latin, Syriac and Coptic versions, read 'water and blood and Spirit', adding the witness of Pentecost to that of the baptism and the passion.

5. The preposition translated 'by' in the first half of the verse is *dia* ('through', 'by means of'); that translated 'with' three times in the second half of the verse is *en* (used in its instrumental sense, which is practically synonymous with *dia* followed by the genitive).

6. J. Calvin takes a different line: 'I do not doubt that by the words "water and blood" he refers to the ancient rites of the Law' (*Commentary on John 11–21 and 1 John*, trans. T. H. L. Parker, Edinburgh, 1961, p. 302).

7. His witness in Scripture is a material factor in the confirmation of the physical death of Jesus in John 19. 36 f.

8. The Latin Vulgate probably bears witness to a text which omitted the second occurrence of 'Spirit' and read: 'And it is the Spirit that bears witness that he (i.e. Christ) is the truth'.

9. The words 'in earth' following 'there are three that bear witness' in AV are a late addition made necessary by the insertion of the spurious text about the three that bear witness 'in heaven' immediately before verse 8. See pp. 129 f.

10. *Die Tradition und der Charakter des ersten Johannesbriefes* (Tübingen, 1957), pp. 147 ff.; cf. T. W. Manson, 'Entry into Membership of the Early Church', *JTS* 48 (1947), pp. 25 ff. Manson points to the case of Cornelius and his household, who received the Spirit (evidenced by their speaking with tongues) before baptism (Acts 10. 44–48; contrast the order in Acts 2. 38; 8. 15 f.; 19. 5 f.), and suggests that Paul regarded the utterance of 'Abba Father!' (Rom. 8. 15 f.; Gal. 4. 6) or 'Jesus is Lord!' (Rom. 10. 9; 1 Cor. 12. 3) as sufficient evidence of reception of the Spirit to satisfy the requirements for baptism.

11. This is a Jewish missionary document of Essene affinities, in which the name of Joseph's Egyptian wife Asenath is given a Hebrew spelling and etymology Aseneth, perhaps to make it mean 'female Essene' ('Esseness'). She is treated as a proselyte, and undergoes an initiation in which 'anointing' (or 'renewal by God's Holy Spirit') is accompanied by the 'eating of the bread of life' and 'the drinking of the blessed cup of immortality'. Apart from the 'anointing', this has little enough relevance to 1 John.

12. In the early Christian recension of the pseudepigraphic *Testament of Levi* (one of the *Testaments of the Twelve Patriarchs*) Levi describes how 'seven men in white raiment' install him in the priestly office: 'the first anointed me with holy oil, . . . the second washed me with pure water and fed me with bread and wine . . .' (8. 4 f.) – in which the influence of this threefold Christian initiation has been detected (cf. T. W. Manson, 'Miscellanea Apocalyptica III', *JTS* 48, 1947, pp. 59 ff.).

13. Gr. *pisteuō eis*, as in John 3. 36, etc.; see notes on 3. 23 (p. 100) and 5. 13 (pp. 122 f.).

14. The reading of AV, RSV, NEB, 'in himself' (Gr. *en hautō* or *en heautō*), is preferable in this context to RV 'in him' (Gr. *en autō*); the difference in Greek may hang on nothing more than the presence or absence of an aspirate, not marked in uncial writing.

15. Manuscript authorities are divided between the present *pisteuēte* ('that you may hold the faith', NEB text) and the aorist *pisteusēte* ('that you may come to believe', NEB margin).

16. Gr. *pisteuō eis*, as in John 1. 12; 2. 23; 3. 18, etc.; see notes on 3. 23 (p. 100) and 5. 10 (p. 121).

17. *Lectures to my Students*, abridged one-volume edition (London, 1954), p. 65.

18. RSV renders 'sin unto death' as 'mortal sin'; NEB as 'deadly sin' – possibly (but not certainly) in allusion to Article XVI: 'Not every deadly sin willingly committed after baptism, is sin against the Holy Ghost, and unpardonable...'.

19. The rendering 'not concerning this do I say that he should make request' is a flagrant example of RV pedantry; it is more appropriate to a schoolboy's 'crib' than to a version of the Bible intended for public use.

20. Yet another suggestion is that he means a sin which, like the 'high-handed' sin of Num. 15. 30, can be expiated only by death; this is improbable.

21. Heb. 6. 4–6; cf. Heb. 10. 26–29. Others have compared the sentence passed by our Lord against those who attributed His power to expel demons to possession by Beelzebul instead of to the Spirit of God (Matt. 12. 28): 'whoever blasphemes against the Holy Spirit never has forgiveness, but is guilty of an eternal sin' (Mark 3. 29). They too were guilty of a deliberate refusal of the witness of God.

22. Similarly TEV: 'We know that no child of God keeps on sinning, for the Son of God keeps him safe, and the Evil One cannot harm him'.

23. Cf. Rom. 8. 19 ff.

24. C. K. Barrett, *The Gospel according to St. John* (London, 1955), p. 130.

25. Are all 'conceptions' of God false, falling under the general ban on 'graven images'? The son of a colleague of mine, directed in his Divinity class at school to write an essay on 'My Concept of God', queried the appropriateness of the subject: 'My father says that any concept of God is an idol', he told his teacher. That is certainly true if we allow any concept or conception of God to take the place of God Himself.

26. The Byzantine witnesses and Received Text add 'Amen' (so AV). This is probably due to liturgical usage when the public reading of the epistle in church was concluded with 'Amen'.

27. Instantius, according to G. Morin, 'Pro Instantio', *Revue Bénédictine* 30 (1913), pp. 153 ff.; but cf. the reply by J. Martin, 'Priscillianus oder Instantius?' in *Historisches Jahrbuch der Dörres-Gesellschaft* 47 (1927), pp. 237 ff. The treatise is the *Liber Apologeticus* (Tract. 1. 4; *CSEL* xvii. 6): 'as John says, "there are three that say witness in earth, the Spirit, the water and the blood, and these three (agree) in one; and there are three that say witness in heaven, the Father, the Word and the Spirit, and these three are one in Christ Jesus"' (from which it will be seen that the intrusive words originally *followed* the authentic text about the three witnesses).

28. In the catalogue of Greek NT minuscules its serial number is now 61.

29. Minuscule 629.

30. A manuscript copy of the Greek text of the Complutensian Polyglot, which included the passage (translated, of course, from Latin) when it was printed in 1513–14.
31. Minuscule 88. See B. M. Metzger, *The Text of the New Testament* (Oxford, 1964), pp. 101 f.
32. This was because of the Vulgate basis of the Confraternity Version of 1941. The revised edition of 1970 – in The New American Bible – is based on the scientifically established Greek text.

THE SECOND EPISTLE OF JOHN

INTRODUCTION AND ANALYSIS

The second and third Epistles of John present us with the closest approximations in the New Testament to the conventional letter-form of the contemporary Graeco-Roman world.[1] The second epistle, which deals with the same general problem as the first epistle, but apparently in reference to the particular situation of one local group or house-church, lends itself readily to the following analysis:

1 Opening salutation (verses 1–3)
2 Occasion of rejoicing (verse 4)
3 Exhortation (verses 5–11)
4 Personal notes (verse 12)
5 Final greeting (verse 13)

TEXT AND EXPOSITION

1 OPENING SALUTATION (verses 1-3)

**V. 1   The elder unto the elect lady and her children, whom
I love in truth; and not I only, but also all they that know the
truth;**

We are confronted immediately by the twin problems of the
identity of the writer and that of the recipients. 'The elder' is the
writer's self-chosen designation both here and in 3 John. We are
hardly to think here of an elder in the sense which the word
presbyteros usually bears in Christian contexts in the New Testament, that is, one who discharges the ministry of eldership in a
local church. In this sense there were several elders in each church,
and it would be strange to find one of them singling himself out
with the designation 'the elder' and addressing other churches
with authority. The word appears in another specialized sense in
second-century Christian literature, of church leaders in the
generation after the apostles, particularly those who were disciples
of apostles or of 'apostolic men', and were therefore guarantors of
the 'tradition' which they received from the apostles and delivered
in turn to their own followers.[2] This sense may have been
borrowed from the Old Testament references to 'the elders who
outlived Joshua' (Josh. 24. 31; Judg. 2. 7). Irenaeus, for example,
mentions what he heard 'from a certain elder (presbyter), who had
heard it from those who had seen the apostles, and from those
who learned it (from them)',[3] and cites him again as 'the elder';[4]
later he quotes 'an elder, a disciple of the apostles',[5] who appears
to have been in even closer touch with the fountain-head of
Christian teaching, and is probably to be identified with one at
whose feet Irenaeus sat in his boyhood, Polycarp of Smyrna, who
in his turn had been acquainted with 'John and the others who had
seen the Lord'.[6] Irenaeus's other 'elder', whose contact with the
apostles was indirect, may have been his predecessor as bishop of

Lyons, Pothinus, who died a martyr in AD 177 when he was over ninety years old.

Papias, bishop of Hierapolis in Phrygia, half a century older than Irenaeus, who calls him 'an ancient (*archaios*) man',[7] and a contemporary of Polycarp, also has something to say of the elders, from whom he eagerly collected whatever they could tell him of the teaching of Jesus. 'If ever a person came my way who had been a companion of the elders', he adds, 'I would enquire about the sayings of the elders: "What did Andrew or Peter, or Philip, or Thomas or James, or John or Matthew or any other of the Lord's disciples say? And what do Aristion and the elder John, the disciples of the Lord, say?" For I did not suppose that what I could get from books was of such great value to me as the utterances of a living and abiding voice'.[8]

The relation between Papias's two references to John has provided material for much inconclusive debate. Does he refer to two men called John, both 'disciples of the Lord' (as such orthodox scholars as J. B. Lightfoot[9] and S. P. Tregelles[10] thought, together with many others since their time), or to one only?[11] Whichever is the true answer to this question, it may have little relevance for the exegesis of this epistle and the following one. Papias also quotes one of his elders as 'the elder' *par excellence*; for example, the information he gives about the origin of the Gospel of Mark is said to be what 'the elder' used to say.[12] This suggests that in Papias's circle there was one senior man who because of his age, experience and authority was referred to in this way. It is quite likely that the self-designation of the writer of 2 and 3 John is to be similarly explained – not that he was *necessarily* identical with Papias's 'elder', but that in the circle in which he was best known he was given the affectionate and respectful title 'the elder' both because he was older than the other members of the circle and because his personal knowledge of the Way went back so much farther than theirs. If to them he was 'the elder', to him they may well have been his 'little children', as the anonymous author of 1 John calls his readers. That all three epistles come from one and the same writer is, in my judgment, scarcely to be doubted.

The identity of the recipients, 'the elect lady and her children', presents a problem of another kind. The *prima facie* picture is of a Christian *materfamilias* some at least of whose children follow the truth in which they were brought up and to whom greetings are sent from her nephews and nieces in the place from which 'the elder' is writing. Attempts have been made to extract her personal name from the designation which the writer gives her – *eklektē kyria*. Might this be rendered 'the elect Kyria' or (less probably) 'the lady Electa'?[13] She is evidently well known to Christians in many places: she is loved by all who 'know the truth'. No individual traits appear throughout the letter, however; in this respect it forms a contrast with 3 John, in which we have vivid thumb-nail sketches of Gaius, the recipient, and of Diotrephes and Demetrius, about whom the writer has something to say. Such considerations have led many interpreters, from the fourth century onwards, to understand 'the elect lady' as a corporate personality. As a city or country was commonly personified as a woman, like 'the daughter of Zion' in the Old Testament prophets or Britannia on British coins[14] (a representation going back to Roman times), so a church might be personified – whether the Church Catholic (portrayed in Rev. 20. 2, 9, 'as a bride adorned for her husband') or a local church (as probably in 1 Pet. 5. 13, where 'she who is at Babylon' is best understood as an elect sister-church of those to whom the letter is addressed). If this interpretation be followed here, then 'the elect lady' is a local church (not the Church Catholic, for the Church Catholic has no sister), 'her children' (*tekna*) are the members of that church, and the 'children' (*tekna*) of her 'elect sister' (v. 13) are the members of the local church in the place where the writer is resident. The weighing up of the probabilities for the individual or corporate character of the 'lady' is part of the exegesis of the letter. If the following exegesis leans to the corporate interpretation, this does not suggest that finality is attainable on this question; so long as either interpretation claims the support of serious students of the document, the question must be treated as an open one.

The 'lady and her children' are assured that the writer loves

them 'in truth' (cf. 3 John 1); this probably means not only that he
loves them truly (cf. 1 John 3. 18) but that he loves them as a
fellow-believer, as one who, together with them, is 'of the truth'
(cf. 1 John 3. 19). And all who are similarly 'of the truth', all who
'know the truth' – the truth as embodied in Him who is the truth
(John 14. 6)[15] – share with the writer in loving them too.

V. 2   for the truth's sake which abideth in us, and it shall be with us for ever:

This language is reminiscent of the words in which our Lord
promises His Spirit to the disciples in the upper room: 'he abides
with you and is (*or* will be)[16] in you' (John 14. 17). There is nothing
surprising if what is said of the Spirit in one place is said of 'the
truth' in another place: 'it is the Spirit that bears witness, because
the Spirit is the truth' (1 John 5. 7). It is through 'the Spirit of
truth' that He who is Truth incarnate dwells perpetually in and
with His people.

V. 3   Grace, mercy, peace shall be with us, from God the Father, and from Jesus Christ, the Son of the Father, in truth and love.

The threefold 'Grace, mercy, peace' in the opening salutation
appears also in 1 and 2 Timothy. Jude has a comparable salutation,
'mercy, peace and love'; the earlier Pauline letters and Titus have
the twofold 'Grace and peace', as also have the two Petrine letters
and John's salutation to the churches of Asia (Rev. 1. 4). The
future indicative 'shall be' is perhaps due to the influence of the
same form in verse 2. According to Westcott, 'the succession
"grace, mercy, peace" marks the order from the first motion of
God to the final satisfaction of man'.[17] The phrase 'Jesus Christ,
the Son of the Father', is unique, but the truth it expresses is
attested throughout the New Testament and is basic to John's
argument (cf. verse 9; 1 John 2. 23). The addition 'Lord' (*kyrios*)
before 'Jesus Christ' in the Received Text and AV is not original;

it is noteworthy that this title is not given to Jesus (nor used in any other sense[18]) anywhere in these three epistles. Where 'truth and love' coexist harmoniously, we have a well-balanced Christian character (cf. Eph. 4. 15).

2 Occasion of Rejoicing (verse 4)

V. 4 I rejoice greatly that I have found *certain* of thy children walking in truth, even as we received commandment from the Father.

'I rejoice' is aorist in Greek (*echarēn*); attention is thus concentrated on the moment when the elder's joy began, but since his joy persists we may follow RV and render by the English present.[19] The phrase '(certain) of thy children' (*tekna*) reflects the Greek use of the preposition *ek* in a partitive sense (*ek tōn teknōn sou*); an indefinite pronoun like 'certain' or 'some' is required to complete the sense in idiomatic modern English, although Greek can dispense with it. Since there is no definite article before 'truth' it may be held that 'walking in truth' here means simply 'conducting themselves in all sincerity', whereas the article would point to the embodiment of truth in Christ. It is doubtful if such a sharp distinction can be maintained; if they conducted themselves in sincerity, they conducted themselves as befits followers of Christ, and since their conduct was in accordance with the 'commandment' given them by the Father, it was as much 'walking in love' as 'walking in truth'. The Father's 'commandment' is communicated through the Son (cf. 1 John 3. 23). John does not necessarily suggest that the elect lady's other children do not so conduct themselves; in using the partitive construction he refers to some of them whom he had actually met, away from the place where the 'lady' was normally resident. His joy at meeting them was such that he determined to write a letter to their 'mother', that is (on the premise adopted in this exposition) to the local church from which they had come.

3 EXHORTATION (verses 5–11)

**V. 5 And now I beseech thee, lady, not as though I wrote
to thee a new commandment, but that which we had from
the beginning, that we love one another. v. 6 And this is love,
that we should walk after his commandments. This is the
commandment, even as ye heard from the beginning, that
ye should walk in it.**

The exhortation follows closely that given in general terms in
the first epistle. Since John was so delighted to find some members
of the community keeping the great commandment, his desire was
that the whole community should continue to keep it. For the
description of the commandment of love as no 'new commandment,'
but one 'which we had from the beginning', cf. 1 John 2. 7.[20] For
the essence of love as the keeping of God's commandments cf.
1 John 5. 3. To 'walk in it' at the end of verse 6 probably means
to walk in love; so RSV: 'that you follow love' (NEB takes 'it' to
refer to 'the commandment': 'This is the command which was
given you from the beginning, to be your rule of life'). We have
the same emphasis on love as in the first epistle, the same identification of love and obedience, the same insistence on what has
been held 'from the beginning'.

V. 7 For many deceivers are gone forth into the world,
even **they that confess not that Jesus Christ cometh in the
flesh. This is the deceiver and the antichrist.**

This repeats the warning against 'many Antichrists' given in 1
John 2. 18 ff.; 4. 1–6. The 'deceivers' (*planoi*) are those who lead
people astray (cf. the verb *planaō* in 1 John 2. 26). They are
described, literally, as those 'who do not acknowledge Jesus
Christ coming in flesh'; the participle is present here (*erchomenon*),
whereas in 1 John 4. 2 it is perfect (*elēlythota*), but the reference
is, as there, to the Docetic denial of our Lord's incarnation; the
Greek construction here may be more freely, but idiomatically,

rendered with RSV: 'men who will not acknowledge[21] the coming of Jesus Christ in the flesh'. The RV rendering, 'they that confess not that Jesus Christ cometh in the flesh', might be misunderstood as a reference to the Second Advent.[22]

V. 8 Look to yourselves, that ye [1]lose not the things which [2]we have wrought, but that ye receive a full reward.

[1] Or, *destroy*.
[2] Many ancient authorities read *ye*.

To pay attention to such deceivers and follow them on the path of error would involve the waste of all their Christian service hitherto and the loss of the fruit properly accruing from it. In place of AV and RV 'we have wrought',[23] which is followed by NEB ('that you may not lose all that we worked for'), there is a variant reading 'you have wrought'[24] (cf. RSV 'you have worked for'), which is more appropriate in the context. If, rejecting the enticement of error, they maintained the teaching which they had heard 'from the beginning' and continued the work they had been doing thus far, they would be paid their reward in full. This exhortation echoes much that is taught in other New Testament writings; compare 1 Cor. 3. 8, 14; Rev. 22. 12.

V. 9 Whosoever [1]goeth onward and abideth not in the teaching of Christ, hath not God: he that abideth in the teaching, the same hath both the Father and the Son. v. 10 If any one cometh unto you, and bringeth not this teaching, receive him not into *your* house, and give him no greeting: v. 11 for he that giveth him greeting partaketh in his evil works.

[1] Or, *taketh the lead*.

The Docetist teacher 'goes on' beyond the apostolic teaching; his 'advanced teaching' is condemned because it is 'advanced' in this sense. The apostolic teaching could be called 'the teaching of Christ' either because it is the teaching which derives from Christ and is vested with His authority[25] or because it is the authoritative and true teaching about Christ. Either interpretation would be

appropriate; whether we accept the former or the latter depends
on our understanding the genitive 'of Christ' as subjective or
objective genitive respectively. There is a strong balance of
probability in favour of the former construction (so Westcott).
Anyone, then, who has advanced beyond this teaching in a Docetic
direction 'has not God', since 'no one who denies the Son has the
Father' (1 John 2. 23a); everyone who 'abides' in it 'has both
the Father and the Son', since 'he who confesses the Son has the
Father also' (1 John 2. 23b). The injunction not to receive any one
who does not bring 'the teaching of Christ' means that no such
person must be accepted as a Christian teacher or as one entitled
to the fellowship of the church. It does not mean that (say) one of
Jehovah's Witnesses should not be invited into the house for a
cup of tea in order to be shown the way of God more perfectly in
the sitting-room than would be convenient on the doorstep. Still
less does it mean that disagreements on church order should be
treated as deviations from 'the teaching of Christ' and used as a
ground of exclusion from social as well as ecclesiastical fellowship,
as was done by Edward Cronin in 1849 in a letter terminating 'an
unbroken intimacy and friendship of twenty-five years' with
Anthony Norris Groves.[26] But for a church, or its responsible
leaders, knowingly to admit within its bounds the propagation of
teaching subversive of the gospel is to participate in what John
describes as 'evil works'. To give one who brings such teaching a
greeting is to say *chaire* to him, to bid him hail when he arrives or
farewell when he leaves – here the former is more probably in
view. It is plain from the early Christian manual called the
Didache or *Teaching of the Twelve Apostles* (a work compiled not
much, if at all, later than the Epistles of John) that travelling
prophets and apostles were well-known figures in church life at
this period, and it was necessary to distinguish the right kind from
the wrong kind. The *Didache* gives priority to the doctrinal
criterion. After summarizing the 'way of life' and the 'way of
death' and the proper procedure for baptism, fasting and the
Eucharist, it goes on: 'Whosoever then comes and teaches you
all these things aforesaid, receive him. If, however, the teacher

himself is perverted and teaches another doctrine to destroy these things, do not listen to him; but if his teaching promotes righteousness and the knowledge of the Lord, receive him as the Lord'.[27] It also lays down some practical and pedestrian rules of thumb ('if he stays three days, he is a false prophet . . . if he asks for money, he is a false prophet').[28] The crucial test has already been laid down in 1 John 4. 1–3, and this is the test which is recommended to 'the elect lady'.

4 PERSONAL NOTES (verse 12)

V. 12 **Having many things to write unto you, I would not *write them* with paper and ink: but I hope to come unto you, and to speak face to face, that your joy may be fulfilled.**

Unfortunately we do not know for sure what the other things were which the Elder wanted to say to these friends; perhaps he wished to deal in greater detail, in reference to specific persons, with those questions which are treated briefly and in principle in the letter. The 'paper' which he mentions is papyrus (Gr. *chartēs*); a short letter like 2 John would be accommodated on one papyrus sheet of normal size. To 'speak face to face' is literally 'to speak mouth to mouth' (Gr. *stoma pros stoma*) – a biblical phrase; God uses it of His converse with Moses in Num. 12. 8.[29] The clause 'that your joy may be fulfilled' is repeated from 1 John 1. 4; in both places there is textual variation between 'your' and 'our' ('our' is read here by AV, RSV and NEB and is probably to be preferred, as in 1 John 1. 4).[30]

5 FINAL GREETING (verse 13)

V. 13 **The children of thine elect sister salute thee.**

The status of the lady's 'elect sister' will be comparable to her own status; if she is a local church, so is her sister (the church in the place where the Elder happens to be at the time of writing). The greetings are sent to the lady by 'the children' of her 'elect sister'; if the sisters are two churches and the 'children' their respective members, then the singular and plural are practically interchangeable. It is useless to speculate why the greetings are sent by the sister's 'children' rather than by herself; the Elder can scarcely be referring to sympathetic members of a church whose official leadership is unsympathetic, for in that case he would hardly describe the church as 'elect'. One minuscule of the eleventh century (Cod. 465) identifies the 'elect sister' as the church of Ephesus; this is a piece of traditional interpretation with no textual authority.[31] But both 'sisters' were probably churches in that neighbourhood.[32]

NOTES

1. Cf. R. W. Funk, 'The Form and Structure of II and III John', *JBL* 86 (1967), pp. 424 ff.
2. Cf. Irenaeus, *Against Heresies* v. 5. 1; 36. 1 f.; *Demonstration* 3; 61; also Hippolytus, passages cited by A. Hamel, *Kirche bei Hippolyt von Rom* (Gütersloh, 1951), pp. 106 f. In *Against Heresies* iv. 27-32 Irenaeus incorporates an anti-Marcionite defence by an 'elder' of the unity of the Creator with the Father revealed by Jesus; the OT and NT quotations woven into it indicate the important part played by such 'elders' in the development of the Canon between Papias and Irenaeus (see G. Bornkamm, in *TDNT* vi, Grand Rapids, 1969, pp. 670 ff., *s.v.* πρέσβυς, πρεσβύτερος).
3. *Against Heresies* iv. 42. 2.
4. *Against Heresies* iv. 46. 1; 47. 1.
5. *Against Heresies* iv. 49. 1.
6. *Letter to Florinus*, quoted by Eusebius, *Hist. Eccl.* v. 20. 6; see p. 22, n. 4. Cf. Irenaeus, *Against Heresies* ii. 22. 5; v. 30. 1; 33. 3 f., for the relation of the 'elders' to 'John, the disciple of the Lord'.
7. *Against Heresies* v. 33. 4 (see p. 22, n. 5). The adjective *archaios* suggests contact with the beginning (*archē*); cf. its application to Mnason in Acts 21. 16.
8. *Exegesis of the Dominical Oracles*, quoted by Eusebius, *Hist. Eccl.* iii. 39. 3 f. See p. 22, n. 5.
9. *Essays on the Work entitled 'Supernatural Religion'* (London, 1889), p. 144.
10. *The Historic Evidence of the Authorship and Transmission of the Books of the New Testament*² (London, 1881), p. 47.
11. E.g. F. W. Farrar, *The Early Days of Christianity* (London, 1882), pp. 618 ff.; G. Salmon, *Historical Introduction to the . . . New Testament*⁴ (London, 1889), pp. 287 ff.; T. Zahn, *Apostel und Apostelschüler in der Provinz Asien* (Leipzig, 1900), pp. 112 ff., and *Introduction to the New Testament* (Edinburgh, 1909), ii, pp. 451 ff.; J. Chapman, *John the Presbyter and the Fourth Gospel* (Oxford, 1911); C. J. Cadoux, *Ancient Smyrna* (Oxford, 1938), pp. 316 f.
12. 'This also the elder used to say: "Mark became Peter's interpreter, and wrote down accurately all that he remembered, whether sayings or doings of Christ - not, however, in order, for he was neither a hearer nor a companion of the Lord, but afterwards, as I said, he accompanied Peter, who adapted his teachings as necessity required, not as though he were

making a compilation of the oracles of the Lord. So then, Mark made no mistake in writing certain things just as he remembered them, for he paid attention to one thing – not to omit anything he had heard, nor to include any false statement among them" ' (quoted by Eusebius, *Hist. Eccl.* iii. 39. 15). (It is possible that the two occurrences of 'he [Mark] remembered' should be rendered 'he [Peter] mentioned'.) It is uncertain if the same elder was Papias's authority for his further statement that 'Matthew compiled the oracles (*logia*) in the Hebrew speech, and everyone translated them as best he could' (*Hist. Eccl.* iii. 39. 16).

13. Clement of Alexandria took Electa (Eklektē) to be the lady's personal name, and (linking this passage with 1 Pet. 5. 13) concluded that she and her children were Babylonians and therefore, in view of the political situation at the time, Parthians (*Adumbrations* iv. 437). Hence the spurious title 'To the Parthians' was affixed to 2 John and then to the three Johannine letters as a group and so to 1 John (see p. 32, n. 1).

14. Cf. also the disconsolate female figure 'Captive Judaea' on Roman coins celebrating the fall of Jerusalem and suppression of the Jewish revolt.

15. Cf. also 1 John 5. 20, 'we know him that is true'.

16. Witnesses to the text read variously *esti* ('is') and *estai* ('will be').

17. *The Epistles of St. John* (London, 1902), p. 225.

18. The nearest approach to *kyrios* in these epistles is the courtesy use of the feminine *kyria* in 2 John 1, 5.

19. AV, RSV 'I rejoiced'; cf. NEB 'I was delighted'. Compare 3 John 3 (p. 148).

20. But see also 1 John 2. 8 (pp. 53 ff.).

21. The rendering 'who will not acknowledge . . .' (rather than 'who do not acknowledge . . .') is probably intended to bring out the force of the negative *mē* (not *ouch*) before the participle *homologountes*.

22. His *parousia* is not 'in flesh' but 'in glory'.

23. So Codex Vaticanus (first hand) with the bulk of Byzantine manuscripts and the Received Text.

24. So Codices Sinaiticus, Alexandrinus, 1739, and the Latin and Syriac versions.

25. See pp. 17 f. with p. 24, n. 14.

26. G. H. Lang, *Anthony Norris Groves* (London, 1939), p. 265.

27. *Didache* 11. 1 f. (cf. p. 149).

28. *Didache* 11. 5 f.

29. But in Deut. 34. 10 the LORD is said to have known him 'face to face' (LXX *prosōpon kata prosōpon*). Another, and more sinister, occurrence of our present idiom is in Jer. 32. 4 (LXX 39. 4), where the captive Zedekiah and his captor Nebuchadrezzar speak 'mouth to mouth'.

30. 'Our' (Gr. *hēmōn*) is the reading of Codex Sinaiticus and the Received Text; 'your' (Gr. *hymōn*) of Codices Vaticanus and Alexandrinus and the majority of manuscripts. See p. 40 with p. 46, n. 10.

31. Compare R. Eisler's identification of the 'elect lady' with the church of Palestine (*The Enigma of the Fourth Gospel*, London, 1938, pp. 170 f.), which lacks even the benefit of tradition. J. V. Bartlet had earlier identified her with the church of Thyatira (*JTS* 6, 1905, pp. 204 ff.) and G. G. Findlay with the church of Pergamum (*Fellowship in the Life Eternal*, London, 1909, pp. 32 ff.).

32. At the end of the epistle a few late manuscripts add 'Grace be with you'; the Byzantine witnesses and Received Text (whence AV) add the liturgical 'Amen'.

THE THIRD EPISTLE OF JOHN

INTRODUCTION AND ANALYSIS

The third Epistle, being addressed by an individual to an individual, approximates even more closely than the second epistle to the regular pattern of letter-writing in the Graeco-Roman world of that day. It may be analysed thus:

1 Opening salutation and good wishes (verses 1–2)
2 Occasion of rejoicing (verses 3–4)
3 Appreciation of help given to travelling teachers (verses 5–8)
4 Diotrephes's unbrotherly conduct (verses 9–10)
5 Exhortation (verse 11)
6 Recommendation of Demetrius (verse 12)
7 Personal notes (verses 13–14)
8 Final greeting (verse 15).

The teaching which the writer wished to see accepted and maintained in the churches for which he felt special responsibility was conveyed not only by himself in person, whether orally or in letters, but also by travelling teachers who visited the churches with his recommendation. Gaius, to whom this letter is written, had shown these messengers hospitality; the church to which Gaius evidently belonged, however, had refused to receive them, at the instigation of one Diotrephes. Gaius is praised for his hospitality, but Diotrephes's unco-operative behaviour is deplored. Another of the writer's messengers, Demetrius, probably the bearer of this letter, is commended to Gaius's friendly interest.

TEXT AND EXPOSITION

1 OPENING SALUTATION AND GOOD WISHES (verses 1–2)

V. 1 The elder unto Gaius the beloved, whom I love in truth.

The significance of the self-designation 'the elder' has been discussed in the note on 2 John 1. Gaius was a common name in the Roman world; it was one of the eighteen names from which Roman parents could choose a *praenomen* for one of their sons. Elsewhere in the New Testament we meet Gaius of Corinth, Paul's host (Rom. 16. 23; 1 Cor. 1. 14), and Gaius of Derbe or (according to the Western text) Doberus, Paul's travelling companion (Acts 19. 29; 20. 4). There is no ground for associating the Gaius of 3 John with any other bearer of the name. The adjective clause, 'whom I love in truth', is practically identical with the wording of 2 John 1 (see the note on that verse).

V. 2 Beloved, I pray that in all things thou mayest prosper and be in health, even as thy soul prospereth.

The convention of wishing one's reader good health at the outset of a letter ('Hoping this finds you well, as it leaves me at present') is one of great antiquity. So regular was this sort of thing in Latin letters that it was customarily expressed by the use of initials, S V B E E V (*si uales, bene est; ego ualeo*, 'if you are well, that is good; I am well'). The elder adapts such conventional good wishes in a manner all his own: he knows from Gaius's way of life that his soul is in a healthy condition, and he prays that his bodily health and general prosperity may match the prosperity of his soul. The late Professor A. Rendle Short remarked that at one time it occurred to him that 3 John 2 would be a suitable text to inscribe over his name in his friends' autograph albums, until he

reflected that, so far as some of them were concerned, a prayer
that their general health might match their spiritual prosperity
could be interpreted as a prayer that they might require his
professional attendance. But if the elder's prayer for Gaius were
answered, health and prosperity would be his in abundance.

2   OCCASION OF REJOICING (verses 3–4)

**V. 3   For I ¹rejoiced greatly, when brethren came and bare
witness unto thy truth, even as thou walkest in truth.**

> ¹ Or, *rejoice greatly, when brethren come and bear witness.*

John's conviction about Gaius's spiritual health is based on the
news about Gaius brought to him by 'brethren' – probably those
whom (according to verses 5–8) Gaius had entertained hospitably.
These men, on their return, told John about Gaius's 'truth' – that
is, the loyalty to Christ and the gospel by which his life was
marked. Like those children of 'the elect lady' mentioned in 2
John 4, Gaius 'walked' – conducted himself – 'in truth'. John
knows that the report about Gaius corresponds to the reality, and
is filled with gladness on this account.[1] (The conjunction 'For' at
the beginning of the sentence is not found in all authorities for
the text,[2] but its presence is apt, as it draws attention to the reason
for John's assurance that Gaius's soul is in a prosperous condition.)

**V. 4   Greater ¹joy have I none than ²this, to hear of my
children walking in truth.**

> ¹ Some ancient authorities read *grace.*
> ² Or, *these* things, *that I may hear.*

For 'joy' (Gr. *charan*) Codex Vaticanus and a few other
witnesses have the less appropriate reading 'grace' (*charin*). (The
same variation occurs in 2 Cor. 1. 15.) The infinitive 'to hear' (so
RV, RSV, NEB) represents Gr. *hina akouō.* Although in classical
Greek *hina* with the subjunctive mood expresses purpose, this is
no longer invariably so in Hellenistic Greek, which provides
sufficient examples like the present (cf. John 17. 3) of the increasing
tendency to use this construction as an equivalent of the infinitive –

a tendency which led to the complete supersession of the original infinitive forms by this construction, as in modern Greek (where *hina* appears in the shortened form *na*). The elder reckons Gaius among his 'children' (*tekna*); this might suggest that Gaius was a convert of his, but in view of his designation of all to whom 1 John was sent as 'my little children', he may mean no more than that Gaius is one of many younger fellow-believers for whom he feels a fatherly concern and affection.

3   Appreciation of Help given to Travelling Teachers (verses 5–8)

V. 5 Beloved, thou doest a faithful work in whatsoever thou doest toward them that are brethren and strangers withal;

The ministry of travelling teachers (sometimes called 'apostles' or 'prophets'), as has been mentioned in the notes on 2 John, was a well-known feature of church life in Western Asia at the end of the first and beginning of the second century. It was a Christian duty – 'a faithful (or loyal) work' – to show such visitors hospitality, and this duty was none the less to be discharged faithfully because the opportunity to profit by it was seized by some charlatans. The *Didache*, in its pedestrian way, underlines the importance of receiving as the Lord Himself 'everyone who comes in the name of the Lord'; every true prophet or teacher is 'worthy of his food'[3] (cf. Matt. 10. 10). One group of such teachers evidently went out with the commendation of the elder and his associates, and it was some of them who spoke so well of Gaius. They were 'strangers', and he took them in, treating them as his *guests* (the same word *xenos* does duty in both senses).

V. 6 who bare witness to thy love before the church: whom thou wilt do well to set forward on their journey worthily of God:

In Gaius's case 'walking in truth' was synonymous with 'walking in love'. He showed his visitors Christian love, and when

they spoke of his reception of them in their report of their journey
to the church from which presumably they had set out (perhaps
the same church as is called 'your elect sister' in 2 John 13),
Gaius's hospitality became a matter of widespread renown. He
did not show hospitality in order to gain this renown – indeed, the
renown probably meant that demands on his hospitality greatly
increased – but thanks to their appreciative report of his kindness
his example has been an encouragement to many others. His
kindness was worthy of the God whom he and they alike served;
it was a reflection of God's own kindness (cf. 2 Sam. 9. 3, 'the
kindness of God'). The words 'thou wilt do well' are an idiomatic
form of conveying a request (cf. NEB: 'Please help them on their
journey') or expressing thanks in advance (cf. a similar expression
in the past tense in Acts 10. 33, where 'you have done well to
come' means 'thank you for coming').

V. 7 because that for the sake of the Name they went forth, taking nothing of the Gentiles.

If the Old Testament contains one or two books which do not
mention the name of God, the New Testament contains one which
does not mention Christ by name – our present epistle. But if
Christ is not mentioned by name here, He is referred to in other
ways: for example, 'the Name' on behalf of which these brethren
'went forth' was the name of Christ, and it was in Christ's name
that Gaius had received them (cf. Mark 9. 37). As in Jewish
parlance 'The Name' is a surrogate for YHWH, so here 'The Name'
is a synonym for Christ. It was for His sake that these men went
forth on their teaching journeys, as it is for His sake that all true
Christian service is done. And when it is known to others that it
is done for His sake, His name is honoured. It was good on one
occasion to hear a Hindu resident in East Africa tell what a blessing
the sisters in a neighbouring mission hospital were to the area in
which they worked, and better still to hear him add: 'and they do
it all for Jesus Christ'. Since these teachers went out on their
journeys for Christ's sake, it was fitting that they should be

supported by Christ's people. Had they accepted hospitality from
'the Gentiles', it might have given the impression that their own
people did not support them adequately. The word rendered
'Gentiles' here is *ethnikoi*, Gentile individuals (as in Matt. 5. 47;
6. 7; 18. 17), not the commoner *ethnē*, Gentile nations. It has been
pointed out that there is in 3 John 'precisely the same *contrast*
between the *ekklēsia* and the *ethnikoi* as in Matt. 18. 17: "If he
refuses to listen even to the church, let him be to you an *ethnikos*".'[4]

V. 8 We therefore ought to welcome such, that we may be fellow-workers with the truth.

The pronoun 'we' is emphatic: since these men refused to seek
help or hospitality from Gentiles, 'we Christians (*hēmeis*) ought to
receive them into our homes and entertain them' (Gr. *hypolambanō*).
If, as 2 John 10 f. says, to harbour a false teacher is to have
fellowship with his 'wicked works', correspondingly to show
hospitality to those who maintain the truth of the gospel is to
co-operate 'with the truth', and to enjoy the fulfilment of our
Lord's promise that 'he who receives a prophet in the name of a
prophet will receive a prophet's reward' (Matt. 10. 41).

4   DIOTREPHES'S UNBROTHERLY CONDUCT (verses 9-10)

V. 9 I wrote somewhat unto the church: but Diotrephes, who loveth to have the preeminence among them, receiveth us not.

The most reliable authorities for the text have 'I wrote somewhat' (Gr. *ti*, 'something'); other readings are 'I would have
written to the church',[5] 'I would have written something to the
church',[6] 'I wrote to the church herself'[7] and 'I wrote unto the
church' (so AV, following the Received Text). Of these variants, 'I
would have written to the church' is the second best attested
reading; if it were accepted, the implication would be that John
is writing to Gaius instead of the church, because he knows that,
thanks to the influence of Diotrephes, a letter to the church would

be fruitless. But if we read (as certainly we should) 'I wrote somewhat', the question arises what he wrote and to which church. The suggestion has been made that here is a reference to 2 John – that, the elect lady herself being unresponsive, John had now to write to one of her children, Gaius.[8] But this is unlikely. The natural inference to draw from John's words here is that he had written earlier to Gaius's home church commending his travelling teachers; but this is not the subject of 2 John. On the other hand, the false teaching about which the writer is concerned in 2 John does not figure here. It is better to conclude that the letter to the church, to which reference is made in the present passage, is lost, although its tenor may be surmised.

However that may be, the letter failed of its intended effect because Diotrephes, a dominant personality in that church, forbade his brethren to comply with the Elder's request. Diotrephes is described as *ho philoprōteuōn autōn*, which RSV renders (quite literally) 'who likes to put himself first' and NEB (more freely) 'their would-be leader'. The language suggests a self-promoted demagogue rather than a constitutional *presbyteros* or *episkopos*. It is conceivable, of course, that even a constitutional leader might have been regarded by the Elder as no better than a trumped-up dictator if he behaved in the way described here. The question has been repeatedly raised of the relation which this reference bears to the monarchical episcopate, which we find beginning to emerge in the churches of Western Asia early in the second century, exemplified in such saints and martyrs as Ignatius of Antioch and Polycarp of Smyrna. C. H. Dodd sums up the alternatives thus: 'It may be (i) that Diotrephes is in fact the first "monarchical bishop" known to history in the province of Asia;[9] . . . it may be (ii) that Diotrephes is a symptom of the disease which the quasi-apostolic ministry of monarchical bishops was designed to relieve.'[10] On the whole, the second is more probable. The first monarchical bishops of whom we know were concerned, just as the Elder himself was, to maintain the apostolic teaching in their churches and to exclude whatever conflicted with it. Diotrephes is not charged with heresy,[11] and his exclusive behaviour may have been due entirely to his determination to allow no teaching or leadership in the church but his own. Twenty centuries of church history have witnessed many of his successors: the lust for power, from whatever form of inner insecurity it may spring, is always a curse, and pre-eminently so in the realm of religion. It is, however, possible that his conduct arose in some degree from his disapproval of the teaching that John and his friends maintained; we cannot be sure. He does not receive us, says John; that is to say, he neither recognized John's authority nor admitted his messengers to the church. The former sense comes to the fore in RSV: 'does not acknowledge my authority' (NEB, more generally, says 'will have nothing to do with us').

V. 10   Therefore, if I come, I will bring to remembrance his works which he doeth, prating against us with wicked words: and not content therewith, neither doth he himself receive the brethren, and them that would he forbiddeth, and casteth *them* **out of the church.**

Diotrephes, however, will have to answer for his behaviour: the Elder is no private individual, but one who is capable of speaking authoritatively to Diotrephes and to the church which he dominates. How far he could be sure of asserting his authority successfully cannot be determined, but presumably if Diotrephes could carry the church with him against the Elder their fellowship with the churches which did acknowledge the Elder's authority would be endangered. C. H. Dodd suggests that the preservation of this letter is an argument of some weight in favour of the view that the Elder's appeal was successful.[12] The charges which Diotrephes brought up against the Elder and his associates amounted to sheer nonsense (the verb *phlyareō*, here rendered 'prate', means 'talk nonsense'), but they were malicious nevertheless, and accompanied by malicious actions, for he backed up his own refusal to receive the messengers by forbidding others to welcome them, and excommunicating[13] them if they did. The same verb *epidechomai* is used for 'receive' in verse 10 as in verse 9; RSV varies its rendering

of the word by translating it 'welcome' in this verse.[14] If 3 John
were indeed written to a member of the congregation addressed in
2 John, we should certainly have a piquant situation: the Elder
urges the church not to accept visitors who do not bring 'the
teaching of Christ' with them, but the visitors who are actually
turned away are the Elder's own delegates![15] It is improbable,
however, that the same church is in question; even so, the boycott
was an ecclesiastical weapon which could be used by more than
one party to a dispute.

5   EXHORTATION (verse 11)

V. 11   **Beloved, imitate not that which is evil, but that
which is good. He that doeth good is of God: he that doeth
evil hath not seen God.**

Diotrephes and persons like him are no fit examples for Gaius
or any one else to follow. Happily, there are better examples –
those who do good and not evil, and show thus that they belong
to the family of God (cf. 1 John 3. 10). The contrast between the
two types is summed up in a characteristic Johannine antithesis,
on the same lines as those laid down in 1 John 3. 4–10 (especially
verse 6). It is in Christ that God is seen, and to see Christ is to
become like Him (John 12. 45; 14. 9; 1 John 3. 2).

6   RECOMMENDATION OF DEMETRIUS (verse 12)

V. 12   **Demetrius hath the witness of all** *men,* **and of the
truth itself: yea, we also bear witness; and thou knowest that
our witness is true.**

If Diotrephes provides an example to be avoided, here is one
whose example can be safely followed. Demetrius is apparently
the bearer of this letter, and the letter incorporates the Elder's
commendation of him. In the circumstances it was useless to give
him a letter commending him to the church in that place, for
Diotrephes would see to it that the letter and its bearer were alike
refused. But John is persuaded that Gaius will live up to his

reputation for hospitality and give Demetrius a welcome. Those referred to as 'all', from whom Demetrius receives a good report, may be the generality of Christians in the region where he is known, but we cannot exclude the probability that, in terms of the qualifications for a 'bishop' specified in 1 Tim. 3. 7, he was 'well thought of by outsiders'. The statement that Demetrius in addition received a good report from 'the truth itself' may mean that, apart from any human voice, the facts themselves testified in his favour; but it is more probable that 'the truth' is here personal, denoting our Lord (cf. John 14. 6) and that we should translate: 'the Truth Himself'. Similar language is used by Papias of Hierapolis, a member of the same school a generation or so later, who tells how he sought out those who had been in touch with companions and eyewitnesses of Jesus, so that he might ascertain and record the commandments 'given to faith by the Lord and proceeding from the Truth Himself'[16] (the same phrase as here). The Elder adds his personal testimony, based on first-hand knowledge of Demetrius, and Gaius knows that the Elder's testimony is trustworthy. The words 'thou knowest that our witness is true' are remarkably similar to those appended as a postscript in John 21. 24, presumably by those associates of the Beloved Disciple who were responsible for publishing the Fourth Gospel: 'we know that his witness is true'.[17]

7   PERSONAL NOTES (verses 13–14)

V. 13   I had many things to write unto thee, but I am unwilling to write *them* to thee with ink and pen: v. 14 but I hope shortly to see thee, and we shall speak face to face.

This note is very similar to that at the end of the previous letter (2 John 12). The imperfect tense 'I had' may be epistolary, in which case it should be rendered 'I have'; but this is not necessarily so. There were no doubt delicate personal and ecclesiastical questions which could more conveniently be discussed orally than in a letter. The phrase 'with ink and pen' takes the place of 'with paper and ink' in 2 John 12; the 'pen' is a reed-pen (Gr. *kalamos*) 'reed'). John's intention to see Gaius 'shortly' or 'immediately' (Gr. *eutheōs*) may best be taken to mean very soon after the arrival of his letter; the letter prepares Gaius for his visit (perhaps he was about to set out on a circuit of the churches in his sphere of interest, including also the church addressed in 2 John). The phrase 'speak face to face' (lit. 'mouth to mouth') is repeated from 2 John 12 and is discussed briefly in the comment on that verse (p. 143).

8   FINAL GREETING (verse 15)

V. 15   **Peace** *be* **unto thee. The friends salute thee. Salute the friends by name.**

'Peace to you' is a common Hebraic and Semitic greeting (Heb. *shalom 'alekha*; Arab. *salaam 'alaika*). The 'friends' who send their greetings are those with whom the Elder found himself at the time of writing – perhaps the members of the church referred to as 'the children of your elect sister' in 2 John 13, if both letters were written at the same time. Correspondingly, the 'friends' to whom greetings are sent – 'by name', that is individually – are those who were with Gaius at the time, probably members of his church who, despite Diotrephes, were well-disposed towards John and his messengers.[18]

NOTES

1. For the tense 'I rejoiced' or 'I rejoice' (Gr. *echarēn*) cf. 2 John 4 (p. 139). Here AV, RSV and NEB agree with RV text in the use of the past tense.
2. Its omission in Codex Sinaiticus and a few other authorities may be due to the analogy of 2 John 4.
3. *Didache* 12. 1; 13. 1 (see pp. 142 f.).
4. J. A. T. Robinson, 'The Destination and Purpose of the Johannine Epistles', *Twelve NT Studies* (London, 1962), p. 132.
5. So the third corrector of Codex Sinaiticus with several other Greek witnesses and the Latin and Syriac versions. This depicting of the letter in question as one which he would have written but did not actually write may have been intended to get rid of the disturbing thought that an apostolic letter was lost.
6. So a corrector of minuscule 424.
7. So a corrector of minuscule 326, reading *autē tē ekklēsia* for *ti tē ekklēsia*.
8. Cf. R. Eisler, *The Enigma of the Fourth Gospel* (London, 1938), pp. 172 f.; for the view that 1 and 2 John were 'dedicatory' or covering letters com-

mending to the readers' acceptance copies of the Gospel of John, which accompanied them; and that it was this Gospel that Diotrephes refused to accept, excommunicating those who did accept it. Diotrephes is characterized by Eisler as 'the first of the *Alogoi*' – a disparaging designation given to a group of people towards the end of the second century who rejected the Fourth Gospel (disparaging because it could mean not only 'devoid of the *logos*' in the sense of John 1. 1–14 but also 'devoid of *logos*' in the sense of 'reason', like the 'irrational animals' of Jude 10; 2 Pet. 2. 12). Eisler's theories were invariably brilliant, but almost invariably unconvincing.

9. So A. Harnack, *Über den dritten Johannesbrief* = *TU* 15, 3 (Leipzig, 1897), pp. 21 ff., followed by R. Bultmann, *The Johannine Epistles* (Philadelphia, 1973, p. 101), according to whom the conflict was between the new episcopate under which local churches asserted their autonomy and the old province-wide missionary organization which was at this time under the leadership of the Elder.

10. *The Johannine Epistles* (London, 1946), p. 164.

11. As against W. Bauer, *Rechtgläubigkeit und Ketzerei im ältesten Christentum*[2] (Tübingen, 1963), p. 97, who calls Diotrephes a heresiarch. Conversely, R. Bultmann (*The Johannine Epistles*, p. 101) agrees with E. Käsemann ('Ketzer und Zeuge', *ZTK* 48, 1951, pp. 292 ff.) that Diotrephes represents an inchoate orthodoxy suspicious of the supposed gnostic tendencies of Johannine theology, but dismisses as fantastic his view that Diotrephes actually excommunicated the Elder.

12. *The Johannine Epistles*, p. 165.

13. The same verb (*ekballō*) is used in John 9. 34 f. for what appears to be expulsion from the synagogue.

14. Similarly NEB varies the rendering and translates here: 'he refuses to receive our friends'.

15. Cf. A. Ehrhardt, *The Framework of the New Testament Stories* (Manchester, 1964), pp. 169 f.; he thinks that Diotrephes refused the Elder and his associates because, in his eyes, they did not bring the 'teaching of Christ' and suggests that the judgment 'prating against us with wicked words' would have been phrased 'very differently had there been an authoritative "Apostles' Creed" to pinpoint Diotrephes's heretical views'.

16. Quoted by Eusebius, *Hist. Eccl.* iii. 39. 3. Cf. p. 136.

17. Cf. what is said in reference to the effusion of blood and water from the pierced side of Jesus on the cross: 'he who saw it has borne witness – his witness is true' (John 19. 35).

18. As at the end of the first and second letters, a few later manuscripts add the liturgical 'Amen', but it is absent from the Received Text, and therefore from AV. (In many editions what is here given as verse 15 appears as the continuation of verse 14.)

INDEX

'Abba' 58, 131
Abel 94
Abomination of desolation 67, 82
Abraham 91
Access 123
Advocate 49f., 80, 90, 125
Agapē 110 (see Love)
Ahab (king) 103
Akiba 85
Alexander, N. 21
Alexandria 19, 20, 22, 23
Alogoi 157
Analysis 31f.
Anointing 70f., 76ff., 82, 126
Antichrist 64ff., 82, 104, 105, 106, 140
Antioch 14, 18, 23, 152
Antiochus IV 67
Antitheses 29, 42ff., 51ff., 78, 92, 121, 154
Apocalypse (of John) 13, 23, 67, 68, 118, 138
Apostasy 125
Apostles 14, 21
Apostolic fellowship, teaching, witness 28, 38f., 42, 53, 69, 74f., 141
Aquila 108
Aramaisms 31
Aristion 22, 136
Arndt, W. F. 61, 102, 115
Aseneth 121, 131
Asherah 103
Asia (proconsular) 13, 14, 17, 18, 22, 25
Athanasius 20
Athens 16
Atonement (propitiation) 46, 50, 80, 109, 111
Augustine 32, 131
Authorship 15, 29ff.

Baal 103
Babylon 137
Baptism 120, 121, 132
Baptism of Jesus 118, 119, 120
Barrett, C. K. 128, 132
Bartlet, J. V. 145
Bauer, W. 61, 102, 115, 157
Beginning, The 34f., 45, 74, 126
Behm, J. 47
Belial, Beliar 67, 82
Blood 43f., 118ff.
Bornkamm, G. 144
Brooke, A. E. 20
Bultmann, R. 21, 29, 32, 157
Bunyan, J. 113

Cadoux, C. J. 144
Caesar 68
Caesarea 14
Cain 94, 96, 114
Calvin, J. 80, 131
Canon 15, 18f., 24, 76, 144

Carrington, P. 80
Carthage 18, 19, 20
Catholic Epistles 20
Cerinthus 16f., 23, 26, 73, 105, 118f.
Chapman, J. 30, 144
Chapman, R. C. 62
Children 48, 50, 57, 58, 59, 64, 77, 80, 83, 84, 85, 87, 93, 126, 136, 139, 143f., 148f.
Chytraeus, D. 49
Cleansing 43f., 46, 99
Clement of Alexandria 19, 23, 115, 145
Coinherence (mutual indwelling) 52f., 75, 78f., 110, 112, 128
Colossae 14
Colossians, Epistle to the 14
Commandment(s) 53f., 99f., 114, 116f., 139, 140
Communion, First 120
Complutensian Polyglot 133
Confession 44f., 111, 125, 130
Confidence 79, 97ff., 113, 115, 123
Conscience 97ff., 102
Corinth 71, 104
Creation 16, 85f.
Cronin, E. 142
Cullmann, O. 21, 24

Daniel, book of 67, 68
Date 31
Demetrius 137, 146, 154f.
Demiurge 23
Deuteronomy 104
Didache 142f., 145, 149
Diognetus, Epistle to 18
Dionysius of Alexandria 20, 22, 23
Diotrephes 17, 137, 146, 151ff., 156, 157
Dittenberger, W. 81
Docetism, Docetists 16, 25, 63, 105, 140ff.
Dodd, C. H. 20, 23, 30, 32, 33, 46, 110, 115, 152, 153
Dualism 16

Ehrhardt, A. 45, 46, 157
Eisler, R. 145, 156
Elder, The 24, 28, 135f.
Elect lady 137, 139
Elijah 103
Enoch, book of 80, 101
Ephesus 13, 14, 18, 21, 22, 23, 144
Epimenides 81
Episcopate 152
Erasmus, D. 129
Eschatology 30f., 33, 54, 64ff., 99
Eucharist 121
Eusebius 18, 19, 21, 22, 23, 24, 144, 157
Eve 94, 101
Excommunication 153
Eyewitness testimony 35, 37f., 46